THE

POETICAL WORKS

OF

WILLIAM WORDSWORTH

THE

Poetical Works

OF

WILLIAM WORDSWORTH

THE EXCURSION

THE RECLUSE

PART I BOOK I

Edited from the manuscripts
with
textual and critical notes
by

E. DE SELINCOURT
and
HELEN DARBISHIRE

OXFORD
AT THE CLARENDON PRESS

Oxford University Press, Ely House, London W. 1

GLASGOW NEW YORK TORONTO MELBOURNE WELLINGTON
CAPE TOWN IBADAN NAIROBI DAR ES SALAAM LUSAKA ADDIS ABABA
DELHI BOMBAY CALCUTTA MADRAS KARACHI LAHORE DACCA
KUALA LUMPUR SINGAPORE HONG KONG TOKYO

FIRST PUBLISHED 1949
REPRINTED IN GREAT BRITAIN
AT THE UNIVERSITY PRESS, OXFORD
BY VIVIAN RIDLER, PRINTER TO THE UNIVERSITY
FROM CORRECTED SHEETS OF THE FIRST EDITION
1959, 1966, 1972

PREFACE

THIS last volume of the collected Works contains *The Excursion*; *The Recluse*, Part I, Book I (in Appendix A); some interesting early passages of blank verse written when Wordsworth was contemplating *The Recluse* (in Appendix B); and *The Tuft of Primroses*, a long desultory poem, from which some lines were lifted into *The Excursion* (in Appendix C). In the notes at the end of the volume will be found some other passages written, but discarded, for *The Excursion*, notably those on the Shepherd of Bield Crag, pp. 461–2, on the life of the Peasant-boy, pp. 432–41, and on the death of the old Woodman, p. 466.

I have added, p. 362, a fragment of a poem on Milton recently discovered.

From a study of the manuscripts I have been able to trace, at any rate in outline, the chronology of the composition of *The Excursion*, and to throw some light on its genesis.

In printing Wordsworth's final text of *The Excursion* from the edition of 1850 I have made a few corrections: I follow Knight and Nowell C. Smith at iii. 617, v. 378 and 679, ix. 679, and Nowell C. Smith at ii. 398 and v. 529; with the support of the poet's manuscripts I have myself corrected *burnt* to *burned* at iii. 744, *borne* to *held* at vii. 343, and I have restored a missing line at iv. 1272.

At the end of the volume I have appended a list of Corrigenda and Addenda for the preceding volumes, and a comprehensive index, applying to all five volumes.

I am indebted for information on many points of local history to Mrs. Rawnsley of Allan Bank, an unrivalled authority on old Grasmere; and to Mr. Roger Coxon for the revelation of the true identity of 'the ingenuous poet', John Edwards, quoted by Wordsworth in his *Essay on Epitaphs* (*v.* p. 449 *infra*).

H. D.

GRASMERE,
March 1949

Note to Second Impression

THE re-issue of this volume enables me to correct some textual and other errors and to restore a right reading at i. 368, p. 20, *vide apparatus criticus* and Addenda, p. 485.

TABLE OF ABBREVIATIONS, ETC., USED IN THE *APPARATUS CRITICUS* AND NOTES

W. or W. W. William Wordsworth.

D. W. Dorothy Wordsworth.

Dora W. Dora Wordsworth.

M. H. or M. W. Mary Wordsworth.

G. G. W. George Gordon Wordsworth, grandson of the poet.

S. H. Sara Hutchinson.

H. C. R. Henry Crabb Robinson.

M. Memoirs of W. W., by Christopher Wordsworth.

E.L. The Early Letters of W. W. and D. W. Oxford, 1935.

M.Y. The Letters of W. W. and D. W. Middle Years (1806–20), 2 vols. Oxford, 1937.

L.Y. The Letters of W. W. and D. W. Later Years (1821–50), 3 vols. Oxford, 1939.

C.R. The Correspondence of Henry Crabb Robinson with the Wordsworth Circle, ed. Edith J. Morley, 1927.

I. F. The notes indicated by W. W. to Isabella Fenwick in 1843.

W. Notes by Wordsworth in the printed editions.

O.E.D. The Oxford English Dictionary.

1815, 1820, first and second editions of *The Excursion*.

1820, 1827, &c. Collective editions of W. W.'s *Poetical Works* in which *The Excursion* was included.

Prel., E. de S. *The Prelude*, edited from the manuscripts by Ernest de Selincourt, 1932.

Prel. 1805, the text printed by E. de S. in the above volume.

K. Professor William Knight, editor of W. W.'s *Poetical Works*, 8 vols. 1896.

Dowden. Professor Edward Dowden, editor of W. W.'s *Poetical Works*, 7 vols. 1892–3.

Hutchinson. Mr. Thomas Hutchinson, editor of the Oxford Wordsworth, the *Lyrical Ballads* (1798), 1898, and the *Poems in Two Volumes* (1807), 1897.

Griggs. Collected Letters of S. T. Coleridge, edited by Earl Leslie Griggs, 2 vols. 1956.

C. A copy of W. W.'s *Poetical Works*, 1836–7, now in the Royal Library at Windsor, formerly in the possession of Lord Coleridge, used by W. for correction and re-drafting of his text.

Q. A copy of *The Excursion*, 1814, first issue, with leaves afterwards cancelled, and manuscript corrections, presented by John Wordsworth, grandson of the poet, to the library of Queen's College, Oxford.

Manuscripts in Dove Cottage

Alf. MS. A note-book used by W. at Alfoxden between 20 Jan. and 5 March 1798, *v. Prel.*, E. de S., p. xxi.

Christabel MS. A note-book used by D. W. to copy poems, and by W. for composition and fair copies: thè first entries 1797–8, the last 1800.

MS. 18A. A similar note-book of D. W.'s containing many of the same poems, and also a version of *The Ruined Cottage*, MS. D, *v.* p. 404 *infra.*

MS. 1800. MS. B of *Recluse*, *v.* p. 475 *infra.*

MSS. X and Y. Manuscripts containing portions of *Prelude* and *Excursion*, *v. Prel.*, E. de S., pp. xxiii, xxiv.

MS. R. A copy of Coleridge's *Poems*, 1796, containing rough drafts by W. (opposite to *Religious Musings*) of passages afterwards incorporated in *The Recluse* and *The Excursion.*

MS. M. A manuscript of Poems, probably transcribed in March 1804, containing a draft of *The Ruined Cottage* (*Excursion*, Book I), *v. Prel.*, E. de S., p. xx.

MS. P. A small note-book containing fair copy of *Exc.* I, II, part of III, and a rough draft of the rest.

MS. 58. A small note-book containing rough drafts of most of *Exc.* IV, and some of II and V.

MS. 60. A note-book containing drafts of passages for *Exc.* III, IV, VI, and IX.

MS. 61. A note-book containing a fair copy of *Exc.* V and rough drafts of passages from V, VI, VII, VIII, and IX.

MS. 62. A manuscript containing drafts of stray passages from V, VI, VII, VIII, and IX.

T. of P. *The Tuft of Primroses v.* Appendix C and note p. 482.

MS. 1, MS. 2, &c., in *Apparatus Criticus* indicate variants from first draft, second draft, &c., of the particular manuscript text.

[ ] indicates a word or words missing from the manuscript.

Words enclosed in [ ] represent a reading from another manuscript or printed text: words enclosed in ( ) a reading from the same manuscript.

17/18 lines found in a manuscript or printed text between line 17 and line 18.

CONTENTS

THE EXCURSION[1]

TO THE RIGHT HONOURABLE
WILLIAM, EARL OF LONSDALE, K.G.,

ETC., ETC.

OFT, through thy fair domains, illustrious Peer!
In youth I roamed, on youthful pleasures bent;
And mused in rocky cell or sylvan tent,
Beside swift-flowing Lowther's current clear.
—Now, by thy care befriended, I appear
Before thee, LONSDALE, and this Work present,
A token (may it prove a monument!)
Of high respect and gratitude sincere.
Gladly would I have waited till my task
Had reached its close; but Life is insecure,
And Hope full oft fallacious as a dream:
Therefore, for what is here produced, I ask
Thy favour; trusting that thou wilt not deem
The offering, though imperfect, premature.

WILLIAM WORDSWORTH.

RYDAL MOUNT, WESTMORELAND,
July 29, 1814.

PREFACE TO THE EDITION OF 1814

THE Title-page announces that this is only a portion of a poem; and
the Reader must be here apprised that it belongs to the second part
of a long and laborious Work, which is to consist of three parts.—
The Author will candidly acknowledge that, if the first of these had
been completed, and in such a manner as to satisfy his own mind, he
should have preferred the natural order of publication, and have
given that to the world first; but, as the second division of the Work
was designed to refer more to passing events, and to an existing state
of things, than the others were meant to do, more continuous exertion
was naturally bestowed upon it, and greater progress made here than
in the rest of the poem; and as this part does not depend upon the
preceding, to a degree which will materially injure its own peculiar
interest, the Author, complying with the earnest entreaties of some
valued Friends, presents the following pages to the Public.

It may be proper to state whence the poem, of which The Excursion
is a part, derives its Title of THE RECLUSE.—Several years ago, when
the Author retired to his native mountains, with the hope of being

---

[1] THE EXCURSION] 1814 *adds* BEING A PORTION OF THE RECLUSE,
A Poem. so 1820–32

enabled to construct a literary Work that might live, it was a reasonable thing that he should take a review of his own mind, and examine how far Nature and Education had qualified him for such employment. As subsidiary to this preparation, he undertook to record, in verse, the origin and progress of his own powers, as far as he was acquainted with them. That Work, addressed to a dear Friend, most distinguished for his knowledge and genius, and to whom the Author's Intellect is deeply indebted, has been long finished; and the result of the investigation which gave rise to it was a determination to compose a philosophical poem, containing views of Man, Nature, and Society; and to be entitled, The Recluse; as having for its principal subject the sensations and opinions of a poet living in retirement.—The preparatory poem is biographical, and conducts the history of the Author's mind to the point when he was emboldened to hope that his faculties were sufficiently matured for entering upon the arduous labour which he had proposed to himself; and the two Works have the same kind of relation to each other, if he may so express himself, as the ante-chapel has to the body of a gothic church. Continuing this allusion, he may be permitted to add, that his minor Pieces, which have been long before the Public, when they shall be properly arranged, will be found by the attentive Reader to have such connection with the main Work as may give them claim to be likened to the little cells, oratories, and sepulchral recesses, ordinarily included in those edifices.

The Author would not have deemed himself justified in saying, upon this occasion, so much of performances either unfinished, or unpublished, if he had not thought that the labour bestowed by him upon what he has heretofore and now laid before the Public, entitled him to candid attention for such a statement as he thinks necessary to throw light upon his endeavours to please and, he would hope, to benefit his countrymen.—Nothing further need be added, than that the first and third parts of The Recluse will consist chiefly of meditations in the Author's own person; and that in the intermediate part (The Excursion) the intervention of characters speaking is employed, and something of a dramatic form adopted.

It is not the Author's intention formally to announce a system: it was more animating to him to proceed in a different course; and if he shall succeed in conveying to the mind clear thoughts, lively images, and strong feelings, the Reader will have no difficulty in extracting the system for himself. And in the meantime the following passage, taken from the conclusion of the first book of The Recluse, may be acceptable as a kind of *Prospectus* of the design and scope of the whole Poem.

"On Man, on Nature, and on Human Life,
Musing in solitude, I oft perceive
Fair trains of imagery before me rise,
Accompanied by feelings of delight
Pure, or with no unpleasing sadness mixed ;   5
And I am conscious of affecting thoughts
And dear remembrances, whose presence soothes
Or elevates the Mind, intent to weigh
The good and evil of our mortal state.
—To these emotions, whencesoe'er they come,   10
Whether from breath of outward circumstance,
Or from the Soul—an impulse to herself—
I would give utterance in numerous verse.
Of Truth, of Grandeur, Beauty, Love, and Hope,
And melancholy Fear subdued by Faith ;   15
Of blessèd consolations in distress ;
Of moral strength, and intellectual Power ;
Of joy in widest commonalty spread ;
Of the individual Mind that keeps her own
Inviolate retirement, subject there   20
To Conscience only, and the law supreme
Of that Intelligence which governs all—
I sing :—'fit audience let me find though few !'

"So prayed, more gaining than he asked, the Bard—
In holiest mood. Urania, I shall need   25
Thy guidance, or a greater Muse,. if such
Descend to earth or dwell in highest heaven !
For I must tread on shadowy ground, must sink
Deep—and, aloft ascending, breathe in worlds
To which the heaven of heavens is but a veil.   30
All strength—all terror, single or in bands,
That ever was put forth in personal form—

2–13 Thinking in solitude, from time to time
     I find sweet passions traversing my soul
     Like music : unto these where'er I may
     I would give etc.   MS. 1 : so MS. 2 corr. but (2, 3) I often feel Delightful
     passions
14/15 Hope for this earth, and hope beyond the grave   MS. 2   15–17
not in MS. 1   15 not in MS. 2   17 Of virtue and of   MS. 2   18
widest] various   MS. 1
20–2   and consists
     With being limitless, the one great Life   MSS. 1, 2
24–5 Fit audience find though few ! Thus pray'd the Bard,
     Holiest of Men   MSS. 1, 2 : 1814 as text, but Holiest of Men
29 Deep, and ascend aloft, and [   ] worlds   MS. 1   32 by per-
sonal Form   MS. 1 : in personal forms   MS. 2

Jehovah—with his thunder, and the choir
Of shouting Angels, and the empyreal thrones—
I pass them unalarmed. Not Chaos, not   35
The darkest pit of lowest Erebus,
Nor aught of blinder vacancy, scooped out
By help of dreams—can breed such fear and awe
As fall upon us often when we look
Into our Minds, into the Mind of Man—   40
My haunt, and the main region of my song.
—Beauty—a living Presence of the earth,
Surpassing the most fair ideal Forms
Which craft of delicate Spirits hath composed
From earth's materials—waits upon my steps;   45
Pitches her tents before me as I move,
An hourly neighbour. Paradise, and groves
Elysian, Fortunate Fields—like those of old
Sought in the Atlantic Main—why should they be
A history only of departed things,   50
Or a mere fiction of what never was ?
For the discerning intellect of Man,
When wedded to this goodly universe
In love and holy passion, shall find these
A simple produce of the common day.   55
—I, long before the blissful hour arrives,
Would chant, in lonely peace, the spousal verse

35–6   The darkest pit
    Of the profoundest Hell, night, chaos, death   MS. 1
39 Us . . . we] me . . . I   MS. 1   40 Into my soul, into the soul of man
MS. 1
42–4 Beauty, whose living home is the green earth
    Surpassing far what hath by special craft
    Of delicate Poets, been call'd forth, and shap'd   MS. 1
47 An] My   MS. 1
48–76 Elysian, blessed island[s] in the deep
    Of choice seclusion, wherefore need they be
    A history, or but a dream when minds
    Once wedded to this outward frame of things
    In love, find these the growth of common day.
    Such pleasant haunts foregoing if my Song
    Must turn elsewhere and travel near the tribes
    And Fellowships of men, and see ill sights
    Of passions ravenous from each other's rage,
    Insult and injury and wrong and strife
    Must hear etc.   MS. 1
48–9 Elysian, fortunate fields, islands like those
    In the deep Ocean, wherefore   MS. 2
50–5 MS. 2 as MS. 1   56 MS. 2 as text but blessed   57 Would sing
in solitude   MS. 2

Of this great consummation:—and, by words
Which speak of nothing more than what we are,
Would I arouse the sensual from their sleep   60
Of Death, and win the vacant and the vain
To noble raptures; while my voice proclaims
How exquisitely the individual Mind
(And the progressive powers perhaps no less
Of the whole species) to the external World   65
Is fitted:—and how exquisitely, too—
Theme this but little heard of among men—
The external World is fitted to the Mind;
And the creation (by no lower name
Can it be called) which they with blended might   70
Accomplish:—this is our high argument.
—Such grateful haunts foregoing, if I oft
Must turn elsewhere—to travel near the tribes
And fellowships of men, and see ill sights
Of madding passions mutually inflamed;   75
Must hear Humanity in fields and groves
Pipe solitary anguish; or must hang
Brooding above the fierce confederate storm
Of sorrow, barricadoed evermore
Within the walls of cities—may these sounds   80
Have their authentic comment; that even these
Hearing, I be not downcast or forlorn!—
Descend, prophetic Spirit! that inspir'st
The human Soul of universal earth,
Dreaming on things to come; and dost possess   85
A metropolitan temple in the hearts
Of mighty Poets: upon me bestow

58–63   would proclaim
    Speaking of nothing more than what we are
    How exquisitely *etc.* MS. 2
64–76 MS. 2 *as text but* 71 my great *for* our high, *and* 75 *as* MS. 1 *v. app.*
crit. 48–76
80–6   to these sounds
    Let me find meaning more akin to that
    Which to God's ear they carry, that even these
    Hearing, I be not heartless or forlorn.
    Come thou, prophetic Spirit, soul of Man
    Thou human Soul of the wide earth, that hast
    Thy metropolitan *etc.* MS. 1: *so* MS. 2 *but* May these sounds . . .
Hearing *as text*
83 Descend] Come thou 1814
87–94   unto me vouchsafe
    Thy foresight, teach me to discern and part
    Inherent things from casual, what is fix'd

A gift of genuine insight; that my Song
With star-like virtue in its place may shine,
Shedding benignant influence, and secure,   90
Itself, from all malevolent effect
Of those mutations that extend their sway
Throughout the nether sphere!—And if with this
I mix more lowly matter; with the thing
Contemplated, describe the Mind and Man   95
Contemplating; and who, and what he was—
The transitory Being that beheld
This Vision; when and where, and how he lived;—
Be not this labour useless. If such theme
May sort with highest objects, then—dread Power!   100
Whose gracious favour is the primal source
Of all illumination,—may my Life
Express the image of a better time,
More wise desires, and simpler manners;—nurse
My Heart in genuine freedom:—all pure thoughts   105
Be with me;—so shall thy unfailing love
Guide, and support, and cheer me to the end!"

From fleeting, that my song may live, and be
Even as a light hung up in heaven to chear
The world in times to come. And if with this
I mingle humbler matter *etc.* MS. 1: *so* MSS. 2, 3 *but* guidance
(*corr. to* succour MS. 2) *for* foresight, verse *for* song, Mankind *for* The world,
and blend more lowly *for* mingle humbler
88–93   that the body of my verse
        By the mutations of the world untouch'd
        And by its ferments undisturbed may shine
        Even as a light hung up in heaven *etc.* MS. 2 *alt. draft*
98/9 With all his little realties of life   MSS. 1, 2, 3
        In part a Fellow-citizen, in part
        An outlaw, and a Borderer of his age   MS. 1
99–107   O great God,
        To less than thee I cannot make this prayer.
        Innocent mighty Spirit let my life
        Express *etc.*
        Desires more wise *etc.*
        My heart *etc.*
        Be with me and uphold me to the end   MS. 1
 100–2 With highest things may [   ] then great God
        Thou who art breath and being, way and guide
        And power, and understanding, may my life   MS. 2: *so* MS. 3 *but*
101   Almighty being who art light and law.
106–7 MS. 2 as MS. 1

THE EXCURSION
BOOK FIRST
THE WANDERER
ARGUMENT

A summer forenoon.—The Author reaches a ruined Cottage upon a
Common, and there meets with a revered Friend, the Wanderer, of whose
education and course of life he gives an account.[1]—The Wanderer, while
resting under the shade of the Trees that surround the Cottage, relates the
History of its last Inhabitant.

'Twas summer, and the sun had mounted high:
Southward the landscape indistinctly glared
Through a pale steam; but all the northern downs,
In clearest air ascending, showed far off
A surface dappled o'er with shadows flung   5
From brooding clouds; shadows that lay in spots
Determined and unmoved, with steady beams
Of bright and pleasant sunshine interposed;
To him most pleasant who on soft cool moss
Extends his careless limbs along the front   10
Of some huge cave, whose rocky ceiling casts
A twilight of its own, an ample shade,

[1] *so* 1837: The Wanderer, of whom he gives an account— 1814–32
    For MSS. B, D *v.* pp. 378–409 *infra*

2–30 Travelling on foot and distant from my home
Several days' journey, over the flat Plain
Of a bare Common, I had toil'd along
With languid steps, and when I stretch'd myself
On the brown earth, my limbs from very heat
Could find no rest, nor my weak arm disperse
The host of insects gathering round my face.
The time was hot, the place was shelterless;
And, rising, right across the open Plain
On to the spot I hasten'd, whither I
Was bound that morning, a small group of Trees
Which midway on the Common stood alone.
I made no second stop, and soon I reach'd
The port that lay before me full in view.
It was a knot of clustering Elms that sprang
As if from the same root, beneath whose shade
I found a Ruin'd House   MS. E
6 *so* 1827: From many a brooding cloud; far as the sight
        Could reach, those many shadows lay in spots   1814–20
9 *so* 1845: Pleasant to him who on the soft cool moss   1814–43

Where the wren warbles, while the dreaming man,
Half conscious of the soothing melody,
With side-long eye looks out upon the scene,   15
By power of that impending covert thrown
To finer distance. Mine was at that hour
Far other lot, yet with good hope that soon
Under a shade as grateful I should find
Rest, and be welcomed there to livelier joy.   20
Across a bare wide Common I was toiling
With languid steps that by the slippery turf
Were baffled; nor could my weak arm disperse
The host of insects gathering round my face,
And ever with me as I paced along.   25

Upon that open moorland stood a grove,
The wished-for port to which my course was bound.
Thither I came, and there, amid the gloom
Spread by a brotherhood of lofty elms,
Appeared a roofless Hut; four naked walls   30
That stared upon each other!—I looked round,
And to my wish and to my hope espied
The Friend I sought; a Man of reverend age,
But stout and hale, for travel unimpaired.
There was he seen upon the cottage-bench,   35
Recumbent in the shade, as if asleep;
An iron-pointed staff lay at his side.

Him had I marked the day before—alone
And stationed in the public way, with face

16–17 *so* 1827: By that impending covert made more soft,
            More low and distant! MS. P, 1814–20
17–20 *so* 1845:   Other lot was mine
            Yet with good hope that soon I should obtain
            As grateful resting-place, and livelier joy MS. P, 1814–43
22 steps that 1827: feet, which 1814–20; turf 1845: ground 1814–43
25–7   paced along,
      Now with eyes turn'd tow'rds the far distant hills
      Now toward a grove that from the wide-spread moor
      Rose up, the port C
26 moorland 1845: level 1814–43   27 course was 1827: steps were
1814–20   33 The Friend 1845: Him whom 1814–43
38–41 *so* 1827: And in the middle of the public way
            Stationed, as if to rest himself, with face
            Turned tow'rds the sun then setting, while that staff

Turned toward the sun then setting, while that staff   40
Afforded, to the figure of the man
Detained for contemplation or repose,
Graceful support; his countenance as he stood
Was hidden from my view, and he remained
Unrecognised; but, stricken by the sight,   45
With slackened footsteps I advanced, and soon
A glad congratulation we exchanged
At such unthought-of meeting.—For the night
We parted, nothing willingly; and now
He by appointment waited for me here,   50
Under the covert of these clustering elms.

We were tried Friends: amid a pleasant vale,
In the antique market-village where was passed
My school-time, an apartment he had owned,
To which at intervals the Wanderer drew,   55
And found a kind of home or harbour there.
He loved me; from a swarm of rosy boys
Singled out me, as he in sport would say,

Afforded to his Figure, as he stood,   1814–20; MS. E *as*
B *ll.* 42–7; P 38–9 *as* 1814, 40–1 *as* B
            Him had I chanc'd to see the day before
            Standing alone in the open public way
            [   ] as a statue, motionless,
            Westward he looked as if his eyes were fixed
            Upon the Sun   C
40 toward   1832: tow'rd   1827: tow'rds   1814–20
42–7 With slacker pace towards him I advanced
      Half wondering who the Man might be, but soon
      As I came up to him, great joy was ours   MS. E
43 *so* 1845: the countenance of the Man   1814–20: his countenance mean-
while   1827–43   47 P *as* E *corr. to text*
51 *so* 1845: Beneath the shelter   1814–43
            Beneath these Elms, we having both a wish
            To travel on together a few days   MS. E
            To turn to profit this good hap, and be
            Companions to each other a few days   MS. E²
52–5 *so* 1845; *so* 1827–43, *but* were passed My school-days:
            We were tried Friends: I from my Childhood up
            Had known him.—In a little Town obscure,
            A market-village, seated in a tract
            Of mountains, where my school-day time was pass'd,
            One room he owned, the fifth part of a house,
            A place to which he drew, from time to time,   1814–20: MS. E
as Addendum IV *to* D (*q.v.*)

For my grave looks, too thoughtful for my years.
As I grew up, it was my best delight   60
To be his chosen comrade. Many a time,
On holidays, we rambled through the woods:
We sate—we walked; he pleased me with report
Of things which he had seen; and often touched
Abstrusest matter, reasonings of the mind   65
Turned inward; or at my request would sing
Old songs, the product of his native hills;
A skilful distribution of sweet sounds,
Feeding the soul, and eagerly imbibed
As cool refreshing water, by the care   70
Of the industrious husbandman, diffused
Through a parched meadow-ground, in time of drought.
Still deeper welcome found his pure discourse:
How precious when in riper days I learned
To weigh with care his words, and to rejoice   75
In the plain presence of his dignity!

Oh! many are the Poets that are sown
By Nature; men endowed with highest gifts,
The vision and the faculty divine;
Yet wanting the accomplishment of verse,   80
(Which, in the docile season of their youth,
It was denied them to acquire, through lack
Of culture and the inspiring aid of books,
Or haply by a temper too severe,
Or a nice backwardness afraid of shame)   85

62–3 *so* 1827:   we wander'd through the woods,
          A pair of random travellers; we sate—
          We walked; he pleas'd me with his sweet discourse   1814–20
66–72   or, in other mood, he sang
     Old songs, and sometimes, too, at my request
     Psalms and religious anthems, sounds sedate
     And soft, and most refreshing to the heart   MS. E: *so* E² and M *but*
                              at my request
     More solemn music which he in his youth
     Had learn'd, religious anthems *etc.*
67 the product of] brought with him from   C
77–89 *This passage first introduced in* MS. E² *but for ll.* 81–9:
          And never being led by accident
          Or circumstance to take unto the height
          (By estimate comparative at least)
          The measure of themselves, live out their time,

Nor having e'er, as life advanced, been led
By circumstance to take unto the height
The measure of themselves, these favoured Beings,
All but a scattered few, live out their time,
Husbanding that which they possess within,				90
And go to the grave, unthought of. Strongest minds
Are often those of whom the noisy world
Hears least; else surely this Man had not left
His graces unrevealed and unproclaimed.
But, as the mind was filled with inward light,				95
So not without distinction had he lived,
Beloved and honoured—far as he was known.
And some small portion of his eloquent speech,
And something that may serve to set in view
The feeling pleasures of his loneliness,				100
His observations, and the thoughts his mind
Had dealt with—I will here record in verse;
Which, if with truth it correspond, and sink
Or rise as venerable Nature leads,
The high and tender Muses shall accept				105
With gracious smile, deliberately pleased,
And listening Time reward with sacred praise.

Among the hills of Athol he was born;
Where, on a small hereditary farm,
An unproductive slip of rugged ground,				110
His Parents, with their numerous offspring, dwelt;

93/4 And sundry others, too, whom I have known   MSS. E², M: Nor
others of like mold *etc.*   MS. P
95–102 Though born in low estate, and earning bread
		By a low calling yet this very Man [mild good man P]
		Was as [Rank'd with P] the prime and choice of sterling minds.
		I honour'd him, respected, nay revered
		And some small portion of his eloquent words [speech P]
		And something that may serve to set in view
		The feeling pleasures of his loneliness
		The doings, observations which his life [mind P]
		Had dealt with, I will here record in verse MSS. M, P
99 *not in* M, P		103 *so* P: *not in* M
108 Athol] Perthshire MSS. E, M, *and* C		109–10 *not in* MSS. E, M
109 Where,   1827: There,   MS. P, 1814–20
111 *so* 1827: His Father dwelt; and died in poverty;
		While He, whose lowly fortune I retrace,
		The youngest of three sons, was yet a Babe,
		A little One—unconscious of their loss.

A virtuous household, though exceeding poor!
Pure livers were they all, austere and grave,
And fearing God; the very children taught
Stern self-respect, a reverence for God's word,   115
And an habitual piety, maintained
With strictness scarcely known on English ground.

From his sixth year, the Boy of whom I speak,
In summer, tended cattle on the hills;
But, through the inclement and the perilous days   120
Of long-continuing winter, he repaired,
Equipped with satchel, to a school, that stood
Sole building on a mountain's dreary edge,
Remote from view of city spire, or sound
Of minster clock! From that bleak tenement   125
He, many an evening, to his distant home
In solitude returning, saw the hills
Grow larger in the darkness; all alone
Beheld the stars come out above his head,
And travelled through the wood, with no one near   130
To whom he might confess the things he saw.

So the foundations of his mind were laid.
In such communion, not from terror free,
While yet a child, and long before his time,
Had he perceived the presence and the power   135
Of greatness; and deep feelings had impressed
So vividly great objects that they lay

But ere he had outgrown his infant days
His widowed Mother, for a second Mate,
Espoused the Teacher of the Village School;
Who on her offspring zealously bestowed
Needful instruction; not alone in arts
Which to his humble duties appertained,
But in the lore of right and [or P] wrong, the rule
Of human kindness, in the peaceful ways
Of honesty, and holiness severe.   MS. P, 1814–20
116–17 And piety scarce known on English Land   MS. P   120–1 But
in the winter time he duly went   MSS. E–P   122 *so* 1827: To his
Step-father's School, that stood alone,   MSS. E–P 1814–20
137–9 *so* 1845: Great objects on his mind, with portraiture
          And colour so distinct, that on his mind
          They lay like substances, and almost seemed
          To haunt the bodily sense. He had received

Upon his mind like substances, whose presence
Perplexed the bodily sense.   He had received
A precious gift; for, as he grew in years,   140
With these impressions would he still compare
All his remembrances, thoughts, shapes, and forms;
And, being still unsatisfied with aught
Of dimmer character, he thence attained
An active power to fasten images   145
Upon his brain; and on their pictured lines
Intensely brooded, even till they acquired
The liveliness of dreams.   Nor did he fail,
While yet a child, with a child's eagerness
Incessantly to turn his ear and eye   150
On all things which the moving seasons brought
To feed such appetite—nor this alone
Appeased his yearning:—in the after-day
Of boyhood, many an hour in caves forlorn,
And 'mid the hollow depths of naked crags   155
He sate, and even in their fixed lineaments,
Or from the power of a peculiar eye,
Or by creative feeling overborne,
Or by predominance of thought oppressed,
Even in their fixed and steady lineaments   160
He traced an ebbing and a flowing mind,
Expression ever varying!
                           Thus informed,
He had small need of books; for many a tale
Traditionary, round the mountains hung,
And many a legend, peopling the dark woods,   165
Nourished Imagination in her growth,
And gave the Mind that apprehensive power
By which she is made quick to recognise
The moral properties and scope of things.
But eagerly he read, and read again,   170

(Vigorous in native genius as he was).   (Vigorous in mind
by nature.   MSS. E, M)   MSS. E, M 1814–20: *so* 1827–43, *but omitting last*
line:
      Upon his mind great objects so distinct
      In portraiture (lineament), in colouring so vivid
      That on his mind they lay like substances
      And almost indistinguishably mixed
      With things of bodily sense.   C
142 *so* MSS. E², M, P: All his ideal stores, his shapes and forms   MS. E

Whate'er the minister's old shelf supplied;
The life and death of martyrs, who sustained,
With will inflexible, those fearful pangs
Triumphantly displayed in records left
Of persecution, and the Covenant—times   175
Whose echo rings through Scotland to this hour!
And there, by lucky hap, had been preserved
A straggling volume, torn and incomplete,
That left half-told the preternatural tale,
Romance of giants, chronicle of fiends,   180
Profuse in garniture of wooden cuts
Strange and uncouth; dire faces, figures dire,
Sharp-kneed, sharp-elbowed, and lean-ankled too,
With long and ghostly shanks—forms which once seen
Could never be forgotten!
                    In his heart,   185
Where Fear sate thus, a cherished visitant,
Was wanting yet the pure delight of love
By sound diffused, or by the breathing air,
Or by the silent looks of happy things,
Or flowing from the universal face   190
Of earth and sky. But he had felt the power
Of Nature, and already was prepared,
By his intense conceptions, to receive
Deeply the lesson deep of love which he,
Whom Nature, by whatever means, has taught   195
To feel intensely, cannot but receive.

    Such was the Boy—but for the growing Youth
What soul was his, when, from the naked top

173-7 Intolerable pangs, and here and there   MS. E
      Intolerable pangs, the cruel time
      Of superstition and the Covenant
      That like an echo *etc.*   E²
      Intolerable pangs, the Records left
      Of Persecution and the Covenant, times
      That like an echo ring through Scotland still.
            Nor haply was there wanting, here and there   MSS. M, P, *but* P   176
as text
186 *not in* MSS. E, M   187 Love was not yet, nor the pure joy of
love   MSS. E, M:
            A milder Spirit yet had found no place.
            Love yet was wanting, the pure joy of love   MS. P
197-9 *so* 1827: From early childhood, even, as hath been said,
      From his sixth year, he had been sent abroad

Of some bold headland, he beheld the sun
Rise up, and bathe the world in light! He looked—　　200
Ocean and earth, the solid frame of earth
And ocean's liquid mass, in gladness lay
Beneath him:—Far and wide the clouds were touched,
And in their silent faces could he read
Unutterable love. Sound needed none,　　205
Nor any voice of joy; his spirit drank
The spectacle: sensation, soul, and form,
All melted into him; they swallowed up
His animal being; in them did he live,
And by them did he live; they were his life.　　210
In such access of mind, in such high hour
Of visitation from the living God,
Thought was not; in enjoyment it expired.
No thanks he breathed, he proffered no request;
Rapt into still communion that transcends　　215
The imperfect offices of prayer and praise,
His mind was a thanksgiving to the power
That made him; it was blessedness and love!

A Herdsman on the lonely mountain-tops,
Such intercourse was his, and in this sort　　220
Was his existence oftentimes _possessed_.
O then how beautiful, how bright, appeared
The written promise! Early had he learned
To reverence the volume that displays
The mystery, the life which cannot die;　　225
But in the mountains did he _feel_ his faith.
All things, responsive to the writing, there

　　　　　In summer to tend herds: such was his task
　　　　　Thenceforward 'till the later day of youth.
　　　　　O then what soul was his, when, on the tops
　　　　　Of the high mountains, he beheld the sun.　1814–20: _so_
MSS. E–P, _but in first line_ as I have said
201–3 The ocean and the earth beneath him lay
　　　　　In gladness and deep joy. The clouds were touched　MSS. E–P
202–3 _so_ 1845: . . . mass, beneath him lay _etc. as_ MSS., 1814–43
214–16 _so_ MS. P: Such hour by prayer or praise was unprofan'd
　　　　　　　　He neither pray'd nor offer'd thanks or praise,　MS. E,
_so_ E² _and_ M, _but omitting second line_
223 _so_ 1827 He had early learned　MSS., 1814–20
227 _so_ 1832: There did he see the writing;—all things there　MSS.
1814–20: Responsive to the writing, all things there　1827

Breathed immortality, revolving life,
And greatness still revolving; infinite:
There littleness was not; the least of things   230
Seemed infinite; and there his spirit shaped
Her prospects, nor did he believe,—he *saw*.
What wonder if his being thus became
Sublime and comprehensive! Low desires,
Low thoughts had there no place; yet was his heart   235
Lowly; for he was meek in gratitude,
Oft as he called those ecstasies to mind,
And whence they flowed; and from them he acquired
Wisdom, which works thro' patience; thence he learned
In oft-recurring hours of sober thought   240
To look on Nature with a humble heart,
Self-questioned where it did not understand,
And with a superstitious eye of love.

So passed the time; yet to the nearest town
He duly went with what small overplus   245
His earnings might supply, and brought away
The book that most had tempted his desires
While at the stall he read. Among the hills
He gazed upon that mighty orb of song,
The divine Milton. Lore of different kind,   250
The annual savings of a toilsome life,
His Schoolmaster supplied; books that explain
The purer elements of truth involved
In lines and numbers, and, by charm severe,
(Especially perceived where nature droops   255
And feeling is suppressed) preserve the mind
Busy in solitude and poverty.
These occupations oftentimes deceived
The listless hours, while in the hollow vale,
Hollow and green, he lay on the green turf   260
In pensive idleness. What could he do,
Thus daily thirsting, in that lonesome life,

240 *so* 1827: In many a calmer hour MSS., 1814–20   244 the nearest
1827: a [the MSS.] neighbouring MSS., 1814–20   247 tempted
MS. M: waken'd MS. E   252 Schoolmaster 1827: Step-father MSS.,
1814–20   258 And thus employ'd he many a time o'erlook'd MSS.
262–3 *so* 1827: The weight of genius was upon his mind *del.* MS. E²
With blind endeavours, in that lonesome life,
Thus thirsting daily? MSS. M, P, 1814–20

With blind endeavours? Yet, still uppermost,
Nature was at his heart as if he felt,
Though yet he knew not how, a wasting power   265
In all things that from her sweet influence
Might tend to wean him. Therefore with her hues,
Her forms, and with the spirit of her forms,
He clothed the nakedness of austere truth.
While yet he lingered in the rudiments   270
Of science, and among her simplest laws,
His triangles—they were the stars of heaven,
The silent stars! Oft did he take delight
To measure the altitude of some tall crag
That is the eagle's birthplace, or some peak   275
Familiar with forgotten years, that shows
Inscribed upon its visionary sides,
The history of many a winter storm,
Or obscure records of the path of fire.

And thus before his eighteenth year was told,   280
Accumulated feelings pressed his heart
With still increasing weight; he was o'erpowered
By Nature; by the turbulence subdued
Of his own mind; by mystery and hope,
And the first virgin passion of a soul   285
Communing with the glorious universe.
Full often wished he that the winds might rage
When they were silent: far more fondly now
Than in his earlier season did he love
Tempestuous nights—the conflict and the sounds   290
That live in darkness. From his intellect
And from the stillness of abstracted thought

264 as if he felt MS. M: and he perceived MS. E   270 rudiments]
elements MSS.
277 so 1845: Inscribed, as with the silence of the thought,
                Upon its bleak and visionary sides, MSS., 1814–43
                Inscribed, for [intercourse ?] with speechless thought C
278–9   of widespread ruin wrought
            By torrent, tempest or departing frost
        Or obscure etc. C
280 told] gone MSS.   280–300 not in MS. E   280–340 v. MS. D:
Addendum v. p. 405 infra.   282 still 1827: an 1814–20   283 By
his own nature, by the turbulence MSS.   284 mind] heart MSS.
285 soul] mind MSS.

He asked repose; and, failing oft to win
The peace required, he scanned the laws of light
Amid the roar of torrents, where they send   295
From hollow clefts up to the clearer air
A cloud of mist, that smitten by the sun
Varies its rainbow hues. But vainly thus,
And vainly by all other means, he strove
To mitigate the fever of his heart.   300

In dreams, in study, and in ardent thought,
Thus was he reared; much wanting to assist
The growth of intellect, yet gaining more,
And every moral feeling of his soul
Strengthened and braced, by breathing in content   305
The keen, the wholesome, air of poverty,
And drinking from the well of homely life.
—But, from past liberty, and tried restraints,
He now was summoned to select the course
Of humble industry that promised best   310
To yield him no unworthy maintenance.
Urged by his Mother, he essayed to teach

293 *so* 1827: He asked repose; and I have heard him say
            That often, failing at this time to gain   1814–20
293–4 He sought repose in vain: I have heard him say
            That at this time he   MSS. E², M, P
297–8 *so* 1827: which in the shining sun *etc.*   MSS. E², M, P:
                        which in the sunshine frames
                        A lasting tablet—for the observer's eye
                        Varying *etc.* 1814–20
302–3 *so* 1827: Thus, even from childhood upward, was he reared;
                        For intellectual progress wanting much,
                        Doubtless, of needful help—yet gaining more, 1814–20
302 *not in* MS. E: *in* MSS. E², M, P *as* 1814
303–6 He wanting much, perhaps (E) Doubtless in want of much, yet
            gaining more
            Breathing a piercing air of poverty   MSS.
308–11 And now growing up (E) brought near [drawing near   M] to man-
            hood he began
            To think about his future life (E) years (M) [life's future course   P]
            and how
            He best might earn his worldly maintenance   MSS.
312–14 *so* 1827: The Mother strove to make her Son perceive
                        With what advantage he might teach a School
                        In the adjoining Village; but the Youth,
                        Who of this service made a short essay,
                        Found that the wanderings of his thought were then
                        A misery to him; that he must resign   MSS., 1814–20

A village-school—but wandering thoughts were then
A misery to him; and the Youth resigned
A task he was unable to perform.   315

That stern yet kindly Spirit, who constrains
The Savoyard to quit his naked rocks,
The freeborn Swiss to leave his narrow vales,
(Spirit attached to regions mountainous
Like their own stedfast clouds) did now impel   320
His restless mind to look abroad with hope.
—An irksome drudgery seems it to plod on,
Through hot and dusty ways, or pelting storm,
A vagrant Merchant under a heavy load
Bent as he moves, and needing frequent rest;   325
Yet do such travellers find their own delight;
And their hard service, deemed debasing now,
Gained merited respect in simpler times;
When squire, and priest, and they who round them dwelt
In rustic sequestration—all dependent   330
Upon the PEDLAR's toil—supplied their wants,
Or pleased their fancies, with the wares he brought.
Not ignorant was the Youth that still no few
Of his adventurous countrymen were led
By perseverance in this track of life   335
To competence and ease:—to him it offered
Attractions manifold;—and this he chose.
—His Parents on the enterprise bestowed

316–37 He had a Brother elder than himself
        Six years, who long before, had left his home
        To journey up and down with Pedlar's wares
        In England where he traffick'd at that time,
        Healthy and prosperous. "What should hinder now,"
        Said he within himself, "but that I go
        And toil in the same calling?" And, in truth,
        This plan, long time had been his favorite thought   MSS. E–P
(cf. D. Add. V)
323 so 1827: Through dusty ways, in storm, from door to door,   1814–20
324 under a heavy 1837: bent beneath his 1814–32́   325 not in
1814–20
338–9 so 1827: He asked his Mother's blessing; he with tears
        Thank'd the good Man, his second Father, ask'd
        From him paternal blessings, and set forth
        A Traveller bound for England. The good Pair
        Offer'd up prayers, and bless'd him; but with hearts MSS.
        He asked his Mother's blessing; and, with tears

Their farewell benediction, but with hearts
Foreboding evil. From his native hills   340
He wandered far; much did he see of men,[1]
Their manners, their enjoyments, and pursuits,
Their passions and their feelings; chiefly those
Essential and eternal in the heart,
That, 'mid the simpler forms of rural life,   345
Exist more simple in their elements,
And speak a plainer language. In the woods,
A lone Enthusiast, and among the fields,
Itinerant in this labour, he had passed
The better portion of his time; and there   350
Spontaneously had his affections thriven
Amid the bounties of the year, the peace
And liberty of nature; there he kept
In solitude and solitary thought
His mind in a just equipoise of love.   355
Serene it was, unclouded by the cares
Of ordinary life; unvexed, unwarped
By partial bondage. In his steady course,
No piteous revolutions had he felt,
No wild varieties of joy and grief.   360
Unoccupied by sorrow of its own,
His heart lay open; and, by nature tuned
And constant disposition of his thoughts
To sympathy with man, he was alive
To all that was enjoyed where'er he went,   365
And all that was endured; for, in himself
Happy, and quiet in his cheerfulness,
He had no painful pressure from within
That made him turn aside from wretchedness
With coward fears. He could *afford* to suffer   370
With those whom he saw suffer. Hence it came
That in our best experience he was rich,
And in the wisdom of our daily life.

[1] See Note, p. 411.

Thanking his second Father, asked from him
Paternal blessings. The good Pair bestowed *etc. as text* 1814–20
351–3 *so* 1827: From day to day had his affections breath'd
    The wholesome air of nature   MSS., 1814–20 *as text, but*
    Upon the bounties of the year, and felt
    The liberty of Nature
368 within MS. B: without 1814–1850

For hence, minutely, in his various rounds,
He had observed the progress and decay   375
Of many minds, of minds and bodies too;
The history of many families;
How they had prospered; how they were o'erthrown
By passion or mischance, or such misrule
Among the unthinking masters of the earth   380
As makes the nations groan.
                              This active course
He followed till provision for his wants
Had been obtained;—the Wanderer then resolved
To pass the remnant of his days, untasked
With needless services, from hardship free.   385
His calling laid aside, he lived at ease:
But still he loved to pace the public roads
And the wild paths; and, by the summer's warmth
Invited, often would he leave his home
And journey far, revisiting the scenes   390
That to his memory were most endeared.
—Vigorous in health, of hopeful spirits, undamped
By worldly-mindedness or anxious care;
Observant, studious, thoughtful, and refreshed
By knowledge gathered up from day to day;   395
Thus had he lived a long and innocent life.

The Scottish Church, both on himself and those
With whom from childhood he grew up, had held
The strong hand of her purity; and still
Had watched him with an unrelenting eye.   400
This he remembered in his riper age
With gratitude, and reverential thoughts.
But by the native vigour of his mind,

380 masters MS. M: Rulers MS. E   381-92 groan. Untouched by
[Pure from all E] taint Of worldly mindedness E-P, *but an addition to*
P *gives draft of the lines of text*
382-3 *so* 1827: Chosen in youth, through manhood he pursued,
                    Till due provision for his modest wants
                    Had been obtained;—and, thereupon, resolved. 1814-20
388-91 *so* 1827: . . . and, when the summer's warmth
                    Invited him, would often leave his home
                    And journey far, revisiting those scenes
                    Which to his memory were most endeared. 1814-20
392 undamped   1827: untouched 1814-20   401 age] years MSS.

By his habitual wanderings out of doors,
By loneliness, and goodness, and kind works,   405
Whate'er, in docile childhood or in youth,
He had imbibed of fear or darker thought
Was melted all away; so true was this,
That sometimes his religion seemed to me
Self-taught, as of a dreamer in the woods;   410
Who to the model of his own pure heart
Shaped his belief, as grace divine inspired,
And human reason dictated with awe.
—And surely never did there live on earth
A man of kindlier nature. The rough sports   415
And teasing ways of children vexed not him;
Indulgent listener was he to the tongue
Of garrulous age; nor did the sick man's tale,
To his fraternal sympathy addressed,
Obtain reluctant hearing.
                          Plain his garb;   420
Such as might suit a rustic Sire, prepared
For sabbath duties; yet he was a man
Whom no one could have passed without remark.
Active and nervous was his gait; his limbs
And his whole figure breathed intelligence.   425
Time had compressed the freshness of his cheek
Into a narrower circle of deep red,
But had not tamed his eye; that, under brows
Shaggy and grey, had meanings which it brought
From years of youth; which, like a Being made   430
Of many Beings, he had wondrous skill
To blend with knowledge of the years to come,
Human, or such as lie beyond the grave.

So was He framed; and such his course of life

406 Whatever in his childhood   MSS.   411–13 *not in* MSS. E, M;
added to P   412 Shaped   1827: Framed   MS. P, 1814–20   413
And   1836: Or   1814–32
415–22 A man of sweeter temper. Birds and beasts
          He lov'd them all, chickens and household dogs,
          And to the kitten of a neighbour's house
          Would carry crumbs [*corr. to* milk   E] and feed it. Poor and plain
          Was his appearance, yet he was a man   MSS.
416/17 Nor could he bid them from his presence, tired
          With questions and importunate demands: 1814–20
434–9 Such was in brief the history of my Friend;

Who now, with no appendage but a staff,   435
The prized memorial of relinquished toils,
Upon that cottage-bench reposed his limbs,
Screened from the sun. Supine the Wanderer lay,
His eyes as if in drowsiness half shut,
The shadows of the breezy elms above   440
Dappling his face. He had not heard the sound
Of my approaching steps, and in the shade
Unnoticed did I stand some minutes' space.
At length I hailed him, seeing that his hat
Was moist with water-drops, as if the brim   445
Had newly scooped a running stream. He rose,
And ere our lively greeting into peace
Had settled, " 'Tis," said I, a "a burning day:
My lips are parched with thirst, but you, it seems,
Have somewhere found relief." He, at the word,   450
Pointing towards a sweet-briar, bade me climb
The fence where that aspiring shrub looked out
Upon the public way. It was a plot
Of garden ground run wild, its matted weeds
Marked with the steps of those, whom, as they passed,   455
The gooseberry trees that shot in long lank slips,
Or currants, hanging from their leafless stems,
In scanty strings, had tempted to o'erleap

So was he fram'd.—Now on the Bench he lay
And of his Pack of merchandize had made
A pillow for his head: his eyes were shut   MSS. D–P: P *corr. last*
three lines to
    And one memorial of his former toils
    A Staff with iron filleted and forked
    Lay at his side
441–3 *so* 1827:   He had not heard my steps
            As I approached ; and near him did I stand
            Unnotic'd in the shade, some minutes' space.   MSS. M, P,
1814–20
447–8 *so* 1827: And ere the joyful greeting which we had
            Was ended, " 'Tis a burning day," said I   MS. E: *so* M,
but pleasant greeting
            And ere the pleasant greeting that ensued
            Was ended, *etc.* MS. P, 1814–20
449 it seems   1827: I see   MS. E: I guess   MS. P, 1814–20
452–3 *so* 1827: The fence hard by, where that aspiring [tall slender   MSS.]
                shrub
            Looked out upon the road. MSS., 1814–20
456–8   that shewed their dwindled fruit
        Hanging in long lank slips, or leafless strings
        Of Currants might have C

The broken wall. I looked around, and there,
Where two tall hedge-rows of thick alder boughs   460
Joined in a cold damp nook, espied a well
Shrouded with willow-flowers and plumy fern.
My thirst I slaked, and, from the cheerless spot
Withdrawing, straightway to the shade returned
Where sate the old Man on the cottage-bench;   465
And, while, beside him, with uncovered head,
I yet was standing, freely to respire,
And cool my temples in the fanning air,
Thus did he speak. "I see around me here
Things which you cannot see: we die, my Friend,   470
Nor we alone, but that which each man loved
And prized in his peculiar nook of earth
Dies with him, or is changed; and very soon
Even of the good is no memorial left.
—The Poets, in their elegies and songs   475
Lamenting the departed, call the groves,
They call upon the hills and streams to mourn,
And senseless rocks; nor idly; for they speak,
In these their invocations, with a voice
Obedient to the strong creative power   480
Of human passion. Sympathies there are
More tranquil, yet perhaps of kindred birth,
That steal upon the meditative mind,
And grow with thought. Beside yon spring I stood,
And eyed its waters till we seemed to feel   485
One sadness, they and I. For them a bond
Of brotherhood is broken: time has been
When, every day, the touch of human hand
Dislodged the natural sleep that binds them up
In mortal stillness; and they ministered   490

459 around] about MSS.   461 espied] I found MSS.   462 Half
cover'd up with willow flowers and grass MSS. E, M (*corr. to* fern P)
463–9 I slak'd my thirst; and soon as to the Bench
    I had return'd, while with uncover'd head
    I stood, to catch the motion of the air,
    The old Man spake MSS. E, M
    My thirst I slaked, and from the chearless spot
    Withdrew, and while beside the shady bench
    Yet was I standing with uncovered head
    Intent to catch the motion of the air,
    The Old Man spoke MS. P
489–90 Disturb'd their stillness, and they ministered MSS. B–E

To human comfort. Stooping down to drink,
Upon the slimy foot-stone I espied
The useless fragment of a wooden bowl,
Green with the moss of years, and subject only
To the soft handling of the elements: 495
There let it lie—how foolish are such thoughts!
Forgive them;—never—never did my steps
Approach this door but she who dwelt within
A daughter's welcome gave me, and I loved her
As my own child. Oh, Sir! the good die first,   500
And they whose hearts are dry as summer dust
Burn to the socket. Many a passenger
Hath blessed poor Margaret for her gentle looks,
When she upheld the cool refreshment drawn
From that forsaken spring; and no one came   505
But he was welcome; no one went away
But that it seemed she loved him. She is dead,
The light extinguished of her lonely hut,
The hut itself abandoned to decay,
And she forgotten in the quiet grave.   510

"I speak," continued he, "of One whose stock
Of virtues bloomed beneath this lowly roof.

491 Stooping down] 1827: When [As 1814] I stooped   MSS., 1814–20
494–8 It mov'd me to the [my very M] heart. The time has been
        When I could never pass this road but she
        Who liv'd within these walls, when I appear'd MSS. E, M
        Green with the moss of years; a pensive sight [a sight it was P]
        That moved my heart!—recalling former days
        When I could never pass that road but She
        Who lived within these walls, at my approach, MS. P, but (when I
            appeared), 1814–20
        Green with the moss of years, a forlorn relic
        There let it lie in memory of days
        Departed; never never did my steps   C¹
        Green with the moss of years. Upon the relique
        As there it lay I could not look unmoved.
        Forgive the weakness—Never did step of mine   C²
        Upon the simple sight I could not look
        Unmoved—never—never did step of mine   C³
494–5 so 1827   496 so 1837   497–8 so 1832
496–8 There let the relic lie—fond thought—vain words!
        Forgive them—never did my steps approach
        This humble door but she who dwelt within   1827 only
508–10 Forgotten in the quiet of the grave   MSS.
511–12 I speak of a poor Woman who dwelt here,

She was a Woman of a steady mind,
Tender and deep in her excess of love;
Not speaking much, pleased rather with the joy   515
Of her own thoughts: by some especial care
Her temper had been framed, as if to make
A Being, who by adding love to peace
Might live on earth a life of happiness.
Her wedded Partner lacked not on his side   520
The humble worth that satisfied her heart:
Frugal, affectionate, sober, and withal
Keenly industrious. She with pride would tell
That he was often seated at his loom,
In summer, ere the mower was abroad   525
Among the dewy grass,—in early spring,
Ere the last star had vanished.—They who passed
At evening, from behind the garden fence
Might hear his busy spade, which he would ply,
After his daily work, until the light   530
Had failed, and every leaf and flower were lost
In the dark hedges. So their days were spent
In peace and comfort; and a pretty boy
Was their best hope, next to the God in heaven.

"Not twenty years ago, but you I think   535
Can scarcely bear it now in mind, there came
Two blighting seasons, when the fields were left
With half a harvest. It pleased Heaven to add
A worse affliction in the plague of war:
This happy Land was stricken to the heart!   540
A Wanderer then among the cottages,
I, with my freight of winter raiment, saw
The hardships of that season: many rich
Sank down, as in a dream, among the poor;
And of the poor did many cease to be,   545
And their place knew them not. Meanwhile, abridged
Of daily comforts, gladly reconciled

This Cottage was her home, and she the best
    Of many thousands who are good and poor. MSS.
520–4 *so* MS. P: She had a husband, an industrious Man
            Sober and frugal [steady MS. D]; I have heard her say
            That he was up and busy at his loom   MSS. D, E, M
526 Among the grass, and in the [oft in P] early Spring MSS.   531
Had failed 1814: Was gone MSS.

To numerous self-denials, Margaret
Went struggling on through those calamitous years
With cheerful hope, until the second autumn,   550
When her life's Helpmate on a sick-bed lay,
Smitten with perilous fever. In disease
He lingered long; and, when his strength returned,
He found the little he had stored, to meet
The hour of accident or crippling age,   555
Was all consumed. A second infant now
Was added to the troubles of a time
Laden, for them and all of their degree,
With care and sorrow: shoals of artisans
From ill-requited labour turned adrift   560
Sought daily bread from public charity,
They, and their wives and children—happier far
Could they have lived as do the little birds
That peck along the hedge-rows, or the kite
That makes her dwelling on the mountain rocks!   565

"A sad reverse it was for him who long
Had filled with plenty, and possessed in peace,
This lonely Cottage. At the door he stood,
And whistled many a snatch of merry tunes
That had no mirth in them; or with his knife   570
Carved uncouth figures on the heads of sticks—
Then, not less idly, sought, through every nook
In house or garden, any casual work
Of use or ornament; and with a strange,

550 . . . but ere the second autumn   MSS., 1814–20
551–2 A fever seized her Husband. In disease   MSS. E, M
     Her husband to a sick-bed was confined
     Labouring with perilous fever. In disease   MS. P
     Her life's true Helpmate *etc. as text*   1814–20
556–61 *so* 1827: Was all consumed. Two children had they now,
          One newly born. As I have said, it was
          A time of trouble; shoals of Artisans
          Were from their daily labour turn'd adrift [away   MSS.
          E, M]
          To seek their bread from public charity,   MSS., 1814–20
564–5 hedge-rows . . . her dwelling   1827: hedges . . . his dwelling   MSS.,
1814–20
566–8 Ill far'd it now with Robert, he who dwelt
     Here in this Cottage. At his door   MSS.
572 Then idly sought about   MSS.

Amusing, yet uneasy, novelty,   575
He mingled, where he might, the various tasks
Of summer, autumn, winter, and of spring.
But this endured not; his good humour soon
Became a weight in which no pleasure was:
And poverty brought on a petted mood   580
And a sore temper: day by day he drooped,
And he would leave his work—and to the town
Would turn without an errand his slack steps;
Or wander here and there among the fields.
One while he would speak lightly of his babes,   585
And with a cruel tongue: at other times
He tossed them with a false unnatural joy:
And 'twas a rueful thing to see the looks
Of the poor innocent children. 'Every smile,'
Said Margaret to me, here beneath these trees,   590
'Made my heart bleed.' "
                    At this the Wanderer paused;
And, looking up to those enormous elms,
He said, " 'Tis now the hour of deepest noon.
At this still season of repose and peace,
This hour when all things which are not at rest   595
Are cheerful; while this multitude of flies
With tuneful hum is filling all the air;
Why should a tear be on an old Man's cheek?
Why should we thus, with an untoward mind,
And in the weakness of humanity,   600
From natural wisdom turn our hearts away;
To natural comfort shut our eyes and ears;
And, feeding on disquiet, thus disturb
The calm of nature with our restless thoughts?"

He spake with somewhat of a solemn tone: 605
But, when he ended, there was in his face
Such easy cheerfulness, a look so mild,
That for a little time it stole away
All recollection; and that simple tale

576 mingled 1837: blended MSS., 1814–32   582 work] home MSS.
583 *so* 1837: Without an errand would he turn his steps MSS. E, M:
would direct his steps   MS. P, 1814–32   591 Wanderer] Old Man
MSS.   597 tuneful] ceaseless *corr. to* tuneful C
597–8 *so* 1845: Is filling all the air with melody;
          Why should a tear be in an Old Man's eye? MSS., 1814–43

Passed from my mind like a forgotten sound.	610
A while on trivial things we held discourse,
To me soon tasteless. In my own despite,
I thought of that poor Woman as of one
Whom I had known and loved. He had rehearsed
Her homely tale with such familiar power,	615
With such an active countenance, an eye
So busy, that the things of which he spake
Seemed present; and, attention now relaxed,
A heart-felt chillness crept along my veins.
I rose; and, having left the breezy shade,	620
Stood drinking comfort from the warmer sun,
That had not cheered me long—ere, looking round
Upon that tranquil Ruin, I returned,
And begged of the old Man that, for my sake,
He would resume his story.

　　　　　　He replied,	625
"It were a wantonness, and would demand
Severe reproof, if we were men whose hearts
Could hold vain dalliance with the misery
Even of the dead; contented thence to draw
A momentary pleasure, never marked	630
By reason, barren of all future good.
But we have known that there is often found
In mournful thoughts, and always might be found,
A power to virtue friendly; wer't not so,
I am a dreamer among men, indeed	635
An idle dreamer! 'Tis a common tale,
An ordinary sorrow of man's life,
A tale of silent suffering, hardly clothed
In bodily form.—But without further bidding
I will proceed.
　　　　　　While thus it fared with them,	640

619-22 *so* 1827: There was a heart-felt chillness in my veins.—
　　　　　　I rose; and, turning from the breezy shade,
　　　　　　Went forth into the open air, and stood
　　　　　　To drink the comfort of the warmer sun.
　　　　　　Long time I had not staid, ere,　MSS., 1814-20
630 passing pleasure felt but　*Alfoxden* MS.
639 *so* MSS. M, P: In bodily form, and to the grosser sense
　　　　　　But ill adapted, scarcely palpable
　　　　　　To him who does not think; but at your bidding　MS. E

To whom this cottage, till those hapless years,
Had been a blessèd home, it was my chance
To travel in a country far remote;
And when these lofty elms once more appeared
What pleasant expectations lured me on   645
O'er the flat Common!—With quick step I reached
The threshold, lifted with light hand the latch;
But, when I entered, Margaret looked at me
A little while; then turned her head away
Speechless,—and, sitting down upon a chair,   650
Wept bitterly. I wist not what to do,
Nor how to speak to her. Poor Wretch! at last
She rose from off her seat, and then,—O Sir!
I cannot *tell* how she pronounced my name:—
With fervent love, and with a face of grief   655
Unutterably helpless, and a look
That seemed to cling upon me, she enquired
If I had seen her husband. As she spake
A strange surprise and fear came to my heart,
Nor had I power to answer ere she told   660
That he had disappeared—not two months gone.
He left his house: two wretched days had past,
And on the third, as wistfully she raised
Her head from off her pillow, to look forth,
Like one in trouble, for returning light,   665
Within her chamber-casement she espied
A folded paper, lying as if placed
To meet her waking eyes. This tremblingly

644-8 *so* 1827: And glad I was, when, halting by yon gate
          That leads from the green lane, once more I saw
          These lofty elm-trees. Long I did not rest:
          With many pleasant thoughts I chear'd my way
          O'er the flat Common.—Having reached the door [At the
              door arrived   MS.]
          I knock'd,—and, when I entered with the hope
          Of usual greeting, Margaret looked at me   MSS., 1814-20
656-7 Unutterable, and a helpless look that seemed
        To cling upon me faltering she   C
661 not] just   MSS.
663-70 And on the third, by the first break of light
          Within her casement full in view she saw
          A letter, as it seemed, which she forthwith
          Open'd, and found no writing, but therein
          Pieces of money carefully wrapp'd up   MSS.

She opened—found no writing, but beheld
Pieces of money carefully enclosed,   670
Silver and gold. 'I shuddered at the sight,'
Said Margaret, 'for I knew it was his hand
That must have placed it there; and ere that day
Was ended, that long anxious day, I learned,
From one who by my husband had been sent   675
With the sad news, that he had joined a troop
Of soldiers, going to a distant land.
—He left me thus—he could not gather heart
To take a farewell of me; for he feared
That I should follow with my babes, and sink   680
Beneath the misery of that wandering life.'

"This tale did Margaret tell with many tears:
And, when she ended, I had little power
To give her comfort, and was glad to take
Such words of hope from her own mouth as served   685
To cheer us both. But long we had not talked
Ere we built up a pile of better thoughts,
And with a brighter eye she looked around
As if she had been shedding tears of joy.
We parted.—'Twas the time of early spring;   690
I left her busy with her garden tools;
And well remember, o'er that fence she looked,
And, while I paced along the foot-way path,
Called out, and sent a blessing after me,
With tender cheerfulness, and with a voice   695
That seemed the very sound of happy thoughts.

"I roved o'er many a hill and many a dale,
With my accustomed load; in heat and cold,

669 beheld   1827: therein   MSS., 1814–20   671 shuddered] trembled
MSS.
673–6 *so* 1837: Which plac'd it there, and on that very day,
                By one who from my Husband had been sent,
                The tidings came that *etc.*   MSS.
                Which placed it there: and ere that day was ended,
                That long and anxious day! I learned from One
                Sent hither by my Husband to impart
                The heavy news,—that *etc.*   1814–32
678 —Poor Man! he had not heart   MSS.   698 With this my weary
load   MSS.

Through many a wood and many an open ground,
In sunshine and in shade, in wet and fair,   700
Drooping or blithe of heart, as might befal;
My best companions now the driving winds,
And now the 'trotting brooks' and whispering trees,
And now the music of my own sad steps,
With many a short-lived thought that passed between,   705
And disappeared.
             I journeyed back this way,
When, in the warmth of midsummer, the wheat
Was yellow; and the soft and bladed grass,
Springing afresh, had o'er the hay-field spread
Its tender verdure. At the door arrived,   710
I found that she was absent. In the shade,
Where now we sit, I waited her return.
Her cottage, then a cheerful object, wore
Its customary look,—only, it seemed,
The honeysuckle, crowding round the porch,   715
Hung down in heavier tufts; and that bright weed,
The yellow stone-crop, suffered to take root
Along the window's edge, profusely grew
Blinding the lower panes. I turned aside,
And strolled into her garden. It appeared   720
To lag behind the season, and had lost
Its pride of neatness. Daisy-flowers and thrift

701 *so* MS. P: Now blithe, now drooping, as it might befal;   MSS. E–M
706 I came this way again   MSS.   707 *so* 1827: Towards the wane
of Summer; when the wheat   MSS., 1814–20   710 Its tender green.
When I had reach'd the door   MSS.
713–19 Her cottage, in its outward look, appear'd
       As chearful as before, in any shew
       Of neatness little chang'd; but that I thought
       The honeysuckle crowded round the door,
       And from the wall hung down in heavier tufts
       And knots of worthless stone-crop started out
       Along the window's edge and grew like weeds
       Against the lower panes.   MSS.
722–8 Its trimness and its pride. The border tufts,
       Daisy and thrift, and lowly camomile
       And thyme had straggl'd out into the path,
       The bindweed with its bells and cumbrous wreaths   MSS. E, M
       Its pride of neatness. From the border lines
       Composed of daisy and resplendent thrift,
       Flowers straggling forth had on those paths encroached
       Which they were used to deck:—Carnations *etc. as text*   MS. P, 1814–20

Had broken their trim border-lines, and straggled
O'er paths they used to deck: carnations, once
Prized for surpassing beauty, and no less   725
For the peculiar pains they had required,
Declined their languid heads, wanting support.
The cumbrous bind-weed, with its wreaths and bells,
Had twined about her two small rows of peas,
And dragged them to the earth.

                        Ere this an hour   730
Was wasted.—Back I turned my restless steps;
A stranger passed; and, guessing whom I sought,
He said that she was used to ramble far.—
The sun was sinking in the west; and now
I sate with sad impatience. From within   735
Her solitary infant cried aloud;
Then, like a blast that dies away self-stilled,
The voice was silent. From the bench I rose;
But neither could divert nor soothe my thoughts.
The spot, though fair, was very desolate—   740
The longer I remained, more desolate:
And, looking round me, now I first observed
The corner stones, on either side the porch,
With dull red stains discoloured, and stuck o'er
With tufts and hairs of wool, as if the sheep,   745
That fed upon the Common, thither came
Familiarly, and found a couching-place
Even at her threshold. Deeper shadows fell
From these tall elms; the cottage-clock struck eight;—
I turned, and saw her distant a few steps.   750
Her face was pale and thin—her figure, too,
Was changed. As she unlocked the door, she said,
'It grieves me you have waited here so long,
But, in good truth, I've wandered much of late;
And, sometimes—to my shame I speak—have need   755
Of my best prayers to bring me back again.'

            Daisy-flowers and thrift
      Had broken their trim lines, and straggled o'er
      The paths they used to deck *etc.* 1827–43
731/2 And, as I walk'd before the door, it chanc'd MSS., 1814–20
737–9 *not in* MSS. E, M; *added to* P
742–3 *so* 1827: And, looking round, I saw the corner stones
            Till then unnotic'd, on either side the door MSS., 1814–20
748–9 Even at her threshold. The house-clock struck eight; MSS.

While on the board she spread our evening meal,
She told me—interrupting not the work
Which gave employment to her listless hands—
That she had parted with her elder child;   760
To a kind master on a distant farm
Now happily apprenticed.—'I perceive
You look at me, and you have cause; to-day
I have been travelling far; and many days
About the fields I wander, knowing this   765
Only, that what I seek I cannot find;
And so I waste my time: for I am changed;
And to myself,' said she, 'have done much wrong
And to this helpless infant. I have slept
Weeping, and weeping have I waked; my tears   770
Have flowed as if my body were not such
As others are; and I could never die.
But I am now in mind and in my heart
More easy; and I hope,' said she, 'that God
Will give me patience to endure the things   775
Which I behold at home.'
                              It would have grieved
Your very soul to see her. Sir, I feel
The story linger in my heart; I fear
'Tis long and tedious; but my spirit clings
To that poor Woman:—so familiarly   780
Do I perceive her manner, and her look,
And presence; and so deeply do I feel
Her goodness, that, not seldom, in my walks
A momentary trance comes over me;
And to myself I seem to muse on One   785
By sorrow laid asleep; or borne away,
A human being destined to awake
To human life, or something very near
To human life, when he shall come again
For whom she suffered. Yes, it would have grieved   790
Your very soul to see her: evermore
Her eyelids drooped, her eyes downward were cast;

758–62 She told me she had lost her elder Child,
          That he for months had been a Serving-boy
          Apprentic'd by the Parish. MSS. (MS. P *corr. to text*)
770 have I 1827: I have MSS., 1814–20   774 God 1832: Heaven
MSS., 1814–27   790 Yes,] Sir MSS.   792 downward were
1845: were downward 1814–43

And, when she at her table gave me food,
She did not look at me. Her voice was low,
Her body was subdued. In every act   795
Pertaining to her house-affairs, appeared
The careless stillness of a thinking mind
Self-occupied; to which all outward things
Are like an idle matter. Still she sighed,
But yet no motion of the breast was seen,   800
No heaving of the heart. While by the fire
We sate together, sighs came on my ear,
I knew not how, and hardly whence they came.

"Ere my departure, to her care I gave,
For her son's use, some tokens of regard,   805
Which with a look of welcome she received;
And I exhorted her to place her trust
In God's good love, and seek his help by prayer.
I took my staff, and, when I kissed her babe,
The tears stood in her eyes. I left her then   810
With the best hope and comfort I could give:
She thanked me for my wish;—but for my hope
It seemed she did not thank me.
                              I returned,
And took my rounds along this road again
When on its sunny bank the primrose flower   815
Peeped forth, to give an earnest of the Spring.
I found her sad and drooping: she had learned
No tidings of her husband; if he lived,
She knew not that he lived; if he were dead,
She knew not he was dead. She seemed the same   820
In person and appearance; but her house
Bespake a sleepy hand of negligence;
The floor was neither dry nor neat, the hearth
Was comfortless, and her small lot of books,

804–7 I gave her for her Son, the Parish Boy,
        A kerchief and a book, wherewith she seem'd
        Pleas'd; and I counsell'd her to have her trust   MSS.
807 place   1827: have   1814–20   813 It seemed   1837: Methought
1814–32   815 When   1845: Ere   MSS., 1814–43   816 *so* MS. M:
Had chronicled the earliest day of spring   MS. E
817–18   drooping: Time had brought
        No tidings which might lead her anxious mind
        To a source of quiet; if her husband lived   C

Which, in the cottage-window, heretofore   825
Had been piled up against the corner panes
In seemly order, now, with straggling leaves
Lay scattered here and there, open or shut,
As they had chanced to fall. Her infant Babe
Had from its mother caught the trick of grief,   830
And sighed among its playthings. I withdrew,
And once again entering the garden saw,
More plainly still, that poverty and grief
Were now come nearer to her: weeds defaced
The hardened soil, and knots of withered grass: 835
No ridges there appeared of clear black mold,
No winter greenness; of her herbs and flowers,
It seemed the better part were gnawed away
Or trampled into earth; a chain of straw,
Which had been twined about the slender stem   840
Of a young apple-tree, lay at its root;
The bark was nibbled round by truant sheep.
—Margaret stood near, her infant in her arms,
And, noting that my eye was on the tree,
She said, 'I fear it will be dead and gone   845
Ere Robert come again.' When to the House
We had returned together, she enquired
If I had any hope:—but for her babe
And for her little orphan boy, she said,
She had no wish to live, that she must die   850
Of sorrow. Yet I saw the idle loom
Still in its place; his Sunday garments hung
Upon the self-same nail; his very staff
Stood undisturbed behind the door.
                                        And when,
In bleak December, I retraced this way,   855
She told me that her little babe was dead,
And she was left alone. She now, released

825 Which, one upon the other, heretofore   MSS.   831-2 *so* 1845:
Once again I turn'd towards the garden-gate, and saw   MSS., 1814-43
834-5 the earth was hard, With weeds defaced   MSS.   846-7 Towards
the house Together we returned; and   MSS., 1814-43   849 orphan]
friendless   MSS.   855 I pass'd this way, beaten by autumn winds
MS. E: This way the ensuing winter I returned   MSS. M, P
857-9 *so* MS. P: She now, I learn'd,
                 After her Infant's death had taken up
                 The employment common hereabouts,   MSS. E, **M**

From her maternal cares, had taken up
The employment common through these wilds, and gained,
By spinning hemp, a pittance for herself;   860
And for this end had hired a neighbour's boy
To give her needful help. That very time
Most willingly she put her work aside,
And walked with me along the miry road,
Heedless how far; and, in such piteous sort   865
That any heart had ached to hear her, begged
That, wheresoe'er I went, I still would ask
For him whom she had lost. We parted then—
Our final parting; for from that time forth
Did many seasons pass ere I returned   870
Into this tract again.
                          Nine tedious years;
From their first separation, nine long years,
She lingered in unquiet widowhood;
A Wife and Widow. Needs must it have been
A sore heart-wasting! I have heard, my Friend,   875
That in yon arbour oftentimes she sate
Alone, through half the vacant sabbath day;
And, if a dog passed by, she still would quit
The shade, and look abroad. On this old bench
For hours she sate; and evermore her eye   880
Was busy in the distance, shaping things
That made her heart beat quick. You see that path,
Now faint,—the grass has crept o'er its grey line;
There, to and fro, she paced through many a day
Of the warm summer, from a belt of hemp   885
That girt her waist, spinning the long-drawn thread
With backward steps. Yet ever as there passed
A man whose garments showed the soldier's red,
Or crippled mendicant in sailor's garb,
The little child who sate to turn the wheel   890
Ceased from his task; and she with faltering voice
Made many a fond enquiry; and when they,
Whose presence gave no comfort, were gone by,

862 To help her in her work   MSS.   864–5 And walked with me a
mile, and in such sort   MSS.   871 Nine] Five   MSS. B–D
876–7 That in yon broken arbour she would sit
     The idle length of half a Sabbath day   MSS.
891/2 Expecting still to hear her Husband's fate,   MSS. E, M

Her heart was still more sad. And by yon gate,
That bars the traveller's road, she often stood,   895
And when a stranger horseman came, the latch
Would lift, and in his face look wistfully:
Most happy, if, from aught discovered there
Of tender feeling, she might dare repeat
The same sad question. Meanwhile her poor Hut   900
Sank to decay; for he was gone, whose hand,
At the first nipping of October frost,
Closed up each chink, and with fresh bands of straw
Chequered the green-grown thatch. And so she lived
Through the long winter, reckless and alone;   905
Until her house by frost, and thaw, and rain,
Was sapped; and while she slept, the nightly damps
Did chill her breast; and in the stormy day
Her tattered clothes were ruffled by the wind,
Even at the side of her own fire. Yet still   910
She loved this wretched spot, nor would for worlds
Have parted hence; and still that length of road,
And this rude bench, one torturing hope endeared,
Fast rooted at her heart: and here, my Friend,—
In sickness she remained; and here she died;   915
Last human tenant of these ruined walls!"

    The old Man ceased: he saw that I was moved;
From that low bench, rising instinctively
I turned aside in weakness, nor had power
To thank him for the tale which he had told.   920
I stood, and leaning o'er the garden wall
Reviewed that Woman's sufferings; and it seemed
To comfort me while with a brother's love
I blessed her in the impotence of grief.
Then towards the cottage I returned; and traced   925

905–6 In objects of her need and of her love
        Made poorer every day till at the last
        The loom was parted with and nothing left
        But naked walls where joyless and alone
        Through the long winter long and desolate
        She linger'd in neglect and unconcern
        Until her house *etc.* MS. E *alt. draft*
921 wall   MS. M: gate   MSS. D–P
925–6 *so* 1837: At length towards the Cottage I returned
                Fondly,—and trac'd with milder interest   MSS. 1814–32
(*but* P *and* 1814–32 interest more mild)

Fondly, though with an interest more mild,
That secret spirit of humanity
Which, 'mid the calm oblivious tendencies
Of nature, 'mid her plants, and weeds, and flowers,
And silent overgrowings, still survived.   930
The old Man, noting this, resumed, and said,
"My Friend! enough to sorrow you have given,
The purposes of wisdom ask no more:
Nor more would she have craved as due to One
Who, in her worst distress, had ofttimes felt   935
The unbounded might of prayer; and learned, with soul
Fixed on the Cross, that consolation springs,
From sources deeper far than deepest pain,
For the meek Sufferer. Why then should we read
The forms of things with an unworthy eye?   940
She sleeps in the calm earth, and peace is here.
I well remember that those very plumes,
Those weeds, and the high spear-grass on that wall,
By mist and silent rain-drops silvered o'er,
As once I passed, into my heart conveyed   945
So still an image of tranquillity,
So calm and still, and looked so beautiful
Amid the uneasy thoughts which filled my mind,
That what we feel of sorrow and despair
From ruin and from change, and all the grief   950
That passing shows of Being leave behind,
Appeared an idle dream, that could maintain,
Nowhere, dominion o'er the enlightened spirit
Whose meditative sympathies repose
Upon the breast of Faith. I turned away,   955
And walked along my road in happiness."

    He ceased. Ere long the sun declining shot
A slant and mellow radiance, which began
To fall upon us, while, beneath the trees,
We sate on that low bench: and now we felt,   960

934-7 Doubt not that oft-times in her soul she felt
       The unbounded might of prayer. Upon her knees
       Was taught that heavenly consolation springs   C
934-40 *so* 1845: Be wise and chearful, and no longer read
                The forms of things with an unworthy eye MSS., 1814-43
945 *so* 1837: did to my heart convey   MSS., 1814-32   952-5 *so*
1845: that could not live Where meditation was.   MSS., 1814-43

Admonished thus, the sweet hour coming on.
A linnet warbled from those lofty elms,
A thrush sang loud, and other melodies,
At distance heard, peopled the milder air.
The old Man rose, and, with a sprightly mien   965
Of hopeful preparation, grasped his staff;
Together casting then a farewell look
Upon those silent walls, we left the shade;
And, ere the stars were visible, had reached
A village-inn,—our evening resting-place.   970

965–6 The old Man rose and hoisted [*corr. to* lifted] up his load   MSS.:
P *corr. to text*

BOOK SECOND

THE SOLITARY
ARGUMENT

The Author describes his travels with the Wanderer, whose character is further illustrated.—Morning scene, and view of a Village Wake.—Wanderer's account of a Friend whom he purposes to visit.—View, from an eminence, of the Valley which his Friend had chosen for his retreat.[1]— Sound of singing from below.—A funeral procession.—Descent into the Valley.—Observations drawn from the Wanderer at sight of a book accidentally discovered in a recess in the Valley.—Meeting with the Wanderer's friend, the Solitary.—Wanderer's description of the mode of burial in this mountainous district.—Solitary contrasts with this, that of the individual carried a few minutes before from the cottage.[2]—The cottage entered.— Description of the Solitary's apartment.—Repast there.—View, from the window, of two mountain summits; and the Solitary's description of the companionship they afford him.—Account of the departed inmate of the cottage.—Description of a grand spectacle upon the mountains, with its effect upon the Solitary's mind.—Leave[3] the house.

> In days of yore how fortunately fared
> The Minstrel! wandering on from hall to hall,
> Baronial court or royal; cheered with gifts
> Munificent, and love, and ladies' praise;
> Now meeting on his road an armed knight,   5
> Now resting with a pilgrim by the side
> Of a clear brook;—beneath an abbey's roof
> One evening sumptuously lodged; the next,
> Humbly in a religious hospital;
> Or with some merry outlaws of the wood;   10
> Or haply shrouded in a hermit's cell.
> Him, sleeping or awake, the robber spared;

II. [1] *so* 1837: retreat—feelings of the Author at the sight of it—1814–32
[2] *so* 1837: cottage—Brief conversation—1814–32   [3] Leave 1837:
Quit 1814–32

---

1 yore] old X   6–7 A pilgrim now within an Abbey lodged X
8 . . . sumptuously, the next perhaps X   12 Him savage robbers
spared, asleep or wake MS.
12–27 Withal from Robbers and from danger safe,
By melody and by the charm of verse,
And with his Harp still pendent at his side
Familiarly as now our Labourers wear
Their Satchels when they plod to distant fields;
Yet such an one so favour'd could not draw
By his glad faculties more earnest bliss

He walked—protected from the sword of war
By virtue of that sacred instrument
His harp, suspended at the traveller's side;   15
His dear companion wheresoe'er he went
Opening from land to land an easy way
By melody, and by the charm of verse.
Yet not the noblest of that honoured Race
Drew happier, loftier, more empassioned, thoughts   20
From his long journeyings and eventful life,
Than this obscure Itinerant had skill
To gather, ranging through the tamer ground
Of these our unimaginative days;
Both while he trod the earth in humblest guise   25
Accoutred with his burthen and his staff;
And now, when free to move with lighter pace.

    What wonder, then, if I, whose favourite school
Hath been the fields, the roads, and rural lanes,
Looked on this guide with reverential love?   30

From the eventful and wayfaring life
Than this same Man uncountenanc'd and obscure,
Accoutred with a Burthen and a Staff,
And nothing better, had the skill to draw
By grace of Heaven from many a ramble, far
And wide protracted, through the tamer land
Of these our unimaginative Days;   X

15 traveller's] Wanderer's   MS.   20 loftier] purer   MS.   21
journeyings] travels   MS.
22-3 *so* 1827: Than this obscure Itinerant (an obscure
        But a high-souled and tender-hearted Man)
        [Accoutred with his burden and his staff,   MS.]
        Had skill to draw from many a ramble, far
        And wide protracted, through the tamer ground   MS.,
        1814-20

25-7 MS. *omits*
28-90 He was a Man whom many sympathies
      Had made me cleave to, and we now pursued
      Our journey beneath favorable Heavens
      At leisure, resting, reading in the shade,
      Or talking of such matters as occurred;
      But when the sun had for the third time risen
      My Fellow-traveller said with earnest voice
      As if the thought were but a moment old
      That, leaving all encumbrances behind,
      The day should be a day of Liberty,
      And I must yield myself without reserve
      To his disposal. Glad was I of this,
      We started and he led towards *etc.*   X
29/30 And pathways winding on from farm to farm   MS., 1814-20

Each with the other pleased, we now pursued
Our journey, under favourable skies.
Turn wheresoe'er we would, he was a light
Unfailing: not a hamlet could we pass,
Rarely a house, that did not yield to him   35
Remembrances; or from his tongue call forth
Some way-beguiling tale. Nor less regard
Accompanied those strains of apt discourse,
Which nature's various objects might inspire;
And in the silence of his face I read   40
His overflowing spirit. Birds and beasts,
And the mute fish that glances in the stream,
And harmless reptile coiling in the sun,
And gorgeous insect hovering in the air,
The fowl domestic, and the household dog—   45
In his capacious mind, he loved them all:
Their rights acknowledging he felt for all.
Oft was occasion given me to perceive
How the calm pleasures of the pasturing herd
To happy contemplation soothed his walk;   50
How the poor brute's condition, forced to run
Its course of suffering in the public road,
Sad contrast! all too often smote his heart
With unavailing pity. Rich in love
And sweet humanity, he was, himself,   55
To the degree that he desired, beloved.
Smiles of good-will from faces that he knew
Greeted us all day long; we took our seats
By many a cottage-hearth, where he received
The welcome of an Inmate from afar,   60

32 under 1837: beneath MS., 1814–32
36–90 Remembrances, while monitory hints
       By nature's various objects were supplied
       For apt discourse, and way-beguiling tales
       Perpetually were flowing from his tongue.
       Greetings and smiles we met with all day long
       From faces that he knew: we took our seats
       By many a cottage hearth, where he received
       The welcome of an Inmate come from far.
       But when the sun . . . led towards *etc.* as X, MS.
39 inspire 1827: supply 1814–20   50/1 Along the field, and in the
shady grove MS., 1814–20   60 from afar 1845: come from far
MS., 1814–43

And I at once forgot, I was a Stranger.
—Nor was he loth to enter ragged huts,
Huts where his charity was blest; his voice
Heard as the voice of an experienced friend.
And, sometimes—where the poor man held dispute   65
With his own mind, unable to subdue
Impatience through inaptness to perceive
General distress in his particular lot;
Or cherishing resentment, or in vain
Struggling against it; with a soul perplexed,   70
And finding in herself no steady power
To draw the line of comfort that divides
Calamity, the chastisement of Heaven,
From the injustice of our brother men—
To him appeal was made as to a judge;   75
Who, with an understanding heart, allayed
The perturbation; listened to the plea;
Resolved the dubious point; and sentence gave
So grounded, so applied, that it was heard
With softened spirit, even when it condemned.   80

Such intercourse I witnessed, while we roved,
Now as his choice directed, now as mine;
Or both, with equal readiness of will,
Our course submitting to the changeful breeze
Of accident. But when the rising sun   85
Had three times called us to renew our walk,
My Fellow-traveller, with earnest voice,
As if the thought were but a moment old,
Claimed absolute dominion for the day.
We started—and he led me toward the hills,   90
Up through an ample vale, with higher hills
Before us, mountains stern and desolate;
But, in the majesty of distance, now

61 *added* 1845   63 *so* 1827: Wherein his MS., 1814–20   71 herself
1827: itself MS., 1814–20   87–9 *so* 1832: 87 *as above* (*see* 28–90),
88 *as text, followed by* That I must yield myself *etc. as above*   1814–27
90 led me toward   1837: led towards MS., 1814–32   92 At dis-
tance, crags austere and desolate,   X *here goes on at l.* 318 (*a version of ll.*
164–317 *being introduced later*)
92–6 *Another MS. has* 92 *as* X, *followed by*
          Now beautiful by morning's radiant light   *corr. to*
          But now array'd in morning's chearful light

Set off, and to our ken appearing fair
Of aspect, with aërial softness clad,   95
And beautified with morning's purple beams.

   The wealthy, the luxurious, by the stress
Of business roused, or pleasure, ere their time,
May roll in chariots, or provoke the hoofs
Of the fleet coursers they bestride, to raise   100
From earth the dust of morning, slow to rise;
And they, if blest with health and hearts at ease,
Shall lack not their enjoyment:—but how faint
Compared with ours! who, pacing side by side,
Could, with an eye of leisure, look on all   105
That we beheld; and lend the listening sense
To every grateful sound of earth and air;
Pausing at will—our spirits braced, our thoughts
Pleasant as roses in the thickets blown,
And pure as dew bathing their crimson leaves.   110

   Mount slowly, sun! that we may journey long,
By this dark hill protected from thy beams!
Such is the summer pilgrim's frequent wish;
But quickly from among our morning thoughts
'Twas chased away: for, toward the western side   115
Of the broad vale, casting a casual glance,
We saw a throng of people;—wherefore met?
Blithe notes of music, suddenly let loose
On the thrilled ear, and flags uprising, yield
Prompt answer; they proclaim the annual Wake,   120
Which the bright season favours.—Tabor and pipe
In purpose join to hasten or reprove
The laggard Rustic; and repay with boons
Of merriment a party-coloured knot,

111-14 *so* 1827: Mount slowly Sun! and may our journey lie
          Awhile within the shadow of this hill,
          This friendly hill, a shelter from thy beams!
          Such is the summer Pilgrim's frequent wish;
          And as that wish, with prevalence of thanks
          For present good o'er fear of future ill,
          Stole in among the morning's blither thoughts,   **MS.**,
          1814–20
115 'Twas banished for towards, *corr. to text with* tow'rds (*so also* 1814–20)
for toward   MS.   119 *so* 1827: ear, did to the [this   **MS.**] question
yield   MS., 1814–20

Already formed upon the village-green.   125
—Beyond the limits of the shadow cast
By the broad hill, glistened upon our sight
That gay assemblage. Round them and above,
Glitter, with dark recesses interposed,
Casement, and cottage-roof, and stems of trees   130
Half-veiled in vapoury cloud, the silver steam
Of dews fast melting on their leafy boughs
By the strong sunbeams smitten. Like a mast
Of gold, the Maypole shines; as if the rays
Of morning, aided by exhaling dew,   135
With gladsome influence could re-animate
The faded garlands dangling from its sides.

Said I, "The music and the sprightly scene
Invite us; shall we quit our road, and join
These festive matins?"—He replied, "Not loth   140
To linger I would here with you partake,
Not one hour merely, but till evening's close,
The simple pastimes of the day and place.
By the fleet Racers, ere the sun be set,
The turf of yon large pasture will be skimmed;   145
There, too, the lusty Wrestlers shall contend:
But know we not that he, who intermits
The appointed task and duties of the day,
Untunes full oft the pleasures of the day;
Checking the finer spirits that refuse   150
To flow, when purposes are lightly changed?
A length of journey yet remains untraced:
Let us proceed." Then, pointing with his staff
Raised toward those craggy summits, his intent
He thus imparted:—
                              "In a spot that lies   155

141 *so* 1845: Here would I linger and   MS., 1814–43
152–3 *so* 1845: We must proceed—a length of journey yet
                    Remains untraced. MS., 1814–43
153–8 As up this Vale we journeyed side by side
        My Fellow-traveller, pointing as he spoke,
        Made known his purpose: To a spot that lies
        Concealed among yon mountain solitudes
        I shall conduct you to receive, I hope,
        Ere noon, a recompense of this day's toil   MS.
154 Raised toward   1832: Towards   1814–27

Among yon mountain fastnesses concealed,
You will receive, before the hour of noon,
Good recompense, I hope, for this day's toil,
From sight of One who lives secluded there,
Lonesome and lost: of whom, and whose past life,   160
(Not to forestall such knowledge as may be
More faithfully collected from himself)
This brief communication shall suffice.

　　"Though now sojourning there, he, like myself,
Sprang from a stock of lowly parentage   165

161 forestall] foretaste MS., *corr. to text*
164–82 There, though sequestered, he was, like myself,
　　　Born in the hills of Scotland—we had this
　　　In common too, that both were sprung from poor
　　　And lowly parentage; his time of youth
　　　In piety and innocence was spent;
　　　And as he shewed in study forward zeal
　　　All helps were sought, all means were strain'd that he,
　　　By due scholastic discipline prepared,
　　　Might to the Ministry be called; which done,
　　　Partly through lack of better hopes, and part,
　　　Perhaps, incited by a curious mind,
　　　In early life the charge he undertook
　　　Of spiritual guide and teacher to a band
　　　Of Highlanders who to the Bagpipes marched
　　　In plaided vest, his fellow-countrymen,
　　　This humble station filling—to the world
　　　Such seemed it, to his Comrades and himself;
　　　But stored with learning and by native power
　　　And force *etc. as text* 179–81. . . vanity, and prompt meanwhile
　　　In every generous feeling, among these
　　　Gay *etc.* MS. 58
164–221 (*v. app. crit. to* 487–91)
　　　Born on the hills of Scotland, we had this
　　　In common, too, that both of us were sprung
　　　From poor and lowly parentage, and hence,
　　　And from some noble personal qualities,
　　　He had awaken'd in me more concern
　　　Than might seem just; yet not so, for his powers
　　　Were bright and rare; but let me be more brief.
　　　In piety and innocence he spent
　　　A studious youth, and after proper course
　　　Of studies to the Ministry was called,
　　　And went abroad for lack of better hopes
　　　As military Chaplain to a band
　　　Of Highlanders, his fellow countrymen.
　　　In knowledge first, in talents far the first,

Among the wilds of Scotland, in a tract
Where many a sheltered and well-tended plant
Bears, on the humblest ground of social life,
Blossoms of piety and innocence.
Such grateful promises his youth displayed: 170
And, having shown in study forward zeal,
He to the Ministry was duly called;
And straight, incited by a curious mind
Filled with vague hopes, he undertook the charge
Of Chaplain to a military troop   175
Cheered by the Highland bagpipe, as they marched
In plaided vest,—his fellow-countrymen.
This office filling, yet by native power
And force of native inclination made
An intellectual ruler in the haunts   180
Of social vanity, he walked the world,
Gay, and affecting graceful gaiety;
Lax, buoyant—less a pastor with his flock
Than a soldier among soldiers—lived and roamed
Where Fortune led:—and Fortune, who oft proves   185
The careless wanderer's friend, to him made known
A blooming Lady—a conspicuous flower,
Admired for beauty, for her sweetness praised;
Whom he had sensibility to love,
Ambition to attempt, and skill to win.   190

Subject to vanities, yet powerful
In every generous feeling, among these
[? Young] ardent, less a pastor with his Flock
Than a soldier among soldiers, many years
He went where Fortune led. But nobler days
Open'd upon him, and a nobler life.
The vision that enchanted all mankind
Save some few selfish hearts, appeared in France,
Him did it rouze to a surpassing joy
Who was by nature fervent to disease.
He broke from out his narrow sphere, repaired
To London, then a fountain of great hopes,
And there with popular talents preach'd the cause
Of Christ and of the new-born Liberty   X
168–9 *so* 1827: Upon the humblest ground of social life,
            Doth at this day, I trust, the blossoms bear
            Of piety and simple innocence   MS., 1814–20
171–4 *so* 1827: 1814–20 *as* MS. *above*   178 yet   1827: and   1814–20
185–215 Where Fortune led. But more ambitious aims
            Opened upon him, and more dazzling views
            The vision *etc*. . . . repaired *as* X

"For this fair Bride, most rich in gifts of mind,
Nor sparingly endowed with worldly wealth,
His office he relinquished ; and retired
From the world's notice to a rural home.
Youth's season yet with him was scarcely past,   195
And she was in youth's prime. How free their love,
How full their joy! Till, pitiable doom!
In the short course of one undreaded year,
Death blasted all. Death suddenly o'erthrew
Two lovely Children—all that they possessed!   200
The Mother followed :—miserably bare
The one Survivor stood ; he wept, he prayed
For his dismissal, day and night, compelled
To hold communion with the grave, and face
With pain the regions of eternity.   205
An uncomplaining apathy displaced
This anguish ; and, indifferent to delight,
To aim and purpose, he consumed his days,
To private interest dead, and public care.
So lived he ; so he might have died.
                              But now,   210
To the wide world's astonishment, appeared
A glorious opening, the unlooked-for dawn,
That promised everlasting joy to France!
Her voice of social transport reached even him!
He broke from his contracted bounds, repaired   215
To the great City, an emporium then
Of golden expectations, and receiving
Freights every day from a new world of hope.
Thither his popular talents he transferred ;
And, from the pulpit, zealously maintained   220
The cause of Christ and civil liberty,

196–7 *so* 1845: . . . How full their joy
           How free their love! nor did [their 1814–20] that love decay
           Nor joy abate till, pitiable doom! 1814–43
204–5 *so* 1845: By pain to turn his thoughts towards the grave
           And face MS., 1814–43
           To commune with the grave, soul-sick, and face   C
212 A glorious 1827: The glorious   MS., 1814–20
213/14 That sudden light had power to pierce the gloom
   In which his Spirit, friendless upon earth,
   In separation dwelt, and solitude.   MS., 1814–20
214 Her] The   MS., 1814–20

As one, and moving to one glorious end.
Intoxicating service! I might say
A happy service; for he was sincere
As vanity and fondness for applause,   225
And new and shapeless wishes, would allow.

    "That righteous cause (such power hath freedom) bound,
For one hostility, in friendly league,
Ethereal natures and the worst of slaves;
Was served by rival advocates that came   230
From regions opposite as heaven and hell.
One courage seemed to animate them all:
And, from the dazzling conquests daily gained
By their united efforts, there arose
A proud and most presumptuous confidence   235
In the transcendent wisdom of the age,
And her discernment; not alone in rights,
And in the origin and bounds of power
Social and temporal; but in laws divine,
Deduced by reason, or to faith revealed.   240
An overweening trust was raised; and fear
Cast out, alike of person and of thing.
Plague from this union spread, whose subtle bane
The strongest did not easily escape;
And He, what wonder! took a mortal taint.   245
How shall I trace the change, how bear to tell

223 I might say] more than that   X
227–8 *so* 1827:   Cause of freedom, did, we know,
              Combine, for one hostility, as friends,   MS., 1814–20: That
righteous and most holy cause, we know, Combined   X
230 by rival] as seemed, by   X   233 dazzling] flattering MS.
233–42 *not in* X   234 arose] sprang forth   MS.
239–43 . . . but in nature's laws
        And in the eternal government of things,
        Religion's high immunity, the grants
        Of faith to chosen lands vouchsafed, or those
        By Deity committed to the heart
        O'er the wide plain of universal earth,
        Man's spiritual hopes, dependencies and needs.
        An overweening confidence was raised
        That cast out fear of person and of thing
        [In well intentioned minds to action raised]
        Plague from this union spread *etc.* MS. 58
 243 Plagues followed on such mixture spreading plagues   X

That he broke faith with them whom he had laid
In earth's dark chambers, with a Christian's hope!
An infidel contempt of holy writ
Stole by degrees upon his mind; and hence   250
Life, like that Roman Janus, double-faced;
Vilest hypocrisy—the laughing, gay
Hypocrisy, not leagued with fear, but pride.
Smooth words he had to wheedle simple souls;
But, for disciples of the inner school,   255
Old freedom was old servitude, and they
The wisest whose opinions stooped the least
To known restraints; and who most boldly drew
Hopeful prognostications from a creed,
That, in the light of false philosophy,   260
Spread like a halo round a misty moon,
Widening its circle as the storms advance.

  "His sacred function was at length renounced;
And every day and every place enjoyed
The unshackled layman's natural liberty;   265
Speech, manners, morals, all without disguise.
I do not wish to wrong him; though the course
Of private life licentiously displayed
Unhallowed actions—planted like a crown
Upon the insolent aspiring brow   270
Of spurious notions—worn as open signs
Of prejudice subdued—still he retained,

249 holy writ] sacred truth   MS. 58   250/1 For him and for his indivi-
dual harm   MS. 58
258–60 To tried authority and known restraints
        Whose creed, with sorrow be it said, [for this at bottom was the
            truth   X]
        Did in the light etc.   MSS
263 Although his sacred function was abjured   MS. 58   263–6 not
in X
267–9 I do not wish to wrong him, though the course
        Of private life was sullied and disgraced
        By evil actions . . .   MS. 58
267–72   for his heart
        Was generously disposed, and he retained   MS. 58 alt.
267–73 I would not wrong him, for he was a man
        Of generous wishes, and retained in midst
        Of such abasement etc.   X
272 so 1837: he still   MS., 1814–32

'Mid much abasement, what he had received
From nature, an intense and glowing mind.
Wherefore, when humbled Liberty grew weak,   275
And mortal sickness on her face appeared,
He coloured objects to his own desire
As with a lover's passion. Yet his moods
Of pain were keen as those of better men,
Nay keener, as his fortitude was less: 280
And he continued, when worse days were come,
To deal about his sparkling eloquence,
Struggling against the strange reverse with zeal
That showed like happiness. But, in despite
Of all this outside bravery, within,   285
He neither felt encouragement nor hope:
For moral dignity, and strength of mind,
Were wanting; and simplicity of life;
And reverence for himself; and, last and best,
Confiding thoughts, through love and fear of Him   290
Before whose sight the troubles of this world
Are vain, as billows in a tossing sea.

"The glory of the times fading away—
The splendor, which had given a festal air
To self-importance, hallowed it, and veiled   295
From his own sight—this gone, he forfeited
All joy in human nature; was consumed,
And vexed, and chafed, by levity and scorn,
And fruitless indignation; galled by pride;
Made desperate by contempt of men who throve   300
Before his sight in power or fame, and won,
Without desert, what he desired; weak men,
Too weak even for his envy or his hate!

273 much   1837: such   MS., 1814–32   275 And when the strength of
liberty decayed   MSS.   287 dignity] fortitude   X
290–2 The love and fear of God, the sense of God
        Sole feeling by the which we can sustain
        True comprehensiveness of intellect.   X
290 through   1827: and   MS., 1814–20
296 so 1827: . . . this gone, therewith he lost   1814–20: From sight of his
own eyes—this gone, he lost   MSS.   298 And toss'd about by levity
and spleen   X   300 throve] gained   X   301 not in X

Tormented thus, after a wandering course
Of discontent, and inwardly opprest   305
With malady—in part, I fear, provoked
By weariness of life—he fixed his home,
Or, rather say, sate down by very chance,
Among these rugged hills; where now he dwells,
And wastes the sad remainder of his hours,   310
Steeped in a self-indulging spleen, that wants not
Its own voluptuousness;—on this resolved,
With this content, that he will live and die
Forgotten,—at safe distance from 'a world
Not moving to his mind.' "
                     These serious words   315
Closed the preparatory notices
That served my Fellow-traveller to beguile
The way, while we advanced up that wide vale.
Diverging now (as if his quest had been
Some secret of the mountains, cavern, fall   320
Of water, or some lofty eminence,
Renowned for splendid prospect far and wide)
We scaled, without a track to ease our steps,
A steep ascent; and reached a dreary plain,
With a tumultuous waste of huge hill tops   325

304–5 *so* 1827: —And thus beset, and finding in himself
          No pleasure nor tranquillity, at last,
          After a wandering course of discontent
          In foreign lands, and *etc.*   MS., 1814–20
304–14 And thus beset . . . at last (*as above*)
          For want of better prospect he withdrew
          Into this place, as farthest from a world   X
311 *so* 1845: In Self-indulging spleen, that doth not want   MS., 1814–43
318–19 X *goes on here* (*from l.* 90)
          Along this Vale till noontide we advanc'd
          When suddenly upturning he began
          To climb upon one side of it, a ridge
          Of steep ascent, his object being, I guessed,   X
319 *so* 1827: Now, suddenly diverging, he began
          To climb upon its western side a ridge
          Pathless and smooth, a long and steep ascent;
          As if the object of his quest had been   1814–20: *as* MS., *but*
upturning *for* diverging *and* one side of it *for* its western side
321 some lofty   1845: some boastful   MS., 1814–43: conspicuous   C
323 Scaled . . . ease   1827: clomb . . . guide   MSS., 1814–20   324 *so*
1827: And, on the summit, reached a heathy plain   MSS., 1814–20

Before us; savage region! which I paced
Dispirited: when, all at once, behold!
Beneath our feet, a little lowly vale,
A lowly vale, and yet uplifted high
Among the mountains; even as if the spot   330
Had been from eldest time by wish of theirs
So placed, to be shut out from all the world!
Urn-like it was in shape, deep as an urn;
With rocks encompassed, save that to the south
Was one small opening, where a heath-clad ridge   335
Supplied a boundary less abrupt and close;
A quiet treeless nook, with two green fields,
A liquid pool that glittered in the sun,
And one bare dwelling; one abode, no more!
It seemed the home of poverty and toil,   340
Though not of want: the little fields, made green
By husbandry of many thrifty years,
Paid cheerful tribute to the moorland house.
—There crows the cock, single in his domain:
The small birds find in spring no thicket there   345
To shroud them; only from the neighbouring vales
The cuckoo, straggling up to the hill tops,
Shouteth faint tidings of some gladder place.

        Ah! what a sweet Recess, thought I, is here!
Instantly throwing down my limbs at ease   350
Upon a bed of heath;—full many a spot
Of hidden beauty have I chanced to espy
Among the mountains; never one like this;
So lonesome, and so perfectly secure;
Not melancholy—no, for it is green,   355
And bright, and fertile, furnished in itself
With the few needful things that life requires.
—In rugged arms how softly does it lie,
How tenderly protected! Far and near
We have an image of the pristine earth,   360
The planet in its nakedness: were this

326-7 . . . and I walked In weariness   MSS., 1814-20
334-6 Encompassed round about with highest rocks
       Which, but in one small opening, to the south
       Sloped gently back; elsewhere abrupt and close.   MSS.
358 softly does it   1837: soft it seems to   MSS., 1814-32

Man's only dwelling, sole appointed seat,
First, last, and single, in the breathing world,
It could not be more quiet: peace is here
Or nowhere; days unruffled by the gale   365
Of public news or private; years that pass
Forgetfully; uncalled upon to pay
The common penalties of mortal life,
Sickness, or accident, or grief, or pain.

On these and kindred thoughts intent I lay   370
In silence musing by my Comrade's side,
He also silent; when from out the heart
Of that profound abyss a solemn voice,
Or several voices in one solemn sound,
Was heard ascending; mournful, deep, and slow   375
The cadence, as of psalms—a funeral dirge!
We listened, looking down upon the hut,
But seeing no one: meanwhile from below
The strain continued, spiritual as before;
And now distinctly could I recognise   380
These words:—"*Shall in the grave thy love be known,
In death thy faithfulness?*"—"God rest his soul!"
Said the old man, abruptly breaking silence,—
"He is departed, and finds peace at last!"

This scarcely spoken, and those holy strains   385
Not ceasing, forth appeared in view a band
Of rustic persons, from behind the hut
Bearing a coffin in the midst, with which
They shaped their course along the sloping side
Of that small valley, singing as they moved;   390
A sober company and few, the men
Bare-headed, and all decently attired!

363/4 Without a fellow, near it or remote   MSS.
370–1 *so* 1827:   On these and other kindred thoughts intent
                In silence by my Comrade's side I lay   MSS., 1814–20
376 funeral dirge] psalm of death   MSS.   377 upon   1827: towards
MSS., 1814–20
382–3   Belike those words
          Said my companion, sighing as he spoke,
          Were chosen by himself. God rest his soul,   C
383 Said the old man   1845: The old Man exclaimed   MSS.: The Wan-
derer cried   1814–43   384 He is then dead, and hath found [God
give him   X]   MSS.   385 He scarce had spoken when   MSS.

Some steps when they had thus advanced, the dirge
Ended; and, from the stillness that ensued
Recovering, to my Friend I said, "You spake,   395
Methought, with apprehension that these rites
Are paid to Him upon whose shy retreat
This day we purposed to intrude."—"I did so.
But let us hence, that we may learn the truth:
Perhaps it is not he but some one else   400
For whom this pious service is performed;
Some other tenant of the solitude."

So, to a steep and difficult descent
Trusting ourselves, we wound from crag to crag,
Where passage could be won; and, as the last   405
Of the mute train, behind the heathy top
Of that off-sloping outlet, disappeared,
I, more impatient in my downward course,
Had landed upon easy ground; and there
Stood waiting for my Comrade. When behold   410
An object that enticed my steps aside!
A narrow, winding entry opened out
Into a platform—that lay, sheepfold-wise,
Enclosed between an upright mass of rock
And one old moss-grown wall;—a cool recess,   415
And fanciful! For where the rock and wall
Met in an angle, hung a penthouse, framed

396–9 I fancied with emotion, as of one
   Who must have been well known to you. He was so,
   But let us to the House, for I would have
   Assurance of the manner of his death   X
398 so. 1814: so, 1820–50   400 He is it not perhaps but   C
405–6 . . . as [while X] the train Who bore the body, having gained
[reach'd X] the top   MSS.   408 so 1827: in the course I took   MSS.,
1814–20   408–9 I landed upon easy ground, and there   X
412 so 1827: It was an Entry, narrow as a door;
               A passage whose brief windings (Which after some short
                     windings) opened out   MSS., 1814–20
413 . . . that by work of chance, As seemed, and not design, lay etc.   MSS.
414 an upright   1827: a single   MSS., 1814–20
415–16 And one stone wall. The floor was smooth and green
   And the small compass of the space within
   Shut out from view of anything but sky
   And passing clouds; and where the rock and wall   MSS.
417 so 1827: . . . hung a tiny roof
               Or penthouse which most quaintly had been framed   MSS.,
1814–20

By thrusting two rude staves into the wall
And overlaying them with mountain sods;
To weather-fend a little turf-built seat   420
Whereon a full-grown man might rest, nor dread
The burning sunshine, or a transient shower;
But the whole plainly wrought by children's hands!
Whose skill had thronged the floor with a proud show
Of baby-houses, curiously arranged;   425
Nor wanting ornament of walks between,
With mimic trees inserted in the turf,
And gardens interposed. Pleased with the sight,
I could not choose but beckon to my Guide,
Who, entering, round him threw a careless glance   430
Impatient to pass on, when I exclaimed,
"Lo! what is here?" and, stooping down, drew forth
A book, that, in the midst of stones and moss
And wreck of party-coloured earthenware,
Aptly disposed, had lent its help to raise   435
One of those petty structures. "His it must be!"   .
Exclaimed the Wanderer, "cannot but be his,
And he is gone!" The book, which in my hand
Had opened of itself (for it was swoln
With searching damp, and seemingly had lain   440
To the injurious elements exposed
From week to week,) I found to be a work

418 staves 1827: sticks MSS., 1814–20
420–2 Screen for a low sod seat beneath, a seat
       On which a man of stature tall might rest
                     [beneath, of width
       And barely so, to hold a full-grown Man,   X]
       Scantily sheltered from a transient shower   MSS.
424 *so* 1827: Whose simple skill had thronged the grassy floor
              With work of frame less solid, a proud show   1814–20
424–31 And here and there the grassy floor was thronged
        With baby-houses, chiefly small loose stones
        Together ranged in circle or in square.
        The old Man who, to my summons giving way,
        Had entered, looked about him carelessly
        And now would have passed on *etc.*   MSS.
430–1 *so* 1827: Who having entered, carelessly looked round,
              And now *etc. as* MS., 1814–20
435 Placed as they came to hand, had helped to make   MS.: Finding a
useful place . . . build   X   436–7 *so* 1845: "Gracious Heaven!" The
Wanderer cried, "it cannot" *etc.* 1814–43; *so* MSS., *but* Cried the Old Man
440–2 With damp and rain) I found to be a book   MS.

In the French tongue, a Novel of Voltaire,
His famous Optimist. "Unhappy Man!"
Exclaimed my Friend: "here then has been to him   445
Retreat within retreat, a sheltering-place
Within how deep a shelter! He had fits,
Even to the last, of genuine tenderness,
And loved the haunts of children; here, no doubt,
Pleasing and pleased, he shared their simple sports,   450
Or sate companionless; and here the book,
Left and forgotten in his careless way,
Must by the cottage-children have been found:
Heaven bless them, and their inconsiderate work!
To what odd purpose have the darlings turned   455
This sad memorial of their hapless friend!"

    "Me," said I, "most doth it surprise, to find
Such book in such a place!"—"A book it is,"
He answered, "to the Person suited well,
Though little suited to surrounding things: 460
'Tis strange, I grant; and stranger still had been
To see the Man who owned it, dwelling here,
With one poor shepherd, far from all the world!—
Now, if our errand hath been thrown away,
As from these intimations I forebode,   465
Grieved shall I be—less for my sake than yours,
And least of all for him who is no more."

450–3 *so* 1827: He sometimes played with them; and here hath sate
                Far oftener by himself. This Book, I guess,
                Hath been forgotten in his careless way;
                Left here when he was occupied in mind;
                And by the Cottage Children has been found. 1814–20; *so*
MSS., *but l.* 453 And so must by the Children have been found
456 This monument of their unhappy Friend! MSS.   457 ... said I "the
device surprizes less, I know not for what reason, than to find   MSS.
459–62 ... not ill suited to the Man
                And I was moved at sight of it; 'tis strange
                I grant, and yet more strange had been to see
                The Man, who was its Owner, dwelling here.   MSS.
461–2 *so* 1827: Nor, with the knowledge which my mind possessed,
                Could I behold it undisturbed: 'tis strange,
                I grant, and stranger still had been to see *etc. as* MSS.,
1814–20
464–6 Our errand has, it seems, been thrown away,
                And I am griev'd, less *etc.*   X

By this, the book was in the old Man's hand;
And he continued, glancing on the leaves
An eye of scorn:—"The lover," said he, "doomed   470
To love when hope hath failed him—whom no depth
Of privacy is deep enough to hide,
Hath yet his bracelet or his lock of hair,
And that is joy to him. When change of times
Hath summoned kings to scaffolds, do but give   475
The faithful servant, who must hide his head
Henceforth in whatsoever nook he may,
A kerchief sprinkled with his master's blood,
And he too hath his comforter. How poor,
Beyond all poverty how destitute,   480
Must that Man have been left, who, hither driven,
Flying or seeking, could yet bring with him
No dearer relique, and no better stay,
Than this dull product of a scoffer's pen,
Impure conceits discharging from a heart   485
Hardened by impious pride!—I did not fear
To tax you with this journey;"—mildly said
My venerable Friend, as forth we stepped
Into the presence of the cheerful light—
"For I have knowledge that you do not shrink   490
From moving spectacles;—but let us on."

So speaking, on he went, and at the word
I followed, till he made a sudden stand:
For full in view, approaching through a gate
That opened from the enclosure of green fields   495
Into the rough uncultivated ground,
Behold the Man whom he had fancied dead!
I knew from his deportment, mien, and dress,
That it could be no other; a pale face,
A meagre person, tall, and in a garb   500

484 dull] vile   C   484–6 Than such a Book as this. I did not fear   X
487–91   . . . journey, as we stepped
        Forth from that covert into open day
        Said chearfully my venerable Friend
        For I . . . spectacles. Few words may serve
        To tell his story   X (which now returns to l. 164 app. crit.—He was,
            like myself etc.)
498 so 1827: from the appearance and the dress   MSS., 1814–20
500 so 1845: A tall and meagre person, in a garb   MS., 1814–43

Not rustic—dull and faded like himself!
He saw us not, though distant but few steps;
For he was busy, dealing, from a store
Upon a broad leaf carried, choicest strings
Of red ripe currants; gift by which he strove,   505
With intermixture of endearing words,
To soothe a Child, who walked beside him, weeping
As if disconsolate.—"They to the grave
Are bearing him, my Little-one," he said,
"To the dark pit; but he will feel no pain;   510
His body is at rest, his soul in heaven."

    More might have followed—but my honoured Friend
Broke in upon the Speaker with a frank
And cordial greeting.—Vivid was the light
That flashed and sparkled from the other's eyes;   515
He was all fire: no shadow on his brow
Remained, nor sign of sickness on his face.
Hands joined he with his Visitant,—a grasp,
An eager grasp; and many moments' space—
When the first glow of pleasure was no more,   520
And, of the sad appearance which at once
Had vanished, much was come and coming back—
An amicable smile retained the life
Which it had unexpectedly received,
Upon his hollow cheek. "How kind," he said,   525
"Nor could your coming have been better timed;
For this, you see, is in our narrow world

504–5 *so* 1827: Which on a leaf he carried in his hand,
           Strings of ripe currants *etc.* MSS., 1814–20
508–8 To chear a weeping Child, a ruddy Boy
           That tottered by his side. MSS.
512–15 *so* 1827: Glad was my Comrade now, though he at first,
           I doubt not, had been more surprized than glad.
           But now, recovered from the shock and calm,
           He soberly advanced; and to the Man
           Gave cheerful greeting.—Vivid was the light
           Which flashed at this from out the Other's eyes; MSS.,
1814–20
516–17 *so* 1845: *so* C, *but l.* 517 No sign of . . . left upon . . .
           He was all fire: the sickness from his face
           Passed like a fancy that is swept away; MSS., 1814–43
521–2 *so* 1840: Long after what was vanished had returned MSS.: And
much of what had vanished was returned 1814–37   527 narrow
1827: little MS., 1814–20

A day of sorrow. I have here a charge"—
And, speaking thus, he patted tenderly
The sun-burnt forehead of the weeping child—   530
"A little mourner, whom it is my task
To comfort;—but how came ye?—if yon track
(Which doth at once befriend us and betray)
Conducted hither your most welcome feet,
Ye could not miss the funeral train—they yet   535
Have scarcely disappeared." "This blooming Child,"
Said the old Man, "is of an age to weep
At any grave or solemn spectacle,
Inly distressed or overpowered with awe,
He knows not wherefore;—but the boy to-day,   540
Perhaps is shedding orphan's tears; you also
Must have sustained a loss."—"The hand of Death,"
He answered, "has been here; but could not well
Have fallen more lightly, if it had not fallen
Upon myself."—The other left these words   545
Unnoticed, thus continuing.—
                                    "From yon crag
Down whose steep sides we dropped into the vale,
We heard the hymn they sang—a solemn sound
Heard anywhere; but in a place like this
'Tis more than human! Many precious rites   550
And customs of our rural ancestry
Are gone, or stealing from us; this, I hope,
Will last for ever. Oft on my way have I
Stood still, though but a casual passenger,
So much I felt the awfulness of life,   555

532–6   . . . which your road,
     You cannot well have missed the funeral train
     They scarcely yet are out of sight." This Child   MS.
536–49   . . . we heard,
     The old man answered, from yon rock above
     Down whose etc. (547)
     The hymn they sang—a solemn sound, in truth,
     Whenever heard, etc.   X
540–1 so 1845: He knows not why;—but he, perchance, this day,
                Is shedding Orphan's tears; and you yourself MS., 1814–43
550 precious] antient   X
553–4 so 1837:   . . . Often have I stopped
                When on my way, I could not chuse but stop,   MS.,
     1814–20, 1832: Often have I stopped   1827
553–6   . . . Who that has a heart

In that one moment when the corse is lifted
In silence, with a hush of decency;
Then from the threshold moves with song of peace,
And confidential yearnings, tow'rds its home,
Its final home on earth. What traveller—who—   560
(How far soe'er a stranger) does not own
The bond of brotherhood, when he sees them go,
A mute procession on the houseless road;
Or passing by some single tenement
Or clustered dwellings, where again they raise   565
The monitory voice? But most of all
It touches, it confirms, and elevates,
Then, when the body, soon to be consigned
Ashes to ashes, dust bequeathed to dust,
Is raised from the church-aisle, and forward borne   570
Upon the shoulders of the next in love,
The nearest in affection or in blood;
Yea, by the very mourners who had knelt
Beside the coffin, resting on its lid
In silent grief their unuplifted heads,   575
And heard meanwhile the Psalmist's mournful plaint,
And that most awful scripture which declares
We shall not sleep, but we shall all be changed!
—Have I not seen—ye likewise may have seen—
Son, husband, brothers—brothers side by side,   580
And son and father also side by side,
Rise from that posture:—and in concert move
On the green turf following the vested Priest,
Four dear supporters of one senseless weight,
From which they do not shrink, and under which   585
They faint not, but advance towards the open grave
Step after step—together, with their firm
Unhidden faces: he that suffers most,

And does not feel the awfulness of life,
   That moment when the corpse is lifted up   X
559 tow'rds 1845: to MS., 1814–43   560 on earth 1837: in earth
MS., 1814–32   560-2 Its final home in God. And when they go   X
563 houseless] lonely X   563/4 As is, I know, the manner in the
hills X
564-5 And pass some single tenement or lot
   Of clustered dwellings, taking up again   X
573–606 *page torn out of* X   586 open grave 1837: grave MS.,
1814–32

He outwardly, and inwardly perhaps,
The most serene, with most undaunted eye!—   590
Oh! blest are they who live and die like these,
Loved with such love, and with such sorrow mourned!''

    "That poor Man taken hence to-day," replied
The Solitary, with a faint sarcastic smile
Which did not please me, "must be deemed, I fear,   595
Of the unblest; for he will surely sink
Into his mother earth without such pomp
Of grief, depart without occasion given
By him for such array of fortitude.
Full seventy winters hath he lived, and mark!   600
This simple Child will mourn his one short hour,
And I shall miss him; scanty tribute! yet,
This wanting, he would leave the sight of men,
If love were his sole claim upon their care,
Like a ripe date which in the desert falls   605
Without a hand to gather it.''
                                        At this
I interposed, though loth to speak, and said,
"Can it be thus among so small a band
As ye must needs be here? in such a place
I would not willingly, methinks, lose sight   610
Of a departing cloud.''—" 'Twas not for love''—
Answered the sick Man with a careless voice—
"That I came hither; neither have I found
Among associates who have power of speech,
Nor in such other converse as is here,   615
Temptation so prevailing as to change
That mood, or undermine my first resolve.''
Then, speaking in like careless sort, he said
To my benign Companion,—"Pity 'tis
That fortune did not guide you to this house   620
A few days earlier; then would you have seen
What stuff the Dwellers in a solitude,
That seems by Nature hollowed out to be

590/1 Nor finally doth care of other hands
     Resign the body to the hollow ground   MS.
614 associates] my comrades   MSS.
622/3 This tempting, smiling [little tempting X] innocent solitude   MSS.
622–4 *so* 1827:   . . . this Solitude
         (That seems by Nature framed to be the seat
         And very bosom of pure innocence)   MS., 1814–20

The seat and bosom of pure innocence,
Are made of; an ungracious matter this!   625
Which, for truth's sake, yet in remembrance too
Of past discussions with this zealous friend
And advocate of humble life, I now
Will force upon his notice; undeterred
By the example of his own pure course,   630
And that respect and deference which a soul
May fairly claim, by niggard age enriched
In what she most doth value, love of God
And his frail creature Man;—but ye shall hear.
I talk—and ye are standing in the sun   635
Without refreshment!''
                    Quickly had he spoken,
And, with light steps still quicker than his words,
Led toward the Cottage. Homely was the spot;
And, to my feeling, ere we reached the door,
Had almost a forbidding nakedness;   640
Less fair, I grant, even painfully less fair,
Than it appeared when from the beetling rock
We had looked down upon it. All within,
As left by the departed company,
Was silent; save the solitary clock   645
That on mine ear ticked with a mournful sound.—
Following our Guide, we clomb the cottage-stairs
And reached a small apartment dark and low,
Which was no sooner entered than our Host

627–34 Of former conversations with my Friend
        I will tell nakedly and undeterred
        By reverence which is due to his grey hairs
        And venerable life; but ye shall hear   MSS.
633 *so* 1845: In what it [she 1827 *etc.*] values most—the love of God 1814–43
636–8 *so* 1837: Saying this he led Towards the Cottage   MSS., 1814–32
638 tow'rds *corr. to* toward C   642 beetling rock   1827: Valley's brink
MSS., 1814–20   644 the   1827: that   1814–20:   As by the funeral
train it had been left MSS.   645 save 1845: and MSS., 1814–43
646 *so* 1845: Ticked, as I thought, with melancholy sound   MSS., 1814–43
646/7 The chairs were in disorder, on a board
        Was seen the remnants of that humble fare
        On which the little Company had fed
        Ere to the distant Church they took their way   MS.
647 We clomb the cottage-stairs, as we were led   X   648 . . . little
room, narrow and dark   X

Said gaily, "This is my domain, my cell,　650
My hermitage, my cabin, what you will—
I love it better than a snail his house.
But now ye shall be feasted with our best."

　So, with more ardour than an unripe girl
Left one day mistress of her mother's stores,　655
He went about his hospitable task.
My eyes were busy, and my thoughts no less,
And pleased I looked upon my grey-haired Friend,
As if to thank him; he returned that look,
Cheered, plainly, and yet serious. What a wreck　660
Had we about us! scattered was the floor,
And, in like sort, chair, window-seat, and shelf,
With books, maps, fossils, withered plants and flowers,
And tufts of mountain moss. Mechanic tools
Lay intermixed with scraps of paper, some　665
Scribbled with verse: a broken angling-rod
And shattered telescope, together linked
By cobwebs, stood within a dusty nook;
And instruments of music, some half-made,
Some in disgrace, hung dangling from the walls.　670
But speedily the promise was fulfilled;
A feast before us, and a courteous Host
Inviting us in glee to sit and eat.
A napkin, white as foam of that rough brook
By which it had been bleached, o'erspread the board; 675

659 . . . he, too, looked and looked　MSS.　　661 *so* 1845: We had
around [about　MS]　MS., 1814–20: Had we around　1827–43
664–5 *so* 1827:　　　　. . . moss; and here and there
　　　　　Lay intermixed with these, mechanic tools
　　　　　And scraps of paper,—some I could perceive　1814–20
664–8 Mechanic tools, the shavings and the dust
　　From woods of divers colours, trinket toys,
　　Loose scraps of paper, some as I could see
　　Scribbled with verse, a broken angling-rod
　　For neighbourhood, a cob-webb'd telescope　X
　　And tufts of mountain moss. Here and there flowers
　　And feathers dropp'd from hawks' and eagles' wings
　　Lay intermixed with these mechanic tools
　　Loose scraps *etc. as* X　MS.
671 But from such entertainment of our eyes
　　And such employment of our thoughts, we soon
　　Were summon'd, for the promise was fulfill'd　X

And was itself half-covered with a store
Of dainties,—oaten bread, curd, cheese, and cream;
And cakes of butter curiously embossed,
Butter that had imbibed from meadow-flowers
A golden hue, delicate as their own   680
Faintly reflected in a lingering stream.
Nor lacked, for more delight on that warm day,
Our table, small parade of garden fruits,
And whortle-berries from the mountain side.
The Child, who long ere this had stilled his sobs,   685
Was now a help to his late comforter,
And moved, a willing Page, as he was bid,
Ministering to our need.
                          In genial mood,
While at our pastoral banquet thus we sate
Fronting the window of that little cell,   690
I could not, ever and anon, forbear
To glance an upward look on two huge Peaks,
That from some other vale peered into this.

676 store   1845: load   MSS., 1814–43   677 curd   1827: curds
MS., 1814–20
678–81 *so* 1832: Butter that had imbibed a golden tinge,
              A hue like that of yellow meadow flowers
              Reflected faintly in a silent pool.   MS., 1814–20
              Butter . . . golden tinge
              From meadow flowers, hue delicate as theirs *etc. as text*   1827
687 Moved, like a   MSS.
688–725   While thus we sate
              Fronting the window ever and anon
              I glanced an upward look (the sight till now
              I had not seen) on two huge mountain peaks
              That from some other vale peep'd into this
              "Those lusty twins and I," exclaimed our Host
              "Are good Companions. Many are the sounds
              Which the wind fashions in his tuneful course
              Among the rocks and heaths and dashing shores.
              These Creatures also of the silent sky
              These also have their harmony, for so,
              So do I call it, though there be no voice,
              Clouds, mists, and shadow, light . . . *as text*
                        , . . sick hearts
              And idle spirits. Here I sit and watch.
              Thoughts are not busier in the mind of man
              Than is the work done here."   X *which ends here but v. note*
to 741–62 *p.* 418
692/3 Right opposite, two giant mountain Peaks   MS.

"Those lusty twins," exclaimed our host, "if here
It were your lot to dwell, would soon become   695
Your prized companions.—Many are the notes
Which, in his tuneful course, the wind draws forth
From rocks, woods, caverns, heaths, and dashing shores;
And well those lofty brethren bear their part
In the wild concert—chiefly when the storm   700
Rides high; then all the upper air they fill
With roaring sound, that ceases not to flow,
Like smoke, along the level of the blast,
In mighty current; theirs, too, is the song
Of stream and headlong flood that seldom fails;   705
And, in the grim and breathless hour of noon,
Methinks that I have heard them echo back
The thunder's greeting. Nor have nature's laws
Left them ungifted with a power to yield
Music of finer tone; a harmony,   710
So do I call it, though it be the hand
Of silence, though there be no voice;—the clouds,
The mist, the shadows, light of golden suns,
Motions of moonlight, all come thither—touch,
And have an answer—thither come, and shape   715
A language not unwelcome to sick hearts
And idle spirits:—there the sun himself,
At the calm close of summer's longest day,
Rests his substantial orb;—between those heights
And on the top of either pinnacle,   720
More keenly than elsewhere in night's blue vault,
Sparkle the stars, as of their station proud.
Thoughts are not busier in the mind of man
Than the mute agents stirring there:—alone
Here do I sit and watch.—"
                              A fall of voice,   725
Regretted like the nightingale's last note,

694–5 *so* 1827: "Those lusty Twins on which your eyes are cast" [you cast
          your eyes   MS.]
               Exclaimed our Host, "if here you dwelt would be   MS.,
               1814–20
704 and the song is theirs   MS.   708–9 . . . greeting, but they also
yield   710 tone   1827: frame   MS., 1814–20
725–8 *so* 1827–50 [*but* rhapsody *for* strain of rapture   1845]
                              With brightening face
          The Wanderer [Old Man   MS.] heard him speaking thus, and said,
          MS., 1814–20

Had scarcely closed this high-wrought strain of rapture
Ere with inviting smile the Wanderer said:
"Now for the tale with which you threatened us!"
"In truth the threat escaped me unawares:⁣   730
Should the tale tire you, let this challenge stand
For my excuse. Dissevered from mankind,
As to your eyes and thoughts we must have seemed
When ye looked down upon us from the crag,
Islanders mid a stormy mountain sea,   735
We are not so;—perpetually we touch
Upon the vulgar ordinances of the world;
And he, whom this our cottage hath to-day
Relinquished, lived dependent for his bread
Upon the laws of public charity.   740
The Housewife, tempted by such slender gains
As might from that occasion be distilled,
Opened, as she before had done for me,
Her doors to admit this homeless Pensioner;
The portion gave of coarse but wholesome fare   745
Which appetite required—a blind dull nook,
Such as she had, the *kennel* of his rest!
This, in itself not ill, would yet have been
Ill borne in earlier life; but his was now
The still contentedness of seventy years.   750
Calm did he sit under the wide-spread tree
Of his old age; and yet less calm and meek,
Winningly meek or venerably calm,

731–3 *so* 1827: I had forgotten it, and 'tis no more
        Than a bare incident of rustic life,
        But ye shall have it. Outcast and cut off
        As we seem here, and must have seemed to you   MS.
        And was forgotten. Let this challenge stand
        For my excuse, if what I shall relate
        Tire your attention.—Outcast and cut off *etc. as* MS.,
            1814–20
735 mid   1845: of   MS., 1814–43   737 ordinances   1837: ordinance
MS., 1814–32   739 lived   1827: was   MS., 1814–20   743 Opened]
Contriv'd   X   744 A place to harbour also this Old man   X   745–6
The portion ... required] Food gave him for his meals   MS.   750 seventy]
eighty   X   751 under   1837: beneath   MS., 1814–32
751–6 And more than that more torpid and more slow
        He moved about beneath a double cloud
        The punishment if punishment it were
        Of spendthrift *etc. as text*   X

Than slow and torpid; paying in this wise
A penalty, if penalty it were,   755
For spendthrift feats, excesses of his prime.
I loved the old Man, for I pitied him!
A task it was, I own, to hold discourse
With one so slow in gathering up his thoughts,
But he was a cheap pleasure to my eyes;   760
Mild, inoffensive, ready in *his* way,
And helpful to his utmost power: and there
Our housewife knew full well what she possessed!
He was her vassal of all labour, tilled
Her garden, from the pasture fetched her kine;   765
And, one among the orderly array
Of hay-makers, beneath the burning sun
Maintained his place; or heedfully pursued
His course, on errands bound, to other vales,
Leading sometimes an inexperienced child   770
Too young for any profitable task.
So moved he like a shadow that performed
Substantial service. Mark me now, and learn
For what reward!—The moon her monthly round
Hath not completed since our dame, the queen   775
Of this one cottage and this lonely dale,
Into my little sanctuary rushed—
Voice to a rueful treble humanised,
And features in deplorable dismay.
I treat the matter lightly, but, alas!   780
It is most serious: persevering rain

755 A lingering penalty, if such it were   MS.   762 *so* 1827: And
useful to the utmost of his power   MS.: 1814–20 *as text but* useful
764–9   . . . labour, nursed
     Her infants, from the Pasture fetched her Kine,
     Her plot of garden ground he delved and dressed,
     And one among the band of Haymakers,
     Well as he might, beneath the burning sun
     Did he maintain his place, with steady pains;
     Errands he went at need *etc.*   MS.
773–5   . . . willingly and well.
     So came and went, uninjured and secure
     From all mishap. Now mark, and I will prove
     That we have here a growth of human hearts
     Unsightly as the worst. Our dame *etc.*   MS.
776/7 At the approach of evening, three weeks past   MS.
781 *so* 1827: from mid-noon the rain   MS., 1814–20

Had fallen in torrents; all the mountain-tops
Were hidden, and black vapours coursed their sides;
This had I seen, and saw; but, till she spake,
Was wholly ignorant that my ancient Friend—   785
Who at her bidding early and alone,
Had clomb aloft to delve the moorland turf
For winter fuel—to his noontide meal
Returned not, and now, haply, on the heights
Lay at the mercy of this raging storm.   790
'Inhuman!'—said I, 'was an old Man's life
Not worth the trouble of a thought?—alas!
This notice comes too late.' With joy I saw
Her husband enter—from a distant vale.
We sallied forth together; found the tools   795
Which the neglected veteran had dropped,
But through all quarters looked for him in vain.
We shouted—but no answer! Darkness fell
Without remission of the blast or shower,
And fears for our own safety drove us home.   800

        "I, who weep little, did, I will confess,
The moment I was seated here alone,
Honour my little cell with some few tears
Which anger and resentment could not dry.
All night the storm endured: and, soon as help   805

784-94   and from her mouth
        Now heard, I heard it with distress of mind,
        That the Old Man alone upon the heights
        Lay somewhere at the mercy of the storm
        Alone, and had been so for many hours.
        'Twas known to her, her only of the house,
        For at her bidding early in the day
        The heights he had ascended to delve turf
        For winter fuel—to the noontide meal
        He came not, nor returned though hours passed by,
        Hour after hour, and still a raging storm.
        "Inhuman," said I, "Why not speak ere this?
        Alas, 'tis now too late." Even at the word
        Her husband entered *etc.* MS.
787 moorland 1827: mountain 1814-20   789 *so* 1827: Came not,
and now perchance upon 1814-20
795-7   . . . found the Spot
        With difficulty found it, where the Old Man
        Had piled his work, but looked for him in vain MS.
804 and 1827: or MS., 1814-20

Had been collected from the neighbouring vale,
With morning we renewed our quest: the wind
Was fallen, the rain abated, but the hills
Lay shrouded in impenetrable mist;
And long and hopelessly we sought in vain:　　　810
Till, chancing on that lofty ridge to pass
A heap of ruin—almost without walls
And wholly without roof (the bleached remains
Of a small chapel, where, in ancient time,
The peasants of these lonely valleys used　　　815
To meet for worship on that central height)—
We there espied the object of our search,
Lying full three parts buried among tufts
Of heath-plant, under and above him strewn,
To baffle, as he might, the watery storm:　　　820
And there we found him breathing peaceably,
Snug as a child that hides itself in sport
'Mid a green hay-cock in a sunny field.
We spake—he made reply, but would not stir
At our entreaty; less from want of power　　　825
Than apprehension and bewildering thoughts.

　　"So was he lifted gently from the ground,
And with their freight homeward the shepherds moved
Through the dull mist, I following—when a step,
A single step, that freed me from the skirts　　　830
Of the blind vapour, opened to my view
Glory beyond all glory ever seen

809 Lay] Were　MS.　　　811 on that　1827: by [on　MS.] yon　MS.,
1814–20
813–17 *so* 1827: And wholly without roof (in ancient time
　　　　　　　It was a Chapel, a small Edifice
　　　　　　　In which the Peasants of these lonely Dells
　　　　　　　For worship met upon that central height)—
　　　　　　　Chancing to pass this wreck of stones, we there
　　　　　　　Espied at last the Object of our search,
　　　　　　　Couched in a nook, and seemingly alive.
　　　　　　　It would have moved you, had you seen the guise
　　　　　　　In which he occupied his chosen bed,　MS., 1814–20
818–19 Lay more than three parts buried under load
　　　　Of heath-plant which he with his hands had pulled
　　　　And spread for a protection from the touch
　　　　Of the cold ground, and heaped the covering high　MS.
827 So did we lift him　MS.　　　828 *so* 1837: the Shepherds homeward
MS., 1814–32

By waking sense or by the dreaming soul!
The appearance, instantaneously disclosed,
Was of a mighty city—boldly say   835
A wilderness of building, sinking far
And self-withdrawn into a boundless depth,
Far sinking into splendor—without end!
Fabric it seemed of diamond and of gold,
With alabaster domes, and silver spires,   840
And blazing terrace upon terrace, high
Uplifted; here, serene pavilions bright,
In avenues disposed; there, towers begirt
With battlements that on their restless fronts
Bore stars—illumination of all gems!   845
By earthly nature had the effect been wrought
Upon the dark materials of the storm
Now pacified; on them, and on the coves
And mountain-steeps and summits, whereunto
The vapours had receded, taking there   850
Their station under a cerulean sky.
Oh, 'twas an unimaginable sight!
Clouds, mists, streams, watery rocks and emerald turf,
Clouds of all tincture, rocks and sapphire sky,
Confused, commingled, mutually inflamed,   855
Molten together, and composing thus,
Each lost in each, that marvellous array
Of temple, palace, citadel, and huge
Fantastic pomp of structure without name,
In fleecy folds voluminous, enwrapped.   860
Right in the midst, where interspace appeared
Of open court, an object like a throne
Under a shining canopy of state

833 living soul   MS.
833/4 Though I am conscious that no power of words
      Can body forth, no hues of speech can paint
      That gorgeous spectacle—too bright and fair
      Even for remembrance; yet the attempt may give
      Collateral interest to this homely Tale,   1814–20 (*not in* MS.)
834–5 A huge and mighty City—boldly say   MS.   837 boundless
MS., 1845: wondrous   1814–43   842 here] and   MS.   843 *not*
in MS.   844 With] And   MS.
863 Under   1837: Beneath   1814–32
863–5 Stood fixed, and shining canopies were seen
      And implements *etc.*   MS.

Stood fixed; and fixed resemblances were seen
To implements of ordinary use,   865
But vast in size, in substance glorified;
Such as by Hebrew Prophets were beheld
In vision—forms uncouth of mightiest power
For admiration and mysterious awe.
This little Vale, a dwelling-place of Man,   870
Lay low beneath my feet; 'twas visible—
I saw not, but I felt that it was there.
That which I *saw* was the revealed abode
Of Spirits in beatitude: my heart
Swelled in my breast.—'I have been dead,' I cried,   875
'And now I live! Oh! wherefore *do* I live?'
And with that pang I prayed to be no more!—
—But I forget our Charge, as utterly
I then forgot him:—there I stood and gazed:
The apparition faded not away,   880
And I descended.

               Having reached the house,
I found its rescued inmate safely lodged,
And in serene possession of himself,
Beside a fire whose genial warmth seemed met
By a faint shining from the heart, a gleam   885
Of comfort, spread over his pallid face.
Great show of joy the housewife made, and truly
Was glad to find her conscience set at ease;
And not less glad, for sake of her good name,
That the poor Sufferer had escaped with life.   890
But, though he seemed at first to have received
No harm, and uncomplaining as before
Went through his usual tasks, a silent change
Soon showed itself: he lingered three short weeks;
And from the cottage hath been borne to-day.   895

    "So ends my dolorous tale, and glad I am
That it is ended." At these words he turned—
And, with blithe air of open fellowship,

---

870 *so* 1845: Below me was the earth; this little Vale   MS., 1814–43
882 I found the Shepherds' burden   MS.
884–6 *so* 1837: Beside a genial fire; that seemed to spread
         A gleam of comfort o'er his pallid face.   MS., 1814–32

Brought from the cupboard wine and stouter cheer,
Like one who would be merry. Seeing this,   900
My grey-haired Friend said courteously—"Nay, nay,
You have regaled us as a hermit ought;
Now let us forth into the sun!"—Our Host
Rose, though reluctantly, and forth we went.

BOOK THIRD

DESPONDENCY

ARGUMENT

Images in the Valley.—Another Recess in it entered and described.—
Wanderer's sensations.—Solitary's excited by the same objects.—Contrast
between these.—Despondency of the Solitary gently reproved.—Conversa-
tion exhibiting the Solitary's past and present opinions and feelings, till he
enters upon his own History at length.—His domestic felicity.—Afflictions.
—Dejection.—Roused by the French Revolution.—Disappointment and
disgust.—Voyage to America.—Disappointment and disgust pursue him.—
His return.—His languor and depression of mind, from want of faith in the
great truths of Religion, and want of confidence in the virtue of Mankind.

A HUMMING BEE—a little tinkling rill—
A pair of falcons wheeling on the wing,
In clamorous agitation, round the crest
Of a tall rock, their airy citadel—
By each and all of these the pensive ear   5
Was greeted, in the silence that ensued,
When through the cottage-threshold we had passed,
And, deep within that lonesome valley, stood
Once more beneath the concave of a blue
And cloudless sky.—Anon exclaimed our Host,   10
Triumphantly dispersing with the taunt
The shade of discontent which on his brow
Had gathered,—"Ye have left my cell,—but see
How Nature hems you in with friendly arms!
And by her help ye are my prisoners still.   15
But which way shall I lead you?—how contrive,
In spot so parsimoniously endowed,
That the brief hours, which yet remain, may reap
Some recompense of knowledge or delight?"
So saying, round he looked, as if perplexed;   20
And, to remove those doubts, my grey-haired Friend
Said—"Shall we take this pathway for our guide?—
Upward it winds, as if, in summer heats,
Its line had first been fashioned by the flock
Seeking a place of refuge at the root   25

9 a blue   1832: the blue   1814–27   9–10 . . . the concave of the
calm, Cerulean sky   MS.   25 so 1837: A place of refuge seeking   MS.,
1814–32

Of yon black Yew-tree, whose protruded boughs
Darken the silver bosom of the crag,
From which she draws her meagre sustenance.
There in commodious shelter may we rest.
Or let us trace this streamlet to its source;   30
Feebly it tinkles with an earthy sound,
And a few steps may bring us to the spot
Where, haply, crowned with flowerets and green herbs,
The mountain infant to the sun comes forth,
Like human life from darkness."—A quick turn   35
Through a strait passage of encumbered ground,
Proved that such hope was vain:—for now we stood
Shut out from prospect of the open vale,
And saw the water, that composed this rill,
Descending, disembodied, and diffused   40
O'er the smooth surface of an ample crag,
Lofty, and steep, and naked as a tower.
All further progress here was barred;—And who,
Thought I, if master of a vacant hour,
Here would not linger, willingly detained?   45
Whether to such wild objects he were led
When copious rains have magnified the stream
Into a loud and white-robed waterfall,
Or introduced at this more quiet time.

Upon a semicirque of turf-clad ground,   50
The hidden nook discovered to our view
A mass of rock, resembling, as it lay
Right at the foot of that moist precipice,
A stranded ship, with keel upturned, that rests
Fearless of winds and waves. Three several stones   55
Stood near, of smaller size, and not unlike
To monumental pillars: and, from these
Some little space disjoined, a pair were seen,
That with united shoulders bore aloft
A fragment, like an altar, flat and smooth: 60

28 she . . . her 1827: it . . . its MS., 1814–20   30 its MS., 1814–27,
1845–50: his 1832–43   35 so 1827: At the word We followed
where [as MS.] he led:—a sudden turn MS., 1814–20   43 progress]
prospect MS.
44 Stranger, or Inmate of the lonesome vale
     What living Man, thought I within myself MS.

Barren the tablet, yet thereon appeared
A tall and shining holly, that had found
A hospitable chink, and stood upright,
As if inserted by some human hand
In mockery, to wither in the sun,   65
Or lay its beauty flat before a breeze,
The first that entered. But no breeze did now
Find entrance;—high or low appeared no trace
Of motion, save the water that descended,
Diffused adown that barrier of steep rock,   70
And softly creeping, like a breath of air,
Such as is sometimes seen, and hardly seen,
To brush the still breast of a crystal lake.

  "Behold a cabinet for sages built,
Which kings might envy!"—Praise to this effect   75
Broke from the happy old Man's reverend lip;
Who to the Solitary turned, and said,
"In sooth, with love's familiar privilege,
You have decried the wealth which is your own.
Among these rocks and stones, methinks, I see   80
More than the heedless impress that belongs
To lonely nature's casual work: they bear
A semblance strange of power intelligent,
And of design not wholly worn away.
Boldest of plants that ever faced the wind,   85
How gracefully that slender shrub looks forth
From its fantastic birthplace! And I own,
Some shadowy intimations haunt me here,

61/2 Conspicuously stationed, one fair Plant,   MS., 1814–20
79 decried the   1827: decried, in no unseemly terms Of modesty, that
MS., 1814–20   88/9 I cannot but incline to a belief   1814–20
88–90 Some shadowy notion hangs upon my mind
        That in the fashion of the smooth flat stone,
        The moss from which the careless Holly sprouts,
        And in the fellowship which thus it holds
        With its untired supporters, and no less
        In those three others, upright and unhewn,
        Each single and yet seemingly allied
        Yea, in that stranded Hulk, or rather call it
        A rugged Temple thatched with living heath
        That punctually renews its splendid flowers
        From year to year, I cannot but incline

That in these shows a chronicle survives
Of purposes akin to those of Man,   90
But wrought with mightier arm than now prevails.
—Voiceless the stream descends into the gulf
With timid lapse;—and lo! while in this strait
I stand—the chasm of sky above my head
Is heaven's profoundest azure; no domain   95
For fickle, short-lived clouds to occupy,
Or to pass through; but rather an abyss
In which the everlasting stars abide;
And whose soft gloom, and boundless depth, might tempt
The curious eye to look for them by day.   100
—Hail Contemplation! from the stately towers,
Reared by the industrious hand of human art
To lift thee high above the misty air
And turbulence of murmuring cities vast;
From academic groves, that have for thee   105
Been planted, hither come and find a lodge
To which thou mayst resort for holier peace,—
From whose calm centre thou, through height or depth,
Mayst penetrate, wherever truth shall lead;
Measuring through all degrees, until the scale   110
Of time and conscious nature disappear,
Lost in unsearchable eternity!"

    A pause ensued; and with minuter care
We scanned the various features of the scene:
And soon the Tenant of that lonely vale   115
With courteous voice thus spake—
                         "I should have grieved
Hereafter, not escaping self-reproach,
If from my poor retirement ye had gone
Leaving this nook unvisited: but, in sooth,
Your unexpected presence had so roused   120
My spirits, that they were bent on enterprise;
And, like an ardent hunter, I forgot,
Or, shall I say?—disdained, the game that lurks
At my own door. The shapes before our eyes

    To a dim faith that in these various shews
    A chronicle survives, a type or remnant
    Of purposes *etc.* MS.
117 *so* 1827: Hereafter, should perhaps have blamed myself MS., 1814–20

And their arrangement, doubtless must be deemed   125
The sport of Nature, aided by blind Chance
Rudely to mock the works of toiling Man.
And hence, this upright shaft of unhewn stone,
From Fancy, willing to set off her stores
By sounding titles, hath acquired the name   130
Of Pompey's pillar; that I gravely style
My Theban obelisk; and, there, behold
A Druid cromlech!—thus I entertain
The antiquarian humour, and am pleased
To skim along the surfaces of things,   135
Beguiling harmlessly the listless hours.
But if the spirit be oppressed by sense
Of instability, revolt, decay,
And change, and emptiness, these freaks of Nature
And her blind helper Chance, do *then* suffice   140
To quicken, and to aggravate—to feed
Pity and scorn, and melancholy pride,
Not less than that huge Pile (from some abyss
Of mortal power unquestionably sprung)
Whose hoary diadem of pendent rocks   145
Confines the shrill-voiced whirlwind, round and round
Eddying within its vast circumference,
On Sarum's naked plain—than pyramid
Of Egypt, unsubverted, undissolved—
Or Syria's marble ruins towering high   150
Above the sandy desert, in the light
Of sun or moon.—Forgive me, if I say
That an appearance which hath raised your minds
To an exalted pitch (the self-same cause
Different effect producing) is for me   155
Fraught rather with depression than delight,
Though shame it were, could I not look around,
By the reflection of your pleasure, pleased.
Yet happier in my judgment, even than you
With your bright transports fairly may be deemed,   160

128–30 Imagination fills the secret [heart ?]
        And hence that upright shaft of unhewn stone
        Hath won from me the venerable name   MS.
128–36 *added to* MS.
156–7 Rather a place of penance than delight
        Though at this moment I can look around me   MS.
157 around   1827: around me   1815–20

The wandering Herbalist,—who, clear alike
From vain, and, that worse evil, vexing thoughts,
Casts, if he ever chance to enter here,
Upon these uncouth Forms a slight regard
Of transitory interest, and peeps round   165
For some rare floweret of the hills, or plant
Of craggy fountain; what he hopes for wins,
Or learns, at least, that 'tis not to be won:
Then, keen and eager, as a fine-nosed hound
By soul-engrossing instinct driven along   170
Through wood or open field, the harmless Man
Departs, intent upon his onward quest!—
Nor is that Fellow-wanderer, so deem I,
Less to be envied, (you may trace him oft
By scars which his activity has left   175
Beside our roads and pathways, though, thank Heaven!
This covert nook reports not of his hand)
He who with pocket-hammer smites the edge
Of luckless rock or prominent stone, disguised
In weather-stains or crusted o'er by Nature   180
With her first growths, detaching by the stroke
A chip or splinter—to resolve his doubts;
And, with that ready answer satisfied,
The substance classes by some barbarous name,
And hurries on; or from the fragments picks   185
His specimen, if but haply intervened
With sparkling mineral, or should crystal cube
Lurk in its cells—and thinks himself enriched,
Wealthier, and doubtless wiser, than before!

161 *so* 1827: Is He (if such have ever entered here)
       The wandering Herbalist,—who, *etc.* MS., 1814–20
163–4 *so* 1827: Casts on these uncouth *etc.* MS., 1814–20
179–81 *so* 1827: Of the hard rocks by weather stains disguised
                Or green and grey with vegetation thin
                Nature's first growth *etc.* MS.
                Of every luckless rock or stone that stands
                Before his sight, by weather-stains disguised,
                Or crusted o'er with vegetation thin,
                Nature's first growth *etc.* 1814–20
184 *so* 1827: Doth to the substance give MS., 1814–20
185 *so* 1827: Then hurries 1814–20: passes MS.   186 *so* 1845: if haply
1814–43   187 cube 1820: tube MS., 1814   188 *so* 1820: Be
lodged therein MS., 1814   189–208 *not in* MS.

Intrusted safely each to his pursuit,   190
Earnest alike, let both from hill to hill
Range; if it please them, speed from clime to clime;
The mind is full—and free from pain their pastime."

"Then," said I, interposing, "One is near,
Who cannot but possess in your esteem   195
Place worthier still of envy. May I name,
Without offence, that fair-faced cottage-boy?
Dame Nature's pupil of the lowest form,
Youngest apprentice in the school of art!
Him, as we entered from the open glen,   200
You might have noticed, busily engaged,
Heart, soul, and hands,—in mending the defects
Left in the fabric of a leaky dam
Raised for enabling this penurious stream
To turn a slender mill (that new-made plaything)   205
For his delight—the happiest he of all!"

"Far happiest," answered the desponding Man,
"If, such as now he is, he might remain!
Ah! what avails imagination high
Or question deep? what profits all that earth,   210
Or heaven's blue vault, is suffered to put forth
Of impulse or allurement, for the Soul
To quit the beaten track of life, and soar
Far as she finds a yielding element
In past or future; far as she can go   215
Through time or space—if neither in the one,
Nor in the other region, nor in aught
That Fancy, dreaming o'er the map of things,
Hath placed beyond these penetrable bounds,
Words of assurance can be heard; if nowhere   220
A habitation, for consummate good,
Or for progressive virtue, by the search
Can be attained,—a better sanctuary
From doubt and sorrow, than the senseless grave?"

191–2 *so* 1827: This earnest Pair may range from hill to hill And   1814–20
193 *so* 1845: —no pain is in their sport   1814–43: their pastime free from
pain C   204 Raised 1827: Framed   1814–20
218–19 That may by pure abstraction be conceived
        To lie beyond *etc.* MS.
222 Or MS., 1814–20, 1845: Nor   1827–43

"Is this," the grey-haired Wanderer mildly said,   225
"The voice, which we so lately overheard,
To that same child, addressing tenderly
The consolations of a hopeful mind?
'*His body is at rest, his soul in heaven.*'
These were your words; and, verily, methinks   230
Wisdom is ofttimes nearer when we stoop
Than when we soar."—
    The Other, not displeased,
Promptly replied—"My notion is the same.
And I, without reluctance, could decline
All act of inquisition whence we rise,   235
And what, when breath hath ceased, we may become.
Here are we, in a bright and breathing world.
Our origin, what matters it? In lack
Of worthier explanation, say at once
With the American (a thought which suits   240
The place where now we stand) that certain men
Leapt out together from a rocky cave;
And these were the first parents of mankind:
Or, if a different image be recalled
By the warm sunshine, and the jocund voice   245
Of insects chirping out their careless lives
On these soft beds of thyme-besprinkled turf,
Choose, with the gay Athenian, a conceit
As sound—blithe race! whose mantles were bedecked
With golden grasshoppers, in sign that they   250
Had sprung, like those bright creatures, from the soil
Whereon their endless generations dwelt.
But stop! these theoretic fancies jar
On serious minds: then, as the Hindoos draw

225 Wanderer   1814: Pedlar   MS.
225–35 *added to* MS.
227 Consoling tenderly the weeping child   MS.
234–5 But I could waive the thought of whence we rise   MS.
246 Of insects sporting in the summer air
  Or chirping out their brief and careless lives   MS.
249–52 *so* 1827: . . . with that blithe race who wore erewhile
    Their golden Grasshoppers, in sign that they
     Had sprung from out the soil whereon they dwelt.   MS.,
    1814–20
254 minds; then   1827: minds; for, doubtless, in one sense,
    The theme *is* serious; then,   MS., 1814–20

Their holy Ganges from a skiey fount,　　　　　255
Even so deduce the stream of human life
From seats of power divine; and hope, or trust,
That our existence winds her stately course
Beneath the sun, like Ganges, to make part
Of a living ocean; or, to sink engulfed,　　　　　260
Like Niger, in impenetrable sands
And utter darkness: thought which may be faced,
Though comfortless!—
　　　　　　　　Not of myself I speak;
Such acquiescence neither doth imply,
In me, a meekly-bending spirit soothed　　　　　265
By natural piety; nor a lofty mind,
By philosophic discipline prepared
For calm subjection to acknowledged law;
Pleased to have been, contented not to be.
Such palms I boast not;—no! to me, who find,　　　　　270
Reviewing my past way, much to condemn,
Little to praise, and nothing to regret,
(Save some remembrances of dream-like joys
That scarcely seem to have belonged to me)
If I must take my choice between the pair　　　　　275
That rule alternately the weary hours,
Night is than day more acceptable; sleep
Doth, in my estimate of good, appear
A better state than waking; death than sleep:
Feelingly sweet is stillness after storm,　　　　　280
Though under covert of the wormy ground!

　　"Yet be it said, in justice to myself,
That in more genial times, when I was free
To explore the destiny of human kind
(Not as an intellectual game pursued　　　　　285
With curious subtilty, from wish to cheat
Irksome sensations; but by love of truth
Urged on, or haply by intense delight
In feeding thought, wherever thought could feed)
I did not rank with those (too dull or nice,　　　　　290

258 her　1827: its　MS., 1814–20
260 *so* 1827: . . . Ocean: or, if such may seem
　　　　　Its tendency, to be engulphed and lost　MS., 1814–20
273–4 *added to* MS.　　　286 from wish　1827: thereby　MS., 1814–20

For to my judgment such they then appeared,
Or too aspiring, thankless at the best)
Who, in this frame of human life, perceive
An object whereunto their souls are tied
In discontented wedlock; nor did e'er,   295
From me, those dark impervious shades, that hang
Upon the region whither we are bound,
Exclude a power to enjoy the vital beams
Of present sunshine.—Deities that float
On wings, angelic Spirits! I could muse   300
O'er what from eldest time we have been told
Of your bright forms and glorious faculties,
And with the imagination rest content,
Not wishing more; repining not to tread
The little sinuous path of earthly care,   305
By flowers embellished, and by springs refreshed.
—'Blow winds of autumn!—let your chilling breath
Take the live herbage from the mead, and strip
The shady forest of its green attire,—
And let the bursting clouds to fury rouse   310
The gentle brooks!—Your desolating sway,
Sheds,' I exclaimed, 'no sadness upon me,
And no disorder in your rage I find.
What dignity, what beauty, in this change
From mild to angry, and from sad to gay,   315
Alternate and revolving! How benign,
How rich in animation and delight,
How bountiful these elements—compared
With aught, as more desirable and fair,
Devised by fancy for the golden age;   320
Or the perpetual warbling that prevails
In Arcady, beneath unaltered skies,
Through the long year in constant quiet bound,
Night hushed as night, and day serene as day!'
—But why this tedious record?—Age, we know,   325

300 Spirits] Virtues MS.   303 rest 1845: be MS., 1814–43
305 sinuous] twining MS.   306 Embellished by sweet flowers, by
springs C   308 live] green MS.   309 The forest of its beauti-
ful attire MS.   312 *so* 1837: Thus I exclaimed, "no sadness sheds
on me MS., 1814–32
325 But, out of matter worthless as myself
    See with what strenuous idleness I spin
    Most wearisome reflections—Age we know MS. (*second draft*)

Is garrulous; and solitude is apt
To anticipate the privilege of Age.
From far ye come; and surely with a hope
Of better entertainment:—let us hence!"

Loth to forsake the spot, and still more loth   330
To be diverted from our present theme,
I said, "My thoughts, agreeing, Sir, with yours,
Would push this censure farther;—for, if smiles
Of scornful pity be the just reward
Of Poesy thus courteously employed   335
In framing models to improve the scheme
Of Man's existence, and recast the world,
Why should not grave Philosophy be styled,
Herself, a dreamer of a kindred stock,
A dreamer yet more spiritless and dull?   340
Yes, shall the fine immunities she boasts
Establish sounder titles of esteem
For her, who (all too timid and reserved
For onset, for resistance too inert,
Too weak for suffering, and for hope too tame)   345
Placed, among flowery gardens curtained round
With world-excluding groves, the brotherhood
Of soft Epicureans, taught—if they
The ends of being would secure, and win
The crown of wisdom—to yield up their souls   350
To a voluptuous unconcern, preferring
Tranquillity to all things. Or is she,"
I cried, "more worthy of regard, the Power,
Who, for the sake of sterner quiet, closed
The Stoic's heart against the vain approach   355
Of admiration, and all sense of joy?"

325–34 Or that Elysium fabled to possess
       Stars and purpureal [? sunshine] of its own
       A place of recompense; for ghostly shades
       Of Heroes, Bards, and Lovers, myrtle crowns.
       Though pleased to listen I was tempted here
       To slide into the stream of his discourse
       With a consenting current; and I said
       "If smiles of pity be the just reward   MS. (*first draft*)
341 *so* 1827: "Yes," said I, "shall the immunities to which
            She doth lay claim, the precepts she bestows,   MS., 1814–20
346 Placed, among *so* 1827: Did place, in   MS., 1814–20

His countenance gave notice that my zeal
Accorded little with his present mind ;
I ceased, and he resumed.—"Ah! gentle Sir,
Slight, if you will, the *means* ; but spare to slight   360
The *end* of those, who did, by system, rank,
As the prime object of a wise man's aim,
Security from shock of accident,
Release from fear ; and cherished peaceful days
For their own sakes, as mortal life's chief good,   365
And only reasonable felicity.
What motive drew, what impulse, I would ask,
Through a long course of later ages, drove,
The hermit to his cell in forest wide ;
Or what detained him, till his closing eyes   370
Took their last farewell of the sun and stars,
Fast anchored in the desert ?—Not alone
Dread of the persecuting sword, remorse,
Wrongs unredressed, or insults unavenged
And unavengeable, defeated pride,   375
Prosperity subverted, maddening want,
Friendship betrayed, affection unreturned,
Love with despair, or grief in agony ;—
Not always from intolerable pangs
He fled ; but, compassed round by pleasure, sighed   380
For independent happiness ; craving peace,
The central feeling of all happiness,
Not as a refuge from distress or pain,
A breathing-time, vacation, or a truce,
But for its absolute self ; a life of peace,   385
Stability without regret or fear ;
That hath been, is, and shall be evermore!—
Such the reward he sought ; and wore out life,
There, where on few external things his heart
Was set, and those his own ; or, if not his,   390
Subsisting under nature's stedfast law.

359 ceased] stopped   MS.
365–6 For their own sakes, the bound of just desires
           As mortal life's chief good and worthiest hope   MS.
367–72 What impulse drove the Hermit to his cell
           And what detained him there till life was spent
           Fast anchored *etc.*   MS. (*T. of P.—v. notes*)
381 happiness] quiet   *T. of P.*   388–9 Therefore on few   *T. of P.*

"What other yearning was the master tie
Of the monastic brotherhood, upon rock
Aërial, or in green secluded vale,
One after one, collected from afar,   395
An undissolving fellowship ?—What but this,
The universal instinct of repose,
The longing for confirmed tranquillity,
Inward and outward ; humble, yet sublime :
The life where hope and memory are as one ;   400
Where earth is quiet and her face unchanged
Save by the simplest toil of human hands
Or seasons' difference ; the immortal Soul
Consistent in self-rule ; and heaven revealed
To meditation in that quietness !—   405
Such was their scheme : and though the wished-for end
By multitudes was missed, perhaps attained
By none, they for the attempt, and pains employed,
Do, in my present censure, stand redeemed
From the unqualified disdain, that once   410
Would have been cast upon them by my voice
Delivering her decisions from the seat
Of forward youth—that scruples not to solve
Doubts, and determine questions, by the rules
Of inexperienced judgment, ever prone   415
To overweening faith ; and is inflamed,
By courage, to demand from real life
The test of act and suffering, to provoke
Hostility—how dreadful when it comes,
Whether affliction be the foe, or guilt !   420

"A child of earth, I rested, in that stage
Of my past course to which these thoughts advert,

399 In small and great, in humble and sublime   *T. of P.*
401–3 *so* 1845 : Earth quiet and unchanged ; the human Soul   MSS., 1814–
43
          Where present time is noiseless as the past
          Or as a thing unborn, the face of earth
          Save *etc. as text but* human *for* immortal   C
406–8 *so* 1845 : . . . thrice happy he who gained
          The end proposed ! And,—though the same were missed
          By multitudes, perhaps obtained by none,—
          They, for the attempt, and for the pains employed,   MS.,
                    1814–43
412 her   1832 : its   MS., 1814–27

Upon earth's native energies; forgetting
That mine was a condition which required
Nor energy, nor fortitude—a calm   425
Without vicissitude; which, if the like
Had been presented to my view elsewhere,
I might have even been tempted to despise.
But no—for the serene was also bright;
Enlivened happiness with joy o'erflowing,   430
With joy, and—oh! that memory should survive
To speak the word—with rapture! Nature's boon,
Life's genuine inspiration, happiness
Above what rules can teach, or fancy feign;
Abused, as all possessions *are* abused   435
That are not prized according to their worth.
And yet, what worth? what good is given to men,
More solid than the gilded clouds of heaven?
What joy more lasting than a vernal flower?—
None! 'tis the general plaint of human kind   440
In solitude: and mutually addressed
From each to all, for wisdom's sake:—This truth
The priest announces from his holy seat:
And, crowned with garlands in the summer grove,
The poet fits it to his pensive lyre.   445
Yet, ere that final resting-place be gained,
Sharp contradictions may arise, by doom
Of this same life, compelling us to grieve
That the prosperities of love and joy
Should be permitted, oft-times, to endure   450
So long, and be at once cast down for ever.
Oh! tremble, ye, to whom hath been assigned
A course of days composing happy months,
And they as happy years; the present still
So like the past, and both so firm a pledge   455
Of a congenial future, that the wheels
Of pleasure move without the aid of hope:

429 *so* 1837: But that which was serene   MS., 1814–32   431 should
survive] still survives   MS.
440–8 And yet by doom of this same life we grieve
      We are compelled to grieve and to repine   MS. (440–6 *added to* MS.)
447–8 *so* 1827: Sharp contradictions hourly shall arise
                 To cross the way; and we, perchance, by doom
                 Of this same life, shall be compelled [constrained   MS.] to
                 grieve   MS., 1814–20

For Mutability is Nature's bane;
And slighted Hope *will* be avenged; and, when
Ye need her favours, ye shall find her not;   460
But in her stead—fear—doubt—and agony!"

This was the bitter language of the heart:
But, while he spake, look, gesture, tone of voice,
Though discomposed and vehement, were such
As skill and graceful nature might suggest   465
To a proficient of the tragic scene
Standing before the multitude, beset
With dark events. Desirous to divert
Or stem the current of the speaker's thoughts,
We signified a wish to leave that place   470
Of stillness and close privacy, a nook
That seemed for self-examination made;
Or, for confession, in the sinner's need,
Hidden from all men's view. To our attempt
He yielded not; but, pointing to a slope   475
Of mossy turf defended from the sun,
And on that couch inviting us to rest,
Full on that tender-hearted Man he turned
A serious eye, and his speech thus renewed.

"You never saw, your eyes did never look   480
On the bright form of Her whom once I loved:—
Her silver voice was heard upon the earth,
A sound unknown to you; else, honoured Friend!
Your heart had borne a pitiable share
Of what I suffered, when I wept that loss,   485
And suffer now, not seldom, from the thought
That I remember, and can weep no more.—

468 *so* 1837: With sorrowful events; and we, who heard
            And saw, were moved. Desirous [Desiring] to divert   MS.,
            1814–20   MS.
472 made   1827: framed   MS., 1814–20   474 view] eyes   MS.
475–6 slope Of mossy turf] bank Or sloping couch   MS.
477–8 By the projecting side of that huge rock
      Which bore the likeness of a stranded hulk
      Or uncouth temple built in some dark age
      For worship, and inviting us to sit
      He turned upon that tender-hearted Man   MS.
478 Full on   1827: Towards   1814–20   479 *so* 1837: and thus his
speech   MS., 1814–32

Stripped as I am of all the golden fruit
Of self-esteem ; and by the cutting blasts
Of self-reproach familiarly assailed ;   490
Yet would I not be of such wintry bareness
But that some leaf of your regard should hang
Upon my naked branches :—lively thoughts
Give birth, full often, to unguarded words ;
I grieve that, in your presence, from my tongue   495
Too much of frailty hath already dropped ;
But that too much demands still more.

                          You know,
Revered Compatriot—and to you, kind Sir,
(Not to be deemed a stranger, as you come
Following the guidance of these welcome feet   500
To our secluded vale) it may be told—

491 *so* 1837: I would not yet be   MS., 1814–32
501 *In place of this one line* MS. *reads:*
       To our secluded Vale) I would discourse
       Of what I have been, to the end that ye,
       By evidence from other lips than mine
       Not to be gained, may judge of what I am,
       And what our common nature is in me.
       Yet how without humiliation speak,
       Though (to the pensive Wanderer this was said)
       Some points between us lie where we may meet
       In fellow feeling, dare I hope to gain
       The requisite indulgence from a Soul
       So widely parted from me, that hath moved,
       Above the unequal ground of hope and fear,
       Along its own peculiar element,
       With the unimpeded motion of a cloud
       Upon the bosom of the etherial deep.
       To that exclusive bower in which we dwell
       How shall I draw so free a spirit down ?
       And if that wish succeed, }
       And by what skill shall I } detain him there
       Till he hath seen, and knows, and understands,
       What love, to souls content with narrow room,
       A secret bounty can bestow, what life
       Can give, and that familiar spectre, Death,
       Insatiably recurring to his task,
       At three tremendous moments take away ?
       Yet, if extremes degrade a living Soul,
       Is any calm so perfect as the calm
       Of the vast ocean, though the same disturbed
       By sudden visitations of the blast
       Frets as if very madness were at large

That my demerits did not sue in vain
To One on whose mild radiance many gazed
With hope, and all with pleasure. This fair Bride—
In the devotedness of youthful love,   505
Preferring me to parents, and the choir
Of gay companions, to the natal roof,
And all known places and familiar sights
(Resigned with sadness gently weighing down
Her trembling expectations, but no more   510
Than did to her due honour, and to me
Yielded, that day, a confidence sublime
In what I had to build upon)—this Bride,
Young, modest, meek, and beautiful, I led
To a low cottage in a sunny bay,   515
Where the salt sea innocuously breaks,
And the sea breeze as innocently breathes,
On Devon's leafy shores ;—a sheltered hold,
In a soft clime encouraging the soil
To a luxuriant bounty!—As our steps   520
Approach the embowered abode—our chosen seat—
See, rooted in the earth, her kindly bed,
The unendangered myrtle, decked with flowers,
Before the threshold stands to welcome us!
While, in the flowering myrtle's neighbourhood,   525

Amid its lowest depths ? Behold in me
How time and solitude together make
A lawless speaker, all incapable
To keep the appointed line. It grieves me now
Tho' here we sit in stillness and cool shade
That we were tempted forth and left that cell
Which, as a lonely shipwrecked Man might say,
Doth harbour me and mine. Upon its walls
An instrument is hung to which my voice
Could sing of pleasures that I dare not speak ;
Composure would at least attend the touch
Of those soft strings, and then I could relate
With progress steady as a flowing stream
How those benignant Spirits that direct
Unsettled Fancies where to fix, were pleased
That my demerits *etc.*

520–1 To a luxuriant bounty. With the Rose
   The jasmine intertwined her slender arms
   Around the windows of our Cot, a weight
   Of Woodbine overcanopied the Porch,   MS.
522 her   1827: its   MS., 1814–20

Not overlooked but courting no regard,
Those native plants, the holly and the yew,
Gave modest intimation to the mind
How willingly their aid they would unite
With the green myrtle, to endear the hours   530
Of winter, and protect that pleasant place.
—Wild were the walks upon those lonely Downs,
Track leading into track; how marked, how worn
Into bright verdure, between fern and gorse,
Winding away its never-ending line   535
On their smooth surface, evidence was none:
But, there, lay open to our daily haunt,
A range of unappropriated earth,
Where youth's ambitious feet might move at large;
Whence, unmolested wanderers, we beheld   540
The shining giver of the day diffuse
His brightness o'er a tract of sea and land
Gay as our spirits, free as our desires;
As our enjoyments, boundless.—From those heights
We dropped, at pleasure, into sylvan combs;   545
Where arbours of impenetrable shade,
And mossy seats, detained us side by side,
With hearts at ease, and knowledge in our hearts
'That all the grove and all the day was ours.'

529 *so* 1827: Of willingness with which   MS., 1814–20
531/2 "Ah! why so full, so perfect, so mature,"
       Exclaim'd my Anna, "no deficience left,
       None where invention might suggest a work
       For our united hands, presumptuous aim
       Such beauty to reform;—to take away
       Is to destroy; and would to thee, dear Spot,
       Be an ungrateful wrong; unkind it were
       To undo what has so happily been done,
       Time, Art, and Nature all consenting here"   MS.
534 between] among   MS.
535/6 How fashion'd first, and by what means preserved,
       Whether by tread of man or beast, or touch
       Of supernatural steps invisible,—   MS.
549/50 Then, ere the measure of repose was full
       Ris'n on the impulse of some sudden thought
       From the dark bower, if gently sloping turf
       Allured, or tangled woodland would permit,
       We took the infant streamlet for our guide.
       One I remember, an indulgent rill
       That oft had moistened Anna's rosy lip

"O happy time! still happier was at hand;   550
For Nature called my Partner to resign
Her share in the pure freedom of that life,

> With its cool waters—this wild wandering Brook
> And others, not less wild, o'er those free tracks
> Conducting us, not seldom were we smit
> By composition, choice of nature's forms
> Remote or near, presenting to the eye
> Tasks for the shading pencil which some day
> More patient in the tenour of its joys
> Should see accomplished. Mid a fearful store
> Of things for years unlooked at I possess
> A work in that far distant time performed
> By Anna's hand—the Canvas represents,
> As in a mirror shown, the first Abode
> Of man, a clay-built Cottage thatch'd with Broom,
> The first which he who with the Rill descends,
> Ere far descended, meets upon the bank
> Of its life-feeding waters. As it grew
> The mimic Piece was quicken'd by my praise.
> Flowers also have I, pictured with a touch
> Of skill as fine; the scentless images
> Of past delights existing in their forms
> And not relinquishing their brilliant hues
> Though in their spirit dead. But all was life
> To us, all Nature, breathing love, was filled
> With fragrance universal. Still, perhaps,
> Still may be seen undwindled, undecayed,
> Some bright originals from which she took
> Those faithful copies in the ground surviving
> Whither transplanted with a tender hand
> They from their various birthplaces were brought
> And throve assembled in our small domain!
> Blest occupation, pastimes innocent.
> Thus, and by other inoffensive ways,
> Thus Love, that through the region of the thoughts
> Can make that purer which was deemed most pure,
> Love that exalts the finest essences
> And brightens brightest hues not only wrought
> In that Enclosure to redress and guard
> And to maintain, but also could find space
> To introduce new touches of his own,
> Heightened the beauties of a finished spot
> Finished and fair as Paradise itself
> Where the first Adam dwelt with sinless Eve.   MS.

550–2 *so* 1845:   But in due season, Nature interfered
> And called my Partner to resign her share
> In the pure freedom of that wedded life.   MS.,   1814–20;
> 1827–43 *as text, but omitting l.* 550, *and with* But *for* For

Enjoyed by us in common.—To my hope,
To my heart's wish, my tender Mate became
The thankful captive of maternal bonds;   555
And those wild paths were left to me alone.
There could I meditate on follies past;
And, like a weary voyager escaped
From risk and hardship, inwardly retrace
A course of vain delights and thoughtless guilt,   560
And self-indulgence—without shame pursued.
There, undisturbed, could think of and could thank
Her whose submissive spirit was to me
Rule and restraint—my guardian—shall I say
That earthly Providence, whose guiding love   565
Within a port of rest had lodged me safe;
Safe from temptation, and from danger far?
Strains followed of acknowledgment addressed
To an Authority enthroned above
The reach of sight; from whom, as from their source,   570
Proceed all visible ministers of good
That walk the earth—Father of heaven and earth,
Father, and king, and judge, adored and feared!
These acts of mind, and memory, and heart,
And spirit—interrupted and relieved   575
By observations transient as the glance
Of flying sunbeams, or to the outward form
Cleaving with power inherent and intense,
As the mute insect fixed upon the plant
On whose soft leaves it hangs, and from whose cup   580
It draws its nourishment imperceptibly—
Endeared my wanderings; and the mother's kiss
And infant's smile awaited my return.

"In privacy we dwelt, a wedded pair,
Companions daily, often all day long;   585
Not placed by fortune within easy reach
Of various intercourse, nor wishing aught
Beyond the allowance of our own fireside,
The twain within our happy cottage born,
Inmates, and heirs of our united love;   590
Graced mutually by difference of sex,
And with no wider interval of time

581 *so* 1845: Draws imperceptibly its nourishment   1814–43
591/2 By the endearing names of nature bound [joined MS.] MS., 1814–43

Between their several births than served for one
To establish something of a leader's sway;
Yet left them joined by sympathy in age;   595
Equals in pleasure, fellows in pursuit.
On these two pillars rested as in air
Our solitude.

598-9   Our solitude. I speak to minds that know
The course of Nature. See we not the Nun
Within a Convent's wiry grate encaged
A Prisoner, though not wanting choice of grave
Or gay Companions, to a Captive Bird
Yield her affections, occupies the time
In delicate attention to its needs
Or fond observance of its antic feats;
And if her lessons raised to higher pitch
Its marvellous accomplishments, she smiles
In triumph, gives caresses and receives,
Nor finds the day too long when so beguiled.
The handy Mariner from Indian shores
Returning homeward, if the Ship convey
A Leopard's cub or brindled Tyger's whelp
Drawn from its native forests, can in them
Find ready solace for his leisure hours,
And in the busiest casts a glance that way.
Who more delighted, more sincerely pleased
Than this ungentle Wanderer of the Deep
While he admires the gambols, and incites
To new exertion, nor perchance forbears
To lull the Favorite in his rugged arms
Till it hath learnt to love him in return?
No otherwise mid Como's chestnut groves
Or on the pineclad steeps of Appenine
The Hermit Monk forth issuing from his cell
Lures down the squirrel from the bough and wins
From the high rock the unrestricted dove
To perch upon his shoulders—Ah, if then
Nature and circumstance, for one effect
Combining, can to such dependence pledge
The human feeling in their several hearts,
Judge of a parent's joy in solitude,
A mother's tenderness, a father's love,
How constant, how habitual, how intense!
The sanguine Chaser of the world's delights
Knows not to measure such affection—He
Moves in the shoals, but never tried its depths.
This universal instinct of mankind
'Tis Solitude that carries to the extreme
Of passion and dominion in the Soul
A strength, a weakness inconceivable.

It soothes me to perceive,
Your courtesy withholds not from my words
Attentive audience. But, oh! gentle Friends,   600
As times of quiet and unbroken peace,
Though, for a nation, times of blessedness,
Give back faint echoes from the historian's page;
So, in the imperfect sounds of this discourse,
Depressed I hear, how faithless is the voice   605
Which those most blissful days reverberate.
What special record can, or need, be given
To rules and habits, whereby much was done,
But all within the sphere of little things;
Of humble, though, to us, important cares,   610
And precious interests ? Smoothly did our life
Advance, swerving not from the path prescribed;
Her annual, her diurnal, round alike
Maintained with faithful care. And you divine
The worst effects that our condition saw   615
If you imagine changes slowly wrought,
And in their progress unperceivable;
Not wished for; sometimes noticed with a sigh,
(Whate'er of good or lovely they might bring)
Sighs of regret, for the familiar good   620
And loveliness endeared which they removed.

"Seven years of occupation undisturbed
Established seemingly a right to hold

> The state of Kings is lonely, for this cause,
> For this cause chiefly is the crowned King
> To a degree unusual among men
> Bless'd with the sight of children, and holds dear
> The company their Innocence affords.
> The Spartan Monarch, once, so Story tells,
> Surprized while busy with a Playmate's part
> Mid his young children, blush'd not, well aware
> That Nature of herself is justified:
> But oh he loved not, could not love like those
> Who far from armies and the pomp of Courts
> Awake to these calm pleasures every day
> On the plain ground of rural privacies,
> As I, even I, cherished and loved my own.
> Your courtesy *etc.* MS.

612 *so* 1837: not swerving MS., 1814–32   617 progress MS., 1814–
45: process 1850 unperceivable 1845: imperceptible MS., 1814–43

That happiness; and use and habit gave
To what an alien spirit had acquired   625
A patrimonial sanctity. And thus,
With thoughts and wishes bounded to this world,
I lived and breathed; most grateful—if to enjoy
Without repining or desire for more,
For different lot, or change to higher sphere,   630
(Only except some impulses of pride
With no determined object, though upheld
By theories with suitable support)—
Most grateful, if in such wise to enjoy
Be proof of gratitude for what we have;   635
Else, I allow, most thankless.—But, at once,
From some dark seat of fatal power was urged
A claim that shattered all.—Our blooming girl,
Caught in the gripe of death, with such brief time
To struggle in as scarcely would allow   640
Her cheek to change its colour, was conveyed
From us to inaccessible worlds, to regions
Where height, or depth, admits not the approach
Of living man, though longing to pursue.
—With even as brief a warning—and how soon,   645

638 A claim that shattered all—the Spoiler fell
        Upon our peace, and robb'd us unforewarned (*but v. notes*)
        Have you espied *etc. as "Maternal Grief" (Vol.* II, *pp.* 51–2), *ll.* 27–38,
with lines in app. crit.:
        Ah, but a Mother saw it, it was seen
        And by a Father felt. Our blooming girl   MS.
642 *so* 1845: From us, to regions inaccessible   MS., 1814–43
645–9   So was the myrtle-shaded Cottage turned
                Into a House of mourning, from whose doors
                All grace and favour were at once withdrawn.
                No light of gladness shone around the Hearth,
                No music rang within the walls, but there
                Silence prevailed and undeparting gloom,
                Suspense of breath and respiration deep,
                Prayers yielding short relief or haply none,
                Wringing of hands, and in the Mother's breast
                Conflicts of agonizing thoughts like these:
                [*Here follows "Maternal Grief", ll.* 1–26, *as in app. crit.*]
                When we were summoned to deplore her loss
                That point she had attained, that single point
                At which those powers are given and only those
                And only in such measure and degree
                That one so furnished may depart from earth

With what short interval of time between,
I tremble yet to think of—our last prop,
Our happy life's only remaining stay—
The brother followed ; and was seen no more!

"Calm as a frozen lake when ruthless winds   650
Blow fiercely, agitating earth and sky,
The Mother now remained ; as if in her,
Who, to the lowest region of the soul,

> And be received into another world
> An untransfigured Spirit, without change
> From grace to be supplied or taint removed
> Or discord needing to be harmonized.
> [*Here follows* "*Characteristics of a Child three years old*" (*as
>   Vol.* I, *p.* 229), *but with verbs in past tense*]
> To my Co-partner in this bitter loss
> Support I could not yield, who did myself
> Require support from others less disturbed,
> Or from the blank and calm of solitude.
> Dark became doubly dark, to outward weight
> Was inward added, wheresoe'er our minds
> In converse met—nor could the Mother lean
> In this affliction on the company
> Of her surviving Child as on a staff *etc. as* "*Maternal Grief*",
>   *ll.* 48–73, *app. crit.*
> If still I linger in these thoughts detained
> Condemn me not—The time no doubt has been
> When strength of passion would have made me boast
> As each enraptured Lover fondly boasts,
> And every Husband happy in his choice,
> And every Parent tender in his love,
> That mine was a peculiar blessedness.
> And when in pride of passion stronger still
> I could have boasted that the Power which shook
> That Pile, and having shaken overthrew,
> To me had dealt a portion of despair
> Unmatch'd on earth, and solitary pain ;
> But no—exception to a common fate
> Had kept me silent ; as a feeble man
> Among a suffering multitude I speak,
> Yet can I tell, how bear to tell, that he
> Who in this sort fortasted of the grave
> Not fearfully, but with delight, and gleams
> Of fancy, scattered among serious thoughts,
> Before those snowdrops with their passing flowers
> Had beautified the mound to which his pains
> Had brought them, that the Innocent was laid
> In the green Churchyard by his sister's side   MS.

Had been erewhile unsettled and disturbed,
This second visitation had no power   655
To shake; but only to bind up and seal;
And to establish thankfulness of heart
In Heaven's determinations, ever just.
The eminence whereon her spirit stood,
Mine was unable to attain. Immense   660
The space that severed us! But, as the sight
Communicates with heaven's ethereal orbs
Incalculably distant; so, I felt
That consolation may descend from far
(And that is intercourse, and union, too,)   665
While, overcome with speechless gratitude,
And, with a holier love inspired, I looked
On her—at once superior to my woes
And partner of my loss.—O heavy change!
Dimness o'er this clear luminary crept   670
Insensibly;—the immortal and divine
Yielded to mortal reflux; her pure glory,
As from the pinnacle of worldly state
Wretched ambition drops astounded, fell
Into a gulf obscure of silent grief,   675
And keen heart-anguish—of itseif ashamed,
Yet obstinately cherishing itself:
And, so consumed, she melted from my arms;
And left me, on this earth, disconsolate!

657–60   And to inspire meek patience and delight
            In heaven's determination ever just,
            And even when most severe, most merciful,
            If so interpreted. Behold, said I,
            Not finding strength within me to attain
            The elevation where she stood alone
            (But not too senseless to admire), behold
            An untranslated Spirit all at once
            Cleansed and made perfect; see in human Form
            Ideal Truth embodied and enshrined,
            The weeds of misery put off, and faith
            Once more by miracle disclosed. O Thou
            Ordained at once the Partner of my woes
            And comforter, eye hast Thou given to hope
            Benighted suddenly, and filled with joy
            The House of mourning. [Nay, ?] Immense   MS.
666–7 . . . with gratitude and filled
       With encrease pure of holiest love   MS.
670 this clear] that bright   MS.

"What followed cannot be reviewed in thought;   680
Much less, retraced in words. If she, of life
Blameless, so intimate with love and joy
And all the tender motions of the soul,
Had been supplanted, could I hope to stand—
Infirm, dependent, and now destitute?   685
I called on dreams and visions, to disclose
That which is veiled from waking thought; conjured
Eternity, as men constrain a ghost
To appear and answer; to the grave I spake
Imploringly;—looked up, and asked the Heavens   690
If Angels traversed their cerulean floors,
If fixed or wandering star could tidings yield
Of the departed spirit—what abode
It occupies—what consciousness retains
Of former loves and interests. Then my soul   695
Turned inward,—to examine of what stuff
Time's fetters are composed; and life was put
To inquisition, long and profitless!
By pain of heart—now checked—and now impelled—
The intellectual power, through words and things,   700
Went sounding on, a dim and perilous way!
And from those transports, and these toils abstruse,
Some trace am I enabled to retain
Of time, else lost;—existing unto me
Only by records in myself not found.   705

    "From that abstraction I was roused,—and how?
Even as a thoughtful shepherd by a flash
Of lightning startled in a gloomy cave
Of these wild hills. For, lo! the dread Bastille,
With all the chambers in its horrid towers,   710
Fell to the ground:—by violence overthrown
Of indignation; and with shouts that drowned

692 If they in truth could any tidings yield   MS.
706–33 MS. *has these lines in the following order*: 706–9, 718–31, *followed by*
            Be rich, by mutual and reflected wealth.
            To mortal men displayed—the Horrid Towers
            Where wretched Mortals, seldom seen or heard
            From age to age had been deposited
            As in a treasure-house—by prime command
            And for the secret joy of sovereign Power—
            Fell to the ground *etc. as* 711–16 (sway.)

The crash it made in falling! From the wreck
A golden palace rose, or seemed to rise,
The appointed seat of equitable law   715
And mild paternal sway. The potent shock
I felt: the transformation I perceived,
As marvellously seized as in that moment
When, from the blind mist issuing, I beheld
Glory—beyond all glory ever seen,   720
Confusion infinite of heaven and earth,
Dazzling the soul. Meanwhile, prophetic harps
In every grove were ringing, 'War shall cease;
Did ye not hear that conquest is abjured ?
Bring garlands, bring forth choicest flowers, to deck   725
The tree of Liberty.'—My heart rebounded;
My melancholy voice the chorus joined;
—'Be joyful all ye nations; in all lands,
Ye that are capable of joy be glad!
Henceforth, whate'er is wanting to yourselves   730
In others ye shall promptly find ;—and all,
Enriched by mutual and reflected wealth,
Shall with one heart honour their common kind.'

  "Thus was I reconverted to the world;
Society became my glittering bride,   735
And airy hopes my children.—From the depths
Of natural passion, seemingly escaped,
My soul diffused herself in wide embrace
Of institutions, and the forms of things;
As they exist, in mutable array,   740
Upon life's surface. What, though in my veins
There flowed no Gallic blood, nor had I breathed
The air of France, not less than Gallic zeal
Kindled and burned among the sapless twigs
Of my exhausted heart. If busy men   745
In sober conclave met, to weave a web

718–19 As marvellously rouz'd as, when involved
        In blinding mist upon the mountain tops
        As hath erewhile been told I reached the skirts
        Of the deep vapour and beheld at once   MS.
722 Meanwhile] For lo!   732–3 *so* 1832: Be rich by mutual and
reflected wealth.   1814–27   737 natural passion] personal feeling
alternative in MS.   738 herself   1827: itself   MS., 1814–20
744 burned   C: burnt   1814–50

Of amity, whose living threads should stretch
Beyond the seas, and to the farthest pole,
There did I sit, assisting. If, with noise
And acclamation, crowds in open air   750
Expressed the tumult of their minds, my voice
There mingled, heard or not. The powers of song
I left not uninvoked; and, in still groves,
Where mild enthusiasts tuned a pensive lay
Of thanks and expectation, in accord   755
With their belief, I sang Saturnian rule
Returned,—a progeny of golden years
Permitted to descend, and bless mankind.
—With promises the Hebrew Scriptures teem:
I felt their invitation; and resumed   760
A long-suspended office in the House
Of public worship, where, the glowing phrase
Of ancient inspiration serving me,
I promised also,—with undaunted trust
Foretold, and added prayer to prophecy;   765
The admiration winning of the crowd;
The help desiring of the pure devout.

    "Scorn and contempt forbid me to proceed!
But History, time's slavish scribe, will tell
How rapidly the zealots of the cause   770
Disbanded—or in hostile ranks appeared;
Some, tired of honest service; these, outdone,
Disgusted therefore, or appalled, by aims
Of fiercer zealots—so confusion reigned,
And the more faithful were compelled to exclaim,   775
As Brutus did to Virtue, 'Liberty,
I worshipped thee, and find thee but a Shade!'

    "Such recantation had for me no charm,
Nor would I bend to it; who should have grieved
At aught, however fair, that bore the mien   780
Of a conclusion, or catastrophe.
Why then conceal, that, when the simply good
In timid selfishness withdrew, I sought

754 tuned] framed MS.   757 golden] happier MS.   760 their]
so 1845: the MS., 1814–43: that C   776 did] spake MS.   782
simply 1827: simple MS., 1814–20

Other support, not scrupulous whence it came;
And, by what compromise it stood, not nice?　　　　　785
Enough if notions seemed to be high-pitched,
And qualities determined.—Among men
So charactered did I maintain a strife
Hopeless, and still more hopeless every hour;
But, in the process, I began to feel　　　　　790
That, if the emancipation of the world
Were missed, I should at least secure my own,
And be in part compensated. For rights,
Widely—inveterately usurped upon,
I spake with vehemence; and promptly seized　　　　　795
All that Abstraction furnished for my needs
Or purposes; nor scrupled to proclaim,
And propagate, by liberty of life,
Those new persuasions. Not that I rejoiced,
Or even found pleasure, in such vagrant course,　　　　　800
For its own sake; but farthest from the walk
Which I had trod in happiness and peace,
Was most inviting to a troubled mind;
That, in a struggling and distempered world,
Saw a seductive image of herself.　　　　　805
Yet, mark the contradictions of which Man
Is still the sport! Here Nature was my guide,
The Nature of the dissolute; but thee,
O fostering Nature! I rejected—smiled
At others' tears in pity; and in scorn　　　　　810
At those, which thy soft influence sometimes drew
From my unguarded heart.—The tranquil shores
Of Britain circumscribed me; else, perhaps
I might have been entangled among deeds,
Which, now, as infamous, I should abhor—　　　　　815
Despise, as senseless: for my spirit relished

787–8 *so* 1827: Ruling such, And with such herding, I maintained a strife
[began to feel MS.]　MS., 1814–20
793–6　　　　　　　. . . Of rights
　　　Usurped upon I argued and adopted
　　　Among the floating tenets of the day
　　　Whate'er Abstraction *etc.*　MS.
796 All that　1837: Whate'er　MS., 1814–32　　　805 *so* 1827: Beheld
a cherished image of itself.　MS., 1814–20　　　811 At those which
treacherous Nature sometimes drew　MS.
816–17 *so* 1827:　　　　　　. . . I strangely relished
　　　　　The exasperated Spirit of that Land　MS., 1814–20

Strangely the exasperation of that Land,
Which turned an angry beak against the down
Of her own breast; confounded into hope
Of disencumbering thus her fretful wings.   820

"But all was quieted by iron bonds
Of military sway. The shifting aims,
The moral interests, the creative might,
The varied functions and high attributes
Of civil action, yielded to a power   825
Formal, and odious, and contemptible.
—In Britain, ruled a panic dread of change;
The weak were praised, rewarded, and advanced;
And, from the impulse of a just disdain,
Once more did I retire into myself.   830
There feeling no contentment, I resolved
To fly, for safeguard, to some foreign shore,
Remote from Europe; from her blasted hopes;
Her fields of carnage, and polluted air.

"Fresh blew the wind, when o'er the Atlantic Main   835
The ship went gliding with her thoughtless crew;
And who among them but an Exile, freed
From discontent, indifferent, pleased to sit
Among the busily-employed, not more
With obligation charged, with service taxed,   840
Than the loose pendant—to the idle wind
Upon the tall mast streaming. But, ye Powers
Of soul and sense mysteriously allied,
O, never let the Wretched, if a choice
Be left him, trust the freight of his distress   845
To a long voyage on the silent deep!
For, like a plague, will memory break out;
And, in the blank and solitude of things,
Upon his spirit, with a fever's strength,
Will conscience prey.—Feebly must they have felt   850
Who, in old time, attired with snakes and whips
The vengeful Furies. *Beautiful* regards
Were turned on me—the face of her I loved;

819–20 *so* 1827: Of its own breast; as if it hoped, thereby,
            To disencumber its impatient wings. MS., 1814–20
840 taxed] tasked MS.   846 on] o'er MS.

The Wife and Mother pitifully fixing
Tender reproaches, insupportable!   855
Where now that boasted liberty ? No welcome
From unknown objects I received ; and those,
Known and familiar, which the vaulted sky
Did, in the placid clearness of the night,
Disclose, had accusations to prefer   860
Against my peace. Within the cabin stood
That volume—as a compass for the soul—
Revered among the nations. I implored
Its guidance ; but the infallible support
Of faith was wanting. Tell me, why refused   865
To One by storms annoyed and adverse winds ;
Perplexed with currents ; of his weakness sick ;
Of vain endeavours tired ; and by his own,
And by his nature's, ignorance, dismayed!

    "Long wished-for sight, the Western World appeared ; 870
And, when the ship was moored, I leaped ashore
Indignantly—resolved to be a man,
Who, having o'er the past no power, would live
No longer in subjection to the past,
With abject mind—from a tyrannic lord   875
Inviting penance, fruitlessly endured:
So, like a fugitive, whose feet have cleared
Some boundary, which his followers may not cross
In prosecution of their deadly chase,
Respiring I looked round.—How bright the sun,   880
The breeze how soft! Can any thing produced
In the old World compare, thought I, for power
And majesty with this gigantic stream,
Sprung from the desert ? And behold a city
Fresh, youthful, and aspiring! What are these   885
To me, or I to them ? As much, at least
As he desires that they should be, whom winds
And waves have wafted to this distant shore,
In the condition of a damaged seed,
Whose fibres cannot, if they would, take root.   890
Here may I roam at large ;—my business is,

881 *so* 1845 : How promising the Breeze! Can aught produced MS., 1814–
43   884 Sprung from] Child of MS.

Roaming at large, to observe, and not to feel
And, therefore, not to act—convinced that all
Which bears the name of action, howsoe'er
Beginning, ends in servitude—still painful,   895
And mostly profitless. And, sooth to say,
On nearer view, a motley spectacle
Appeared, of high pretensions—unreproved
But by the obstreperous voice of higher still;
Big passions strutting on a petty stage;   900
Which a detached spectator may regard
Not unamused.—But ridicule demands
Quick change of objects; and, to laugh alone,
At a composing distance from the haunts
Of strife and folly, though it be a treat   905
As choice as musing Leisure can bestow;
Yet, in the very centre of the crowd,
To keep the secret of a poignant scorn,
Howe'er to airy Demons suitable,
Of all unsocial courses, is least fit   910
For the gross spirit of mankind,—the one
That soonest fails to please, and quickliest turns
Into vexation.   Let us, then, I said,
Leave this unknit Republic to the scourge
Of her own passions; and to regions haste,   915
Whose shades have never felt the encroaching axe,
Or soil endured a transfer in the mart
Of dire rapacity. There, Man abides,
Primeval Nature's child. A creature weak
In combination, (wherefore else driven back   920
So far, and of his old inheritance
So easily deprived?) but, for that cause,
More dignified, and stronger in himself;
Whether to act, judge, suffer, or enjoy.
True, the intelligence of social art   925
Hath overpowered his forefathers, and soon
Will sweep the remnant of his line away;

892 To observe whate'er I may MS.   903/4 In woods and wilds, or
any lonely place MS., 1814–20
909–10 so 1827: May suit an airy Demon; but, of all
               Unsocial courses, 'tis the one least fit MS., 1814–20
914 this . . . Republic] these . . . Republics MS.   915 her 1827:
their MS.: its 1814–20   918 dire] their MS.

But contemplations, worthier, nobler far
Than her destructive energies, attend
His independence, when along the side   930
Of Mississippi, or that northern stream
That spreads into successive seas, he walks;
Pleased to perceive his own unshackled life,
And his innate capacities of soul,
There imaged: or when, having gained the top   935
Of some commanding eminence, which yet
Intruder ne'er beheld, he thence surveys
Regions of wood and wide savannah, vast
Expanse of unappropriated earth,
With mind that sheds a light on what he sees;   940
Free as the sun, and lonely as the sun,
Pouring above his head its radiance down
Upon a living and rejoicing world!

"So, westward, tow'rd the unviolated woods
I bent my way; and, roaming far and wide,   945
Failed not to greet the merry Mocking-bird;
And, while the melancholy Muccawiss
(The sportive bird's companion in the grove)
Repeated o'er and o'er his plaintive cry,
I sympathised at leisure with the sound;   950
But that pure archetype of human greatness,
I found him not. There, in his stead, appeared
A creature, squalid, vengeful, and impure;
Remorseless, and submissive to no law
But superstitious fear, and abject sloth.   955

"Enough is told! Here am I—ye have heard
What evidence I seek, and vainly seek;

928–30 But can the oppressor show an inward soul
          That shall with his compare. How bright, how clear,
          How lofty, how serene when by the side   MS.
933 And not obscurely feels his power of mind   MS.   934 innate]
sublime   MS.
945–50 I bent my way, and verily was cheared
          By the blithe mocking-bird, and heard [? the cry]
          ⎧ The melancholy cry of Whip-poor-will,
          ⎩ The plaintive cry repeated Whip-poor-will   MS.
956–69   What need of more? Here am I, and the course
          Which my life holds this parallel will shew;
          Say how you stood etc.   MS.

What from my fellow-beings I require,
And either they have not to give, or I
Lack virtue to receive; what I myself,   960
Too oft by wilful forfeiture, have lost
Nor can regain. How languidly I look
Upon this visible fabric of the world,
May be divined—perhaps it hath been said:—
But spare your pity, if there be in me   965
Aught that deserves respect: for I exist,
Within myself, not comfortless.—The tenour
Which my life holds, he readily may conceive
Whoe'er hath stood to watch a mountain brook
In some still passage of its course, and seen,   970
Within the depths of its capacious breast,
Inverted trees, rocks, clouds, and azure sky;
And, on its glassy surface, specks of foam,
And conglobated bubbles undissolved,
Numerous as stars; that, by their onward lapse,   975
Betray to sight the motion of the stream,
Else imperceptible. Meanwhile, is heard
A softened roar, or murmur; and the sound
Though soothing, and the little floating isles
Though beautiful, are both by Nature charged   980
With the same pensive office; and make known
Through what perplexing labyrinths, abrupt
Precipitations, and untoward straits,
The earth-born wanderer hath passed; and quickly,
That respite o'er, like traverses and toils   985
Must he again encounter.—Such a stream
Is human Life; and so the Spirit fares
In the best quiet to her course allowed;
And such is mine,—save only for a hope
That my particular current soon will reach   990
The unfathomable gulf, where all is still!''

959-61 *so* 1845: And cannot find; what I myself have lost   1814-43
971 capacious] unruffled MS.   972 rocks, clouds,   1837: and rocks,
MS., 1814-32   973 . . . its surface, specks of silver foam   MS.
974/5 A company of little floating Isles   MS.   978 *so* 1837: Per-
chance, a roar or murmur   MS., 1814-20; A softened roar, a murmur
1827-32   979 little floating isles] specks of silver foam   MS.   986
so 1845: Must be again encountered—   MS., 1814-43

BOOK FOURTH
DESPONDENCY CORRECTED

ARGUMENT

State of feeling produced by the foregoing Narrative.—A belief in a superintending Providence the only adequate support under affliction.—Wanderer's ejaculation.[1]—Acknowledges the difficulty of a lively faith.—Hence immoderate sorrow.[2]—Exhortations.—How received.—Wanderer applies[3] his discourse to that other cause of dejection in the Solitary's mind.—Disappointment[4] from the French Revolution.—States[5] grounds of hope, and insists on the necessity of patience and fortitude with respect to the course of great revolutions.[6]—Knowledge the source of tranquillity.—Rural Solitude favourable to[7] knowledge of the inferior Creatures; Study of their habits and ways recommended;[8] exhortation to bodily exertion and communion[9] with Nature.—Morbid Solitude pitiable.[10]—Superstition better than apathy.—Apathy and destitution unknown in the infancy of society.—The various modes of Religion prevented it.—Illustrated in the Jewish, Persian, Babylonian, Chaldean, and Grecian modes of belief.—Solitary interposes.—Wanderer[11] points out the influence of religious and imaginative feeling[12] in the humble ranks of society, illustrated from present and past times.—These principles[13] tend to recal exploded superstitions and Popery.—Wanderer rebuts this charge, and contrasts the dignities of the Imagination with the presumptuous littleness of certain modern Philosophers.—Recommends[14] other lights and guides.—Asserts the power of the Soul to regenerate herself; Solitary asks how.[15]—Reply.—Personal appeal.[16]—Exhortation to activity of body renewed.—How to commune

[1] so 1837: ejaculation to the supreme Being—Account of his own devotional feelings in youth involved in it—Implores that he may retain in age the power to find repose among enduring and eternal things—What these are 1814–20; 1827–32 . . . involved *as* 1814, *but omitting* to . . . Being, *and after* involved *as* 1837   [2] so 1837: sorrow—but doubt or despondence not therefore to be inferred—And proceeds to administer consolation to the Solitary 1814–32, *but* 1827–32 *omit* but *and* And . . . administer   [3] so 1827: resumes—and applies 1814–20   [4] so 1827: the disappointment of his expectations from 1814–20   [5] so 1827: states the rational grounds 1814–20   [6] so 1827: of the great revolutions of the world 1814–20   [7] so 1827: Rural life and solitude particularly favourable to a 1814–20   [8] so 1827: recommended for its influence on the affections and the imagination 1814–20   [9] so 1827: an active Communion 1814–20   [10] so 1827: a pitiable thing—If the elevated imagination cannot be exerted—try the humbler fancy 1814–20   [11] so 1827: Wanderer in answer 1814–20   [12] so 1827: on the mind in the humble ranks of Society, in rural life especially—This illustrated 1814–20   [13] so 1827: Observation that these principles 1814–20   [14] so 1827: Philosophers, whom the Solitary appears to esteem—Recommends to him 1814–20   [15] so 1827: agitated, and asks how 1814–20   [16] so 1837: Happy for us that the imagination and affections in our own despite

with Nature.[17]—Wanderer concludes with a legitimate union of the imagina-
tion,[18] affections,[18] understanding, and[18] reason.—Effect of his discourse.—
Evening; Return to the Cottage.

HERE closed the Tenant of that lonely vale
His mournful narrative—commenced in pain,
In pain commenced, and ended without peace:
Yet tempered, not unfrequently, with strains
Of native feeling, grateful to our minds;   5
And yielding surely some relief to his,
While we sate listening with compassion due.
A pause of silence followed; then, with voice
That did not falter though the heart was moved,
The Wanderer said:—
                         "One adequate support   10
For the calamities of mortal life
Exists—one only; an assured belief
That the procession of our fate, howe'er
Sad or disturbed, is ordered by a Being
Of infinite benevolence and power;   15
Whose everlasting purposes embrace
All accidents, converting them to good.
—The darts of anguish *fix* not where the seat
Of suffering hath been thoroughly fortified
By acquiescence in the Will supreme   20
For time and for eternity; by faith,
Faith absolute in God, including hope,
And the defence that lies in boundless love
Of his perfections; with habitual dread
Of aught unworthily conceived, endured   25
Impatiently, ill-done, or left undone,
To the dishonour of his holy name.
Soul of our Souls, and safeguard of the world!
Sustain, thou only canst, the sick of heart;
Restore their languid spirits, and recal   30
Their lost affections unto thee and thine!"

mitigate the evils of that state of intellectual Slavery which the calculating
understanding is so apt to produce— 1814–20; 1827–32 *omit* in our own
despite, state of, *and* so   [17] *so* 1827: How Nature is to be communed
with.—Wanderer concludes with a prospect of a 1814–20   [18] *so* 1827:
1814–20 *add* the
  6 yielding surely 1845: doubtless yielding 1814–43   8–9 *so* 1845:
Such pity yet surviving, with firm voice *etc. as* 1845, 1814–32; 1837–43
clear *for* firm, *and l.* 9 That falter'd not, albeit *etc.*

Then, as we issued from that covert nook,
He thus continued, lifting up his eyes
To heaven:—"How beautiful this dome of sky;
And the vast hills, in fluctuation fixed   35
At thy command, how awful! Shall the Soul,
Human and rational, report of thee
Even less than these!—Be mute who will, who can,
Yet I will praise thee with impassioned voice:
My lips, that may forget thee in the crowd,   40
Cannot forget thee here; where thou hast built,
For thy own glory, in the wilderness!
Me didst thou constitute a priest of thine,
In such a temple as we now behold
Reared for thy presence: therefore, am I bound   45
To worship, here, and everywhere—as one
Not doomed to ignorance, though forced to tread,
From childhood up, the ways of poverty;
From unreflecting ignorance preserved,
And from debasement rescued.—By thy grace   50
The particle divine remained unquenched;
And, 'mid the wild weeds of a rugged soil,
Thy bounty caused to flourish deathless flowers,
From paradise transplanted: wintry age
Impends; the frost will gather round my heart;   55
If the flowers wither, I am worse than dead!
—Come, labour, when the worn-out frame requires
Perpetual sabbath; come, disease and want;
And sad exclusion through decay of sense;
But leave me unabated trust in thee—   60
And let thy favour, to the end of life,
Inspire me with ability to seek
Repose and hope among eternal things—
Father of heaven and earth! and I am rich,
And will possess my portion in content!   65

And what are things eternal?—powers depart,"
The grey-haired Wanderer stedfastly replied,
Answering the question which himself had asked,
"Possessions vanish, and opinions change,
And passions hold a fluctuating seat: 70
But, by the storms of circumstance unshaken,

56 If the flowers   1837: And, if they   1814–32

And subject neither to eclipse nor wane,
Duty exists ;—immutably survive,
For our support, the measures and the forms,
Which an abstract intelligence supplies ;   75
Whose kingdom is, where time and space are not.
Of other converse which mind, soul, and heart,
Do, with united urgency, require,
What more that may not perish ?—Thou, dread source,
Prime, self-existing cause and end of all   80
That in the scale of being fill their place ;
Above our human region, or below,
Set and sustained ;—thou, who didst wrap the cloud
Of infancy around us, that thyself,
Therein, with our simplicity awhile   85
Might'st hold, on earth, communion undisturbed ;
Who from the anarchy of dreaming sleep,
Or from its death-like void, with punctual care,
And touch as gentle as the morning light,
Restor'st us, daily, to the powers of sense   90
And reason's stedfast rule—thou, thou alone
Art everlasting, and the blessed Spirits,
Which thou includest, as the sea her waves :
For adoration thou endur'st ; endure
For consciousness the motions of thy will ;   95
For apprehension those transcendent truths
Of the pure intellect, that stand as laws
(Submission constituting strength and power)
Even to thy Being's infinite majesty !
This universe shall pass away—a work   100
Glorious ! because the shadow of thy might,
A step, or link, for intercourse with thee.
Ah ! if the time must come, in which my feet
No more shall stray where meditation leads,
By flowing stream, through wood, or craggy wild,   105
Loved haunts like these ; the unimprisoned Mind
May yet have scope to range among her own,
Her thoughts, her images, her high desires.

72 nor   1827: or 1814–20
87–91 Whose care doth [chase ?] the Anarch that disturbs
    Our dreams, and doth restore us every day
    To reason's blessed light   MS.
100 work   1827: frame   1814–20

If the dear faculty of sight should fail,
Still, it may be allowed me to remember   110
What visionary powers of eye and soul
In youth were mine; when, stationed on the top
Of some huge hill—expectant, I beheld
The sun rise up, from distant climes returned
Darkness to chase, and sleep; and bring the day   115
His bounteous gift! or saw him toward the deep
Sink, with a retinue of flaming clouds
Attended; then, my spirit was entranced
With joy exalted to beatitude;
The measure of my soul was filled with bliss,   120
And holiest love; as earth, sea, air, with light,
With pomp, with glory, with magnificence!

"Those fervent raptures are for ever flown;
And, since their date, my soul hath undergone
Change manifold, for better or for worse: 125
Yet cease I not to struggle, and aspire
Heavenward; and chide the part of me that flags,
Through sinful choice; or dread necessity
On human nature from above imposed.
'Tis, by comparison, an easy task   130
Earth to despise; but, to converse with heaven—
This is not easy:—to relinquish all
We have, or hope, of happiness and joy,
And stand in freedom loosened from this world,
I deem not arduous; but must needs confess   135
That 'tis a thing impossible to frame
Conceptions equal to the soul's desires;
And the most difficult of tasks to *keep*
Heights which the soul is competent to gain.
—Man is of dust: ethereal hopes are his,   140
Which, when they should sustain themselves aloft,
Want due consistence; like a pillar of smoke,
That with majestic energy from earth
Rises; but, having reached the thinner air,
Melts, and dissolves, and is no longer seen.   145
From this infirmity of mortal kind

116 toward 1832: tow'rds 1814–20: tow'rd 1827   126 and 1827:
and to   1814–20

Sorrow proceeds, which else were not; at least,
If grief be something hallowed and ordained,
If, in proportion, it be just and meet,
Yet, through this weakness of the general heart,   150
Is it enabled to maintain its hold
In that excess which conscience disapproves.
For who could sink and settle to that point
Of selfishness; so senseless who could be
As long and perseveringly to mourn   155
For any object of his love, removed
From this unstable world, if he could fix
A satisfying view upon that state
Of pure, imperishable, blessedness,
Which reason promises, and holy writ   160
Ensures to all believers ?—Yet mistrust
Is of such incapacity, methinks,
No natural branch; despondency far less;
And, least of all, is absolute despair.
—And, if there be whose tender frames have drooped 165
Even to the dust; apparently, through weight
Of anguish unrelieved, and lack of power
An agonizing sorrow to transmute;
Deem not that proof is here of hope withheld
When wanted most; a confidence impaired   170
So pitiably, that, having ceased to see
With bodily eyes, they are borne down by love
Of what is lost, and perish through regret.
Oh! no, the innocent Sufferer often sees
Too clearly; feels too vividly; and longs   175
To realize the vision, with intense
And over-constant yearning;—there—there lies
The excess, by which the balance is destroyed.
Too, too contracted are these walls of flesh,

147-52 And pitiable weakness of man's heart
      Sorrow and grief proceed which else were not;
      Or would exist only to sanctify
      The spirit and invigorate the mind
      Being themselves controlled while they chastise   C
150-1 *so* 1837: Through this, 'tis able to maintain its hold,   1814–32
154/5 In passing estimates of loss and gain,   1814–20   163 less;
1837: less.   1814–32   164 *added* 1837   169 *so* 1837: Infer not
hence a hope from those withheld   1814–32   174 *so* 1837: ... full
oft the innocent Sufferer sees   1814–32

This vital warmth too cold, these visual orbs,   180
Though inconceivably endowed, too dim
For any passion of the soul that leads
To ecstasy; and, all the crooked paths
Of time and change disdaining, takes its course
Along the line of limitless desires.   185
I, speaking now from such disorder free,
Nor rapt, nor craving, but in settled peace,
I cannot doubt that they whom you deplore
Are glorified; or, if they sleep, shall wake
From sleep, and dwell with God in endless love.   190
Hope, below this, consists not with belief
In mercy, carried infinite degrees
Beyond the tenderness of human hearts:
Hope, below this, consists not with belief
In perfect wisdom, guiding mightiest power,   195
That finds no limits but her own pure will.

"Here then we rest; not fearing for our creed
The worst that human reasoning can achieve,
To unsettle or perplex it: yet with pain
Acknowledging, and grievous self-reproach,   200
That, though immovably convinced, we want
Zeal, and the virtue to exist by faith
As soldiers live by courage; as, by strength
Of heart, the sailor fights with roaring seas.
Alas! the endowment of immortal power   205
Is matched unequally with custom, time,[1]
And domineering faculties of sense
In *all*; in most with superadded foes,
Idle temptations; open vanities,
Ephemeral offspring of the unblushing world;   210
And, in the private regions of the mind,
Ill-governed passions, ranklings of despite,
Immoderate wishes, pining discontent,

[1] See Note, p. 424.

187 rapt   1820: sleep [*sic*]   1814   196 her   1827: its   1814–20
197–9 *so* 1827:   . . . not fearing to be left
                    In undisturbed possession of our creed
                    For aught that human reasoning can achieve
                    To unsettle or perplex us   1814–20.
209/10 Of dissipation; countless, still-renewed,   1814–20

Distress and care. What then remains ?—To seek
Those helps for his occasions ever near   215
Who lacks not will to use them ; vows, renewed
On the first motion of a holy thought ;
Vigils of contemplation ; praise ; and prayer—
A stream, which, from the fountain of the heart
Issuing, however feebly, nowhere flows   220
Without access of unexpected strength.
But, above all, the victory is most sure
For him, who, seeking faith by virtue, strives
To yield entire submission to the law
Of conscience—conscience reverenced and obeyed,   225
As God's most intimate presence in the soul,
And his most perfect image in the world.
—Endeavour thus to live ; these rules regard ;
These helps solicit ; and a stedfast seat
Shall then be yours among the happy few   230
Who dwell on earth, yet breathe empyreal air,
Sons of the morning. For your nobler part,
Ere disencumbered of her mortal chains,
Doubt shall be quelled and trouble chased away ;
With only such degree of sadness left   235
As may support longings of pure desire ;
And strengthen love, rejoicing secretly
In the sublime attractions of the grave."

    While, in this strain, the venerable Sage
Poured forth his aspirations, and announced   240
His judgments, near that lonely house we paced
A plot of green-sward, seemingly preserved
By nature's care from wreck of scattered stones,
And from encroachment of encircling heath :
Small space ! but, for reiterated steps,   245
Smooth and commodious ; as a stately deck
Which to and fro the mariner is used
To tread for pastime, talking with his mates,
Or haply thinking of far-distant friends,
While the ship glides before a steady breeze.   250
Stillness prevailed around us : and the voice
That spake was capable to lift the soul
Toward regions yet more tranquil. But, methought,

253 Toward 1832 : Tow'rds 1814 : Tow'rd 1827

That he, whose fixed despondency had given
Impulse and motive to that strong discourse,   255
Was less upraised in spirit than abashed;
Shrinking from admonition, like a man
Who feels that to exhort is to reproach.
Yet not to be diverted from his aim,
The Sage continued:—
      "For that other loss,   260
The loss of confidence in social man,
By the unexpected transports of our age
Carried so high, that every thought, which looked
Beyond the temporal destiny of the Kind,
To many seemed superfluous—as, no cause   265
Could e'er for such exalted confidence
Exist; so, none is now for fixed despair:
The two extremes are equally disowned
By reason: if, with sharp recoil, from one
You have been driven far as its opposite,   270
Between them seek the point whereon to build
Sound expectations. So doth he advise
Who shared at first the illusion; but was soon
Cast from the pedestal of pride by shocks
Which Nature gently gave, in woods and fields;   275
Nor unreproved by Providence, thus speaking
To the inattentive children of the world:
'Vain-glorious Generation! what new powers
On you have been conferred? what gifts, withheld
From your progenitors, have ye received,   280
Fit recompense of new desert? what claim
Are ye prepared to urge, that my decrees
For you should undergo a sudden change;
And the weak functions of one busy day,
Reclaiming and extirpating, perform   285
What all the slowly-moving years of time,
With their united force, have left undone?
By nature's gradual processes be taught;

266 *so* 1845: For such exalted confidence could e'er   1814–43
267 fixed 1827: such 1814–20   268 disowned 1827: remote 1814–20
269–71 *so* 1827: From Truth and Reason;—do not, then, confound
    One with the other, but reject them both;
     And choose the middle point, *etc.*   1814–20
272 So 1827: This 1814–20

By story be confounded! Ye aspire
Rashly, to fall once more; and that false fruit,   290
Which, to your overweening spirits, yields
Hope of a fight celestial, will produce
Misery and shame. But Wisdom of her sons
Shall not the less, though late, be justified.'

 "Such timely warning," said the Wanderer, "gave   295
That visionary voice; and, at this day,
When a Tartarean darkness overspreads
The groaning nations; when the impious rule,
By will or by established ordinance,
Their own dire agents, and constrain the good   300
To acts which they abhor; though I bewail
This triumph, yet the pity of my heart
Prevents me not from owning, that the law,
By which mankind now suffers, is most just.
For by superior energies; more strict   305
Affiance in each other; faith more firm
In their unhallowed principles; the bad
Have fairly earned a victory o'er the weak,
The vacillating, inconsistent good.
Therefore, not unconsoled, I wait—in hope   310
To see the moment, when the righteous cause
Shall gain defenders zealous and devout
As they who have opposed her; in which Virtue
Will, to her efforts, tolerate no bounds
That are not lofty as her rights; aspiring   315
By impulse of her own ethereal zeal.
That spirit only can redeem mankind;
And when that sacred spirit shall appear,
Then shall *our* triumph be complete as theirs.
Yet, should this confidence prove vain, the wise   320
Have still the keeping of their proper peace;
Are guardians of their own tranquillity.
They act, or they recede, observe, and feel;
'Knowing the heart of man is set to be[1]
The centre of this world, about the which   325
Those revolutions of disturbances

------

[1] See Note, p. 424.

324/5 "Knowing"—(to adopt the energetic words
Which a time-hallowed Poet hath employed)   1814-20

Still roll; where all the aspècts of misery
Predominate; whose strong effects are such
As he must bear, being powerless to redress;
And that unless above himself he can   330
Erect himself, how poor a thing is Man![1]

"Happy is he who lives to understand,
Not human nature only, but explores
All natures,—to the end that he may find
The law that governs each; and where begins   335
The union, the partition where, that makes
Kind and degree, among all visible Beings;
The constitutions, powers, and faculties,
Which they inherit,—cannot step beyond,—
And cannot fall beneath; that do assign   340
To every class its station and its office,
Through all the mighty commonwealth of things;
Up from the creeping plant to sovereign Man.
Such converse, if directed by a meek,
Sincere, and humble spirit, teaches love: 345
For knowledge is delight; and such delight
Breeds love: yet, suited as it rather is
To thought and to the climbing intellect,
It teaches less to love, than to adore;
If that be not indeed the highest love!"   350

"Yet," said I, tempted here to interpose,
"The dignity of life is not impaired

---

[1] Daniel.

333–7 Observes, explores, for this that he may find
       The law, and what it is, and where begins
       The union and disunion, that which makes
       Degree or kind in every shape of being   MS. R
339–41 And habits and enjoyments that assign
       To every class its office or abode   MS. R
343 creeping] stone or   MS. R   344 meek] mild   MS.
344–5 Such converse, if but fervent, teaches love   MS. R
347 Breeds] Is   MS. R
351–7 Yet something hangs about our daily life (And yet a something to
       our nature cleaves)
       Not to be (Which is not) satisfied with this, and he
       Is yet a happier . . . descends (*as text*)
       At Nature's call in Reason's leisure hours
       And his affections gently entertains   MS.

By aught that innocently satisfies
The humbler cravings of the heart; and he
Is still a happier man, who, for those heights   355
Of speculation not unfit, descends;
And such benign affections cultivates
Among the inferior kinds; not merely those
That he may call his own, and which depend,
As individual objects of regard,   360
Upon his care, from whom he also looks
For signs and tokens of a mutual bond;
But others, far beyond this narrow sphere,
Whom, for the very sake of love, he loves.
Nor is it a mean praise of rural life   365
And solitude, that they do favour most,
Most frequently call forth, and best sustain,
These pure sensations; that can penetrate
The obstreperous city; on the barren seas
Are not unfelt; and much might recommend,   370
How much they might inspirit and endear,
The loneliness of this sublime retreat!"

   "Yes," said the Sage, resuming the discourse
Again directed to his downcast Friend,
"If, with the froward will and grovelling soul   375
Of man, offended, liberty is here,
And invitation every hour renewed,
To mark *their* placid state, who never heard
Of a command which they have power to break,
Or rule which they are tempted to transgress: 380
These with a soothed or elevated heart,
May we behold; their knowledge register;
Observe their ways; and, free from envy, find
Complacence there:—but wherefore this to you?
I guess that, welcome to your lonely hearth,   385
The redbreast, ruffled up by winter's cold
Into a 'feathery bunch,' feeds at your hand:
A box, perchance, is from your casement hung
For the small wren to build in;—not in vain,

355 Is still a   1850: Is a still   1814–45: Is yet a   MS.   364/5 And
takes the after-knowledge as it comes   MS. R   371 ... endear and
recommend   MS.   386–7 *so* 1837: The Redbreast feeds in winter
from your hand   MSS., 1814–32

The barriers disregarding that surround   390
This deep abiding place, before your sight
Mounts on the breeze the butterfly; and soars,
Small creature as she is, from earth's bright flowers,
Into the dewy clouds. Ambition reigns
In the waste wilderness: the Soul ascends   395
Drawn towards her native firmament of heaven,
When the fresh eagle, in the month of May,
Upborne, at evening, on replenished wing,
This shaded valley leaves; and leaves the dark
Empurpled hills, conspicuously renewing   400
A proud communication with the sun
Low sunk beneath the horizon!—List!—I heard,
From yon huge breast of rock, a voice sent forth
As if the visible mountain made the cry.
Again!''—The effect upon the soul was such   405
As he expressed: from out the mountain's heart
The solemn voice appeared to issue, startling
The blank air—for the region all around
Stood empty of all shape of life, and silent
Save for that single cry, the unanswer'd bleat   410
Of a poor lamb—left somewhere to itself,
The plaintive spirit of the solitude!
He paused, as if unwilling to proceed,

395 waste] blank MS.   396 Drawn towards 1837: Towards 1814–32
399 shaded 1820: shady MS., 1814
402 . . . horizon. While I trace
    Or strive at least imperfectly to trace
    These obligations of the human soul
    Mysteriously sustained, even now I hear MS.
403 *so* 1845: a solemn bleat;
    Sent forth as if it were the Mountain's voice, MS., 1814–43
405–11 And hark! again that solemn bleat, there is
    No other, and the region, all around
    Is silent, empty of all shape of life.
    It is a Lamb—*etc.* MS.
405–6 Again! In the surrounding vacancy
    The effect upon the soul was verily such
    As he expressed for from the mountain's self C
406–11 *so* 1845: . . . for, from the mountain's heart
    The solemn bleat appeared to come; there was
    No other—and the region all around
    Stood silent, empty of all shape of life.
    —It was a Lamb—*etc.* 1814–20: 1827–43

Through consciousness that silence in such place
Was best, the most affecting eloquence.   415
But soon his thoughts returned upon themselves,
And, in soft tone of speech, thus he resumed.

"Ah! if the heart, too confidently raised,
Perchance too highly occupied, or lulled
Too easily, despise or overlook   420
The vassalage that binds her to the earth,
Her sad dependence upon time, and all
The trepidations of mortality,
What place so destitute and void—but there
The little flower her vanity shall check;   425
The trailing worm reprove her thoughtless pride?

"These craggy regions, these chaotic wilds,
Does that benignity pervade, that warms
The mole contented with her darksome walk
In the cold ground; and to the emmet gives   430
Her foresight, and intelligence that makes
The tiny creatures strong by social league;
Supports the generations, multiplies
Their tribes, till we behold a spacious plain
Or grassy bottom, all, with little hills—   435
Their labour, covered, as a lake with waves;
Thousands of cities, in the desert place
Built up of life, and food, and means of life!
Nor wanting here, to entertain the thought,
Creatures that in communities exist   440
Less, as might seem, for general guardianship
Or through dependence upon mutual aid,
Than by participation of delight
And a strict love of fellowship, combined.
What other spirit can it be that prompts   445
The gilded summer flies to mix and weave
Their sports together in the solar beam,
Or in the gloom of twilight hum their joy?
More obviously the self-same influence rules
The feathered kinds; the fieldfare's pensive flock,   450

417 thus he   1837: he thus   1814–32   431 intelligence   1827: the
intelligence   1814–20   432 creatures] emmet   MS.   436 lake]
sea   MS.   450 flock   1827: flocks   1814–20

The cawing rooks, and sea-mews from afar,
Hovering above these inland solitudes,
By the rough wind unscattered, at whose call
Up through the trenches of the long-drawn vales
Their voyage was begun: nor is its power   455
Unfelt among the sedentary fowl
That seek yon pool, and there prolong their stay
In silent congress; or together roused
Take flight; while with their clang the air resounds.
And, over all, in that ethereal vault,   460
Is the mute company of changeful clouds;
Bright apparition, suddenly put forth,
The rainbow smiling on the faded storm;
The mild assemblage of the starry heavens;
And the great sun, earth's universal lord!   465

"How bountiful is Nature! he shall find
Who seeks not; and to him, who hath not asked,
Large measures shall be dealt. Three sabbath-days
Are scarcely told, since, on a service bent
Of mere humanity, you clomb those heights;   470
And what a marvellous and heavenly show
Was suddenly revealed!—the swains moved on,
And heeded not: you lingered, you perceived
And felt, deeply as living man could feel.
There is a luxury in self-dispraise;   475
And inward self-disparagement affords
To meditative spleen a grateful feast.
Trust me, pronouncing on your own desert,
You judge unthankfully: distempered nerves
Infect the thoughts: the languor of the frame   480

451-3 Rooks cawing loud, or, as they pass or light
        Announced by shadows gliding on the ground
        In multitudes; and sea-mews from afar
        Which at some boisterous time when fleets of ships
        Upon the angry surface of the main
        Are broken and confounded, steer their course
        And hover o'er the troubled Element
        Unscattered by the wind, at whose loud call   MS. 58
453 *so* 1827; 1814-20 *as* MS.   454 *added* 1837   455 was begun]
they began C   460 vault 1832: arch MS., 1814-27   461 Is
the mute] The fleecy MS.   472 suddenly 1827: to your sight MS.,
1814-32   473 you perceived 1837: and perceived MS., 1814-32
474 *added* 1837

Depresses the soul's vigour. Quit your couch—
Cleave not so fondly to your moody cell;
Nor let the hallowed powers, that shed from heaven
Stillness and rest, with disapproving eye
Look down upon your taper, through a watch   485
Of midnight hours, unseasonably twinkling
In this deep Hollow, like a sullen star
Dimly reflected in a lonely pool.
Take courage, and withdraw yourself from ways
That run not parallel to nature's course.   490
Rise with the lark! your matins shall obtain
Grace, be their composition what it may,
If but with hers performed; climb once again,
Climb every day, those ramparts; meet the breeze
Upon their tops, adventurous as a bee   495
That from your garden thither soars, to feed
On new-blown heath; let yon commanding rock
Be your frequented watch-tower; roll the stone
In thunder down the mountains; with all your might
Chase the wild goat; and if the bold red deer   500
Fly to those harbours, driven by hound and horn
Loud echoing, add your speed to the pursuit;
So, wearied to your hut shall you return,
And sink at evening into sound repose."

The Solitary lifted toward the hills   505
A kindling eye:—accordant feelings rushed
Into my bosom, whence these words broke forth:
"Oh! what a joy it were, in vigorous health,

483–4 Nor let the spirits that maintain repose
        In heaven and earth *etc*. MS. 58
493–8 . . .   Climb once again
        These ramparts, daily climb, and ranging round
        Their wide circumference, inhale thereon
        Celestial air, the clefts and caverns seek
        Fill'd with the strife of waters; roll the stone   MS. 58
495–7 Upon their tops; and haply you shall there
        Pass in your wanderings an adventurous bee
        From your own garden, murmuring in the beds
        Of blooming heath   MS. 58
501 those   1837: these   MS., 1814–32   504 sound repose] timely
sleep   MS.   505–7 *om*. Q
506–7 *so* 1845: An animated eye; and thoughts were mine
                Which this ejaculation clothed in words—   1814–20;
                1827–43 *as text, but* poetic *for* accordant

To have a body (this our vital frame
With shrinking sensibility endued,   510
And all the nice regards of flesh and blood)
And to the elements surrender it
As if it were a spirit!—How divine,
The liberty, for frail, for mortal, man
To roam at large among unpeopled glens   515
And mountainous retirements, only trod
By devious footsteps; regions consecrate
To oldest time! and, reckless of the storm
That keeps the raven quiet in her nest,
Be as a presence or a motion—one   520
Among the many there; and while the mists
Flying, and rainy vapours, call out shapes
And phantoms from the crags and solid earth
As fast as a musician scatters sounds
Out of an instrument; and while the streams   525
(As at a first creation and in haste
To exercise their untried faculties)
Descending from the region of the clouds,
And starting from the hollows of the earth
More multitudinous every moment, rend   530
Their way before them—what a joy to roam
An equal among mightiest energies;
And haply sometimes with articulate voice,
Amid the deafening tumult, scarcely heard
By him that utters it, exclaim aloud,   535
'Rage on, ye elements! let moon and stars
Their aspects lend, and mingle in their turn
With this commotion (ruinous though it be)
From day to night, from night to day, prolonged!' "

513–15 . . . spirit, from mischance
          Secure, and unobnoxious to distress!
          What joy to wander in unpeopled Vales   MS. 58
518 reckless] careless   MS.
536–41 Be this continued so from month to month.
          Whoe'er hath known such transports—even in youth   MS. Q
536–9 *so* 1845: Be this continued so from day to day,
                    Nor let it have an end from month to month!"   1814–20
                    Be this *etc.*
                    Nor let the fierce commotion have an end,
                    Ruinous though it be, from month to month!   1827–43

"Yes," said the Wanderer, taking from my lips   540
The strain of transport, "whosoe'er in youth
Has, through ambition of his soul, given way
To such desires, and grasped at such delight,
Shall feel congenial stirrings late and long,
In spite of all the weakness that life brings,   545
Its cares and sorrows; he, though taught to own
The tranquillizing power of time, shall wake,
Wake sometimes to a noble restlessness—
Loving the sports which once he gloried in.

"Compatriot, Friend, remote are Garry's hills,   550
The streams far distant of your native glen;
Yet is their form and image here expressed
With brotherly resemblance. Turn your steps
Wherever fancy leads; by day, by night,
Are various engines working, not the same   555
As those with which your soul in youth was moved,
But by the great Artificer endowed
With no inferior power. You dwell alone;
You walk, you live, you speculate alone;
Yet doth remembrance, like a sovereign prince,   560
For you a stately gallery maintain
Of gay or tragic pictures. You have seen,
Have acted, suffered, travelled far, observed
With no incurious eye; and books are yours,
Within whose silent chambers treasure lies   565
Preserved from age to age; more precious far
Than that accumulated store of gold
And orient gems, which, for a day of need,
The Sultan hides deep in ancestral tombs.
These hoards of truth you can unlock at will: 570

544 congenial stirrings 1827: the stirrings of them MS., 1814–20
546–7 His disappointments, griefs, and vexing cares,
        And heavier sorrows, he shall lift the load
        Of his despondency, shall hear and wake MS. 58
549 sports MS., 1827: spots [*sic*] 1814–20   552/3 As by a dupli-
cate, at least set forth MS., 1814–20   553 By a fraternal likeness
MS. 58   556 with 1837: by MS., 1814–32   557 endowed 1837:
endued MS., 1814–32   558 power. You] power. Though not de-
prived The sight of human face, you MS.
565–71 Where lay the treasures of antiquity
        Entombed, and music waits upon your touch MS.
569 deep in 1837: within 1814–32

And music waits upon your skilful touch,
Sounds which the wandering shepherd from these heights
Hears, and forgets his purpose ;—furnished thus,
How can you droop, if willing to be upraised ?

"A piteous lot it were to flee from Man—   575
Yet not rejoice in Nature. He, whose hours
Are by domestic pleasure uncaressed
And unenlivened ; who exists whole years
Apart from benefits received or done
'Mid the transactions of the bustling crowd ;   580
Who neither hears, nor feels a wish to hear,
Of the world's interests—such a one hath need
Of a quick fancy and an active heart,
That, for the day's consumption, books may yield
Food not unwholesome ; earth and air correct   585
His morbid humour, with delight supplied
Or solace, varying as the seasons change.
—Truth has her pleasure-grounds, her haunts of ease
And easy contemplation ; gay parterres,
And labyrinthine walks, her sunny glades   590
And shady groves in studied contrast—each,
For recreation, leading into each :
These may he range, if willing to partake
Their soft indulgences, and in due time
May issue thence, recruited for the tasks   595

574 upraised 1837: raised   MS., 1814–32   579/80 Distress relieved
or injury sustained   MS. 58   580 the bustling crowd] a bustling
world   MS.
581–602 Cut off from its discoveries and fears
        And baby passions, such a man has need
        Of a quick fancy and a lively heart
        That Books for his consumption may provide
        A daily food of wholesome quality
        And earth and air inspire him with delight,
        Else what awaits him but the yew-tree shade
        Of black and unproductive melancholy,
        Within its circuit killing grass and flowers
        The whole year through and banishing the sun
        And the soft music of the shepherd's pipe   MS. 58
585–7 *so* 1845: A not unwholesome food, and earth and air
              Supply his morbid [pensive MS.] humour with delight
              MS., 1814–32: 1837–43 *as text but omitting l.* 587, *added
              in* 1845
591–2 *so* 1837: And shady groves, for recreation framed   MS., 1814–32

And course of service Truth requires from those
Who tend her altars, wait upon her throne,
And guard her fortresses. Who thinks, and feels,
And recognizes ever and anon
The breeze of nature stirring in his soul,   600
Why need such man go desperately astray,
And nurse 'the dreadful appetite of death ?'
If tired with systems, each in its degree
Substantial, and all crumbling in their turn,
Let him build systems of his own, and smile   605
At the fond work, demolished with a touch ;
If unreligious, let him be at once,
Among ten thousand innocents, enrolled
A pupil in the many-chambered school,
Where superstition weaves her airy dreams.   610

    "Life's autumn past, I stand on winter's verge ;
And daily lose what I desire to keep :
Yet rather would I instantly decline
To the traditionary sympathies
Of a most rustic ignorance and take   615
A fearful apprehension from the owl
Or death-watch : and as readily rejoice,
If two auspicious magpies crossed my way ;—
To this would rather bend than see and hear
The repetitions wearisome of sense,   620
Where soul is dead, and feeling hath no place ;
Where knowledge, ill begun in cold remark
On outward things, with formal inference ends ;
Or, if the mind turn inward, she recoils
At once—or, not recoiling, is perplexed—   625
Lost in a gloom of uninspired research ;
Meanwhile, the heart within the heart, the seat
Where peace and happy consciousness should dwell,
On its own axis restlessly revolving,
Seeks, yet can nowhere find, the light of truth.   630

614–15 To the simplicities of childish days Or a *etc.*   MS. 58   **619** *so*
1827 : This rather would I do   MS., 1814–20   621/2 For purposes
of wisdom and delight   MS. 58   624–5 *so* 1837 : Or if the Mind turn
inward, 'tis perplexed   MS., 1814–32   628 . . . conscience ought to
dwell   MS.   629–30 *so* 1845 : . . . restlessly revolves Yet nowhere
finds the cheering light of truth   MS., 1814–43

"Upon the breast of new-created earth
Man walked; and when and wheresoe'er he moved,
Alone or mated, solitude was not.
He heard, borne on the wind, the articulate voice
Of God; and Angels to his sight appeared   635
Crowning the glorious hills of paradise;
Or through the groves gliding like morning mist
Enkindled by the sun. He sate—and talked
With wingèd Messengers; who daily brought
To his small island in the ethereal deep   640
Tidings of joy and love.—From those pure heights
(Whether of actual vision, sensible
To sight and feeling, or that in this sort
Have condescendingly been shadowed forth
Communications spiritually maintained,   645
And intuitions moral and divine)
Fell Human-kind—to banishment condemned
That flowing years repealed not: and distress
And grief spread wide; but Man escaped the doom
Of destitution;—solitude was not.   650
—Jehovah—shapeless Power above all Powers,
Single and one, the omnipresent God,
By vocal utterance, or blaze of light,
Or cloud of darkness, localised in heaven;
On earth, enshrined within the wandering ark;   655
Or, out of Sion, thundering from his throne
Between the Cherubim—on the chosen Race
Showered miracles, and ceased not to dispense
Judgments, that filled the land from age to age
With hope, and love, and gratitude, and fear;   660

632–3 Man walked alone or mated and where'er
    In that first blissful garden he reposed,
    Or lodged, or wandered, solitude was not   MS. 58
634 borne on   1837: upon   MS., 1814–32
639–40 With Heaven's ambassador, familiar guest
    In his green bower and heard of [   ]   MS. 58
641 those   1837: these   MS., 1814–32
647–50 Fell the first Parent; banishment ensued
    For all the race, and sorrow and distress
    Were spread by him (And grief spread wide), and Man for Man's
        Estate
    Had cause to mourn; but solitude was not   MS. 58
653 By speaking voice   MS. 58

And with amazement smote;—thereby to assert
His scorned, or unacknowledged, sovereignty.
And when the One, ineffable of name,
Of nature indivisible, withdrew
From mortal adoration or regard,   665
Not then was Deity engulfed; nor Man,
The rational creature, left, to feel the weight
Of his own reason, without sense or thought
Of higher reason and a purer will,
To benefit and bless, through mightier power:—   670
Whether the Persian—zealous to reject
Altar and image, and the inclusive walls
And roofs of temples built by human hands—
To loftiest heights ascending, from their tops,
With myrtle-wreathed tiara on his brow,   675
Presentèd sacrifice to moon and stars,
And to the winds and mother elements,
And the whole circle of the heavens, for him
A sensitive existence, and a God,
With lifted hands invoked, and songs of praise: 680
Or, less reluctantly to bonds of sense
Yielding his soul, the Babylonian framed
For influence undefined a personal shape;
And, from the plain, with toil immense, upreared
Tower eight times planted on the top of tower,   685
That Belus, nightly to his splendid couch
Descending, there might rest; upon that height
Pure and serene, diffused—to overlook
Winding Euphrates, and the city vast
Of his devoted worshippers, far-stretched,   690
With grove and field and garden interspersed;
Their town, and foodful region for support
Against the pressure of beleaguering war.

      "Chaldean Shepherds, ranging trackless fields,
Beneath the concave of unclouded skies   695

664 Of 1827: In MS., 1814–20   675 brow 1827: brows MS.,
1814–20
683–4 Metal or stone idolatrously served
        And by their labour from the plain upreared MS. 58
687–8 *so* 1827: . . . and from that Height
                Pure and serene, the Godhead overlook MS., 1814–20

Spread like a sea, in boundless solitude,
Looked on the polar star, as on a guide
And guardian of their course, that never closed
His stedfast eye. The planetary Five
With a submissive reverence they beheld;   700
Watched, from the centre of their sleeping flocks,
Those radiant Mercuries, that seemed to move
Carrying through ether, in perpetual round,
Decrees and resolutions of the Gods;
And, by their aspects, signifying works   705
Of dim futurity, to Man revealed.
—The imaginative faculty was lord
Of observations natural; and, thus
Led on, those shepherds made report of stars
In set rotation passing to and fro,   710
Between the orbs of our apparent sphere
And its invisible counterpart, adorned
With answering constellations, under earth,
Removed from all approach of living sight
But present to the dead; who, so they deemed,   715
Like those celestial messengers beheld
All accidents, and judges were of all.

"The lively Grecian, in a land of hills,
Rivers and fertile plains, and sounding shores,—
Under a cope of sky more variable,   720
Could find commodious place for every God,
Promptly received, as prodigally brought,
From the surrounding countries, at the choice

696 Spread like a sea, their life's support, and [? home],   MS. 58
699 His stedfast eye, nor could mislead their steps
     If danger press'd; the planetary five   MS. 58
704 Decrees and resolutions] The purposes and counsels   MS.
707–9 These primitive astronomers pursued
     The motions nightly traceable in heaven
     Urged from within they made report of stars   MS. 58
708–9 Of observations natural, led on
     To moral inquisition bolder still
     Thus nightly from within enjoined and urged
     Those first astronomers intermingling dreams
     Of their religion made report of stars   MS. 58 (*alt. draft*)
710 set] apt   MS.   714 Veiled, nor approachable by living Man
MS. 58   718 lively] spritely   MS. 58   720 *so* 1837: Under a
cope of variegated sky   MS., 1814–32

Of all adventurers. With unrivalled skill,
As nicest observation furnished hints   725
For studious fancy, his quick hand bestowed
On fluent operations a fixed shape;
Metal or stone, idolatrously served.
And yet—triumphant o'er this pompous show
Of art, this palpable array of sense,   730
On every side encountered; in despite
Of the gross fictions chanted in the streets
By wandering Rhapsodists; and in contempt
Of doubt and bold denial hourly urged
Amid the wrangling schools—a SPIRIT hung,   735
Beautiful region! o'er thy towns and farms,
Statues and temples, and memorial tombs;
And emanations were perceived; and acts
Of immortality, in Nature's course,
Exemplified by mysteries, that were felt   740
As bonds, on grave philosopher imposed
And armèd warrior; and in every grove
A gay or pensive tenderness prevailed,
When piety more awful had relaxed.
—'Take, running river, take these locks of mine'—   745
Thus would the Votary say—'this severed hair,
My vow fulfilling, do I here present,
Thankful for my belovèd child's return.
Thy banks, Cephisus, he again hath trod,
Thy murmurs heard; and drunk the crystal lymph   750
With which thou dost refresh the thirsty lip,
And, all day long, moisten these flowery fields!'
And, doubtless, sometimes, when the hair was shed

724–7   His genius gave
      With new invention and unrivall'd skill
      To fluent operations personal form   MS. 58
726 *so* 1837: did his hand bestow   1814–32   730 palpable] tangible
MS. 58   734 denial   MS., 1837: denials   1814–32
740–3 And in her laws and mysteries being held
      As Bonds, by grave Philosopher and [   ]
      And armed warrior, chearfulness prevailed   MS. 58
746–9 Thus might a Votary say, the severed hair
      Presenting humbly to his native stream,
      "The consecrated gift has been thy due
      Since first a child upon thy banks I played,   MS. 58
752 *so* 1845: And moisten all day long   MS., 1814–43
752/3 Accept the offering, and be ever kind
      My prayers [to] grant, my wishes to fulfill.'

Upon the flowing stream, a thought arose
Of Life continuous, Being unimpaired;   755
That hath been, is, and where it was and is
There shall endure,—existence unexposed
To the blind walk of mortal accident;
From diminution safe and weakening age;
While man grows old, and dwindles, and decays;   760
And countless generations of mankind
Depart; and leave no vestige where they trod.

"We live by Admiration, Hope, and Love;
And, even as these are well and wisely fixed,
In dignity of being we ascend.   765
But what is error?"—"Answer he who can!"
The Sceptic somewhat haughtily exclaimed:
"Love, Hope, and Admiration—are they not
Mad Fancy's favourite vassals? Does not life
Use them, full oft, as pioneers to ruin,   770
Guides to destruction? Is it well to trust
Imagination's light when reason's fails,
The unguarded taper where the guarded faints?
—Stoop from those heights, and soberly declare
What error is; and, of our errors, which   775
Doth most debase the mind; the genuine seats
Of power, where are they? Who shall regulate,
With truth, the scale of intellectual rank?"

"Methinks," persuasively the Sage replied,
"That for this arduous office you possess   780
Some rare advantages. Your early days
A grateful recollection must supply
Of much exalted good by Heaven vouchsafed

Such frame of words the Votary might use,
And thus perhaps might silently prolong
His inward meditation, while he stood
And eyed the current as it passed along.   MS. 58
757 *so* 1827: There shall be,—seen, and heard, and felt, and known,
          And recognized,—existence *etc.*   MS., 1814–20
763 Hope and] and by   MS.   765/6 As they are placed erroneously we
fall   MS. 58   766–75 But what is error? and of errors which   MS. 58
782–90 A feeling recollection may supply
          Of much exalted good that may attend
          Upon a humble state. You well must know
          That on the lap religion may be learned   MS. 58
783–4 *so* 1827: . . . that may attend Upon the very humblest *etc.*   1814–20

To dignify the humblest state.—Your voice
Hath, in my hearing, often testified   785
That poor men's children, they, and they alone,
By their condition taught, can understand
The wisdom of the prayer that daily asks
For daily bread. A consciousness is yours
How feelingly religion may be learned   790
In smoky cabins, from a mother's tongue—
Heard while the dwelling vibrates to the din
Of the contiguous torrent, gathering strength
At every moment—and, with strength, increase
Of fury; or, while snow is at the door,   795
Assaulting and defending, and the wind,
A sightless labourer, whistles at his work—
Fearful; but resignation tempers fear,
And piety is sweet to infant minds.
—The Shepherd-lad, that in the sunshine carves,   800
On the green turf, a dial—to divide
The silent hours; and who to that report
Can portion out his pleasures, and adapt,
Throughout a long and lonely summer's day
His round of pastoral duties, is not left   805
With less intelligence for *moral* things
Of gravest import. Early he perceives,
Within himself, a measure and a rule,
Which to the sun of truth he can apply,
That shines for him, and shines for all mankind.   810
Experience daily fixing his regards
On nature's wants, he knows how few they are,
And where they lie, how answered and appeased.
This knowledge ample recompense affords
For manifold privations; he refers   815

791 tongue] voice   MS. 58
792–5 Its music blending with the lonesome wind
        While showers descend, or snow is at the door   MS.
793–5 . . . torrent, swoln with rains
        And furious, or while snow is at the door.   MS. 58 (*later draft*)
804 *added* 1837
811–13 He, by experience taught, can understand
        And feel the wisdom of the prayer that asks
        For daily bread, he knows that Nature's wants
        Are few and plain, yet not to be appeased
        But by endeavours keeping pace with time.   MS. 58

His notions to this standard; on this rock
Rests his desires; and hence, in after life,
Soul-strengthening patience, and sublime content.
Imagination—not permitted here
To waste her powers, as in the worldling's mind,   820
On fickle pleasures, and superfluous cares,
And trivial ostentation—is left free
And puissant to range the solemn walks
Of time and nature, girded by a zone
That, while it binds, invigorates and supports.   825
Acknowledge, then, that whether by the side
Of his poor hut, or on the mountain-top,
Or in the cultured field, a Man so bred
(Take from him what you will upon the score
Of ignorance or illusion) lives and breathes   830
For noble purposes of mind: his heart
Beats to the heroic song of ancient days;
His eye distinguishes, his soul creates.
And those illusions, which excite the scorn
Or move the pity of unthinking minds,   835
Are they not mainly outward ministers
Of inward conscience? with whose service charged
They came and go, appeared and disappear,
Diverting evil purposes, remorse
Awakening, chastening an intemperate grief,   840
Or pride of heart abating: and, whene'er
For less important ends those phantoms move,
Who would forbid them, if their presence serve,
On thinly-peopled mountains and wild heaths,
Filling a space, else vacant, to exalt   845
The forms of Nature, and enlarge her powers?

"Once more to distant ages of the world
Let us revert, and place before our thoughts
The face which rural solitude might wear
To the unenlightened swains of pagan Greece.   850

828 so bred 1827: like this MS., 1814–20   838 came . . . appeared
1827: come . . . appear 1814–20
844 so 1845: Among wild mountains and unpeopled heaths, 1814–43
          Among wild hills and thinly peopled shores, C
847 Let us revert and contemplate the face
    Which Nature in her solitudes might wear
    To the unenlightened sons . . . C

—In that fair clime, the lonely herdsman, stretched
On the soft grass through half a summer's day,
With music lulled his indolent repose:
And, in some fit of weariness, if he,
When his own breath was silent, chanced to hear   855
A distant strain, far sweeter than the sounds
Which his poor skill could make, his fancy fetched,
Even from the blazing chariot of the sun,
A beardless Youth, who touched a golden lute,
And filled the illumined groves with ravishment.   860
The nightly hunter, lifting a bright eye
Up towards the crescent moon, with grateful heart
Called on the lovely wanderer who bestowed
That timely light, to share his joyous sport:
And hence, a beaming Goddess with her Nymphs,   865
Across the lawn and through the darksome grove,
Not unaccompanied with tuneful notes
By echo multiplied from rock or cave,
Swept in the storm of chase; as moon and stars
Glance rapidly along the clouded heaven,   870
When winds are blowing strong. The traveller slaked
His thirst from rill or gushing fount, and thanked
The Naiad. Sunbeams, upon distant hills
Gliding apace, with shadows in their train,
Might, with small help from fancy, be transformed   875
Into fleet Oreads sporting visibly.
The Zephyrs fanning, as they passed, their wings,
Lacked not, for love, fair objects whom they wooed
With gentle whisper. Withered boughs grotesque,
Stripped of their leaves and twigs by hoary age,   880

861–2 *so* 1837: . . . lifting up his eyes Towards the   MS., 1814–32
870 heaven   1827: heavens   1814–20
871–2   The youthful Maid
   Or if not she the Lover at her side
   Looking with earnest eye into the depth
   Of a still lake amid the glimmering [groves ?]
   Of plants that there were nourished would create
   Helped by reflection of (a human face) her own fair face
   Some beautiful Inhabitant who there
   Might dwell in calm security unknown
   To mortal creature: Hence the green-haired brood
   Of Water Nymphs. And tempted to repose (readily induced)
   In(To) like belief the Traveller, when he slaked
   His thirst from rill or gushing fount would thank   C

From depth of shaggy covert peeping forth
In the low vale, or on steep mountain-side;
And, sometimes, intermixed with stirring horns
Of the live deer, or goat's depending beard,—
These were the lurking Satyrs, a wild brood   885
Of gamesome Deities; or Pan himself,
The simple shepherd's awe-inspiring God!"

    The strain was aptly chosen; and I could mark
Its kindly influence, o'er the yielding brow
Of our Companion, gradually diffused;   890
While, listening, he had paced the noiseless turf,
Like one whose untired ear a murmuring stream
Detains; but tempted now to interpose,
He with a smile exclaimed:—
                  " 'Tis well you speak
At a safe distance from our native land,   895
And from the mansions where our youth was taught.
The true descendants of those godly men
Who swept from Scotland, in a flame of zeal,
Shrine, altar, image, and the massy piles
That harboured them,—the souls retaining yet   900
The churlish features of that after-race
Who fled to woods, caverns, and jutting rocks,
In deadly scorn of superstitious rites,
Or what their scruples construed to be such—
How, think you, would they tolerate this scheme   905
Of fine propensities, that tends, if urged
Far as it might be urged, to sow afresh
The weeds of Romish phantasy, in vain
Uprooted; would re-consecrate our wells
To good Saint Fillan and to fair Saint Anne;   910

888 *so* 1845: No apter Strain could have been chosen: I marked   1814–20:
        As this apt strain proceeded, I could mark   1827–43
889 o'er   1827: on   1814–20
888–94   The pale Recluse who hitherto had sate
    On the grey stone, hearkening in silent mood
    Like one who listens to a murmuring stream
    Untired, was tempted here to interpose
    And with a smile *etc.*   MS. 58
902 *so* 1837: to caves and clefts of hollow rock   MS.: to caves, and woods,
and naked rocks,   1814–32
910 To fair S^t. Helen and to good S^t. Anne   MS. 58

And from long banishment recal Saint Giles,
To watch again with tutelary love
O'er stately Edinborough throned on crags ?
A blessed restoration, to behold
The patron, on the shoulders of his priests,   915
Once more parading through her crowded streets
Now simply guarded by the sober powers
Of science, and philosophy, and sense!''

    This answer followed.—"You have turned my thoughts
Upon our brave Progenitors, who rose   920
Against idolatry with warlike mind,
And shrunk from vain observances, to lurk
In woods, and dwell under impending rocks
Ill-sheltered, and oft wanting fire and food ;
Why ?—for this very reason that they felt,   925
And did acknowledge, wheresoe'er they moved,
A spiritual presence, ofttimes misconceived,
But still a high dependence, a divine
Bounty and government, that filled their hearts
With joy, and gratitude, and fear, and love ;   930
And from their fervent lips drew hymns of praise,
That through the desert rang. Though favoured less,
Far less, than these, yet such, in their degree,
Were those bewildered Pagans of old time.
Beyond their own poor natures and above   935
They looked ; were humbly thankful for the good
Which the warm sun solicited, and earth
Bestowed ; were gladsome,—and their moral sense
They fortified with reverence for the Gods ;
And they had hopes that overstepped the Grave.   940

    "Now, shall our great Discoverers," he exclaimed,
Raising his voice triumphantly, "obtain

923–4 *so* 1845 (*and* 1837–43, *but* beneath *for* under):
    In caves, and woods, and under dismal rocks,
    Deprived of shelter, covering, fire, and food ; 1814–32 ; *so* MS., *but* In
        caves and in the clefts of ;
932 *so* 1827: With which the desarts   MS., 1814–20
937–9 Which they received at Nature's hand, their will
    They check[ed] and fortified their moral sense,
    Their hopes by chearful reverence for the Gods   MS. 58
941–79   Now shall profound (our sage) Philosophers be poor
    Compared with these. Shall Men for whom our age

From sense and reason less than these obtained,
Though far misled ? Shall men for whom our age
Unbaffled powers of vision hath prepared,   945
To explore the world without and world within,
Be joyless as the blind ? Ambitious spirits—
Whom earth, at this late season, hath produced
To regulate the moving spheres, and weigh
The planets in the hollow of their hand ;   950
And they who rather dive than soar, whose pains
Have solved the elements, or analysed
The thinking principle—shall they in fact
Prove a degraded Race ? and what avails
Renown, if their presumption make them such ?   955
Oh! there is laughter at their work in heaven!
Enquire of ancient Wisdom; go, demand
Of mighty Nature, if 'twas ever meant
That we should pry far off yet be unraised ;
That we should pore, and dwindle as we pore,   960
Viewing all objects unremittingly
In disconnexion dead and spiritless;
And still dividing, and dividing still,
Break down all grandeur, still unsatisfied
With the perverse attempt, while littleness   965
May yet become more little ; waging thus
An impious warfare with the very life
Of our own souls!
            And if indeed there be
An all-pervading Spirit, upon whom
Our dark foundations rest, could he design   970
That this magnificent effect of power,

The optic glass of Science hath prepared,
Both for the world within and world without,
Be joyless as the blind ? Ambitious souls
Whom Earth as if to recompense her loss
Of bodily Stature, has produced at length
To wage with heaven a second war, to weigh
The planets in the hollow of their hand
And tame the elements—shall they, in fact,
Be but a dwindled race. Accuse me not
Of boldness, unknown Wanderer as I am   MS. 58
947 spirits   1837: Souls   1814–32   952–3 elements or our bodily
life Traced to its fountain   MS. (*another draft*) 958–68 *v. note p.* 428 *and
Addendum to MS. B of* "*The Ruined Cottage*", *ll.* 58–68, *p.* 402   970/1 Or
will his rites and services permit,   1814–20

The earth we tread, the sky that we behold
By day, and all the pomp which night reveals;
That these—and that superior mystery
Our vital frame, so fearfully devised,   975
And the dread soul within it—should exist
Only to be examined, pondered, searched,
Probed, vexed, and criticised ?—Accuse me not
Of arrogance, unknown Wanderer as I am,
If, having walked with Nature threescore years,   980
And offered, far as frailty would allow,
My heart a daily sacrifice to Truth,
I now affirm of Nature and of Truth,
Whom I have served, that their DIVINITY
Revolts, offended at the ways of men   985
Swayed by such motives, to such ends employed;
Philosophers, who, though the human soul
Be of a thousand faculties composed,
And twice ten thousand interests, do yet prize
This soul, and the transcendent universe,   990
No more than as a mirror that reflects
To proud Self-love her own intelligence;
That one, poor, finite object, in the abyss
Of infinite Being, twinkling restlessly!

"Nor higher place can be assigned to him   995
And his compeers—the laughing Sage of France.—
Crowned was he, if my memory do not err,
With laurel planted upon hoary hairs,
In sign of conquest by his wit achieved
And benefits his wisdom had conferred;   1000
His stooping body tottered with wreaths of flowers

983–8 I do pronounce them such. A worthier name
    Can they deserve who, while the human soul
    Is of a thousand *etc.* MS. 58
986 ends   1837: end   1814–32   987–8 though . . . Be   1827: when
. . . Is   1814–20
989–90 . . . prize the frame
    Of nature, this transcendent universe   MS. 58
994 Of Mind and Being   MS. 58
995–6 Nor higher title would I yield to him
    And his compeers—the shrewd, the laughing Sage   MS. 58
997 do   1827: doth   MS., 1814–20
1001 *so* 1840: His tottering Body was oppressed with flowers; MS., 1814–
20 . . . was with wreaths of flowers Opprest *as text* 1827–37

Opprest, far less becoming ornaments
Than Spring oft twines about a mouldering tree;
Yet so it pleased a fond, a vain, old Man,
And a most frivolous people. Him I mean	1005
Who penned, to ridicule confiding faith,
This sorry Legend; which by chance we found
Piled in a nook, through malice, as might seem,
Among more innocent rubbish."—Speaking thus,
With a brief notice when, and how, and where,	1010
We had espied the book, he drew it forth;
And courteously, as if the act removed,
At once, all traces from the good Man's heart
Of unbenign aversion or contempt,
Restored it to its owner. "Gentle Friend,"	1015
Herewith he grasped the Solitary's hand,
"You have known lights and guides better than these.
Ah! let not aught amiss within dispose
A noble mind to practise on herself,
And tempt opinion to support the wrongs	1020
Of passion: whatsoe'er be felt or feared,
From higher judgment-seats make no appeal
To lower: can you question that the soul
Inherits an allegiance, not by choice
To be cast off, upon an oath proposed	1025
By each new upstart notion? In the ports
Of levity no refuge can be found,
No shelter, for a spirit in distress.

1002–3 *so* 1827: Far less becoming ornaments than those
      With which Spring often decks a mouldering Tree! 1814–20
so MS., *but* withered *for* mouldering
1006 penned   1827: framed   MS., 1814–20   1017 *so* 1845: You have
known better Lights and Guides than these   MS., 1814–43
1019–23 A noble mind to traffic with itself
      To invest authority and make appeal
      From high to lower judgment-seats; whate'er
      Looking before or after you perceive,
      Tempt not opinion to promote the work
      Of passion and engage a faithless will
      In services which conscience disapproves
      Or shrinks from. Can you *etc.*   MS. 58
1021 be   1827: is   1814–20
1028/9 Laugh, but sincerely, with mirth's genuine spirit,
      Meet scorn with scorn, but seek for truth elsewhere.   MS. 58

He, who by wilful disesteem of life
And proud insensibility to hope,   1030
Affronts the eye of Solitude, shall learn
That her mild nature can be terrible;
That neither she nor Silence lack the power
To avenge their own insulted majesty.

"O blest seclusion! when the mind admits   1035
The law of duty; and can therefore move
Through each vicissitude of loss and gain,
Linked in entire complacence with her choice;
When youth's presumptuousness is mellowed down,
And manhood's vain anxiety dismissed;   1040
When wisdom shows her seasonable fruit,
Upon the boughs of sheltering leisure hung
In sober plenty; when the spirit stoops
To drink with gratitude the crystal stream
Of unreproved enjoyment; and is pleased   1045
To muse, and be saluted by the air
Of meek repentance, wafting wall-flower scents
From out the crumbling ruins of fallen pride
And chambers of transgression, now forlorn.
O, calm contented days, and peaceful nights!   1050
Who, when such good can be obtained, would strive
To reconcile his manhood to a couch
Soft, as may seem, but, under that disguise,
Stuffed with the thorny substance of the past
For fixed annoyance; and full oft beset   1055
With floating dreams, black and disconsolate,
The vapoury phantoms of futurity?

"Within the soul a faculty abides,
That with interpositions, which would hide
And darken, so can deal that they become   1060
Contingencies of pomp; and serve to exalt
Her native brightness. As the ample moon,
In the deep stillness of a summer even
Rising behind a thick and lofty grove,

1036 *so* 1827: and thereby can live,   MS., 1814–20   1048 crumbling]
mouldered   MS. 58   1056 *so* 1837: disconsolate and black   MS.,
1814–32
1062 Her native brightness. As to the eye of him
Who pauses on his way, the ample moon   MS. 58

Burns, like an unconsuming fire of light,   1065
In the green trees; and, kindling on all sides
Their leafy umbrage, turns the dusky veil
Into a substance glorious as her own,
Yea, with her own incorporated, by power
Capacious and serene. Like power abides   1070
In man's celestial spirit; virtue thus
Sets forth and magnifies herself; thus feeds
A calm, a beautiful, and silent fire,
From the encumbrances of mortal life,
From error, disappointment—nay, from guilt;   1075
And sometimes, so relenting justice wills,
From palpable oppressions of despair."

The Solitary by these words was touched
With manifest emotion, and exclaimed;
"But how begin? and whence?—'The Mind is free— 1080
Resolve,' the haughty Moralist would say,
'This single act is all that we demand.'
Alas! such wisdom bids a creature fly
Whose very sorrow is, that time hath shorn
His natural wings!—To friendship let him turn   1085
For succour; but perhaps he sits alone
On stormy waters, tossed in a little boat
That holds but him, and can contain no more!
Religion tells of amity sublime
Which no condition can preclude; of One   1090
Who sees all suffering, comprehends all wants,
All weakness fathoms, can supply all needs:
But is that bounty absolute?—His gifts,
Are they not, still, in some degree, rewards
For acts of service? Can his love extend   1095

1069–72 Yea, with its own embodied by a power
        Capacious and serene. Like influence dwells
        In Man's immortal spirit, to pervade
        And to subdue, incorporate and absorb.
        Desert and virtue cannot even exist
        But in the neighbourhood and by the touch
        Of evil which they overcome, and feed   MS. 58
1087 stormy] the wild   MS.: tossed *added* 1837
1088 him] one   MS.
1095 For service done. [As a Friend?] who doth need
        Reciprocal observance, will he own
        The heart that owns not him   MS. 58

To hearts that own not him ? Will showers of grace,
When in the sky no promise may be seen,
Fall to refresh a parched and withered land ?
Or shall the groaning Spirit cast her load
At the Redeemer's feet ?"

                      In rueful tone,   1100
With some impatience in his mien, he spake:
Back to my mind rushed all that had been urged
To calm the Sufferer when his story closed;
I looked for counsel as unbending now;
But a discriminating sympathy   1105
Stooped to this apt reply:—

                   "As men from men
Do, in the constitution of their souls,
Differ, by mystery not to be explained;
And as we fall by various ways, and sink
One deeper than another, self-condemned   1110
Through manifold degrees of guilt and shame;
So manifold and various are the ways
Of restoration, fashioned to the steps
Of all infirmity, and tending all
To the same point, attainable by all—   1115
Peace in ourselves, and union with our God.
For you, assuredly, a hopeful road
Lies open: we have heard from you a voice
At every moment softened in its course
By tenderness of heart; have seen your eye,   1120
Even like an altar lit by fire from heaven,
Kindle before us.—Your discourse this day,
That, like the fabled Lethe, wished to flow
In creeping sadness, through oblivious shades
Of death and night, has caught at every turn   1125
The colours of the sun. Access for you
Is yet preserved to principles of truth,
Which the imaginative Will upholds
In seats of wisdom, not to be approached

1100–6 In rueful . . . reply *so* 1827; *not in* MS.
              In rueful tones,
  With some impatience in his mien, he spake;
  And this reply was given.—"As Men . . .   1814–20
1109 And as we fall from right by various ways MS.   1117 *so* 1827:
For Him, to whom I speak, an easy road MS., 1814–20   1129 In
seats of power that cannot MS.

By the inferior Faculty that moulds,   1130
With her minute and speculative pains,
Opinion, ever changing!
                               I have seen
A curious child, who dwelt upon a tract
Of inland ground, applying to his ear
The convolutions of a smooth-lipped shell;   1135
To which, in silence hushed, his very soul
Listened intensely; and his countenance soon
Brightened with joy; for from within were heard
Murmurings, whereby the monitor expressed
Mysterious union with its native sea.   1140
Even such a shell the universe itself
Is to the ear of Faith; and there are times,
I doubt not, when to you it doth impart
Authentic tidings of invisible things;
Of ebb and flow, and ever-during power;   1145
And central peace, subsisting at the heart
Of endless agitation. Here you stand,
Adore, and worship, when you know it not;
Pious beyond the intention of your thought;
Devout above the meaning of your will.   1150
—Yes, you have felt, and may not cease to feel.
The estate of man would be indeed forlorn
If false conclusions of the reasoning power
Made the eye blind, and closed the passages
Through which the ear converses with the heart.   1155
Has not the soul, the being of your life,
Received a shock of awful consciousness,
In some calm season, when these lofty rocks
At night's approach bring down the unclouded sky,
To rest upon their circumambient walls;   1160
A temple framing of dimensions vast,

1135 smooth-lipped] purple   MS. 58
1138–9 *so* 1845: . . . for murmurings from within
            Were heard, sonorous cadences! whereby,
            To his belief the Monitor *etc*.   MS. 58, 1814–43 (*but* MS.
                by which *for* whereby)
            Murmurs by which as they would rise or fall
            The monitor to his belief expressed   C¹
            Sonorous intonations, rising or falling
            Were heard by which the monitor expressed   C²
1158 Mild yet deep searching, when   MS.   1159 unclouded] cloud-·
less   MS.   1161 In peace a Temple framing vast and huge   MS.

And yet not too enormous for the sound
Of human anthems,—choral song, or burst
Sublime of instrumental harmony,
To glorify the Eternal! What if these   1165
Did never break the stillness that prevails
Here,—if the solemn nightingale be mute,
And the soft woodlark here did never chant
Her vespers,—Nature fails not to provide
Impulse and utterance. The whispering air   1170
Sends inspiration from the shadowy heights,
And blind recesses of the caverned rocks;
The little rills, and waters numberless,
Inaudible by daylight, blend their notes
With the loud streams: and often, at the hour   1175
When issue forth the first pale stars, is heard,
Within the circuit of this fabric huge,
One voice—the solitary raven, flying
Athwart the concave of the dark blue dome,
Unseen, perchance above all power of sight—   1180
An iron knell! with echoes from afar
Faint—and still fainter—as the cry, with which
The wanderer accompanies her flight
Through the calm region, fades upon the ear,
Diminishing by distance till it seemed   1185

1162 enormous] gigantic   MS.
1166–76 Be wanting, Nature fails not to provide
        Impulse and utterance, to the solemn scene
        And to the holy passions of the soul
        Accordant, chiefly then, when at such hour
        Of stillness, dimness, and repose, is heard   MS.
1166–8 Be wanting, if the nightingale be mute
        And the soft woodlark never chanted here   MS.
1170 whispering] passing   MS.   1171 Murmurs devoutly   MS.
1175–6 . . . streams; and oftentimes is heard   MS.   1180 all   1827:
the   1814–20
1180–3 Unseen, and high above all power of sight
        The Raven's voice, an iron knell renewed
        At intervals with echoes from afar
        Fainter and fainter echoes as the cry
        With which the bird accompanies his flight   MS.
1185 By distance and yet dies not. All is still
        Save those celestial lamps the living stars
        That twinkle in their stations self-disturbed.
                                All is still
        Earth, air, and water are at peace, no form

To expire ; yet from the abyss is caught again,
And yet again recovered !
              But descending
From these imaginative heights, that yield
Far-stretching views into eternity,
Acknowledge that to Nature's humbler power   1190
Your cherished sullenness is forced to bend
Even here, where her amenities are sown
With sparing hand. Then trust yourself abroad
To range her blooming bowers, and spacious fields,
Where on the labours of the happy throng   1195
She smiles, including in her wide embrace
City, and town, and tower,—and sea with ships
Sprinkled ;—be our Companion while we track
Her rivers populous with gliding life ;
While, free as air, o'er printless sands we march,   1200
Or pierce the gloom of her majestic woods ;
Roaming, or resting under grateful shade
In peace and meditative cheerfulness ;
Where living things, and things inanimate,

Memorial, intimation, vestige, thought
Or image (breathing) of disquietude appears
Save in the blue unfathomable sky
Whence those celestial *etc.* Are twinkling *etc. as above* MS. (*alt. version*)
1190–207 By long experience taught (With earnest heart once more) I
          recommend
       Those humbler sympathies with things that hold
       An inarticulate language . . . *corr. to*
                      I recommend
       As a support for chearfulness and ease
       For hearts if not too heavily oppressed
       Those softer renovations that proceed
       From general Nature's mild appearances,
       Those humbler sympathies with living things
       Or things inanimate that from morn to eve
       Do speak to eye and ear in every grove *corr. to*
                      I recommend
       As a resource for indolence and ease
       A charm for care, an opportune relief
       For hearts *etc.*
       An intercourse habitually maintained
       With general *etc.*
       And humble *etc.* . . . grove.
       And speak to social Reason's inner sense MS.
1201 Or   1827: And   1814–20
1204–97 *v. note p.* 430 *infra*

Do speak, at Heaven's command, to eye and ear,   1205
And speak to social reason's inner sense,
With inarticulate language.
                              For, the Man—
Who, in this spirit, communes with the Forms
Of nature, who with understanding heart
Both knows and loves such objects as excite   1210
No morbid passions, no disquietude,
No vengeance, and no hatred—needs must feel
The joy of that pure principle of love
So deeply, that, unsatisfied with aught
Less pure and exquisite, he cannot choose   1215
But seek for objects of a kindred love
In fellow-natures and a kindred joy.
Accordingly he by degrees perceives
His feelings of aversion softened down;
A holy tenderness pervade his frame.   1220
His sanity of reason not impaired,
Say rather, all his thoughts now flowing clear,
From a clear fountain flowing, he looks round
And seeks for good; and finds the good he seeks:
Until abhorrence and contempt are things   1225
He only knows by name; and, if he hear,
From other mouths, the language which they speak,
He is compassionate; and has no thought,
No feeling, which can overcome his love.

        "And further; by contemplating these Forms   1230
In the relations which they bear to man,
He shall discern, how, through the various means
Which silently they yield, are multiplied
The spiritual presences of absent things.
Trust me, that for the instructed, time will come   1235
When they shall meet no object but may teach
Some acceptable lesson to their minds
Of human suffering, or of human joy.
So shall they learn, while all things speak of man,

1207 An universal language MS.   1207–97 *For early draft of these
lines v. Addendum* B *to* "*The Ruined Cottage*", *ll.* 1–110, *p.* 400 *infra, and
notes pp.* 431–2   1210 *so* 1837: Doth know and love 1814–20
1234/5 Convoked by knowledge; and for his delight
          Still ready to obey the gentle call 1814–20
1239–40 *so* 1827: For them shall all things speak of Man, they read
                    Their duties in all forms; 1814–20

Their duties from all forms; and general laws,   1240
And local accidents, shall tend alike
To rouse, to urge; and, with the will, confer
The ability to spread the blessings wide
Of true philanthropy. The light of love
Not failing, perseverance from their steps   1245
Departing not, for them shall be confirmed
The glorious habit by which sense is made
Subservient still to moral purposes,
Auxiliar to divine. That change shall clothe
The naked spirit, ceasing to deplore   1250
The burthen of existence. Science then
Shall be a precious visitant; and then,
And only then, be worthy of her name:
For then her heart shall kindle; her dull eye,
Dull and inanimate, no more shall hang   1255
Chained to its object in brute slavery;
But taught with patient interest to watch
The processes of things, and serve the cause
Of order and distinctness, not for this
Shall it forget that its most noble use,   1260
Its most illustrious province, must be found
In furnishing clear guidance, a support
Not treacherous, to the mind's *excursive* power.
—So build we up the Being that we are;
Thus deeply drinking-in the soul of things,   1265
We shall be wise perforce; and, while inspired
By choice, and conscious that the Will is free,
Shall move unswerving, even as if impelled
By strict necessity, along the path
Of order and of good. Whate'er we see,   1270
Or feel, shall tend to quicken and refine

1246 *so* 1827: ... they shall at length obtain   1814–20   1268 *so*
1837: Unswerving shall we move, as if impelled   1814–32
1270–4 *so* C and Q MS.: *so* 1845, *but omitting* The humblest functions of
corporeal sense:
            ... Whate'er we see,
            Whate'er we feel, by agency direct
            Or indirect shall tend to feed and nurse
            Our faculties, shall fix in calmer seats
            Of moral strength, and raise to loftier heights
            Of love divine, our intellectual Soul.   1814–43; *but* 1837–43
transpose by ... indirect *and* shall ... nurse

The humblest functions of corporeal sense;
Shall fix, in calmer seats of moral strength,
Earthly desires; and raise, to loftier heights
Of divine love, our intellectual soul.''   1275

    Here closed the Sage that eloquent harangue,
Poured forth with fervour in continuous stream,
Such as, remote, 'mid savage wilderness,
An Indian Chief discharges from his breast
Into the hearing of assembled tribes,   1280
In open circle seated round, and hushed
As the unbreathing air, when not a leaf
Stirs in the mighty woods.—So did he speak:
The words he uttered shall not pass away
Dispersed, like music that the wind takes up   1285
By snatches, and lets fall, to be forgotten;
No—they sank into me, the bounteous gift
Of one whom time and nature had made wise,
Gracing his doctrine with authority
Which hostile spirits silently allow;   1290
Of one accustomed to desires that feed
On fruitage gathered from the tree of life;
To hopes on knowledge and experience built;
Of one in whom persuasion and belief
Had ripened into faith, and faith become   1295
A passionate intuition; whence the Soul,
Though bound to earth by ties of pity and love,
From all injurious servitude was free.

    The Sun, before his place of rest were reached,
Had yet to travel far, but unto us,   1300
To us who stood low in that hollow dell,
He had become invisible,—a pomp
Leaving behind of yellow radiance spread
Over the mountain-sides, in contrast bold
With ample shadows, seemingly, no less   1305

1278–89 Like a grave Elder among Indian tribes
    Whom Time and lonely Nature have made wise,
    . Gracing etc.   MS.
1280 assembled   1827: the assembled   1814–20   1285–6 added 1837
1287 No—   1837: For   1814–32   1289 doctrine   1837: language
MS., 1814–32   1304 Over   1837: Upon   1814–32

Than those resplendent lights, his rich bequest;
A dispensation of his evening power.
—Adown the path that from the glen had led
The funeral train, the Shepherd and his Mate
Were seen descending:—forth to greet them ran   1310
Our little Page: the rustic pair approach;
And in the Matron's countenance may be read
Plain indication that the words, which told
How that neglected Pensioner was sent
Before his time into a quiet grave,   1315
Had done to her humanity no wrong:
But we are kindly welcomed—promptly served
With ostentatious zeal.—Along the floor
Of the small Cottage in the lonely Dell
A grateful couch was spread for our repose;   1320
Where, in the guise of mountaineers, we lay,
Stretched upon fragrant heath, and lulled by sound
Of far-off torrents charming the still night,
And, to tired limbs and over-busy thoughts,
Inviting sleep and soft forgetfulness.   1325

1308 that   1827: which   1814–20   1310 to greet them   1827: in
transport   1814–20   1312 countenance   1845: aspect   1814–43
1313 *so* 1845: A plain assurance   1814–43   1321 lay   1845: slept
1814–43
1325 Inviting ease and quietness [profound ?]
    Till every thought as gently as a flower,
    That shuts its eyes at fall of evening dew,
    Had folded up itself in dreamless sleep   C

BOOK FIFTH
THE PASTOR
ARGUMENT

Farewell to the Valley.—Reflections.—A large and populous Vale de-
scribed.[1]—The Pastor's Dwelling, and some account of him.—Church[2] and
Monuments.—The Solitary musing, and where.—Roused.—In the Church-
yard the Solitary communicates the thoughts which had recently passed
through his mind.—Lofty tone of the Wanderer's discourse of yesterday
adverted to.—Rite of Baptism, and the professions accompanying it, con-
trasted with the real state of human life.—Apology for the Rite.[3]—Incon-
sistency of the best men.—Acknowledgment that practice falls far below
the injunctions of duty as existing in the mind.—General complaint of a
falling-off in the value of life after the time of youth.—Outward appearances
of content and happiness in degree illusive.—Pastor approaches.—Appeal
made to him.—His answer.—Wanderer in sympathy with him.—Suggestion
that the least ambitious enquirers may be most free from error.—The
Pastor is desired to give some portraits of the living or dead from his own
observation of life among these Mountains—and for what purpose.—Pastor
consents.—Mountain cottage.—Excellent qualities of its Inhabitants.—
Solitary expresses his pleasure; but denies the praise of virtue to worth of
this kind.—Feelings of the Priest before he enters upon his account of
persons interred in the Churchyard.—Graves of unbaptized Infants.[4]—
Funeral and sepulchral observances, whence.—Ecclesiastical Establish-
ments, whence derived.—Profession of belief in the doctrine of Immortality.

"FAREWELL, deep Valley, with thy one rude House,
And its small lot of life-supporting fields,
And guardian rocks!—Farewell, attractive seat!
To the still influx of the morning light
Open, and day's pure cheerfulness, but veiled   5
From human observation, as if yet
Primeval forests wrapped thee round with dark
Impenetrable shade; once more farewell,
Majestic circuit, beautiful abyss,
By Nature destined from the birth of things   10
For quietness profound!"
                                    Upon the side

---

[1] *so* 1837: Sight of a large and populous Vale—Solitary consents to go
forward—Vale described   1814–32   [2] *so* 1837: The Churchyard—
Church   1814–32   [3] Apology for the Rite *added* 1837   [4] *so*
1837: Infants—What sensations they excite—   1814–32

1 one rude] lonesome   MS.   2 supporting] sustaining   MS.
3 *so* 1827: And guardian rocks!—With unreverted eyes
          I cannot pass thy bounds, attractive Seat!   1814–20
4–9 *not in* MS.

Of that brown ridge, sole outlet of the vale
Which foot of boldest stranger would attempt,
Lingering behind my comrades, thus I breathed
A parting tribute to a spot that seemed   15
Like the fixed centre of a troubled world.
Again I halted with reverted eyes;
The chain that would not slacken, was at length
Snapt,—and, pursuing leisurely my way,
How vain, thought I, is it by change of place   20
To seek that comfort which the mind denies;
Yet trial and temptation oft are shunned
Wisely; and by such tenure do we hold
Frail life's possessions, that even they whose fate
Yields no peculiar reason of complaint   25
Might, by the promise that is here, be won
To steal from active duties, and embrace
Obscurity, and undisturbed repose.

12 *so* 1837: The sole commodious outlet   MS.: Of that green Slope, the
outlet   1814–20: brown Slope   1827–32   14/15 In a hushed voice, and
with reverted eyes   MS.
16 *After this line an early draft continues:*
            Backward I looked and looked again with hope
            To imprint a final Image on my mind
            That should not fade. Even they methought whose life
            Yields no peculiar reason for complaint
            By this allurement might be led to quit
            The road of active duty and embrace
            Obscure delights and calm forgetfulness.
            What impulse drove the Hermit to his cell
            And what detained him there till life was spent
            Fast anchored in the desert, not alone
            Dread of the persecuting sword, remorse
            Wrongs unredress'd or insults unavenged
            And unavengeable . . . *as* III. 375–7
            Love with despair (*cetera desunt*)   MS. 58
17–19 *so* 1837: Thence the smooth bank ascending with slow step
                And now, pursuing leisurely my way,   MS.: 1814–32 *last
                    line only*
23 tenure]   1827: tenor   MS., 1814–20
24 they] some   MS.
28 undisturbed repose   1845: calm forgetfulness   MS., 1814–43
28/9   Once more I stopp'd to cast a backward look
        On that profound recess; and while I gazed
        From my full heart a livelier strain broke forth,
        Transition such as animates the grove
        In springtime, when a Bird, that for a while

—Knowledge, methinks, in these disordered times,
Should be allowed a privilege to have   30
Her anchorites, like piety of old;
Men, who, from faction sacred, and unstained
By war, might, if so minded, turn aside
Uncensured, and subsist, a scattered few
Living to God and nature, and content   35
With that communion. Consecrated be
The spots where such abide! But happier still
The Man, whom, furthermore, a hope attends
That meditation and research may guide
His privacy to principles and powers   40
Discovered or invented; or set forth,
Through his acquaintance with the ways of truth,
In lucid order; so that, when his course
Is run, some faithful eulogist may say,
He sought not praise, and praise did overlook   45
His unobtrusive merit; but his life,
Sweet to himself, was exercised in good
That shall survive his name and memory.

Hath soothed himself with notes subdued and low
Into a lofty pitch mounts suddenly.
(On that recess: and like a Bird of Song
That from a low key passes suddenly
Thus with a livelier impulse I exclaimed)
O happy Britain! heaven protected Isle!
From that immense Metropolis through all
Thy humbler cities, towns, and villages
To the bare rock upon thy sounding shores
And thy remotest Dwelling-places, blest!
Oh my beloved Country, favoured, blest
Above all Countries, enviably blest
When with thy neighbour, haughty France, compared;
For justice rules thy wide domain—the voice
Of Liberty is heard throughout thy bounds.
Dells deep as this the Mountains of Auvergne
Include, and gay Burgundia's vine-clad Hills
Hold many a green and habitable nook
Of Beauty more luxuriant, nor less safe,
Perchance, from notice and intrusive feet,
But what avails allurement in a Land
Where none are free to chuse? Whose Sons, if cross'd
By aught which they would fly from, may not flee?
Predestined all to works of violence,
Born to be slaves and ripened for the sword.   MS.
33/4 In age, in manhood, or in ardent youth   MS.
34 Uncensured] Unthwarted   MS.

Acknowledgments of gratitude sincere
Accompanied these musings; fervent thanks   50
For my own peaceful lot and happy choice;
A choice that from the passions of the world
Withdrew, and fixed me in a still retreat;
Sheltered, but not to social duties lost,
Secluded, but not buried; and with song   55
Cheering my days, and with industrious thought;
With the ever-welcome company of books;
With virtuous friendship's soul-sustaining aid,
And with the blessings of domestic love.

Thus occupied in mind I paced along,   60
Following the rugged road, by sledge or wheel
Worn in the moorland, till I overtook
My two Associates, in the morning sunshine
Halting together on a rocky knoll,
Whence the bare road descended rapidly   65
To the green meadows of another vale.

Here did our pensive Host put forth his hand
In sign of farewell. "Nay," the old Man said,
"The fragrant air its coolness still retains;
The herds and flocks are yet abroad to crop   70
The dewy grass; you cannot leave us now,
We must not part at this inviting hour."
He yielded, though reluctant; for his mind
Instinctively disposed him to retire
To his own covert; as a billow, heaved   75
Upon the beach, rolls back into the sea.
—So we descend: and winding round a rock
Attain a point that showed the valley—stretched

49–50 Nor would I, as a Patriot and a Man,
        The harbour quit whose stillness had inspired
        These farewell musings without fervent thanks   MS.
57 the ever-welcome   MS., 1814–20, 1837–50: ever-welcome   1827–32
58 With   1837: By   MS., 1814–32   65 *so* 1845: From which the
road *etc.*   MS., 1814–43
69–72 "The air its dewy freshness still retains,
        Pleasant and cool; you must not leave us yet."   MS.
72/3 To that [this MS.] injunction, earnestly expressed,   MS., 1814–20
77–8 So we descend and at the bottom gain
        A jutting crag, and winding round its base,
        We reach *etc.*   MS.

In length before us; and, not distant far,
Upon a rising ground a grey church-tower,   80
Whose battlements were screened by tufted trees.
And towards a crystal Mere, that lay beyond
Among steep hills and woods embosomed, flowed
A copious stream with boldly-winding course;
Here traceable, there hidden—there again   85
To sight restored, and glittering in the sun.
On the stream's bank, and everywhere, appeared
Fair dwellings, single, or in social knots;
Some scattered o'er the level, others perched
On the hill-sides, a cheerful quiet scene,   90
Now in its morning purity arrayed.

     "As 'mid some happy valley of the Alps,"
Said I, "once happy, ere tyrannic power,
Wantonly breaking in upon the Swiss,
Destroyed their unoffending commonwealth,   95
A popular equality reigns here,
Save for yon stately House beneath whose roof
A rural lord might dwell."—"No feudal pomp,
Or power," replied the Wanderer, "to that House
Belongs, but there in his allotted Home   100
Abides, from year to year, a genuine Priest,
The shepherd of his flock; or, as a king
Is styled, when most affectionately praised,
The father of his people. Such is he;
And rich and poor, and young and old, rejoice   105
Under his spiritual sway. He hath vouchsafed
To me some portion of a kind regard;
And something also of his inner mind

81 tufted] peaceful MS.
96–101 so 1845: A popular equality doth seem
                    Here to prevail; and yet a House of State
                    Stands yonder, one beneath whose roof, methinks,
                    A rural Lord might dwell." "No feudal pomp,"
                    Replied our Friend, a Chronicler who stood
                    Where'er he moved upon familiar ground,
                    Nor feudal power is there; but there abides,
                        In his allotted Home, a genuine Priest,   MS., 1814–20;
96–8, 1827–43, as text but one for yon   99–101 as MS.
106 so 1827: . . . sway, collected round him
                    In this sequestered Realm. He hath vouchsafed   MS., 1814–20
107 so 1827: his kind   MS., 1814–20

Hath he imparted—but I speak of him
As he is known to all.
              The calm delights   110
Of unambitious piety he chose,
And learning's solid dignity; though born
Of knightly race, nor wanting powerful friends.
Hither, in prime of manhood, he withdrew
From academic bowers. He loved the spot—   115
Who does not love his native soil ?—he prized
The ancient rural character, composed
Of simple manners, feelings unsupprest
And undisguised, and strong and serious thought;
A character reflected in himself,   120
With such embellishment as well beseems
His rank and sacred function. This deep vale
Winds far in reaches hidden from our sight,
And one a turreted manorial hall
Adorns, in which the good Man's ancestors   125
Have dwelt through ages—Patrons of this Cure.
To them, and to his own judicious pains,
The Vicar's dwelling, and the whole domain,
Owes that presiding aspect which might well
Attract your notice; statelier than could else   130
Have been bestowed, through course of common chance,
On an unwealthy mountain Benefice."

    This said, oft pausing, we pursued our way;
Nor reached the village-churchyard till the sun
Travelling at steadier pace than ours, had risen   135
Above the summits of the highest hills,
And round our path darted oppressive beams.

110 calm delights] tranquil joys MS.   113/14 This good to reap,
these pleasures to secure, MS., 1814–20   120 A character] And
these are all MS.
123–7 *so* 1837: Is lengthened out by many a winding reach,
          Not visible to us; and one of these
          A turretted manorial Hall adorns;
          In which the good Man's Ancestors have dwelt
          From age to age, the Patrons of this Cure.
          To them, and to his decorating [and more to his adorning
            MS.] hand, MS., 1814–20; 1827–32 *as text, but* eyes *for*
            sight
131 in course MS., 1814–20   133 pausing 1837: halting MS., 1814–32

As chanced, the portals of the sacred Pile
Stood open; and we entered. On my frame,
At such transition from the fervid air,   140
A grateful coolness fell, that seemed to strike
The heart, in concert with that temperate awe
And natural reverence which the place inspired.
Not raised in nice proportions was the pile,
But large and massy; for duration built;   145
With pillars crowded, and the roof upheld
By naked rafters intricately crossed,
Like leafless underboughs, in some thick wood,
All withered by the depth of shade above.
Admonitory texts inscribed the walls,   150
Each, in its ornamental scroll, enclosed;
Each also crowned with wingèd heads—a pair
Of rudely-painted Cherubim. The floor
Of nave and aisle, in unpretending guise,
Was occupied by oaken benches ranged   155
In seemly rows; the chancel only showed
Some vain distinctions, marks of earthly state
By immemorial privilege allowed;
Though with the Encincture's special sanctity
But ill according. An heraldic shield,   160
Varying its tincture with the changeful light,
Imbued the altar-window; fixed aloft
A faded hatchment hung, and one by time
Yet undiscoloured. A capacious pew
Of sculptured oak stood here, with drapery lined;   165
And marble monuments were here displayed
Thronging the walls; and on the floor beneath
Sepulchral stones appeared, with emblems graven

---

140 fervid] sunny MS.   142 concert] union MS.   144 raised in
1827: framed to MS., 1814–20   148 in ... wood 1845: in ['mid 1827–
43] ... grove MS., 1814–43
157–64 *so* 1845: Some inoffensive marks of earthly state
                        And vain distinction. MS., 1814–43
                        Some vain distinctions, an heraldic shield,
                        In tincture varying as the sun might shine,
                        Imbued its eastern window, and aloft
                        A faded hatchment hung and one by time
                        Yet undiscolour'd, marks of earthly state C
167 Thronging 1827: Upon MS., 1814–20   168 Sepulchral] Sculp-
tural MS.

And foot-worn epitaphs, and some with small
And shining effigies of brass inlaid.   170

    The tribute by these various records claimed,
Duly we paid, each after each, and read
The ordinary chronicle of birth,
Office, alliance, and promotion—all
Ending in dust; of upright magistrates,   175
Grave doctors strenuous for the mother-church,
And uncorrupted senators, alike
To king and people true. A brazen plate,
Not easily deciphered, told of one
Whose course of earthly honour was begun   180
In quality of page among the train
Of the eighth Henry, when he crossed the seas
His royal state to show, and prove his strength
In tournament, upon the fields of France.
Another tablet registered the death,   185
And praised the gallant bearing, of a Knight
Tried in the sea-fights of the second Charles.
Near this brave Knight his Father lay entombed;
And, to the silent language giving voice,
I read,—how in his manhood's earlier day   190
He, 'mid the afflictions of intestine war
And rightful government subverted, found
One only solace—that he had espoused
A virtuous Lady tenderly beloved
For her benign perfections; and yet more   195
Endeared to him, for this, that, in her state
Of wedlock richly crowned with Heaven's regard,
She with a numerous issue filled his house,
Who throve, like plants, uninjured by the storm
That laid their country waste. No need to speak   200
Of less particular notices assigned
To Youth or Maiden gone before their time,
And Matrons and unwedded Sisters old;

169 On the smooth slab, and   MS.   172 *so* 1845: Without reluctance
did we pay;   MS., 1814–43: We paid to each with due respect   C   190
manhood's] youth and   MS.
193–4 This only solace—that a gentle Dame
      He had espoused, a Lady most beloved   MS.
195–8 *so* 1827: . . . and for this, That she with numerous *etc.*   MS.; and for
this Yet more endeared to him, that *etc. as text*   1814–20

Whose charity and goodness were rehearsed
In modest panegyric.
                              "These dim lines,   205
What would they tell?" said I,—but, from the task
Of puzzling out that faded narrative,
With whisper soft my venerable Friend
Called me; and, looking down the darksome aisle,
I saw the Tenant of the lonely vale   210
Standing apart; with curvèd arm reclined
On the baptismal font; his pallid face
Upturned, as if his mind were rapt, or lost
In some abstraction;—gracefully he stood,
The semblance bearing of a sculptured form   215
That leans upon a monumental urn
In peace, from morn to night, from year to year.

Him from that posture did the Sexton rouse;
Who entered, humming carelessly a tune,
Continuation haply of the notes   220
That had beguiled the work from which he came,
With spade and mattock o'er his shoulder hung;
To be deposited, for future need,
In their appointed place. The pale Recluse
Withdrew; and straight we followed,—to a spot   225
Where sun and shade were intermixed; for there
A broad oak, stretching forth its leafy arms
From an adjoining pasture, overhung
Small space of that green churchyard with a light
And pleasant awning. On the moss-grown wall   230
My ancient Friend and I together took
Our seats; and thus the Solitary spake,
Standing before us:—
                              "Did you note the mien
Of that self-solaced, easy-hearted churl,
Death's hireling, who scoops out his neighbour's grave, 235
Or wraps an old acquaintance up in clay,

207 faded] broken   C   211 Our comrade, standing with his arm re-
clined   MS.
215–16 Fixed without motion like a sculptured form
          Leaning upon a monumental urn   MS. 58
224 appointed] appropriate   MS.
232/3 On the smooth platform of this churchyard ground   MS.
235 hireling, who scoops out] minister who digs   MS.

All unconcerned as he would bind a sheaf,
Or plant a tree. And did you hear his voice ?
I was abruptly summoned by the sound
From some affecting images and thoughts,   240
Which then were silent; but crave utterance now.

"Much," he continued, with dejected look,
"Much, yesterday, was said in glowing phrase
Of our sublime dependencies, and hopes
For future states of being; and the wings   245
Of speculation, joyfully outspread,
Hovered above our destiny on earth:
But stoop, and place the prospect of the soul
In sober contrast with reality,
And man's substantial life. If this mute earth   250
Of what it holds could speak, and every grave
Were as a volume, shut, yet capable
Of yielding its contents to eye and ear,
We should recoil, stricken with sorrow and shame,
To see disclosed, by such dread proof, how ill   255
That which is done accords with what is known
To reason, and by conscience is enjoined;
How idly, how perversely, life's whole course,
To this conclusion, deviates from the line,
Or of the end stops short, proposed to all   260
At her aspiring outset.
                    Mark the babe
Not long accustomed to this breathing world;
One that hath barely learned to shape a smile,
Though yet irrational of soul, to grasp
With tiny finger—to let fall a tear;   265
And, as the heavy cloud of sleep dissolves,
To stretch his limbs, bemocking, as might seem,
The outward functions of intelligent man;
A grave proficient in amusive feats
Of puppetry, that from the lap declare   270

237–8 *so* 1837: As unconcerned as when he plants a tree ?   MS., 1814–32
239 the sound   1837: his voice   MS., 1814–32   241 And from the
company of serious words   MS., 1814–43   242 *added* 1837
248–9 But what more differ than the human Soul,
    The powers and prospects in the human Soul   MS.
255–6 ill . . . accords with] far . . . falls short of   MS.   261 her
1827: its   MS., 1814–20   265 finger   1837: fingers   MS., 1814–32

His expectations, and announce his claims
To that inheritance which millions rue
That they were ever born to! In due time
A day of solemn ceremonial comes;
When they, who for this Minor hold in trust   275
Rights that transcend the loftiest heritage
Of mere humanity, present their Charge,
For this occasion daintily adorned,
At the baptismal font. And when the pure
And consecrating element hath cleansed   280
The original stain, the child is there received
Into the second ark, Christ's church, with trust
That he, from wrath redeemed, therein shall float
Over the billows of this troublesome world
To the fair land of everlasting life.   285
Corrupt affections, covetous desires,
Are all renounced; high as the thought of man
Can carry virtue, virtue is professed;
A dedication made, a promise given
For due provision to control and guide,   290
And unremitting progress to ensure
In holiness and truth."
                         "You cannot blame,"
Here interposing fervently I said,
"Rites which attest that Man by nature lies
Bedded for good and evil in a gulf   295
Fearfully low; nor will your judgment scorn

273–4   . . . But the day
        Of solemn ceremonial is announced   MS.
275 Minor] Infant   MS.   276 loftiest   1845: unblest   MS., 1814–20:
humblest   1827–43
292–4 . . . truth.   No brighter gleams,
        Kindled at dawn among the leaden clouds
        In summer's stillest hour, precede the Sun,
        A yet invisible Traveller on his path
        Behind the eastern hill, and yet how soon
        The radiant prospect shall be brushed away
        Or shatter'd; 'tis dependent on a breath;
        Even while we gaze, a dimness or decay
        Hath reach'd it.   Deem not, Sir, that I condemn
        The rites by which your ministry attests,
        Echoing the assurance of the inmost heart,
        That unregenerate Man by Nature lies   MS.
296 . . . or that my judgment scorns   MS.

Those services, whereby attempt is made
To lift the creature toward that eminence
On which, now fallen, erewhile in majesty
He stood; or if not so, whose top serene   300
At least he feels 'tis given him to descry;
Not without aspirations, evermore
Returning, and injunctions from within
Doubt to cast off and weariness; in trust
That what the Soul perceives, if glory lost,   305
May be, through pains and persevering hope,
Recovered; or, if hitherto unknown,
Lies within reach, and one day shall be gained."

"I blame them not," he calmly answered—"no;
The outward ritual and established forms   310
With which communities of men invest
These inward feelings, and the aspiring vows
To which the lips give public utterance
Are both a natural process; and by me
Shall pass uncensured; though the issue prove,   315
Bringing from age to age its own reproach,
Incongruous, impotent, and blank.—But, oh!
If to be weak is to be wretched—miserable,
As the lost Angel by a human voice
Hath mournfully pronounced, then, in my mind,   320
Far better not to move at all than move
By impulse sent from such illusive power,—
That finds and cannot fasten down; that grasps
And is rejoiced, and loses while it grasps;
That tempts, emboldens—for a time sustains,   325
And then betrays; accuses and inflicts
Remorseless punishment; and so retreads
The inevitable circle: better far
Than this, to graze the herb in thoughtless peace,
By foresight, or remembrance, undisturbed!   330

"Philosophy! and thou more vaunted name
Religion! with thy statelier retinue,

298 toward 1832: tow'rds 1814–20: tow'rd 1827   309–20 *not in*
MS.   321 Ah, *for* Far MS.   325 *so* 1837: doth a while sustain,
MS., 1814–32   330 By foresight undisturbed and vain regret. MS.
330/1 Yet if the upright form and countenance reared
        Aloft, as if to the heavens it would present

Faith, Hope, and Charity—from the visible world
Choose for your emblems whatsoe'er ye find
Of safest guidance or of firmest trust—   335
The torch, the star, the anchor; nor except
The cross itself, at whose unconscious feet
The generations of mankind have knelt
Ruefully seized, and shedding bitter tears,
And through that conflict seeking rest—of you,   340
High-titled Powers, am I constrained to ask,
Here standing, with the unvoyageable sky
In faint reflection of infinitude
Stretched overhead, and at my pensive feet
A subterraneous magazine of bones,   345
In whose dark vaults my own shall soon be laid,
Where are your triumphs ? your dominion where ?
And in what age admitted and confirmed ?
—Not for a happy land do I enquire,
Island or grove, that hides a blessed few   350
Who, with obedience willing and sincere,
To your serene authorities conform ;
But whom, I ask, of individual Souls,
Have ye withdrawn from passion's crooked ways,
Inspired, and thoroughly fortified ?—If the heart   355
Could be inspected to its inmost folds
By sight undazzled with the glare of praise,
Who shall be named—in the resplendent line
Of sages, martyrs, confessors—the man

A more magnificent impress than their own,
Forbid that discontent should stoop thus low,
Then welcome reason's least ambitious course,
And envied be without reproof their lot
Who, to and fro, from morn to evening pace
The narrow avenue of daily toil
For daily bread. Praise to the sturdy plough
And patient spade, and shepherd's simple crook
Nor be the light mechanic tool ungraced
With honour, which encasing by its power
Through long companionship, the artist's hand,
With indurated substance like itself,
Cuts off that hand, with all its world of nerves,
From a too busy commerce with the heart. MS. (*cf. ll.* 599–610,
    infra)
335 or 1845: and MS., 1814–43   357 the glare of praise] external
fame MS.

Whom the best might of faith, wherever fix'd,   360
For one day's little compass, has preserved
From painful and discreditable shocks
Of contradiction, from some vague desire
Culpably cherished, or corrupt relapse
To some unsanctioned fear ?"
                    "If this be so,   365
And Man," said I, "be in his noblest shape
Thus pitiably infirm; then, he who made,
And who shall judge the creature, will forgive
—Yet, in its general tenor, your complaint
Is all too true; and surely not misplaced: 370
For, from this pregnant spot of ground, such thoughts
Rise to the notice of a serious mind
By natural exhalation. With the dead
In their repose, the living in their mirth,
Who can reflect, unmoved, upon the round   375
Of smooth and solemnized complacencies,
By which, on Christian lands, from age to age
Profession mocks performance ? Earth is sick,
And Heaven is weary, of the hollow words
Which States and Kingdoms utter when they talk   380
Of truth and justice. Turn to private life
And social neighbourhood; look we to ourselves;
A light of duty shines on every day
For all; and yet how few are warmed or cheered!
How few who mingle with their fellow-men   385
And still remain self-governed, and apart,
Like this our honoured Friend; and thence acquire
Right to expect his vigorous decline,
That promises to the end a blest old age!"

  "Yet," with a smile of triumph thus exclaimed   390
The Solitary, "in the life of man,

360 faith, wherever fix'd   1845: Conscience, Faith, and Hope   MS.;
Conscience, Truth, and Hope 1814–43   361 For one day's little
space, suffice to ease   MS.   363 vague] false   MS.   364 Culpably]
Sinfully   MS.
365 If this be so] Then hail once more
    The inglorious implements of rustic toil *etc. as ll.* 612–19, *infra, but*
those *for* ye (612, 615), they *for* ye (616), baffling *for* ceaseless (617), Which
they preclude in that contented race, Who to their *etc.* (618–19)   MS.,
which continues as ll. 87–149 *of draft quoted in notes*, pp. 434–6   378 per-
formance ?] performance.   MS., 1814–50

If to the poetry of common speech
Faith may be given, we see as in a glass
A true reflection of the circling year,
With all its seasons. Grant that Spring is there,   395
In spite of many a rough untoward blast,
Hopeful and promising with buds and flowers;
Yet where is glowing Summer's long rich day,
That *ought* to follow faithfully expressed ?
And mellow Autumn, charged with bounteous fruit,   400
Where is she imaged ? in what favoured clime
Her lavish pomp, and ripe magnificence ?
—Yet, while the better part is missed, the worse
In man's autumnal season is set forth
With a resemblance not to be denied,   405
And that contents him; bowers that hear no more
The voice of gladness, less and less supply
Of outward sunshine and internal warmth;
And, with this change, sharp air and falling leaves,
Foretelling aged Winter's desolate sway.   410

"How gay the habitations that bedeck
This fertile valley! Not a house but seems
To give assurance of content within;
Embosomed happiness, and placid love;
As if the sunshine of the day were met   415
With answering brightness in the hearts of all
Who walk this favoured ground. But chance-regards,
And notice forced upon incurious ears;
These, if these only, acting in despite
Of the encomiums by my Friend pronounced   420
On humble life, forbid the judging mind
To trust the smiling aspect of this fair
And noiseless commonwealth. The simple race
Of mountaineers (by nature's self removed
From foul temptations, and by constant care   425
Of a good shepherd tended, as themselves
Do tend their flocks) partake man's general lot
With little mitigation. They escape,

410 *so* 1845: *so* 1840, *but* dreary *for* desolate: Foretelling total Winter,
blank and cold. MS., 1814–37: Prelude to coming Winter's desolate sway
C   411 bedeck 1827: adorn MS., 1814–20
427 partake 1827: These share MS., 1814–20

Perchance, the heavier woes of guilt; feel not
The tedium of fantastic idleness: 430
Yet life, as with the multitude, with them
Is fashioned like an ill-constructed tale;
That on the outset wastes its gay desires,
Its fair adventures, its enlivening hopes,
And pleasant interests—for the sequel leaving   435
Old things repeated with diminished grace;
And all the laboured novelties at best
Imperfect substitutes, whose use and power
Evince the want and weakness whence they spring."

While in this serious mood we held discourse,   440
The reverend Pastor toward the churchyard gate
Approached; and, with a mild respectful air
Of native cordiality, our Friend
Advanced to greet him. With a gracious mien
Was he received, and mutual joy prevailed.   445
Awhile they stood in conference, and I guess
That he, who now upon the mossy wall
Sate by my side, had vanished, if a wish
Could have transferred him to the flying clouds,
Or the least penetrable hiding-place   450
In his own valley's rocky guardianship.
—For me, I looked upon the pair, well pleased:
Nature had framed them both, and both were marked
By circumstance, with intermixture fine
Of contrast and resemblance. To an oak   455
Hardy and grand, a weather-beaten oak,

429 *so* 1837: Perchance, guilt's heavier woes; and do not feel   MS., 1814–32
439/40 Here see, no less than in the wider world,
    See for the gushing fount's continuous stream
    The toiling engine's interrupted gifts,
    Or joyless Cistern's hoard that fears the sun,
    The sail that caught the help of every wind,
    The sail abandoned for the creeping oar!
    This barter, these exchanges manhood brings,
    Proud of his charge, and thus we prove a scheme
    Well rounded and compleat, a promise kept
    A heighth attained, a noble growth matured.   MS.
440 serious mood] pensive way   MS.   441 toward   1832: tow'rds
1814–20: tow'rd   1827
449–51 *so* 1837:   . . . to his lonely House
      Within the circuit of those guardian rocks. MS., 1814–32
453 Like and unlike, by nature framed and marked   MS.

Fresh in the strength and majesty of age,
One might be likened: flourishing appeared,
Though somewhat past the fulness of his prime,
The other—like a stately sycamore,   460
That spreads, in gentle pomp, its honied shade.

A general greeting was exchanged; and soon
The Pastor learned that his approach had given
A welcome interruption to discourse
Grave, and in truth too often sad.—"Is Man   465
A child of hope? Do generations press
On generations, without progress made?
Halts the individual, ere his hairs be grey,
Perforce? Are we a creature in whom good
Preponderates, or evil? Doth the will   470
Acknowledge reason's law? A living power
Is virtue, or no better than a name,
Fleeting as health or beauty, and unsound?
So that the only substance which remains,
(For thus the tenor of complaint hath run)   475
Among so many shadows, are the pains
And penalties of miserable life,
Doomed to decay, and then expire in dust!
—Our cogitations this way have been drawn,
These are the points," the Wanderer said, "on which   480
Our inquest turns.—Accord, good Sir! the light
Of your experience to dispel this gloom:
By your persuasive wisdom shall the heart
That frets, or languishes, be stilled and cheered."

"Our nature," said the Priest, in mild reply,.   485
"Angels may weigh and fathom: they perceive,
With undistempered and unclouded spirit,
The object as it is; but, for ourselves,
That speculative height we may not reach.
The good and evil are our own; and we   490
Are that which we would contemplate from far.

461 gentle   1837 gentler   MS., 1814–32:   465 too   1827: full   MS.,
1814–20   480 Wanderer] Pedlar MS.
491/2 For since by passion only we can act
     The Almighty Wisdom hath ordained that Man
     In all the intimate concerns of life,
     Its joys and pains, should see but as he feels,
     Judging, yet never an indifferent judge.   MS.

Knowledge, for us, is difficult to gain—
Is difficult to gain, and hard to keep—
As virtue's self; like virtue is beset
With snares; tried, tempted, subject to decay.   495
Love, admiration, fear, desire, and hate,
Blind were we without these: through these alone
Are capable to notice or discern
Or to record; we judge, but cannot be
Indifferent judges. 'Spite of proudest boast,   500
Reason, best reason, is to imperfect man
An effort only, and a noble aim;
A crown, an attribute of sovereign power,
Still to be courted—never to be won.
—Look forth, or each man dive into himself;   505
What sees he but a creature too perturbed;
That is transported to excess; that yearns,
Regrets, or trembles, wrongly, or too much;
Hopes rashly, in disgust as rash recoils;
Battens on spleen, or moulders in despair?   510
Thus comprehension fails, and truth is missed;
Thus darkness and delusion round our path
Spread, from disease, whose subtle injury lurks
Within the very faculty of sight.

"Yet for the general purposes of faith   515
In Providence, for solace and support,
We may not doubt that who can best subject
The will to reason's law, can strictliest live
And act in that obedience, he shall gain
The clearest apprehension of those truths,   520
Which unassisted reason's utmost power
Is too infirm to reach. But, waiving this,
And our regards confining within bounds
Of less exalted consciousness, through which
The very multitude are free to range,   525
We safely may affirm that human life
Is either fair and tempting, a soft scene
Grateful to sight, refreshing to the soul,

507 transported] exalted MS.   513 injury] spirit MS.
516/17 And for those hopes without whose blessed aid
          Duty would be a burthen; for these ends MS.
521-2 which Reason cannot fathom. But waiving that MS.
528 By sight of which the Spirit is refreshed MS.

Or a forbidding tract of cheerless view;
Even as the same is looked at, or approached.   530
Thus, when in changeful April fields are white.
With new-fallen snow, if from the sullen north
Your walk conduct you hither, ere the sun
Hath gained his noontide height, this churchyard, filled
With mounds transversely lying side by side   535
From east to west, before you will appear
An unillumined, blank, and dreary, plain,
With more than wintry cheerlessness and gloom
Saddening the heart. Go forward, and look back;
Look, from the quarter whence the lord of light,   540
Of life, of love, and gladness doth dispense
His beams; which, unexcluded in their fall,
Upon the southern side of every grave
Have gently exercised a melting power;
Then will a vernal prospect greet your eye,   545
All fresh and beautiful, and green and bright,
Hopeful and cheerful:—vanished is the pall
That overspread and chilled the sacred turf,
Vanished or hidden; and the whole domain,
To some, too lightly minded, might appear   550

529 forbidding   MS., 1814, 1827–43: forbidden   1820, 1845, 1850
530/1 —The Priest continued—"I am tempted here
          To use an illustration of my thought,
          Drawn from the very spot on which we stand.   MS.
          "Permit me", said the Priest continuing, "here *etc. as* MS., 1814–20
531–5 *so* 1837: —In changeful April, when, as he is wont,
          Winter has reassumed a short-lived sway
          And whitened all the surface of the fields,
          If—from the sullen region of the North
          Towards the circuit of this holy ground
          Your walk conducts you, ere the vigorous sun,
          High climbing, hath attained his noon-tide height—
          These Mounds,"   MS., 1814–20
          In changeful April when with frost and snow
          Winter, as he is wont, has re-assumed
          A short-lived sway returning unawares *etc. as* 1814, MS.
alt. version; 1827–32 *as text, but* 531–2 Thus, when in changeful April snow
has fallen And fields are white;
537 *so* 1827: A dreary plain of unillumined snow   MS., 1814–20
539/40 On the same circuit of this Church-yard ground   MS., 1814–20
543–4 Have reach'd the turf-clad slope of every grave And gently   MS.
547 pall   1837: snow   MS., 1814–32   548 *added* 1837

A meadow carpet for the dancing hours.
—This contrast, not unsuitable to life,
Is to that other state more apposite,
Death and its two-fold aspect! wintry—one,
Cold, sullen, blank, from hope and joy shut out;   555
The other, which the ray divine hath touched,
Replete with vivid promise, bright as spring."

"We see, then, as we feel," the Wanderer thus
With a complacent animation spake,
"And in your judgment, Sir! the mind's repose   560
On evidence is not to be ensured
By act of naked reason. Moral truth
Is no mechanic structure, built by rule;
And which, once built, retains a stedfast shape
And undisturbed proportions; but a thing   565
Subject, you deem, to vital accidents;
And, like the water-lily, lives and thrives,
Whose root is fixed in stable earth, whose head
Floats on the tossing waves. With joy sincere
I re-salute these sentiments confirmed   570
By your authority. But how acquire
The inward principle that gives effect
To outward argument; the passive will
Meek to admit; the active energy,
Strong and unbounded to embrace, and firm   575
To keep and cherish? how shall man unite
With self-forgetting tenderness of heart
An earth-despising dignity of soul?
Wise in that union, and without it blind!"

"The way," said I, "to court, if not obtain   580
The ingenuous mind, apt to be set aright;
This, in the lonely dell discoursing, you
Declared at large; and by what exercise
From visible nature, or the inner self
Power may be trained, and renovation brought   585
To those who need the gift. But, after all,
Is aught so certain as that man is doomed

552 . . . which to life may be applied MS. 558 Wanderer] Pedlar
MS. 569 tossing] restless MS. 577–8 With . . . An 1827–50:
A . . . And MS., 1814–20 582–3 This, while we conversed in the
lonely dell, You shewed MS.

To breathe beneath a vault of ignorance?
The natural roof of that dark house in which
His soul is pent! How little can be known—   590
This is the wise man's sigh; how far we err—
This is the good man's not unfrequent pang!
And they perhaps err least, the lowly class
Whom a benign necessity compels
To follow reason's least ambitious course;   595
Such do I mean who, unperplexed by doubt,
And unincited by a wish to look
Into high objects farther than they may,
Pace to and fro, from morn till eventide,
The narrow avenue of daily toil   600
For daily bread."
                         "Yes," buoyantly exclaimed
The pale Recluse—"praise to the sturdy plough,
And patient spade; praise to the simple crook,
And ponderous loom—resounding while it holds
Body and mind in one captivity;   605
And let the light mechanic tool be hailed
With honour; which, encasing by the power
Of long companionship, the artist's hand,
Cuts off that hand, with all its world of nerves,
From a too busy commerce with the heart!   610
—Inglorious implements of craft and toil,
Both ye that shape and build, and ye that force,
By slow solicitation, earth to yield
Her annual bounty, sparingly dealt forth
With wise reluctance; you would I extol,   615
Not for gross good alone which ye produce,
But for the impertinent and ceaseless strife
Of proofs and reasons ye preclude—in those
Who to your dull society are born,
And with their humble birthright rest content.   620
—Would I had ne'er renounced it!"
                                    A slight flush
Of moral anger previously had tinged
The old Man's cheek; but, at this closing turn
Of self-reproach, it passed away. Said he,

599–610 *v. app. crit.* 330/1 *supra*   603 praise to the   1837: and shep-
herd's   MS., 1814–32   611–19 *v. app. crit.* 365 *supra*

"That which we feel we utter; as we think   625
So have we argued; reaping for our pains
No visible recompense. For our relief
You," to the Pastor turning thus he spake,
"Have kindly interposed. May I entreat
Your further help? The mine of real life   630
Dig for us; and present us, in the shape
Of virgin ore, that gold which we, by pains
Fruitless as those of aery alchemists,
Seek from the torturing crucible. There lies
Around us a domain where you have long   635
Watched both the outward course and inner heart:
Give us, for our abstractions, solid facts;
For our disputes, plain pictures. Say what man
He is who cultivates yon hanging field;
What qualities of mind she bears, who comes,   640
For morn and evening service, with her pail,
To that green pasture; place before our sight
The family who dwell within yon house
Fenced round with glittering laurel; or in that
Below, from which the curling smoke ascends.   645
Or rather, as we stand on holy earth,
And have the dead around us, take from them
Your instances; for they are both best known,
And by frail man most equitably judged.
Epitomise the life; pronounce, you can,   650
Authentic epitaphs on some of these
Who, from their lowly mansions hither brought,
Beneath this turf lie mouldering at our feet:
So, by your records, may our doubts be solved;
And so, not searching higher, we may learn   655
To prize the breath we share with human kind;
And look upon the dust of man with awe."

    The Priest replied—"An office you impose
For which peculiar requisites are mine;
Yet much, I feel, is wanting—else the task   660
Would be most grateful. True indeed it is
That they whom death has hidden from our sight

635/6 Held spiritual sway, have guided and consoled, MS., 1814–20
636 And watched MS., 1814–20   644 Fenced round with] Em-
bowered in MS.   645 the peering shrubs ascend. MS.   656–7
MS., 1814–20 *no italics*

Are worthiest of the mind's regard; with these
The future cannot contradict the past:
Mortality's last exercise and proof   665
Is undergone; the transit made that shows
The very Soul, revealed as she departs.
Yet, on your first suggestion, will I give,
Ere we descend into these silent vaults,
One picture from the living.
                              You behold,   670
High on the breast of yon dark mountain, dark
With stony barrenness, a shining speck
Bright as a sunbeam sleeping till a shower
Brush it away, or cloud pass over it;
And such it might be deemed—a sleeping sunbeam;   675
But 'tis a plot of cultivated ground,
Cut off, an island in the dusky waste;
And that attractive brightness is its own.
The lofty site, by nature framed to tempt
Amid a wilderness of rocks and stones   680
The tiller's hand, a hermit might have chosen,
For opportunity presented, thence
Far forth to send his wandering eye o'er land
And ocean, and look down upon the works,
The habitations, and the ways of men,   685
Himself unseen! But no tradition tells
That ever hermit dipped his maple dish
In the sweet spring that lurks 'mid yon green fields;
And no such visionary views belong
To those who occupy and till the ground,   690
High on that mountain where they long have dwelt
A wedded pair in childless solitude.
A house of stones collected on the spot,
By rude hands built, with rocky knolls in front,
Backed also by a ledge of rock, whose crest   695
Of birch-trees waves over the chimney top;

667 she   1827: it   MS., 1814–20   677 dusky] barren   MS.   679
site   MS., 1814–45: sight [*sic*]   1850   691 *so* 1845: And on the bosom
of the mountain dwell   MS., 1814–43
693–8 A hut of rough materials rudely built,
        And in a vegetable garb disguised
    Of fern self-planted on the roof and walls,
    In shape, in size, in colour such a Hut
    As in the unsettled time of Border war   MS.

A rough abode—in colour, shape, and size,
Such as in unsafe times of border-war
Might have been wished for and contrived, to elude
The eye of roving plunderer—for their need   700
Suffices; and unshaken bears the assault
Of their most dreaded foe, the strong South-west
In anger blowing from the distant sea.
—Alone within her solitary hut;
There, or within the compass of her fields,   705
At any moment may the Dame be found,
True as the stock-dove to her shallow nest
And to the grove that holds it. She beguiles
By intermingled work of house and field
The summer's day, and winter's; with success   710
Not equal, but sufficient to maintain,
Even at the worst, a smooth stream of content,
Until the expected hour at which her Mate
From the far-distant quarry's vault returns;
And by his converse crowns a silent day   715
With evening cheerfulness. In powers of mind,
In scale of culture, few among my flock
Hold lower rank than this sequestered pair:
But true humility descends from heaven;
And that best gift of heaven hath fallen on them;   720
Abundant recompense for every want.
—Stoop from your height, ye proud, and copy these!
Who, in their noiseless dwelling-place, can hear
The voice of wisdom whispering scripture texts
For the mind's government, or temper's peace;   725
And recommending for their mutual need,
Forgiveness, patience, hope, and charity!"

"Much was I pleased," the grey-haired Wanderer said,
"When to those shining fields our notice first
You turned; and yet more pleased have from your lips 730
Gathered this fair report of them who dwell
In that retirement; whither, by such course
Of evil hap and good as oft awaits

697 *so* 1827: In shape, in size, and colour, an abode   1814–20   700
plunderer] traveller   MS.   701 protects them from the assault   MS.
719 true humility   1845: humbleness of heart   MS., 1814–43   729
shining] lonely   MS.   731 them   1827: those   1814–20

A tired way-faring man, once *I* was brought
While traversing alone yon mountain-pass.　　　　735
Dark on my road the autumnal evening fell,
And night succeeded with unusual gloom,
So hazardous that feet and hands became
Guides better than mine eyes—until a light
High in the gloom appeared, too high, methought,　740
For human habitation; but I longed
To reach it, destitute of other hope.
I looked with steadiness as sailors look
On the north star, or watch-tower's distant lamp,
And saw the light—now fixed—and shifting now—　745
Not like a dancing meteor, but in line
Of never-varying motion, to and fro.
It is no night-fire of the naked hills,
Thought I—some friendly covert must be near.
With this persuasion thitherward my steps　　　750
I turn, and reach at last the guiding light;
Joy to myself! but to the heart of her
Who there was standing on the open hill,
(The same kind Matron whom your tongue hath praised)
Alarm and disappointment! The alarm　　　　755
Ceased, when she learned through what mishap I came,
And by what help had gained those distant fields.

734 tired . . . once *I*] lone . . . I once MS.
734–6 *so* 1827: A lone way-faring Man, I once was brought.
　　　　　Dark on my road the autumnal evening fell
　　　　　While I was traversing yon mountain-pass MS., 1814–20
738 *so* 1845: So that my feet and hands at length became　MS., 1814–43
749 Thought 1827: Said MS., 1814–20
751–4 I turned, and floundering over pathless wastes
　　　　Attained the object of that toil at last
　　　　Joy to myself but to a female's heart MS.
757–68 And to the spot how guided, words addressed
　　　　Even to the Matron whom your tongue has praised.
　　　　There was she standing on the open hill
　　　　Drawn from her neighbouring cottage by an act
　　　　Of anxious duty which the lofty Site
　　　　By nothing led to but a few faint paths
　　　　Imposes. With a lantern in her hand
　　　　Alone she stood, and paced, as she is wont,
　　　　By this unwearied signal kenned afar
　　　　To guide her husband home, if any chance
　　　　(Such chance is rare) detains him till the night
　　　　Falls dark upon the Hills. But come, she said,

Drawn from her cottage, on that aëry height,
Bearing a lantern in her hand she stood,
Or paced the ground—to guide her Husband home,   760
By that unwearied signal, kenned afar;
An anxious duty! which the lofty site,
Traversed but by a few irregular paths,
Imposes, whensoe'er untoward chance
Detains him after his accustomed hour   765
Till night lies black upon the ground. 'But come,
Come,' said the Matron, 'to our poor abode;
Those dark rocks hide it!' Entering, I beheld
A blazing fire—beside a cleanly hearth
Sate down; and to her office, with leave asked,   770
The Dame returned.
                       Or ere that glowing pile
Of mountain turf required the builder's hand
Its wasted splendour to repair, the door
Opened, and she re-entered with glad looks,
Her Helpmate following. Hospitable fare,   775
Frank conversation, made the evening's treat:
Need a bewildered traveller wish for more?
But more was given; I studied as we sate
By the bright fire, the good Man's form, and face
Not less than beautiful; an open brow   780
Of undisturbed humanity; a cheek

Come let me lead you to our poor Abode.
Behind these rocks it stands, as if it shunned
In churlishness the eye of all mankind.
But the few guests who seek the door receive
Most hearty welcome—Entering I beheld   MS.
758 aery   1837: open   MS., 1814–32
763 so 1827: Far from all Public road or beaten way
          And traversed only by a few faint paths   1814–20
765–8 so 1832: so 1827 but 766 When night . . . hills; 1814–20 as MS. but
black for dark   771 Or ere] Before   MS.   777/8 Escaped from
darkness and uncertain toil   MS.
778–85 so 1845: . . . the eye, the mind, the heart
          Found exercise in noting, as we sate
          By the bright fire, the good Man's face, composed
          Of features elegant, the countenance mild,
          A brow of undisturbed humanity;
          And as the course of conversation changed,
          Expression slowly varying   MS.
778–80 1814–20 as MS. but from 780 an open brow as text: 1827–43 has 778
as text, 779–80 as 1814

Suffused with something of a feminine hue;
Eyes beaming courtesy and mild regard;
But, in the quicker turns of the discourse,
Expression slowly varying, that evinced   785
A tardy apprehension. From a fount
Lost, thought I, in the obscurities of time,
But honoured once, those features and that mien
May have descended, though I see them here.
In such a man, so gentle and subdued,   790
Withal so graceful in his gentleness,
A race illustrious for heroic deeds,
Humbled, but not degraded, may expire.
This pleasing fancy (cherished and upheld
By sundry recollections of such fall   795
From high to low, ascent from low to high,
As books record, and even the careless mind
Cannot but notice among men and things)
Went with me to the place of my repose.

"Roused by the crowing cock at dawn of day,   800
I yet had risen too late to interchange
A morning salutation with my Host,
Gone forth already to the far-off seat
Of his day's work. 'Three dark mid-winter months
Pass', said the Matron, 'and I never see,   805
Save when the sabbath brings its kind release,
My helpmate's face by light of day. He quits
His door in darkness, nor till dusk returns.
And, through Heaven's blessing, thus we gain the bread
For which we pray; and for the wants provide   810
Of sickness, accident, and helpless age.
Companions have I many; many friends,
Dependants, comforters—my wheel, my fire,

788 those 1837–50: these MS., 1814–32   788–90 and that mien . . .
In such] may descend In such MS.   794–5 . . . fancy that derived
support From sundry MS.
799 Sweetened for me our mutual goodnight
          Nor left me on a lowly pallat stretch'd
          Till slumber had given way to dreamless sleep   C
799/800 Where every thought as gently as a flower
          That shuts its eyes at fall of evening dew
          Soon folded up itself in dreamless sleep   C
809 Heaven's] God's   C

All day the house-clock ticking in mine ear,
The cackling hen, the tender chicken brood,   815
And the wild birds that gather round my porch.
This honest sheep-dog's countenance I read;
With him can talk; nor blush to waste a word
On creatures less intelligent and shrewd.
And if the blustering wind that drives the clouds   820
Care not for me, he lingers round my door,
And makes me pastime when our tempers suit;—
But, above all, my thoughts are my support,
My comfort:—would that they were oftener fixed
On what, for guidance in the way that leads   825
To heaven, I know, by my Redeemer taught.'
The Matron ended—nor could I forbear
To exclaim—'O happy! yielding to the law
Of these privations, richer in the main!—
While thankless thousands are opprest and clogged   830
By ease and leisure; by the very wealth
And pride of opportunity made poor;
While tens of thousands falter in their path,
And sink, through utter want of cheering light;
For you the hours of labour do not flag;   835
For you each evening hath its shining star,
And every sabbath-day its golden sun.' "

  "Yes!" said the Solitary with a smile
That seemed to break from an expanding heart,
"The untutored bird may found, and so construct,   840
And with such soft materials line, her nest
Fixed in the centre of a prickly brake,
That the thorns wound her not; they only guard.
Powers not unjustly likened to those gifts
Of happy instinct which the woodland bird   845
Shares with her species, nature's grace sometimes
Upon the individual doth confer,
Among her higher creatures born and trained
To use of reason. And, I own that, tired

818 nor blush to   1827: and often   MS.: nor seldom   1814–20
824–6 *added* 1845   830 clogged] cloyed   MS.   840–1 The
little bird, by happy instinct taught, Can   MS.
844–7 What on the species Nature doth confer
    Is sometimes to the Individual given   MS.

Of the ostentatious world—a swelling stage   850
With empty actions and vain passions stuffed,
And from the private struggles of mankind
Hoping far less than I could wish to hope,
Far less than once I trusted and believed—
I love to hear of those, who, not contending   855
Nor summoned to contend for virtue's prize,
Miss not the humbler good at which they aim,
Blest with a kindly faculty to blunt
The edge of adverse circumstance, and turn
Into their contraries the petty plagues   860
And hindrances with which they stand beset.
In early youth, among my native hills,
I knew a Scottish Peasant who possessed
A few small crofts of stone-encumbered ground;
Masses of every shape and size, that lay   865
Scattered about under the mouldering walls
Of a rough precipice; and some, apart,
In quarters unobnoxious to such chance,
As if the moon had showered them down in spite.
But he repined not. Though the plough was scared   870
By these obstructions, 'round the shady stones
A fertilising moisture,' said the Swain,
'Gathers, and is preserved; and feeding dews
And damps, through all the droughty summer day
From out their substance issuing, maintain   875
Herbage that never fails: no grass springs up
So green, so fresh, so plentiful, as mine!'
But thinly sown these natures; rare, at least,
The mutual aptitude of seed and soil
That yields such kindly product. He, whose bed   880
Perhaps yon loose sods cover, the poor Pensioner
Brought yesterday from our sequestered dell
Here to lie down in lasting quiet, he,
If living now, could otherwise report
Of rustic loneliness: that grey-haired Orphan—   885

853 far 1837: for MS., 1814–32   861/2 Though this is rather
Nature's praise than theirs. MS.   866 under 1832: beneath MS.,
1814–27   872–3 Gather, said he, the dews; and feeding dews MS.
877/8 See in this well-conditioned Soul, a Third
        To match with your good Couple that put forth
        Their homely graces on the Mountain side. MS., 1814–20

So call him, for humanity to him
No parent was—feelingly could have told,
In life, in death, what solitude can breed
Of selfishness, and cruelty, and vice;
Or, if it breed not, hath not power to cure.　　890
—But your compliance, Sir! with our request
My words too long have hindered."
　　　　　　　　　　　　　　Undeterred,
Perhaps incited rather, by these shocks,
In no ungracious opposition, given
To the confiding spirit of his own　　895
Experienced faith, the reverend Pastor said,
Around him looking; "Where shall I begin?
Who shall be first selected from my flock
Gathered together in their peaceful fold?"
He paused—and having lifted up his eyes　　900
To the pure heaven, he cast them down again
Upon the earth beneath his feet; and spake:—

　"To a mysteriously-united pair
This place is consecrate; to Death and Life,
And to the best affections that proceed　　905
From their conjunction; consecrate to faith
In him who bled for man upon the cross;
Hallowed to revelation; and no less
To reason's mandates; and the hopes divine
Of pure imagination;—above all,　　910
To charity, and love, that have provided,
Within these precincts, a capacious bed
And receptacle, open to the good

887 feelingly could　1832: could feelingly　MS., 1814-27
898-9 Whose hallowed sleep shall such [? unusual] voice
　　Disturb, though speaking in parental tone.
　　Who shall be first selected . . . fold.
　　This said, the Reverend Pastor silent stood
　　In thoughtful hesitation, on the ground
　　Looking, upon the graves that nearest lay,
　　Then on the mounds that rose on either hand.
　　This noticing the Itinerant interposing said
　　I wonder not that meditative awe
　　Hath seized you doubting to uplift the scale
　　(To stand in judgment and uplift the scale)
　　And weigh albeit in a spiritual . . . *cetera desunt*　MS.
903 united　1845: consorted　MS., 1814-43

And evil, to the just and the unjust;
In which they find an equal resting-place: 915
Even as the multitude of kindred brooks
And streams, whose murmur fills this hollow vale,
Whether their course be turbulent or smooth,
Their waters clear or sullied, all are lost
Within the bosom of yon crystal Lake,   920
And end their journey in the same repose!

"And blest are they who sleep; and we that know,
While in a spot like this we breathe and walk,
That all beneath us by the wings are covered
Of motherly humanity, outspread   925
And gathering all within their tender shade,
Though loth and slow to come! A battlefield,
In stillness left when slaughter is no more,
With this compared, makes a strange spectacle!
A dismal prospect yields the wild shore strewn   930
With wrecks, and trod by feet of young and old
Wandering about in miserable search
Of friends or kindred, whom the angry sea
Restores not to their prayer! Ah! who would think

926 within] beneath MS.   929 makes 1845: is 1814–32: yields
1837–43
930–3 *so* 1837: A rueful sight the wild shore strewn with wrecks
                And trod by people in afflicted quest
                Of friends and kindred, MS., 1814–32
934–43   ... The contrast yet
        A little longer may our thoughts pursue.
        Behold, and where? where, but in polished realms
        For arts and arms and luxury renowned,
        That to our minds present this sight of truth?
        Mark him who shuts and opens his sad eyes
        In some sepulchral dungeon's trickling vault,
        Buried where scarcely he can note or feel
        The several qualities of night and day,
        To lull a Tyrant's fear or please his will,
        And in the end and quietness of all
        The bones remaining when the breath expired.
        From this dire truth which polished Realms afford
        Turn to the region of the East, and see
        Where sandy desarts to the walls extend
        Of some proud City, which the Turbaned chief
        Rules with his scymitar—a fainting wretch;
        Yea more, a Company of either sex
        Crawled forth and thankfully set down to take

That all the scattered subjects which compose　　　　935
Earth's melancholy vision through the space
Of all her climes—these wretched, these depraved,
To virtue lost, insensible of peace,
From the delights of charity cut off,
To pity dead, the oppressor and the opprest;　　　　940
Tyrants who utter the destroying word,
And slaves who will consent to be destroyed—
Were of one species with the sheltered few,
Who, with a dutiful and tender hand,

> The gaunt Hyena's leavings, they themselves
> Destined, perhaps, ere morning's light return
> To be the wild Beasts' prey. Behold, and this
> This, though a sight (effect) of keener wretchedness,
> Perhaps our bodily eyes have often seen,
> While the heart knew not what they looked upon,
> One out of many in our Christian land
> Who, hopeless of relief, and unrelieved
> (Retire like Birds to holes and corners chased
> By pitiless winter, Miserable Men)
> Is marching forward through the crowded street
> In some unheeded corner to lie down
> Making that place his home where he can die.
> Track where you may the course of those who bent
> On strange adventures, or desiring gain,
> Or urged by thirst of knowledge, wander on
> Restless, encountering with their own free choice
> All shapes of danger and unsolaced death,
> Wherever foot can go. Before your mind
> Place, if you can, a City to the flames
> Of war delivered, and the [?]
> Or to a field of battle turn once more,
> But ere the fight begin, and there behold
> A mighty number taught by pride of heart
> And martial discipline to stand or move
> Firm and compact as with one soul inspired,
> Till irresistibly the storm break in
> And sever them, like green leaves from the boughs
> By summer whirlwinds torn! Ah, who would think
> That they who issue the destroying word,
> And they who thus consent to be destroyed,
> What Man, or Angel looking from the height
> Of tranquil pity, in his heart could deem
> That all the scattered subjects which compose
> Earth's melancholy vision, wretched some,
> Some careless. desperate these, and these depraved,
> Tyrants, and slaves who will consent [　　　]
> Were of one species etc. MS.

Lodged, in a dear appropriated spot,   945
This file of infants; some that never breathed
The vital air; others, which, though allowed
That privilege, did yet expire too soon,
Or with too brief a warning, to admit
Administration of the holy rite   950
That lovingly consigns the babe to the arms
Of Jesus, and his everlasting care.
These that in trembling hope are laid apart;
And the besprinkled nursling, unrequired
Till he begins to smile upon the breast   955
That feeds him; and the tottering little-one
Taken from air and sunshine when the rose
Of infancy first blooms upon his cheek;
The thinking, thoughtless, school-boy; the bold youth
Of soul impetuous, and the bashful maid   960
Smitten while all the promises of life
Are opening round her; those of middle age,
Cast down while confident in strength they stand,
Like pillars fixed more firmly, as might seem,
And more secure, by very weight of all   965
That, for support, rests on them; the decayed
And burthensome; and lastly, that poor few
Whose light of reason is with age extinct;
The hopeful and the hopeless, first and last,
The earliest summoned and the longest spared—   970
Are here deposited, with tribute paid
Various, but unto each some tribute paid;
As if, amid these peaceful hills and groves,
Society were touched with kind concern,
And gentle 'Nature grieved, that one should die;'   975
Or, if the change demanded no regret,
Observed the liberating stroke—and blessed.

    "And whence that tribute? wherefore these regards?
Not from the naked *Heart* alone of Man

945 *so* 1837: Did lodge, in an appropriated spot   1814–32   947 *so*
1837: and others, who, allowed   MS., 1814–32   960 Exulting and
impetuous and the Maid   MS.
964–6 As if more firmly fixed by very weight
        Of those that rest upon them   MS.
967 and that unconscious few   C

(Though claiming high distinction upon earth   980
As the sole spring and fountain-head of tears,
His own peculiar utterance for distress
Or gladness)—No," the philosophic Priest
Continued, " 'tis not in the vital seat
Of feeling to produce them, without aid   985
From the pure soul, the soul sublime and pure;
With her two faculties of eye and ear,
The one by which a creature, whom his sins
Have rendered prone, can upward look to heaven;
The other that empowers him to perceive   990
The voice of Deity, on height and plain,
Whispering those truths in stillness, which the WORD,
To the four quarters of the winds, proclaims.
Not without such assistance could the use
Of these benign observances prevail: 995
Thus are they born, thus fostered, thus maintained;
And by the care prospective of our wise
Forefathers, who, to guard against the shocks,
The fluctuation and decay of things,
Embodied and established these high truths   1000
In solemn institutions:—men convinced
That life is love and immortality,
The being one, and one the element.
There lies the channel, and original bed,
From the beginning, hollowed out and scooped   1005
For Man's affections—else betrayed and lost,
And swallowed up 'mid deserts infinite!
This is the genuine course, the aim, and end
Of prescient reason; all conclusions else
Are abject, vain, presumptuous, and perverse.   1010
The faith partaking of those holy times,
Life, I repeat, is energy of love
Divine or human; exercised in pain,
In strife, in tribulation; and ordained,
If so approved and sanctified, to pass,   1015
Through shades and silent rest, to endless joy."

980 claiming   1827: framed to   MS., 1814–20   983–6 Or gladness)
no, but from the soul sublime   MS.   987 faculties] ministers   MS.
989 upward can   C   996 fostered, thus   1837: fostered, and   1814–32:
Proceeding thence thereby they are maintained,   MS.   1001 con-
vinced] believing   MS.   1004–7 not in MS.   1008–11 added
to MS. on separate page

BOOK SIXTH

THE CHURCHYARD AMONG THE MOUNTAINS

ARGUMENT

Poet's Address to the State and Church of England.—The Pastor not inferior to the ancient Worthies of the Church.—He begins his Narratives with an instance of unrequited Love.—Anguish of mind subdued, and how.— —The lonely Miner.—An instance of perseverance.—Which leads by contrast to an example of abused talents, irresolution, and weakness.—Solitary, applying this covertly to his own case, asks for an instance of some Stranger, whose dispositions may have led him to end his days here.—Pastor, in answer, gives an account of the harmonising influence of Solitude upon two men of opposite principles, who had encountered agitations in public life.— The rule by which Peace may be obtained expressed, and where.—Solitary hints at an overpowering Fatality.—Answer of the Pastor.—What subjects he will exclude from his Narratives.—Conversation upon this.—Instance of an unamiable character, a Female,[1] and why given.—Contrasted with this, a meek sufferer, from unguarded and betrayed love.—Instance of heavier guilt, and its consequences to the Offender.—With this instance of a Marriage Contract broken is contrasted one of a Widower, evidencing his faithful affection towards his deceased wife by his care of their female Children.[2]

HAIL to the crown by Freedom shaped—to gird
An English Sovereign's brow! and to the throne
Whereon he sits! Whose deep foundations lie
In veneration and the people's love;
Whose steps are equity, whose seat is law.   5
—Hail to the State of England! And conjoin
With this a salutation as devout,
Made to the spiritual fabric of her Church;
Founded in truth; by blood of Martyrdom
Cemented; by the hands of Wisdom reared   10
In beauty of holiness, with ordered pomp,
Decent and unreproved. The voice, that greets
The majesty of both, shall pray for both;
That, mutually protected and sustained,
They may endure long as the sea surrounds   15
This favoured Land, or sunshine warms her soil.

[1] Woman   C   [2] —Second Marriage of a Widower prudential and happy.   1814–20

15 *so* 1832: as long as sea   MS., 1814–27   16 Land] Isle   MS.

And O, ye swelling hills, and spacious plains!
Besprent from shore to shore with steeple-towers,
And spires whose "silent finger points to heaven;"
Nor wanting, at wide intervals, the bulk   20
Of ancient minster lifted above the cloud
Of the dense air, which town or city breeds
To intercept the sun's glad beams—may ne'er
That true succession fail of English hearts,
Who, with ancestral feeling, can perceive   25
What in those holy structures ye possess
Of ornamental interest, and the charm
Of pious sentiment diffused afar,
And human charity, and social love.
—Thus never shall the indignities of time   30
Approach their reverend graces, unopposed;
Nor shall the elements be free to hurt
Their fair proportions; nor the blinder rage
Of bigot zeal madly to overturn;
And, if the desolating hand of war   35
Spare them, they shall continue to bestow,
Upon the thronged abodes of busy men
(Depraved, and ever prone to fill the mind
Exclusively with transitory things)
An air and mien of dignified pursuit;   40
Of sweet civility, on rustic wilds.

The Poet, fostering for his native land
Such hope, entreats that servants may abound
Of those pure altars worthy; ministers
Detached from pleasure, to the love of gain   45
Superior, insusceptible of pride,
And by ambitious longings undisturbed;
Men, whose delight is where their duty leads
Or fixes them; whose least distinguished day

21 lifted] rising, *corr. to* reared   MS.
25 *so* 1827: That can perceive, not less than heretofore
        Our Ancestors did feelingly perceive   MS., 1814–20
31 Approach those reverend Fabrics   MS.   32 hurt] mar   MS.
35–6 if . . . they shall] may . . . and they   MS.   38 the mind   1837:
their minds   MS., 1814–32
42–3 Thus wishing, can the Poet fail to add
        An earnest prayer that   MS.
47 ambition's   1814–20

Shines with some portion of that heavenly lustre   50
Which makes the sabbath lovely in the sight
Of blessèd angels, pitying human cares.
—And, as on earth it is the doom of truth
To be perpetually attacked by foes
Open or covert, be that priesthood still,   55
For her defence, replenished with a band
Of strenuous champions, in scholastic arts
Thoroughly disciplined; nor (if in course
Of the revolving world's disturbances
Cause should recur, which righteous Heaven avert!   60
To meet such trial) from their spiritual sires
Degenerate; who, constrained to wield the sword
Of disputation, shrunk not, though assailed
With hostile din, and combating in sight
Of angry umpires, partial and unjust;   65
And did, thereafter, bathe their hands in fire,
So to declare the conscience satisfied:
Nor for their bodies would accept release;
But, blessing God and praising him, bequeathed
With their last breath, from out the smouldering flame, 70
The faith which they by diligence had earned,
Or, through illuminating grace, received,
For their dear countrymen, and all mankind.
O high example, constancy divine!

Even such a Man (inheriting the zeal   75
And from the sanctity of elder times
Not deviating,—a priest, the like of whom,
If multiplied, and in their stations set,
Would o'er the bosom of a joyful land
Spread true religion and her genuine fruits)   80
Before me stood that day; on holy ground
Fraught with the relics of mortality,
Exalting tender themes, by just degrees
To lofty raised; and to the highest, last;
The head and mighty paramount of truths,—   85
Immortal life, in never-fading worlds,
For mortal creatures, conquered and secured.

---

54 attacked] assailed MS.   55–7 . . . may that Priesthood yield . . .
a never failing Band Of zealous MS.

That basis laid, those principles of faith
Announced, as a preparatory act
Of reverence done to the spirit of the place,   90
The Pastor cast his eyes upon the ground ;
Not, as before, like one oppressed with awe,
But with a mild and social cheerfulness ;
Then to the Solitary turned, and spake.

"At morn or eve, in your retired domain,   95
Perchance you not unfrequently have marked
A Visitor—in quest of herbs and flowers ;
Too delicate employ, as would appear,
For one, who, though of drooping mien, had yet
From nature's kindliness received a frame   100
Robust as ever rural labour bred."

The Solitary answered : "Such a Form
Full well I recollect. We often crossed
Each other's path ; but, as the Intruder seemed
Fondly to prize the silence which he kept,   105
And I as willingly did cherish mine,
We met, and passed, like shadows. I have heard,
From my good Host, that being crazed in brain
By unrequited love, he scaled the rocks,
Dived into caves, and pierced the matted woods,   110
In hope to find some virtuous herb of power
To cure his malady !"
                          The Vicar smiled,—
"Alas ! before to-morrow's sun goes down
His habitation will be here : for him
That open grave is destined."
                                "Died he then   115

90 done] *added* 1845
97 *so* 1827 : A Visitor—intent upon the task
          Of prying, low and high, for herbs and flowers MS., 1814–20
97/8 You cannot but have noticed him—he ranged
      Through two years' space these mountains, every flower
      Collecting as successively they blow
      On rock, in dells, or by the plashy springs   MS.
103 Often we crossed   C
108–9 *so* 1837 :   that he was crazed in brain
              By unrequited love ; and scaled the rocks, [clomb the crags
                  MS.] MS., 1814–32

Of pain and grief ?" the Solitary asked,
"Do not believe it; never could that be!"

"He loved," the Vicar answered, "deeply loved,
Loved fondly, truly, fervently; and dared
At length to tell his love, but sued in vain;   120
Rejected, yea repelled; and, if with scorn
Upon the haughty maiden's brow, 'tis but
A high-prized plume which female Beauty wears
In wantonness of conquest, or puts on
To cheat the world, or from herself to hide   125
Humiliation, when no longer free.
That he could brook, and glory in;—but when
The tidings came that she whom he had wooed
Was wedded to another, and his heart
Was forced to rend away its only hope;   130
Then, Pity could have scarcely found on earth
An object worthier of regard than he,
In the transition of that bitter hour!
Lost was she, lost; nor could the Sufferer say
That in the act of preference he had been   135
Unjustly dealt with; but the Maid was gone!
Had vanished from his prospects and desires;
Not by translation to the heavenly choir
Who have put off their mortal spoils—ah no!
She lives another's wishes to complete,—   140
'Joy be their lot, and happiness,' he cried,
'His lot and hers, as misery must be mine!'

"Such was that strong concussion; but the Man,
Who trembled, trunk and limbs, like some huge oak
By a fierce tempest shaken, soon resumed   145
The stedfast quiet natural to a mind
Of composition gentle and sedate,

117 *so* 1837: "Believe it not—Oh! never could that be!" MS., 1814–32
119 fervently] hopelessly MS.   119–20 *so* 1827: and pined When
he had told his love, and MS., 1814–20
124–6 *added* 1827
136/7 She, whose dear name with unregarded sighs
He long had blessed, whose Image was preserved—
Shrined in his breast with fond idolatry, MS., 1814–20
137/8 Happy her Husband was, and wretched He MS. *del.*
142 must be 1845: is MS., 1814–43: misery henceforth is mine C
146 stedfast] outward MS.

And, in its movements, circumspect and slow.
To books, and to the long-forsaken desk,
O'er which enchained by science he had loved   150
To bend, he stoutly re-addressed himself,
Resolved to quell his pain, and search for truth
With keener appetite (if that might be)
And closer industry. Of what ensued
Within the heart no outward sign appeared   155
Till a betraying sickliness was seen
To tinge his cheek; and through his frame it crept
With slow mutation unconcealable;
Such universal change as autumn makes
In the fair body of a leafy grove   160
Discoloured, then divested.   'Tis affirmed
By poets skilled in nature's secret ways
That Love will not submit to be controlled
By mastery:—and the good Man lacked not friends
Who strove to instil this truth into his mind,   165
A mind in all heart-mysteries unversed.
'Go to the hills,' said one, 'remit a while
This baneful diligence:—at early morn
Court the fresh air, explore the heaths and woods;
And, leaving it to others to foretell,   170

149–53 *so* 1827: Of rustic Parents bred, (born MS.) He had been trained, (So prompted their aspiring wish) to skill

In numbers and the sedentary art
Of penmanship,—with pride professed, and taught
By his endeavours in the mountain dales.
Now, those sad tidings weighing on his heart,
To books, and papers, and the studious desk,
He stoutly readdressed himself—resolved
To quell his pain, and enter on the path
Of old pursuits with keener appetite
And closer industry 1814–20

and the labours of the pen
Mute sedentary arts by which he earned,
Teaching the swains, his maintenance; and now

To books, and papers, and the studious desk,
He stoutly readdressed himself—resolved
To quell his pain, or if not quell, deceive,
By entering on the path of old pursuits
With keener appetite. MS.

155 the heart 1827: his soul MS., 1814–20   157 To o'erspread his cheek MS.   158 not to be concealed MS.   168 This most injurious diligence, at morn MS.

By calculations sage, the ebb and flow
Of tides, and when the moon will be eclipsed,
Do you, for your own benefit, construct
A calendar of flowers, plucked as they blow
Where health abides, and cheerfulness, and peace.'   175
The attempt was made;—'tis needless to report
How hopelessly; but innocence is strong,
And an entire simplicity of mind
A thing most sacred in the eye of Heaven;
That opens, for such sufferers, relief   180
Within the soul, fountains of grace divine;
And doth commend their weakness and disease
To Nature's care, assisted in her office
By all the elements that round her wait
To generate, to preserve, and to restore;   185
And by her beautiful array of forms
Shedding sweet influence from above; or pure
Delight exhaling from the ground they tread."

     "Impute it not to impatience, if," exclaimed
The Wanderer, "I infer that he was healed   190
By perseverance in the course prescribed."

     "You do not err: the powers, that had been lost
By slow degrees, were gradually regained;
The fluttering nerves composed; the beating heart
In rest established; and the jarring thoughts   195
To harmony restored.—But yon dark mould
Will cover him, in the fulness of his strength,
Hastily smitten by a fever's force;
Yet not with stroke so sudden as refused
Time to look back with tenderness on her   200
Whom he had loved in passion; and to send
Some farewell words—with one, but one, request;
That, from his dying hand, she would accept
Of his possessions that which most he prized;

181 the soul, fountains 1837: their souls, a fount MS., 1814–32
189–90 Ascribe . . . here exclaimed . . . if I guess MS.   192–3 powers
that . . . were] strength which . . . was MS.
195–6 Established in tranquillity, the heart
     Brought back to Reason's sway— MS.
197 so 1832: in height [pride MS.] of strength—to earth MS., 1814–27
202 so 1827: . . . words; and, with those words, a prayer, MS., 1814–20

A book, upon whose leaves some chosen plants,   205
By his own hand disposed with nicest care,
In undecaying beauty were preserved;
Mute register, to him, of time and place,
And various fluctuations in the breast;
To her, a monument of faithful love   210
Conquered, and in tranquillity retained!

"Close to his destined habitation, lies
One who achieved a humbler victory,
Though marvellous in its kind. A place there is
High in these mountains, that allured a band   215
Of keen adventurers to unite their pains
In search of precious ore: they tried, were foiled—
And all desisted, all, save him alone.
He, taking counsel of his own clear thoughts,
And trusting only to his own weak hands,   220
Urged unremittingly the stubborn work,
Unseconded, uncountenanced; then, as time
Passed on, while still his lonely efforts found
No recompense, derided; and at length,
By many pitied, as insane of mind;   225
By others dreaded as the luckless thrall
Of subterranean Spirits feeding hope
By various mockery of sight and sound;
Hope after hope, encouraged and destroyed.
—But when the lord of seasons had matured   230
The fruits of earth through space of twice ten years,
The mountain's entrails offered to his view
And trembling grasp the long-deferred reward.
Not with more transport did Columbus greet

205–6 *so* 1827: ... the surface of whose leaves Some chosen plants, 1814–20:
within whose leaves the forms of plants   MS., *omitting l.* 206   208
of tenderest thoughts   MS.
213–14 *so* 1827: One whose Endeavours did at length achieve
        A victory less worthy of regard,
        Though marvellous in its kind. A Place exists   1814–20
217 *so* 1827 (*but* who *for* they   1827–32):
    In search of treasure there by Nature formed,
    And there concealed: but they who tried were foiled   1814–20
232–3 *so* 1827:   ... the view
       Of the Old Man, and to his trembling grasp
       His bright, his long-deferred, his dear reward.   1814–20

A world, his rich discovery! But our Swain,   235
A very hero till his point was gained,
Proved all unable to support the weight
Of prosperous fortune. On the fields he looked
With an unsettled liberty of thought,
Wishes and endless schemes; by daylight walked   240
Giddy and restless; ever and anon
Quaffed in his gratitude immoderate cups;
And truly might be said to die of joy!
He vanished; but conspicuous to this day
The path remains that linked his cottage-door   245
To the mine's mouth; a long and slanting track,
Upon the rugged mountain's stony side,
Worn by his daily visits to and from
The darksome centre of a constant hope.
This vestige, neither force of beating rain,   250
Nor the vicissitudes of frost and thaw
Shall cause to fade, till ages pass away;
And it is named, in memory of the event,
The PATH OF PERSEVERANCE."
                                        "Thou from whom
Man has his strength," exclaimed the Wanderer, "oh! 255
Do thou direct it! To the virtuous grant
The penetrative eye which can perceive
In this blind world the guiding vein of hope;
That, like this Labourer, such may dig their way,
'Unshaken, unseduced, unterrified;'   260
Grant to the wise *his* firmness of resolve!"

   "That prayer were not superfluous," said the Priest,
"Amid the noblest relics, proudest dust,
That Westminster, for Britain's glory, holds
Within the bosom of her awful pile,   265
Ambitiously collected. Yet the sigh,
Which wafts that prayer to heaven, is due to all,
Wherever laid, who living fell below
Their virtue's humbler mark; a sigh of *pain*
If to the opposite extreme they sank.   270
How would you pity her who yonder rests;
Him, farther off; the pair, who here are laid;
But, above all, that mixture of earth's mould

240 *so* 1837: Of schemes and wishes; in the day-light walked   1814-32

Whom sight of this green hillock to my mind
Recals!

      He lived not till his locks were nipped   275
By seasonable frost of age; nor died
Before his temples, prematurely forced
To mix the manly brown with silver grey,
Gave obvious instance of the sad effect
Produced, when thoughtless Folly hath usurped   280
The natural crown that sage Experience wears.
Gay, volatile, ingenious, quick to learn,
And prompt to exhibit all that he possessed
Or could perform; a zealous actor, hired
Into the troop of mirth, a soldier, sworn   285
Into the lists of giddy enterprise—
Such was he; yet, as if within his frame
Two several souls alternately had lodged,
Two sets of manners could the Youth put on;
And, fraught with antics as the Indian bird   290
That writhes and chatters in her wiry cage,
Was graceful, when it pleased him, smooth and still
As the mute swan that floats adown the stream,
Or, on the waters of the unruffled lake,
Anchors her placid beauty. Not a leaf,   295
That flutters on the bough, lighter than he;
And not a flower, that droops in the green shade,
More winningly reserved! If ye enquire
How such consummate elegance was bred
Amid these wilds, this answer may suffice;   300
'Twas Nature's will; who sometimes undertakes,
For the reproof of human vanity,
Art to outstrip in her peculiar walk.
Hence, for this Favourite—lavishly endowed
With personal gifts, and bright instinctive wit,   305

275   . . . Near the Turf
    Which hides that strenuous Labourer's furrowed brow
    Lies one who lived not *etc.* MS.
296 lighter 1840: more light MS., 1814–37   299–300 How in these
wilds such elegance was bred Mid rustic swains MS.
300 *so* 1827: Amid these wilds; a Composition framed
                Of qualities so adverse—to diffuse,
                Where'er he moved, diversified delight;
                A simple answer may suffice, even this, MS., 1814–20

While both, embellishing each other, stood
Yet farther recommended by the charm
Of fine demeanour, and by dance and song,
And skill in letters—every fancy shaped
Fair expectations; nor, when to the world's   310
Capacious field forth went the Adventurer, there
Were he and his attainments overlooked,
Or scantily rewarded; but all hopes,
Cherished for him, he suffered to depart,
Like blighted buds; or clouds that mimicked land   315
Before the sailor's eye; or diamond drops
That sparkling decked the morning grass; or aught
That *was* attractive, and hath ceased to be!

  "Yet, when this Prodigal returned, the rites
Of joyful greeting were on him bestowed,   320
Who, by humiliation undeterred,
Sought for his weariness a place of rest
Within his Father's gates.—Whence came he?—clothed
In tattered garb, from hovels where abides
Necessity, the stationary host   325
Of vagrant poverty; from rifted barns
Where no one dwells but the wide-staring owl
And the owl's prey; from these bare haunts, to which
He had descended from the proud saloon,
He came, the ghost of beauty and of health,   330
The wreck of gaiety! But soon revived
In strength, in power refitted, he renewed
His suit to Fortune; and she smiled again
Upon a fickle Ingrate. Thrice he rose,
Thrice sank as willingly. For he—whose nerves   335
Were used to thrill with pleasure, while his voice
Softly accompanied the tuneful harp,
By the nice finger of fair ladies touched
In glittering halls—was able to derive
No less enjoyment from an abject choice.   340
Who happier for the moment—who more blithe
Than this fallen Spirit? in those dreary holds

309 shaped] framed MS.
328 *so* 1827: And the Owl's Prey; none permanently house
                But many harbour; from these Haunts, to which MS., 1814-
          20
334 fickle] faithless MS.   335-6 nerves Were] heart Was MS.

His talents lending to exalt the freaks
Of merry-making beggars,—now, provoked
To laughter multiplied in louder peals   345
By his malicious wit; then, all enchained
With mute astonishment, themselves to see
In their own arts outdone, their fame eclipsed,
As by the very presence of the Fiend
Who dictates and inspires illusive feats,   350
For knavish purposes! The city, too,
(With shame I speak it) to her guilty bowers
Allured him, sunk so low in self-respect
As there to linger, there to eat his bread,
Hired minstrel of voluptuous blandishment;   355
Charming the air with skill of hand or voice,
Listen who would, be wrought upon who might,
Sincerely wretched hearts, or falsely gay.
—Such the too frequent tenour of his boast
In ears that relished the report;—but all   360
Was from his Parents happily concealed;
Who saw enough for blame and pitying love.
They also were permitted to receive
His last, repentant breath; and closed his eyes,
No more to open on that irksome world   365
Where he had long existed in the state
Of a young fowl beneath one mother hatched,
Though from another sprung, different in kind:
Where he had lived, and could not cease to live,
Distracted in propensity; content   370
With neither element of good or ill;
And yet in both rejoicing; man unblest;
Of contradictions infinite the slave,
Till his deliverance, when Mercy made him
One with himself, and one with them that sleep."   375

" 'Tis strange," observed the Solitary, "strange
It seems, and scarcely less than pitiful,
That in a land where charity provides
For all that can no longer feed themselves,

359 *so* 1827: —Truths I record to many known, for each
         The not infrequent tenor MS., 1814–20
362 for pity and for love MS.   365 irksome] vexing MS.
368 *so* 1837: of different race MS.: of different kind 1814–32
375 *so* 1837: those who MS., 1814–20: them who 1827–32

A man like this should choose to bring his shame   380
To the parental door; and with his sighs
Infect the air which he had freely breathed
In happy infancy. He could not pine
Through lack of converse; no—he must have found
Abundant exercise for thought and speech,   385
In his dividual being, self-reviewed,
Self-catechised, self-punished.—Some there are
Who, drawing near their final home, and much
And daily longing that the same were reached,
Would rather shun than seek the fellowship   390
Of kindred mould.—Such haply here are laid?"

   "Yes," said the Priest, "the Genius of our hills—
Who seems, by these stupendous barriers cast
Round his domain, desirous not alone
To keep his own, but also to exclude   395
All other progeny—doth sometimes lure,
Even by his studied depth of privacy,
The unhappy alien hoping to obtain
Concealment, or seduced by wish to find,
In place from outward molestation free,   400
Helps to internal ease. Of many such
Could I discourse; but as their stay was brief,
So their departure only left behind
Fancies, and loose conjectures. Other trace
Survives, for worthy mention, of a pair   405
Who, from the pressure of their several fates,
Meeting as strangers, in a petty town

381 parental] paternal MS.   383/4 (Whence e'er rejected, howsoe'er
forlorn) MS., 1814–20   393 Who might appear by these stern bar-
riers cast MS.   397 *so* 1845: this very depth MS.: this studied
depth 1814–43   399 Needful concealment or a hope to find MS.
404–12 . . . conjectures. Yet this vale
   Retains no faint remembrance of a pair
   Who driven at separate times, by diverse fates (*corr. to text*)
   Here met as strangers, and remained as Friends
   Content; and finally did leave in sign
   Of friendship and of genial gratitude,
   For hospitable kindness left their bones
   In this green spot, unscutcheoned and remote, MS. *last 4 lines corr. to*
   True to their choice; and as a last effect
   And evidence of friendship and a sign
   Of a participated gratitude.
   For local recollections gave their bones *etc. as text*

Whose blue roofs ornament a distant reach
Of this far-winding vale, remained as friends
True to their choice; and gave their bones in trust   410
To this loved cemetery, here to lodge
With unescutcheoned privacy interred
Far from the family vault.—A Chieftain one
By right of birth; within whose spotless breast
The fire of ancient Caledonia burned: 415
He, with the foremost whose impatience hailed
The Stuart, landing to resume, by force
Of arms, the crown which bigotry had lost,
Aroused his clan; and, fighting at their head,
With his brave sword endeavoured to prevent   420
Culloden's fatal overthrow. Escaped
From that disastrous rout, to foreign shores
He fled; and when the lenient hand of time
Those troubles had appeased, he sought and gained,
For his obscured condition, an obscure   425
Retreat, within this nook of English ground.

."The other, born in Britain's southern tract,
Had fixed his milder loyalty, and placed
His gentler sentiments of love and hate,
There, where *they* placed them who in conscience prized 430
The new succession, as a line of kings
Whose oath had virtue to protect the land
Against the dire assaults of papacy
And arbitrary rule. But launch thy bark
On the distempered flood of public life,   435
And cause for most rare triumph will be thine
If, spite of keenest eye and steadiest hand,
The stream, that bears thee forward, prove not, soon
Or late, a perilous master. He—who oft,
Beneath the battlements and stately trees   440
That round his mansion cast a sober gloom,
Had moralised on this, and other truths
Of kindred import, pleased and satisfied—

431-2 . . . succession, as their best defence,
    The House of Brunswick as their country's shield   MS.
436-9 And to thy peril thou shalt surely find
    That spite of watchful eye and stediest hand
    The flood will be its master   MS.
440 Beneath   1837: Under   MS., 1814-32

Was forced to vent his wisdom with a sigh
Heaved from the heart in fortune's bitterness,   445
When he had crushed a plentiful estate
By ruinous contest, to obtain a seat
In Britain's senate. Fruitless was the attempt:
And while the uproar of that desperate strife
Continued yet to vibrate on his ear,   450
The vanquished Whig, under a borrowed name,
(For the mere sound and echo of his own
Haunted him with sensations of disgust

443 pleased] soothed   MS.
446–64 When he had served his Country—to the loss
Of a most plentiful and fair Estate
His old Inheritance! Imagine not
That I deride the Patriot's worthy aim (strife of civic zeal)
With (And) needful efforts in a generous cause,
Virtue forbid, sweet Liberty reject
A sneer so senseless with thy prouder scorn,
I but repeat the censure which, 'tis said,
The mild good man would pass upon himself
Most freely when recovered from his heat
Of blood and giddiness of brain, he heard
Far more distinctly than his living ear
Had ever heard the intelligible sounds
Of his devoted followers.   MS. *draft* i *deleted*
When he had served . . . Estate *as above*
An honoured birthright fruitlessly dispersed
        (An honoured birthright in his own despite
        Consumed by an insatiable crowd
        Of Partizans, good wishes bawling forth
        For all the precious rights of Church and State
        And these their staunch defenders. But at length
        The Contest closed and then he might have seen   *draft* iii)
For when the contest closed, he might have seen
His Tory Rival, bowing thanks, and smiles
Of triumph shedding from the uplifted Chair
Throne dearly bought, by mutual ruin gained.
Forthwith the din of that protracted (uproar of that desperate)
        strife
Not ceasing yet to hang upon his ear,
Vex'd, beggar'd and discomfited, the Whig
Slunk to the shade, beneath a borrowed name,
The very sound and echo of his own
So much disgusted him. And here they met
Like adverse Planets—flaming Jacobite
And sullen Hanoverian. I have heard
My grey-haired Sire relate that mid the peace   MS. *draft* ii
451 under   1837: beneath   1814–32

That he was glad to lose) slunk from the world
To the deep shade of those untravelled Wilds; 455
In which the Scottish Laird had long possessed
An undisturbed abode. Here, then, they met,
Two doughty champions; flaming Jacobite
And sullen Hanoverian! You might think
That losses and vexations, less severe 460
Than those which they had severally sustained,
Would have inclined each to abate his zeal
For his ungrateful cause; no,—I have heard
My reverend Father tell that, 'mid the calm
Of that small town encountering thus, they filled, 465
Daily, its bowling-green with harmless strife;
Plagued with uncharitable thoughts the church;
And vexed the market-place. But in the breasts
Of these opponents gradually was wrought,
With little change of general sentiment, 470
Such leaning towards each other, that their days
By choice were spent in constant fellowship;
And if, at times, they fretted with the yoke,
Those very bickerings made them love it more.

"A favourite boundary to their lengthened walks 475
This Churchyard was. And, whether they had come
Treading their path in sympathy and linked
In social converse, or by some short space
Discreetly parted to preserve the peace,
One spirit seldom failed to extend its sway 480
Over both minds, when they awhile had marked
The visible quiet of this holy ground,

455 those   1837: these   1814–32
467–8 And church and market suffered from the feud
      By them excited. But within the breasts   MS.
471 leaning   1845: change   1814–43
471–4 Such change towards each other that they bare
      The yoke of fellowship from morn to night,
      Companions, friends inseparably dear
      Their very bickering knotting them more close.   MS.
477–8 . . . in cordial intercourse
      And sympathizing converse, or at worst   MS.
481–3   . . . breathed,
      Together seated in this holy place,
      Its tranquillizing air   MS.

And breathed its soothing air;—the spirit of hope
And saintly magnanimity; that—spurning
The field of selfish difference and dispute,   485
And every care which transitory things,
Earth and the kingdoms of the earth, create—
Doth, by a rapture of forgetfulness,
Preclude forgiveness, from the praise debarred,
Which else the Christian virtue might have claimed.   490

    "There live who yet remember here to have seen
Their courtly figures, seated on the stump
Of an old yew, their favourite resting-place.
But as the remnant of the long-lived tree
Was disappearing by a swift decay,   495
They, with joint care, determined to erect,
Upon its site, a dial, that might stand
For public use preserved, and thus survive
As their own private monument: for this
Was the particular spot, in which they wished   500
(And Heaven was pleased to accomplish the desire)
That, undivided, their remains should lie.
So, where the mouldered tree had stood, was raised
Yon structure, framing, with the ascent of steps
That to the decorated pillar lead,   505
A work of art more sumptuous than might seem
To suit this place; yet built in no proud scorn
Of rustic homeliness; they only aimed
To ensure for it respectful guardianship.
Around the margin of the plate, whereon   510
The shadow falls to note the stealthy hours,
Winds an inscriptive legend."—At these words
Thither we turned; and gathered, as we read,
The appropriate sense, in Latin numbers couched:
"Time flies; it is his melancholy task   515

497–8 *so* 1827:   . . . which should stand
              For public use; and also might survive   1814–20
                        . . . a little work of art
              For public use, which also might survive   MS.
504 structure] Dial   MS.
506–7 *so* 1827:   . . . as might seem,
              Than suits this Place   MS., 1814–20
506–8 A sumptuous Structure built in no proud scorn
        Of homely rustic taste, but thus they hope   MS.

To bring, and bear away, delusive hopes,
And re-produce the troubles he destroys.
But, while his blindness thus is occupied,
Discerning Mortal! do thou serve the will
Of Time's eternal Master, and that peace,   520
Which the world wants, shall be for thee confirmed!"

"Smooth verse, inspired by no unlettered Muse,"
Exclaimed the Sceptic, "and the strain of thought
Accords with nature's language;—the soft voice
Of yon white torrent falling down the rocks   525
Speaks, less distinctly, to the same effect.
If, then, their blended influence be not lost
Upon our hearts, not wholly lost, I grant,
Even upon mine, the more are we required
To feel for those among our fellow-men,   530
Who, offering no obeisance to the world,
Are yet made desperate by 'too quick a sense
Of constant infelicity,' cut off
From peace like exiles on some barren rock,
Their life's appointed prison; not more free   535
Than sentinels, between two armies, set,
With nothing better, in the chill night air,
Than their own thoughts to comfort them. Say why
That ancient story of Prometheus chained
To the bare rock, on frozen Caucasus;   540
The vulture, the inexhaustible repast
Drawn from his vitals? Say what meant the woes
By Tantalus entailed upon his race,
And the dark sorrows of the line of Thebes?
Fictions in form, but in their substance truths,   545
Tremendous truths! familiar to the men
Of long-past times, nor obsolete in ours.
Exchange the shepherd's frock of native grey
For robes with regal purple tinged; convert
The crook into a sceptre; give the pomp   550
Of circumstance; and here the tragic Muse
Shall find apt subjects for her highest art.
Amid the groves, under the shadowy hills,
The generations are prepared; the pangs,
The internal pangs, are ready; the dread strife   555

540 *added* 1845   553 under   1837: beneath   1814–32

Of poor humanity's afflicted will
Struggling in vain with ruthless destiny."

"Though," said the Priest in answer, "these be terms
Which a divine philosophy rejects,
We, whose established and unfailing trust   560
Is in controlling Providence, admit
That, through all stations, human life abounds
With mysteries;—for, if Faith were left untried,
How could the might, that lurks within her, then
Be shown? her glorious excellence—that ranks   565
Among the first of Powers and Virtues—proved?
Our system is not fashioned to preclude
That sympathy which you for others ask;
And I could tell, not travelling for my theme
Beyond these humble graves, of grievous crimes   570
And strange disasters; but I pass them by,
Loth to disturb what Heaven hath hushed in peace.
—Still less, far less, am I inclined to treat
Of Man degraded in his Maker's sight
By the deformities of brutish vice: 575
For, in such portraits, though a vulgar face
And a coarse outside of repulsive life
And unaffecting manners might at once
Be recognised by all—" "Ah! do not think,"
The Wanderer somewhat eagerly exclaimed,   580
"Wish could be ours that you, for such poor gain,
(Gain shall I call it?—gain of what?—for whom?)
Should breathe a word tending to violate
Your own pure spirit. Not a step we look for
In slight of that forbearance and reserve   585
Which common human-heartedness inspires,
And mortal ignorance and frailty claim,
Upon this sacred ground, if nowhere else."

570-1 *so* 1827: Beyond the limits of these humble graves, Of *etc.* 1814-20
573-6 Whom shall we turn to next? Ye asked for truth
       And unadulterate truth shall ye receive.
       But vice, depravity and low desires
       These will creep in wherever man is found
       And out of such material might be framed
       Harsh Portraiture, in which a vulgar face   MS.
576 *so* 1827: For, though from these materials *etc. as* MS., 1814-20

    "True," said the Solitary, "be it far
From us to infringe the laws of charity.   590
Let judgment here in mercy be pronounced;
This, self-respecting Nature prompts, and this
Wisdom enjoins; but if the thing we seek
Be genuine knowledge, bear we then in mind
How, from his lofty throne, the sun can fling   595
Colours as bright on exhalations bred
By weedy pool or pestilential swamp,
As by the rivulet sparkling where it runs,
Or the pellucid lake."
                 "Small risk," said I,
"Of such illusion do we here incur;   600
Temptation here is none to exceed the truth;
No evidence appears that they who rest
Within this ground, were covetous of praise,
Or of remembrance even, deserved or not.
Green is the Churchyard, beautiful and green,   605
Ridge rising gently by the side of ridge,
A heaving surface, almost wholly free
From interruption of sepulchral stones,
And mantled o'er with aboriginal turf
And everlasting flowers. These Dalesmen trust   610
The lingering gleam of their departed lives
To oral record, and the silent heart;
Depositories faithful and more kind
Than fondest epitaph: for, if those fail,
What boots the sculptured tomb? And who can blame, 615
Who rather would not envy, men that feel
This mutual confidence; if, from such source,
The practice flow,—if thence, or from a deep
And general humility in death?

---

589 Solitary] pensive sceptic   MS.
594–8 Be what the understanding shall respect
     As truth and knowledge, bear we then in mind
     How from his lofty seat the sun can paint
     Colours as bright on exhalations risen
     From pestilential bog or noisome swamp
     As from *etc. as text*   MS.
607 A heaving] An undulating *corr. to* A billowy   MS.   611–13 record
. . . Depositories . . . if those fail   1837: records . . . Depository . . . if it
fail   MS., 1814–20: *so* 1827–32 *but* if that fail   615 tomb] stone   MS.

Nor should I much condemn it, if it spring   620
From disregard of time's destructive power,
As only capable to prey on things
Of earth, and human nature's mortal part.

    "Yet—in less simple districts, where we see
Stone lift its forehead emulous of stone   625
In courting notice; and the ground all paved
With commendations of departed worth;
Reading, where'er we turn, of innocent lives,
Of each domestic charity fulfilled,
And sufferings meekly borne—I, for my part,   630
Though with the silence pleased that here prevails,
Among those fair recitals also range,
Soothed by the natural spirit which they breathe.
And, in the centre of a world whose soil
Is rank with all unkindness, compassed round   635
With such memorials, I have sometimes felt,
It was no momentary happiness
To have *one* Enclosure where the voice that speaks
In envy or detraction is not heard;
Which malice may not enter; where the traces   640
Of evil inclinations are unknown;
Where love and pity tenderly unite
With resignation; and no jarring tone
Intrudes, the peaceful concert to disturb
Of amity and gratitude."
                                "Thus sanctioned,"   645
The Pastor said, "I willingly confine
My narratives to subjects that excite
Feelings with these accordant; love, esteem,
And admiration; lifting up a veil,
A sunbeam introducing among hearts   650
Retired and covert; so that ye shall have
Clear images before your gladdened eyes
Of nature's unambitious underwood,

621 destructive] consuming MS.   623 mortal] earthly MS.
625–9 Upon the front of each memorial stone
      Conspicuous attestation, in a stream
      Unvaried, of integrity and worth;
      Religious duties zealously performed,
      And each *etc*. MS.

And flowers that prosper in the shade. And when
I speak of such among my flock as swerved   655
Or fell, those only shall be singled out
Upon whose lapse, or error, something more
Than brotherly forgiveness may attend;
To such will we restrict our notice, else
Better my tongue were mute.
                     And yet there are,   660
I feel, good reasons why we should not leave
Wholly untraced a more forbidding way.
For, strength to persevere and to support,
And energy to conquer and repel—
These elements of virtue, that declare   665
The native grandeur of the human soul—
Are oft-times not unprofitably shown
In the perverseness of a selfish course:
Truth every day exemplified, no less
In the grey cottage by the murmuring stream   670
Than in fantastic conqueror's roving camp,
Or 'mid the factious senate unappalled
Whoe'er may sink, or rise—to sink again,
As merciless proscription ebbs and flows.

  "There," said the Vicar, pointing as he spake,   675
"A woman rests in peace; surpassed by few
In power of mind, and eloquent discourse.
Tall was her stature; her complexion dark
And saturnine; her head not raised to hold
Converse with heaven, nor yet deprest towards earth, 680
But in projection carried, as she walked

656 will I single out MS., 1814–32
661/2 For passionate regards of love and hate,
    Magnanimous disdain and courage high MS.
663 For] And MS.   671 in 1827: the 1814–20   672 'mid
1827: in 1814–20   673 added 1845   674 As 1845: While
MS., 1843
674/5 Shifting its course as no one can forsee
    And Power almighty only may controul C
675 Vicar, pointing] Priest, and pointed MS.
676 . . . distinguished above all
    Of her estate whom I have chanced to know MS.
679 so 1827: And saturnine; her port erect, her head
    Not absolutely raised, as if to hold MS., 1814–20
681 Save only that the head, the Citadel
    And watchtower of the meditative mind
    Stooped and projected firmly as she walked MS.

For ever musing. Sunken were her eyes;
Wrinkled and furrowed with habitual thought
Was her broad forehead; like the brow of one
Whose visual nerve shrinks from a painful glare   685
Of overpowering light.—While yet a child,
She, 'mid the humble flowerets of the vale,
Towered like the imperial thistle, not unfurnished
With its appropriate grace, yet rather seeking
To be admired, than coveted and loved.   690
Even at that age she ruled, a sovereign queen,
Over her comrades; else their simple sports,
Wanting all relish for her strenuous mind,
Had crossed her only to be shunned with scorn.
—Oh! pang of sorrowful regret for those   695
Whom, in their youth, sweet study has enthralled,
That they have lived for harsher servitude,
Whether in soul, in body, or estate!
Such doom was hers; yet nothing could subdue
Her keen desire of knowledge, nor efface   700
Those brighter images by books imprest
Upon her memory, faithfully as stars
That occupy their places, and, though oft
Hidden by clouds, and oft bedimmed by haze,
Are not to be extinguished, nor impaired.   705

"Two passions, both degenerate, for they both
Began in honour, gradually obtained
Rule over her, and vexed her daily life;

683–4 Her ample forehead by habitual thought
      Furrowed and wrinkled   MS.
689 seeking   1827: framed   MS., 1814–20   691 ruled, a   1832:
ruled as   MS., 1814–27   692 so 1832: Among her Playmates etc.
1814–20: 'Mid her companions   1827: Among her comrades yet was she
herself   MS.
693–4 so 1827: Had wanted power to occupy a mind
                Held in subjection by a strong controul
                Of studious application, self-imposed.
                Books were her creditors; to them she paid,
                With pleasing, anxious eagerness, the hours
                Which they exacted; were it time allowed,
                Or seized upon by stealth, or fairly won,
                By stretch of industry, from other tasks.   1814–20, so
MS., but without first line, and In turn subjected for Held in subjection
695 those   1827: them   MS., 1814–20   700 nor   1827: or   MS.,
1814–20   705 nor   1832: or   MS., 1814–27

An unremitting, avaricious thrift;
And a strange thraldom of maternal love,   710
That held her spirit, in its own despite,
Bound—by vexation, and regret, and scorn,
Constrained forgiveness, and relenting vows,
And tears, in pride suppressed, in shame concealed—
To a poor dissolute Son, her only child.   715
—Her wedded days had opened with mishap,
Whence dire dependence. What could she perform
To shake the burthen off? Ah! there was felt,
Indignantly, the weakness of her sex.
She mused, resolved, adhered to her resolve;   720
The hand grew slack in alms-giving, the heart
Closed by degrees to charity; heaven's blessing
Not seeking from that source, she placed her trust
In ceaseless pains—and strictest parsimony
Which sternly hoarded all that could be spared,   725
From each day's need, out of each day's least gain.

   "Thus all was re-established, and a pile
Constructed, that sufficed for every end,
Save the contentment of the builder's mind;
A mind by nature indisposed to aught   730
So placid, so inactive, as content;
A mind intolerant of lasting peace,
And cherishing the pang her heart deplored.
Dread life of conflict! which I oft compared
To the agitation of a brook that runs   735
Down a rocky mountain, buried now and lost

709 unremitting 1837: unrelenting MS., 1814–32   710 bondage *corr.*
to passion *corr. to* thraldom   MS.
712–13 Bound by forgiveness and by tender thought,
        Mortification and regret and scorn,   MS.
720–3 *so* 1827: The injustice of her low estate.—She mused;
                Resolved, adhered to her resolve; her heart
                Closed by degrees to charity; and, thence
                Expecting not Heaven's blessing, placed her trust   MS.,
1814–20, *but* MS. God's *for* Heaven's
724–6 *so* 1837: . . . parsimonious care
                Which got, and sternly hoarded each day's gain.   MS.,
                1814–32
733 her heart 1837: that it   MS.: which it   1814–32   734 Dread]
A   MS.   736 *so* 1837: . . . rocky mountains   MS., 1814–32

In silent pools, now in strong eddies chained;
But never to be charmed to gentleness:
Its best attainment fits of such repose
As timid eyes might shrink from fathoming.   740

  "A sudden illness seized her in the strength
Of life's autumnal season.—Shall I tell
How on her bed of death the Matron lay,
To Providence submissive, so she thought;
But fretted, vexed, and wrought upon, almost   745
To anger, by the malady that griped
Her prostrate frame with unrelaxing power,
As the fierce eagle fastens on the lamb?
She prayed, she moaned;—her husband's sister watched
Her dreary pillow, waited on her needs;   750
And yet the very sound of that kind foot
Was anguish to her ears! 'And must she rule,'
This was the death-doomed Woman heard to say
In bitterness, 'and must she rule and reign,
Sole Mistress of this house, when I am gone?   755
Tend what I tended, calling it her own!'
Enough;—I fear, too much.—One vernal evening,
While she was yet in prime of health and strength,
I well remember, while I passed her door
Alone, with loitering step, and upward eye   760
Turned towards the planet Jupiter that hung
Above the centre of the Vale, a voice
Roused me, her voice; it said, 'That glorious star
In its untroubled element will shine
As now it shines, when we are laid in earth   765
And safe from all our sorrows.' With a sigh

737 *so* 1832: . . . unfathomably deep   MS., 1814–20: and now in eddies
chained   1827
738–40 *so* 1827: Now, in a moment, starting forth again
                    With violence, and proud of its escape;—
                    Until it sink once more, by slow degrees,
                    Or instantly, into as dark [deep MS.] repose. MS., 1814–20
753 death-doomed   1845: dying   MS., 1814–43: suffering   C   755/6
Sit by my fire—possess what I possessed—   MS., 1814–43   °   757 *so*
1827: . . . much. Of nobler feeling Take this example—One autumnal
evening   MS., 1814–20   760 Alone   1845: Musing   MS., 1814–43
761 Fixed on   MS.   766–74 *so* 1845: And safe from all our sorrows."
She is safe   MS., 1814–43
766–8   with that sigh
        Mingled I question not sustaining faith

She spake, yet, I believe, not unsustained
By faith in glory that shall far transcend
Aught by these perishable heavens disclosed
To sight or mind. Nor less than care divine   770
Is divine mercy. She, who had rebelled,
Was into meekness softened and subdued;
Did, after trials not in vain prolonged,
With resignation sink into the grave;
And her uncharitable acts, I trust,   775
And harsh unkindnesses are all forgiven,
Tho', in this Vale, remembered with deep awe."

———————

The Vicar paused; and toward a seat advanced,
A long stone-seat, fixed in the Churchyard wall;
Part shaded by cool sycamore, and part   780
Offering a sunny resting-place to them
Who seek the House of worship, while the bells
Yet ring with all their voices, or before
The last hath ceased its solitary knoll.
Beneath the shade we all sate down; and there   785
His office, uninvited, he resumed.

"As on a sunny bank, a tender lamb
Lurks in safe shelter from the winds of March,
Screened by its parent, so that little mound
Lies guarded by its neighbour; the small heap   790
Speaks for itself; an Infant there doth rest;

In revelation, for the immortal Soul
Guides unto glory that shall far transcend *etc.* C
770 care] love C
778–81 *so* 1827: The Vicar paused; and tow'rds a seat advanced,
                 A long stone-seat, framed in the Church-yard wall;
                 Part under shady sycamore, and part
                 Offering a place of rest in pleasant sunshine,
                 Even as may suit the comers old or young MS., 1814–20
                     (*but* MS. ceased *for* paused)
782 seek] reach MS.
785 Beneath 1837: Under 1827–32:
                 To this commodious resting-place he led;
                 Where, by his side, we all *etc.* MS., 1814–20
787 As on a greenhill slope MS.
789–90 Screen'd by its nursing parent, in such sort,
                 Even so, methinks, that little hillock lies
                 Protected by *etc.* MS.

The sheltering hillock is the Mother's grave.
If mild discourse, and manners that conferred
A natural dignity on humblest rank;
If gladsome spirits, and benignant looks,   795
That for a face not beautiful did more
Than beauty for the fairest face can do;
And if religious tenderness of heart,
Grieving for sin, and penitential tears
Shed when the clouds had gathered and distained   800
The spotless ether of a maiden life;
If these may make a hallowed spot of earth
More holy in the sight of God or Man;
Then, o'er that mould, a sanctity shall brood
Till the stars sicken at the day of doom.   805

          "Ah! what a warning for a thoughtless man,
Could field or grove, could any spot of earth,
Show to his eye an image of the pangs
Which it hath witnessed; render back an echo
Of the sad steps by which it hath been trod!   810
There, by her innocent Baby's precious grave,
And on the very turf that roofs her own,
The Mother oft was seen to stand, or kneel
In the broad day, a weeping Magdalene.
Now she is not; the swelling turf reports   815
Of the fresh shower, but of poor Ellen's tears
Is silent; nor is any vestige left
Of the path worn by mournful tread of her
Who, at her heart's light bidding, once had moved

792–4 The Mother at its side in fearless peace;
        If natural manners, and discourse that gave
        A genuine dignity to lowest rank   MS.
804 O'er that mould   1827: on that mold   1814–20:
        Then on this humble grave, upon that pair
        Of humble graves *etc*.   MS.
807 Where'er he might be found, could earth present,
        Could any pleasant field or grove of earth   MS.: Could field or grove
              or   1814–27
812. *so* 1845: Yea, doubtless, on the turf   MS., 1814–43   816 Ellen's]
Emma's   MS., *and so throughout the story*
818–19 *so* 1827: Upon the pathway, of her mournful tread;
                    Nor of that pace with which she once had moved   MS.,
              1814–20

In virgin fearlessness, with step that seemed   820
Caught from the pressure of elastic turf
Upon the mountains gemmed with morning dew,
In the prime hour of sweetest scents and airs.
—Serious and thoughtful was her mind ; and yet,
By reconcilement exquisite and rare,   825
The form, port, motions, of this Cottage-girl
Were such as might have quickened and inspired
A Titian's hand, addrest to picture forth
Oread or Dryad glancing through the shade
What time the hunter's earliest horn is heard   830
Startling the golden hills.
                  A wide-spread elm
Stands in our valley, named THE JOYFUL TREE ;
From dateless usage which our peasants hold
Of giving welcome to the first of May
By dances round its trunk.—And if the sky   835
Permit, like honours, dance and song, are paid
To the Twelfth Night, beneath the frosty stars
Or the clear moon. The queen of these gay sports,
If not in beauty yet in sprightly air,
Was hapless Ellen.—No one touched the ground   840
So deftly, and the nicest maiden's locks
Less gracefully were braided ;—but this praise,

820 with   1827 : a   MS., 1814–20   822 gemmed   1827 : wet   MS.,
1814–20
830–1 *so* 1827 : When first the Hunter's startling horn is heard
                    Upon the golden hills. A spreading Elm [Oak MS.]   MS.,
                    1814–20
832/3 An Elm [Oak MS.] distinguished by that festive name, MS., 1814–20
833 From ancient   MS.
833–8 Time out of mind distinguished by that name
      For from each nook of that sequester'd glen
      Maiden and Youth, by annual custom, meet
      At sunrise, and give welcome to the May
      By dances round its trunk: and if the sky
      Permit, like honours, dance and song are paid
      To the Twelfth Night, beneath its gloomy depths
      Of leafless boughs, twinkling with frosty stars,
      Or on the shadow-chequered floor of moss
      The revelry proceeds, what time the Tree
      Is silver'd o'er with acceptable light
      From the clear Moon. MS. *draft* i
840 hapless Ellen] Emma Dalton   MS.

Methinks, would better suit another place.

"She loved, and fondly deemed herself beloved.
—The road is dim, the current unperceived,   845
The weakness painful and most pitiful,
By which a virtuous woman, in pure youth,
May be delivered to distress and shame.
Such fate was hers.—The last time Ellen danced,
Among her equals, round THE JOYFUL TREE,   850
She bore a secret burthen; and full soon
Was left to tremble for a breaking vow,—
Then, to bewail a sternly-broken vow,
Alone, within her widowed Mother's house.
It was the season of unfolding leaves,   855
Of days advancing toward their utmost length,
And small birds singing happily to mates
Happy as they. With spirit-saddening power
Winds pipe through fading woods; but those blithe notes
Strike the deserted to the heart; I speak   860
Of what I know, and what we feel within.
—Beside the cottage in which Ellen dwelt
Stands a tall ash-tree; to whose topmost twig
A thrush resorts, and annually chants,
At morn and evening from that naked perch,   865
While all the undergrove is thick with leaves,
A time-beguiling ditty, for delight
Of his fond partner, silent in the nest.
—'Ah why,' said Ellen, sighing to herself,
'Why do not words, and kiss, and solemn pledge,   870
And nature that is kind in woman's breast,
And reason that in man is wise and good,
And fear of him who is a righteous judge;
Why do not these prevail for human life,
To keep two hearts together, that began   875
Their spring-time with one love, and that have need

855–9 *so* 1837: It was the season sweet, of budding leaves,
          Of days advancing tow'rds [tow'rd   1832] their utmost
               length,
          And small birds singing to their happy mates.
          Wild is the music of the autumnal wind
          Among the faded woods; but these blithe notes   MS.,
               1814–32
864 chants] sings   MS.   871 that is] ever   MS.

Of mutual pity and forgiveness, sweet
To grant, or be received; while that poor bird—
O come and hear him! Thou who hast to me
Been faithless, hear him, though a lowly creature,   880
One of God's simple children that yet know not
The universal Parent, how he sings
As if he wished the firmament of heaven
Should listen, and give back to him the voice
Of his triumphant constancy and love;   885
The proclamation that he makes, how far
His darkness doth transcend our fickle light!'

"Such was the tender passage, not by me
Repeated without loss of simple phrase,
Which I perused, even as the words had been   890
Committed by forsaken Ellen's hand
To the blank margin of a Valentine,
Bedropped with tears. 'Twill please you to be told
That, studiously withdrawing from the eye
Of all companionship, the Sufferer yet   895
In lonely reading found a meek resource:
How thankful for the warmth of summer days,
When she could slip into the cottage-barn,
And find a secret oratory there;
Or, in the garden, under friendly veil   900
Of their long twilight, pore upon her book
By the last lingering help of the open sky
Until dark night dismissed her to her bed!
Thus did a waking fancy sometimes lose
The unconquerable pang of despised love.   905

"A kindlier passion opened on her soul
When that poor Child was born. Upon its face
She gazed as on a pure and spotless gift
Of unexpected promise, where a grief

878 or to receive   MS.   897 And she was thankful for the summer
days   MS.
898–901 *so* 1827: And their long twilight!—friendly to that stealth
                    With which she slipped into the Cottage-barn,
                    And found a secret oratory there;
                    Or, in the garden, pored upon her book   MS., 1814–20
900 garden] Orchard   MS.   902 the open   1845: open   MS., 1814–43
903 Until   1845: Till the   MS., 1814–43   908 gazed   1845: looked
MS., 1814–43

Or dread was all that had been thought of,—joy   910
Far livelier than bewildered traveller feels,
Amid a perilous waste that all night long
Hath harassed him toiling through fearful storm,
When he beholds the first pale speck serene
Of day-spring, in the gloomy east, revealed,   915
And greets it with thanksgiving. 'Till this hour,'
Thus, in her Mother's hearing Ellen spake,
'There was a stony region in my heart;
But He, at whose command the parchèd rock
Was smitten, and poured forth a quenching stream,   920
Hath softened that obduracy, and made
Unlooked-for gladness in the desert place,
To save the perishing; and, henceforth, I breathe
The air with cheerful spirit, for thy sake,
My Infant! and for that good Mother dear,   925
Who bore me; and hath prayed for me in vain;—
Yet not in vain; it shall not be in vain.'
She spake, nor was the assurance unfulfilled;
And if heart-rending thoughts would oft return,
They stayed not long.—The blameless Infant grew;   930
The Child whom Ellen and her Mother loved
They soon were proud of; tended it and nursed;
A soothing comforter, although forlorn;
Like a poor singing-bird from distant lands;
Or a choice shrub, which he, who passes by   935
With vacant mind, not seldom may observe
Fair-flowering in a thinly-peopled house,
Whose window, somewhat sadly, it adorns.

"Through four months' space the Infant drew its food
From the maternal breast; then scruples rose;   940
Thoughts, which the rich are free from, came and crossed
The fond affection. She no more could bear
By her offence to lay a twofold weight

911–13 livelier . . . that . . . Hath etc. 1827: sweeter . . . where . . .
Through darkness he hath toiled and etc. MS., 1814–20   919 parchèd]
barren MS.   923–4 so 1845 . . . look Upon the light with (in   MS.)
cheerfulness, for thee. MS., 1814–43   925 Infant] Baby MS.
928–30 Then followed other workings; self-reproach
        Grief for a human being born to shame,
        And fatherless and friendless in the world.
        What need of more ? The etc. MS.
936 With mind at ease MS.   942 fond 1837: sweet MS., 1814–32

On a kind parent willing to forget
Their slender means: so, to that parent's care   945
Trusting her child, she left their common home,
And undertook with dutiful content
A Foster-mother's office.
                            'Tis, perchance,
Unknown to you that in these simple vales
The natural feeling of equality   950
Is by domestic service unimpaired;
Yet, though such service be, with us, removed
From sense of degradation, not the less
The ungentle mind can easily find means
To impose severe restraints and laws unjust,   955
Which hapless Ellen now was doomed to feel:
For (blinded by an over-anxious dread
Of such excitement and divided thought
As with her office would but ill accord)
The pair, whose infant she was bound to nurse,   960

945–51   How slender are their means. With this regard
            She shrank not from a painful sacrifice,
            And trusting to her Mother's care the Child,
            For that occasion weaned from her own breast,
            She left her home and chearfully became
            A Foster-parent in a neighbouring farm.
            Perchance ye may not know, for 'tis, I think,
            Peculiar to these simple vales, that here
            Domestic service takes not from the mind
            The natural feeling of equality.
            No haughtiness the Master thence derives,
            The servant no abasement. Youth and Man
            Go forth, constrained or of free choice, and take
            The hire of strangers or of nearest kin
            Within their native or some neighbouring glen
            Even as may chance. Meanwhile they see and learn,
            Their eyes are quickened and their minds prepared
            For future duties—process not unlike
            To that of old (if the rude commonwealth
            And its inglorious arts may be compared
            To the proud world) when Youths of gentle blood,
            Many of the noblest stock, were duly sent
            To undertake the office of a Page
            In house of Prelate or exalted Peer,
            There to be disciplined in goodly *thewes*.   MS.
947 *so* 1845: And with contented spirit undertook   1814–43
957–9 *so* 1827: In selfish blindness, for I will not say
                    In naked and deliberate cruelty,   MS., 1814–20

Forbad her all communion with her own:
Week after week, the mandate they enforced.
—So near! yet not allowed upon that sight
To fix her eyes—alas! 'twas hard to bear!
But worse affliction must be borne—far worse;   965
For 'tis Heaven's will—that, after a disease
Begun and ended within three days' space,
Her child should die; as Ellen now exclaimed,
Her own—deserted child!—Once, only once,
She saw it in that mortal malady;   970
And, on the burial-day, could scarcely gain
Permission to attend its obsequies.
She reached the house, last of the funeral train;
And some one, as she entered, having chanced
To urge unthinkingly their prompt departure,   975
'Nay,' said she, with commanding look, a spirit
Of anger never seen in her before,
'Nay, ye must wait my time!' and down she sate,
And by the unclosed coffin kept her seat
Weeping and looking, looking on and weeping,   980
Upon the last sweet slumber of her Child,
Until at length her soul was satisfied.

"You see the Infant's Grave; and to this spot,
The Mother, oft as she was sent abroad,
On whatsoever errand, urged her steps: 985
Hither she came; here stood, and sometimes knelt
In the broad day, a rueful Magdalene!
So call her; for not only she bewailed
A mother's loss, but mourned in bitterness
Her own transgression; penitent sincere   990
As ever raised to heaven a streaming eye!
—At length the parents of the foster-child,
Noting that in despite of their commands
She still renewed and could not but renew
Those visitations, ceased to send her forth;   995
Or, to the garden's narrow bounds, confined.

961/2 They argued that such meeting would disturb
     The Mother's mind, distract her thoughts, and thus
     Unfit her for her duty [office MS.]—in which dread, MS., 1814–20
962 they 1827: was MS., 1814–20   985 On whatsoever 1837:
And whatsoe'er the MS., 1814–32   986 so 1832: and here she stood,
or knelt MS., 1814–27
995/6 And she remained a prisoner: to the house MS.

I failed not to remind them that they erred;
For holy Nature might not thus be crossed,
Thus wronged in woman's breast: in vain I pleaded—
But the green stalk of Ellen's life was snapped, 1000
And the flower drooped; as every eye could see,
It hung its head in mortal languishment.
—Aided by this appearance, I at length
Prevailed; and, from those bonds released, she went
Home to her mother's house.

              The Youth was fled; 1005
The rash betrayer could not face the shame
Or sorrow which his senseless guilt had caused;
And little would his presence, or proof given
Of a relenting soul, have now availed;
For, like a shadow, he was passed away 1010
From Ellen's thoughts; had perished to her mind
For all concerns of fear, or hope, or love,
Save only those which to their common shame,
And to his moral being appertained:
Hope from that quarter would, I know, have brought 1015
A heavenly comfort; there she recognised
An unrelaxing bond, a mutual need;
There, and, as seemed, there only.

                 She had built,
Her fond maternal heart had built, a nest
In blindness all too near the river's edge; 1020
That work a summer flood with hasty swell
Had swept away; and now her Spirit longed
For its last flight to heaven's security.
—The bodily frame wasted from day to day;
Meanwhile, relinquishing all other cares, 1025
Her mind she strictly tutored to find peace
And pleasure in endurance. Much she thought,
And much she read; and brooded feelingly
Upon her own unworthiness. To me,

997 When this was known by me I did not fail
    To admonish and remind *etc.* MS.
1018 built 1827: raised MS., 1814–20
1021–2 That dear abiding-place of tranquil thought
    Of binding duties and of tender cares
    A hasty summer flood had swept away
    And thus deprived her homeless Spirit . . . MS.
1024 *so* 1845: was wasted day by day MS., 1814–43

As to a spiritual comforter and friend,   1030
Her heart she opened; and no pains were spared
To mitigate, as gently as I could,
The sting of self-reproach, with healing words.
Meek Saint! through patience glorified on earth!
In whom, as by her lonely hearth she sate,   1035
The ghastly face of cold decay put on
A sun-like beauty, and appeared divine!
May I not mention—that, within those walls,
In due observance of her pious wish,
The congregation joined with me in prayer   1040
For her soul's good? Nor was that office vain.
—Much did she suffer: but, if any friend,
Beholding her condition, at the sight
Give way to words of pity or complaint,
She stilled them with a prompt reproof, and said,   1045
'He who afflicts me knows what I can bear;
And, when I fail, and can endure no more,
Will mercifully take me to himself.'
So, through the cloud of death, her Spirit passed
Into that pure and unknown world of love   1050
Where injury cannot come:—and here is laid
The mortal Body by her Infant's side."

        The Vicar ceased; and downcast looks made known
That each had listened with his inmost heart.
For me, the emotion scarcely was less strong   1055
Or less benign than that which I had felt
When seated near my venerable Friend,
Under those shady elms, from him I heard
The story that retraced the slow decline
Of Margaret, sinking on the lonely heath   1060
With the neglected house to which she clung.
—I noted that the Solitary's cheek
Confessed the power of nature.—Pleased though sad,

1038 those 1827: these MS., 1814–20   1038–9 . . . at her desire,
Her pious wish within these holy walls   MS.
1053 . . . nor did his audience fail
        To shew by silence and by downcast looks   MS.
1057–8 Two days before when, seated with my Friend, Beneath etc.   MS.
1058 Under 1845: Beneath 1814–43   1061 so 1827: . . . house in
which she dwelt MS., 1814–20

More pleased than sad, the grey-haired Wanderer sate;
Thanks to his pure imaginative soul   1065
Capacious and serene; his blameless life,
His knowledge, wisdom, love of truth, and love
Of human kind! He was it who first broke
The pensive silence, saying:—
                              "Blest are they
Whose sorrow rather is to suffer wrong   1070
Than to do wrong, albeit themselves have erred.
This tale gives proof that Heaven most gently deals
With such, in their affliction.—Ellen's fate,
Her tender spirit, and her contrite heart,
Call to my mind dark hints which I have heard   1075
Of one who died within this vale, by doom
Heavier, as his offence was heavier far.
Where, Sir, I pray you, where are laid the bones
Of Wilfred Armathwaite?"
                          The Vicar answered,
"In that green nook, close by the Churchyard wall,   1080
Beneath yon hawthorn, planted by myself
In memory and for warning, and in sign
Of sweetness where dire anguish had been known,
Of reconcilement after deep offence—
There doth he rest. No theme his fate supplies   1085

1064 Wanderer] Pedlar MS. 1071 albeit 1837: although MS., 1814–32
1085–6 There doth he lie—In this his native Vale
        He owned and tilled a little plot of land;
        Here with his Consort etc. as MS. infra, 1814–20
1085–93 so 1827:
Yon Cottage, would that it could tell a part
Of its own story. Thousands might give ear,
Might hear it, and blush deep. These few years past
In this his native Valley, dwelt a Man,
The Master of a little plot of ground
A Man of mild deportment and discourse
A scholar also (as the phrase is here)
For he drew much delight from these few books
That lay within his reach and for this cause
Was by his Fellow-dalesmen honoured more,
A Shepherd and a Tiller of the ground
Studious withal, and healthy in his frame
Of body, and of just and placid mind.
He with his Consort and his Children, saw
Days that were seldom crossed by petty strife
Years safe from large misfortune; long (and   1814–20) maintained

For the smooth glozings of the indulgent world;
Nor need the windings of his devious course
Be here retraced;—enough that, by mishap
And venial error, robbed of competence,
And her obsequious shadow, peace of mind,   1090
He craved a substitute in troubled joy;
Against his conscience rose in arms, and, braving
Divine displeasure, broke the marriage-vow.
That which he had been weak enough to do
Was misery in remembrance; he was stung,   1095
Stung by his inward thoughts, and by the smiles
Of wife and children stung to agony.
Wretched at home, he gained no peace abroad;

That cause which men the wisest and most pure (. . . minds, of insight not
    too keen, 1814–20)
Might look on with complacency. And yet (. . . with entire complacency.
    1814–20)
Within himself and near him there were faults (Yet, in himself *etc.* 1814–20)
At work to undermine his happiness (. . . his happy state 1814–20)
By little and by little (By sure, though tardy progress. 1814–20) Active,
    prompt
And lively was the Housewife; in the Vale
None more industrious; but her industry
Was of that specious kind which tended more (Ill-judged, full oft, and
    specious 1814–20)
To splendid neatness, to a shewy, trim,
And over laboured purity of house;
Than to substantial thrift. He, on his part,
Generous and easy-minded, was not free
From carelessness; and there, in course (lapse 1814–20) of time
These joint infirmities, combined, perchance ⎫ infirmities induced decay
With other cause less obvious, brought decay ⎭ 1814–20
Of worldly substance; and distress of mind,
Which to a thoughtful Man was hard to shun
And which he could not cure. A blooming Girl
Served them, an Inmate of the House. Alas!
(Served in the house, a Favourite that had grown
Beneath his eye, encouraged by his care. 1814–20)
Poor now in tranquil pleasure he gave way
To thoughts of troubled pleasure; he became
A lawless Suitor to the Maid; and she
Yielded unworthily. Unhappy Man! MS1800, and 1814–20
1097/8 His temper urged him not to seek relief
        Amid the noise of revellers, nor from draughts
        Of lonely stupefaction, he himself
        A rational and suffering Man, himself
        Was his own world, without a resting-place. MS1800

Ranged through the mountains, slept upon the earth,
Asked comfort of the open air, and found   1100
No quiet in the darkness of the night,
No pleasure in the beauty of the day.
His flock he slighted: his paternal fields
Became a clog to him, whose spirit wished
To fly—but whither! And this gracious Church,   1105
That wears a look so full of peace and hope
And love, benignant mother of the vale,
How fair amid her brood of cottages!
She was to him a sickness and reproach.
Much to the last remained unknown: but this   1110
Is sure, that through remorse and grief he died;
Though pitied among men, absolved by God,
He could not find forgiveness in himself;
Nor could endure the weight of his own shame.

        "Here rests a Mother. But from her I turn   1115
And from her grave.—Behold—upon that ridge,
That, stretching boldly from the mountain side,
Carries into the centre of the vale
Its rocks and woods—the Cottage where she dwelt;
And where yet dwells her faithful Partner, left   1120
(Full eight years past) the solitary prop
Of many helpless Children. I begin
With words that might be prelude to a tale
Of sorrow and dejection; but I feel
No sadness, when I think of what mine eyes   1125
See daily in that happy family.

1105 this] yon   MS1800   1106 wears] has   MS1800
1110–14 I speak conjecturing from the little-known
        The much that to the last remain'd unknown,
        But this is sure; he died of his own grief,
        He could not bear the weight of his own shame.   MS1800
1117–21 That ridge which elbowing from the mountain side
        Carries into the Plain its rocks and woods,
        Conceals a cottage where a Father dwells
        In widowhood whose Life's Co-partner died
        Long since, and left him solitary prop   MS1800
1118–20 Carries into the plain its rocks and woods
        Behold the Cottage where she dwelt, where now
        Her husband dwells in widowhood, whom she left   MS.
1124/5 Though in the midst of sadness, as might seem,   MS1800
1126–8 Have seen in that delightful family.
        —Bright garland make they for their Father's brows   MS1800

—Bright garland form they for the pensive brow
Of their undrooping Father's widowhood,
Those six fair Daughters, budding yet—not one,
Not one of all the band, a full-blown flower.   1130
Deprest, and desolate of soul, as once
That Father was, and filled with anxious fear,
Now, by experience taught, he stands assured,
That God, who takes away, yet takes not half
Of what he seems to take; or gives it back,   1135
Not to our prayer, but far beyond our prayer;
He gives it—the boon produce of a soil
Which our endeavours have refused to till,
And hope hath never watered. The Abode,

1131-4 Go to the dwelling, there shall ye have proof
      That He *etc.*   MS1800
1139-42   . . . watered.—As the spot
    Chosen for the Raven's nest—the nest itself
    And all the unsightly spoil around it spread,
    Proclaim the savage nature of the Bird
    Which there inhabits, so that humble Lodge
    In which that rustic family abides
    Leaves not uncertain to a transient glance
    That 'tis a covert of content and peace
    And unreproved enjoyment. Thither turn,
    The antient Cottage (at such distance seen)
    Appears in no distinction *etc.*   MS.
1139-60   . . . watered. Ye shall see
    A House which at small distance will appear
    In no distinction to have passed beyond
    Its Fellows, will appear, like them, to have grown
    Out of the native rock, but nearer view
    Will shew it not so grave in outward mien
    And soberly array'd as for the most
    Are those rude mountain-dwellings, Nature's care,
    Mere friendless Nature's, but a studious work
    Of many fancies, and of many hands
    A plaything and a pride, for such the air
    And aspect which the little Spot maintains,
    In spite of lonely winter's nakedness.
    They have their jasmine resting on the porch
    Their rose trees, strong in health, that will be soon
    Roof-high, and here and there the garden wall
    Is topped with simple stones, a shewy pile
    Curious for shape or hue, some round, like Balls
    Worn smooth and round by fretting of the Brook
    From which they have been gathered, others bright
    And sparry, the rough scatterings of the hills.
    These ornaments the cottage chiefly owes
    To one, a hardy Girl, who mounts the rocks,

Whose grateful owner can attest these truths,   1140
Even were the object nearer to our sight,
Would seem in no distinction to surpass
The rudest habitations. Ye might think
That it had sprung self-raised from earth, or grown
Out of the living rock, to be adorned   1145
By nature only; but, if thither led,
Ye would discover, then, a studious work
Of many fancies, prompting many hands.

"Brought from the woods the honeysuckle twines
Around the porch, and seems, in that trim place,   1150
A plant no longer wild; the cultured rose
There blossoms, strong in health, and will be soon
Roof-high; the wild pink crowns the garden-wall,
And with the flowers are intermingled stones
Sparry and bright, rough scatterings of the hills.   1155
These ornaments, that fade not with the year,
A hardy Girl continues to provide;
Who, mounting fearlessly the rocky heights,
Her Father's prompt attendant, does for him
All that a boy could do, but with delight   1160
More keen and prouder daring; yet hath she,
Within the garden, like the rest, a bed
For her own flowers and favourite herbs, a space,
By sacred charter, holden for her use.

Such is her choice; she fears not the bleak wind;
Companion of her Father, does for him
Where'er he wanders in his pastoral course
The service of a Boy, and with delight   MS1800
1164–76 Holden by sacred charter, and I guess
She also helped to frame that tiny plot
Of garden ground which one day 'twas my chance
To find among the woody rocks that rise
Above the House, a slip of smoother earth
Planted with gooseberry bushes, and in one,
Right in the centre of the prickly shrub,
A mimic bird-nest, fashion'd by the hand,
Was stuck, a staring thing of twisted hay,
And one quaint Fir-tree tower'd above the whole.
But in the darkness of the night, then most
This Dwelling charms me, covered by the gloom;
Then, heedless of good manners, I stop short,
And (who could help it?) feed *etc.*   MS1800
1164–76 Holden by sacred charter. Thither go

—These, and whatever else the garden bears   1165
Of fruit or flower, permission asked or not,
I freely gather; and my leisure draws
A not unfrequent pastime from the hum
Of bees around their range of sheltered hives
Busy in that enclosure; while the rill,   1170
That sparkling thrids the rocks, attunes his voice
To the pure course of human life which there
Flows on in solitude. But, when the gloom
Of night is falling round my steps, then most
This Dwelling charms me; often I stop short,   1175
(Who could refrain?) and feed by stealth my sight
With prospect of the company within,
Laid open through the blazing window:—there
I see the eldest Daughter at her wheel
Spinning amain, as if to overtake   1180
The never-halting time; or, in her turn,
Teaching some Novice of the sisterhood
That skill in this or other household work,
Which, from her Father's honoured hand, herself,
While she was yet a little-one, had learned.   1185
Mild Man! he is not gay, but they are gay;
And the whole house seems filled with gaiety.

And the trim outside of this low abode
Will please you more than sight of lordliest dome,
Or choicest work of nature mid these hills
Embosomed, lake, or headlong waterfall,
In quest of which the Traveller comes from far.
For 'tis a little volume to all eyes
Laid open, a fair picture; among trees
The Cottage stands, hard by a plenteous stream
That sparkling thrids the rocks, and tunes its voice
To the pure course of human life which there
Flows on in solitude from year to year.
But at the closing-in of night, then most
This Dwelling charms me, covered by the gloom,
Then, in my walks, I oftentimes stop short,
(Who could refrain?) and feed *etc.*   MS.
1168-70 *so* 1845:   ... from the sight
          Of the Bees murmuring round their sheltered hives
          In that Enclosure; while the mountain rill,   1814-43
1173-6 *so* 1827: 1814-20 *as last* 4 *lines* of MS. *supra*
1187/8 Now have ye not received good recompense
          For that distressful tale which last I told?
          These fruits (so God, the poor man's Friend ordains)
          Shall deck the board of innocence and love

—Thrice happy, then, the Mother may be deemed,
The Wife, from whose consolatory grave
I turned, that ye in mind might witness where,   1190
And how, her Spirit yet survives on earth!"

MS., 1814–20 *add the following lines, omitted in later editions :*
The next three Ridges—those upon the left—
By close connexion with our present thoughts
Tempt me to add, in praise of humble worth,
Their brief and unobtrusive history.   1195
—One Hillock, ye may note, is small and low,
Sunk almost to a level with the plain
By weight of time ; the Others, undepressed,
Are bold and swelling. There a Husband sleeps,
Deposited, in pious confidence   1200
Of glorious resurrection with the just,
Near the loved Partner of his early days ;
And, in the bosom of that family mold,
A second Wife is gathered to his side ;
The approved Assistant of an arduous course   1205
From his mid noon of manhood to old age!
He also of his Mate deprived, was left
Alone—'mid many Children: One a Babe
Orphaned as soon as born. Alas! 'tis not
In course of nature that a Father's wing   1210
Should warm these Little-ones ; and can he *feed* ?
That was a thought of agony more keen.
For, hand in hand with Death, by strange mishap
And chance-encounter on their diverse road,
The ghastlier shape of Poverty had entered   1215
Into that House, unfeared and unforeseen.
He had stepped forth, in time of urgent need,
The generous Surety of a Friend: and now

Where œconomic wisdom doth not fail,
Within doors or without, such the reward
Of conjugal fidelity through life
And partnership when Death has interfered   MS.
1189 *so* 1832: The Wife, who rests beneath that turf, from which   MS.,
1814–27   1195 unobtrusive] uneventful MS.   1205 Associate
MS.
1207–8 He too was left the solitary prop
        Of many helpless Children   MS.
1209 born. Alas] born. His life's dear help Is taken from him, and alas
MS.
1217–18 His generous mind had urged him to stand forth
         In surety for a Brother, who, I fear,
         Ill merited such proof of love, and now   MS.

The widowed Father found that all his rights
In his paternal fields were undermined.   1220
Landless he was and pennyless.—The dews
Of night and morn that wet the mountain sides,
The bright stars twinkling on their dusky tops,
Were conscious of the pain that drove him forth
From his own door, he knew not when—to range   1225
He knew not where; distracted was his brain,
His heart was cloven; and full oft he prayed,
In blind despair, that God would take them all.
—But suddenly, as if in one kind moment
To encourage and reprove, a gleam of light   1230
Broke from the very bosom of that cloud
Which darkened the whole prospect of his days.
For He who now possessed the joyless right
To force the Bondsman from his house and lands,
In pity, and by admiration urged   1235
Of his unmurmuring and considerate mind
Meekly submissive to the law's decree,
Lightened the penalty with liberal hand.
—The desolate Father raised his head and looked
On the wide world in hope. Within these walls,   1240
In course of time was solemnized the vow
Whereby a virtuous Woman, of grave years
And of prudential habits, undertook
The sacred office of a wife to him,
Of Mother to his helpless family.   1245

1221-6   These hills,
        The dews of night and morn that wet their sides,
        The solitary stars upon their tops,
        Were conscious of his anguish, for he left
        His hopeless door to range, he knew not where,
        He knew not when   MS.
1229 But with a sudden burst, as if at once   MS.   1235 urged]
stirred   MS.   1236 his] that
1237-8 With which the Sufferer shewed himself prepared
        For prompt obedience to the voice of law,
        Remitted, in free grace, a weighty sum
        The fifth part of the total penalty.
        At this forbearance shewn, this kindness done   MS.
1240-3 . . . hope. Few words may serve
        To tell the rest. With calm prudential choice
        He made his suit to one who in his House
        Had served, and tended now his new-born Babe,
        A Matron of grave years. To her he sued.
        Within these walls were solemnized the rites
        By which the virtuous Woman undertook   MS.

—Nor did she fail, in nothing did she fail,
Through various exercise of twice ten years,
Save in some partial fondness for that Child
Which at the birth she had received, the Babe
Whose heart had known no Mother but herself.   1250
—By mutual efforts; by united hopes;
By daily-growing help of boy and girl,
Trained early to participate that zeal
Of industry, which runs before the day
And lingers after it; by strong restraint   1255
Of an economy which did not check
The heart's more generous motions tow'rds themselves
Or to their neighbours; and by trust in God;
This Pair insensibly subdued the fears
And troubles that beset their life: and thus   1260
Did the good Father and his second Mate
Redeem at length their plot of smiling fields.
These, at this day, the eldest Son retains:
The younger Offspring, through the busy world,
Have all been scattered wide, by various fates;   1265
But each departed from the native Vale,
In beauty flourishing, and moral worth."

1247 twice ten] twenty   MS.   1256 Of prudence which, however,
MS.   1261 the good Father] Gawain Loveredge   MS.   1264–5
The rest are scattered wide by various fates.   MS.   1266 the] their
MS.

BOOK SEVENTH

THE CHURCHYARD AMONG THE MOUNTAINS (*continued*)

ARGUMENT

Impression of these Narratives upon the Author's mind.—Pastor invited to give account of certain Graves that lie apart.—Clergyman and his Family. —Fortunate influence of change of situation.—Activity in extreme old age.—Another Clergyman, a character of resolute Virtue.—Lamentations over mis-directed applause.—Instance of less exalted excellence in a deaf man.—Elevated character of a blind man.—Reflection upon Blindness.— Interrupted by a Peasant who passes—his animal cheerfulness and careless vivacity.—He occasions a digression on the fall of beautiful and interesting Trees.—A female Infant's Grave.—Joy at her Birth.—Sorrow at her Departure.—A youthful Peasant—his patriotic enthusiasm and distinguished qualities—his[1] untimely death.—Exultation of the Wanderer, as a patriot, in this Picture.—Solitary how affected.—Monument of a Knight.—Traditions concerning him.—Peroration of the Wanderer on the transitoriness of things and the revolutions of society.—Hints at his own past Calling.— Thanks the Pastor.

WHILE thus from theme to theme the Historian passed,
The words he uttered, and the scene that lay
Before our eyes, awakened in my mind
Vivid remembrance of those long-past hours;
When, in the hollow of some shadowy vale,   5

[1] *so* 1837: his patriotic enthusiasm—distinguished qualities—and 1814–32

1–9 Once more did looks of pleasure and of praise
Or words express our thanks. And for myself
I said "Your promise, Sir, so kindly given
Hath been, in truth, most movingly fulfilled.
Oft in the quiet (stillness) of a green recess
Lonesome and deep, beneath the craggy top
Of Cader *etc.*
My very soul hath listened with delight   MS. *corr. to*
Once more with *etc.*
Or speech of no unmeaning (uncertain) courtesy,
To him from whose pure lips these truths had flowed
We all expressed our thanks, *etc. to* fulfilled
The words which you have uttered, and the scene
Before our eyes awakens in my mind
A lively (pleasant) recollection of those hours
When in the quiet *etc.*
5–7 When in a vale whose depth the setting sun
Had ceased to illuminate, though yet his beams
Lay beautiful on Snowdon's craggy top   MS.

(What time the splendour of the setting sun
Lay beautiful on Snowdon's sovereign brow,
On Cader Idris, or huge Penmanmaur)
A wandering Youth, I listened with delight
To pastoral melody or warlike air,   10
Drawn from the chords of the ancient British harp
By some accomplished Master, while he sate
Amid the quiet of the green recess,
And there did inexhaustibly dispense
An interchange of soft or solemn tunes,
Tender or blithe; now, as the varying mood
Of his own spirit urged,—now, as a voice
From youth or maiden, or some honoured chief
Of his compatriot villagers (that hung
Around him, drinking in the impassioned notes   20
Of the time-hallowed minstrelsy) required
For their heart's ease or pleasure. Strains of power
Were they, to seize and occupy the sense;
But to a higher mark than song can reach
Rose this pure eloquence. And, when the stream   25
Which overflowed the soul was passed away,
A consciousness remained that it had left,
Deposited upon the silent shore
Of memory, images and precious thoughts,
That shall not die, and cannot be destroyed.   30

    "These grassy heaps lie amicably close,"
Said I, "like surges heaving in the wind

7 sovereign brow   1827: craggy top   1814–20
14–15 Dispensing an unwearied interchange
    Of soft or solemn tunes, severe or grave   MS., *corr. to*
    And inexhaustibly, as bird that sings
    In leafy bower, an interchange dispensed
    Of soft *etc.*
20–1 drinking in the festal flood Of his   MS.
22–7   Sweet those strains
    But yours are sweeter far; for, while they move,
    They teach, and when that overflowing stream
    Is passed away I feel that it hath left   MS.
31–3 Did you not say that three contiguous vales
    Do each possess within this hallow'd ground
    Its own Compartment ? Yet, from side to side
    Save in the vacant corner of the North
    The grassy heaps rise (lie) amicably close
    Like surges heaving in a gentle wind
    On the small surface *etc.*   MS.

Along the surface of a mountain pool:
Whence comes it, then, that yonder we behold
Five graves, and only five, that rise together   35
Unsociably sequestered, and encroaching
On the smooth play-ground of the village-school?"

The Vicar answered,—"No disdainful pride
In them who rest beneath, nor any course
Of strange or tragic accident, hath helped   40
To place those hillocks in that lonely guise.
—Once more look forth, and follow with your sight
The length of road that from yon mountain's base
Through bare enclosures stretches, 'till its line
Is lost within a little tuft of trees;   45
Then, reappearing in a moment, quits
The cultured fields; and up the heathy waste,
Mounts, as you see, in mazes serpentine,
Led towards an easy outlet of the vale.
That little shady spot, that sylvan tuft,   50
By which the road is hidden, also hides
A cottage from our view; though I discern
(Ye scarcely can) amid its sheltering trees
The smokeless chimney-top.—

              All unembowered
And naked stood that lowly Parsonage   55
(For such in truth it is, and appertains
To a small Chapel in the vale beyond)
When hither came its last Inhabitant.
Rough and forbidding were the choicest roads
By which our northern wilds could then be crossed;   60
And into most of these secluded vales

33 Along 1837: Upon 1814–32   34 we] I MS.
35–6 *so* 1827:   that lie apart,
        Unsociable company and sad;
          And, furthermore, appearing to encroach MS., 1814–20
42 sight 1827: eyes MS., 1814–20   43 that 1827: which MS.,
1814–20   45 within 1827: amid MS.: among 1814–20
46–8 Then, reappearing, quits the cultured fields
    And through the heath-empurpled waste ascends
    Towards yon easy *etc.* MS.
49 Led towards 1837: Towards MS., 1814–32
52–3 The body of a cottage from our view,
    And seated here we scarcely can discern MS.

Was no access for wain, heavy or light.
So, at his dwelling-place the Priest arrived
With store of household goods, in panniers slung
On sturdy horses graced with jingling bells,   65
And on the back of more ignoble beast;
That, with like burthen of effects most prized
Or easiest carried, closed the motley train.
Young was I then, a schoolboy of eight years;
But still, methinks, I see them as they passed   70
In order, drawing toward their wished-for home.
—Rocked by the motion of a trusty ass
Two ruddy children hung, a well-poised freight,
Each in his basket nodding drowsily;
Their bonnets, I remember, wreathed with flowers,   75
Which told it was the pleasant month of June;
And, close behind, the comely Matron rode,
A woman of soft speech and gracious smile,
And with a lady's mien.—From far they came,
Even from Northumbrian hills; yet theirs had been   80
A merry journey, rich in pastime, cheered
By music, prank, and laughter-stirring jest;
And freak put on, and arch word dropped—to swell
The cloud of fancy and uncouth surmise

62 Access was rare MS.   71 toward   1837: tow'rds   1814–20:
tow'rd   1832
72–4 Each in his several pannier, in the pack
    Of a stout ass the rosy children hung   MS.
76 it was   1827: that 'twas   MS., 1814–20   77 Matron] Mother
MS.   81–2 . . . wanting no delight Of gamesome prank or   MS.
83–110 Or freak put on, a dark word dropped, to raise
    Uncouth surmises in the curious mind
    Of Boor or Burgher as they passed along.
    Whence do they come? upon what errand bent?
    And of what calling? Drugs have they to vend,
    Or will they act the Children of the Wood
    At the next village? Hearing this, you guess
    That in their sage migration all the band
    Priest, wife, and servants smiled or laughed with joy;
    Of which adventures oft the pair would tell
    With undiminished etc. MS. (draft i); draft ii, ll. 91–2 as text followed
        by
    And oftimes earnest questions of like drift
    By traveller halting in his own despite
    Were boldly put to them, whereat ye guess
    That etc. as (i) but grave for sage

That gathered round the slowly-moving train.   85
—'Whence do they come ? and with what errand charged ?
Belong they to the fortune-telling tribe
Who pitch their tents under the green-wood tree ?
Or Strollers are they, furnished to enact
Fair Rosamond, and the Children of the Wood,   90
And, by that whiskered tabby's aid, set forth
The lucky venture of sage Whittington,
When the next village hears the show announced
By blast of trumpet ?' Plenteous was the growth
Of such conjectures, overheard, or seen   95
On many a staring countenance portrayed
Of boor or burgher, as they marched along.
And more than once their steadiness of face
Was put to proof, and exercise supplied
To their inventive humour, by stern looks,   100
And questions in authoritative tone,
From some staid guardian of the public peace,
Checking the sober steed on which he rode,
In his suspicious wisdom ; oftener still,
By notice indirect, or blunt demand   105
From traveller halting in his own despite,
A simple curiosity to ease:
Of which adventures, that beguiled and cheered
Their grave migration, the good pair would tell,
With undiminished glee, in hoary age.   110

    "A Priest he was by function ; but his course
From his youth up, and high as manhood's noon,
(The hour of life to which he then was brought)
Had been irregular, I might say, wild ;
By books unsteadied, by his pastoral care   115
Too little checked. An active, ardent mind ;
A fancy pregnant with resource and scheme
To cheat the sadness of a rainy day ;
Hands apt for all ingenious arts and games ;
A generous spirit, and a body strong   120
To cope with stoutest champions of the bowl ;
Had earned for him sure welcome, and the rights
Of a prized visitant, in the jolly hall

88 under 1837: beneath 1814–32   89 *so* 1837: Or are they Strollers
1814–32

Of country 'squire; or at the statelier board
Of duke or earl, from scenes of courtly pomp   125
Withdrawn,—to while away the summer hours
In condescension among rural guests.

"With these high comrades he had revelled long,
Frolicked industriously, a simple Clerk
By hopes of coming patronage beguiled   130
Till the heart sickened. So, each loftier aim
Abandoning and all his showy friends,
For a life's stay (slender it was, but sure)
He turned to this secluded chapelry;
That had been offered to his doubtful choice   135
By an unthought-of patron. Bleak and bare
They found the cottage, their allotted home;
Naked without, and rude within; a spot
With which the Cure not long had been endowed:
And far remote the chapel stood,—remote,   140
And, from his Dwelling, unapproachable,
Save through a gap high in the hills, an opening
Shadeless and shelterless, by driving showers
Frequented, and beset with howling winds.
Yet cause was none, whate'er regret might hang   145
On his own mind, to quarrel with the choice
Or the necessity that fixed him here;
Apart from old temptations, and constrained
To punctual labour in his sacred charge.
See him a constant preacher to the poor!   150
And visiting, though not with saintly zeal,

126 ... to pass the vacant summer hours   MS.   129 so 1827: Had
frolicked many a year   MS., 1814–20
131–4 so 1837: and so 1827 but l. 133 as 1814–20:
     And vexed, until the weary heart grew sick
     And so, abandoning each higher aim
     And all his showy Friends, at length he turned
     For a life's stay, though slender yet assured,
     To this remote and humble Chapelry;   1814–20 so MS., but l. 131 all
higher aims and l. 133 For an assured though scanty livelihood.
136 By . . . patron] From . . . quarter   MS.
139–44 so 1837: With which the scantily-provided Cure
                Not long had been endowed; and far remote
                The Chapel stood, divided from that House
                By an unpeopled tract of mountain waste.   MS., 1814–32
147 Which fix'd him in this lonely solitude   MS.   148/9 If not to
arduous labour, yet at least   MS.

Yet, when need was, with no reluctant will,
The sick in body, or distrest in mind;
And, by as salutary change, compelled
To rise from timely sleep, and meet the day   155
With no engagement, in his thoughts, more proud
Or splendid than his garden could afford,
His fields, or mountains by the heath-cock ranged,
Or the wild brooks; from which he now returned
Contented to partake the quiet meal   160
Of his own board, where sat his gentle Mate
And three fair Children, plentifully fed
Though simply, from their little household farm;
Nor wanted timely treat of fish or fowl
By nature yielded to his practised hand;—   165
To help the small but certain comings-in
Of that spare benefice. Yet not the less
Theirs was a hospitable board, and theirs
A charitable door.

          So days and years
Passed on;—the inside of that rugged house   170
Was trimmed and brightened by the Matron's care,
And gradually enriched with things of price,
Which might be lacked for use or ornament.
What, though no soft and costly sofa there
Insidiously stretched out its lazy length,   175
And no vain mirror glittered upon the walls,
Yet were the windows of the low abode
By shutters weather-fended, which at once
Repelled the storm and deadened its loud roar.
Their snow-white curtains hung in decent folds;   180
Tough moss, and long-enduring mountain-plants,
That creep along the ground with sinuous trail,
Were nicely braided; and composed a work
Like Indian mats, that with appropriate grace

154/5 Month after month, in that obscure Abode MS., 1814–20   157/8
To an industrious and a lonely spade MS.   159 Or the 1827: Or
these MS., 1814–20   160–1 so 1827: Contentedly, to take a temperate
meal At MS., 1814–20   164 so 1837: With acceptable treat MS.,
1814–32   165/6 In hours of eager sport by these supplied MS.
176 upon 1845: on MS., 1814–43   180 decent] plenteous MS.
181–4 And long-enduring mountain plants that creep
          Close to the ground with thick and sinuous trail,
          In sign of neatness, with appropriate grace MS.

Lay at the threshold and the inner doors;   185
And a fair carpet, woven of homespun wool
But tinctured daintily with florid hues,
For seemliness and warmth, on festal days,
Covered the smooth blue slabs of mountain-stone
With which the parlour-floor, in simplest guise   190
Of pastoral homesteads, had been long inlaid.

"Those pleasing works the Housewife's skill produced:
Meanwhile the unsedentary Master's hand
Was busier with his task—to rid, to plant,
To rear for food, for shelter, and delight;   195
A thriving covert! And when wishes, formed
In youth, and sanctioned by the riper mind,
Restored me to my native valley, here
To end my days; well pleased was I to see
The once-bare cottage, on the mountain-side,   200
Screen'd from assault of every bitter blast;
While the dark shadows of the summer leaves
Danced in the breeze, chequering its mossy roof.
Time, which had thus afforded willing help
To beautify with nature's fairest growths   205
This rustic tenement, had gently shed,
Upon its Master's frame, a wintry grace;
The comeliness of unenfeebled age.

"But how could I say, gently? for he still
Retained a flashing eye, a burning palm,   210
A stirring foot, a head which beat at nights
Upon its pillow with a thousand schemes.
Few likings had he dropped, few pleasures lost;
Generous and charitable, prompt to serve;

186 fair] fresh   MS.   188 festal   1827: festive   MS., 1814–20
191 Of these old pastoral Homesteads, was inlaid.   MS.   192 These
were the Mother's and her daughters' care   MS. Those   1837: These
1814–32
196   . . . when humble wish
    And hopes which with Heaven's blessing have not failed   MS.
203 chequering   1837: upon   MS., 1814–32   205 growths   1837:
growth   MS., 1814–32   211 a head   1827: and head   1814–20
212/13 Though like old Men, comparing present power
        With past, he sometimes yielded to complaints,   MS.
213/14 Of those that speed the day or chear the mind;   MS.

And still his harsher passions kept their hold—   215
Anger and indignation. Still he loved
The sound of titled names, and talked in glee
Of long-past banquetings with high-born friends:
Then, from those lulling fits of vain delight
Uproused by recollected injury, railed   220
At their false ways disdainfully,—and oft
In bitterness, and with a threatening eye
Of fire, incensed beneath its hoary brow.
—Those transports, with staid looks of pure good-will,
And with soft smile, his consort would reprove.   225
She, far behind him in the race of years,
Yet keeping her first mildness, was advanced
Far nearer, in the habit of her soul,
To that still region whither all are bound.
Him might we liken to the setting sun   230
As seen not seldom on some gusty day,
Struggling and bold, and shining from the west
With an inconstant and unmellowed light;
She was a soft attendant cloud, that hung
As if with wish to veil the restless orb;   235
From which it did itself imbibe a ray
Of pleasing lustre.—But no more of this;
I better love to sprinkle on the sod
That now divides the pair, or rather say,
That still unites them, praises, like heaven's dew,   240
Without reserve descending upon both.

　　　"Our very first in eminence of years
　　This old Man stood, the patriarch of the Vale!

216–23　　　　　　　　　. . . Still his tongue
　　Talked of those old exalted friends with glee,
　　And railed with pride at their deceitful ways,
　　And all too oft in words of bitter scorn
　　　From which no time could shield them, nor the grave.　MS., *corr.*
to text, but genial *for* lulling
224 Those　1837: These　MS., 1814–32　　　　　231 *so* 1827: As I have
seen it *etc.*　MS., 1814–20　　　233 inconstant] unquiet　MS.　　238
For I would rather　MS.　　　239–40 That . . . That　1827: Which . . .
Which　MS., 1814–20　　　241 *so* 1827: Without distinction falling
MS., 1814–20
241/2　—Yoke-fellows were they long and well approved
　　　To endure and to perform.
　　　　　　　　　　　With frugal pains,
　　Yet in a course of generous discipline,

And, to his unmolested mansion, death
Had never come, through space of forty years;   245
Sparing both old and young in that abode.
Suddenly then they disappeared: not twice
Had summer scorched the fields; not twice had fallen,
On those high peaks, the first autumnal snow,
Before the greedy visiting was closed,   250
And the long-privileged house left empty—swept
As by a plague. Yet no rapacious plague
Had been among them; all was gentle death,
One after one, with intervals of peace.
A happy consummation! an accord   255
Sweet, perfect, to be wished for! save that here
Was something which to mortal sense might sound
Like harshness,—that the old grey-headed Sire,
The oldest, he was taken last, survived
When the meek Partner of his age, his Son,   260
His Daughter, and that late and high-prized gift,
His little smiling Grandchild, were no more.

    " 'All gone, all vanished! he deprived and bare,
How will he face the remnant of his life?

Did this poor Churchman and his Consort rear
Their progeny.—Of three—sent forth to try
The paths of fortune in the open world,
One, not endowed with firmness to resist
The suit of pleasure, to his native Vale
Returned, and humbly tilled his Father's glebe.
—The youngest Daughter, too, in duty stayed
To lighten her declining Mother's care.
But, ere the bloom was passed away which health
Preserved to adorn a cheek no longer young,
Her heart, in course of nature, finding place
For new affections, to the holy state
Of wedlock they conducted her; but still
The Bride adhering to those filial cares
Dwelt with her Mate beneath her Father's roof.   MS., 1814–20
244–6 Death to the happy house in which they dwelt
    Had given a long reprieve of forty years   *Tuft of Primroses* (*v. note*)
249 The first white snow upon Helvellyn's top   *T. of P.*   255 A
consummation and a harmony   *T. of P.*   255/6 Though framed of
sharp and melancholy notes   MS.   257–8 . . . sounding to our mortal
sense Like discord   *T. of P.*
260–2 When the dear Partner of his manhood's prime
    His Son and Daughter, then a blooming wife,
    And little *etc.*   *T. of P.*

What will become of him ?' we said, and mused   265
In sad conjectures—'Shall we meet him now
Haunting with rod and line the craggy brooks ?
Or shall we overhear him, as we pass,
Striving to entertain the lonely hours
With music ?' (for he had not ceased to touch   270
The harp or viol which himself had framed,
For their sweet purposes, with perfect skill.)
'What titles will he keep ? will he remain
Musician, gardener, builder, mechanist,
A planter, and a rearer from the seed ?   275
A man of hope and forward-looking mind
Even to the last!'—Such was he, unsubdued.
But Heaven was gracious; yet a little while,
And this Survivor, with his cheerful throng
Of open projects, and his inward hoard   280
Of unsunned griefs, too many and too keen,
Was overcome by unexpected sleep,
In one blest moment. Like a shadow thrown
Softly and lightly from a passing cloud,
Death fell upon him, while reclined he lay   285
For noontide solace on the summer grass,
The warm lap of his mother earth: and so,
Their lenient term of separation past,
That family (whose graves you there behold)

266 sad] vain   *T. of P.*   267 craggy] rocky   *T. of P.*
268–70 And mountain tarns, or shall we, as we pass,
          Hear him alone, and solacing his ear
          With music, for he in the fitful hours
          Of his tranquillity had not ceased to touch   *T. of P.*
272 And fitted to their tasks *etc.*   *T. of P.*
278–80 'Twas but a little patience, and his term
          Of solitude was spent—the aged One
          Our very first in eminence of years (*v. ll.* 242–3)
          The Patriarch of the vale; a busy hand,
          Nay more, a burning palm, a flashing eye
          A restless foot, a head that beat at nights
          Upon his pillow with a thousand schemes—
          A Planter, and a Rearer from the Seed,
          Builder had been but scanty means forbad—
          A man of hope *etc. as l.* 276
          Even to the last, he and his cheerful throng
          Of open schemes and all his inward hoard   *T. of P.*
280 *so* 1837: 1814–32 *as T. of P.*   286 noontide] ease and   *T. of P.*
289 That family, the five whose graves you see   *T. of P.*

By yet a higher privilege once more   290
Were gathered to each other."
                              Calm of mind
And silence waited on these closing words;
Until the Wanderer (whether moved by fear
Lest in those passages of life were some
That might have touched the sick heart of his Friend 295
Too nearly, or intent to reinforce
His own firm spirit in degree deprest
By tender sorrow for our mortal state)
Thus silence broke:—"Behold a thoughtless Man
From vice and premature decay preserved   300
By useful habits, to a fitter soil
Transplanted ere too late.—The hermit, lodged
Amid the untrodden desert, tells his beads,
With each repeating its allotted prayer,
And thus divides and thus relieves the time;   305
Smooth task, with *his* compared, whose mind could string,
Not scantily, bright minutes on the thread
Of keen domestic anguish; and beguile
A solitude, unchosen, unprofessed;
Till gentlest death released him.
                              Far from us   310
Be the desire—too curiously to ask
How much of this is but the blind result
Of cordial spirits and vital temperament,
And what to higher powers is justly due.
But you, Sir, know that in a neighbouring vale   315
A Priest abides before whose life such doubts
Fall to the ground; whose gifts of nature lie
Retired from notice, lost in attributes
Of reason, honourably effaced by debts
Which her poor treasure-house is content to owe,   320
And conquests over her dominion gained,
To which her frowardness must needs submit.
In this one Man is shown a temperance—proof
Against all trials; industry severe
And constant as the motion of the day;   325
Stern self-denial round him spread, with shade

294 those 1827: these 1814–20   303 Amid 1837: In MS., 1814–
32   304 allotted] appointed C   310–11 Far ... ask] Who shall
say MS.   315 But in the compass of these pastoral Vales MS.

That might be deemed forbidding, did not there
All generous feelings flourish and rejoice;
Forbearance, charity in deed and thought,
And resolution competent to take   330
Out of the bosom of simplicity
All that her holy customs recommend,
And the best ages of the world prescribe.
—Preaching, administering, in every work
Of his sublime vocation, in the walks   335
Of worldly intercourse between man and man,
And in his humble dwelling, he appears
A labourer, with moral virtue girt,
With spiritual graces, like a glory, crowned."

"Doubt can be none," the Pastor said, "for whom   340
This portraiture is sketched. The great, the good,
The well-beloved, the fortunate, the wise,—
These titles emperors and chiefs have held,
Honour assumed or given: and him, the WONDERFUL,
Our simple shepherds, speaking from the heart,   345
Deservedly have styled.—From his abode
In a dependent chapelry that lies
Behind yon hill, a poor and rugged wild,
Which in his soul he lovingly embraced,
And, having once espoused, would never quit;   350
Into its graveyard will ere long be borne
That lowly, great, good Man. A simple stone
May cover him; and by its help, perchance,
A century shall hear his name pronounced,
With images attendant on the sound;   355
Then, shall the slowly-gathering twilight close
In utter night; and of his course remain
No cognizable vestiges, no more
Than of this breath, which shapes itself in words
To speak of him, and instantly dissolves."   360

336 between 1837: 'twixt MS., 1814–32   343 chiefs] Kings MS.
held C: borne 1814–50 v. note
351–2 so C and 1845: Hither, erelong, that lowly, great, good Man
                    Will be conveyed. An unelaborate Stone MS., 1814–43
357/8 Even in these peaceful mountain solitudes C del.
359 shapes 1827: frames MS., 1814–20

The Pastor pressed by thoughts which round his theme
Still linger'd, after a brief pause, resumed;
"Noise is there not enough in doleful war,
But that the heaven-born poet must stand forth,
And lend the echoes of his sacred shell,   365
To multiply and aggravate the din ?
Pangs are there not enough in hopeless love—
And, in requited passion, all too much
Of turbulence, anxiety, and fear—
But that the minstrel of the rural shade   370
Must tune his pipe, insidiously to nurse
The perturbation in the suffering breast,
And propagate its kind, far as he may ?
—Ah who (and with such rapture as befits
The hallowed theme) will rise and celebrate   375
The good man's purposes and deeds; retrace
His struggles, his discomfitures deplore,
His triumphs hail, and glorify his end;
That virtue, like the fumes and vapoury clouds
Through fancy's heat redounding in the brain,   380
And like the soft infections of the heart,
By charm of measured words may spread o'er field,
Hamlet, and town; and piety survive
Upon the lips of men in hall or bower;
Not for reproof, but high and warm delight,   385
And grave encouragement, by song inspired ?
—Vain thought! but wherefore murmur or repine ?
The memory of the just survives in heaven:
And, without sorrow, will the ground receive
That venerable clay. Meanwhile the best   390
Of what lies here confines us to degrees
In excellence less difficult to reach,
And milder worth: nor need we travel far
From those to whom our last regards were paid,

361–2 *added in* 1845   373 far as   1832: where'er   MS., 1814–27
374–9 Ah, who would take upon him to rehearse
          The good Man's praise in lyric strain or hymn
          That virtue *etc.*   MS.
376 purposes and deeds   1837: deeds and purposes   1814–32
382–3 *so* 1827: through fields And cottages;   MS., 1814–20   389
the ground   1845: this ground   1814–43   391 *so* 1845: Of what it
holds   MS., 1814–43

For such example.
                    Almost at the root   395
Of that tall pine, the shadow of whose bare
And slender stem, while here I sit at eve,
Oft stretches toward me, like a long straight path
Traced faintly in the greensward; there, beneath
A plain blue stone, a gentle Dalesman lies,   400
From whom, in early childhood, was withdrawn
The precious gift of hearing. He grew up
From year to year in loneliness of soul;
And this deep mountain-valley was to him
Soundless, with all its streams. The bird of dawn   405
Did never rouse this Cottager from sleep
With startling summons; not for his delight
The vernal cuckoo shouted; not for him
Murmured the labouring bee. When stormy winds
Were working the broad bosom of the lake   410
Into a thousand thousand sparkling waves,
Rocking the trees, or driving cloud on cloud
Along the sharp edge of yon lofty crags,
The agitated scene before his eye
Was silent as a picture: evermore   415
Were all things silent, wheresoe'er he moved.
Yet, by the solace of his own pure thoughts
Upheld, he duteously pursued the round
Of rural labours; the steep mountain-side
Ascended, with his staff and faithful dog;   420
The plough he guided, and the scythe he swayed;
And the ripe corn before his sickle fell
Among the jocund reapers. For himself,
All watchful and industrious as he was,
He wrought not: neither field nor flock he owned: 425
No wish for wealth had place within his mind;
Nor husband's love, nor father's hope or care.

   "Though born a younger brother, need was none
That from the floor of his paternal home
He should depart, to plant himself anew.   430

395-400 Beneath that pine which rears its dusky head
        Aloft, and covered by a plain blue stone
        Briefly inscribed, a gentle Dalesman lies. *Essay on Epitaphs* III
398 toward 1837: tow'rds 1814-32   417 pure] calm MS.
427 No husband's MS.

And when, mature in manhood, he beheld
His parents laid in earth, no loss ensued
Of rights to him; but he remained well pleased,
By the pure bond of independent love,
An inmate of a second family;   435
The fellow-labourer and friend of him
To whom the small inheritance had fallen.
—Nor deem that his mild presence was a weight
That pressed upon his brother's house; for books
Were ready comrades whom he could not tire;   440
Of whose society the blameless Man
Was never satiate. Their familiar voice,
Even to old age, with unabated charm
Beguiled his leisure hours; refreshed his thoughts;
Beyond its natural elevation raised   445
His introverted spirit; and bestowed
Upon his life an outward dignity
Which all acknowledged. The dark winter night,
The stormy day, each had its own resource;
Song of the muses, sage historic tale,   450
Science severe, or word of holy Writ
Announcing immortality and joy
To the assembled spirits of just men
Made perfect, and from injury secure.
—Thus soothed at home, thus busy in the field,   455
To no perverse suspicion he gave way,
No languor, peevishness, nor vain complaint:
And they, who were about him, did not fail
In reverence, or in courtesy; they prized
His gentle manners: and his peaceful smiles,   460
The gleams of his slow-varying countenance,
Were met with answering sympathy and love.

"At length, when sixty years and five were told,
A slow disease insensibly consumed
The powers of nature: and a few short steps   465
Of friends and kindred bore him from his home
(Yon cottage shaded by the woody crags)
To the profounder stillness of the grave.
—Nor was his funeral denied the grace

449 each had   1837: had each   1814–32   453–4 *so* 1837: the just
From imperfection and decay secure. MS., 1814–32

Of many tears, virtuous and thoughtful grief;   470
Heart-sorrow rendered sweet by gratitude.
And now that monumental stone preserves
His name, and unambitiously relates
How long, and by what kindly outward aids,
And in what pure contentedness of mind,   475
The sad privation was by him endured.
—And yon tall pine-tree, whose composing sound
Was wasted on the good Man's living ear,
Hath now its own peculiar sanctity;
And, at the touch of every wandering breeze,   480
Murmurs, not idly, o'er his peaceful grave.

"Soul-cheering Light, most bountiful of things!
Guide of our way, mysterious comforter!
Whose sacred influence, spread through earth and heaven,
We all too thanklessly participate,   485
Thy gifts were utterly withheld from him
Whose place of rest is near yon ivied porch.
Yet, of the wild brooks ask if he complained;
Ask of the channelled rivers if they held
A safer, easier, more determined, course.   490
What terror doth it strike into the mind
To think of one, blind and alone, advancing
Straight toward some precipice's airy brink!
But, timely warned, *He* would have stayed his steps,
Protected, say enlightened, by his ear;   495
And on the very edge of vacancy
Not more endangered than a man whose eye
Beholds the gulf beneath.—No floweret blooms
Throughout the lofty range of these rough hills,

490/1 Than that wherein he moved from morn to even   MS.
491–500 To them his ways were known, with them he walked,
    No other company required, the sport
    Following in darkness which their streams supplied.
    On mountain height, in wood or shady dell,
    Flowers have we none that could from him conceal *corr. to*
    With them he oftimes walked from morn to even
    Nor other *etc. to* supplied *as above.*
    Or floweret bloom throughout the lofty range
    Of these rough hills, in open field or wood
    There could be none that could from him conceal   MS.
492 *so* 1845: who cannot see, advancing   1814–43   493 Straight
toward   1837: Towards   1814–27: Toward   1832
496 edge   1827: brink   1814–20

Nor in the woods, that could from him conceal 500
Its birthplace; none whose figure did not live
Upon his touch. The bowels of the earth
Enriched with knowledge his industrious mind;
The ocean paid him tribute from the stores
Lodged in her bosom; and, by science led, 505
His genius mounted to the plains of heaven.
—Methinks I see him—how his eye-balls rolled,
Beneath his ample brow, in darkness paired,—
But each instinct with spirit; and the frame
Of the whole countenance alive with thought, 510
Fancy, and understanding; while the voice
Discoursed of natural or moral truth
With eloquence, and such authentic power,
That, in his presence, humbler knowledge stood
Abashed, and tender pity overawed." 515

"A noble—and, to unreflecting minds,
A marvellous spectacle," the Wanderer said,
"Beings like these present! But proof abounds
Upon the earth that faculties, which seem
Extinguished, do not, *therefore*, cease to be. 520
And to the mind among her powers of sense
This transfer is permitted,—not alone
That the bereft their recompense may win;
But for remoter purposes of love

500 Nor   1837: Or   1814–32
502–22   Nay, further (to such height
The grateful wonder mounts) he could peruse
The dappled skin of each familiar beast
That serves in House or field, and every spot
Could tell, by nature painted on the coat
Of all the little creatures slim and sleek
Who hide in clefts or burrow in the ground (*corr. to* under earth)
Shy as the guilty; and the feathered Bird,
Admired for sight with variegated hues,
Brought to his tutored hand appeared to yield
Those subtle colours to some inward sense.
Such conquest heaven permits; and not alone   MS.
512 or   1827: and   1814–20
521 From such example Reason may be taught
Her pride to check, her foolishness to warn,
Affections prone to grovel and descend
May be upraised. Among the powers of sense   MS.
523 *so* 1827: . . . may win their recompense   1814–20

And charity; nor last nor least for this,   525
That to the imagination may be given
A type and shadow of an awful truth;
How, likewise, under sufferance divine,
Darkness is banished from the realms of death,
By man's imperishable spirit, quelled.   530
Unto the men who see not as we see
Futurity was thought, in ancient times,
To be laid open, and they prophesied.
And know we not that from the blind have flowed
The highest, holiest, raptures of the lyre;   535
And wisdom married to immortal verse?"

Among the humbler Worthies, at our feet
Lying insensible to human praise,
Love, or regret,—*whose* lineaments would next
Have been portrayed, I guess not; but it chanced   540
That, near the quiet churchyard where we sate,
A team of horses, with a ponderous freight
Pressing behind, adown a rugged slope,
Whose sharp descent confounded their array,
Came at that moment, ringing noisily.   545

"Here," said the Pastor, "do we muse, and mourn
The waste of death; and lo! the giant oak
Stretched on his bier—that massy timber wain;
Nor fail to note the Man who guides the team."

He was a peasant of the lowest class: 550
Grey locks profusely round his temples hung
In clustering curls, like ivy, which the bite
Of winter cannot thin; the fresh air lodged
Within his cheek, as light within a cloud;
And he returned our greeting with a smile.   555
When he had passed, the Solitary spake;
"A Man he seems of cheerful yesterdays
And confident to-morrows; with a face

530 spirit] Being   MS.   541 That, near] That our attention now
was drawn aside, For, near   MS.
542–5 A team of horses slackened and confused
      By the rough slope down which their ponderous freight
      Was following them, came ringing noisily   MS.
549 But mark the Man who guides the jolly team   MS.   550 lowest]
humblest   MS.

Not worldly-minded, for it bears too much
Of Nature's impress,—gaiety and health,   560
Freedom and hope; but keen, withal, and shrewd.
His gestures note,—and hark! his tones of voice
Are all vivacious as his mien and looks.''

 The Pastor answered, "You have read him well.
Year after year is added to his store   565
With *silent* increase: summers, winters—past,
Past or to come; yea, boldly might I say,
Ten summers and ten winters of a space
That lies beyond life's ordinary bounds,
Upon his sprightly vigour cannot fix   570
The obligation of an anxious mind,
A pride in having, or a fear to lose;
Possessed like outskirts of some large domain,
By any one more thought of than by him
Who holds the land in fee, its careless lord!   575
Yet is the creature rational, endowed
With foresight; hears, too, every sabbath day,
The Christian promise with attentive ear;
Nor will, I trust, the Majesty of Heaven
Reject the incense offered up by him,   580
Though of the kind which beasts and birds present
In grove or pasture; cheerfulness of soul,
From trepidation and repining free.
How many scrupulous worshippers fall down
Upon their knees, and daily homage pay   585
Less worthy, less religious even, than his!

 "This qualified respect, the old Man's due,
Is paid without reluctance; but in truth,''
(Said the good Vicar with a fond half-smile)

576-81   ... a Man
  Endowed with sacred reason, and he hears
  The Christian promises on sabbath days
  Nor disbelieves the tidings which he hears.
  Meanwhile the incense *etc.*
  Is of the kind *etc.* MS.
579-81 *so* 1827: 1814-20 *as* MS. *supra*
579-83 The incense which he offers up to him
  Is of the kind that Bird and beast present
  To the great father, chearfulness of soul
  In which repining finds no place MS. *fragment*

"I feel at times a motion of despite   590
Towards one, whose bold contrivances and skill,
As you have seen, bear such conspicuous part
In works of havoc; taking from these vales,
One after one, their proudest ornaments.
Full oft his doings leave me to deplore   595
Tall ash-tree, sown by winds, by vapours nursed,
In the dry crannies of the pendent rocks;
Light birch, aloft upon the horizon's edge,
A veil of glory for the ascending moon;
And oak whose roots by noontide dew were damped,   600
And on whose forehead inaccessible
The raven lodged in safety.—Many a ship
Launched into Morecamb-bay, to *him* hath owed
Her strong knee-timbers, and the mast that bears
The loftiest of her pendants; He, from park   605
Or forest, fetched the enormous axle-tree
That whirls (how slow itself!) ten thousand spindles:
And the vast engine labouring in the mine,

591 Towards] Tow'rds   MS.   594 And the steep crags, their proudest
ornaments   MS.
595–623 Wherever tree might grow of name or note
        He bought, he chaffered, and with words of skill
        Suited to various tempers and estates
        Plied the reluctant Owner till he gained
        Full oft his purpose. The tall household fir
        A not unfrequent ornament and guard
        Of our old Homesteads, providently placed
        To break the onset of the fierce north winds,
        The honied sycamore in whose cool shade
        Year after year the bleating flock are shorn,
        The elm round which the lasses dance in May
        And the Lord's Oak, not one would he have spared
        For dignity for old acquaintance sake,
        For antient custom or distinguished name.
        Him, as I said, the season's difference
        Distress'd not, and the noisy world's report
        Of tumults, wars, and victories and defeats   MS. (*draft* i)
598/9 A texture thin of leaves and twigs that make   MS.: Transparent tex-
ture, framing in the East 1814–20   599/600 In the pure confines of the
cerulean sky   MS.   603 ... Morecamb-bay, from him receives   MS.:
hath owed to him   1814–20
605–7 *so* 1827:   ... Help he gives
        To lordly mansion rising far or near;
        The enormous wheel that turns ten thousand spindles MS.,
        1814–20

Content with meaner prowess, must have lacked
The trunk and body of its marvellous strength,   610
If his undaunted enterprise had failed
Among the mountain coves.
                            Yon household fir,
A guardian planted to fence off the blast,
But towering high the roof above, as if
Its humble destination were forgot—   615
That sycamore, which annually holds
Within its shade, as in a stately tent
On all sides open to the fanning breeze,
A grave assemblage, seated while they shear
The fleece-encumbered flock—the JOYFUL ELM,   620
Around whose trunk the maidens dance in May—
And the LORD'S OAK—would plead their several rights
In vain, if he were master of their fate;
His sentence to the axe would doom them all.
But, green in age and lusty as he is,   625
And promising to keep his hold on earth
Less, as might seem, in rivalship with men
Than with the forest's more enduring growth,
His own appointed hour will come at last;
And, like the haughty Spoilers of the world,   630
This keen Destroyer, in his turn, must fall.

  "Now from the living pass we once again:
From Age," the Priest continued, "turn your thoughts;
From Age, that often unlamented drops,
And mark that daisied hillock, three spans long!   635
—Seven lusty Sons sate daily round the board

610 its   1827: their   MS., 1814–20
612–23 And his keen search among the coves and woods
      In forest, heath, or chase. The fir that fends
      His neighbour's Cottage from the cutting blast
      Would fall if he were master of its doom.
      The Elm etc. as draft i to name   MS.
612 coves. Yon   1827: coves, or keen research
      In forest, park, or chase. Yon   1814–20
621 maidens   1827: lasses   1814–20
623/4 Not one would have his pitiful regard
      For prized accomodation, pleasant use,
      For dignity for . . . name (as MS. 595–623 supra)   1814–20
625–31 v. note, p. 466, infra   626 so 1827 to stand a hundred years
MS.: . . . from year to year   1814–20   629–31 His fatal hour will come,
and he must fall   MS.   633–4 not in MS.   635 Turn to etc.   MS.

Of Gold-rill side; and, when the hope had ceased
Of other progeny, a Daughter then
Was given, the crowning bounty of the whole;
And so acknowledged with a tremulous joy   640
Felt to the centre of that heavenly calm
With which by nature every mother's soul
Is stricken in the moment when her throes
Are ended, and her ears have heard the cry
Which tells her that a living child is born;   645
And she lies conscious, in a blissful rest,
That the dread storm is weathered by them both.

  "The Father—him at this unlooked-for gift
A bolder transport seizes. From the side
Of his bright hearth, and from his open door,   650
Day after day the gladness is diffused
To all that come, almost to all that pass;
Invited, summoned, to partake the cheer
Spread on the never-empty board, and drink
Health and good wishes to his new-born girl,   655
From cups replenished by his joyous hand.
—Those seven fair brothers variously were moved
Each by the thoughts best suited to his years:
But most of all and with most thankful mind
The hoary grandsire felt himself enriched;   660
A happiness that ebbed not, but remained
To fill the total measure of his soul!
—From the low tenement, his own abode,
Whither, as to a little private cell,
He had withdrawn from bustle, care, and noise,   665
To spend the sabbath of old age in peace,
Once every day he duteously repaired
To rock the cradle of the slumbering babe:
For in that female infant's name he heard
The silent name of his departed wife;   670
Heart-stirring music! hourly heard that name;

639 crowning bounty 1827: crown and glory MS., 1814–20
640–1 *so* 1827: Welcomed with joy, whose penetrating power
                  Was not unfelt amid MS., 1814–20
650/1 And from the laurel-shaded seat thereby 1814–20
653–5 Invited to partake the festal chear
                  And drink good wishes to his new-born girl MS.
657 seven] six MS.

Full blest he was, 'Another Margaret Green,'
Oft did he say, 'was come to Gold-rill side.'

"Oh! pang unthought of, as the precious boon
Itself had been unlooked-for; oh! dire stroke   675
Of desolating anguish for them all!
—Just as the Child could totter on the floor,
And, by some friendly finger's help upstayed
Range round the garden walk, while she perchance
Was catching at some novelty of spring,   680
Ground-flower, or glossy insect from its cell
Drawn by the sunshine—at that hopeful season
The winds of March, smiting insidiously,
Raised in the tender passage of the throat
Viewless obstruction; whence, all unforewarned,   685
The household lost their pride and soul's delight.
—But time hath power to soften all regrets,
And prayer and thought can bring to worst distress
Due resignation. Therefore, though some tears
Fail not to spring from either Parent's eye   690
Oft as they hear of sorrow like their own,
Yet this departed Little-one, too long
The innocent troubler of their quiet, sleeps
In what may now be called a peaceful bed.

"On a bright day—so calm and bright, it seemed   695
To us, with our sad spirits, heavenly-fair—
These mountains echoed to an unknown sound;
A volley, thrice repeated o'er the Corse
Let down into the hollow of that grave,
Whose shelving sides are red with naked mould.   700
Ye rains of April, duly wet this earth!

679–83 *so* 1827:
    Range round the garden walk, whose low ground (winter MS.)-flowers
    Were peeping forth, shy messengers of spring,—
    Even at that hopeful time,—the winds of March,
    One sunny day, smiting insidiously   MS., 1814–20
686 pride   MS., 1814–20: hope   1827
687 *so* 1827: —But Providence, that gives and takes away
                By his own law is merciful and just;
                Time wants not *etc.*   MS., 1814–20
694 bed   1827: grave   MS., 1814–20
695–7 *so* 1827: On a bright day, the brightest of the year,
                These mountains echoed with *etc.*   1814–20

Spare, burning sun of midsummer, these sods,
That they may knit together, and therewith
Our thoughts unite in kindred quietness!
Nor so the Valley shall forget her loss.   705
Dear Youth, by young and old alike beloved,
To me as precious as my own!—Green herbs
May creep (I wish that they would softly creep)
Over thy last abode, and we may pass
Reminded less imperiously of thee;—   710
The ridge itself may sink into the breast
Of earth, the great abyss, and be no more;
Yet shall not thy remembrance leave our hearts,
Thy image disappear!
     The Mountain-ash
No eye can overlook, when 'mid a grove   715
Of yet unfaded trees she lifts her head
Decked with autumnal berries, that outshine
Spring's richest blossoms; and ye may have marked,
By a brook-side or solitary tarn,
How she her station doth adorn: the pool   720
Glows at her feet, and all the gloomy rocks
Are brightened round her. In his native vale
Such and so glorious did this Youth appear;
A sight that kindled pleasure in all hearts
By his ingenuous beauty, by the gleam   725
Of his fair eyes, by his capacious brow,
By all the graces with which nature's hand
Had lavishly arrayed him. As old bards
Tell in their idle songs of wandering gods,
Pan or Apollo, veiled in human form: 730
Yet, like the sweet-breathed violet of the shade,
Discovered in their own despite to sense
Of mortals (if such fables without blame
May find chance-mention on this sacred ground)
So, through a simple rustic garb's disguise,   735
And through the impediment of rural cares,
In him revealed a scholar's genius shone;
And so, not wholly hidden from men's sight,

715–16 *so* 1827: *not in* 1814–20
718 *so* 1827: Spring's richest blossoms, yields a splendid show,
    Amid the leafy woods; and ye have seen 1814–20
728 lavishly 1827: bounteously 1814–20

In him the spirit of a hero walked
Our unpretending valley.—How the quoit   740
Whizzed from the Stripling's arm! If touched by him,
The inglorious football mounted to the pitch
Of the lark's flight,—or shaped a rainbow curve,
Aloft, in prospect of the shouting field!
The indefatigable fox had learned   745
To dread his perseverance in the chase.
With admiration would he lift his eyes
To the wide-ruling eagle, and his hand
Was loth to assault the majesty he loved:
Else had the strongest fastnesses proved weak   750
To guard the royal brood. The sailing glead,
The wheeling swallow, and the darting snipe,
The sportive sea-gull dancing with the waves,
And cautious water-fowl, from distant climes,
Fixed at their seat, the centre of the Mere,   755
Were subject to young Oswald's steady aim,
And lived by his forbearance.

        From the coast
Of France a boastful Tyrant hurled his threats;
Our Country marked the preparation vast
Of hostile forces; and she called—with voice   760
That filled her plains, that reached her utmost shores,
And in remotest vales was heard—to arms!
—Then, for the first time, here you might have seen
The shepherd's grey to martial scarlet changed,
That flashed uncouthly through the woods and fields. 765
Ten hardy Striplings, all in bright attire,
And graced with shining weapons, weekly marched,
From this lone valley, to a central spot
Where, in assemblage with the flower and choice
Of the surrounding district, they might learn   770

745–6 The fox, in mazy wiles however versed
   Or confident in strength for onward flight
   Over hill, vale, and stream was taught to dread
   His voice, and indefatigable feet
   Still foremost, longest in the obstinate chase, C
747 would he 1827: he could 1814–20   756 aim, 1837: aim.
1814–32   757–8 so 1837: From Gallia's coast a Tyrant's threats were
hurled 1814–20: . . . a Tyrant hurled his threats 1827–32   759 pre-
paration 1827: preparations 1814–20   761 so 1832: plains and
1814–27

The rudiments of war; ten—hardy, strong,
And valiant; but young Oswald, like a chief
And yet a modest comrade, led them forth
From their shy solitude, to face the world,
With a gay confidence and seemly pride;   775
Measuring the soil beneath their happy feet
Like Youths released from labour, and yet bound
To most laborious service, though to them
A festival of unencumbered ease;
The inner spirit keeping holiday,   780
Like vernal ground to sabbath sunshine left.

"Oft have I marked him, at some leisure hour,
Stretched on the grass, or seated in the shade,
Among his fellows, while an ample map
Before their eyes lay carefully outspread,   785
From which the gallant teacher would discourse,
Now pointing this way, and now that.—'Here flows,'
Thus would he say, 'the Rhine, that famous stream!
Eastward, the Danube toward this inland sea,
A mightier river, winds from realm to realm;   790
And, like a serpent, shows his glittering back
Bespotted—with innumerable isles:
Here reigns the Russian, there the Turk; observe
His capital city!' Thence, along a tract
Of livelier interest to his hopes and fears,   795
His finger moved, distinguishing the spots
Where wide-spread conflict then most fiercely raged;
Nor left unstigmatized those fatal fields
On which the sons of mighty Germany
Were taught a base submission.—'Here behold   800
A nobler race, the Switzers, and their land,

782-801   . . . seated on the wall
        Of that rude bridge with map in hand and so
        Discoursing with his Fellows. There the Rhine,
        Here flows the Danube; then, along the tract
        His fingers moved, where at that moment war
        Was raging, and the last fields had been fought,
        To Austerlitz he pointed, and to the plain
        Of Jena, upon which—O shame O pride
        For where no Country is, there man is not—
        A battle lost an Empire. Here behold
        Southward the Switzers land, a nobler race   MS.
789 toward   1837: tow'rds   1814-20: tow'rd   1827-32

Vales deeper far than these of ours, huge woods,
And mountains white with everlasting snow!'
—And, surely, he, that spake with kindling brow,
Was a true patriot, hopeful as the best   805
Of that young peasantry, who, in our days,
Have fought and perished for Helvetia's rights—
Ah, not in vain!—or those who, in old time,
For work of happier issue, to the side
Of Tell came trooping from a thousand huts,   810
When he had risen alone! No braver Youth
Descended from Judean heights, to march
With righteous Joshua; nor appeared in arms
When grove was felled, and altar was cast down,
And Gideon blew the trumpet, soul-inflamed,   815
And strong in hatred of idolatry."

The Pastor, even as if by these last words
Raised from his seat within the chosen shade,
Moved towards the grave;—instinctively his steps
We followed; and my voice with joy exclaimed: 820
"Power to the Oppressors of the world is given,
A might of which they dream not. Oh! the curse,
To be the awakener of divinest thoughts,
Father and founder of exalted deeds;
And, to whole nations bound in servile straits,   825
The liberal donor of capacities

804–5 And surely he that spake, and he whose brow
        Had crimsoned like a rock on [   ] side
        When from the west the sun through stormy clouds
        Hath smitten it with gleams sudden and deep—
        He was a patriot *etc.* MS.
807 Have perished for Helvetia's antient rights *corr. to* Perished by thou-
sands for *etc. as text* MS.   811/12 None more inclined to good and
glorious acts MS.   812 Judean 1827: Judea's 1814–20   813
nor 1837: or MS., 1814–32
817–20 *so* 1837: This spoken, from his seat the Pastor rose,
                And moved towards the grave;—instinctively
                His steps we followed; and my voice exclaimed, 1814–32
822 might] Power MS.
823–4 Forth sallying in a blind distemper'd rage,
        To be in good men's hearts a scorn that shakes,
        That nourishes and strengthens while it shakes,
        A spark that gives existence to a flame
        Which else had never kindled, I might say
        To be the father of divinest thoughts MS.

More than heroic! this to be, nor yet
Have sense of one connatural wish, nor yet
Deserve the least return of human thanks;
Winning no recompense but deadly hate   830
With pity mixed, astonishment with scorn!"

When this involuntary strain had ceased,
The Pastor said: "So Providence is served;
The forkèd weapon of the skies can send
Illumination into deep, dark holds,   835
Which the mild sunbeam hath not power to pierce.
Ye Thrones that have defied remorse, and cast
Pity away, soon shall ye quake with *fear!*
For, not unconscious of the mighty debt
Which to outrageous wrong the sufferer owes,   840
Europe, through all her habitable bounds,
Is thirsting for *their* overthrow, who yet
Survive, as pagan temples stood of yore,
By horror of their impious rites, preserved;
Are still permitted to extend their pride   845
Like cedars on the top of Lebanon
Darkening the sun.
                        But less impatient thoughts,
And love 'all hoping and expecting all,'
This hallowed grave demands, where rests in peace
A humble champion of the better cause;   850
A Peasant-youth, so call him, for he asked
No higher name; in whom our country showed,
As in a favourite son, most beautiful.
In spite of vice, and misery, and disease,
Spread with the spreading of her wealthy arts,   855
England, the ancient and the free, appeared
In him to stand before my swimming eyes,
Unconquerably virtuous and secure.
—No more of this, lest I offend his dust:
Short was his life, and a brief tale remains.   860

832 this . . . strain   1837: these . . . words   1814–32   837–8 *so*
1837: Why do ye quake, intimidated Thrones ?   1814–32   841 bounds
1837: Seats   1814–32
842–5 *so* 1837:   . . . who still
            Exist, as Pagan Temples stood of old,
            By very horror of their impious rites
            Preserved; are suffered to *etc.*   1814–32

"One day—a summer's day of annual pomp
And solemn chase—from morn to sultry noon
His steps had followed, fleetest of the fleet,
The red-deer driven along its native heights
With cry of hound and horn; and, from that toil   865
Returned with sinews weakened and relaxed,
This generous Youth, too negligent of self,
Plunged—'mid a gay and busy throng convened
To wash the fleeces of his Father's flock—
Into the chilling flood. Convulsions dire   870
Seized him, that self-same night; and through the space
Of twelve ensuing days his frame was wrenched,
Till nature rested from her work in death.
To him, thus snatched away, his comrades paid
A soldier's honours. At his funeral hour   875
Bright was the sun, the sky a cloudless blue—
A golden lustre slept upon the hills;
And if by chance a stranger, wandering there,
From some commanding eminence had looked
Down on this spot, well pleased would he have seen   880
A glittering spectacle; but every face
Was pallid: seldom hath that eye been moist
With tears, that wept not then; nor were the few,
Who from their dwellings came not forth to join
In this sad service, less disturbed than we.   885
They started at the tributary peal
Of instantaneous thunder, which announced,
Through the still air, the closing of the Grave;
And distant mountains echoed with a sound
Of lamentation, never heard before!"   890

The Pastor ceased.—My venerable Friend
Victoriously upraised his clear bright eye;
And, when that eulogy was ended, stood
Enrapt, as if his inward sense perceived

---

861 *so* 1845: One summer's day, a day of annual pomp   1814–43
868–70 *so* 1827: (A natural failing which maturer years
　　　　　　　　Would have subdued) took fearlessly—and kept—
　　　　　　　　His wonted station in the chilling flood,
　　　　　　　　Among a busy company convened
　　　　　　　　To wash his Father's flock. Convulsions dire 1814–20
894–5 Listening as if another voice yet spake
　　　　The confirmation, or in still response

The prolongation of some still response,   895
Sent by the ancient Soul of this wide land,
The Spirit of its mountains and its seas,
Its cities, temples, fields, its awful power,
Its rights and virtues—by that Deity
Descending, and supporting his pure heart   900
With patriotic confidence and joy.
And, at the last of those memorial words,
The pining Solitary turned aside;
Whether through manly instinct to conceal
Tender emotions spreading from the heart   905
To his worn cheek; or with uneasy shame
For those cold humours of habitual spleen
That, fondly seeking in dispraise of man
Solace and self-excuse, had sometimes urged
To self-abuse a not ineloquent tongue.   910
—Right toward the sacred Edifice his steps
Had been directed; and we saw him now
Intent upon a monumental stone,
Whose uncouth form was grafted on the wall,
Or rather seemed to have grown into the side   915
Of the rude pile; as oft times trunks of trees,
Where nature works in wild and craggy spots,
Are seen incorporate with the living rock—
To endure for aye. The Vicar, taking note
Of his employment, with a courteous smile   920
Exclaimed—
              "The sagest Antiquarian's eye
That task would foil;" then, letting fall his voice
While he advanced, thus spake: "Tradition tells
That, in Eliza's golden days, a Knight
Came on a war-horse sumptuously attired,   925
And fixed his home in this sequestered vale.
'Tis left untold if here he first drew breath,
Or as a stranger reached this deep recess,
Unknowing and unknown. A pleasing thought

Such as the echoes utter'd, render'd back
That funeral tribute from their quiet cells   MS.
905–6 Nature's involuntary workings felt On etc.   MS.   911 toward
1827: tow'rds 1814–20   914 form] frame MS.   915 into] out
of MS.   919 taking note] with a smile MS.   920 not in MS.
922–3 so 1827: And, with these added words He thitherward [towards the
spot MS.] advanced) MS., 1814–20

I sometimes entertain, that haply bound   930
To Scotland's court in service of his Queen,
Or sent on mission to some northern Chief
Of England's realm, this vale he might have seen
With transient observation; and thence caught
An image fair, which, brightening in his soul   935
When joy of war and pride of chivalry
Languished beneath accumulated years,
Had power to draw him from the world, resolved
To make that paradise his chosen home
To which his peaceful fancy oft had turned.   940

   "Vague thoughts are these; but, if belief may rest
Upon unwritten story fondly traced
From sire to son, in this obscure retreat
The Knight arrived, with spear and shield, and borne
Upon a Charger gorgeously bedecked   945
With broidered housings. And the lofty Steed—
His sole companion, and his faithful friend,
Whom he, in gratitude, let loose to range
In fertile pastures—was beheld with eyes
Of admiration and delightful awe,   950
By those untravelled Dalesmen. With less pride,
Yet free from touch of envious discontent,
They saw a mansion at his bidding rise,
Like a bright star, amid the lowly band
Of their rude homesteads. Here the Warrior dwelt;   955
And, in that mansion, children of his own,
Or kindred, gathered round him. As a tree
That falls and disappears, the house is gone;
And, through improvidence or want of love
For ancient worth and honourable things,   960
The spear and shield are vanished, which the Knight

933–4   . . . he might have passed this way
      And from this Valley caught with transient glance   MS.
936–7 *so* 1827: When years admonished him of failing strength
          And he no more rejoiced in war's delights,   MS., 1814–20
938 from the world] to this Vale   MS.
943 retreat] recess   MS.
944–6 *so* 1845:   . . . with pomp of spear and shield,
          And borne upon a Charger covered o'er
          With gilded housings.   MS., 1814–43
955 homesteads] dwellings   MS.

Hung in his rustic hall. One ivied arch
Myself have seen, a gateway, last remains
Of that foundation in domestic care
Raised by his hands. And now no trace is left   965
Of the mild-hearted Champion, save this stone,
Faithless memorial! and his family name
Borne by yon clustering cottages, that sprang
From out the ruins of his stately lodge:
These, and the name and title at full length,—   970
𝕾𝖎𝖗 𝕬𝖑𝖋𝖗𝖊𝖉 𝕵𝖗𝖙𝖍𝖎𝖓𝖌, with appropriate words
Accompanied, still extant, in a wreath
Or posy, girding round the several fronts
Of three clear-sounding and harmonious bells,
That in the steeple hang, his pious gift."   975

    "So fails, so languishes, grows dim, and dies,"
The grey-haired Wanderer pensively exclaimed,
"All that this world is proud of. From their spheres
The stars of human glory are cast down;
Perish the roses and the flowers of kings,   980
Princes, and emperors, and the crowns and palms
Of all the mighty, withered and consumed!
Nor is power given to lowliest innocence
Long to protect her own. The man himself
Departs; and soon is spent the line of those   985
Who, in the bodily image, in the mind,
In heart or soul, in station or pursuit,
Did most resemble him. Degrees and ranks,
Fraternities and orders—heaping high
New wealth upon the burthen of the old,   990
And placing trust in privilege confirmed
And re-confirmed—are scoffed at with a smile
Of greedy foretaste, from the secret stand

969 lodge] House MS.   972 in] like MS.   982 blasted or
decayed MS.
989–99 Classes and orders, all are swept away,
        Their virtues, service, happiness and state,
        Their monuments and their memory. *etc.* MS. *draft* i
990–9 Wealth heap'd on wealth and privilege confirm'd
        And re-confirmed are shattered and dispersed
        As with a breath and Ruin overwhelms.
        And finally green grass [sweet ?] Nature's robe
        Humanity's appointed shroud enwraps
        Their monuments *etc.* MS. *draft* ii

Of Desolation, aimed: to slow decline
These yield, and these to sudden overthrow: 995
Their virtue, service, happiness, and state
Expire; and nature's pleasant robe of green,
Humanity's appointed shroud, enwraps
Their monuments and their memory. The vast Frame
Of social nature changes evermore 1000
Her organs and her members, with decay
Restless, and restless generation, powers
And functions dying and produced at need,—
And by this law the mighty whole subsists:
With an ascent and progress in the main; 1005
Yet, oh! how disproportioned to the hopes
And expectations of self-flattering minds!

"The courteous Knight, whose bones are here interred,
Lived in an age conspicuous as our own
For strife and ferment in the minds of men; 1010
Whence alteration in the forms of things,
Various and vast. A memorable age!
Which did to him assign a pensive lot—
To linger 'mid the last of those bright clouds
That, on the steady breeze of honour, sailed 1015
In long procession calm and beautiful.
He who had seen his own bright order fade,
And its devotion gradually decline,
(While war, relinquishing the lance and shield,
Her temper changed, and bowed to other laws) 1020
Had also witnessed, in his morn of life,
That violent commotion, which o'erthrew,
In town and city and sequestered glen,
Altar, and cross, and church of solemn roof,
And old religious house—pile after pile; 1025
And shook their tenants out into the fields,
Like wild beasts without home! Their hour was come;
But why no softening thought of gratitude,
No just remembrance, scruple, or wise doubt?
Benevolence is mild; nor borrows help, 1030

1007 minds] hearts   MS.
1009–14 Lived at a time when 'twas his pensive lot
        To linger etc.   MS.
1019 While war, compelled to assume a different shape   MS. 1021
life] youth   MS.   1026 their   1837: the   MS., 1814–32

Save at worst need, from bold impetuous force,
Fitliest allied to anger and revenge.
But Human-kind rejoices in the might
Of mutability; and airy hopes,
Dancing around her, hinder and disturb   1035
Those meditations of the soul that feed
The retrospective virtues. Festive songs
Break from the maddened nations at the sight
Of sudden overthrow; and cold neglect
Is the sure consequence of slow decay.   1040

   "Even," said the Wanderer, "as that courteous Knight,
Bound by his vow to labour for redress
Of all who suffer wrong, and to enact
By sword and lance the law of gentleness,
(If I may venture of myself to speak,   1045
Trusting that not incongruously I blend
Low things with lofty) I too shall be doomed
To outlive the kindly use and fair esteem
Of the poor calling which my youth embraced
With no unworthy prospect. But enough;   1050
—Thoughts crowd upon me—and 'twere seemlier now
To stop, and yield our gracious Teacher thanks
For the pathetic records which his voice
Hath here delivered; words of heartfelt truth,
Tending to patience when affliction strikes;   1055
To hope and love; to confident repose
In God; and reverence for the dust of Man."

1035 Prevent, around her dancing giddily,   MS.
1042-4 Who, unattended, came to wear out here
     The last and better portion of life's day
     As in a Convent's hallowed privacy   MS.
1049-50 Of my own humble calling. But enough   MS.   1052-3
. . . to our gracious Teacher yield Thanks for the moving lessons which   MS.

BOOK EIGHTH
THE PARSONAGE

ARGUMENT

Pastor's apology and[1] apprehensions that he might have detained his Auditors too long, with the Pastor's[2] invitation to his house.—Solitary disinclined to comply—rallies the Wanderer—and playfully[3] draws a comparison between his itinerant profession and that of the Knight-errant—which leads to Wanderer's giving an account of changes in the Country from the manufacturing spirit.—Favourable effects.—The other side of the picture, and chiefly as it has affected the humbler classes.—Wanderer asserts the hollowness of all national grandeur if unsupported by moral worth.[4]—Physical science unable to support itself.—Lamentations over an excess of manufacturing industry among the humbler Classes of Society.—Picture of a Child employed in a Cotton-mill.—Ignorance and degradation of Children among the agricultural Population reviewed.—Conversation broken off by a renewed Invitation from the Pastor.—Path leading to his House.—Its appearance described.—His Daughter.—His Wife.—His Son (a Boy) enters with his Companion.—Their happy appearance.—The Wanderer how affected by the sight of them.

THE pensive Sceptic of the lonely vale
To those acknowledgments subscribed his own,
With a sedate compliance, which the Priest
Failed not to notice, inly pleased, and said:—
"If ye, by whom invited I began   5
These narratives of calm and humble life,
Be satisfied, 'tis well,—the end is gained;
And in return for sympathy bestowed
And patient listening, thanks accept from me.
—Life, death, eternity! momentous themes   10
Are they—and might demand a seraph's tongue,
Were they not equal to their own support;
And therefore no incompetence of mine
Could do them wrong. The universal forms
Of human nature, in a spot like this,   15

---

[1] apology and *added*   1837   [2] with the Pastor's *added*   1837
[3] *so* 1837: somewhat playfully   1814–32   [4] *so* 1837: worth—gives
Instances   1814–32

---

5 began   1837: commenced   MS., 1814–32   6 These   1827: Those
MS., 1814–20   9 accept] are due   MS.   10 Life] Time   MS.
11 they   MS., 1827: these   1814–20   demand] require   MS.
13–16 And the main outline and the general form
       Of man's condition in a spot like this
       Presents itself *etc.*   MS.

Present themselves at once to all men's view:
Ye wished for act and circumstance, that make
The individual known and understood;
And such as my best judgment could select
From what the place afforded, have been given;   20
Though apprehensions crossed me that my zeal
To his might well be likened, who unlocks
A cabinet stored with gems and pictures—draws
His treasures forth, soliciting regard
To this, and this, as worthier than the last,   25
Till the spectator, who awhile was pleased
More than the exhibitor himself, becomes
Weary and faint, and longs to be released.
—But let us hence! my dwelling is in sight,
And there—"
            At this the Solitary shrunk   30
With backward will; but, wanting not address
That inward motion to disguise, he said
To his Compatriot, smiling as he spake;
—"The peaceable remains of this good Knight
Would be disturbed, I fear, with wrathful scorn,   35
If consciousness could reach him where he lies
That one, albeit of these degenerate times,
Deploring changes past, or dreading change
Foreseen, had dared to couple, even in thought,
The fine vocation of the sword and lance   40
With the gross aims and body-bending toil
Of a poor brotherhood who walk the earth
Pitied, and, where they are not known, despised.

"Yet, by the good Knight's leave, the two estates
Are graced with some resemblance. Errant those,   45

21-4 *so* 1837: Though apprehensions crossed me, in the course
        Of this self-pleasing exercise, that Ye
        My zeal to his would liken, who, possessed
        Of some rare gems, or pictures finely wrought,
        Unlocks his Cabinet, and draws them forth
        One after one,—soliciting regard   1814-20
        Yet there were times, I frankly will confess,
        When apprehensions, *etc. as* 1814,   MS.
        My zeal to his would liken, who unlocks
        A Cabinet with gems or pictures stored,
        And draws them forth—soliciting regard   1827: 21-2 *as*
          1837, 23-4 *as* 1827,   1832

Exiles and wanderers—and the like are these;
Who, with their burthen, traverse hill and dale,
Carrying relief for nature's simple wants.
—What though no higher recompense be sought
Than honest maintenance, by irksome toil   50
Full oft procured, yet may they claim respect,
Among the intelligent, for what this course
Enables them to be and to perform.
Their tardy steps give leisure to observe,
While solitude permits the mind to feel;   55
Instructs, and prompts her to supply defects
By the division of her inward self
For grateful converse: and to these poor men
Nature (I but repeat your favourite boast)
Is bountiful—go wheresoe'er they may;   60
Kind nature's various wealth is all their own.
Versed in the characters of men; and bound,
By ties of daily interest, to maintain
Conciliatory manners and smooth speech;
Such have been, and still are in their degree,   65
Examples efficacious to refine
Rude intercourse; apt agents to expel,
By importation of unlooked-for arts,
Barbarian torpor, and blind prejudice;
Raising, through just gradation, savage life   70
To rustic, and the rustic to urbane.

46 these] ye   MS.   47–8 . . . your burthen, among these lonely
wilds Pass for relief of MS.   48/9 Cheered by good fortune,—to mishap
exposed   MS.   49 be sought   1837: they seek   1814–32   51
may they] 1837: such may   MS., 1814–32   54 Yet your slow steps
MS.   56 *so* 1827: And doth instruct her   MS., 1814–20
59–60 *so* 1837: (As I have heard you boast with honest pride)
              Nature is bountiful, where'er they go,   MS., 1814–32
60/1 For them, if not for others more at ease
     Birds warble, rivers run, and fragrant smells
     Rise from the bosom of the stedfast earth,
     Or pass and meet them, wafted on the breeze   MS.
63 ties 1832: tie   MS., 1814–20
66–71 Apt instruments to soften and refine
      Rude minds, and savage torpor to dispel
      By importation of unlook'd for arts
      And penetrating force of new desires. MS.
      ⎧ Apt instruments for raising savage life
      ⎨ To rustic and the rustic to urbane MS. *alt.*
67 agents to expel 1827: Instruments to excite   1814–20

—Within their moving magazines is lodged
Power that comes forth to quicken and exalt
Affections seated in the mother's breast,
And in the lover's fancy; and to feed   75
The sober sympathies of long-tried friends.
—By these Itinerants, as experienced men,
Counsel is given; contention they appease
With gentle language; in remotest wilds,
Tears wipe away, and pleasant tidings bring;   80
Could the proud quest of chivalry do more?"

　　"Happy," rejoined the Wanderer, "they who gain
A panegyric from your generous tongue!
But, if to these Wayfarers once pertained
Aught of romantic interest, it is gone.   85
Their purer service, in this realm at least,
Is past for ever.—An inventive Age
Has wrought, if not with speed of magic, yet
To most strange issues. I have lived to mark
A new and unforeseen creation rise   90
From out the labours of a peaceful Land
Wielding her potent enginery to frame
And to produce, with appetite as keen
As that of war, which rests not night or day,
Industrious to destroy! With fruitless pains   95
Might one like me *now* visit many a tract
Which, in his youth, he trod, and trod again,
A lone pedestrian with a scanty freight,
Wished-for, or welcome, wheresoe'er he came—
Among the tenantry of thorpe and vill;   100
Or straggling burgh, of ancient charter proud,
And dignified by battlements and towers
Of some stern castle, mouldering on the brow
Of a green hill or bank of rugged stream.

---

74 Affections 1827: The affections 1814–20: The pure affections in the
mother's breast MS.   79 *so* 1827: With healing words; and, in
remotest Wilds MS., 1814–20   81 What could the pride MS.
85 it is 1837: 'tis MS., 1814–32
95–7   . . . fruitless search
　　Now might I look for many a rugged path
　　And horse-track wild, and formidable lane
　　Which not unthankfully in youth I trod MS.
99 he] I MS.   100–6 *added to* MS.

The foot-path faintly marked, the horse-track wild,   105
And formidable length of plashy lane,
(Prized avenues ere others had been shaped
Or easier links connecting place with place)
Have vanished—swallowed up by stately roads
Easy and bold, that penetrate the gloom   110
Of Britain's farthest glens. The Earth has lent
Her waters, Air her breezes; and the sail
Of traffic glides with ceaseless intercourse,
Glistening along the low and woody dale;
Or, in its progress, on the lofty side   115
Of some bare hill, with wonder kenned from far.

"Meanwhile, at social Industry's command,
How quick, how vast an increase! From the germ
Of some poor hamlet, rapidly produced
Here a huge town, continuous and compact,   120
Hiding the face of earth for leagues—and there,
Where not a habitation stood before,
Abodes of men irregularly massed
Like trees in forests,—spread through spacious tracts,
O'er which the smoke of unremitting fires   125
Hangs permanent, and plentiful as wreaths
Of vapour glittering in the morning sun.
And, wheresoe'er the traveller turns his steps,
He sees the barren wilderness erased,
Or disappearing; triumph that proclaims   130
How much the mild Directress of the plough
Owes to alliance with these new-born arts!
—Hence is the wide sea peopled,—hence the shores
Of Britain are resorted to by ships
Freighted from every climate of the world   135
With the world's choicest produce. Hence that sum
Of keels that rest within her crowded ports,
Or ride at anchor in her sounds and bays;

107 These prized when other avenue was none   MS.   109–10 . . .
giving way to ample roads Stately *etc.*   MS.   111 Britain's   1827:
England's   MS., 1814–20   113 intercourse   1837: interchange   MS.,
1814–32   115–16 *so* 1837: Or on the naked mountain's lofty side.
MS., 1814–32   123 *so* 1827: The abodes   MS., 1814–20   133–4 and
the shores Of Britain hence are sought by gallant Ships   MS.   133
hence 1827: and   1814–20   136/7 Of maritime grandeur and internal
wealth,   MS.   137 The keels that rest at anchor in her ports   MS.

That animating spectacle of sails
That, through her inland regions, to and fro   140
Pass with the respirations of the tide,
Perpetual, multitudinous! Finally,
Hence a dread arm of floating power, a voice
Of thunder daunting those who would approach
With hostile purposes the blessèd Isle,   145
Truth's consecrated residence, the seat
Impregnable of Liberty and Peace.

      "And yet, O happy Pastor of a flock
Faithfully watched, and, by that loving care
And Heaven's good providence, preserved from taint! 150
With you I grieve, when on the darker side
Of this great change I look; and there behold
Such outrage done to nature as compels
The indignant power to justify herself;
Yea, to avenge her violated rights,   155
For England's bane.—When soothing darkness spreads
O'er hill and vale," the Wanderer thus expressed
His recollections, "and the punctual stars,
While all things else are gathering to their homes,
Advance, and in the firmament of heaven   160
Glitter—but undisturbing, undisturbed;
As if their silent company were charged
With peaceful admonitions for the heart
Of all-beholding Man, earth's thoughtful lord;
Then, in full many a region, once like this   165
The assured domain of calm simplicity
And pensive quiet, an unnatural light
Prepared for never-resting Labour's eyes
Breaks from a many-windowed fabric huge;
And at the appointed hour a bell is heard,   170
Of harsher import than the curfew-knoll

139 That] An   MS.   152/3 Through strong temptation of these self-
same arts   MS.: *so* 1814–20 *but* those gainful *for* these self-same
157–8 O'er hill and valley and the Punctual Stars   MS.
164–5 Now that another of his toilsome days
        Is past, and Time has left another step
        To be recorded in his noiseless march
        Towards Eternity, and sweet Repose
        Scatters her weary blessing, and by thanks
        And Prayer preceded holy sleep descends,   MS.

That spake the Norman Conqueror's stern behest—
A local summons to unceasing toil!
Disgorged are now the ministers of day;
And, as they issue from the illumined pile,   175
A fresh band meets them, at the crowded door—
And in the courts—and where the rumbling stream,
That turns the multitude of dizzy wheels,
Glares, like a troubled spirit, in its bed
Among the rocks below. Men, maidens, youths,   180
Mother and little children, boys and girls,
Enter, and each the wonted task resumes
Within this temple, where is offered up
To Gain, the master idol of the realm,
Perpetual sacrifice. Even thus of old   185
Our ancestors, within the still domain
Of vast cathedral or conventual church,
Their vigils kept; where tapers day and night
On the dim altar burned continually,
In token that the House was evermore   190
Watching to God. Religious men were they;
Nor would their reason, tutored to aspire
Above this transitory world, allow
That there should pass a moment of the year,
When in their land the Almighty's service ceased.   195

     "Triumph who will in these profaner rites
Which we, a generation self-extolled,
As zealously perform! I cannot share
His proud complacency:—yet do I exult,
Casting reserve away, exult to see   200
An intellectual mastery exercised
O'er the blind elements; a purpose given,
A perseverance fed; almost a soul
Imparted—to brute matter. I rejoice,

175 And, at the portals of   MS.   182 To their accustomed services
repair   MS., *corr. to text*   194 That a single moment of the year
should pass   C
198–202   . . . I too will share
     Thus far his proud complacency—[with him?]
     Casting reserve away will I rejoice
     To see an intellectual Aim imposed
     On the . . .   MS.
199 *so* 1837: yet I exult   1814–32

Measuring the force of those gigantic powers   205
That, by the thinking mind, have been compelled
To serve the will of feeble-bodied Man.
For with the sense of admiration blends
The animating hope that time may come
When, strengthened, yet not dazzled, by the might   210
Of this dominion over nature gained,
Men of all lands shall exercise the same
In due proportion to their country's need;
Learning, though late, that all true glory rests,
All praise, all safety, and all happiness,   215
Upon the moral law. Egyptian Thebes,
Tyre, by the margin of the sounding waves,
Palmyra, central in the desert, fell;
And the Arts died by which they had been raised.
—Call Archimedes from his buried tomb   220
Upon the grave of vanished Syracuse,
And feelingly the Sage shall make report
How insecure, how baseless in itself,
Is the Philosophy whose sway depends
On mere material instruments;—how weak   225
Those arts, and high inventions, if unpropped
By virtue.—He, sighing with pensive grief,
Amid his calm abstractions, would admit
That not the slender privilege is theirs
To save themselves from blank forgetfulness!"   230

When from the Wanderer's lips these words had fallen,
I said, "And, did in truth those vaunted Arts
Possess such privilege, how could we escape
Sadness and keen regret, we who revere,
And would preserve as things above all price,   235
The old domestic morals of the land,

207 will] needs   MS.
208-9 Yet should I deem this [?] too dearly bought
        Unless I dared to hope that time may come   MS.
221 grave   1837: plain   MS., 1814-32   224-5 *so* 1827: sway is
framed For   MS., 1814-20   227 sighing with   1845: with sighs of
MS., 1814-43
231-4 Meanwhile shall we give way to empty joy
        And inconsiderate boasting, who revere   MS.
232 those   1837: these   1814-32   234 *so* 1837: Regret and painful
sadness, who revere   1814-32

Her simple manners, and the stable worth
That dignified and cheered a low estate ?
Oh! where is now the character of peace,
Sobriety, and order, and chaste love,   240
And honest dealing, and untainted speech,
And pure good-will, and hospitable cheer;
That made the very thought of country-life
A thought of refuge, for a mind detained
Reluctantly amid the bustling crowd ?   245
Where now the beauty of the sabbath kept
With conscientious reverence, as a day
By the almighty Lawgiver pronounced
Holy and blest ? and where the winning grace
Of all the lighter ornaments attached   250
To time and season, as the year rolled round ?"

"Fled!" was the Wanderer's passionate response,
"Fled utterly! or only to be traced
In a few fortunate retreats like this;
Which I behold with trembling, when I think   255
What lamentable change, a year—a month—
May bring; that brook converting as it runs
Into an instrument of deadly bane
For those, who, yet untempted to forsake
The simple occupations of their sires,   260
Drink the pure water of its innocent stream
With lip almost as pure.—Domestic bliss
(Or call it comfort, by a humbler name,)
How art thou blighted for the poor Man's heart!
Lo! in such neighbourhood, from morn to eve,   265
The habitations empty! or perchance
The Mother left alone,—no helping hand
To rock the cradle of her peevish babe;
No daughters round her, busy at the wheel,

237-9 . . . manners, yet are doomed to see
        The objects of our reverential love
        Perish as Victims, and Oblations brought
        To an insatiate Idol whom the State
        Worships with sanction for that worship drawn
        From treacherous Thievery. O where is now
        The worth, the stable worth, that dignified
        A low estate, the character of peace,   MS.
252 *not in* MS.   265 Lo! in the fields and hamlets all day long   MS.

Or in dispatch of each day's little growth   270
Of household occupation; no nice arts
Of needle-work; no bustle at the fire,
Where once the dinner was prepared with pride;
Nothing to speed the day, or cheer the mind;
Nothing to praise, to teach, or to command!   275

"The Father, if perchance he still retain
His old employments, goes to field or wood,
No longer led or followed by the Sons;
Idlers perchance they were,—but in *his* sight;
Breathing fresh air, and treading the green earth;   280
Till their short holiday of childhood ceased,
Ne'er to return! That birthright now is lost.
Economists will tell you that the State
Thrives by the forfeiture—unfeeling thought,
And false as monstrous! Can the mother thrive   285
By the destruction of her innocent sons
In whom a premature necessity
Blocks out the forms of nature, preconsumes
The reason, famishes the heart, shuts up
The infant Being in itself, and makes   290
Its very spring a season of decay!
The lot is wretched, the condition sad,
Whether a pining discontent survive,

278 the Sons 1820: his Sons MS., 1814
283-7 There is a law severe of penury
        Which bends the Cottage boy to early thought,
        To thought whose premature necessity MS. 18ᴬ
292-302 Oh miserable lot! condition sad!
        Which terminates the hour of careless joy
        So soon, that it is lost to memory,
        To the old Man a time that never was,
        And even if on some week-day festival
        Or by the sabbath fire the parent's heart
        Turn with a fond good-humoured tenderness
        To days that are long past, the Stripling hears
        The tale of that sweet season, what he said,
        And what he did, his marvellous feats and freaks,
        His wisdom and his wit,—he hears them all
        With languid interest as a thing detached
        From his own life—O miserable state!
        Then liberty is not and cannot be,
        But wheresoe'er he turns his steps the boy MS. 18ᴬ

And thirst for change; or habit hath subdued
The soul deprest, dejected—even to love   295
Of her close tasks, and long captivity.

"Oh, banish far such wisdom as condemns
A native Briton to these inward chains,
Fixed in his soul, so early and so deep;
Without his own consent, or knowledge, fixed!   300
He is a slave to whom release comes not,
And cannot come. The boy, where'er he turns,
Is still a prisoner; when the wind is up
Among the clouds, and roars through the ancient woods;
Or when the sun is shining in the east,   305
Quiet and calm. Behold him—in the school
Of his attainments? no; but with the air
Fanning his temples under heaven's blue arch.
His raiment, whitened o'er with cotton-flakes
Or locks of wool, announces whence he comes.   310
Creeping his gait and cowering, his lip pale,
His respiration quick and audible;
And scarcely could you fancy that a gleam
Could break from out those languid eyes, or a blush
Mantle upon his cheek. Is this the form,   315
Is that the countenance, and such the port,
Of no mean Being? One who should be clothed
With dignity befitting his proud hope;
Who, in his very childhood, should appear
Sublime from present purity and joy!   320
The limbs increase; but liberty of mind

296 *so* 1837: Of her (those MS.) dull tasks and close captivity 1814–32
297 Oh guard me from   MS.   298 A Briton born to these internal
chains   MS.   304 roars through 1837: in   MSS., 1814–32   305
so 1827: rising in the heavens   MSS., 1814–20   306–15 (*middle*) *not
in* MS. 18ᴬ
306–9 On path or public road, his raiment soiled
          And whitened o'er with cotton flakes re[?]   MS.
314 *so* 1837: From out those languid eyes could (From out those eyes could
ever   MS.) break, or blush   MS., 1814–32   315 Are these the looks,
MSS.
321–2 *so* 1845: 1837–43 *omit* liberty . . . and, *and for* joyful *read* gladsome
          The limbs increase, but while with freedom lost
          Thought pines and dwindles this organic frame   C

Is gone for ever; and this organic frame,
So joyful in its motions, is become
Dull, to the joy of her own motions dead;
And even the touch, so exquisitely poured   325
Through the whole body, with a languid will
Performs its functions; rarely competent
To impress a vivid feeling on the mind
Of what there is delightful in the breeze,
The gentle visitations of the sun,   330
Or lapse of liquid element—by hand,
Or foot, or lip, in summer's warmth—perceived.
—Can hope look forward to a manhood raised
On such foundations?"
                              "Hope is none for him!"
The pale Recluse indignantly exclaimed,   335
"And tens of thousands suffer wrong as deep.
Yet be it asked, in justice to our age,
If there were not, before those arts appeared,
These structures rose, commingling old and young,
And unripe sex with sex, for mutual taint;   340
If there were not, *then*, in our far-famed Isle,
Multitudes, who from infancy had breathed
Air unimprisoned, and had lived at large;
Yet walked beneath the sun, in human shape,
As abject, as degraded? At this day,   345
Who shall enumerate the crazy huts
And tottering hovels, whence do issue forth
A ragged Offspring, with their upright hair

322–3 *so* 1845: Thus gone for ever, this organic Frame
               Which from Heaven's bounty we receive, instinct
               With light and gladsome motions, soon becomes 1814–20:
1837 *as* 1845 *but* gladsome *for* joyful
322 Is gone for ever, and the avenues
     Of sense impeded, (are clogg'd and MS. 18ᴬ) ˙ this organic frame MSS.
323 its 1837: her 1827   324 her] its MSS.   327 its 1814, 1820,
1837–50: her 1827–32
327–32 Performs its functions, in the basking hour
        Scarce carrying to the brain a torpid sense
        Of what there is delightful in the breeze
        The sunshine or the changeful elements MS. 18ᴬ
328 To impress a faint perception on the brain MS.   341 *so* 1837:
Then if there were not 1814–32: and are not at this day MS.   347
Or clay-built hovels MS.   348 upright 1837: own blanched MS.,
1814–32

Crowned like the image of fantastic Fear;
Or wearing, (shall we say ?) in that white growth   350
An ill-adjusted turban, for defence
Or fierceness, wreathed around their sunburnt brows,
By savage Nature ? Shrivelled are their lips;
Naked, and coloured like the soil, the feet
On which they stand; as if thereby they drew   355
Some nourishment, as trees do by their roots,
From earth, the common mother of us all.
Figure and mien, complexion and attire,
Are leagued to strike dismay; but outstretched hand
And whining voice denote them supplicants   360
For the least boon that pity can bestow.
Such on the breast of darksome heaths are found;
And with their parents occupy the skirts
Of furze-clad commons; such are born and reared
At the mine's mouth under impending rocks;   365
Or dwell in chambers of some natural cave;
Or where their ancestors erected huts,
For the convenience of unlawful gain,
In forest purlieus; and the like are bred,
All England through, where nooks and slips of ground 370
Purloined, in times less jealous than our own,
From the green margin of the public way,
A residence afford them, 'mid the bloom
And gaiety of cultivated fields.
Such (we will hope the lowest in the scale)   375
Do I remember oft-times to have seen
'Mid Buxton's dreary heights. In earnest watch,
Till the swift vehicle approach, they stand;
Then, following closely with the cloud of dust,
An uncouth feat exhibit, and are gone   380

350 *so* 1837: wearing, we might say, 1814–32   353 *so* 1837: By
savage Nature's unassisted care. MS., 1814–32   359 *so* 1827: Are
framed . . . but the outstretched MS., 1814–20   363 occupy
1837: dwell upon 1814–32
363–77 In forest pastures and in sheltered lanes
          Among the pride of cultivated fields
          And such do I remember to have seen
          On Buxton's dreary heights. Upon the watch MS.
364 such 1827: and 1814–20   365 under 1837: beneath 1814–
32   366 dwell in 1837: in the 1814–32   377 *so* 1837: Upon
the watch MS., 1814–32

Heels over head, like tumblers on a stage.
—Up from the ground they snatch the copper coin,
And, on the freight of merry passengers
Fixing a steady eye, maintain their speed;
And spin—and pant—and overhead again,   385
Wild pursuivants! until their breath is lost,
Or bounty tires—and every face, that smiled
Encouragement, hath ceased to look that way.
—But, like the vagrants of the gipsy tribe,
These, bred to little pleasure in themselves,   390
Are profitless to others.
                              Turn we then
To Britons born and bred within the pale
Of civil polity, and early trained
To earn, by wholesome labour in the field,
The bread they eat. A sample should I give   395
Of what this stock hath long produced to enrich
The tender age of life, ye would exclaim,
'Is this the whistling plough-boy whose shrill notes
Impart new gladness to the morning air!'
Forgive me if I venture to suspect   400
That many, sweet to hear of in soft verse,
Are of no finer frame. Stiff are his joints;
Beneath a cumbrous frock, that to the knees
Invests the thriving churl, his legs appear,
Fellows to those that lustily upheld   405
The wooden stools for everlasting use,
Whereon our fathers sate. And mark his brow!
Under whose shaggy canopy are set
Two eyes—not dim, but of a healthy stare—
Wide, sluggish, blank, and ignorant, and strange—   410
Proclaiming boldly that they never drew
A look or motion of intelligence
From infant-conning of the Christ-cross-row,
Or puzzling through a primer, line by line,

386 till they have lost their breath   MS.   392 To such as fairly born
MS.
396–7 *so* 1837:   . . . produces to enrich
                  And beautify the tender age of life,
                  A sample fairly called, MS., 1814–20: produces to enrich
                          The tender age of life 1827–32
402 *so* 1837: frame:—his joints are stiff MS., 1814–32   409 healthy]
vacant C   410 *line added in* C *and* 1840

Till perfect mastery crown the pains at last.   415
—What kindly warmth from touch of fostering hand,
What penetrating power of sun or breeze,
Shall e'er dissolve the crust wherein his soul
Sleeps, like a caterpillar sheathed in ice ?
This torpor is no pitiable work   420
Of modern ingenuity ; no town
Nor crowded city can be taxed with aught
Of sottish vice or desperate breach of law,
To which (and who can tell where or how soon ?)
He may be roused. This Boy the fields produce: 425
His spade and hoe, mattock and glittering scythe,
The carter's whip that on his shoulder rests
In air high-towering with a boorish pomp,
The sceptre of his sway ; his country's name,
Her equal rights, her churches and her schools—   430
What have they done for him ? And, let me ask,
For tens of thousands uninformed as he ?
In brief, what liberty of *mind* is here ?"

    This ardent sally pleased the mild good Man,
To whom the appeal couched in its closing words   435
Was pointedly addressed ; and to the thoughts
That, in assent or opposition, rose
Within his mind, he seemed prepared to give
Prompt utterance ; but the Vicar interposed
With invitation urgently renewed.   440
—We followed, taking as he led, a path
Along a hedge of hollies dark and tall,
Whose flexile boughs low bending with a weight
Of leafy spray, concealed the stems and roots

420 pitiable] lamentable MS.   422 can 1837: may MS., 1814–32
424–6 *so* 1837: To which in after years he may be roused.
                —This Boy the Fields produce: his spade and hoe, MS.,
                    1814–32
434 ardent 1827: cheerful MS., 1814–20   435 its 1827: those
MS., 1814–20 closing] final MS.
439 *so* 1837:   . . . rising from our seat
                Beneath the umbrage of those Church-yard trees
                The hospitable Vicar interposed MS., *so* 1814–32, *but omitting*
                    middle line
440 urgently 1827: earnestly MS., 1814–20   442 *so* 1827: stately
hollies framed MS., 1814–20   443 low bending 1837: descending
MS., 1814–32

That gave them nourishment. When frosty winds   445
Howl from the north, what kindly warmth, methought,
Is here—how grateful this impervious screen!
—Not shaped by simple wearing of the foot
On rural business passing to and fro
Was the commodious walk: a careful hand   450
Had marked the line, and strewn its surface o'er
With pure cerulean gravel, from the heights
Fetched by a neighbouring brook.—Across the vale
The stately fence accompanied our steps;
And thus the pathway, by perennial green   455
Guarded and graced, seemed fashioned to unite,
As by a beautiful yet solemn chain,
The Pastor's mansion with the house of prayer.

    Like image of solemnity, conjoined
With feminine allurement soft and fair,   460
The mansion's self displayed;—a reverend pile
With bold projections and recesses deep;
Shadowy, yet gay and lightsome as it stood
Fronting the noontide sun. We paused to admire
The pillared porch, elaborately embossed;   465
The low wide windows with their mullions old;
The cornice, richly fretted, of grey stone;
And that smooth slope from which the dwelling rose,
By beds and banks Arcadian of gay flowers
And flowering shrubs, protected and adorned: 470
Profusion bright! and every flower assuming
A more than natural vividness of hue
From unaffected contrast with the gloom
Of sober cypress, and the darker foil
Of yew, in which survived some traces, here   475
Not unbecoming, of grotesque device

445-7 *so* 1827:   How sweet methought,
    When the fierce wind comes howling from the north,
    How grateful this impenetrable screen! MS., 1814-20
450-3   . . . walk (that wound along
As through a pleasure ground, from field to field)
For here a careful Hand had been employed
To mark the line and strew the surface o'er
With purest gravel from the mountain brook MS.
451, 453 its . . . a 1837: the . . . the MS., 1814-32   471 *not in*
MS.   473 The bright flowers took from contrast MS.

And uncouth fancy. From behind the roof
Rose the slim ash and massy sycamore,
Blending their diverse foliage with the green
Of ivy, flourishing and thick, that clasped   480
The huge round chimneys, harbour of delight
For wren and redbreast,—where they sit and sing
Their slender ditties when the trees are bare.
Nor must I leave untouched (the picture else
Were incomplete) a relique of old times   485
Happily spared, a little Gothic niche
Of nicest workmanship; that once had held
The sculptured image of some patron-saint,
Or of the blessèd Virgin, looking down
On all who entered those religious doors.   490

But lo! where from the rocky garden-mount
Crowned by its antique summer-house—descends,
Light as the silver fawn, a radiant Girl;
For she hath recognised her honoured friend,
The Wanderer ever welcome! A prompt kiss   495
The gladsome child bestows at his request;
And, up the flowery lawn as we advance,
Hangs on the old Man with a happy look,
And with a pretty restless hand of love.
—We enter—by the Lady of the place   500
Cordially greeted. Graceful was her port:
A lofty stature undepressed by time,
Whose visitation had not wholly spared
The finer lineaments of form and face;
To that complexion brought which prudence trusts in 505
And wisdom loves.—But when a stately ship
Sails in smooth weather by the placid coast
On homeward voyage,—what if wind and wave,

477 uncouth] antique   MS.
484-5 *so* 1827:   . . . pass unnoticed (leaving else
          The picture incomplete, as it appeared
          Before our eyes)   MS., 1814-20
500-1 *so* 1827: We enter;—need I tell the courteous guise
          In which the Lady of the place received
          Our little Band, with salutation meet
          To each accorded ? Graceful *etc.*   1814-20
503 *so* 1827: had not spared to touch   1814-20   504 form   1827:
frame   1814-20

And hardship undergone in various climes,
Have caused her to abate the virgin pride,   510
And that full trim of inexperienced hope
With which she left her haven—not for this,
Should the sun strike her, and the impartial breeze
Play on her streamers, fails she to assume
Brightness and touching beauty of her own,   515
That charm all eyes. So bright, so fair, appeared
This goodly Matron, shining in the beams
Of unexpected pleasure.—Soon the board
Was spread, and we partook a plain repast.

    Here, resting in cool shelter, we beguiled   520
The mid-day hours with desultory talk;
From trivial themes to general argument
Passing, as accident or fancy led,
Or courtesy prescribed. While question rose
And answer flowed, the fetters of reserve   525
Dropping from every mind, the Solitary
Resumed the manners of his happier days;
And in the various conversation bore
A willing, nay, at times, a forward part;
Yet with the grace of one who in the world   530
Had learned the art of pleasing, and had now
Occasion given him to display his skill,
Upon the stedfast 'vantage-ground of truth.
He gazed, with admiration unsuppressed,
Upon the landscape of the sun-bright vale,   535
Seen, from the shady room in which we sate,

514 fails she   1827: doth she fail   1814–20   516 so fair   1827: to us
1814–20
520 *so* 1827: Here in cool shelter, while the scorching heat
         Oppressed the fields, we sate, and entertained   1814–20
520–45 But now when we had ended our repast
     And one was looking leisurely abroad
     Upon the living scene, hills, woods, and lake
     Bright in the sun, and one, perhaps, content
     To scan the internal comeliness and grace
     Of that antique apartment where we sate,
     Its shining furniture and portraits old
     Till suddenly our willing eyes were called
     To other entertainment, for the door
     Opening, with eager haste two lusty boys   MS.
526 *so* 1827: Dropped from our minds; and even the shy Recluse   1814–20

In softened pérspective; and more than once
Praised the consummate harmony serene
Of gravity and elegance, diffused
Around the mansion and its whole domain;   540
Not, doubtless, without help of female taste
And female care.—"A blessed lot is yours!"
The words escaped his lip, with a tender sigh
Breathed over them: but suddenly the door
Flew open, and a pair of lusty Boys   545
Appeared, confusion checking their delight.
—Not brothers they in feature or attire,
But fond companions, so I guessed, in field,
And by the river's margin—whence they come,
Keen anglers with unusual spoil elated.   550
One bears a willow-pannier on his back,
The boy of plainer garb, whose blush survives
More deeply tinged. Twin might the other be
To that fair girl who from the garden-mount
Bounded:—triumphant entry this for him!   555
Between his hands he holds a smooth blue stone,
On whose capacious surface see outspread
Large store of gleaming crimson-spotted trouts;
Ranged side by side, and lessening by degrees
Up to the dwarf that tops the pinnacle.   560
Upon the board he lays the sky-blue stone
With its rich freight; their number he proclaims;

543–5 so 1827: He said, and with that exclamation breathed
          A tender sigh;—but suddenly the door etc. as MS. supra,
          1814–20
549–50 so 1836: And by the river-side—from which they came
          A pair of Anglers, laden with their spoil.   MS., 1814–20
          And by the river's margin—whence they came
          Anglers elated with unusual spoil.   1827–32
552–5 so 1827: The Boy of plainer garb, and more abashed
          In countenance,—more distant and retired.
          Twin might the Other be to that fair Girl
          Who bounded tow'rds (towards 1820) us from the garden
          mount.
          Triumphant entry this to him!—for see,   1814–20; so MS.,
but In look at least more shy and more retired
557 see   1827: is   1814–20
559 so 1827: Ranged side by side, in regular ascent,
          (The lordliest first, and then of smaller size   MS.)
          One after one, still lessening by degrees   MS., 1814–20
562 freight   1827: spoil   MS., 1814–20

Tells from what pool the noblest had been dragged;
And where the very monarch of the brook,
After long struggle, had escaped at last—   565
Stealing alternately at them and us
(As doth his comrade too) a look of pride:
And, verily, the silent creatures made
A splendid sight, together thus exposed;
Dead—but not sullied or deformed by death,   570
That seemed to pity what he could not spare.

But O, the animation in the mien
Of those two boys! yea in the very words
With which the young narrator was inspired,
When, as our questions led, he told at large   575
Of that day's prowess! Him might I compare,
His looks, tones, gestures, eager eloquence,
To a bold brook that splits for better speed,
And at the self-same moment, works its way
Through many channels, ever and anon   580
Parted and re-united: his compeer
To the still lake, whose stillness is to sight
As beautiful—as grateful to the mind.
—But to what object shall the lovely Girl
Be likened? She whose countenance and air   585
Unite the graceful qualities of both,
Even as she shares the pride and joy of both.

My grey-haired Friend was moved; his vivid eye
Glistened with tenderness; his mind, I knew,
Was full; and had, I doubted not, returned,   590
Upon this impulse, to the theme—erewhile
Abruptly broken off. The ruddy boys
Withdrew, on summons to their well-earned meal;
And He—to whom all tongues resigned their rights
With willingness, to whom the general ear   595

567 As . . . too] Nor . . . less MS.   577 looks 1837: look 1814–32
582 to sight 1827: to the eye MS., 1814–20
587 Even as to spurious sensibility
    Untrained, she shares etc. MS.
593 so 1827: Did now withdraw to take MS., 1814–20

Listened with readier patience than to strain
Of music, lute or harp, a long delight
That ceased not when his voice had ceased—as One
Who from truth's central point serenely views
The compass of his argument—began   600
Mildly, and with a clear and steady tone.

599 Who from an Eminence   MS.

BOOK NINTH

DISCOURSE OF THE WANDERER AND AN EVENING VISIT TO THE LAKE

ARGUMENT

Wanderer asserts that an active principle pervades the Universe, its noblest seat the human soul.—How lively this principle is in Childhood.—Hence the delight in old Age of looking back upon Childhood.—The dignity, powers, and privileges of Age asserted.—These not to be looked for generally but under a just government.—Right of a human Creature to be exempt from being considered as a mere Instrument.[1]—The condition of multitudes deplored.[2]—Former conversation recurred to, and the Wanderer's opinions set in a clearer light.[3]—Truth placed within reach of the humblest.—Equality.[4]—Happy state of the two Boys again adverted to.—Earnest wish expressed for a System of National Education established universally by Government.—Glorious effects of this foretold.[5]—Walk to the Lake.—Grand spectacle from the side of a hill.—Address of Priest to the Supreme Being—in the course of which he contrasts with ancient Barbarism the present appearance of the scene before him.—The change ascribed to Christianity.—Apostrophe to his flock, living and dead.—Gratitude to the Almighty.—Return over the Lake.—Parting with the Solitary.—Under what circumstances.

"To every Form of being is assigned,"
Thus calmly spake the venerable Sage,
"An *active* Principle:—howe'er removed
From sense and observation, it subsists
In all things, in all natures; in the stars   5
Of azure heaven, the unenduring clouds,
In flower and tree, in every pebbly stone
That paves the brooks, the stationary rocks,
The moving waters, and the invisible air.
Whate'er exists hath properties that spread   10

[1] *so* 1837: Instrument—Vicious inclinations are best kept under by giving good ones an opportunity to shew themselves   1814–32.

[2] *so* 1837: deplored from want of due respect to this truth on the part of their superiors in society   1814–32.   [3] *so* 1837: light—Genuine principles of equality   1814–32.   [4] Equality *added*   1837.

[5] *so* 1837: foretold—Wanderer breaks off—Walk to the Lake—embark. Description of scenery and amusements   1814–32.

1–7 There is an active principle alive
      In all things, in all natures, in the flowers
      And in the trees *etc.*   MS. 18ᴬ
10–12 All beings have their properties which spread
      Beyond themselves, a power by which they make
      Some other being conscious of their life,   MS. 18ᴬ

Beyond itself, communicating good,
A simple blessing, or with evil mixed;
Spirit that knows no insulated spot,
No chasm, no solitude; from link to link
It circulates, the Soul of all the worlds.   15
This is the freedom of the universe;
Unfolded still the more, more visible,
The more we know; and yet is reverenced least,
And least respected in the human Mind,
Its most apparent home. The food of hope   20
Is meditated action; robbed of this
Her sole support, she languishes and dies.
We perish also; for we live by hope
And by desire; we see by the glad light
And breathe the sweet air of futurity;   25
And so we live, or else we have no life.
To-morrow—nay perchance this very hour
(For every moment hath its own to-morrow!)
Those blooming Boys, whose hearts are almost sick
With present triumph, will be sure to find   30
A field before them freshened with the dew
Of other expectations;—in which course
Their happy year spins round. The youth obeys
A like glad impulse; and so moves the man
'Mid all his apprehensions, cares, and fears,—   35
Or so he ought to move. Ah! why in age
Do we revert so fondly to the walks
Of childhood—but that there the Soul discerns
The dear memorial footsteps unimpaired
Of her own native vigour; thence can hear   40
Reverberations; and a choral song,

11 Beyond itself, for evil or for good   MS.   20 apparent] conspi-
cuous   MS.
24 And by desire; they are the very blood
  By which we move, we see by the sweet light   MS. 18ᴬ
27–128 And 'tis expressed in colours of the sun
        That we were never made to be content
        With simple abstinence from ill, for chains,
        For shackles and for bonds, but to be bound
        By laws in which there is a generating soul
        Allied to our own nature, and we know   MS. 18ᴬ
28 hath   1820: has   MS., 1814   40 thence can hear   1827:—but
for this, That it is given her thence in age to hear   MS., 1814–20

Commingling with the incense that ascends,
Undaunted, toward the imperishable heavens,
From her own lonely altar ?
                          Do not think
That good and wise ever will be allowed,   45
Though strength decay, to breathe in such estate
As shall divide them wholly from the stir
Of hopeful nature. Rightly it is said
That Man descends into the VALE of years;
Yet have I thought that we might also speak,   50
And not presumptuously, I trust, of Age,
As of a final EMINENCE; though bare
In aspect and forbidding, yet a point
On which 'tis not impossible to sit
In awful sovereignty; a place of power,   55
A throne, that may be likened unto his,
Who, in some placid day of summer, looks
Down from a mountain-top,—say one of those
High peaks, that bound the vale where now we are.
Faint, and diminished to the gazing eye,   60
Forest and field, and hill and dale appear,
With all the shapes over their surface spread:
But, while the gross and visible frame of things
Relinquishes its hold upon the sense,
Yea almost on the Mind herself, and seems   65
All unsubstantialized,—how loud the voice
Of waters, with invigorated peal
From the full river in the vale below,
Ascending! For on that superior height
Who sits, is disencumbered from the press   70
Of near obstructions, and is privileged
To breathe in solitude, above the host
Of ever-humming insects, 'mid thin air
That suits not them. The murmur of the leaves

43 toward   1837: tow'rds MS., 1814–20: tow'rd   1827–32   45
ever will   1832: will ever   MS., 1814–27   48 it is   1850: is it   MS.,
1814–45   56 that   1827: which MS., 1814–20   57 placid]
gentle MS.   61 Of one so stationed, hill *etc.* MS.   62 over
1845: upon   1814–43   65 herself 1827: itself MS., 1814–20
68 From Brook and River   MS.   69–72 Ascending—for he stands
above the host   MS. *corr. to*
                . . . for who gains that lofty point
                Is privileged : he stands above the host

Many and idle, visits not his ear: 75
This he is freed from, and from thousand notes
(Not less unceasing, not less vain than these,)
By which the finer passages of sense
Are occupied; and the Soul, that would incline
To listen, is prevented or deterred.   80

"And may it not be hoped, that, placed by age
In like removal, tranquil though severe,
We are not so removed for utter loss;
But for some favour, suited to our need?
What more than that the severing should confer   85
Fresh power to commune with the invisible world,
And hear the mighty stream of tendency
Uttering, for elevation of our thought,
A clear sonorous voice, inaudible
To the vast multitude; whose doom it is   90
To run the giddy round of vain delight,
Or fret and labour on the Plain below.

"But, if to such sublime ascent the hopes
Of Man may rise, as to a welcome close
And termination of his mortal course;   95
Them only can such hope inspire whose minds
Have not been starved by absolute neglect;
Nor bodies crushed by unremitting toil;
To whom kind Nature, therefore, may afford
Proof of the sacred love she bears for all;   100
Whose birthright Reason, therefore, may ensure.
For me, consulting what I feel within
In times when most existence with herself
Is satisfied, I cannot but believe,
That, far as kindly Nature hath free scope   105
And Reason's sway predominates; even so far,
Country, society, and time itself,

That saps the individual's bodily frame,
And lays the generations low in dust,
Do, by the almighty Ruler's grace, partake   110
Of one maternal spirit, bringing forth
And cherishing with ever-constant love,
That tires not, nor betrays. Our life is turned
Out of her course, wherever man is made
An offering, or a sacrifice, a tool   115
Or implement, a passive thing employed
As a brute mean, without acknowledgment
Of common right or interest in the end;
Used or abused, as selfishness may prompt.
Say, what can follow for a rational soul   120
Perverted thus, but weakness in all good,
And strength in evil? Hence an after-call
For chastisement, and custody, and bonds,
And oft-times Death, avenger of the past,
And the sole guardian in whose hands we dare   125
Entrust the future.—Not for these sad issues
Was Man created; but to obey the law
Of life, and hope, and action. And 'tis known
That when we stand upon our native soil,
Unelbowed by such objects as oppress   130
Our active powers, those powers themselves become
Strong to subvert our noxious qualities:

110–11 Have one maternal *etc*. MS.   112 ever-constant] never
wearied MS.   113 tires] faints MS.
126–9   . . . But the genuine law
'Tis one that prompts and urges and ⎫ Is that which is an impulse, yea,
impels,   ⎪   a soul
A law of life and action—for 'tis known ⎬ Akin to our own nature, for we
That when *etc*.   ⎭   know MSS.
130 oppress] constrain MS. 18ᴬ: distort MS.
132–40 Subversive of our noxious qualities,
          And by the substitution of delight,
          And by new influxes of strength suppress
          All evil, then the Being spreads abroad
          His branches to the wind, and all who see
          Bless him rejoicing in his neighbourhood.
          There is one only liberty, 'tis his
          Who by beneficence is circumscribed,
          'Tis his to whom the power of doing good
          Is law and statute, penalty and bond,
          His prison and his warder, his who finds
          His freedom in the joy of virtuous thoughts:
          Then sorrow to the many they in whom MS.

They sweep distemper from the busy day,
And make the chalice of the big round year
Run o'er with gladness; whence the Being moves   135
In beauty through the world; and all who see
Bless him, rejoicing in his neighbourhood."

"Then," said the Solitary, "by what force
Of language shall a feeling heart express
Her sorrow for that multitude in whom   140
We look for health from seeds that have been sown
In sickness, and for increase in a power
That works but by extinction? On themselves
They cannot lean, nor turn to their own hearts
To know what they must do; their wisdom is   145
To look into the eyes of others, thence
To be instructed what they must avoid:
Or rather, let us say, how least observed,
How with most quiet and most silent death,
With the least taint and injury to the air   150
The oppressor breathes, their human form divine,
And their immortal soul, may waste away."

The Sage rejoined, "I thank you—you have spared
My voice the utterance of a keen regret,
A wide compassion which with you I share.   155
When, heretofore, I placed before your sight
A Little-one, subjected to the arts
Of modern ingenuity, and made
The senseless member of a vast machine,
Serving as doth a spindle or a wheel;   160
Think not, that, pitying him, I could forget
The rustic Boy, who walks the fields, untaught;
The slave of ignorance, and oft of want,
And miserable hunger. Much, too much,
Of this unhappy lot, in early youth   165

133–5 *so* 1827–50 (*but* Vessel *for* chalice   1827):
　　　They sweep away infection from the heart;
　　　And, by the substitution of delight,
　　　Suppress all evil   1814–20
138 force   1827: power   1814–20   146/7 It is their virtue and their
discipline   MS. 18ᴬ   151 oppressor] rich man   MS. 18ᴬ
152 immortal] eternal   MS. 18ᴬ   MS. *v. notes*   156/7 A most familiar
object of our days,   MS., 1814–20

We both have witnessed, lot which I myself
Shared, though in mild and merciful degree:
Yet was the mind to hinderances exposed,
Through which I struggled, not without distress
And sometimes injury, like a lamb enthralled   170
'Mid thorns and brambles; or a bird that breaks
Through a strong net, and mounts upon the wind,
Though with her plumes impaired. If they, whose souls
Should open while they range the richer fields
Of merry England, are obstructed less   175
By indigence, their ignorance is not less,
Nor less to be deplored. For who can doubt
That tens of thousands at this day exist
Such as the boy you painted, lineal heirs
Of those who once were vassals of her soil,   180
Following its fortunes like the beasts or trees
Which it sustained. But no one takes delight
In this oppression; none are proud of it;
It bears no sounding name, nor ever bore;
A standing grievance, an indigenous vice   185
Of every country under heaven. My thoughts
Were turned to evils that are new and chosen,
A bondage lurking under shape of good,—
Arts, in themselves beneficent and kind,
But all too fondly followed and too far;—   190
To victims, which the merciful can see
Nor think that they are victims—turned to wrongs,
By women, who have children of their own,
Beheld without compassion, yea with praise!
I spake of mischief by the wise diffused   195
With gladness, thinking that the more it spreads
The healthier, the securer, we become;
Delusion which a moment may destroy!
Lastly I mourned for those whom I had seen
Corrupted and cast down, on favoured ground,   200
Where circumstance and nature had combined
To shelter innocence, and cherish love;

168 the mind   1827: my mind   1814–20: my youth   MS.   170 lamb
1827: Sheep   MS., 1814–20
186–7 Of every age and country under heaven,
    I spoke of cherished evils new and chosen,   MS.
193–4 By ... Beheld   1827: Which ... Regard   MS., 1814–20

Who, but for this intrusion, would have lived,
Possessed of health, and strength, and peace of mind;
Thus would have lived, or never have been born.   205

"Alas! what differs more than man from man!
And whence that difference ? Whence but from himself ?
For see the universal Race endowed
With the same upright form!—The sun is fixed,
And the infinite magnificence of heaven   210
Fixed, within reach of every human eye;
The sleepless ocean murmurs for all ears;
The vernal field infuses fresh delight
Into all hearts. Throughout the world of sense,
Even as an object is sublime or fair,   215
That object is laid open to the view
Without reserve or veil; and as a power
Is salutary, or an influence sweet,
Are each and all enabled to perceive
That power, that influence, by impartial law.   220
Gifts nobler are vouchsafed alike to all;
Reason, and, with that reason, smiles and tears;
Imagination, freedom in the will;
Conscience to guide and check; and death to be
Foretasted, immortality conceived   225
By all,—a blissful immortality,
To them whose holiness on earth shall make
The Spirit capable of heaven, assured.
Strange, then, nor less than monstrous, might be deemed
The failure, if the Almighty, to this point   230
Liberal and undistinguishing, should hide
The excellence of moral qualities
From common understanding; leaving truth
And virtue, difficult, abstruse, and dark;
Hard to be won, and only by a few;   235
Strange, should He deal herein with nice respects,
And frustrate all the rest! Believe it not:
The primal duties shine aloft—like stars;
The charities that soothe, and heal, and bless,

204/5 And all their old hereditary rights MS.   211 *so* 1827: Within
the reach MS., 1814–20   225 conceived 1845: presumed MS.,
1814–43   226–8 *added* 1845   231 Liberal] Bountiful C   233
understanding] observation MS.

Are scattered at the feet of Man—like flowers.   240
The generous inclination, the just rule,
Kind wishes, and good actions, and pure thoughts—
No mystery is here! Here is no boon
For high—yet not for low; for proudly graced—
Yet not for meek of heart. The smoke ascends   245
To heaven as lightly from the cottage-hearth
As from the haughtiest palace. He, whose soul
Ponders this true equality, may walk
The fields of earth with gratitude and hope;
Yet, in that meditation, will he find   250
Motive to sadder grief, as we have found;
Lamenting ancient virtues overthrown,
And for the injustice grieving, that hath made
So wide a difference between man and man.

"Then let us rather fix our gladdened thoughts   255
Upon the brighter scene. How blest that pair
Of blooming Boys (whom we beheld even now)
Blest in their several and their common lot!
A few short hours of each returning day
The thriving prisoners of their village-school: 260
And thence let loose, to seek their pleasant homes
Or range the grassy lawn in vacancy;
To breathe and to be happy, run and shout
Idle,—but no delay, no harm, no loss;
For every genial power of heaven and earth,   265
Through all the seasons of the changeful year,
Obsequiously doth take upon herself
To labour for them; bringing each in turn
The tribute of enjoyment, knowledge, health,
Beauty, or strength! Such privilege is theirs,   270
Granted alike in the outset of their course
To both; and, if that partnership must cease,
I grieve not," to the Pastor here he turned,
"Much as I glory in that child of yours,

243 here! Here is no 1837: here; no special MS., 1814–32   244–5
yet . . . Yet 1837: and . . . And MS., 1814–32   247 haughtiest
1837: proudest *corr. to* haughty MS.: haughty 1814–32   253 And
sorrowing for the injustice MS.   254 between 1837: betwixt MS.,
1814–32   255 Then 1837: But MS., 1814–27: fix MS., 1814–20,
1837: turn: 1827–32: gladdened] happy MS.   261 pleasant] chearful
MS.   272 and if hereafter they must part MS.

Repine not for his cottage-comrade, whom   275
Belike no higher destiny awaits
Than the old hereditary wish fulfilled;
The wish for liberty to live—content
With what Heaven grants, and die—in peace of mind,
Within the bosom of his native vale.   280
At least, whatever fate the noon of life
Reserves for either, sure it is that both
Have been permitted to enjoy the dawn;
Whether regarded as a jocund time,
That in itself may terminate, or lead   285
In course of nature to a sober eve.
Both have been fairly dealt with; looking back
They will allow that justice has in them
Been shown, alike to body and to mind."

He paused, as if revolving in his soul   290
Some weighty matter; then, with fervent voice
And an impassioned majesty, exclaimed—

"O for the coming of that glorious time
When, prizing knowledge as her noblest wealth
And best protection, this imperial Realm,   295
While she exacts allegiance, shall admit
An obligation, on her part, to *teach*
Them who are born to serve her and obey;
Binding herself by statute to secure
For all the children whom her soil maintains   300
The rudiments of letters, and inform
The mind with moral and religious truth,
Both understood and practised,—so that none,

275–80   . . . the fair-faced peasant boy,
His lowly Comrade, destined here, perchance, (perhaps,)
To live and die in calm obscurity (humble innocence)   MS.
282 sure it is   1837: this is sure   MS., 1814–32   284 jocund] care-
less   MS.
293–6 O for that happy period, ages past
Not unforseen nor unprepared, though Heaven,
A saintly (Royal) Youth removing from his throne
Before his cherished purpose was fulfilled,
Did to this Land's unworthiness refuse
The pretious boon—to think the time were come (that era I invoke)
Too long deferred, when this enlightened Realm,
On knowledge resting as her surest prop,
While she *etc.*   MSS.

However destitute, be left to droop
By timely culture unsustained; or run   305
Into a wild disorder; or be forced
To drudge through a weary life without the help
Of intellectual implements and tools;
A savage horde among the civilised,
A servile band among the lordly free!   310
This sacred right, the lisping babe proclaims
To be inherent in him, by Heaven's will,
For the protection of his innocence;
And the rude boy—who, having overpast
The sinless age, by conscience is enrolled,   315
Yet mutinously knits his angry brow,
And lifts his wilful hand on mischief bent,
Or turns the godlike faculty of speech
To impious use—by process indirect
Declares his due, while he makes known his need.   320
—This sacred right is fruitlessly announced,
This universal plea in vain addressed,
To eyes and ears of parents who themselves
Did, in the time of their necessity,
Urge it in vain; and, therefore, like a prayer   325
That from the humblest floor ascends to heaven,
It mounts to reach the State's parental ear;

300–7 To all, at least place within reach of all
         The Rudiments of learning, so that none
         As they grow up, however desolate,
         (However needy, poor or destitute)
         Shall be compelled to drudge without the aid   MSS.
307 a weary . . . help   1837: weary . . . aid   1814–32
311 *so* 1827: This right, as sacred almost as the right
                To exist and be supplied with sustenance
                And means of life, the lisping Babe proclaims   MSS., 1814–20
312–16 To be invested (inherent) in his innocence;
                And the rude Lad (Boy) who knits his sullen (angry) brow   MSS.
317 wilful] untaught (unchecked) MS.   318 godlike 1827: sacred
MS., 1814–20
321–2 In vain the right of Nature is announced
         The discipline of slavery is unknown
         To England, hence the more doth she require
         The discipline of Virtue, how can else
         Order exist, security or peace ? (*v. ll.* 351–4)
         The plea is universal—the demand
         A just demand of human nature, yet
         It is, and must be, fruitlessly addressed   MS.

Who, if indeed she own a mother's heart,
And be not most unfeelingly devoid
Of gratitude to Providence, will grant   330
The unquestionable good—which, England, safe
From interference of external force,
May grant at leisure; without risk incurred
That what in wisdom for herself she doth,
Others shall e'er be able to undo.   335

    "Look! and behold, from Calpe's sunburnt cliffs
To the flat margin of the Baltic sea,
Long-reverenced titles cast away as weeds;
Laws overturned; and territory split,
Like fields of ice rent by the polar wind,   340
And forced to join in less obnoxious shapes
Which, ere they gain consistence, by a gust
Of the same breath are shattered and destroyed.
Meantime the sovereignty of these fair Isles
Remains entire and indivisible: 345
And, if that ignorance were removed, which breeds
Within the compass of their several shores
Dark discontent, or loud commotion, each
Might still preserve the beautiful repose
Of heavenly bodies shining in their spheres.   350
—The discipline of slavery is unknown
Among us,—hence the more do we require
The discipline of virtue; order else
Cannot subsist, nor confidence, nor peace.
Thus, duties rising out of good possest   355
And prudent caution needful to avert
Impending evil, equally require
That the whole people should be taught and trained.
So shall licentiousness and black resolve
Be rooted out, and virtuous habits take   360

329–31 Must grant what England consciously secure   MS.   342
Which   1845, MS., 1814–32: That   1837–43   346 breeds   1827:
acts   MS., 1814–20
348–9 *so* 1827: To breed commotion and disquietude,
                Each might preserve *etc.*   MS., 1814–20
357 equally] obviously   MS.
357–8 *so* 1827:   . . . do alike require
                That permanent provision should be made
                For the whole people to be *etc.*   MS., 1814–20

Their place; and genuine piety descend,
Like an inheritance, from age to age.

"With such foundations laid, avaunt the fear
Of numbers crowded on their native soil,
To the prevention of all healthful growth   365
Through mutual injury! Rather in the law
Of increase and the mandate from above
Rejoice!—and ye have special cause for joy.
—For, as the element of air affords
An easy passage to the industrious bees   370
Fraught with their burthens; and a way as smooth
For those ordained to take their sounding flight
From the thronged hive, and settle where they list
In fresh abodes—their labour to renew;
So the wide waters, open to the power,   375
The will, the instincts, and appointed needs
Of Britain, do invite her to cast off
Her swarms, and in succession send them forth;
Bound to establish new communities
On every shore whose aspect favours hope   380
Or bold adventure; promising to skill
And perseverance their deserved reward.

"Yes," he continued, kindling as he spake,
"Change wide, and deep, and silently performed,
This Land shall witness; and as days roll on,   385
Earth's universal frame shall feel the effect;
Even till the smallest habitable rock,
Beaten by lonely billows, hear the songs
Of humanised society; and bloom
With civil arts, that shall breathe forth their fragrance, 390
A grateful tribute to all-ruling Heaven.
From culture, unexclusively bestowed

361/2 Upon the humblest member (subject) of the State,   C
386/7 Through her broad Continents and scattered Isles   MS.   388
That Ocean beats (lulls) with solitary waves   MS.   389–91 *not in* MS.
390 *so* 1845: With civil arts, and (that 1827–43) send their fragrance forth
1814–43
392–3 *so* 1827:
  From Culture, universally bestowed
  On Britain's (Upon a MS.) noble Race in freedom born;
  From (True MS.) Education, from that humble source   MS., 1814–20

On Albion's noble Race in freedom born,
Expect these mighty issues: from the pains
And faithful care of unambitious schools   395
Instructing simple childhood's ready ear:
Thence look for these magnificent results!
—Vast the circumference of hope—and ye
Are at its centre, British Lawgivers;
Ah! sleep not there in shame! Shall Wisdom's voice   400
From out the bosom of these troubled times
Repeat the dictates of her calmer mind,
And shall the venerable halls ye fill
Refuse to echo the sublime decree?
Trust not to partial care a general good;   405
Transfer not to futurity a work
Of urgent need.—Your Country must complete
Her glorious destiny. Begin even now,
Now, when oppression, like the Egyptian plague
Of darkness, stretched o'er guilty Europe, makes   410
The brightness more conspicuous that invests
The happy Island where ye think and act;
Now, when destruction is a prime pursuit,
Show to the wretched nations for what end
The powers of civil polity were given."   415

　　Abruptly here, but with a graceful air,
The Sage broke off. No sooner had he ceased

395 faithful 1827: quiet MS., 1814–20
398–407 So from the virtues of a petty seed,
　　　　Which in his thievish bill the flying Crow
　　　　Transports without encumbrance, are evolved
　　　　Trunk, limbs, and umbrage of the giant oak
　　　　Darkening the noontide, so from some still fount,
　　　　Which the exulting Traveller bestrides
　　　　With sportive ease and proud complacency,
　　　　Proceeds the state of Ganges, or the Nile.
　　　　Awake, ye Rulers of these favoured Realms,
　　　　Awake! assist your Country to fulfill   MS.
411–12 　　　　　　　　. . . conspicuous appear
　　　　In which we move about and think and act   MS.
413/14 And with the anxieties of beastly war
　　　　Your minds are through necessity oppressed   MS.
416–17 At once descending from the height of zeal
　　　　Here gracefully the impassioned Sage broke off
　　　　By apprehension checked lest his discourse
　　　　Might tire the Listener's patience and exhaust
　　　　His sympathy. No sooner etc.   MS.

Than, looking forth, the gentle Lady said,
"Behold the shades of afternoon have fallen
Upon this flowery slope; and see—beyond—   420
The silvery lake is streaked with placid blue;
As if preparing for the peace of evening.
How temptingly the landscape shines! The air
Breathes invitation; easy is the walk
To the lake's margin, where a boat lies moored   425
Under a sheltering tree."—Upon this hint
We rose together: all were pleased; but most
The beauteous girl, whose cheek was flushed with joy.
Light as a sunbeam glides along the hills
She vanished—eager to impart the scheme   430
To her loved brother and his shy compeer.
—Now was there bustle in the Vicar's house
And earnest preparation.—Forth we went,
And down the vale along the streamlet's edge
Pursued our way, a broken company,   435
Mute or conversing, single or in pairs.
Thus having reached a bridge, that overarched
The hasty rivulet where it lay becalmed
In a deep pool, by happy chance we saw
A twofold image; on a grassy bank   440
A snow-white ram, and in the crystal flood
Another and the same! Most beautiful,
On the green turf, with his imperial front
Shaggy and bold, and wreathèd horns superb,
The breathing creature stood; as beautiful,   445
Beneath him, showed his shadowy counterpart.
Each had his glowing mountains, each his sky,
And each seemed centre of his own fair world:
Antipodes unconscious of each other,
Yet, in partition, with their several spheres,   450
Blended in perfect stillness, to our sight!

"Ah! what a pity were it to disperse,
Or to disturb, so fair a spectacle,

---

421 *so* 1837: The lake, though bright, is of a placid blue; MS., 1814–32:
The silvery lake streaked with a placid hue   C   423/4 Whose fervent
heat already is allayed   MS.   426 Under a   1845: Beneath its MS.:
Beneath her   1814–43   434 *so* 1827: And down the Valley on the
Streamlet's bank   MS., 1814–20   437–48 *v. notes*   439 By a flat
meadow, at a glance I saw   MS.   441 crystal] peaceful   MS.

And yet a breath can do it!"

                These few words
The Lady whispered, while we stood and gazed   455
Gathered together, all in still delight,
Not without awe. Thence passing on, she said
In like low voice to my particular ear,
"I love to hear that eloquent old Man
Pour forth his meditations, and descant   460
On human life from infancy to age.
How pure his spirit! in what vivid hues
His mind gives back the various forms of things,
Caught in their fairest, happiest, attitude!
While he is speaking, I have power to see   465
Even as he sees; but when his voice hath ceased,
Then, with a sigh, sometimes I feel, as now,
That combinations so serene and bright
Cannot be lasting in a world like ours,
Whose highest beauty, beautiful as it is,   470
Like that reflected in yon quiet pool,
Seems but a fleeting sunbeam's gift, whose peace
The sufferance only of a breath of air!"

    More had she said—but sportive shouts were heard
Sent from the jocund hearts of those two Boys,   475

461/2 Far back as he remembers, and as far
    As he looks forward cheered by pensive hope
    And wide in compass as a tender heart
    Hath by experience taught him to observe
    Or strong Imagination to conceive.   MS.
462 How bright the picture, in what vivid (living) hues
    Doth he reflect the character of things
    { Even like that image in the silent pool }
    { A mirror faithful as that silent pool }   MS.
467 *so* 1832: I sometimes feel   1814–27
468 so divinely fair   MS.
469–73 *so* 1845:
  Cannot be lasting in a world like ours
  To great and small disturbances exposed;
  But him they shake not—hardly seem to touch.   MS.: 1814–32 *have the
first two of these lines, preceded by* Like those reflected (*etc.* 471):
        Like those reflected in yon silent pool
        Cannot be lasting in a world whose pleasure
        (And whose best beauty, beautiful as it is)
        Seems *etc. as text*, 1837: 1840–3 *as text but* l. 470 One whose
           best beauty *etc.*
475 jocund] merry   MS.

Who, bearing each a basket on his arm,
Down the green field came tripping after us.
With caution we embarked; and now the pair
For prouder service were addrest; but each,
Wishful to leave an opening for my choice,　　　　480
Dropped the light oar his eager hand had seized.
Thanks given for that becoming courtesy,
Their place I took—and for a grateful office
Pregnant with recollections of the time
When, on thy bosom, spacious Windermere!　　　　485
A Youth, I practised this delightful art;
Tossed on the waves alone, or 'mid a crew
Of joyous comrades. Soon as the reedy marge
Was cleared, I dipped, with arms accordant, oars
Free from obstruction; and the boat advanced　　　　490
Through crystal water, smoothly as a hawk,
That, disentangled from the shady boughs
Of some thick wood, her place of covert, cleaves
With correspondent wings the abyss of air.
—"Observe," the Vicar said, "yon rocky isle　　　　495
With birch-trees fringed; my hand shall guide the helm,
While thitherward we shape our course; or while

478–83 *so* 1837: Our company embarked, and orders given
　　　　　　　　And requisite authority put forth,
　　　　　　　　Those inexperienced voyagers were hushed
　　　　　　　　Into secure composure. Looks and words
　　　　　　　　Expressed the wishes of that youthful pair,
　　　　　　　　But an inexorable law forbade,
　　　　　　　　And each resigned the oar which he had seized.
　　　　　　　　Whereat with willing hand I undertook
　　　　　　　　The oarsman's labour, pleasant task to me　MS.
　　　　　　　　When we had cautiously embarked, the Pair
　　　　　　　　Now for a prouder service were addrest;
　　　　　　　　But an inexorable *etc. as* MS. *but* needful *for* oarsman's *and*
　　　　　　　　　　grateful *for* pleasant　1814–32
487–8　　　　　　　　　　. . . mid a band
　　Of happy Comrades. "Towards yon rocky Isle
　　Clothed with transparent birch-trees bend your course"
　　The Vicar said, and pointed as he spoke,
　　"Or tow'rds that other on the western shore.　MS., *draft* i, (488–94
　　　　(Soon . . . air) *added later*)
488–9 *so* 1837: Now, the reedy marge
　　　　　　　　Cleared, with a strenuous arm I dipped the oar　1814–32
490 Free from] Without　MS.　　491 crystal] the clear　MS.　　497
shape　1837: bend　1814–32

We seek that other, on the western shore;
Where the bare columns of those lofty firs,
Supporting gracefully a massy dome   500
Of sombre foliage, seem to imitate
A Grecian temple rising from the Deep."

"Turn where we may," said I, "we cannot err
In this delicious region."—Cultured slopes,
Wild tracts of forest-ground, and scattered groves,   505
And mountains bare, or clothed with ancient woods,
Surrounded us; and, as we held our way
Along the level of the glassy flood,
They ceased not to surround us; change of place,
From kindred features diversely combined,   510
Producing change of beauty ever new.
—Ah! that such beauty, varying in the light
Of living nature, cannot be portrayed
By words, nor by the pencil's silent skill;
But is the property of him alone   515
Who hath beheld it, noted it with care,
And in his mind recorded it with love!
Suffice it, therefore, if the rural Muse
Vouchsafe sweet influence, while her Poet speaks
Of trivial occupations well devised,   520
And unsought pleasures springing up by chance;
As if some friendly Genius had ordained
That, as the day thus far had been enriched
By acquisition of sincere delight,
The same should be continued to its close.   525

One spirit animating old and young,
A gipsy-fire we kindled on the shore

501 sombre] darksome C   505 Rich fields and sylvan slopes, and
rugged rocks MS.   508 surface of the crystal MS.   510
diversely] variously MS.
513 Of living Nature and presented thus
    In smooth succession cannot etc. MS.
518–19 Yet if of willing auditors secure,
       Much could the Poet tell of objects seen
       With admiration fervent and sincere corr. to
       Suppressing, therefore, all desire to aim
       At that which is not in his power to reach
       It shall suffice the Poet if he speak MS.
523–4 replete With pure enjoyment and serene delight MS.

Of the fair Isle with birch-trees fringed—and there,
Merrily seated in a ring, partook
A choice repast—served by our young companions   530
With rival earnestness and kindred glee.
Launched from our hands the smooth stone skimmed the lake;
With shouts we raised the echoes;—stiller sounds
The lovely Girl supplied—a simple song,
Whose low tones reached not to the distant rocks   535
To be repeated thence, but gently sank
Into our hearts; and charmed the peaceful flood.
Rapaciously we gathered flowery spoils
From land and water; lilies of each hue—
Golden and white, that float upon the waves,   540
And court the wind; and leaves of that shy plant,
(Her flowers were shed) the lily of the vale,
That loves the ground, and from the sun withholds
Her pensive beauty; from the breeze her sweets.

    Such product, and such pastime, did the place   545
And season yield; but, as we re-embarked,
Leaving, in quest of other scenes, the shore
Of that wild spot, the Solitary said
In a low voice, yet careless who might hear,
"The fire, that burned so brightly to our wish,   550
Where is it now?—Deserted on the beach—
Dying, or dead! Nor shall the fanning breeze
Revive its ashes. What care we for this,
Whose ends are gained? Behold an emblem here
Of one day's pleasure, and all mortal joys!   555
And, in this unpremeditated slight
Of that which is no longer needed, see
The common course of human gratitude!"

528 Of that fair Island, and beneath its trees MS.   530 by youthful
Pages served C   530–1 *so* 1837: The beverage drawn from China's
fragrant herb MS., 1814–32   533 raised 1837: roused MS., 1814–32
536 thence 1827: there MS., 1814–20   541–2 leaves . . . shed *not*
in MS.   544/5 Shyest of plants (flowers) yet social to (with) her kind
MS.   552 Dying or dead 1837: It seems extinct MS., 1814–32
554 Whose needs are served MS.
556–8 Of that whereof we have no human need
    An emblem too of human gratitude
    That kindles promptly and as soon expires MS.

This plaintive note disturbed not the repose
Of the still evening. Right across the lake   560
Our pinnace moves; then, coasting creek and bay,
Glades we behold, and into thickets peep,
Where couch the spotted deer; or raised our eyes
To shaggy steeps on which the careless goat
Browsed by the side of dashing waterfalls;   565
And thus the bark, meandering with the shore,
Pursued her voyage, till a natural pier
Of jutting rock invited us to land.

Alert to follow as the Pastor led,
We clomb a green hill's side; and, as we clomb,   570
The Valley, opening out her bosom, gave
Fair prospect, intercepted less and less,
O'er the flat meadows and indented coast
Of the smooth lake, in compass seen:—far off,
And yet conspicuous, stood the old Church-tower,   575
In majesty presiding over fields
And habitations seemingly preserved
From all intrusion of the restless world
By rocks impassable and mountains huge.

Soft heath this elevated spot supplied,   580
And choice of moss-clad stones, whereon we couched

560–74 . . . evening. Southward now we steered
　　　And by assistance of a jutting rock
　　　That framed a natural pier we landed all
　　　On the main shore, and climbing the steep side
　　　Of a green hill that from the water's edge
　　　Rose with a bold ascent we there attained
　　　Slowly, a less and less obstructed sight
　　　Of the whole lake *etc.*   MS.
566–7 *so* 1837: Thus did . . . Pursue   1814–32
567–8 *so* 1827: . . . till a point was gained
　　　　　Where a projecting line of rock, that framed
　　　　　A natural pier, invited us to land.   1814–20
570–4 *so* 1827: side; and thence obtained Slowly *etc. as* MS., 1814–20   573
O'er 1837: Of MS., 1814–32   574 smooth 1827: whole 1814–20
576–7 *so* 1827: o'er the Vale And all her dwellings MS., 1814–20   578
all . . . the 1845: the . . . a MS., 1814–43
580–4 Upon this elevated spot we stood
　　　Lingering well pleased, admiring quietly
　　　And each not seldom eager to point out   MS.
581–4 *so* 1827: With resting-place of mossy stone;—and there
　　　　　We sate reclined—admiring quietly

Or sate reclined; admiring quietly
The general aspect of the scene; but each
Not seldom over anxious to make known
His own discoveries; or to favourite points   585
Directing notice, merely from a wish
To impart a joy, imperfect while unshared.
That rapturous moment never shall I forget
When these particular interests were effaced
From every mind!—Already had the sun,   590
Sinking with less than ordinary state,
Attained his western bound; but rays of light—
Now suddenly diverging from the orb
Retired behind the mountain-tops or veiled
By the dense air—shot upwards to the crown   595
Of the blue firmament—aloft, and wide:
And multitudes of little floating clouds,
Through their ethereal texture pierced—ere we,
Who saw, of change were conscious—had become
Vivid as fire; clouds separately poised,—   600
Innumerable multitude of forms
Scattered through half the circle of the sky;
And giving back, and shedding each on each,
With prodigal communion, the bright hues
Which from the unapparent fount of glory   605
They had imbibed, and ceased not to receive.
That which the heavens displayed, the liquid deep
Repeated; but with unity sublime!

The frame and general aspect of the scene;
  And each not seldom eager to make known   1814–20
588 never   1837: ne'er   1814–32
588–90 Until these acts of mutual regard
    And little separate notices were lost
    In one impression that possessed the soul
    Of all who saw. Already *etc.*   MS.
    Until these signs of mutual regard
    And small particular interests were effaced
    By one impression that possessed the soul
    Of all who saw.   MS. *alt.*
594–5 Behind the summit of the [? western] hill
    Withdrawn or veiled, shot *etc.*   MS.
598 *so* 1837: Pierced through their thin etherial mould, ere we,   MS.,
1814–20: Ere we, who saw, of change were conscious, pierced   1827–32
599 *so* MS., 1814–20, 1837: Through their etherial texture, had become
1827–32

While from the grassy mountain's open side
We gazed, in silence hushed, with eyes intent   610
On the refulgent spectacle, diffused
Through earth, sky, water, and all visible space,
The Priest in holy transport thus exclaimed:

"Eternal Spirit! universal God!
Power inaccessible to human thought,   615
Save by degrees and steps which thou hast deigned
To furnish; for this effluence of thyself,
To the infirmity of mortal sense
Vouchsafed; this local transitory type
Of thy paternal splendours, and the pomp   620
Of those who fill thy courts in highest heaven,
The radiant Cherubim;—accept the thanks
Which we, thy humble Creatures, here convened,
Presume to offer; we, who—from the breast
Of the frail earth, permitted to behold   625
The faint reflections only of thy face—
Are yet exalted, and in soul adore!
Such as they are who in thy presence stand
Unsullied, incorruptible, and drink
Imperishable majesty streamed forth   630
From thy empyreal throne, the elect of earth
Shall be—divested at the appointed hour
Of all dishonour, cleansed from mortal stain.
—Accomplish, then, their number; and conclude
Time's weary course! Or if, by thy decree,   635
The consummation that will come by stealth
Be yet far distant, let thy Word prevail,
Oh! let thy Word prevail, to take away
The sting of human nature. Spread the law,
As it is written in thy holy book,   640
Throughout all lands: let every nation hear
The high behest, and every heart obey;
Both for the love of purity, and hope

615 Through every region of the spatious earth
    And through all worlds where'er the light of life
    Is kindled, and intelligence abides
    Adored and dreaded. Being infinite
    And inaccessible *etc.* MS.
617 effluence] 1827: Image 1814–20   617–18 For this material
image of thyself MS.   623 Which we] Of us MS., *omitting* 624–7

Which it affords, to such as do thy will
And persevere in good, that they shall rise,   645
To have a nearer view of thee, in heaven.
—Father of good! this prayer in bounty grant,
In mercy grant it, to thy wretched sons.
Then, nor till then, shall persecution cease,
And cruel wars expire. The way is marked,   650
The guide appointed, and the ransom paid.
Alas! the nations, who of yore received
These tidings, and in Christian temples meet
The sacred truth to acknowledge, linger still;
Preferring bonds and darkness to a state   655
Of holy freedom, by redeeming love
Proffered to all, while yet on earth detained.

    "So fare the many; and the thoughtful few,
Who in the anguish of their souls bewail
This dire perverseness, cannot choose but ask,   660
Shall it endure?—Shall enmity and strife,
Falsehood and guile, be left to sow their seed;
And the kind never perish? Is the hope
Fallacious, or shall righteousness obtain
A peaceable dominion, wide as earth,   665
And ne'er to fail? Shall that blest day arrive
When they, whose choice or lot it is to dwell
In crowded cities, without fear shall live
Studious of mutual benefit; and he,
Whom Morn awakens, among dews and flowers   670
Of every clime, to till the lonely field,
Be happy in himself?—The law of faith
Working through love, such conquest shall it gain,
Such triumph over sin and guilt achieve?
Almighty Lord, thy further grace impart!   675

652-4 But they who knew—the nations who of yore
    Heard, and erected temples where they meet
    Do in their souls' perverseness linger still   MS.
658-66 Shall this be so? And shall the misery
    Deceit and guile be left to sow their seed
    And the kind never perish? Is the hope
    Fallacious, or will that blest day arrive
    When righteousness shall win and hold the world
    In peaceable dominion ne'er to fail   MS.
668/9 Of public outrages and private wrong   MS.   670 so 1837:
Whom morning wakes, among sweet dews and flowers   MS., 1814-32

And with that help the wonder shall be seen
Fulfilled, the hope accomplished ; and thy praise
Be sung with transport and unceasing joy.

"Once," and with mild demeanour, as he spake,
On us the venerable Pastor turned   680
His beaming eye that had been raised to Heaven,
"Once, while the Name, Jehovah, was a sound
Within the circuit of this sea-girt isle
Unheard, the savage nations bowed the head
To Gods delighting in remorseless deeds ;   685
Gods which themselves had fashioned, to promote
Ill purposes, and flatter foul desires.
Then, in the bosom of yon mountain-cove,
To those inventions of corrupted man
Mysterious rites were solemnised ; and there—   690
Amid impending rocks and gloomy woods—
Of those terrific Idols some received
Such dismal service, that the loudest voice
Of the swoln cataracts (which now are heard
Soft murmuring) was too weak to overcome,   695
Though aided by wild winds, the groans and shrieks
Of human victims, offered up to appease
Or to propitiate. And, if living eyes

679 mild 1827–45: wild 1850   679–81 *added* 1827
681 that Heavenward had been raised C   683 Amid the forests of
etc. MS.   684 the head 1827: their heads MS., 1814–20
688 Then, mid these mountainous retreats (mountain fastnesses), (for here
    May yet be seen memorials of that age
    In unmolested solitude preserved) MS.
690–1   . . . in groves
    Gloomy and still, selected from the depths
    Of deepest forests, Nature's silent holds
    And awe-inspiring fastnesses ; secure
    From all intrusion, till by steel and flame
    They were laid waste—the consecrated oaks
    Felled to the ground and altars overturned MS.
692 *so* 1827 : dread Idols some, perchance, 1814–20 terrific] accursed MS.
694–5 Of the perpetual streams (which now are heard
    Soft murmuring) in the season of their rage
    And highest fury were too weak to drown MS.
698–703 Or to propitiate—and this wide-spread mere
    Oft in the quiet of a summer eve
    Reddened from shore to shore with streaming blaze (ghastly light)
    Flung from the heart of those devouring fires MS.

Had visionary faculties to see
The thing that hath been as the thing that is,   700
Aghast we might behold this crystal Mere
Bedimmed with smoke, in wreaths voluminous,
Flung from the body of devouring fires,
To Taranis erected on the heights
By priestly hands, for sacrifice performed   705
Exultingly, in view of open day
And full assemblage of a barbarous host;
Or to Andates, female Power! who gave
(For so they fancied) glorious victory.
—A few rude monuments of mountain-stone   710
Survive; all else is swept away.—How bright
The appearances of things! From such, how changed
The existing worship; and with those compared,
The worshippers how innocent and blest!
So wide the difference, a willing mind   715
Might almost think, at this affecting hour,
That paradise, the lost abode of man,
Was raised again: and to a happy few,
In its original beauty, here restored.

"Whence but from thee, the true and only God,   720
And from the faith derived through Him who bled
Upon the cross, this marvellous advance
Of good from evil; as if one extreme
Were left, the other gained.—O ye, who come
To kneel devoutly in yon reverend Pile,   725
Called to such office by the peaceful sound
Of sabbath bells; and ye, who sleep in earth,
All cares forgotten, round its hallowed walls!
For you, in presence of this little band
Gathered together on the green hill-side,   730
Your Pastor is emboldened to prefer
Vocal thanksgivings to the eternal King;
Whose love, whose counsel, whose commands, have made

701 crystal 1827: spacious 1814-20
710-14 And mark the appearances of things—how changed
       From such the worship; and with that compare
       The worshipper MS.
716 so 1837: At this affecting hour, might almost think MS., 1814-32
727/8 Living or dead an undivided flock MS.

Your very poorest rich in peace of thought
And in good works; and him, who is endowed   735
With scantiest knowledge, master of all truth
Which the salvation of his soul requires.
Conscious of that abundant favour showered
On you, the children of my humble care,
And this dear land, our country, while on earth   740
We sojourn, have I lifted up my soul,
Joy giving voice to fervent gratitude.
These barren rocks, your stern inheritance;
These fertile fields, that recompense your pains;
The shadowy vale, the sunny mountain-top;   745
Woods waving in the wind their lofty heads,
Or hushed; the roaring waters, and the still—
They see the offering of my lifted hands,
They hear my lips present their sacrifice,
They know if I be silent, morn or even: 750
For, though in whispers speaking, the full heart
Will find a vent; and thought is praise to him,
Audible praise, to thee, omniscient Mind,
From whom all gifts descend, all blessings flow!"

This vesper-service closed, without delay,   755
From that exalted station to the plain
Descending, we pursued our homeward course,
In mute composure, o'er the shadowy lake,
Under a faded sky. No trace remained
Of those celestial splendours; grey the vault—   760
Pure, cloudless, ether; and the star of eve
Was wanting; but inferior lights appeared
Faintly, too faint almost for sight; and some
Above the darkened hills stood boldly forth
In twinkling lustre, ere the boat attained   765
Her mooring-place; where, to the sheltering tree,
Our youthful Voyagers bound fast her prow,
With prompt yet careful hands. This done, we paced

740-2 *so* 1827:
   On your Abodes, and this beloved Land,
   Our birthplace, home, and Country, while on Earth
   We sojourn,—loudly do I utter thanks
   With earnest joy, that will not be suppressed.   MS., 1814-20
743-7 Rocks, rivers, mountains, woods, and watry Plains   MS.   759
Under   1837: Beneath   MS., 1814-32   remained] was left   MS.

The dewy fields; but ere the Vicar's door
Was reached, the Solitary checked his steps;   770
Then, intermingling thanks, on each bestowed
A farewell salutation; and, the like
Receiving, took the slender path that leads
To the one cottage in the lonely dell:
But turned not without welcome promise made   775
That he would share the pleasures and pursuits
Of yet another summer's day, not loth
To wander with us through the fertile vales,
And o'er the mountain-wastes. "Another sun,"
Said he, "shall shine upon us, ere we part;   780
Another sun, and peradventure more;
If time, with free consent, be yours to give,
And season favours."
                    To enfeebled Power,
From this communion with uninjured Minds,
What renovation had been brought; and what   785
Degree of healing to a wounded spirit,
Dejected, and habitually disposed
To seek, in degradation of the Kind,
Excuse and solace for her own defects;
How far those erring notions were reformed;   790
And whether aught, of tendency as good
And pure, from further intercourse ensued;
This—if delightful hopes, as heretofore,
Inspire the serious song, and gentle Hearts
Cherish, and lofty Minds approve the past—   795
My future labours may not leave untold.

770-5 . . . the Solitary turned aside,
    That single path inviting him that leads
    To the one Cottage in the dell profound
    His chosen residence. He turned aside,
    But not till welcome promise had been given   MS.
774-5 *so* 1845; and 1827-43 *but with* given *for* made
775 His chosen residence. But, ere he turned
    Aside, a welcome promise had been given   1814-20
775-6 His chosen Residence. He turned aside
    But not before an acceptable word
    Of unexpected promise had been given
    That by the morning light he would return
    And share the random pleasures *etc.* MS.
777-8 *so* 1845: consumed In wandering with us through the Vallies fair
MS., 1814-43: given up To wandering with us through the fertile vales   C
782 be MS., 1814-20, 1845: is 1827-43

APPENDIX A

THE RECLUSE. Part First. Book First.

Home at Grasmere

Once to the verge of yon steep barrier came
A roving School-boy; what the Adventurer's age
Hath now escaped his memory—but the hour,
One of a golden summer holiday,
He well remembers, though the year be gone.   5
Alone and devious from afar he came;
And, with a sudden influx overpowered
At sight of this seclusion, he forgot
His haste, for hasty had his footsteps been
As boyish his pursuits; and, sighing said,   10
"What happy fortune were it here to live!
And, if a thought of dying, if a thought
Of mortal separation, could intrude
With paradise before him, here to die!"
No Prophet was he, had not even a hope,   15
Scarcely a wish, but one bright pleasing thought,
A fancy in the heart of what might be
The lot of Others, never could be his.

    The Station whence he look'd was soft and green,
Not giddy yet aerial, with a depth   20
Of Vale below, a height of hills above.
For rest of body, perfect was the Spot,
All that luxurious nature could desire,
But stirring to the Spirit; who could gaze
And not feel motions there? He thought of clouds   25
That sail on winds; of Breezes that delight
To play on water, or in endless chase

1–3 Once to (on) the (grassy) brow of yon steep hill I came (stopped)
    While I was yet a School-boy (of what age
    I cannot well remember B, *with* I, my, *for* he, his *to* l. 45
4, 6 *not in* B   7 overpowered D: overcome B   10/11 As on
the summit of the hill I stood B *deleted*   13 intrude B *corr.*, D:
come in B   19 The place from which B (*corr.*)
21/2 Long did I halt, I could have made it even
    My business and my errand so to halt B
    On the cool turf I stretch'd my limbs at ease
    And halted long B *alt. draft*
22 perfect was the spot B *corr.*: 'twas a perfect place B   24 stir-
ring B *corr.*: tempting B   gaze B   look D

Pursue each other through the yielding plain
Of grass or corn, over and through and through,
In billow after billow, evermore   30
Disporting. Nor unmindful was the Boy
Of sunbeams, shadows, butterflies and birds,
Of fluttering Sylphs, and softly-gliding Fays,
Genii, and winged Angels that are Lords
Without restraint of all which they behold.   35
The illusion strengthening as he gazed, he felt
That such unfettered liberty was his,
Such power and joy; but only for this end,
To flit from field to rock, from rock to field,
From shore to island, and from isle to shore,   40
From open ground to covert, from a bed
Of meadow-flowers into a tuft of wood;
From high to low, from low to high, yet still
Within the bound of this high Concave; here
Must be his Home, this Valley be his World.   45

    Since that day forth the place to him—*to me*
(For I who live to register the truth
Was that same young and happy Being) became
As beautiful to thought, as it had been,
When present, to the bodily sense; a haunt   50
Of pure affections, shedding upon joy
A brighter joy; and through such damp and gloom
Of the gay mind, as ofttimes splenetic Youth
Mistakes for sorrow, darting beams of light
That no self-cherished sadness could withstand: 55
And now 'tis mine, perchance for life, dear Vale,
Beloved Grasmere (let the Wandering Streams

28 yielding plain D: liquid depths B   31 *so* D *corr.*: He sported.
Like Companionship, his fancy D *deleted*: *not in* B   33 fluttering
D *corr.*: aery BD   34 Genii and winged Angels B *corr.*, D: Angels
and winged Creatures B
36–7 I sate and moved (stirr'd) in fancy (spirit), as I look'd
    I seem'd to feel such liberty was mine B
41 ground D *corr.*: place BD   45 Must D *corr.*: Should BD
46–8 From that time forward was the place to me B   48 became
D *corr.*; stood forth D   50 the . . . sense D *corr.*: my . . . eyes B
51 pure D *corr.*: my BD
51–5 *So* D: Of my affections, oftentimes in joy
            A brighter joy, in sorrow—but of that
            I have known little—in such gloom at least
            Such damp of the gay mind as stood to me
            In place of sorrow, 'twas a gleam of light B

Take up, the cloud-capt hills repeat, the Name),
One of thy lowly Dwellings is my Home.

And was the cost so great ? and could it seem 60
An act of courage, and the thing itself
A conquest ? who must bear the blame ? sage Man
Thy prudence, thy experience—thy desires,
Thy apprehensions—blush thou for them all.

Yes, the realities of life so cold, 65
So cowardly, so ready to betray,
So stinted in the measure of their grace
As we pronounce them, doing them much wrong,
Have been to me more bountiful than hope,
Less timid than desire—but that is passed. 70

57–8 *not in* B   68 pronounce D: report B
70–9 Less timid than desire—oh bold indeed,
They have been, bold and bounteous unto me
Who have myself been bold, not wanting trust
Nor resolution, nor at last the hope
Which is of wisdom, for I feel it is.

And did it cost so much, and did it ask (*v.* 60–4)
Such length of discipline, and could it seem
An act of courage, and the thing itself
A conquest ? shame that this was ever so,—
Not to the Boy or Youth, but shame to thee,
Sage Man, thou Sun in its meridian strength,
Thou flower in its full blow, thou King and Crown
Of human Nature, shame to thee, sage Man,
Thy prudence, thy experience, thy desires,
Thy apprehensions—blush thou for them all.
But I am safe, yes, one at least is safe,
What once was deem'd so difficult is now
Smooth, easy, without obstacle, what once
Did to my blindness seem a sacrifice,
The same is now a choice of the whole heart.
If e'er the acceptance of such dower was deem'd
A condescention or a weak indulgence
To a sick fancy, it is now an act
Of reason that exultingly aspires.
This solitude is mine, the distant thought
Is fetch'd out of the heaven in which it was.
The unappropriated bliss hath found
An owner, and that owner I am he.
The Lord of this enjoyment is on Earth
And in my breast. What wonder if I speak
With fervour, am exalted with the thought
Of my possessions, of my genuine wealth

On Nature's invitation do I come,
By Reason sanctioned—Can the choice mislead,
That made the calmest, fairest spot of earth,
With all its unappropriated good,
My own; and not mine only, for with me   75
Entrenched, say rather peacefully embowered,
Under yon Orchard, in yon humble Cot,
A younger Orphan of a Home extinct,
The only Daughter of my Parents, dwells.

Aye, think on that, my Heart, and cease to stir,   80
Pause upon that, and let the breathing frame
No longer breathe, but all be satisfied.
—Oh if such silence be not thanks to God
For what hath been bestowed, then where, where then
Shall gratitude find rest ? Mine eyes did ne'er   85
Fix on a lovely object, nor my mind
Take pleasure in the midst of happy thoughts,
But either She whom now I have, who now
Divides with me this loved Abode, was there,
Or not far off. Where'er my footsteps turned,   90
Her Voice was like a hidden Bird that sang,
The thought of her was like a flash of light,
Or an *unseen* companionship, a breath,
Or fragrance independent of the wind.
In all my goings, in the new and old   95
Of all my meditations, and in this
Favorite of all, in this the most of all.
—What Being, therefore, since the birth of Man

Inward and outward, what I keep, have gain'd,
Shall gain, must gain, if sound be my belief
From past and present, rightly understood,
That in my day of Childhood I was less
The mind of Nature, less, take all in all,
Whatever may be lost, than I am now.
For proof behold this Valley, and behold
Yon Cottage, where with me my Emma dwells.   B
71–9 Henceforth the unappropriated bliss
Showered on this beautiful domain hath found
An owner, and that owner I am he.
On Nature's *etc. as* 71–2
That made the calmest fairest purest spot
On earth the object of my daily sight
Through every change of season; my Abode
Yon Cottage where with me my Emma dwells.   B *2nd draft*
77 *so* D *corr.*: Under its rocky Orchard, where with me   D   86 Fix
D *corr.*: Rest   BD

Had ever more abundant cause to speak
Thanks, and if favours of the heavenly Muse   100
Make him more thankful, then to call on verse
To aid him, and in Song resound his joy.
The boon is absolute; surpassing grace
To me hath been vouchsafed; among the bowers
Of blissful Eden this was neither given,   105
Nor could be given, possession of the good
Which had been sighed for, ancient thought fulfilled
And dear Imaginations realized
Up to their highest measure, yea and more.

    Embrace me then, ye Hills, and close me in,   110
Now in the clear and open day I feel
Your guardianship; I take it to my heart;
'Tis like the solemn shelter of the night.
But I would call thee beautiful, for mild
And soft, and gay, and beautiful thou art,   115,
Dear Valley, having in thy face a smile
Though peaceful, full of gladness. Thou art pleased,
Pleased with thy crags, and woody steeps, thy Lake,
Its one green Island and its winding shores;
The multitude of little rocky hills,   120
Thy Church and Cottages of mountain stone
Clustered like stars some few, but single most,
And lurking dimly in their shy retreats,
Or glancing at each other chearful looks,
Like separated stars with clouds between.   125
What want we? have we not perpetual streams,
Warm woods, and sunny hills, and fresh green fields,
And mountains not less green, and flocks, and herds,
And thickets full of songsters, and the voice
Of lordly birds, an unexpected sound   130
Heard now and then from morn till latest eve,
Admonishing the man who walks below
Of solitude, and silence in the sky?
These have we, and a thousand nooks of earth
Have also these, but no where else is found,   135
No where (or is it fancy?) can be found
The one sensation that is here; 'tis here,
Here as it found its way into my heart
In childhood, here as it abides by day,
By night, here only; or in chosen minds   140
That take it with them hence, where'er they go.

100 *so* D *corr.*: music and the power of song BD   101 verse D *corr.*:
these BD   102 in Song D *corr.*: with these BD

'Tis, but I cannot name it, 'tis the sense
Of majesty, and beauty, and repose,
A blended holiness of earth and sky,
Something that makes this individual Spot,   145
This small Abiding-place of many Men,
A termination, and a last retreat,
A Centre, come from wheresoe'er you will,
A Whole without dependence or defect,
Made for itself; and happy in itself,   150
Perfect Contentment, Unity entire.

151/2 Long is it since we met, to part no more,
Since I and Emma heard each other's call
And were companions once again, like Birds
Which by the intruding Fowler had been scar'd,
Two of a scatter'd brood that could not bear
To live in loneliness; 'tis long since we,
Remembering much and hoping more, found means
To walk abreast tho' in a narrow path
With undivided steps. Our home was sweet;
Could it be less? if we were forc'd to change,
Our home again was sweet; but still, for Youth,
Strong as it seems and bold, is inly weak
And diffident, the destiny of life
Remain'd unfix'd, and therefore we were still   *so* B,
which here has a page of about twenty-four lines missing. All but six, however,
are found in A, *which begins thus:*
We will be free and as we mean to live
In culture of divinity and truth
Will chuse the noblest Temple that we know,—
Not in mistrust or ignorance of the mind,
And of the power she has within herself
To ennoble all things, made we this resolve,
Far less from any momentary fit
Of inconsiderate fancy, light and vain,
But that we deemed it wise to take the help
Which lay within our reach; and here we knew
Help could be found of no mean sort; the spirit
Of singleness, and unity, and peace.
In this majestic self-sufficing world,
This all in all of nature, it will suit,
We said, no other [   ] on earth so well,
Simplicity of purpose, love intense,
Ambition not aspiring to the prize
Of outward things, but for the prize within   A
                    (*Here* B *begins again*)
Highest ambition; in the daily walks
Of business 'twill be harmony and grace
For the perpetual pleasure of the sense,
And for the Soul—I do not say too much,

Bleak season was it, turbulent and bleak,
When hitherward we journeyed, side by side,
Through bursts of sunshine and through flying showers,
Paced the long Vales, how long they were, and yet   155
How fast that length of way was left behind,
Wensley's rich Vale and Sedbergh's naked heights.
The frosty wind, as if to make amends
For its keen breath, was aiding to our steps,
And drove us onward like two ships at sea,   160
Or like two Birds, companions in mid air,
Parted and re-united by the blast.
Stern was the face of Nature; we rejoiced
In that stern countenance, for our Souls thence drew
A feeling of their strength. The naked Trees,   165
The icy brooks, as on we passed, appeared
To question us. "Whence come ye ? to what end ?"
They seemed to say; "What would ye," said the shower,
"Wild Wanderers, whither through my dark domain ?"
The sunbeam said, "be happy." When this Vale   170

Though much be said, an image for the soul
A habit of Eternity and God.
    Nor have we been deceived, thus far the effect
Falls not below the loftiest of our hopes. AB
152 When Emma journeyed with me from afar
    To this selected region (appointed covert) on we pass'd
                            B, *another draft*
153 side by side D: and on foot AB   154 showers D: snow AB
155-7 How fast we left that length of way behind
        Each vale far-winding and bleak naked heights
                            B, *another draft*
157 rich D: long AB   159 steps D *corr.*: course ABD   161-2
not in AB   164 thence drew D: had thence AB   166 pass'd
B: went A
170-1 When this Vale . . . entered D: They were mov'd
        All things were mov'd, they round us as we went,
        We in the midst of them. And when the trance
        Came to us, as we stood by Hart-leap Well,
        The intimation of the milder day
        Which is to be (come), the fairer world than this,
        And rais'd us up, dejected as we were,
        Among the records of that doleful place,
        By sorrow for the hunted Beast who there
        Had yielded up his breath, the awful trance
        The vision of humanity, and of God
        The Mourner, God the Sufferer, when the heart
        Of his poor Creatures suffers wrongfully—
        Both in the sadness and the joy we found
        A promise and an earnest that we twain,

We entered, bright and solemn was the sky
That faced us with a passionate welcoming,
And led us to our threshold. Daylight failed
Insensibly, and round us gently fell
Composing darkness, with a quiet load   175
Of full contentment, in a little Shed
Disturbed, uneasy in itself as seemed,
And wondering at its new inhabitants.
It loves us now, this Vale so beautiful
Begins to love us! By a sullen storm,   180
Two months unwearied of severest storm,
It put the temper of our minds to proof,
And found us faithful through the gloom, and heard
The Poet mutter his prelusive songs
With chearful heart, an unknown voice of joy,   185
Among the silence of the woods and hills;
Silent to any gladsomeness of sound
With all their Shepherds.

                            But the gates of Spring
Are opened; churlish Winter hath given leave
That she should entertain for this one day,   190
Perhaps for many genial days to come,
His guests, and make them jocund. They are pleased,
But most of all the Birds that haunt the flood,
With the mild summons; inmates though they be
Of Winter's household, they keep festival   195
This day, who drooped, or seemed to droop, so long;
They shew their pleasure, and shall I do less?
Happier of happy though I be, like them

A pair receding from the common world,
Might in that hallow'd spot to which our steps
Were tending, in that individual nook,
Might, even thus early, for ourselves secure,
And in the midst of these unhappy times,
A portion of the blessedness which love
And knowledge, will, we trust, hereafter give
To all the vales of Earth and all mankind.
  Thrice hath the winter moon been filled with light
Since that dear day when Grasmere, our dear Vale,
Received us;   AB
173–4 Daylight failed . . . fell   D: to a home
Within a home, which was to be, and soon
Our love within a love, then darkness came   AB
175 a quiet   D: its quiet   AB   181–2 *So* MS. A *corr.*, B: It put us
to the proof, two months of storm   A   190 one sweet day   A
192 jocund   D: happy   AB   195 keep festival   D *corr.*: are jubilant
A–D

I cannot take possession of the sky,
Mount with a thoughtless impulse, and wheel there,   200
One of a mighty multitude, whose way
Is a perpetual harmony, and dance
Magnificent. Behold, how with a grace
Of ceaseless motion, that might scarcely seem
Inferior to angelical, they prolong   205
Their curious pastime, shaping in mid air,
And sometimes with ambitious wing that soars
High as the level of the mountain tops,
A circuit ampler than the lake beneath,
Their own domain;—but ever, while intent   210
On tracing and retracing that large round,
Their jubilant activity evolves
Hundreds of curves and circlets, to and fro,
Upwards and downwards, progress intricate
Yet unperplexed, as ,if one spirit swayed   215
Their indefatigable flight. 'Tis done—
Ten times and more, I fancied it had ceased;
But lo! the vanished company again
Ascending, they approach—I hear their wings
Faint, faint at first; and then an eager sound   220
Passed in a moment—and as faint again!
They tempt the sun to sport among their plumes;
Tempt the smooth water, or the gleaming ice,
To shew them a fair image,—'tis themselves,
Their own fair forms, upon the glimmering plain,   225
Painted more soft and fair as they descend,
Almost to touch;—then up again aloft,
Up with a sally, and a flash of speed,
As if they scorned both resting-place and rest!

    This day is a thanksgiving, 'tis a day   230
Of glad emotion and deep quietness;

202 *so* D *corr.*: And motion is a harmony A–D: *for version of* 1827 *v. note*
203–15 *so* D *corr.*:   Behold them how they shape
        Orb after orb, their course still round and round
        Above the area (circuit) of the Lake, their own
        Adopted region, girding it about
        In wanton repetition, yet therewith
        With that large circle evermore renew'd:
        Hundreds of curves and circlets high and low
        Backwards and forwards, progress intricate,
        As if one spirit was (*corr. to* dwelt) in all, and sway'd
        A–D
219 they approach D *corr.*: list, again A–D
230–1 *so* B *corr.*: Spring, for this day belongs to thee, rejoice **AB**

Not upon me alone hath been bestowed,
Me rich in many onward-looking thoughts,
The penetrating bliss; oh surely these
Have felt it, not the happy Quires of Spring,   235
Her own peculiar family of love
That sport among green leaves, a blither train.

　　But two are missing—two, a lonely pair
Of milk-white Swans, wherefore are they not seen
Partaking this day's pleasure? From afar   240
They came, to sojourn here in solitude,
Chusing this Valley, they who had the choice
Of the whole world. We saw them day by day,
Through those two months of unrelenting storm,
Conspicuous at the centre of the Lake,   245
Their safe retreat; we knew them well, I guess
That the whole Valley knew them; but to us
They were more dear than may be well believed,
Not only for their beauty, and their still
And placid way of life, and constant love   250
Inseparable, not for these alone,
But that their state so much resembled ours,
They having also chosen this abode;
They strangers, and we strangers; they a pair,
And we a solitary pair like them.   255
They should not have departed; many days
Did I look forth in vain, nor on the wing
Could see them, nor in that small open space
Of blue unfrozen water, where they lodged,
And lived so long in quiet, side by side.   260
Shall we behold them, consecrated friends,
Faithful Companions, yet another year
Surviving, they for us, and we for them,

233 rich in B *corr.*: blest with AB
234–6 *so* B *corr.*: This sunshine and mild air—Oh surely these
　　　　　　　Are grateful, not the happy Quires of love,
　　　　　　　Thine own peculiar family sweet Spring, AB
237 a blither D *corr.*: so blithe a A–D
239–40 *so* D: . . . Ah why are these not here
　　　　　　　These above all, ah, why are they not here
　　　　　　　To share in AB
241 *so* D *corr.*: They came like Emma and myself to live
　　　　　　　Together here in peace and solitude A–D
250 constant D *corr.*: faithful A–D   257–8 *so* D *corr.*: I've looked
for them . . . Have seen A–D
261–2 *so* D: Companions, partners, consecrated Friends,
　　　　　　　Shall we behold them AB

And neither pair be broken ? Nay perchance
It is too late already for such hope,   265
The Dalesmen may have aimed the deadly tube,
And parted them; or haply both are gone
One death, and that were mercy given to both.
Recal my song the ungenerous thought; forgive,
Thrice favoured Region, the conjecture harsh   270
Of such inhospitable penalty,
Inflicted upon confidence so pure.
Ah, if I wished to follow where the sight
Of all that is before my eyes, the voice
Which speaks from a presiding Spirit here,   275
Would lead me, I should whisper to myself;
They who are dwellers in this holy place
Must needs themselves be hallowed, they require
No benediction from the Stranger's lips,
For they are blest already. None would give   280
The greeting "peace be with you" unto them,
For peace they have, it cannot but be theirs,
And mercy, and forbearance. Nay—not these,
Their healing offices a pure good-will
Precludes, and charity beyond the bounds   285
Of charity—an overflowing love,
Not for the Creature only, but for all
That is around them, love for every thing
Which in this happy Region they behold!

266 Dalesmen D corr.: Shepherd A–D; aimed D: seized AB
267 so D corr.: And parted them, incited by a prize
                Which for the sake of those (her) he loves at home
                And for the Lamb upon the mountain tops
                He should have spared; A–C, but C omits third line
269–73 so D corr.: I cannot look upon this favoured Vale
                But that I seem, by harbouring this thought,
                To wrong it, such unworthy recompense
                Imagining of confidence so pure
                Ah, if etc. AB
                And could a Poet harbour such a thought,
                Imagine such unworthy recompence
                Of confidence so pure ? More natural were it
                To follow without scruple where the sight D
275 speaks from D: is as AB   276–7 I should whisper to myself:
They who are BD corr.: . . . say unto myself etc. A: and not wronging what
he sees, Whisper "the dwellers' B corr. and D
284–5 so D corr.: There is no call for these; that office Love
                Performs, and charity A–D
286 an overflowing BD: a heart-delighting A   289 region B corr.:
valley AB

Thus do we soothe ourselves, and when the thought 290
Is pass'd we blame it not for having come.
What, if I floated down a pleasant Stream
And now am landed, and the motion gone,
Shall I reprove myself? Ah no, the Stream
Is flowing, and will never cease to flow, 295
And I shall float upon that Stream again.
By such forgetfulness the Soul becomes,
Words cannot say, how beautiful; then hail,
Hail to the visible Presence, hail to thee,
Delightful Valley, habitation fair! 300
And to whatever else of outward form
Can give us inward help, can purify,
And elevate, and harmonise, and soothe,
And steal away, and for a while deceive
And lap in pleasing rest, and bear us on 305
Without desire in full complacency,
Contemplating perfection absolute
And entertained as in a placid sleep.

But not betrayed by tenderness of mind
That feared, or wholly overlook'd the truth, 310
Did we come hither, with romantic hope
To find, in midst of so much loveliness,
Love, perfect love; of so much majesty
A like majestic frame of mind in those
Who here abide, the persons like the place. 315
Not from such hope, or aught of such belief
Hath issued any portion of the joy
Which I have felt this day. An awful voice,
'Tis true, hath in my walks been often heard,
Sent from the mountains or the sheltered fields, 320
Shout after shout—reiterated whoop
In manner of a bird that takes delight
In answering to itself; or like a hound
Single at chase among the lonely woods,
His yell repeating; yet it was in truth 325
A human voice—a Spirit of coming night,
How solemn when the sky is dark, and earth
Not dark, nor yet enlightened, but by snow
Made visible, amid a noise of winds

309 But neither lull'd nor lost nor rapt away A *corr.*   310 wholly
overlook'd A *corr.*: utterly forgot A   313 perfect BD: purest A
326–9 *so* B *corr.*: A human voice how awful in the gloom
                Of coming night amid A

And bleatings manifold of mountain sheep,   330
Which in that iteration recognize
Their summons, and are gathering round for food,
Devoured with keenness ere to grove or bank
Or rocky *bield* with patience they retire.

    That very voice, which, in some timid mood   335
Of superstitious fancy, might have seemed
Awful as ever stray Demoniac uttered,
His steps to govern in the Wilderness;
Or as the Norman Curfew's regular beat,
To hearths when first they darkened at the knell: 340
That Shepherd's voice, it may have reached mine ear
Debased and under profanation, made
The ready Organ of articulate sounds
From ribaldry, impiety, or wrath
Issuing when shame hath ceased to check the brawls   345
Of some abused Festivity—so be it.
I came not dreaming of unruffled life,
Untainted manners; born among the hills,
Bred also there, I wanted not a scale
To regulate my hopes. Pleased with the good,   350
I shrink not from the evil with disgust,
Or with immoderate pain. I look for Man,
The common Creature of the brotherhood,
Differing but little from the Man elsewhere,
For selfishness, and envy, and revenge,   355
Ill neighbourhood—pity that this should be—
Flattery and double-dealing, strife and wrong.

    Yet is it something gained, it is in truth
A mighty gain, that Labour here preserves
His rosy face, a Servant only here   360
Of the fire-side, or of the open field,
A Freeman, therefore, sound and unimpaired;
That extreme penury is here unknown,
And cold and hunger's abject wretchedness,
Mortal to body, and the heaven-born mind;   365

330–4 mountain sheep . . . retire D: sheep that know
        Their summons, and are gathering round for food,
        That voice the same, the very same that breath
        Which was an utterance awful as the wind
        Or any sound the mountains ever heard AB
335–40 *not in* AB
343–6 *so* D: An organ for the sounds articulate
        Of ribaldry and blasphemy, and wrath
        When drunkenness hath kindled senseless frays AB

That they who want, are not too great a weight
For those who can relieve. Here may the heart
Breathe in the air of fellow-suffering
Dreadless, as in a kind of fresher breeze
Of her own native element, the hand   370
Be ready and unwearied without plea
From tasks too frequent, or beyond its power
For languor, or indifference, or despair.
And as these lofty barriers break the force
Of winds, this deep Vale,—as it doth in part   375
Conceal us from the Storm,—so here abides
A Power and a protection for the mind,
Dispensed indeed to other solitudes,
Favored by noble privilege like this,
Where kindred independence of estate   380
Is prevalent, where he who tills the field,
He, happy Man! is Master of the field,
And treads the mountains which his Fathers trod.

     Not less than half-way up yon Mountain's side
Behold a dusky spot, a grove of Firs,   385
That seems still smaller than it is; this grove
Is haunted—by what ghost? a gentle Spirit
Of memory faithful to the call of love;
For, as reports the Dame, whose fire sends up
Yon curling smoke from the grey cot below,   390
The trees (her first-born Child being then a babe)
Were planted by her husband and herself,
That ranging o'er the high and houseless ground

376   so here there is
       Or seems to be for it befits [me ?] yet
       New comer as I am to speak in doubt A *which ends here*
383/4 Hence, and from other local circumstance
     In this enclosure many of the old
     Substantial virtues have a firmer tone
       Than in the bare and ordinary world *so* B, *followed by the two stories*
given in Excursion vi. 1080–1190 *q.v. app. crit.; then*
                 From yonder [   ] grey stone that stands alone
                 Not less than half-way up the mountain side
                 Close to the foaming stream look up and see
                 A dusky spot, a little grove of Firs (385)
387–92 *so* D: As from the dame I learn'd who dwells below,
                 Just six weeks younger than her eldest boy,
                 Was planted B
393–8 *so* D *corr.*: For a convenient shelter which in storm
                     Their sheep might draw to, "and they knew it well",
                     Said she, "for thither do we bear their food BD

Their sheep might neither want (from perilous storms
Of winter, nor from summer's sultry heat)   395
A friendly covert. "And they knew it well,"
Said she, "for thither as the trees grew up,
We to the patient creatures carried food
In times of heavy snow." She then began
In fond obedience to her private thoughts   400
To speak of her dead Husband: is there not
An art, a music, and a strain of words
That shall be life, the acknowledged voice of life,
Shall speak of what is done among the fields,
Done truly there, or felt, of solid good   405
And real evil, yet be sweet withal,
More grateful, more harmonious than the breath,
The idle breath of softest pipe attuned
To pastoral fancies? Is there such a stream,
Pure and unsullied, flowing from the heart   410
With motions of true dignity and grace?
Or must we seek that stream where Man is not?
Methinks I could repeat in tuneful verse,
Delicious as the gentlest breeze that sounds
Through that aerial fir-grove, could preserve   415
Some portion of its human history
As gathered from the Matron's lips, and tell
Of tears that have been shed at sight of it,
And moving dialogues between this Pair,
Who in their prime of wedlock, with joint hands   420
Did plant the grove, now flourishing, while they
No longer flourish, he entirely gone,
She withering in her loneliness. Be this
A task above my skill; the silent mind
Has her own treasures, and I think of these,   425
Love what I see, and honour humankind.

   No, we are not alone, we do not stand,
My Sister, here misplaced and desolate,
Loving what no one cares for but ourselves;
We shall not scatter through the plains and rocks   430
Of this fair Vale, and o'er its spacious heights
Unprofitable kindliness, bestowed
On objects unaccustomed to the gifts
Of feeling, which were chearless and forlorn

412 that stream D *corr.*: these things BD
427–8 No I am not alone, we do not stand
      My Emma in a solitary world R
428 Sister D: Emma RB

But few weeks past, and would be so again   435
Were we not here; we do not tend a lamp
Whose lustre we alone participate,
Which shines dependent upon us alone,
Mortal though bright, a dying, dying flame.
Look where we will, some human heart has been   440
Before us with its offering; not a tree
Sprinkles these little pastures but the same
Hath furnished matter for a thought; perchance,
For some one serves as a familiar friend.
Joy spreads, and sorrow spreads; and this whole Vale, 445
Home of untutored Shepherds as it is,
Swarms with sensation, as with gleams of sunshine,
Shadows or breezes, scents or sounds. Nor deem
These feelings, though subservient more than ours
To every day's demand for daily bread,   450
And borrowing more their spirit, and their shape
From self-respecting interests, deem them not
Unworthy therefore, and unhallowed: no,
They lift the animal being, do themselves
By Nature's kind and ever-present aid   455
Refine the selfishness from which they spring,
Redeem by love the individual sense
Of anxiousness with which they are combined.
And thus it is that fitly they become
Associates in the joy of purest minds,   460
They blend therewith congenially: meanwhile,
Calmly they breathe their own undying life
Through this their mountain sanctuary; long,
Oh long may it remain inviolate,
Diffusing health and sober chearfulness,   465
And giving to the moments as they pass

436 *so* D *corr.*: If we were not; RBD   438 shines D *corr.*: is RBD
440 heart RB: hand D   442 Sprinkles] Stands in R   444
For . . serves D: To . . is RB   447 sunshine BD: light R
450 To the necessities of daily life R
454–6 *so* B *corr.*: Many are pure, the best of them are pure,
                    The best, and these, remember, most abound,
                    Are fit associates of the worthiest joy,
                    Joy of the highest and the purest minds RB
462/3 Lowly and unassuming as it is RB
463–70 Labour they sweeten, and they soften care
       Diffusing through this mountain sanctuary
       —O long may it remain inviolate—
       Health, innocence, and sober chearfulness
       And little boons of animating thought,
       As faithfully as morning comes with light R

Their little boons of animating thought
That sweeten labour, make it seen and felt
To be no arbitrary weight imposed,
But a glad function natural to Man.   470

   Fair proof of this, Newcomer though I be,
Already have I gained.' The inward frame
Though slowly opening, opens every day
With process not unlike to that which chears
A pensive Stranger, journeying at his leisure   475
Through some Helvetian dell, when low-hung mists
Break up, and are beginning to recede ;
How pleased he is where thin and thinner grows
The veil, or where it parts at once, to spy
The dark pines thrusting forth their spiky heads ;   480
To watch the spreading lawns with cattle grazed,
Then to be greeted by the scattered huts,
As they shine out ; and *see* the streams whose murmur
Had soothed his ear while they were hidden : how pleased
To have about him, which way e'er he goes,   485
Something on every side concealed from view,
In every quarter something visible,
Half-seen or wholly, lost and found again,
Alternate progress and impediment,
And yet a growing prospect in the main.   490

   Such pleasure now is mine, albeit forced,
Herein less happy than the Traveller
To cast from time to time a painful look
Upon unwelcome things, which unawares

472 gained D: seen RB
474–6 *so* D *corr.*: Nor am I less delighted with the show
          As it unfolds itself, now here, now there,
          Than is the passing Traveller, when his way
          Lies through some region then first trod by him
          (Say this fair valley's self) when low-hung mists RBD
478–82 *so* D *corr.*: How pleased he is to greet the rocks and lawns
        As they put off their Veil; the spiky Pines
        As they thrust forth their heads ; the scatter'd Huts *etc.* D
478–85 How pleased he is to hear the murmuring streams
        The many voices, whence he knows not, pleased
        To have about him *etc.* RB
490 *so* B, D *corr.*: Yet in the main a prospect spread and spreading B *corr.*,
D
491–3 *so* B *corr.*: Such pleasure now is mine, and what if I,
        Less happy than the Traveller in this
        Am sometimes forced to cast a painful look RB

Reveal themselves; not therefore is my heart   495
Depressed, nor does it fear what is to come,
But confident, enriched at every glance.
The more I see the more delight my mind
Receives, or by reflexion can create.
Truth justifies herself, and as she dwells   500
With Hope, who would not follow where she leads ?

Nor let me pass unheeded other loves
Where no fear is, and humbler sympathies.
Already hath sprung up within my heart
A liking for the small grey horse that bears   505
The paralytic Man, and for the brute—
In Scripture sanctified—the patient brute,
On which the cripple, in the Quarry maim'd,
Rides to and fro: I know them and their ways.
The famous Sheep-dog, first in all the Vale,   510
Though yet to me a Stranger, will not be
A Stranger long; nor will the blind man's guide,
Meek and neglected thing, of no renown!
Soon will peep forth the primrose; ere it fades
Friends shall I have at dawn, blackbird and thrush   515
To rouse me, and a hundred Warblers more;

495 heart B *corr.*, D: mind RB   498–500 *so* B *corr.*: . . . the more
is my delight, Truth, *etc.* RB   499 create D *corr.*: extract BD
502 pass unheeded B *corr.*: overlook those B
502–4 Nor is it a mean praise of rural life
    And solitude that they do favour most,
    Most frequently call forth and best sustain
    These mild and pure affections, and to me
    How much do they endear the quietness
    Of this sublime retirement. I begin
    Already to inscribe upon my heart R
503/4 That have to me endeared the quietness
    Of this sublime retirement. I begin— B (*deleted*)
504 hath sprung up within D *corr.*: is inscribed upon BD   506 for
the brute B *corr.*, D: I know the Ass RB   507 *not in* R; sancti-
fied D *corr.*: glorified BD
514–20 *so* D *corr.*: Whoever liv'd a winter in one place,
    Beneath the shelter of one Cottage roof,
    And has not had his Redbreast or his Wren ?
    I have them both, and I shall have my Thrush
    In spring-time, and a hundred Warblers more
    And if the banish'd Eagle pair return,
    Helvellyn's Eagles to their antient Hold
    Then shall I see, shall claim with those two Birds
    Acquaintance, as they soar amid the Heavens RB (D *partly illegible*)

And if those Eagles to their ancient Hold
Return, Helvellyn's Eagles! with the Pair
From my own door I shall be free to claim
Acquaintance as they sweep from cloud to cloud.   520
The Owl that gives the name to Owlet-Crag
Have I heard whooping, and he soon will be
A chosen one of my regards. See there
The Heifer in yon little croft belongs
To one who holds it dear; with duteous care   525
She reared it, and in speaking of her charge
I heard her scatter some endearing words
Domestic, and in spirit motherly
She being herself a Mother, happy Beast
If the caresses of a human voice   530
Can make it so, and care of human hands.

And ye as happy under Nature's care,
Strangers to me, and all men, or at least
Strangers to all particular amity,
All intercourse of knowledge or of love   535
That parts the individual from his kind,
Whether in large communities ye keep
From year to year, not shunning Man's abode,
A settled residence, or be from far,
Wild creatures, and of many homes, that come   540
The gift of winds, and whom the winds again
Take from us at your pleasure—yet shall ye
Not want, for this, your own subordinate place
In my affections. Witness the delight
With which erewhile I saw that multitude   545
Wheel through the sky, and see them now at rest,

522 whooping D *corr.*: shouting RBD   527 once a word or two RB
528 A term domestic yea and motherly R   539 Your stationary
homes R   543/4 According to your claims, an under-place RB
544–9 Bright shines the Sun; a wintry stillness blends
Its pensive influence with the warmth of Spring,
Spring's vital warmth pervading earth and air,
And chearingly reflected from the folds
And fleecy skirts of clouds, that keeping each
Their form and station decorate the front
Of the clear sky; and from the naked rocks
And stony Hills imbued with tender light.
That multitude which through the [?] peace
Of the past day were seen to soar aloft
And in the azure element repeat
Their evolution are assembled now
Right at the centre of the glassy lake:
There have they settled from disturbance safe

Yet not at rest, upon the glassy lake.
They *cannot* rest, they gambol like young whelps;
Active as lambs, and overcome with joy,
They try all frolic motions; flutter, plunge,   550
And beat the passive water with their wings.
Too distant are they for plain view, but lo!
Those little fountains, sparkling in the sun,
Betray their occupation, rising up,
First one and then another silver spout,   555
As one or other takes the fit of glee,
Fountains and spouts, yet somewhat in the guise
Of play-thing fire-works, that on festal nights
Sparkle about the feet of wanton boys.
—How vast the compass of this theatre,   560
Yet nothing to be seen but lovely pomp
And silent majesty; the birch-tree woods
Are hung with thousand thousand diamond drops
Of melted hoar-frost, every tiny knot
In the bare twigs, each little budding-place   565
Cased with its several bead, what myriads there
Upon one tree, while all the distant grove
That rises to the summit of the steep
Shows like a mountain built of silver light.
See yonder the same pageant, and again   570
Behold the universal imagery
Inverted, all its sun-bright features touched
As with the varnish, and the gloss of dreams;
Dreamlike the blending also of the whole
Harmonious landscape; all along the shore   575
The boundary lost, the line invisible
That parts the image from reality;
And the clear hills, as high as they ascend
Heavenward, so piercing deep the lake below.
Admonished of the days of love to come   580
The raven croaks, and fills the upper air

But through the uneasy spirit of delight
They cannot rest, they gambol like young whelps
Active as lambs *etc. alt. draft on verso* B
554 *so* D: Which tell what they are doing, which rise up RB   554/5
Spend their short lives appear and disappear B *deleted*   559 Hop
skip about the feet of merry boys. RB   569 Shows B *corr.*, D: Is RB
572–9 Inverted . . . below *so* D: At what a depth, deep in the Lake below
RB
574–5 *so* D *corr.*: Dreamlike the blending too; along the shore
            The boundary (landmark) lost—the line invisible D
581 upper D: sunny RB

With a strange sound of genial harmony;
And in and all about that playful band,
Incapable although they be of rest,
And in their fashion very rioters,   585
There is a stillness, and they seem to make
Calm revelry in that their calm abode.
Them leaving to their joyous hours I pass,
Pass with a thought the life of the whole year
That is to come, the throng of woodland flowers,   590
And lillies that will dance upon the waves.

   Say boldly then that solitude is not
Where these things are: he truly is alone,
He of the multitude whose eyes are doomed
To hold a vacant commerce day by day   595
With objects wanting life, repelling love;
He by the vast Metropolis immured,
Where pity shrinks from unremitting calls,
Where numbers overwhelm humanity,
And neighbourhood serves rather to divide   600
Than to unite. What sighs more deep than his,
Whose nobler will hath long been sacrificed;
Who must inhabit, under a black sky,
A City where, if indifference to disgust
Yield not, to scorn, or sorrow, living Men   605
Are ofttimes to their fellow-men no more
Than to the Forest Hermit are the leaves
That hang aloft in myriads—nay, far less,
For they protect his walk from sun and shower,
Swell his devotion with their voice in storms,   610
And whisper while the stars twinkle among them
His lullaby. From crowded streets remote,

588 *so* D *corr.*: I leave them to their pleasure and I pass RBD   590
woodland D *corr.*: mountain RBD   591 waves D: lake RB
592 *so* D *corr.*: Then boldly say D *corr.*, RB
596–606 *so* D *corr.*: With that which he can neither know nor love,
        Dead things, or living men to him no more D
        With that which he can neither know nor love,
        Dead things, to him thrice dead, or worse than this
        With swarms of life, and worse than all, of men,
        His fellow men that are to him no more RB
601 *so* D *corr.*:   Yes, yes there is a weight
        Of loneliness, *he* can report of it D
608–15 *so* D *corr.*:   nay far less
      Far less for aught that comforts or defends
      Or lulls or chears. Society is here
      The true community, the noblest *etc.* B (D *pasted over*)

Far from the living and dead wilderness
Of the thronged World, Society is here
A true Community, a genuine frame   615
Of many into one incorporate.
That must be looked for here, paternal sway,
One household, under God, for high and low,
One family, and one mansion; to themselves
Appropriate, and divided from the world   620
As if it were a cave, a multitude
Human and brute, possessors undisturbed
Of this Recess, their legislative Hall,
Their Temple, and their glorious Dwelling-place.

Dismissing therefore, all Arcadian dreams,   625
All golden fancies of the golden Age,
The bright array of shadowy thoughts from times
That were before all time, or are to be
Ere time expire, the pageantry that stirs
And will be stirring when our eyes are fixed   630
On lovely objects, and we wish to part
With all remembrance of a jarring world,
—Take we at once this one sufficient hope,
What need of more ? that we shall neither droop,
Nor pine for want of pleasure in the life   635
Scattered about us, nor through dearth of aught
That keeps in health the insatiable mind;
That we shall have for knowledge and for love
Abundance; and that, feeling as we do
How goodly, how exceeding fair, how pure   640
From all reproach is yon ethereal vault,

623 Recess] deep vale R
625–31 Dismiss[ing] therefore all Arcadian dreams
        All golden fancies shadows from the times
        That were before all time, that perfect age
        How dear to think of when we long to part R
628 are BD: is D *corr.*   629 *so* D *corr.*: When time is not RBD
632/3 Give entrance to this sober truth, avow
        That Nature to this favoured (favourite B) spot of ours
        Yields no exemption but her awful rights
        Enforces to the utmost, and exacts
        Her tribute of inevitable pain
        And that the sting is added, man himself
        For ever busy to afflict himself,
        Yet temper this with one sufficient hope, (633) RB
636 Scattered D *corr.*: Which is RBD   641 yon . vault B *corr.*,
D: this . frame B

And this deep Vale its earthly counterpart,
By which, and under which, we are enclosed
To breathe in peace, we shall moreover find
(If sound, and what we ought to be ourselves,   645
If rightly we observe and justly weigh)
The Inmates not unworthy of their home
The Dwellers of their Dwelling.
                                    And if this
Were otherwise, we have within ourselves
Enough to fill the present day with joy,   650
And overspread the future years with hope,
Our beautiful and quiet home, enriched
Already with a Stranger whom we love
Deeply, a Stranger of our Father's House,
A never-resting Pilgrim of the Sea,   655
Who finds at last an hour to his content
Beneath our roof. And others whom we love
Will seek us also, Sisters of our hearts,
And One, like them, a Brother of our hearts,
Philosopher and Poet, in whose sight   660
These Mountains will rejoice with open joy.
—Such is our wealth; O Vale of Peace, we are
And must be, with God's will, a happy Band.

    Yet 'tis not to enjoy that we exist,
For that end only; something must be done.   665
I must not walk in unreproved delight
These narrow bounds, and think of nothing more,
No duty that looks further, and no care.
Each Being has his office, lowly some
And common, yet all worthy if fulfilled   670
With zeal, acknowledgment that with the gift
Keeps pace a harvest answering to the seed—
Of ill-advised Ambition and of Pride
I would stand clear, but yet to me I feel
That an internal brightness is vouchsafed   675
That must not die, that must not pass away.
Why does this inward lustre fondly seek,

649 *so* D *corr.*: Were not, we have enough BD
648–60   And if this
        Were not, our habitation will be sought
        By kindred spirits, Sisters of our hearts
        And Brothers of our love [by whose aspect ?]
        By whose example aided we shall strive
        To make our minds as lovely as the scene
        Which we behold, as fit as fair abode B *another draft*

And gladly blend with outward fellowship ?
Why do *they* shine around me whom I love ?
Why do they teach me whom I thus revere ?   680
Strange question, yet it answers not itself.
That humble Roof embowered among the trees,
That calm fire-side, it is not even in them,
Blest as they are, to furnish a reply,
That satisfies and ends in perfect rest.   685
Possessions have I that are solely mine,
Something within which yet is shared by none,
Not even the nearest to me and most dear,
Something which power and effort may impart,
I would impart it, I would spread it wide,   690
Immortal in the world which is to come.
Forgive me if I add another claim,
And would not wholly perish even in this,
Lie down and be forgotten in the dust,
I and the modest Partners of my days   695
Making a silent company in death ;
Love, Knowledge, all my manifold delights
All buried with me without monument
Or profit unto any but ourselves.
It must not be, if I, divinely taught,   700
Be privileged to speak as I have felt
Of what in man is human or divine.

While yet an innocent Little-one, with a heart
That doubtless wanted not its tender moods,
I breathed (for this I better recollect)   705
Among wild appetites and blind desires,
Motions of savage instinct my delight
And exaltation. Nothing at that time
So welcome, no temptation half so dear
As that which urged me to a daring feat.   710
Deep pools, tall trees, black chasms, and dizzy crags,
And tottering towers ; I loved to stand and read
Their looks forbidding, read and disobey,
Sometimes in act, and evermore in thought.
With impulses that scarcely were by these   715
Surpassed in strength, I heard of danger, met
Or sought with courage ; enterprize forlorn
By one, sole keeper of his own intent,
Or by a resolute few who for the sake

679 *so* D: Why shine they round me thus whom thus I love ?   B
715 that scarcely   D: which only   B

Of glory, fronted multitudes in arms.   720
Yea to this hour I cannot read a tale
Of two brave Vessels matched in deadly fight,
And fighting to the death, but I am pleased
More than a wise man ought to be. I wish,
Fret, burn, and struggle, and in soul am there;   725
But me hath Nature tamed, and bade to seek
For other agitations, or be calm;
Hath dealt with me as with a turbulent Stream,
Some nursling of the mountains, whom she leads
Through quiet meadows, after he has learnt   730
His strength, and had his triumph and his joy,
His desperate course of tumult and of glee.
That which in stealth by Nature was performed
Hath Reason sanctioned. Her deliberate Voice
Hath said, "Be mild and cleave to gentle things,   735
Thy glory and thy happiness be there.
Nor fear, though thou confide in me, a want
Of aspirations that *have* been, of foes
To wrestle with, and victory to complete,
Bounds to be leapt, darkness to be explored,   740
All that inflamed thy infant heart, the love,
The longing, the contempt, the undaunted quest,
All shall survive—though changed their office, all
Shall live,—it is not in their power to die."

Then farewell to the Warrior's schemes, farewell   745
The forwardness of Soul which looks that way
Upon a less incitement than the cause
Of Liberty endangered, and farewell
That other hope, long mine, the hope to fill
The heroic trumpet with the Muse's breath!   750
Yet in this peaceful Vale we will not spend
Unheard-of days, though loving peaceful thoughts.

721 *so* D *corr.*: Yea to this day I swell with like desire.
          I cannot at this moment read   BD
725 I burn, I struggle B   729 whom B *corr.*: which BD   730 he
B *corr.*, D: it B   735 cleave to D *corr.*: love all BD
729–32 Nursed in the darkness of some mountain cave
          And trained and exercised in rocky strath
          And headlong steeps, which after it has run
          Its desperate course, triumphantly she leads
          Through flowery meadows and embowering groves.
                                        another draft B
745 schemes D *corr.*:: shield D: deeds B   749 *so* D: All hope which
once and long was mine, to fill B   752 Unheard of D: Inglorious B

A Voice shall speak, and what will be the Theme ?
On Man on Nature and on Human life
Musing in Solitude

[*For the concluding lines v. "Prospectus" of "The Excursion"*
(*p. 3 supra*).]

754—   MS. B's *version is as follows*:
On Man on Nature and on human life
Thinking in solitude, from time to time
I feel sweet passions traversing my soul
Like Music, unto these, where'er I may
I would give utterance in numerous verse:
Of truth, of grandeur, beauty love and hope
Hope for this earth and hope beyond the grave
Of virtue and of intellectual power
Of blessed consolations in distress
Of joy in widest commonalty spread
Of the individual mind that keeps its own
Inviolate retirement, and consists
With being limitless, the one great Life
I sing, fit audience let me find though few—
Fit audience find tho' few, thus pray'd the Bard
Holiest of Men. Urania I shall need
Thy guidance or a greater Muse if such
Descend to earth or dwell in highest heaven
For I must tread on shadowy ground must sink
Deep, and aloft ascending breathe in worlds
To which the Heaven of Heavens is but a veil.
All strength, all terror, single or in bands
That ever was put forth in personal forms,
Jehovah with his thunder and the quire
Of shouting Angels and the empyreal thrones
I pass them unalarmed. The darkest Pit
Of the profoundest Hell and chaos, night,
Nor aught of [   ] vacancy scoop'd out
By help of dreams can breed such fear and awe
As fall upon us often when we look
Into our minds, into the Mind of Man,
My haunt and the main region of my song.
Beauty whose living home is the green earth
Surpassing the most fair ideal Forms
Which craft of delicate spirits hath compos'd
From earth's materials waits upon my steps
Pitches her tents before me where I move
An hourly Neighbour. Paradise and groves
Elysian, fortunate (islands) fields like those
In the deep ocean wherefore should they be
A History or but a dream, when minds
Once wedded to this outward frame of things
In love find these the growth of common day.

I, long before the blessed hour arrives,
Would sing in solitude the spousal verse
Of this great consummation, would proclaim
Speaking of nothing more than what we are
How exquisitely the individual Mind,
And the progressive powers perhaps no less
Of the whole species to the external world
Is fitted, and how exquisitely too,
Theme this but little heard of among men,
The external world is fitted to the mind
And the creation, (by no lower name
Can it be call'd), which they with blended might
Accomplish: this is my great argument
Such [   ] foregoing if I oft
Must turn elsewhere and travel near the tribes
And fellowships of men and see ill sights
Of passions ravenous from each other's rage
Must hear humanity in fields and groves
Pipe solitary anguish or must hang
Brooding above the fierce confederate storm
Of Sorrow barricadoed evermore
Within the walls of Cities, may these sounds
Have their authentic comment that even these
Hearing, I be not heartless or forlorn.
Come thou prophetic Spirit, Soul of Man
Thou human Soul of the wide earth that hast
Thy metropolitan Temple in the hearts
Of mighty Poets, unto me vouchsafe
Thy guidance, teach me to discern and part
Inherent things from casual, what is fixed
From fleeting, that my verse may live and be
Even as a light hung up in heaven to chear
Mankind in times to come. And if with this
I blend more lowly matter with the thing
Contemplated describe the mind and man
Contemplating and who and what he was
The transitory Being that beheld
This vision when and where and how he lived
With all his little realties of life
Be not the labour useless: if such theme
With highest things may [mingle   MS. 1] then great God
Thou who art breath and being, way and guide
And power and understanding, may my life
Express the image of a better time
More wise desires and simple manners, nurse
My heart in genuine freedom, all pure thoughts
Be with me and uphold me to the end.

APPENDIX B

FRAGMENTS of blank verse akin to *The Prelude* and *The Excursion*, written at a time when Wordsworth was contemplating *The Recluse*, or working at *The Ruined Cottage* and *The Pedlar*. For other fragments *v. Prel.* E. de S., pp. lvi, 525, 545, 571–8, 581–3, 612, 620–8.

I

From the verso of a loose foolscap sheet on which an early draft of
"The Old Cumberland Beggar" *is written*

YET once again do I behold the forms
Of these huge mountains, and yet once again,
Standing beneath these elms, I hear thy voice,
Beloved Derwent, that peculiar voice
Heard in the stillness of the evening air,
Half-heard and half-created.

II

Fragments from the Alfoxden note-book

i

there would he stand
In the still covert of some [? lonesome] rock,
Or gaze upon the moon until its light
Fell like a strain of music on his soul
And seem'd to sink into his very heart.

ii

Why is it we feel
So little for each other, but for this,
That we with nature have no sympathy,
Or with such things as have no power to hold
Articulate language ?
And never for each other shall we feel
As we may feel, till we have sympathy
With nature in her forms inanimate,
With objects such as have no power to hold
Articulate language. In all forms of things
There is a mind.

iii

Of unknown modes of being which on earth,
Or in the heavens, or in the heavens and earth

Exist by mighty combinations, bound
Together by a link, and with a soul
Which makes all one.

iv

To gaze
On that green hill and on those scattered trees
And feel a pleasant consciousness of life
In the impression of that loveliness
Until the sweet sensation called the mind
Into itself, by image from without
Unvisited, and all her reflex powers
Wrapped in a still dream [of] forgetfulness.

I lived without the knowledge that I lived
Then by those beauteous forms brought back again
To lose myself again as if my life
Did ebb and flow with a strange mystery.

v

solemn dreams,
Dreams beautiful as the fair hues that lie
About the moon in clouds of various depth,
In many clouds about the full-orb'd moon.
Why cannot they be still those barking curs
That so disturb the stillness of the moon
And make the [   ] restless ?

vi

and beneath the star
Of evening let the steep and lonely path
The steep path of the rocky mountain side
Among the stillness of the mountains hear
The panting of thy breath.

vii

lovely as the fairy day
Which one hour after sunset the sea gains
From the bright west when, on the bare hill-top,
Scarce distant twenty paces, the sheep bleats
Unseen, and darkness covers all the vales.

viii

these populous slopes
With all their groves and with their murmurous woods,
Giving a curious feeling to the mind
Of peopled solitude.

ix

where truth
Like some fair fabric in romantic glory
Built by the charm of sounds and symphonies
Uplifts her fair proportions at the call
Of pleasure her best minister.

III

THERE was a spot,
My favourite station when the winds were up,
Three knots of fir-trees, small and circular,
Which with smooth space of open plain between
Stood single, for the delicate eye of taste   5
Too formally arranged. Right opposite
The central clump I loved to stand and hear
The wind come on and touch the several groves
Each after each, and thence in the dark night
Elicit all proportions of sweet sounds   10
As from an instrument. "The strains are passed,"
Thus often to myself I said, "the sounds
Even while they are approaching are gone by,
And now they are more distant, more and more.
O listen, listen, how they wind away   15
Still heard they wind away, heard yet and yet,
While the last touch they leave upon the sense
Is sweeter than whate'er was heard before,
And seems to say that they can never die."

IV

Fragments (1798–9) *from a note-book containing the first extant MS. of*
"Christabel"

i

THOU issuest from a fissure in the rock
Compact into one individual stream,
A small short stream not longer than the blade
Of a child's coral, then, upon the face
Of the steep crag diffused, thou dost flow down
Wide, weak and glimmering, and so thin withal
Thy course is like the brushing of a breeze
Upon a calm smooth lake. A few bold drops
Are there, these regularly starting forth
Strike somewhere on the rocks and stones beneath
And are thy voice, for thou wert silent else.

III 4–5 And for the poet's or the painter's eye   *Alf.* MS.   7 clump]
grove   *Alf.* MS.

ii

The leaves stir not,
They all are steady as the cloudless sky;
How deep the Quiet: all is motionless,
As if the life of the vast world was hushed
Into a breathless dream.

iii

Oh 'tis a joy divine on summer days
When not a breeze is stirring, not a cloud,
To sit within some solitary wood,
Far in some lonely wood, and hear no sound
Which the heart does not make, or else so fit[s]
To its own temper that in external things
No longer seem internal difference
All melts away, and things that are without
Live in our minds as in their native home.

iv

The clouds are standing still in the mid heavens;
A perfect quietness is in the air;
The ear hears not; and yet, I know not how,
More than the other senses does it hold
A manifest communion with the heart.

v

The sl[ender ?] dandelion bows his head
With graceful [motion ?]; touched by the same breeze
The low geranium shivers wantonly.
Child art thou of the mountains, infant [stream ?]
A Brother of the stormy breeze; these flowers
Are they not all thy neighbours ? yet with thee
Do they maintain no visible fellowship,
Nor can I say that aught which they possess,
Of garb or colour is a gift of thine.

vi

There is creation in the eye,
Nor less in all the other senses; powers
They are that colour, model, and combine
The things perceived with such an absolute
Essential energy that we may say   5
That those most godlike faculties of ours
At one and the same moment are the mind
And the mind's minister. In many a walk
At evening or by moonlight, or reclined
At midday upon beds of forest moss,   10

Have we to Nature and her impulses
Of our whole being made free gift, and when
Our trance had left us, oft have we, by aid
Of the impressions which it left behind,
Looked inward on ourselves, and learned, perhaps,   15
Something of what we are. Nor in those hours
Did we destroy [   ]
The original impression of delight,
But by such retrospect it was recalled
To yet a second and a second life,
While in this excitation of the mind   20
A vivid pulse of sentiment and thought
Beat palpably within us, and all shades
Of consciousness were ours.

vii

Long had I stood and looked into the west,
Where clouds and mountain tops and gleams of light,
Children of glory all [   ]
Made one society and seemed to be
Of the same nature; long I stood and looked,   5
But when my thoughts began to fail, I turned
Towards a grove, a spot which well I knew,
For oftentimes its sympathies had fallen
Like a refreshing dew upon my heart;
I stretch[ed] myself beneath the shade   10
And soon the stirring and inquisitive mind
Was laid asleep; the godlike senses gave
Short impulses of life that seemed to tell
Of our existence, and then passed away.

viii

The moon is in the East, I see her not;
But to the summit of the arch of heaven
She whitens o'er the azure of the sky
With thin and milky gleams of visible light.

ix

For let the impediment be what it may
His hands must clothe and nourish them, and [thence ?]
From hour to hour so constantly he feels
An obligation pressing him with weight
Inevitable, that all offices   5
Which want this single tendency appear
Or trivial or redundant; hence remains
So little to be done that can assume

The appearance of a voluntary act,
That his affections in their very core 10
Are false, there is no freedom in his love.
Nor would he err perhaps who should assert
That this perceiv'd necessity creates
The same constriction of the heart, the same
[   ] in those with whom he lives, 15
His wife and children. What then can we hope
From one who is the worst of slaves, the slave
Of his own home ? The light that shines abroad,
How can it lead him to an act of love ?
Whom can he comfort ? Will the afflicted turn 20
Their steps to him, or will the eye of grief
And sorrow seek him ? Is the name of friend
Known to the poor man ? Whence is he to hear
The sweet creative voice of gratitude ?

V

From MS. 18 A, *the note-book containing MS.* D *of*
"The Ruined Cottage" *etc.* (*v. p.* 404)

i

THERE are who tell us that in recent times
We have been great discoverers, that by dint
Of nice experience we have lately given
To education principles as fixed
And plain as those of a mechanic trade;
Fair books and pure have been composed, that act
Upon the infant mind as does the sun
Upon a flower. In the corrected scheme
Of modern days all error is block'd out
So jealously, that wisdom thrives apace,
And in our very boyhood we become
Familiar friends with cause and consequence.
Great feats have been performed, a smooth high-way,
So they assert, has lately overbridged
The random chaos of futurity,
Hence all our steps are firm, and we are made
Strong in the power of knowledge. Ample cause
Why we, now living in this happy age,
Should bless ourselves. For, briefly, 'tis maintained
We now have rules and theories so precise
That by the inspection of unwearied eyes
We can secure infallible results.
But if the shepherd to his flock should point
The herb which each should feed on, were it not

Service redundant and ridiculous ?
And they, the tutors of our youth, our guides
And Masters, Wardens of our faculties,
And stewards of our labour, watchful men
And skilful in the usury of time,
Sages who in their prescience would coerce
All accidents, and tracing in their map
The way we ought to tread, would chain us down
Like engines, *etc. as Prelude* (1805), V. 383–8.
My playmates! brothers! nurs'd by the same years,
And fellow-children of the self-same hills,
Though we are moulded now by various fates
To various characters, I do not think
That there is one of us who cannot tell
How manifold the expedients, how intense
The unwearied passion with which nature toils
To win us to herself, and to impress
Our careless hearts with beauty and with love.
There was a Boy *etc. as Prelude* (1805), V. 389 *et seq.*

ii
Fragment with heading "Redundance"

Not the more
Failed I to lengthen out my watch. I stood
Within the area of the frozen vale,
Mine eye subdued and quiet as the ear
Of one that listens, for even yet the scene,
Its fluctuating hues and surfaces,
And the decaying vestiges of forms,
Did to the dispossessing power of night
Impart a feeble visionary sense
Of movement and creation doubly felt

VI

Fragment found in a note-book containing a few early drafts of "The Excursion" *and of the* "Guide to the Lakes"

As when, upon the smooth pacific deep
Dense fogs, to sight impervious, have withheld
A gallant vessel from some bold Emprize
Day after day deferred, till anxious hope
Yields to despair, if chance a sudden breeze
Spring up and dissipate the veil, all hearts
Throb at the change, and every sail is spread
To speed her course along the dazzling waves
For recompense of glorious conquest soon
To be atchieved upon the astonish'd foe.

VII

Fragments extracted by K. (Life, i, p. 389; *Poems of Wordsworth,* vol. viii, p. 263) *"from the miscellaneous jottings of D. W.'s Journals".*
[Composed 1800–6. First printed 1889.]

i

ALONG the mazes of this song I go
As inward motions of the wandering thought
Lead me, or outward circumstance impels.
Thus do I urge a never-ending way
Year after year, with many a sleep between,
Through joy and sorrow; if my lot be joy
More joyful if it be with sorrow sooth'd.

ii

Witness thou
The dear companion of my lonely walk,
My hope, my joy, my sister, and my friend,
Or something dearer still, if reason knows
A dearer thought, or in the heart of love
There be a dearer name.

iii

To the Evening Star over Grasmere Water [July 1800 ?]

The Lake is thine
The mountains too are thine, some clouds there are,
Some little feeble stars, but all is thine
Thou, thou art king, and sole proprietor,
A moon among her stars.

iv

A mighty vale,
Fresh as the freshest field, scoop'd out, and green
As is the greenest billow of the sea:
The multitude of little rocky hills,
Rocky or green, that do like islands rise
From the flat meadow lonely there—
Embowering mountains, and the dome of Heaven
And waters in the midst, a second Heaven

APPENDIX C

THE TUFT OF PRIMROSES

ONCE more I welcome Thee, and Thou, fair Plant,
Fair Primrose, hast put forth thy radiant Flowers
All eager to be welcomed once again.
O pity if the faithful Spring beguiled
By her accustomed hopes had come to breathe   5
Upon the bosom of this barren crag
And found thee not; but Thou art here, reviv'd
And beautiful as ever like a Queen
Smiling from thy imperishable throne,
And so shall keep for ages yet untold   10
Frail as Thou art, if the prophetic Muse
Be rightly trusted, so shalt Thou maintain
Conspicuously thy solitary state
In splendour unimpaired. For Thou art safe
From most adventurous bound of mountain sheep   15
By keenest hunger press'd, and from approach
Of the wild Goat still bolder, nor more cause,
Though in that sunny and obtrusive crag,
Hast thou to dread the desolating grasp
Of Child or Schoolboy, and though hand perchance   20
Of taller Passenger might want not power
To win thee, yet a thought would intervene
Though Thou be tempting, and that thought of love
Would hold him back, check'd in the first conceit
And impulse of such rapine. A benign   25
A good and friendly Spirit Thee hath watched
Thus far, and shall continue to preserve
Less for thy beauty's sake, though that might claim
All favour, than for pleasure which Thou shed'st
Down-looking and far-looking all day long   30
From that thy sunny and obtrusive seat
Upon the Travellers that do hourly climb
This steep, new gladness yielding to the glad,
And genial promises to those who droop
Sick, poor, or weary, or disconsolate,   35
Brightening at once the winter of their souls.

    I have a Friend, whom Seasons as they pass'd
All pleased: they in her bosom damp'd no joy

1–2 See there our [   ] fair Primrose of the rock
    Put forth once more her tuft of radiant flowers *alt.*
2 Fair primrose tuft hast put forth thy bright Flowers MS. A
4–7 Oh Pity if the spring had breathed in vain
    On the bare crag, but see the plant revives *alt.*

And from her light step took no liberty,
When suddenly as lightning from a cloud 40
Came danger with disease; Came suddenly
And linger'd long, and this commanding Hill
Which with its rocky chambers heretofore
Had been to her a range of dear resort,
The palace of her freedom, now, sad change, 45
Was interdicted ground, a place of fear
For her, a melancholy Hill for us
Constrain'd to think and ponder for her sake.

Fair primrose, lonely and distinguished Flower
Well worthy of that honourable place 50
That holds thy beauty up to public view,
For ever parted from all neighbourhood,
In a calm course of meditative years,
Oft have I hail'd thee with serene delight;
This greeting is far more—it is the voice 55
Of a surpassing joyance. She herself
With her own eyes shall bless thee, ere Thou fade
The Prisoner shall come forth, and all the toil
And labours of this sharp ascent shall melt
Before thy mild assurances, and pain 60
And weakness shall pass from her like a sleep
Chas'd by a bright glimpse of the morning Sun.

Farewell, yet turning from thee, happy Flower,
With these dear thoughts, not therefore are old claims
Unrecognised, nor have I languid sense 65
Of what thy reappearance would have been
Without this further joy, have been to me

42 commanding] high climbing MS. A   46 Was a forbidden haunt, a
thought MS. A
49 O primrose-tuft, fair sisterhood of flowers,
    One although many, many and yet one MS. *alt.* *so* MS. A, *followed by*
    With what delight I hail thee, she herself, *followed by* 58, 59 *as text.*
MS. A
59–62 And labour of this road shall melt away
    Before thy mild assurances, and pain
    And weakness shall pass from her like a dream.
    Thus have I not, thou bright imperial Flower,
    Queen, prophet, precurser, abundant cause
    Now above all to greet thee, long beloved
    With a surpassing joy. *cetera desunt.* MS. A
65–7 . . . nor therefore is the sense
    Less vivid of that pleasure which to me
    Thy punctual re-appearance would have given MS. *alt.*
67 further] cause of *alt.*

In its pure self. For often when I pass
This way, while thou art in thy winter sleep,
Or the rank Summer hides thee from my view   70
Even then I think of thee. Alas how much,
Since I beheld and loved thee first, how much
Is gone, though thou be left. I would not speak
Of best Friends dead, or other deep heart-loss
Bewail'd with weeping, but by River sides   75
And in broad fields how many gentle loves,
How many mute memorials pass'd away.
Stately herself, though of a lowly kind
That little Flower remains and has survived
The lofty band of Firs that overtopp'd   80
Their antient neighbour the old Steeple Tower,
That consecrated File which had so oft
Swung in the blast, mingling their solemn strain
Of music with the one determined voice
From the slow funeral bell, a symphony   85
Most awful and affecting to the ear
Of him who pass'd beneath; or had dealt forth
Soft murmurs like the cooing of a Dove
Ere first distinguishably heard, and cast
Their dancing shadows on the flowery turf   90
While through the Churchyard tripp'd the bridal train
In festive Ribbands deck'd, and those same trees
By moonlight in their stillness and repose
Deep'n'd the silence of a hundred graves.
Ah what a welcome! when from absence long   95
Returning, on the centre of the Vale
I look'd a first glad look, and saw them not!
Was it a dream? th' aerial grove, no more
Right in the centre of the lovely Vale
Suspended like a stationary cloud,   100
Had vanish'd like a cloud—yet say not so
For here and there a straggling Tree was left
To mourn in blanc and monumental grief,
To pine and wither for its fellows gone.
—Ill word that laid them low—unfeeling Heart   105
Had He who could endure that they should fall,
Who spared not them, nor spar'd that Sycamore high,
The universal glory of the Vale,
And did not spare the little avenue
Of lightly-stirring Ash-trees that sufficed   110
To dim the glare of Summer, and to blunt
The strong Wind turn'd into a gentle breeze
Whose freshness cheared the pavèd walk beneath,

That antient walk, which from the Vicar's door
Led to the Church-yard gate. Then, Grasmere, then   115
Thy sabbath mornings had a holy grace,
That incommunicable sanctity
Which Time and nature only can bestow
When from his plain abode the rustic Priest
Did issue forth glistening in best attire,   120
And down that consecrated visto paced
Towards the Churchyard where his ready Flock
Were gathered round in sunshine or in shade;
While Trees and mountains echoed to the Voice
Of the glad bells, and all the murmuring streams   125
United their Soft chorus with the Song.

Now stands the Steeple naked and forlorn
And from the Haven, the "last Central Home",
To which all change conducts the Thought, looks round
Upon the changes of this peaceful Vale.   131
What sees the old grey Tower, through high or low
Of his domain, that calls for more regret
Than yon small Cottage? there it is aloft
And nearest to the flying clouds of three
Perched each above the other on the side   135
Of the vale's northern outlet—from below
And from afar,—yet say not from afar
For all things in this little world of ours
Are in one bosom of close neighbourhood.
The hoary steeple now beholds that roof   140
Laid open to the glare of Common day,
And marks five graves beneath his feet, in which
Divided by a breadth of smooth green space
From nearer neighbourhood they who were erewhile
The Inmates of that Cottage are at rest.   145
Death to the happy House in which they dwelt
Had given a long reprieve of forty years:
Suddenly then they disappeared—not twice
Had Summer scorch'd the fields, not twice had fallen
The first white snow upon Helvellyn's top   150
Before the greedy visiting was closed
And the long-priviledged House left empty, swept
As by a plague; yet no rapacious plague

133-40 Than yon small Cottage. Gentle Auditor
Who hast a heart at leisure to receive
The mild enjoyments of this pensive lay,
Look thou, and thou alone behold . . .   MS. *alt.*

Had been among them, all was gentle death,
One after one with intervals of peace,   155
A consummation, and a harmony
Sweet, perfect, to be wish'd for, save that here
Was something sounding to our mortal sense
Like harshness, that the old grey headed sire,
The oldest, he was taken last, 'survived   160
When the dear Partner of his manhood's prime,
His Son, and Daughter, then a blooming Wife,
And little smiling Grandchild were no more.
(Methinks that Emma hears the murmuring song
And the pure Ether of her Maiden soul   165
Is overcast, and thy maternal eyes,
Mary, are wet, but not with tears of grief.)
'Twas but a little patience and his term
Of solitude was spent—the aged One
Our very first in Eminence of years   170
The Patriarch of the Vale; a busy Hand
Yea more, a burning palm, a flashing eye
A restless foot, a head that beat at nights
Upon its pillow with a thousand schemes,
A Planter, and a Rearer from the Seed,   175
Builder had been but scanty means forbad.
A Man of Hope, a forward-looking Mind
Even to the last, he and his chearful throng
Of open schemes, and all his inward hoard
Of unsunn'd griefs, too many and too keen,   180
Fell with the body into gentle sleep
In one blest moment, and the family
By yet a higher privilege once more
Were gathered to each other.
                          Yet I own,
Though I can look on their associate graves   185
With nothing but still thoughts, that I repine,
It costs me something like a pain to feel
That after them so many of their works
Which round that Dwelling covertly preserved
The History of their unambitious lives   190
Have perish'd, and so soon! the Cottage-Court
Spread with blue gravel from the torrent's side
And gay with shrubs, the garden, bed and walk
His own creation; that embattled Host
Of garish tulips, fruit-trees choice and rare   195
And roses of all colours, which he sought

159 harshness] discord MS. *alt.*

Most curiously, as generously dispers'd
Their kinds, to beautify his neighbours' grounds,
Trees of the forest, too, a stately fence
Planted for shelter in his manhood's prime,   200
And small Flowers watered by his wrinkled hand,—
That all are ravaged—that his Daughter's bower
Is creeping into shapelessness, self lost
In the wild wood, like a neglected image
Or Fancy which hath ceased to be recalled.   205
The jasmine, her own charge, which she had trained
To climb the wall, and of one flowery spray
Had made an Inmate, luring it from sun
And breeze, and from its fellows, to pervade
The inside of her chamber with its sweet,   210
I grieve to see that jasmine on the ground
Stretching it's desolate length, mourn that these works
Of love and diligence and innocent care
Are sullied and disgrac'd ; or that a gulf
Hath swallowed them which renders nothing back   215
That they so quickly in a cave are hidden
Which cannot be unlock'd ; upon their bloom
That a perpetual winter should have fallen.
Meanwhile the little Primrose of the rock
Remains, in sacred beauty, without taint   220
Of injury or decay, lives to proclaim
Her charter in the blaze of noon ; salutes
Not unobserved the Early Shepherd-Swain
Or Labourer plodding at the accustomed hour
Home to his distant hearth, and will be seen   225
Long as the fullness of her bloom endures,
Once with an instantaneous chear of mind
By stranger in late travel ; as I myself
Have often seen her, when the last lone Thrush
Hath ceas'd his Vesper hymn, piercing the gloom   230
Of Twilight with the vigor of a star ;
Or rather say, hung from the shadowy Rock
Like the broad Moon, with lustre somewhat dimm'd
Lovely and bright, and as the Moon secure.

Oh for some band of guardian spirits prompt   235
As were those human Ministers of old
Who daily, nightly, under various names
With various service stood or walked their rounds

227 With one short instantaneous *alt.*   232 Say, rather, shining
from her station bold *alt.*   234 Large as the Moon, *alt.*

Through the wide Forest, to protect from harm
The wild Beast with her young, and from the touch   240
Of waste the green-leav'd thicket to defend,
Her secret couching-place, and stately tree
Her canopy, and berry-bearing shrub
And grassy lawn, their pasture's pleasant range,
Continual and firm peace from outrage safe   245
And all annoyance, till the Sovereign comes
Heading his train, and through that franchise high
Urges the chase with clamorous Hound and horn.
O grant some wardenship of spirits pure
As duteous in their office to maintain   250
Inviolate for nobler purposes,
These individual precincts, to protect
Here, if here only, from despoil and wrong
All growth of nature and all frame of Art
By, and in which the blissful pleasures live.   255
Have not th' incumbent Mountains looks of awe
In which their mandate may be read, the streams
A Voice that pleads, beseeches, and implores ?
In vain: the deafness of the world is here
Even here, and all too many of the haunts   260
Which Fancy most delights in, and the best
And dearest resting-places of the heart
Vanish beneath an unrelenting doom.

What impulse drove the Hermit to his Cell,
And what detain'd him there till life was spent   265
Fast anchored in the desart ? Not alone
Dread of the persecuting sword, remorse,
Wrongs unredress'd, and insults unaveng'd
And unavengeable, defeated pride,
Prosperity subverted, maddening want,   270
Love with despair or grief in agony.
Not always from intolerable pangs
He fled ; but compassed round by pleasure sighed
For independent quiet, craving peace,
The central feeling of all happiness,   275
Not as a refuge from distress or pain
A breathing time, vacation, or a truce,
But for its absolute self, a life of peace,
Stability without regret or fear,
That hath been, is, and shall be evermore.   280
Therefore on few external things his heart

263 Vanish] Perish *alt.*   273 but in the height of pleasure *alt.*

Was set, and those his own, or if not his
Subsisting under nature's stedfast law.
What other yearning was the master tie
Of the monastic brotherhood, upon rock   285
Aerial or in Green secluded Vale
One after one collected from afar
An undissolving fellowship ? What but this
The universal instinct of repose
The longing for confirm'd tranquillity   290
In small and great, in humble and sublime,
The life where hope and memory are as one,
Earth quiet and unchanged, the human soul
Consistent in self-rule, and heaven revealed
To meditation in that quietness.   295

Thus tempted, thus inspired, St. Basil left
(Man as he was of noble blood, high born,
High station'd, and elaborately taught)
The vain felicities of Athens, left
Her throng of Sophists glorying in their snares,   300
Her Poets, and conflicting Orators,
Abandon'd Alexandria's splendid Halls,
Antioch and Cesarea, and withdrew
To his delicious Pontic solitude,
Remembering with deep thankfulness meanwhile   305
Those exhortations of a female voice
Pathetically urg'd, his Sister's voice,
Macrina, pious Maid, most beautiful
And in the gentleness of woman wise,
By whom admonish'd, He, while yet a youth   310
And a triumphant Scholar, had dismiss'd
That loftiness and to the way inclined
Of virtue, self restraint and privacy,
Virtue severe and absolute Restraint,
Which, when he chose, erelong he found the same   315
Beyond the utmost of its promise, rich
In dignity, sincere content, and joy.

Mark! for the Picture to this hour remains,
With what luxuriant fondness he pourtrays
The lineaments and image of that spot   320

312–17   That loftiness and bent his dearest hopes
         To a strict life of virtuous privacy
         Which sequestration, when he chose, erelong
         He found the same beyond all promise rich
         In dignity   alt.

In which upon a Mount, sylvan and high,
And at the boldest jutting in its side,
His cell was fix'd, a Mount with towering Hills
Girt round, and vallies intricate and deep,
Which, leaving one blind entrance to a plain   325
Of fertile meadow-ground that lay beneath
Fronting the cell, had from all quarters else
Forbidden all approach; by rocks abrupt,
Or rampart as effectual of huge woods
Neither austere nor gloomy to behold   330
But in gay prospect lifting to the Sun
Majestic beds of diverse foliage, fruits
And thousand laughing blossoms; and the plain
Stretched out beneath the high-perch'd cell was bright
With herbs and flowers and tufts of flowering plants,   335
The choicest which the lavish East pours forth,
And sober-headed cypress interspersed,
And grac'd with presence of a famous stream
The Rapid Iris, journeying from remote
Armenian Mountains to his Euxine bourne,   340
Sole Traveller by the guarded mount; and He
To enter there had leapt with thunderous voice
Down a steep rock, and through the secret place,
Not without many a lesser bound advanc'd
Self-chear'd with song to keep his onward course   345
Like a belated Pilgrim.
                        "Come, O Friend,"
Thus did St. Basil fervently break forth,
Thus call upon the man he held most dear:
"Come Nazianzen to these fortunate Isles,
This blest Arcadia, to these purer fields   350
Than those which Pagan superstition feigned
For mansions of the happy dead—O come
To this Enduring Paradise, these walks
Of Contemplation, piety and love,
Coverts serene of bless'd mortality.   355
What if the Roses and the flowers of Kings,
Princes and Emperors, and the crowns and palms
Of all the great are blasted, or decay;
What if the meanest of their subjects, each
Within the narrow region of his cares,   360
Tremble beneath a sad uncertainty?

323–5 His cell was fix'd aloft! yet overtopped,
    Far overtopped by circumambient hills
    Which, *alt.*

There is a priviledge to plead, there is;
Renounce, and thou shalt find that priviledge here.
No loss lamenting, no privation felt,
Disturb'd by no vicissitudes, unscared   365
By civil faction, by religious broils
Unplagu'd, forgetting and forgotten here
May'st thou possess thy own invisible nest
Like one of those small birds that round us chaunt
In multitudes; their warbling will be thine,   370
And freedom to unite thy voice with theirs
When they at morn or dewy evening praise
High heaven in sweet and solemn services.
Here may'st thou dedicate thyself to God,
And acceptably fill the votive hours   375
Not only as these Creatures of the grove
That need no rule, and live but to enjoy;
Not only lifted often to the calm
Of that entire beatitude in which
The Angels serve, but when thou must descend   380
From the pure vision, and thy soul admit
A salutary glow of hope and fear,
Searching in patience and humility
Among the written mysteries of faith
The will divine; or when thou would'st assume   385
The burthen and the seasonable yoke
Befitting our frail nature, would'st be tamed
By vigils, abstinence and prayer with tears,
What place so fit ?—a deeper solitude
Thebais or the Syrian Wilderness   390
Contains not in its dry and barren round.
For not a human form is seen this way
Unless some straggling Hunter led by chance;
Him, if the graver duties be performed,
Or overwrought with study if the mind   395
Be haunted by a vain disquietude
And gladly would be taken from itself;
Or if it be the time when thoughts are blithe,
Him may'st thou follow to the hills, or mount
Alone, as fancy prompts, equipp'd with bow   400
And shafts and quiver, not for perilous aim
At the gaunt wolf, the lion or the Pard,—
These lurk not in our bounds, but Deer and Goat
And other kinds as peaceable are there

393 straggling] devious *alt.*   396 Be restless under vain disturbances
alt.

In readiness for inoffensive chase.   405
The River also owns his harmless tribes,
And tempts thee to like sport; labour itself
Is pastime here; for generous is the sun,
And cool airs blowing from the mountain top
Refresh the brow of him who in plain field   410
Or garden presses his industrious spade.
Or if a different exercise thou chuse
And from boon nature rather would'st receive
Food for the day, behold the fruits that hang
In the primæval woods; the Wells and Springs   415
Have each a living garland of green herbs
From which they to the rifling hand will yield
Ungrudgingly supply that never fails,
Bestowed as freely as their waters pure,
To deck thy temperate board."
                              From theme to theme   420
Transported in this sort by fervent zeal
That stopp'd not here, the venerable man
Holy and great his invitation breathed—
And Nazianzen fashion'd a reply
Ingenious and rhetorical, with taunts   425
Of wit and gay good-humoured ridicule
Directed both against the life itself
And that strong passion for those fortunate Isles
For the Arcadia of a golden dream.
But in his inward council-seat, his soul   430
Was mov'd, was rapt and fill'd with seriousness,
Nor was it long ere broken loose from ties
Of the world's business he the call obey'd.
And Amphilochius came, and numbers more,
Men of all tempers, qualities, estates,   435
Came with one spirit, like a troop of fowl
That single or in clusters, at a sign
Given by their leader, settle on the breast
Of some broad pool, green field, or loftiest tree
In harmony and undisturbed repose;   440
Or as a brood of eager younglings flock
Delighted, to the mother's outspread wings
And shelter there in unity and love.

An intellectual Champion of the faith,
Accomplish'd above all who then appeared   445
Or, haply, since victoriously have stood
In opposition to the desperate course
Of Pagan rites or impious heresies,

St. Basil, after lapse of years, went forth
To a station of authority and power 450
Upon an urgent summons, and resigned,
Ah! not without regret, the heavenly Mount,
The sheltering valley, and his lov'd Compeers.
He parted from them, but their common life,
If neither first nor singular, at least 455
More beautiful than any of like frame
That hitherto had been conceived, a life
To which by written institutes and rules
He gave a solid being, did not fail
Nor die with him, and hung through many an age 460
In bright remembrance, like a shining cloud
O'er the vast regions of the western Church;
Whence those communities of holy men,
That spread so far, to shrouded quietness
Devoted, and of saintly Virgins pure. 465

Fallen in a thousand vales the stately Towers
And branching windows gorgeously array'd
And aisles and roofs magnificent that thrill'd
With halleluiahs, and the strong-ribb'd vaults
Are crush'd; and buried under weeds and earth 470
The cloistral avenues—they that heard the voice
Of Rhone or Loire or some sequester'd brook
Soft murmuring among woods and olive bowers
And tilth and vineyard, and the Piles that rose
On British lawns by Severn, Thames, or Tweed, 475
And saw their pomp reflected in the stream,
As Tintern saw; and, to this day beholds
Her faded image in the depths of Wye;
Of solemn port smitten but unsubdued
She stands; nor less tenacious of her rights 480
Stands Fountains Abbey, glorious in decay,
Before the pious Traveller's lifted eye
Threatening to outlive the ravages of Time
And bear the cross till Christ shall come again.
So cleave they to the earth in monument 485
Of Revelation, nor in memory less
Of nature's pure religion, as in line
Uninterrupted it hath travelled down
From the first man who heard a howling storm
Or knew a troubled thought or vain desire, 490
Or in the very sunshine of his joy

472 Of some sequester'd brook in Gallia's vales

Was saddened at a perishable bliss
Or languish'd idly under fond regrets
That would not be subdued . . . [Methinks I hear,
Not from these woods, but from some merry grove   495
That lies I know not where, the spritely blast
Of the clear bugle, and from thicket green
Of hollies sparkling in an April sun
Forth, in a moment, issues to the glade
A Troop of green-clad Foresters in arms   500
Blithe Outlaws with their Chieftain, Would they rouze
The Stag, dislodge the Hart; or will they keep
Their oath in presence of Maid Marian sworn
And with a cloud of shafts this day confound
The royal Officers? Let them on, and yield   505
Even at their pleasure to the boisterous drift
Of pastime or adventure—let them on
I love them better when at ease]

                       "And is thy doom
Pronounc'd" (I said, a stripling at that time   510
Who with a Fellow-pilgrim had been driv'n
Through madding France before a joyous gale
And to the solemn haven of Chartreuse
Repaired for timely rest) "and are we twain
The last, perchance the very last, of men   515
Who shall be welcom'd here, whose limbs shall find
Repose within these modest cells, whose hearts
Receive a comfort from these awful spires?
Alas! for what I see, the flash of arms,
O Sorrow! and yon military glare;   520
And hark, those Voices! let us hide in gloom
Profoundest of St. Bruno's wood—these sighs
These whispers that pursue or meet me, whence
[   ] are they but a common [   ]
From the two Sister streams of Life and Death,   525
Or are they by the parting Genius sent
Unheard till now and to be heard no more"?

   Yes, I was moved and to this hour am moved;
What Man would bring to nothing if he might
A natural power or element? and who,   530
If the ability were his, would dare
To kill a species of insensate life,
Or to the bird of meanest wing would say,
Thou and thy kind must perish? Even so

494–508 Methinks . . . ease: *deleted in* MS.

So consecrated, almost, might he deem   535
That power, that organ, that transcendent frame
Of social being.—"Stay your impious hand":
Such was the vain injunction of that hour
By Nature uttered from her Alpine throne:
"O leave in quiet this embodied dream   540
This substance by which mortal men have clothed,
Humanly cloth'd, the ghostliness of things
In silence visible and perpetual calm,
Let this one Temple last—be this one spot
Of Earth devoted to Eternity."—   545
I heard or seemed to hear, and thus the Voice
Proceeded: "Honour to the Patriot's zeal
Glory and life to new-born liberty—
All hail ye mighty Passions of the Time,
The vengeance and the transport and the hope,   550
But spare, if past and future be the wings
On whose support harmoniously conjoined
Moves the great Spirit of human knowledge, spare
This House, these courts of mystery, where a step
Between the Portals of the shadowy rocks   555
Leaves far behind the vanities of life;
Where, if a peasant enter or a king,
One holy thought, a single holy thought
Has power to initiate. Let it be redeem'd
With all its blameless priesthood for the sake   560
Of Heaven-descended truth; and humbler claim
Of these majestic floods, my noblest boast,
These shining cliffs, pure as their home, the sky,
These forests unapproachable by death
That shall endure as long as Man endures   565
To think, to hope, to worship and to feel;
To struggle,—to be lost within himself
In trepidation,—from the dim abyss
To look with bodily eyes, and be consoled."
Such repetition of that [   ]   570
My thoughts demanded; now an humbler task
Awaits us for the unwearied Song will lead
Into a lonely Vale the mild abode
Of female Votaries—No [   ] plain
Blank as the Arabian wilderness defends   575
This chosen spot nor is it [   ]
By rocks like those of Caucasus or Alps
Shapes untransmuted of successive worlds,
Nor can it boast a massy structure huge
Founded and built by hands with arch and towers,   580

Pillar and pinnacle and glittering spire
Sublime as if in Emulation reared
Of the eternal Architect—these signs
These tokens, admonitions to recall,
Curbs to restrain, or stays to lean upon,   585
Such food to nourish or appease the Soul
The gentle Beings who found harbour here
Required not—Them a lowly Edifice
Embraced by [?] grounds that did not aim
To overshadow but to screen and hide,   590
Contented; and an unassuming brook
Working between these hills its careless way
Through meadow, chestnut woods and olive-bowers
And tilth and vineyard
                    cetera desunt

ADDENDUM

Fragment of an intended poem on Milton, written in the copy of
Paradise Lost *which belonged to Wordsworth at Cambridge*

                    ON Religion's holy hill
He built an altar, and the fire from heaven
Came down upon it. Round the growing flames
That filled the sense with fragrance gently rose
Sounds and [1] and all the while were heard
Airs of high melody from solemn harp,
And voice of Angel in accordance sweet.
Anon the trump of God, with dreadful blast
Rock'd all the mountain; on their flashing clouds
The silent cherubs trembled; undismayed
Stood the blind prophet and   *cetera desunt*

                    1 *left blank*

NOTES

Preface to the Edition of 1814:

The Recluse *and the genesis of* The Excursion

"Several years ago, when the Author retired to his native mountains, with the hope of being enabled to construct a literary Work that might live, it was a reasonable thing that he should take a review of his own mind, and examine how far Nature and Education had qualified him for such employment. As subsidiary to this preparation he undertook to record, in verse, the origin and progress of his own powers. That Work, addressed to a dear Friend, most distinguished for his knowledge and genius, . . . has been long finished ;[1] and the result of the investigation which gave rise to it was a determination to compose a philosophical poem, containing views of Man, Nature, and Society ; and to be entitled *The Recluse*. . . ."

This paragraph gives an account of the genesis of *The Recluse, The Excursion* "being a portion of *The Recluse*",[2] and of *The Prelude*, which is not strictly accurate. Wordsworth did not retire to Grasmere till December 1799. The scheme for the great philosophical poem to be called "The Recluse" was embraced early in 1798 at Alfoxden, Somerset (*v.* Letters of Wordsworth written March 1798, *E.L.*, pp. 188–90). The relation between *The Prelude, The Excursion*, and *The Recluse* is somewhat obscured by the fact that W. first used *The Recluse* as a covering title for all the blank verse which he was writing in the early years with a view to the great philosophical poem. Some of this verse was incorporated in *The Prelude*, his poetical autobiography (completed in its first form in 1805) some in *The Excursion*. As this preface shows, he conceived *The Prelude* as subsidiary and preparatory to *The Recluse* ; and he now, in 1814, planned *The Recluse* as a tripartite poem, of which he had written Book I of Part I (*v.* Appendix A) and of which *The Excursion* was to form Part II.

From his letters and MS. note-books, and from Dorothy Wordsworth's journals and letters, the emergence of *The Excursion* from the original plan of *The Recluse* can be traced.

March 6, 1798. "I have written 1300 lines of a poem in which I contrive to convey most of the knowledge of which I am possessed. My object is to give pictures of Nature, Man and Society. Indeed I know not anything which will not come within the scope of my plan" (W. W. to James Tobin: *E.L.*, p. 188).

March 11. "I have written 1300 lines of a poem which I hope to make of considerable utility. Its title will be *The Recluse; or, views of Nature, Man, and Society*" (W. W. to James Losh: *E.L.*, p. 190).

[1] *The Prelude*, published 1850.

[2] Thus it is described on the title-page of 1814.

A first draft of the lines "On Man, on Nature, and on Human Life" afterwards printed as Prospectus to *The Recluse* was probably written at this time. The resolve to compose his autobiography rather than embark straightway upon the great poem was perhaps formed in the winter of 1798–9.

Coleridge was the prime mover in the scheme for the great philosophic poem. "I looked forward to 'The Recluse' as the first and only true philosophical poem in existence" (letter of S. T. C. to W. W., May 30, 1815). Wordsworth kept the task before him for many years, finding himself increasingly reluctant for it, and at first turning to Coleridge for stimulus and assistance.

March 6, 1804. "I am very anxious to have your notes for *The Recluse*. I cannot say how much importance I attach to this: if it should please God that I survive you, I should reproach myself for ever in writing the work if I had neglected to procure this help" (W. W. to S. T. C.[1] *E.L.*, p. 368).

Coleridge's comment on *The Excursion*, recorded in his *Table Talk*, July 31, 1832, reveals the original design of *The Recluse*:

"I cannot help regretting that Wordsworth did not first publish his thirteen books on the growth of an individual mind—superior, as I used to think, upon the whole, to *The Excursion*. You may judge how I felt about them by my own poem upon the occasion. Then the plan laid out, and, I believe, partly suggested by me, was, that Wordsworth should assume the station of a man in mental repose, one whose principles were made up, and so prepared to deliver upon authority a system of philosophy. He was to treat man as man—a subject of eye, ear, touch, and taste, in contact with external nature, and informing the senses from the mind, and not compounding a mind out of the senses; then he was to describe the pastoral and other states of society, assuming something of the Juvenalian spirit as he approached the high civilization of cities and towns, and opening a melancholy picture of the present state of degeneracy and vice; thence he was to infer and reveal the proof of, and necessity for, the whole state of man and society being subject to, and illustrative of, a redemptive process in operation, showing how this idea reconciled all the anomalies, and promised future glory and restoration. Something of this sort was, I think, agreed on. It is, in substance, what I have been all my life doing in my system of philosophy.

"I think Wordsworth possessed more of the genius of a great philosophic poet than any man I ever knew, or, as I believe, has existed in England since Milton; but it seems to me that he ought never to have abandoned the contemplative position, which is peculiarly—

---

[1] W. never received the notes. From a letter of S. T. C. to W. W. of May 1, 1805, D. W. transcribes the following: "my Ideas respecting your *Recluse* were burnt as a Plague-garment, and all my long letters to you and Sir George Beaumont sunk to the bottom of the Sea!" *E.L.*, p. 508.

perhaps I might say exclusively—fitted for him. His proper title is *Spectator ab extra.*"

March 6, 1804. "I am now writing a poem on my own earlier life. This Poem will not be published . . . till I have finished a larger and more important work to which it is tributary. Of this larger work I have written one Book and several scattered fragments, it is a moral and philosophical Poem; the subject whatever I find most interesting in Nature, Man and Society. . . . To this work I mean to devote the prime of my life and the chief force of my mind. I have also arranged the plan of a narrative Poem; and if I live to finish these three principal works I shall be content. . . . They are all to be in blank verse." (W. W. to De Quincey: *E.L.*, p. 370.)

But to take up his station "as a man in mental repose", and "deliver upon authority a system of philosophy" according to Coleridge's plan, was what Wordsworth found he could not do. The "one book" which he told De Quincey he had written was entitled *The Recluse*, Part First, Book First, *Home at Grasmere*.¹ Composed early in 1800 it ends with the eloquent passage already referred to, "On Man, on Nature, and on Human Life", which he was to quote in his Preface to *The Excursion* as "a kind of Prospectus of the design and scope of the whole Poem" (*The Recluse*), but the substance of the Book, well described in its title *Home at Grasmere*, is an intimate record of his impressions of the Vale and its inhabitants during his first months of residence at Dove Cottage: it is in fact a continuation of his poetical autobiography from the place where *The Prelude* leaves off. *The Excursion*, which he published with the sub-title "*a Portion of The Recluse*", took the poetic form of philosophic dialogue on a slender dramatic basis, interlarded with narrative: it had its starting-point not in Coleridge's conception of the philosophical poem but in a tale in blank verse, *The Ruined Cottage*, written at Racedown before Wordsworth's intimacy with Coleridge began.

June 1797. "The first thing that was read after he (Coleridge) came was W.'s new poem *The Ruined Cottage*, with which he was much delighted" (D. W. to M. H. (?): *E.L.*, p. 169).

Though no complete MS. survives of the earliest draft of *The Ruined Cottage*, it must have contained a short bare narrative of unrelieved distress. The earliest MS. of portions of it (MS. A) seems to have been written in 1795 (*v. infra*). In a letter to J. P. Estlin in June 1797² Coleridge quotes the last lines of it, ending "Last human tenant of these ruined walls"³ (corresponding with MS. B *infra*, ll. 705–42, and *Exc.* i. 871–916). Its theme was expressly the Ruined Cottage, found by the poet in his wanderings and haunting him by

¹ *The Recluse*. Home at Grasmere. First published in 1888. *Vide* Appendix A, p. 313 *supra*, and note, p. 475.

² *Collected Letters of S. T. C.*, edited Griggs, vol. i, p. 327.

³ In the two earliest complete MSS. B and D the poem ends at this line.

the human appeal of its abandoned walls and garden, and its disused well:[1] and the poem must have told how on one of his visits to the place he met by chance a Pedlar, who, when questioned, told him the story of the "last human tenant of the ruined walls". In the following March D. W. writes to Mary Hutchinson:

March 5, 1798. "You desire me to send you a copy of *The Ruined Cottage*. This is impossible for it has grown to the length of 900 lines.[2] I will however send you a copy of that part which is immediately and solely connected with the Cottage. The Pedlar's character now makes a very, certainly the *most*, considerable part of the Poem."

By March 1798, as we know from a letter of Coleridge written in that month[3] the philosophical tail-piece had been added (*v.* Addendum to MS. B *infra*). The character of the philosophic Pedlar and his relation with the young Poet, his interlocutor, were evidently a new feature: in the version of the closing lines quoted by Coleridge in June 1797 the interlocutor had been addressed by the narrator of the tale as "Stranger"; he has become "my friend" in the later version (MS. B 740 (*v. infra*, p. 399); *Exc.* i. 914).

From Dec. 1801 to March 1802 there are many references in Dorothy Wordsworth's journal to *The Pedlar* as the expanded story is now entitled, and she speaks of it as a poem in three parts. It covered roughly the ground of *Exc.* Book I, divided, as it still is, into three parts at l. 433 and l. 604.

On Oct. 9, 1800, Coleridge had written to Sir H. Davy: "We mean to publish *Christabel* with a long blank verse poem of W's entitled *The Pedlar*"; and on March 10, 1802, Dorothy Wordsworth writes in her journal: "W. has been talking about publishing the Yorkshire Wolds poem (i.e. *Peter Bell*) with *The Pedlar*."[4] At what date precisely Wordsworth ceased to regard *The Pedlar* as a separate poem and began to plan *The Excursion* as a development of it is not revealed; but it is evident that he found in the philosophic pedlar, later to be called the Wanderer, whose character took on a special significance for him, an effective starting-point for this portion of his great philosophical poem, and by the end of 1804 he is writing of *The Pedlar* as a part of *The Recluse*.

Dec. 25, 1804. "I do not know if you are exactly acquainted with the plan of my poetical labour: it is twofold; first, a Poem, to be called *The Recluse*, in which it will be my object to express in verse my most interesting feelings concerning Man, Nature, and society; and next, a Poem (in which I am at present principally engaged) on my earlier life. . . . This latter work I expect to have finished before the month

---

[1] *v.* the first fragmentary MS., A, described *infra* p. 377.

[2] This revised form of the poem has survived in MS. B.

[3] *Collected Letters of S. T. C.*, edited Griggs, i. 397.

[4] *v.* also D. W.'s journal for Feb. 13 where *The Pedlar* and *The Recluse* are referred to as two poems.

of May; and then I purpose to fall with all my might on the former, which is the chief object upon which my thoughts have been fixed these many years. Of this poem, that of "The Pedlar", which Coleridge read you, is part, and I may have written of it altogether about 2,000 lines. It will consist I hope of almost 10, or 12 thousand." (W. to Sir G. Beaumont.)

June 3, 1805. "I have the pleasure to say that I finished my poem [The Prelude] about a fortnight ago. . . . This work may be considered as a sort of *portico* to *The Recluse*, part of the same building, which I hope to be able, ere long, to begin with in earnest." (W. to Sir G. B.)

He was to make the composition of *The Excursion* his principal work for the next nine years: it was published under the title of *The Excursion, Being a Portion of The Recluse* in 1814. His unfulfilled promise of *The Recluse* lay on his conscience and engaged the hopes of his friends for the rest of his life.* Twice he had turned aside from

---

* *Nov. 10, 1806.* I am going to Press with a volume . . . it will consist entirely of small pieces, and I publish with great reluctance; but the day when my long work will be finished seems farther and farther off. (W. W. to Walter Scott.)

Feb. 18, 1815. W. has had one of his weeks of rest and we now begin to wish that he was at work again, but as he intends completely to plan the first part of *The Recluse* before he begins the composition, he must read many Books before he will fairly set to labour again. (D. W. to S. H.)

Oct. 16, 1817. . . . he intends to work hard at *The Recluse* in Winter. (D. W. to C. Clarkson.)

June 7, 1819. If, as you say, The Waggoner in some sort came at my call, Oh for a potent voice to call forth *The Recluse* from his profound dormitory, where he sleeps forgetful of his foolish charge—the world! (C. Lamb to W. W.)

March 27, 1821. W. is quite well, and very busy, though he has not looked at *The Recluse* or the poem on his own life; and this disturbs us. After 50 years of age there is no time to spare, and unfinished works should not if possible be left behind. This he feels, but the will never governs *his* labours. (D. W. to C. Clarkson.)

April 20, 1822. *The Recluse* has had a long sleep, save in my thoughts; my MSS. are so ill-penned and blurred that they are useless to all but myself; and at present I cannot face them. (W. W. to W. S. Landor.)

Dec. 13, 1824. My Brother has not yet looked at *The Recluse*; he seems to feel the task so weighty that he shrinks from beginning with it . . . yet knows that he has now no time to loiter if another great work is to be accomplished by him—I say another—for I consider *The Excursion* as one work though the Title-page tells that it is but a *part* of one that has another Title. (D. W. to H. C. R.)

1826. I hope we shall have the remainder of *The Recluse* ere long. (Hartley Coleridge to Derwent.)

Dec. 18, 1826. He has lately written some very good sonnets. I wish I could add that *The Recluse* was brought from his hiding-place. (D. W. to H. C. R.)

Jan. 22, 1830. For your head (I do not flatter) is not a nob or the end of

his central task. Of the great philosophical poem on Coleridge's plan, to which he still endeavoured to be faithful (he says in the Preface to *The Excursion* that "the first and third parts of *The Recluse* will consist chiefly of meditations in the Author's own person"), all that finally survived, apart from one Book, was a Prelude to the main theme and an Excursion from it. It is clear from the letters and the MSS. that there was from the start a divergence between Wordsworth's own idea of *The Recluse* and Coleridge's plan. Coleridge intended a philosophical discourse delivered authoritatively from the mouth of the poet. Wordsworth early defined his object as "to give *pictures* of Nature, Man, and Society", and the early note-books of the Alfoxden period, 1797–8, show that the "scattered fragments" of which he speaks later were jottings in blank verse falling into three categories: (1) descriptions of natural scenes and images that impressed him, (2) human tales and character sketches, and (3) philosophical reflections rising out of both. Wordsworth was right to follow his own bent: his poetic thought sprang out of the living body of his experience, and could only be delivered through images and incidents and characters

a ninepin—unless a Vulcanian hammer could fairly batter a Recluse out of it, then would I bid the smirch'd God knock and knock lustily, the two-handed skinker. (Lamb to W. W.)

Aug. 1830. I am afraid there is little hope at present of another portion of *The Recluse*. (Hartley Coleridge to Derwent.)

Sept. 28, 1836. We hope . . . that the Poet may leave home with a perfect holiday before him—and, but I dare not say so—return to *The Recluse*; and let me charge you, not to encourage the Muse to *vagrant* subjects. (M. W. to H. C. R.)

Dec. 17, 1836. Oh! continue *The Recluse*. I wish I was Moxon. I would make you such an offer for it as could ruin me and enrich my children. . . . I really think from what Murray said to me, two or three years ago, he would give you £1,000 for the rest of *The Recluse*. (Barron Field to W. W., *unpublished letter*.)

[It is noteworthy that in correcting his last fair copy of *The Prelude* (MS. E) in 1839 (or possibly a little later), he omitted the line which concludes a tentative passage on the senses counteracting each other: *But this is matter for another Song* (*Prel.* 1805, xi. 185). Clearly he had still contemplated up to that time working out some of these ideas in *The Recluse*.]

June 25, 1841. He [Wordsworth] says that the "Recluse" has never been written except a few passages—and probably never will. (Aubrey de Vere to his sister.)

Jan. 12, 1843. . . . if I could hope to see the conclusion of *The Excursion* it would be worth living for—I am sure I should live longer if I could only have the hope of seeing a portion of it. . . . (C. Clarkson to H. C. R.)

Feb. 16, 1845. I am sorry to see him [the poet] entering into politics or political economy. . . . He does not shine in such subjects. . . . I wish he would either complete *The Recluse* or lock up his desk. (Barron Field to H. C. R.)

which belonged to the life of Man and Nature as he knew it ; the auto-
biographic form of *The Prelude* and, in a less degree, the dramatic and
narrative form of *The Excursion* fitted his genius.

Chronology of the Composition of The Excursion

The chronology of the composition of *The Excursion* can be traced
in outline from a study of the MSS. and letters and other evidence.
It is clear that W.'s habit was to compose in detached passages, which
he afterwards worked into the fabric of his poem. Certain passages
of *The Excursion* were written in the early years when he was con-
templating *The Recluse*, and had started upon *The Prelude*, and before
he had set to work upon *The Excursion* as a separate publication. I
append a list with approximate dates:

1795. W. says that the lines first written were "those beginning
'Nine tedious years' and ending 'Last human tenant of these
ruined walls' [*Exc.* i. 871–916]. These were composed in '95 at
Racedown".—I. F. But MS. A of *The Ruined Cottage*, which
must belong to 1795 *circa*, has the central part of Margaret's story,
the unhappy events leading to her husband's breakdown, MS. B,
348–413 and 430–9 (*v.* pp. 389–92 *infra*), *Exc.* i. 502–70, 582–91.

1797. In June 1797 S. T. C. quotes *Exc.* i. 880–916 in a letter.

1797–8. Passages describing "Margaret during her affliction"
(*v.* I. F.). W. places next in date, as composed at Racedown or
Alfoxden, lines at the close of Book IV "For the man who in this
spirit . . . intellectual soul" [*Exc.* iv. 1207–75]—I. F. This
passage appears first in Addendum to MS. B, 3–58, 92–9 (*v.*
pp. 400–3 *infra*), and is quoted by S. T. C. in a letter of March
1798. In MS. B the passage included *Exc.* iv. 958–68.

MS. B and B 2 of *The Ruined Cottage* (*v. infra*) belong to the
winter 1797–8. In the *Alfoxden* note-book which W. used
between Jan. 20 and March 5, 1798, there are jottings for the
pedlar's character (*v.* note to *Exc.* i. 422–33) and for "Objects
that have no power to hold articulate language", *Exc.* iv. 1204–7
(*v.* note).

1798–9. In the *Christabel* note-book lines corresponding to *Exc.* iii.
69–73 (*v.* Appendix B, IV. i *supra*, p. 342) probably belong
to late Spring 1798. MS. 18A contains a fragment about the
factory lad corresponding to *Exc.* viii. 292–305, 315–33 (*v. app.
crit.* and note) and a fragment "There is an active principle
. . ." corresponding to *Exc.* ix. 1–26, 124–52 (*v. app. crit.* and
note).

The lines used as Prospectus to *Exc.*, "On Man, on Nature,
and on human life . . .", were probably written in 1798.

1799–1800. MS. 2 of *Peter Bell* has lines describing Margaret of
R. C. (*Exc.* i. 513), including some hitherto unpublished (*v.* note
pp. 413–14. *infra*).

1800. MS. R, which comprises rough drafts for *Recluse* i, written early in 1800, includes "Happy is he who lives . . ." (*Exc.* iv. 332–72) and the two stories introduced in *Exc.* vi. 1080–187, those of W. Armathwaite (complete), and the widowed family from l. 1149.

1804 (or earlier). MS. Y, containing chiefly passages for *Prel.*, has (*a*) *Exc.* ii. 1–26 originally written as opening of *Prel.* viii (*v. Prel.*, E. de S., p. lii); (*b*) deleted passage written for *Prel.* viii. 497 *et seq.* (*v. Prel.*, E. de S., p. 581), incident of solitary lamb, *Exc.* iv. 402–12; (*c*) description of snow-white ram reflected in pool, *Exc.* ix. 437–48 (*v.* note *infra*); (*d*) first draft of "We live by admiration hope and love", *Exc.* iv. 763 *et seq.* (*v.* note *infra*); (*e*) lines about the Indian looking out from an eminence, *Exc.* iii. 928–40 (*v.* note *infra*).

When in 1804 W. began to shape in his mind the section of *The Recluse* which was in the issue to be published as *The Excursion*, he had decided to use *The Pedlar* as his starting-point; *v.* his letter to Sir G. Beaumont of Dec. 25, 1804: "Of this poem [*The Recluse*] that of the Pedlar is part, and I may have written of it altogether about 2,000 lines." These 2,000 lines would be accounted for by *The Ruined Cottage*, just under 1,000, and the first book of *The Recluse* (*v.* Appendix A), a little over 1,000 (the last line of *Recl.* MS. B is numbered 1047; *v.* p. 476 *infra*).

In June 1805 *The Prelude* was finished, but he was slow to get under way with *The Recluse*, and did not get to work in earnest upon it till the summer of 1806, as the following evidence from letters shows:

(1) Aug. 7, 1805. "My Brother has not resumed his great work since the finishing of the poem on his own life, and he now begins to be anxious to get forward again." (D. W. to Lady Beaumont.)

(2) Dec. 25, 1805. ". . . He is very anxious to get forward with *The Recluse* and is reading for the nourishment of his mind, preparatory to beginning." (D. W. to Lady Beaumont.)

(3) Jan. 19, 1806. "My Brother, though not actually employed in his great work, is not idle, for he almost daily produces something, and his thoughts are employed upon *The Recluse.*" (D. W. to Lady Beaumont.)

(4) July 23, 1806. "Wm. goes on rapidly with *The Recluse.*" (D. W. to C. Clarkson.)

(5) Aug. 1, 1806. "Within this last month I have returned to *The Recluse* and have written 700 additional lines." (W. W. to Sir G. Beaumont.)

(6) Sept. 8, 1806. "I have been busily employed lately; I wrote one book of *The Recluse* nearly 1,000 lines, then had a rest, last week began again, and have written 300 more: I hope all tolerably well, and certainly with good views." (W. W. to Sir G. Beaumont; *v. M.Y.*, p. 62.)

It is not clear whether the 700 lines mentioned in (5) are to be included in the 1,000 mentioned in (6). I incline to think, after long study of the MSS., that they are additional to the 1,000. The precise reference to "one book", and the 300 more lines written in the first week of September (6), would fit very closely the first constructive draft of Book II and the lines 1–324 of Book III of which there is a consecutive fair copy in MS. P.(*v. infra*, p. 410), followed by a more or less rough draft of the rest of Book III. What, then, would the 700 additional lines of (5) represent ? I believe these would be the rough drafts of passages of Book IV found in MS. 58, a small note-book similar in form to MS. X and MS. Y of *The Prelude* (*v. Prel.*, E. de S., pp. xxxi and xxxii). It is mainly occupied with these rough drafts, in separate groups, of lines afterwards incorporated in Book IV, but pages near the beginning contain drafts of v. 1–225, and at the end drafts of ii. 152–320, in a version earlier than MS. P. These have clearly been written in *after* the passages of Book IV. We may suppose then that W. was occupied in July, and earlier, with the planning of Books II, III, and IV and had written, in the rough, a good deal of these three books ; and further that in August and September he wrote a first constructive draft of Book II and the first 300 lines of Book III.

After this bout of work he seems to have done very little to *The Excursion* for the next three years. He was diverted from it by many distractions : Coleridge's return and the anxieties consequent upon it ; the removal to Coleorton (Nov. 1806) ; the preparation for press of the volumes of 1807 and the composition of some of their contents, including *Song at the Feast of Brougham Castle* ; the return to Gras-mere (June 1807) ; the composition of *The White Doe of Rylstone* (winter 1807–8) ; a visit to London (March 1808) ; the removal to Allan Bank (June 1808) ; his excited interest in the Spanish War and his composition of his pamphlet on the Convention of Cintra (winter of 1808) ; his translation of epitaphs of Chiabrera, and the writing of two essays for *The Friend* (1809–10). But on Feb. 28, 1810, D. W. wrote to Lady Beaumont: "He is deeply engaged in composition. Before he turns to any other labour I hope he will have finished three books of *The Recluse*. He seldom writes less than 50 lines every day." In the same letter she writes: "The essay [on Epitaphs in the *The Friend*] of this week is by my brother·. . . he has written two more essays on the same subject which will appear when there is need." The subject matter of Books V, VI, and VII of *The Excursion*, the "authentic epitaphs" (v. 651), given by the Pastor of some of his parishioners, is clearly related to W.'s broodings over the general subject of Epitaphs, and it is significant that he appended his first essay on Epitaphs as a note to Book V, and that in his third essay (publ. by Grosart, 1876) he quotes the Pastor's account of the Deaf Man (*v.* note to vii. 395).

His second bout of constructive work dates then from the winter of 1809–1810, and was continued through 1811–13. The final pulling together and revision was going on early in 1814 (*v.* D. W.'s letter to C. Clarkson, April 24, 1814; *M.Y.*, p. 590). Conjectural chronology of the separate books is given in the introductory notes to these, *infra.*

Apart from the labour he devoted to composition, shown in draft after draft of particular passages in the MSS., he spent much pains throughout his life in revising the printed text of *The Excursion*. The more important revisions were made in the editions of 1827, 1837, and 1845. On Oct. 24, 1828, he wrote to Barron Field: "I am much pleased that you think the alterations of *The Excursion* improvements. My sister thinks them so invariably" (*L.Y.*, p. 313). For his alterations for *ed.* 1845 *v.* notes to I. 51, 792 and 934–55, *infra.*

p. 3. *Prospectus*: On Man, on Nature, and on Human Life, *etc.*] Of the *Prospectus* there are three extant MSS. MS. 1 is found, as an independent fragment, in a small note-book, with thin blue cardboard cover, similar to those used for drafts of *The Prelude*. This note-book was used in 1808 for accounts of the money expended on the Green Family (*v. George and Sarah Green*, by D. W., Oxford, 1936, p. 11). The date of the MS. is uncertain, but it represents an earlier stage of the text than MS. 2, and thus was probably written before the rest of *The Recluse* Book I. It is quite likely that it is a fair copy of a draft of lines written as early as 1798, at Alfoxden.

MS. 2 is found in MS. B of *The Recluse*, of which it forms the conclusion (*v.* Appendix A, p. 338, where this version is given in full). It probably dates from the early months of 1800. MS. 3, only fragmentary, is preserved on a loose sheet, on the back of which is a quotation from Milton and the motto of *The Prioress's Tale* (probably added later). Those lines which it contains are very nearly identical with MS. 2, with which it is probably contemporary.

13. numerous verse] *Paradise Lost*, v. 150.

23. "fit audience let me find though few!"] from Milton's address to Urania, *P.L.* vii. 30–1:

> still govern thou my Song
> Urania, and fit audience find, though few.

34. empyreal thrones] *P.L.* ii. 43: "O progeny of Heaven, empyreal thrones."

79. cf. *P.L.* viii. 241:   fast shut

> The dismal Gates, and barricado'd strong.

83–5. Descend, prophetic Spirit . . . things to come]:

> "Not my own fears, nor the prophetic Soul
> Of the wide world dreaming on things to come." Shakespeare's
>   *Sonnets.*—W.

90–3. Shedding benignant influence . . . sphere] Cf. Milton, *P.L.* vii. 375:

the Pleiades before him danc'd
Shedding sweet influence.

The rest of the passage is reminiscent of *P.L.* x. 660–2.

THE EXCURSION

"Something must now be said of this poem, but chiefly, as has been done through the whole of these notes, with reference to my personal friends, and especially to her who has perseveringly taken them down from my dictation. Towards the close of the first book stand the lines that were first written, beginning, "Nine tedious years," and ending, "Last human tenant of these ruined walls." These were composed in '95 at Racedown; and for several passages describing the employment and demeanour of Margaret during her affliction, I was indebted to observations made in Dorsetshire, and afterwards at Alfoxden in Somersetshire, where I resided in '97 and '98. The lines towards the conclusion of the fourth book, "Despondency corrected", beginning, "For the man who in this spirit," to the words "intellectual soul"—were in order of time composed the next, either at Racedown or Alfoxden, I do not remember which. The rest of the Poem was written in the vale of Grasmere, chiefly during our residence at Allan Bank. The long Poem on my own education was, together with many minor Poems, composed while we lived at the cottage at Town End. Perhaps my purpose of giving an additional interest to these my Poems in the eyes of my nearest and dearest Friends may be promoted by saying a few words upon the character of the Wanderer, the Solitary, and the Pastor, and some other of the persons introduced—and first, of the principal one, the Wanderer. My lamented friend Southey (for this is written a month after his decease) used to say that had he been born a papist, the course of life which would in all probability have been his was the one for which he was most fitted and most to his mind, that of a Benedictine Monk in a convent, furnished, as many once were and some still are, with an inexhaustible Library. *Books*, as appears from many passages in his writings, and as was evident to those who had opportunities of observing his daily life, were in fact *his passion*; and *wandering*, I can with truth affirm, was *mine*; but this propensity in me was happily counteracted by inability from want of fortune to fulfil my wishes. But, had I been born in a class which would have deprived me of what is called a liberal education, it is not unlikely that, being strong in body, I should have taken to a way of life such as that in which my Pedlar passed the greater part of his days. At all events, I am here called upon freely to acknowledge that the character I have represented in his person is chiefly an idea of what I fancied my own character might have become in his circumstances. Nevertheless, much of what he says and does had an external existence that fell under my own youthful and subsequent observation. An individual named Patrick, by birth and education a Scotchman, followed this humble occupation for many years, and afterwards settled in the Town of Kendal. He married a kinswoman of my wife's, and her sister Sarah was brought up from early childhood under this good man's eye.[1] My own imaginations I was happy to find clothed in reality, and fresh ones suggested, by what she reported of this man's tenderness of heart, his strong and pure imagination, and his solid attainments in literature, chiefly religious whether in prose or verse. At Hawkshead also, while I was a schoolboy, there occasionally resided a Packman (the name then generally given to [persons of] this calling) with whom I had frequent conversations upon what had befallen him, and what he had observed, during his wandering life; and, as was natural, we took much to each other: and, upon the subject of *Pedlarism* in general, as *then* followed, and its favourableness to an intimate knowledge of human concerns, not merely among the humbler classes of society, I need say nothing here in addition to what is to be found in *The Excursion*, and a note attached to it.

"Now for the Solitary. Of him I have much less to say. Not long after we took up our abode at Grasmere, came to reside there, from what motive I either never knew or have forgotten, a Scotchman a little past the middle of life, who had for many years been Chaplain to a Highland regiment. He was in no respect as far as I know, an interesting character, though in his appearance there was a good deal that attracted attention, as if he had been shattered in fortune and not happy in mind. Of his quondam position I availed myself, to connect with the Wanderer, also a Scotchman, a character suitable to my purpose, the elements of which I drew from several persons with whom I had been connected, and who fell under my observation during frequent residences in London at the beginning of the French Revolution. The chief of these was, one may *now* say, a Mr. Fawcett, a preacher at a dissenting meeting-house at the Old Jewry. It happened to me several times to be one of his congregation through my connection with Mr. Nicholson of Cateaton Street, Strand, who at a time, when I had not many acquaintances in London, used often to

---

[1] eye *corr. in pencil by* M. W. *to* roof *with the note* "Sarah went to Kendal on our Mother's death, but Mr. P. died in the course of a year or two.— M. W." In notes about the family made by M. W. for her son William she writes of "James Patrick of Kendal, the intellectual Pedlar, whose character suggested to your Father that of the Wanderer in the 1st Book of the Excursion—the details of which he gathered from conversations with your Aunt Sarah, who was taken by her sister's godmother (Mrs. Patrick) from her home upon the death of our Mother, when she was 8 years old—she went to School in Kendal, but the most important part of her education was gathered from the stores of that good man's mind". G. G. W. notes, "Mrs. Hutchinson died March 31, 1783." James Patrick died March 27, 1787, aged 71 years.

invite me to dine with him on Sundays; and I took that opportunity (Mr. N. being a Dissenter) of going to hear Fawcett, who was an able and eloquent man. He published a Poem on War, which had a good deal of merit, and made me think more about him than I should otherwise have done. But his Christianity was probably never very deeply rooted; and, like many others in those times of like shewy talents, he had not strength of character to withstand the effects of the French Revolution, and of the wild and lax opinions which had done so much towards producing it, and far more in carrying it forward in its extremes. Poor Fawcett, I have been told, became pretty much such a person as I have described; and early disappeared from the stage, having fallen into habits of intemperance, which I have heard (though I will not answer for the fact) hastened his death. Of him I need say no more: there were many like him at that time, which the world will never be without, but which were more numerous then for reasons too obvious to be dwelt upon.

"*The Pastor*. To what is said of the Pastor in the Poem I have little to add but what may be deemed superfluous. It has ever appeared to me highly favourable to the beneficial influence of the Church of England upon all gradations and classes of society, that the patronage of its benefices is in numerous instances attached to the estates of noble families of ancient gentry; and accordingly I am gratified by the opportunity afforded me in *The Excursion*, to portray the character of a country clergyman of more than ordinary talents, born and bred in the upper ranks of society so as to partake of their refinements, and at the same time brought by his pastoral office and his love of rural life into intimate connection with the peasantry of his native district. To illustrate the relation which in my mind this Pastor bore to the Wanderer, and the resemblance between them, or rather the points of community in their nature, I likened one to an oak and the other to a sycamore; and, having here referred to this comparison, I need only add, I had no one individual in my mind, wishing rather to embody this idea than to break in upon the simplicity of it, by traits of individual character or of any peculiarity of opinion.

"And now for a few words upon the scene where these interviews and conversations are supposed to occur. The scene of the first book of the Poem is, I must own, laid in a tract of country not sufficiently near to that which soon comes into view in the second book, to agree with the fact. All that relates to Margaret and the ruined cottage etc., was taken from observations made in the South-West of England, and certainly it would require more than seven-league boots to stretch in one morning from a common in Somersetshire or Dorsetshire to the heights of Furness Fells and the deep valleys they embosom. For thus dealing with space I need make, I trust, no apology, but my friends may be amused by the truth.

"In the Poem, I suppose that the Pedlar and I ascended from a

plain country up the vale of Langdale, and struck off a good way
above the chapel to the western side of the vale. We ascended the
hill and thence looked down upon the circular recess in which lies
Blea Tarn, chosen by the Solitary for his retreat. After we quit his
cottage, passing over a low ridge we descend into another vale, that
of Little Langdale, towards the head of which stands, embowered or
partly shaded by yews and other trees, something between a cottage
and a mansion or gentleman's house such as they once were in this
country. This I convert into the Parsonage, and at the same time
and as by the waving of a magic wand, I turn the comparatively
confined vale of Langdale, its Tarn, and the rude Chapel which once
adorned the valley, into the stately and comparatively spacious vale
of Grasmere, its Lake, and its ancient Parish Church; and upon the
side of Loughrigg Fell, at the foot of the Lake, and looking down upon
it and the whole vale and its encompassing mountains, the Pastor is
supposed by me to stand, when at sunset he addresses his companions
in words which I hope my readers will remember, or I should not have
taken the trouble of giving so much in detail the materials on which
my mind actually worked.

"Now for a few particulars of *fact* respecting the persons whose
stories are told or characters are described by the different speakers.
To Margaret I have already alluded. I will add here, that the lines
beginning, 'She was a woman of a steady mind . . . live on earth a life
of happiness', faithfully delineate, as far as they go, the character
possessed in common by many women whom it has been my happiness
to know in humble life; and that several of the most touching things
which she is represented as saying and doing are taken from actual
observation of the distresses and trials under which different persons
were suffering, some of them strangers to me, and others daily under
my notice. I was born too late to have a distinct remembrance of the
origin of the American war, but the state in which I represent Robert's
mind to be I had frequent opportunities of observing at the com-
mencement of our rupture with France in '93, opportunities of which
I availed myself in the story of the Female Vagrant, as told in the
poem on Guilt and Sorrow."—I. F. (*The rest of the* I. F. *note is given
in the appropriate places in the notes that follow.*)

BOOK I

This book was completed in its first form as an independent poem
entitled *The Ruined Cottage* in the spring of 1798. This poem had
been read to Coleridge in a shorter form in June 1797, but some
portions of it had been written as early as 1795: *v.* I. F. note to *The
Excursion*, in which W. says that ll. 871–916 of Book I were the first
written of the whole poem, and were composed at Racedown. From
a study of the extant MSS. to which I refer as A, B, B², D, E, M, and
P, it is possible to trace the stages of its development. In addition to

these MSS., drafts of isolated passages occur in the *Alfoxden* and *Christabel* note-books to which I have already referred (*v*. p. 369 *supra*).

MS. A is a folio sheet with watermark 1795, inscribed in W. W.'s hand. It contains fragmentary drafts of passages closely corresponding to the following lines of MS. B, 348–413, *v*. p. 389–92 *infra*, connected by the words "for half a day He then would leave" with ll. 430–9 (*Exc*. i. 502–70, 582–91); and also passages describing the ruined cottage, which add to the picture given in MS. B, ll. 354–66, details closely corresponding to lines 1–7 and 13–22 of *Incipient Madness* (*v*. Vol. I, p. 314):

(*a*) A cold bare wall whose top you see is trick'd
    With weeds and the rank spear-grass—from this casement
    You see the swallow's nest has dropp'd away,
    A wretched covert 'tis for man or beast
    And when the poor man's horse that shelters there
    Turns from the beating wind and open sky
    The iron links with which his feet are clogg'd
    Mix their dull clanking with the heavy sound
    Of falling rain, a melancholy thing
    To any man who has a heart to feel

There are several attempts:

(*b*) But two nights gone I cross'd this dreary moor
    Just as the moon was rising
    The poor man's horse that feeds along the lanes
    Had hither come within these roofless walls
    To weather out the storm

(*c*)   The poor man's horse
    That feeds along the lanes, from cold night showers
    Finds shelter now within the chimney wall
    I heard him turning from the beating rain
    And open sky, and as he turn'd I heard. . . .

(*d*) But two nights gone I cross'd this dreary moor
    In the still moonlight, when I reached the hut
    I looked within and all was still and dark
    Only within the ruin I beheld
    At a small distance on the dusky ground
    A broken pane which glitter'd to the moon.

The inception of the two poems, *The Ruined Cottage* and *Incipient Madness*, must belong to the same period of spiritual gloom, possibly 1795, and must refer to the same incident, a visit to a desolate ruined cottage.

Next we must presuppose a MS., A², of *The Ruined Cottage* comprising the Story of Margaret read to Coleridge in June 1797 and to

Mary Hutchinson during her visit to Racedown, March–June of the
same year. That it was a very much shorter narrative than that
developed in MS. B is proved by D. W.'s letter to M. H., March 5,
1798, quoted below. One important difference is betrayed by a
variant in l. 740 as transcribed in Coleridge's letter of June 1797:
the Pedlar is here addressed as "Stranger", instead of "my friend"
as in MS. B, where, however, "Stranger", mechanically copied from
the earlier version, has been deleted. This clearly shows that in the
first version of the tale the Pedlar was a person unknown to the poet,
casually met on the road near the cottage, and not, as he became
later, his old friend.

   MS. B consists of 52 octavo sheets roughly stitched together,
written in a clear hand by D. W. on one side of the paper. It has a
few corrections by W. W. and on the versos some additions by him.
It can be dated Jan.–Feb. 1798. For on March 5 D. W. wrote to
M. H.: "You desire me, my dear Mary, to send you a copy of *The
Ruined Cottage*. This is impossible, for it has grown to length of 900
lines. I will, however, send you a copy of that part which is imme-
diately and solely connected with the Cottage. The Pedlar's character
now makes a very, certainly the *most*, considerable part of the poem."
Her transcript (MS. B²) was clearly taken from MS. B which it
follows in its readings and its occasional defective lines; and her letter
shows that B had only just been finished. The *Alfoxden* note-book in
which entries were made between Jan. 20 and March 5, 1798 (*v. Prel.*
E. de S., p. xxv) contains a preliminary draft of *Exc.* i. 457–93 MS. B
and various suggestions for the character of the Pedlar; *v.* note to
ll. 422–33 *infra*.

   As B is the first complete draft of what was to become Book I of
The Excursion it seems worth while to reproduce it *in extenso*. It is
to be noted that this version divides the poem into two parts (at
l. 605 *Exc.* i), that it concludes with l. 916, and that an early draft of
most of *Exc.* i. 916–end is found in an *Addendum*.[1] The MS. clearly
shows that at the time it was written, winter and spring 1797–8,
Wordsworth had emerged from the slough of despond in which he
first conceived the poem; he makes the wise old Pedlar interpret the
story, and it is in the light of his faith that we are to read it. *v.* lines
added at l. 366 (*app. crit. infra*), and the first attempts at a final
reconciling passage at the end, as well as the Addendum *infra*. In
the *apparatus criticus* I have given the variants found in A, B², and
D.[2] The numbers placed in brackets on the right-hand side of the
page indicate the corresponding lines in W.'s final text of *Exc.* i.

   [1] Written before April 1798, when Coleridge quotes the opening lines;
v. footnote, p. 401, *infra*.
   [2] For description of D, *v.* p. 404, *infra*.

THE RUINED COTTAGE

A Poem

GIVE me a spark of Nature's fire,
'Tis the best learning I desire

. . . . .

My Muse though homely in attire
May touch the heart. Burns.

Part 1st

'Twas Summer, and the sun was mounted high,
Along the south the uplands feebly glared
Through a pale steam, and all the northern downs
In clearer air ascending shewed far off
5   Their surfaces on which the shadows lay
Of many clouds far as the sight could reach
Along the horizon's edge, that lay in spots
Determined and unmoved; with steady beams
Of clear and pleasant sunshine interposed;
10 Pleasant to him who on the soft cool grass
Extends his careless limbs beside the root   (10)
Of some huge oak whose aged branches make
A twilight of their own, a dewy shade
Where the wren warbles, while the dreaming man,
15 Half conscious of that soothing melody,   (14)
With sidelong eye looks out upon the scene
By those impending branches made [more soft]
More soft and distant. Other lot was mine;   (18)
Across a bare wide Common I had toiled
20 With languid feet which by the slippery ground
Were baffled still; and when I stretched myself
On the brown earth, my limbs from very heat
Could find no rest, nor my weak arm disperse
The insect host which gathered round my face   (24)
25 And joined their murmurs to the tedious noise
Of seeds of bursting gorse which crackled round.
I rose and turned towards a group of trees
Which midway in that level stood alone,
And thither come at length beneath a shade
30 Of clustering elms that sprang from the same root
I found a ruined Cottage—four clay walls   (30)

5–7 Their surfaces with shadows dappled o'er
    Of deep embattled clouds: far as the sight
    Could reach those many shadows lay in spots B *originally and* D
17 more soft: *supplied from* D   27 I turned my steps B *del.,* B²
30–1 A ruin'd cottage four bare shapeless walls
    That midway on that level stood alone *Alfoxden* MS.
31 house, four naked walls D

That stared upon each other. 'Twas a spot
The wandering gypsey in a stormy night
Would pass it with his moveables to house
35 On the open plain beneath the imperfect arch
Of a cold lime-kiln. As I looked around
Beside the door I saw an aged Man
Stretched on a bench whose edge with short bright moss
Was green, and studded o'er with fungus flowers.
40 An iron-pointed staff lay at his side. (37)
Him had I seen the day before, alone
And in the middle of the public way
Standing to rest himself. His eyes were turned
Towards the setting sun, while, with that staff
45 Behind him fixed, he propped a long white pack
Which crossed his shoulders; wares for maids who live
In lonely villages or straggling huts.
I knew him—he was born of lowly race
On Cumbrian hills, and I have seen the tear
50 Stand in his luminous eye when he described
The house in which his early youth was passed
And found I was no stranger to the spot.
I loved to hear him talk of former days
And tell how when a child, ere yet of age
55 To be a shepherd, he had learned to read
His bible in a school that stood alone,
Sole building on a mountain's dreary edge, (123)
Far from the sight of city spire, or sound
Of Minster clock. [He from his native hills (125) (340)
60 Had wandered far, much had he seen of men,
Their manners, their enjoyments and pursuits,
Their passions and their feelings, chiefly those
Essential and eternal in the heart
Which mid the simpler forms of rural life (345)

32–6 'Twas . . . As *not in* D *which has* I looked round, And near the door
I saw, *etc.*
38–9 Alone, and stretched upon the cottage bench *verso and* D
After 40 With instantaneous joy I recognized
       That pride of nature and of lowly life
       The venerable Armytage, a friend
       As dear to me as is the setting sun.
       He lay, his pack of rustic merchandize
       Pillowing his head, *etc. verso and* D (cf. 303)
42 And on the middle of the heath B² *corr. to text*
59 After "Minster Clock" there is a mark which clearly brackets the follow-
ing 10½ lines, 59–69, so that the MS. runs on "From that bleak tene-
ment . . .", l. 70 *infra*. The bracketed lines are to be inserted at l. (264) *infra*.

65 Exist more simple in their elements
   And speak a plainer language. He possessed   (347)
   No vulgar mind, though he had passed his life
   In this poor occupation, first assumed
   From impulses of curious thought from such]
   [*Bottom of page in MS.; the next page begins:*]
70   From that bleak tenement   (125)
   He many an evening to his distant home
   In solitude returning saw the hills
   Grow larger in the darkness, all alone
   Beheld the stars come out above his head,
75 And travelled through the wood, no comrade near,   (130)
   To whom he might confess the things he saw.
   So the foundations of his mind were laid
   In such communion, not from terror free.
   While yet a child, and long before his time
80 He had perceived the presence and the power   (135)
   Of greatness, and deep feelings had impressed
   Great objects on his mind, with portraiture
   And colour so distinct [that on his mind]
   They lay like substances, and almost seemed
85 To haunt the bodily sense. He had received   (140)
   A precious gift, for as he grew in years
   With these impressions would he still compare
   All his ideal stores, his shapes and forms,
   And being still unsatisfied with aught
90 Of dimmer character, he thence attained
   An *active* power to fasten images   (145)
   Upon his brain, and on their pictured lines
   Intensely brooded, even till they acquired
   The liveliness of dreams. Nor did he fail,
95 While yet a child, with a child's eagerness,
   Incessantly to turn his ear and eye   (150)
   On all things which the rolling seasons brought
   To feed such appetite. Nor this alone
   Appeased his yearning; in the after day
100 Of boyhood, many an hour in caves forlorn
   And in the hollow depth of naked crags   (155)
   He sate, and even in their fixed lineaments,
   Or from the power of a peculiar eye,
   Or by creative feeling overborne,
105 Or by predominance of thought oppressed,

82 Great objects with outline and portraiture *verso*   83 that on his
mind] *supplied from* D   88 All shapes and forms that came into his
mind *verso*
92–3 Upon his thought, retouch'd till they acquired *verso*

Even in their fixed and steady lineaments   (160)
He traced an ebbing and a flowing mind,
Expression ever varying. In his heart
Love was not yet, nor the pure joy of love,
110 By sound diffused, or by the breathing air,   (188)
Or by the silent looks of happy things,
Or flowing from the universal face   (190)
Of earth and sky. But he had felt the power
Of nature, and already was prepared
115 By his intense conceptions to receive
Deeply the lesson deep of love, which he
Whom Nature, by whatever means, has taught   (195)
To feel intensely, cannot but receive.
        Ere his ninth summer he was sent abroad
120 To tend his father's sheep, such was his task
Henceforward till the later day of youth.
Oh! then what soul was his when on the tops
Of the high mountains he beheld the sun
Rise up and bathe the world in light. He looked,   (200)
125 The ocean and the earth beneath him lay
In gladness and deep joy. The clouds were touched
And in their silent faces did he read
Unutterable love. Sound needed none   (205)
Nor any voice of joy: his spirit drank
130 The spectacle. Sensation, soul and form
All melted into him. They swallowed up
His animal being; in them did he live
And by them did he live. They were his life.   (210)
In such access of mind, in such high hour
135 Of visitation from the living God,
He did not feel the God; he felt his works;
Thought was not. In enjoyment it expired.
Such hour by prayer or praise was unprofaned,
He neither prayed, nor offered thanks or praise,   (216)
140 His mind was a thanksgiving to the power
That made him. It was blessedness and love.
A shepherd on the lonely mountain tops
Such intercourse was his, and in this sort   (220)
Was his existence oftentimes possessed.
145 Ah! *then* how beautiful, how bright appeared
The written promise; he had early learned
To reverence the volume which displays
The mystery, the life which cannot die;   (225)
But in the mountains did he *feel* his faith
150 There did he see the writing—All things there
Looked immortality, revolving life,

And greatness still revolving, infinite ;
There littleness was not, the least of things   (230)
Seemed infinite, and there his spirit shaped
155   Her prospects, nor did he *believe*—he saw,
What wonder if his being thus became
Sublime and comprehensive. Low desires
Low thoughts had there no place, yet was his heart   (235)
Lowly ; for he was meek in gratitude
160   Oft as he called to mind those ecstacies,
And whence they flowed, and from them he acquired
Wisdom which works through patience ; thence he learned
In many a calmer hour of sober thought   (240)
To look on nature with an humble heart
165   Self-questioned where it did not understand,
And with a superstitious eye of love.
Small need had he of books ; for many a tale   (163)
Traditionary round the mountains hung,
And many a legend peopling the dark woods
170   Nourished Imagination in her growth,
And gave the mind that apprehensive power
By which she is made quick to recognize
The moral properties and scope of things.
Yet greedily he read and read again   (170)
175   Whate'er the rustic Vicar's shelf supplied,
The life and death of Martyrs who sustained
Intolerable pangs, and here and there
A straggling volume torn and incomplete   (177)
Which left half-told the preternatural tale,
180   Romance of giants, chronicle of fiends
Profuse in garniture of wooden cuts
Strange and uncouth, dire faces, figures dire,
Sharp-kneed, sharp-elbowed, and lean-ankled too
With long and ghostly shanks, forms which once seen   (184)
185   Could never be forgotten. Things though low
Though low and humble, not to be despised
By such as have observed the curious links
With which the perishable hours of life

166 eye of love. *Here is added, on verso:*
                Thus passed the time yet to the neighbouring town   (244)
                He often went with what small overplus
                His earnings might supply, and brought away
                The book which most had tempted his desires
                While at the stall he read. Among the hills
                He gazed upon that mighty orb of song
                The divine Milton. Other lore *so* D, *but* Lore of   (250)
                                different kind, *going on at* l. 191

Are bound together, and the world of thought
190   Exists and is sustained. A different store,   (250)
The annual savings of a toilsome life,
The Schoolmaster supplied ; books that explain
The purer elements of truth involv'd
In lines and numbers, and by charm severe,
195   Especially perceived where Nature droops   (255)
And feeling is suppress'd, preserve the mind
Busy, in solitude and poverty.
And thus employed he many a time forgot
The listless (creeping) hours when in the hollow vale,
200   Hollow and green, he lay on the green turf   (260)
In lonesome idleness. What could he do ?
Nature was at his heart, and he perceived
Though yet he knew not how, a wasting power   (265)
In all things which from her sweet influence
205   Might tend to wean him, therefore with her hues
Her forms and with the spirit of her forms
He cloathed the nakedness of austere truth.
While yet he linger'd in the elements   (270)
Of science, and among her simplest laws,
210   His triangles, they were the stars of heaven,
The *silent* stars ; his altitudes the crag
Which is the eagle's birthplace ; or some peak   (275)
Familiar with forgotten years, which shews,
Inscribed, as with the silence of the thought,
215   Upon its bleak and visionary sides,
The history of many a winter storm,
Or obscure records of the path of fire.   (279)
Yet with these lonesome sciences he still
Continued to amuse the heavier hours
220   Of solitude, and solitary thought.
But now, before his twentieth year was pass'd   (280)
Accumulated feelings press'd his heart
With an encreasing weight ; he was o'er power'd
By Nature, and his mind became disturbed,
225   And many a time he wished the winds might rage   (287)
When they were silent : from his intellect,

217/18   Or of the day of vengeance, when the sea
Rose like a giant from his sleep, and smote
The hills, and when the firmament of heaven
Rained darkness which the race of men beheld
Yea all the men that lived and had no hope   *on verso*
224 . . . and his spirit was on fire With restless thoughts—his eye became
disturb'd   *verso* D
226 . . . silent ; far more fondly now
Than in his earlier season did he love

And from the stillness of abstracted thought,
In vain he sought repose, in vain he turned,   (292)
To science for a cure. I have heard him say
230 That at this time he scann'd the laws of light
With a strange pleasure of disquietude
Amid the din of torrents, when they send   (295)
From hollow clefts, up to the clearer air
A cloud of mist which in the shining sun
235 Varies its rainbow hues. But vainly thus
And vainly by all other means he strove
To mitigate the fever of his heart.   (300)
From Nature and her overflowing soul   (*Prelude, Text* A, ii. 416–34)
He had received so much, that all his thoughts
240 Were steeped in feeling. He was only then
Contented, when, with bliss ineffable
He felt the sentiment of being, spread
O'er all that moves, and all that seemeth still,
O'er all which, lost beyond the reach of thought,
245 And human knowledge, to the human eye
Invisible, yet liveth to the heart,
O'er all that leaps, and runs, and shouts, and sings,
Or beats the gladsome air, o'er all that glides
Beneath the wave, yea in the wave itself
250 And mighty depth of waters. Wonder not
If such his transports were; for in all things
He saw one life, and felt that it was joy.
One song they sang, and it was audible,
Most audible then, when the fleshly ear
255 O'ercome by grosser prelude of that strain,
Forgot its functions, and slept undisturbed.
These things he had sustained in solitude
Even till his bodily strength began to yield
Beneath their weight. The mind within him burnt
260 And he resolved to quit his native hills.
He asked his father's blessing, and assumed
This lowly occupation. The old man

Tempestuous nights the uproar and the sounds
That live in darkness; from his intellect   *verso* D
260/1 The Father strove to make his son perceive
As clearly as the old man did himself
With what advantage he might teach a school   (312)
In the adjoining village. But the youth
Who of this service made a short essay
Found that the wandrings of his thought were then
A misery to him, that he must resign
A task he was unable to perform.   *verso* D   (315)

        Bless'd him and prayed for him, yet with a heart
264   Foreboding evil.* [He from his native hills
        Had wandered far, much had he seen of men
        Their manners, their enjoyments and pursuits
        Their passions and their feelings, chiefly those
        Essential and eternal in the heart
        Which mid the simpler forms of rural life   (345)
        Exist more simple in their elements
        And speak a plainer language.† He possessed

   * Here is a blank space which is clearly meant to be filled by ll. 59–69
supra.
     † The following passage is written on the next three versos:
                                        Many a year
        Of lonesome meditation and impelled
        By curious thought he was content to toil
        In this poor calling which he now pursued
        From habit and necessity. He walked
        Among the [   ]¹ haunts of vulgar men
        Unstained; the talisman of constant thought
        And kind² sensations in a gentle heart
        Preserv'd him; every shew of vice to him
        Was a remembrancer of what he knew
        Or a fresh seed of wisdom, or produced
        That tender interest which the virtuous feel
        Among the wicked, which when truly felt
        May bring the bad man nearer to the good,
        But, innocent of evil, cannot sink
        The good man to the bad. Among the woods   (347)
        A lone enthusiast, and among the hills
        Itinerant in this labour (In this way-wandering business) he had passed
        The better portion of his time, and there   (350)
        From day to day had his affections breathed
        The wholesome air of nature; there he kept
        In solitude, and solitary thought,
        So pleasant were those comprehensive views,
        His mind in a just equipoise of love.   (355)
        Serene it was, unclouded by the cares
        Of ordinary life, unvexed, unwarped
        By partial bondage. In his steady course
        No piteous evolutions had he felt,
        No wild varieties of joy or grief,   (360)
        Unoccupied by sorrow of its own
        His heart lay open and by nature tuned
        And constant disposition of his thoughts
        To sympathy with Man, he was alive
        To all that was enjoyed where'er he went,   (365)

_____

            ¹ *blank in* B: impure D   ² pure *corr. to* kind B

No vulgar mind though he had passed his life
In this poor occupation, first assumed
From impulses of curious thought, from such]
265 Continued many a year and now pursued
From habit and necessity. His eye
Flashing poetic fire he would repeat

And all that was endured and in himself
Happy and quiet in his chearfulness
He had no painful pressure from within
Which made him turn away from wretchedness
With coward fears. He could afford to suffer   (370)
With those whom he saw suffer. Hence it was
That in our best experience he was rich
The home-felt wisdom of our daily life.
He had observ'd the progress and decay   (375)
Of many minds, of minds and bodies too
The history of many families,
And how they prosper'd, how they lived in peace
And happiness, and how they were o'erthrown
By passion or mischance, or such misrule
Among the [unthinking D] masters of the earth   (380)
As makes the nations groan. He was a man   (422)
One whom you could not pass without remark—
If you had met him on a rainy day
You [would] have stopped to look at him, Robust
Active and nervous was his gait, his limbs
And his whole figure breathed intelligence,   (425)
His Body, tall and shapely, shewed in front
A faint line of the hollowness of age,
Or, rather, what appeared the curvature
Of toil, his head looked up steady and fixed;
Age had condensed[1] the rose upon his cheek
But had not tamed his eye, which, under brows
Of hoary grey, had meanings which it brought
From years of youth which, like a being made   (430)
Of many beings, he had wondrous skill
To blend with meanings of the years to come,
Human or such as lie beyond the grave—   (433)
Long had I loved him—Oh! it was most sweet
To hear him tell of things which he had seen,
To hear him teach in unambitious style
Reasoning and thought, by painting as he did
The manners and the passions. Many a time
He made a holyday and left his pack
Behind, and we two wandered through the hills
A pair of random Travellers—His eye (v. 266)

---

[1] compressed MS. D

The songs of Burns and as we trudged along
Together did we make the hollow grove
270   Ring with our transports: though he was untaught,
In the dead lore of schools undisciplined,
Why should he grieve ? he was a chosen son   (*Prelude, Text* A, iii. 82)
To him was given an ear which deeply felt
The voice of Nature in the obscure wind
275   The sounding mountain and the running stream.
To every natural form, rock, fruit and flower   (*Prelude, Text* A,
Even the loose stones that cover the highway   [iii. 124)
He gave a moral life, he saw them feel
Or linked them to some feeling. In all shapes
280   He found a secret and mysterious soul,
A fragrance and a spirit of strange meaning.   (*ib.* 134)
Though poor in outward shew he was most rich,   (*ib.* 141)
He had a world about him, 'twas his own
He made it, for it only lived to him
285   And to the God who looked into his mind.
Such sympathies would often bear him far
In outward gesture, and in visible look,
Beyond the common seeming of mankind.
Some called it madness—such it might have been   (*ib.* 147)
290   But that he had an eye that evermore
Looked deep into the shades of difference   (*ib.* 158)
As they lie hid in all exterior forms
Near or remote, minute or vast, an eye
Which from a stone, a tree, a withered leaf,
295   To the broad ocean and the azure heavens
Spangled with kindred multitudes of stars
Could find no surface where its power might sleep,
Which spake perpetual logic to his soul,   (*ib.* 165)
And by an unrelenting agency
300   Did bind his feelings even as in a chain.   (*ib.* 167)
    So was he framed. Now on the Bench he lay   (434)
Stretched at his ease (length), and with that weary load
Pillowed his head. I guess he had no thought
Of his way-wandering life. His eyes were shut,   (440)
305   The shadows of the breezy elms above
Dappled his face. With thirsty heat oppressed
At length I hailed him, glad to see his hat
Bedewed with water-drops, as if the brim   (445)
Had newly scooped a running stream. He rose

268 . . . Burns or many a ditty wild
     Which he had fitted to the moorland harp,
     His own sweet verse, and as we   *verso and* D

310 And, pointing to a sun-flower, bade me climb   (451)
    The [   ] wall where that same gaudy flower
    Looked out upon the road. It was a plot
    Of garden ground now wild, its matted weeds
    Marked with the steps of those whom as they pass'd   (455)
315 The gooseberry trees that shot in long [lank slips]
    Or currants hanging from their leafless stems
    In scanty strings had tempted to o'erleap
    The broken wall. Within that cheerless spot
    Where two tall hedgrows of thick willow boughs   (460)
320 Joined in a damp cold nook I found a well
    Half choaked
    I slaked my thirst and to the shady bench
    Returned, and while I stood unbonneted   (466)
    To catch the current of the breezy air
325 The old man said "I see around me [here]
    Things which you cannot see. We die, my Friend,   (470)
    Nor we alone, but that which each man loved
    And prized in his peculiar nook of earth
    Dies with him or is changed, and very soon
330 Even of the good is no memorial left.   (474)
    The Waters of that spring if they could feel   (485)
    Might mourn. They are not as they were, the bond
    Of brotherhood is broken; time has been
    When every day the touch of human hand
335 Disturbed their stillness, and they ministered   (490)
    To human comfort. As I stooped to drink
    Few minutes gone at that deserted well
    What feelings came to me! A spider's web
    Across its mouth hung to the water's edge
340 And on the wet and slimy foot-stone lay
    The useless fragment of a wooden bowl.   (493)
    It moved my very heart. The day has been
    When I would never pass this road but she
    Who lived within these walls, when I appeared,
345 A daughter's welcome gave me, and I loved her   (499)
    As my own child. Oh Sir! The good die first
    And they whose hearts are dry as summer dust
    Burn to the socket. Many a passenger

311 [   ]; *a blank in both* B *and* D   315 lank slips] *supplied from*
D   318–25 *A draft of these lines is in the Alfoxden* MS.   319
willow *corr. to* alder D   321 Half (choked *deleted*) covered up with
willow-flowers and grass *added to* D   324 motion of the cooler air
D   325 here] *supplied from* D   331–2 D *as Exc.* i. 475–86
342–61 *A draft of these lines is in Alfoxden* MS.

Has blessed poor Margaret for her gentle looks
350   When she upheld the cool refreshment drawn
From that forsaken well, and no one came   (505)
But he was welcome—no one went away
But that it seemed she loved him. She is dead,
The worm is on her cheek, and this poor hut
355   Stripped of its outward garb of household flowers
Of rose and sweetbriar (jasmine) offers to the wind
A cold bare wall whose earthy top is tricked
With weeds and the rank spear-grass; she is dead
And nettles rot and adders sun themselves
360   Where we have sate together while she nursed
Her infant at her bosom. The wild colt
The unstalled heifer and the Potter's ass
Find shelter now within the chimney wall
Where I have seen her evening hearth-stone blaze
365   And through the window spread upon the road
Its chearful light. You will forgive me, Sir,
I feel I play the truant with my tale.
She had a husband, an industrious man   (520)
Sober and steady. I have heard her say

351 well] spring D *and* B *alt.*   356 sweet-briar] jasmine   A: wood-
bine B²
358 . . . spear-grass; from this casement
   You see the swallow's nest has dropp'd away   A   and *Christabel* MS.
360–1 Upon the floor where I have seen [her] sit
         And rock her baby in its Cradle   A
         Where we have sat together while she rock'd
         Her baby in its cradle   *Christabel* MS.
361 breast. The unshod colt D   361–3 *For readings of* A   *v. p.* 377
supra   362 unstalled] wandring D
366–7 *A later draft written on verso of previous page in* W. W.'s *hand runs:*
                        But I have spoken thus
         With an ungrateful temper and have read
         The forms of things with an unworthy eye
         She sleeps in the calm earth and peace is here.
         I well remember that those very plumes
         Those weeds and the high spear-grass on that wall
etc. as addendum to MS. B *infra* 124–34 *and Exc.* i (1814), 944–55
         . . . Appeared an idle dream that could not live
         Where meditation was. I turned away
         And walked along the road (my path) in happiness.
         You will forgive me, Sir. I feel I play
         The truant with my tale—Poor Margaret
367 But often on this cottage do I muse
      As on a picture, till my wiser mind
      Sinks, yielding to the foolishness of grief. D

370 That he was up and busy at his loom
In summer ere the mower's scythe had swept   (525)
The dewy grass, and in the early spring
Ere the last star had vanished. They who passed
At evening from behind the garden fence
375 Might hear his busy spade which he would ply
After his daily work till the day-light   (530)
Was gone, and every leaf and flower were lost
In the dark hedges. So they pass'd their days
In peace and comfort, and two pretty babes
380 Were their best hope next to the God in Heaven.
—You may remember, now some ten years gone,   (535)
Two blighting seasons, when the fields were left
With half a harvest (tillage) ; it pleased heaven to add
A worse affliction in the plague of war.
385 A happy land was stricken to the heart.   (540)
'Twas a sad time of sorrow and distress.
A wanderer among the cottages
I with my pack of winter raiment saw
The hardships of that season ; many rich
390 Sank down as in a dream among the poor,
And of the poor did many cease to be,   (545)
And their place knew them not. Meanwhile abridged
Of daily comforts, gladly reconciled
To numerous self-denials, Margaret
395 Went struggling on through those calamitous years
With chearful hope, but ere the second spring   (550)
A fever seized her husband. In disease
He lingered long, and when his strength returned
He found the little he had stored to meet
400 The hour of accident or crippling age   (555)
Was all consumed. As I have said, 'twas now
A time of trouble—shoals of artizans
Were from their daily labour turned away   (560)
To hang for bread on parish charity
405 They and their wives and children, happier far
Could they have lived as do the little birds
That peck along the hedges, or the kite
That makes his dwelling in the mountain rocks.   (565)
Ill fared it now with Robert, he who dwelt
410 In this poor cottage ; at his door he stood

389 What the poor suffer'd—Many of the rich   A   396 spring]
autumn   D
392–7   'Twas at this time
        As Margaret told me on this very bench
        A Fever, *etc.*   A

And whistled many a snatch of merry tunes
That had no mirth in them, or with his knife   (570)
Carved uncouth figures on the heads of sticks,
Then idly sought about through every nook
415   Of house or garden any casual task
Of use or ornament, and with a strange
Amusing but uneasy novelty   (575)
He blended where he might the various tasks
Of summer, autumn, winter, and of spring.
420   The passenger might see him at the door
With his small hammer on the threshold stone
Pointing lame buckle-tongues and rusty nails,
The treasured store of an old household box,
Or braiding cords or weaving bells and caps
425   Of rushes, playthings for his babes.
But this endured not, his good-humour soon
Became a weight in which no pleasure was
And poverty brought on a petted mood   (580)
And a sore temper, day by day he drooped,
430   And he would leave his home, and to the town
Without an errand would he turn his steps,
Or wander here and there among the fields.
One while he would speak lightly of his babes   (585)
And with a cruel tongue, at other times
435   He played with them wild freaks of merriment;
And 'twas a piteous thing to see the looks
Of the poor innocent children. 'Every smile',
Said Margaret to me, here beneath these trees,   (590)
'Made my heart bleed.'" At this the old man paused
440   And looking up to those enormous elms
He said, "'tis now the hour of deepest noon,
At this still season of repose and peace,
This hour when all things which are not at rest   (595)
Are chearful, while this multitude of flies
445   Fills all the air with happy melody,
Why should a tear be in an old Man's eye?
Why should we thus with an untoward mind,
And in the weakness of humanity,   (600)
From natural wisdom turn our hearts away,
450   To natural comfort shut our eyes and ears,
And, feeding on disquiet, thus disturb
[The calm] of Nature with our restless thoughts?"   (604)

420–5 *not in* D: *struck out in* B   452 calm] *supplied from* D:
tone B²

2nd Part

	He spake with somewhat of a solemn tone	(605)
	But when he ended there was in his face	
455	Such easy chearfulness, a look so mild	
	That for a little time it stole away	
	All recollection and that simple tale	
	Passed from my mind like a forgotten sound.	(610)
	A while on trivial things we held discourse	
460	To me soon tasteless. In my own despite	
	I thought of that poor woman as of one	
	Whom I had known and loved. He had rehearsed	
	Her homely tale with such familiar power	(615)
	With such a tender countenance, an eye	
465	So busy, that the things of which he spake	
	Seemed present, and attention now relaxed	
	There was a heartfelt chillness in my veins.	
	I rose and turning from that breezy shade	(620)
	Went out into the open air, and stood	
470	To drink the comfort of the warmer sun.	
	Long time I had not stayed ere looking round	
	Upon that tranquil ruin, and impelled	
	By a mild form of curious pensiveness	
	I begg'd of the old man that for my sake	
475	He would resume his story. He replied	(625)
	It were a wantonness, and would demand	
	Severe reproof, if we were men whose hearts	
	Could hold vain dalliance with the misery	
	Even of the dead, contented thence to draw	
480	A momentary pleasure, never marked	(630)
	By reason, barren of all future good.	
	But we have known that there is often found	
	In mournful thoughts, and always might be found,	
	A power to virtue friendly; were't not so	
485	I am a dreamer among men—indeed	(635)
	An idle dreamer. 'Tis a common tale	
	By moving accidents uncharactered	
	A tale of silent suffering, hardly clothed	
	In bodily form, and to the grosser sense	
490	But ill adapted, scarcely palpable	
	To him who does not think. But at your bidding	
	I will proceed.	
	While thus it fared with them	(640)

457–93 *Alfoxden* MS. *has a preliminary draft of these lines*   460 I
was depressed and   *Alfoxden* MS.   472–4 and impelled . . . I] I returned
And D
917.17 **V**   C C

To whom this Cottage till that hapless year
Had been a blessed home, it was my chance
495 To travel in a country far remote,
And glad I was when, halting by yon gate
Which leads from the green lane, again I saw
These lofty elm-trees. Long I did not rest,
With many pleasant thoughts I cheared my way   (645)
500 O'er the flat common. At the door arrived
I knocked, and when I entered with the hope
Of usual greeting Margaret looked at me
A little while, then turned her head away
Speechless, and sitting down upon a chair   (650)
505 Wept bitterly. I wist not what to do
Or how to speak to her. Poor wretch! at last
She rose from off her seat, and then, Oh Sir!
I cannot *tell* how she pronounced my name,
With fervent love and with a face of grief   (655)
510 Unutterably helpless, and a look
That seemed to cling upon me, she inquired
If I had seen her husband. As she spake
A strange surprize and fear came to my heart,
And I could make no answer. Then she told   (660)
515 That he had disappeared; just two months gone
He left his house; two wretched days had passed,
And on the third by the first break of light   (665)
Within her casement full in view she saw
A purse of gold. 'I trembled at the sight,'   (671)
520 Said Margaret, 'for I knew it was his hand
That placed it there, and on that very day
By one a stranger, from my husband sent,   (675)
The tidings came that he had joined a troop
Of soldiers going to a distant land.
525 He left me thus. Poor Man! he had not heart
To take a farewell of me, and he feared
That I should follow with my babes and sink   (680)
Beneath the misery of a soldier's life.'
This tale did Margaret tell with many tears;
530 And when she ended I had little power
To give her comfort, and was glad to take
Such words of hope from her own mouth as served   (685)
To chear us both; but long we had not talked
Ere we built up a pile of better thoughts
535 And with a brighter eye she looked around
As if she had been shedding tears of joy.

514 Nor had I power to answer D

We parted. It was then the early spring;   (690)
I left her busy with her garden tools;
And well remember, o'er that fence she looked,
540   And while I paced along the foot-way path,
Called out, and sent a blessing after me,
With tender chearfulness, and with a voice   (695)
That seemed the very sound of happy thoughts.
    I roved o'er many a hill and many a dale
545   With this my weary load, in heat and cold,
Through many a wood, and many an open ground
In sunshine or in shade, in wet or fair,   (700)
Now blithe, now drooping, as it might befal,
My best companions now the driving winds
550   And now the 'trotting' brooks and whispering trees,
And now the music of my own sad steps,
With many a short-lived thought that passed between   (705)
And disappeared. I measured back this road
Towards the wane of summer, when the wheat
555   Was yellow, and the soft and bladed grass
Sprung up afresh and o'er the hay-field spread
Its tender green. When I had reached the door   (710)
I found that she was absent. In the shade
Where now we sit I waited her return.
560   Her cottage in its outward look appeared
As chearful as before; in any shew   .
Of neatness little changed, but that I thought
The honeysuckle crowded round the door   (715)
And from the wall hung down in heavier loads
565   And knots of worthless stone-crop started out
Along the window's edge, and grew like weeds
Against the lower panes. I turned aside
And strolled into her garden. It was changed,   (720)
The unprofitable bindweed spread his bells   (728)
570   From side to side, and with unwieldy wreaths
Had dragged the rose from its sustaining wall
And bent it down to earth; the border tufts,
Daisy, and thrift, and lowly camomile   (722)
And thyme had straggled out into the paths
575   Which they were used to deck. Ere this an hour   (730)
Was wasted, back I turned my restless steps
And as I walked before the door it chanced
A stranger passed, and guessing whom I sought
He said that she was used to ramble far.

553 came this way again B (*alternative*), D   564 loads] tufts B²:
wreaths *corr. to* tufts D

580 The sun was sinking in the west, and now
     I sate with sad impatience. From within   (735)
     Her solitary infant cried aloud ;
     The spot though fair seemed very desolate   (740)
     The longer I remained more desolate.
585 And looking round I saw the corner stones
     Till then unmarked, on either side the door
     With dull red stains discoloured, and stuck o'er
     With tufts and hairs of wool as if the sheep   (745)
     That feed upon the commons thither came
590 As to a couching-place and rubbed their sides
     Even at her threshold. The church-clock struck eight,
     I turned and saw her distant a few steps.   (750)
     Her face was pale and thin, her figure too
     Was changed. As she unlocked the door she said
595 'It grieves me you have waited here so long
     But in good truth I've wandered much of late ;
     And sometimes, to my shame I speak, have need   (755)
     Of my best prayers to bring me back again.'
     While on the board she spread our evening meal
600 She told me she had lost her elder child,   (760)
     That he for months had been a serving boy
     Apprenticed by the parish. 'I am changed,
     And to myself,' said she, 'have done much wrong,
     And to this helpless infant. I have slept
605 Weeping, and weeping have I waked ; my tears   (770)
     Have flowed as if my body were not such
     As others are, and I could never die.
     But I am now in mind and in my heart
     More easy, and I hope,' said she, 'that heaven
610 Will give me patience to endure the things   (775)
     Which I behold at home.' It would have grieved
     Your very soul to see her. Sir, I feel
     The story linger in my heart. I fear
     'Tis long and tedious, but my spirit clings
615 To that poor woman, so familiarly   (780)
     Do I perceive her manner and her look
     And presence, and so deeply do I feel

590 Familiarly, and found a couching place D   591 church-clock]
house-clock D
602 parish. I]:   ... parish. I perceive
                  You look at me, and you have cause. To-day
                  I have been travelling far, and many days
                  About the fields I wander, knowing this
                  Only, that what I seek I cannot find
                  And so I waste my time, for I   D

Her goodness that a vision of the mind,
A momentary trance comes over me
620 And to myself I seem to muse on one (785)
By sorrow laid asleep, or borne away,
A human being destined to awake
To human life or something very near
To human life, when he shall come again
625 For whom she suffered. Sir, it would have grieved (790)
Your very heart to see her, evermore
Her eyelids drooped, her eyes were downward cast,
And when she at her table gave me food
She did not look at me, her voice was low,
630 Her body was subdued. In every act (795)
Pertaining to her house-affairs appeared
The careless stillness which a thinking soul
Gives to an idle matter. Still she sighed,
But yet no motion of the breast was seen, (800)
635 No heaving of the heart. While by the fire
We sate together, sighs came on my ear
I knew not how, and scarcely whence they came. (803)
I took my staff, and when I kissed her babe
The tears were in her eyes. I left her then (810)
640 With the best hope and comfort I could give.
She thanked me for my will, but for my hope
It seemed she did not thank me. I returned,
And took my rounds along this road again.
Ere on its sunny bank the primrose flower (815)
645 Had chronicled the earliest day of spring.
I found her sad and drooping; she had learned
No tidings of her husband, if he lived
She knew not that he lived; if he were dead
She knew not he was dead. She seemed not changed (820)
650 In person or appearance, but her house
Bespoke a sleepy hand of negligence,
The floor was neither dry nor neat, the hearth
Was comfortless
The windows they were dim, and her few books
655 Which one upon the other heretofore (825)
Had been piled up against the corner panes
In seemly order, now with straggling leaves
Lay scattered here and there, open or shut,
As they had chanced to fall. Her infant babe
660 Had from its mother caught the trick of grief, (830)
And sighed among its playthings; once again

618 Her goodness, that not seldom in my walks D 649 not
changed] the same D 654 they] too D

I turned towards the garden gate, and saw
More plainly still that poverty and grief
Were now come nearer to her; the earth was hard
665 With weeds defaced and knots of withered grass;   (835)
No ridges there appeared of clear black mould,
No winter greenness. Of her herbs and flowers
It seemed the better part were gnawed away
Or trampled on the earth; a chain of straw
670 Which had been twisted round the tender stem   (840)
Of a young apple-tree lay at its root,
The bark was nibbled round by truant sheep.
Margaret stood near, her infant in her arms
And seeing that my eye was on the tree
675 She said, 'I fear it will be dead and gone   (845)
Ere Robert come again'. Towards the house
Together we returned and she enquired
If I had any hope. But for her babe
And for her little friendless Boy, she said,
680 She had no wish to live, that she must die   (850)
Of sorrow. Yet I saw the idle loom
Still in its place. His Sunday garments hung
Upon the self-same nail—his very staff
Stood undisturbed behind the door, and when
685 I passed this way, beaten by autumn winds,   (855)
She told me that her little babe was dead
And she was left alone. That very time,
I yet remember, through the miry lane
She walked with me a mile when the bare trees
690 Trickled with foggy damps, and in such sort   (865)
That any heart had ached to hear her, begged
That wheresoe'r I went I still would ask
For him whom she had lost. We parted then,
Our final parting, for from that time forth
695 Did many seasons pass ere I return'd   (870)
Into this tract again. Five tedious years
She lingered in unquiet widowhood
A wife and widow. Needs must it have been
A sore heart-wasting. I have heard, my Friend,   (875)
700 That in that broken arbour she would sit
The idle length of half a sabbath day
There—where you see the toadstool's lazy head,
And when a dog passed by she still would quit

681–96 *A draft of these lines is in Alfoxden* MS.   689 She went B²
696/7 From their first separation, five long years   D   699 Master I
have heard   B *del.*

The shade and look abroad. On this old Bench
705 For hours she sate, and evermore, her eye[1]   (880)
Was busy in the distance, shaping things
Which made her heart beat quick. Seest thou that path ?
The greensward now has broken its grey line ;
There to and fro she paced through many a day
710 Of the warm summer, from a belt of flax   (885)
That girt her waist spinning the long-drawn thread
With backward steps—yet ever as there passed
A Man whose garments shewed the Soldier's red
Or crippled Mendicant in Sailor's garb
715 The little child who sate to turn the wheel   (890)
Ceased from his toil, and she with faltering voice
Expecting still to learn her husband's fate,
Made many a fond enquiry, and when they,
Whose presence gave no comfort, were gone by
720 Her heart was still more sad. And by yon gate
Which bars the traveller's road she often stood   (895)
And when a stranger horseman came, the latch
Would lift, and in his face look wistfully
Most happy if from aught discovered there
725 Of tender feeling she might dare repeat
The same sad question. Meanwhile her poor hut   (900)
Sank to decay, for he was gone, whose hand
At the first nippings of October frost
Closed up each chink, and with fresh bands of straw
730 Chequered the green-grown thatch. And so she lived
Through the long winter, reckless and alone ;   (905)
Till this reft house, by frost, and thaw, and rain
Was sapped, and, when she slept, the nightly damps
Did chill her breast, and in the stormy day
735 Her tattered clothes were ruffled by the wind
Even at the side of her own fire. Yet still   (910)
She loved this wretched spot, nor would for worlds
Have parted hence, and still that length of road
And this rude bench one torturing hope endeared,
740 Fast rooted at her heart ; and here, my friend,
In sickness she remained, and here she died,   (915)
Last human tenant of these ruined walls."

The End.

[1] These lines from "her eye" to the end, 705–42, are quoted by S. T. C.
in a letter to the Rev. J. P. Estlin from Racedown, June 1797 ; Griggs, i. 327.

740 and, Stranger, here   S. T. C.'s letter June 1797 *and* B *del.*

On the two next pages W. has made three different attempts at
a reconciling passage for the close of the poem:

1. The old man ceased: he saw that I was moved.
   From that low bench rising instinctively
   I turned away in weakness, and my heart
   Went back into the tale which he had told,
   And when at last returning from my mind
   I looked around, the cottage and the elms,
   The road, the pathway, and the garden wall
   Which old and loose and mossy o'er the road
   Hung bellying, all appeared, I know not how
   But to some eye within me all appeared
   Colours and forms of a strange discipline.
   The trouble which they sent into my thought
   Was sweet, I looked and looked again, and to myself
   I seemed a better and a wiser man.

2. And when at length the silence of my grief
   By some irregular fancy from within
   Or by some chance impression from without
   Was first disturbed I looked around, the road
   The door the pathway and the garden wall
                            and then
   I well remember what I felt,—the road
   The door, the pathway . . .
   I turned to the old man, and said, my friend
   Your words have consecrated many things.
   And for the tale which you have told I think
   I am a better and a wiser man.

3. How sweetly breathes the air—it breathes most sweet
   And my heart feels it, how divinely fair
   Are yon huge clouds, how lovely are these elms
   That shew themselves with all their verdant leaves
   And all the myriad veins of those green leaves
   A luminous prospect fashioned by the sun,
   The very sunshine spread upon the dust
   Is beautiful.

He struck out these passages and returned to the lines rejected at
l. 366 (v. app. crit. 366–7 supra), making them the culmination of a
long reflective argument (much of which was afterwards incorporated
in the Exc. Book IV) as follows:

[Addendum to MS. B]
                  Not useless do I deem
These quiet sympathies with things that hold
An inarticulate language; for the man   (Exc. iv. 1207)
Once taught to love such objects as excite

5   No morbid passions no disquietude
     No vengeance, and no hatred needs must feel
     The joy of that pure principle of love
     So deeply that unsatisfied with aught
     Less pure and exquisite he cannot choose
10   But seek for objects of a kindred love
     In fellow-natures and a kindred joy.
     Accordingly he by degrees perceives
     His feelings of aversion softened down
     A holy tenderness pervade his frame   (iv. 1220)
15   His sanity of reason not impaired
     Say rather all his thoughts now flowing clear
     From a clear fountain flowing he looks round
     He seeks for good and finds the good he seeks[1]
     Till execration and contempt are things
20   He only knows by name and if he hears
     From other mouths the language which they speak
     He is compassionate and has no thought
     No feeling which can overcome his love.
        And further, by contemplating these forms   (iv. 1230)
25   In the relations which they bear to man
     We shall discover what a power is theirs
     To stimulate our minds, and multiply
     The spiritual presences of absent things.   (iv. 1234)
     Then weariness shall cease. We shall acquire
30   The [   ] habit by which sense is made
     Subservient still to moral purposes   (iv. 1248)
     A vital essence, and a saving power.
     Nor shall we meet an object but may read
     Some sweet and tender lesson to our minds
35   Of human suffering or of human joy.
     All things shall speak of Man, and we shall read
     Our duties in all forms, and general laws
     And local accidents shall tend alike
     To quicken and to rouze, and give the will   (iv. 1242)
40   And power which by a [   ] chain of good
     Shall link us to our kind. No naked hearts,
     No naked minds shall then be left to mourn   (iv. 1250)
     The burthen of existence. Science then *etc.*,
                          as Exc. iv. 1252–6, *followed by*
     But better taught, and mindful of its use

---

[1] Coleridge quotes the first 18 lines of this passage (*but with* shadowy *for*
quiet in 2) in a letter dated March 1798.

---

30 *blank space for omitted word in* B *and* D   40 a chain of benefits
D

50   Legitimate and its peculiar power
     While with a patient interest it shall watch
     The processes of things, and serve the cause   (iv. 1258)
     Of order and distinctness; not for this
     Shall it forget that its most noble end   (iv. 1260)
55   Its most illustrious province must be found
     In ministering to the excursive power
     Of intellect and thought. So build we up   (iv. 1264)
     The being that we are. For was it meant
     That we should pore, and dwindle as we pore,   (iv. 960)
60   For ever dimly pore on things minute,
     On solitary objects, still beheld
     In disconnection dead and spiritless,
     And still dividing and dividing still,
     Break down all grandeur, still unsatisfied
65   With our unnatural toil, while littleness   (iv. 965)
     May yet become more little, waging thus
     An impious warfare with the very life
     Of our own souls? Or was it ever meant   (iv. 968)
     That this majestic imagery, the clouds
70   The ocean and the firmament of heaven
     Should lie a barren picture on the mind?
     Never for ends of vanity and pain
     And sickly wretchedness were we endued
     Amid this world of feeling and of life
75   With apprehension, reason, will and thought,
     Affections, organs, passions. Let us rise
     From this oblivious sleep, these fretful dreams
     Of feverish nothingness. Thus disciplined
     All things shall live in us and we shall live
80   In all things that surround us. This I deem
     Our tendency, and thus shall every day
     Enlarge our sphere of pleasure and of power,
     For thus the senses and the intellect
     Shall each to each supply a mutual aid,
85   Invigorate and sharpen and refine
     Each other with a power that knows no bound,
     And forms and feelings acting thus, and thus
     Reacting, they shall each acquire
     A living spirit and a character
90   Till then unfelt, and each be multiplied
     With a variety that knows no end.
     Thus deeply drinking in the soul of things   (iv. 1265)
     We shall be wise perforce, and we shall move

82 power]   D: B *reads* pain, *clearly a copyist's error*

From strict necessity along the path
95   Of order and of good. Whate'er we see   (iv. 1270)
Whate'er we feel, by agency direct
Or indirect, shall tend to feed and nurse
Our faculties, and raise to loftier heights
Our intellectual soul. The old man ceased   (iv. 1275)
100   The words he uttered shall not pass away
They had sunk into me, but not as sounds   (iv. 1285)
To be expressed by visible characters,
For while he spake my spirit had obeyed
The presence of his eye, my ear had drunk
105   The meanings of his voice. He had discoursed
Like one who in the slow and silent works,
The manifold conclusions of his thought,
Had brooded till Imagination's power
Condensed them to a passion whence she drew   (iv. 1295)
110   Herself new energies, resistless force.
      Yet still towards the cottage did I turn   (i. 925)
Fondly, and trace with nearer interest
That secret spirit of humanity
Which, 'mid the calm oblivious tendencies
115   Of Nature, 'mid her plants, her weeds and flowers,
And silent overgrowings, still survived.   (930)
The old man, seeing this, resumed, and said
My Friend, enough to sorrow have you given,
The purposes of Wisdom ask no more,   (933)
120   Be wise and chearful, and no longer read
The forms of things with an unworthy eye.
She sleeps in the calm earth and peace is here.   (941)
I well remember that those very plumes,
Those weeds and the high spear-grass on that wall,
125   By mist and silent rain-drops silvered o'er,
As once I passed, did to my mind convey   (945)
So still an image of tranquillity,
So calm and still, and looked so beautiful,
Amid the uneasy thoughts which filled my mind,
130   That what we feel of sorrow and despair
From ruin and from change, and all the grief   (950)
The passing shews of being leave behind
Appeared an idle dream that could not live
Where meditation was. I turned away   (955)
135   And walked along my road in happiness.
He ceased, and now the sun declining shot

103 my mind and heart obeyed D   104 my ear drunk in D
106 silent] patient D

> A slant and mellow radiance, which began
> To fall upon us when beneath the trees
> We sate on that low bench; and now we felt   (960)
> 140 Admonished thus, the sweet hour coming on;
> A linnet warbled from those lofty elms
> A thrush sang loud, and other melodies
> At distance heard, peopled the milder air.
> The old man rose and hoisted up his load;   (965)
> 145 Together casting then a farewell look
> Upon those silent walls we left the shade
> And chearfully pursued our evening way.

146–7   . . . we turned away
   And pleasantly did we pursue our road   B *del.*
147 And ere the stars were visible attained
   A rustic inn, our evening resting-place   D

MS. D, headed *The Ruined Cottage*, may have been copied in 1799. It is contained in a small octavo note-book bound in red leather, MS. 18 A, in which are also found, among other poems, *Adventures on Salisbury Plain*, parts of *Prelude* i and v, *Nutting*, and some of the *Matthew* poems. It is in D. W.'s neatest hand, with occasional corrections by W. In the main D follows B, making a few corrections, filling in most of the blanks and incorporating in the text many of the additional passages written on the versos. It concludes the poem by adding after the original last line ("Last human tenant of these ruined walls") lines corresponding with *Exc.* i. 917–24 followed by ll. 111–47 of *Addendum* to B with slight variations. But when it was copied W. seems to have become uneasy about the double-barrelled form the poem was taking; and to have contemplated the publication of *The Ruined Cottage* without the lines on the Pedlar's character and background which made their first appearance in B. For it omits from the text ll. 41–303, and after adopting the four lines added to B after l. 40 (*v. app. crit.*), it goes on:

> He lay, his pack of rustic merchandize
> Pillowing his head. I guess he had no thought
>
>   *as* B 303 ff.

This leaves a compact poem, rightly entitled *The Ruined Cottage*: Part I has 197 lines, Part II 320.

The omitted lines are given as *Addenda*, evidently reserved for use in some other place, but rearranged more in accordance with the order in which they are found in *Exc.* i. Thus:

Addendum i:

41–59. MS. B (Minster clock).

70 (From that bleak tenement)**–108** (ever varying) *after which it goes on*:

> Thus informed
> He had small need of books *etc., as* 167–90

108 (Within his heart)**–166** (eye of love) *followed by lines on verso of* B *after* 166 (*v. app. crit.*), *but with* Lore of other kind *for* Other lore.

191–220. (Of solitude.) *but running on*

> Of solitude. Yet not the less he found
> In cold relation and the lifelessness
> Of truth, by oversubtlety dislodged
> From grandeur and from love, an idle toy,
> The dullest of all toys. He saw in truth
> A holy spirit and a breathing soul;
> He reverenced her and trembled at her look
> When, with a moral beauty in her face,
> She led him through the worlds.

W. has written *out* against this passage.

221 (But now)**–60** (native hills) *followed by lines on verso of* B (260/1); **261–4**;

60–6. *followed by passage on versos of* B *after* 264 (*v. app. crit.*) (Many a year . . . His eye)

267–70. (transports).

Here a blank space is left in the MS., and it is clear that what follows is rejected from the text and reserved for use elsewhere:

Addendum ii:

270 (though he was untaught)**–300** (chain), *but with* l. 273 He yet retained *for* To him was given, *and* 275/6

> From deep analogies by thought supplied
> Or consciousnesses not to be subdued

Addendum iii is Addendum to B 1–110, p. 400 *supra*

Addendum iv. Between the main text of *The Ruined Cottage* and the Addenda described above, but obviously added to the note-book later, on a space till then left blank, and probably, as I suggest in my account of MS. E *infra*, in 1801–2, is another draft which, beginning with 41–7 of B, goes on to give a new origin and antecedents to the Pedlar. The name Armytage is changed to Patrick Drummond, and instead of being born on the Cumbrian hills and brought up as a shepherd, he is now a Scotsman, who in boyhood tended cattle on the hills of Perthshire, but in later life made his pedlar's headquarters at Hawkshead, when the poet was a schoolboy. It runs thus:

> He stood, his back towards me, but as soon
> As I drew near to him great joy was ours
> At this unthought-of meeting. For the night
> We parted nothing willingly, and now
> 5   He by appointment waited for me here
> Beneath these elms, it being our joint wish
> To travel on together a few days.
> —We were dear Friends; I from my childhood up

Had known him, in a nook of Furness Fells
10   At Hawkshead, where I went to school nine years.
One room he had, the fifth part of a house,
A place to which he drew from time to time
And found a kind of home or harbour there.
He was the best Old Man! and often I
15   Delight to recollect him, and his looks,
And think of him and his affectionate ways.
In that same Town of Hawkshead where we dwelt
There was a little girl ten years of age,
But tiny for her years, a pretty dwarf,
20   Fair-hair'd, fair-fac'd, and though of stature small
In heart as forward as a lusty child.
Oft to his tenement this Girl would come
To play with the good Man, and he was wont
To tell her stories of his early life,
25   And often have I listen'd to their talk—
"Nay"—would she answer him, unsaying thus
All he had said to her, "you never could
Be a poor ragged little Boy, and hir'd
To the poor Man you talk [of] to herd Cattle
30   On a hill-side for forty [pence] a year"—
All which did to the Girl appear so strange
She could not credit it; and when she us'd
To doubt his words, as I remember well,
Spite of himself the good Man smile[d], and held
35   His hand up to his face to hide his smiles,
Because he knew that if the little Girl
Once spi'd them, she would then be sure, past doubt,
That he was joking. She being thus perplex'd
He was far better pleas'd to sing to her
40   Scotch songs, sometimes, but oftener to repeat
Scotch poetry, old ballads, and old tales,
Love-Gregory, *William Wallace* and *Rob Roy*.
All this while she was sitting on a stool
Between his knees, and oft would she stand up
45   Upon her stool, and coax him with a kiss
To tell her more, and often times would he
Cry over her, and she would wonder why.
This, standing at his threshold, have I seen

10 ten *corr. to* nine   5–82 *A shorter draft of these lines appears in*
Alfoxden MS.
17/18 There was a little Girl (and though in truth
        This incident be something like a nook
        Or pleasant corner which from my right path
        Diverts me, yet I cannot pass it by) MS. E 2

Yea, many times, when he had little thought
That any one was near. And for myself
He lov'd me, out of many rosy Boys
Singled out me, as he in sport would say
For my grave looks, too thoughtful for my years.
His name was Drummond: the bare truth it was
Which he had told the Girl, that he had been
A Herd-Callan for forty pence a year,
Among the hills of Perthshire he was born   (*i.* 107)
His Father died and left behind three sons
                    (ere he was four years old)
And Patrick was the youngest of the three.
His Mother married for a second Mate
A School-master who taught the Boys to read
And bred them up and gave them as he could
Needful instruction, teaching them the ways
Of honesty and holiness severe.
Patrick as soon as he was six years old   (*i.* 118)
Served as a Herd-Boy all the summer through
But in the winter months he duly went
To his Step-Father's school that stood alone
Sole building on a mountain's dreary edge   (*i.* 123)
Far from the sight of City spire or sound
Of minster clock. From this bleak tenement
He in the evening sometimes to his home
In solitude return'd and saw the hills
Grow larger in the darkness; all alone
Beheld the stars come out above his head,
And travell'd through the wood with no one near   (*i.* 130)
To whom he might confess the things he saw.
He had small need of Books *etc.*   (*i.* 163)
His history I from himself have heard
Full often after I grew up and he
Found in my heart as he would kindly say
A kindred heart to his. His father died,
Could never be forgotten.
                    Thus was he
Bred up among the fields, and in a house
Virtuous, and wanting little to the growth   (*i.* 112)
Of a strong mind, although exceeding poor.
Pure livers were they all, austere and grave
And fearing God, the very children taught
Stern self-respect, a reverence for God's word   (*i.* 115)
And piety, scarce known on English land.
And thus did Patrick gather when a Boy
Some gloomy notions which in later life

50

55

60

65

70

75

80

85

90

Would come to him at times, but from his birth
He had a gracious nature, genial blood
95   Flow'd in him, and the region of the heart
Even from the first was sensitive and kind.
Never had living man a gentler creed,
For love was his, and the pure joy of love,   (*i.* 187)
By sound diffus'd, or by the breathing air,
100   Or by the silent looks of happy things,
Or flowing from the universal face   (*i.* 190)
Of earth and sky; for he had early felt
The power of nature, early had been taught
By his intense conceptions to receive
105   Deeply the lesson deep of love which he
Whom Nature by whatever means has taught   (*i.* 195)
To feel intensely cannot but receive.
      He was a man of genius and yet more
A man of science too; among the hills,
110   While he was a hired Labourer tending herds
He gaz'd upon that mighty orb of song
The divine Milton. Lore of different kind   (*i.* 250)
His step-father supplied, books that explain'd[1]
             cetera desunt

Addendum v. At another place in the note-book are found the follow-
ing lines, intended as an alternative to B 220–64:

Of solitude, but now the time was come
When he, approaching to a man's estate
Began to think about his way of life
In future, and his worldly maintenance.
His mother strove *etc.*, *as verso to* B 260/1
His eldest Brother, elder than himself
Six years had travelled southward long before
To carry up and down a Pedlar's Pack
In England where he traded at that time
Healthy and prosperous—"I to him will go"
Said Patrick "I am stout as he, can bear
A Load with ease the weight of twenty stone"—
This plan, long time, had been his favourite thought.
He ask'd his Mother's blessing, and with tears
Thank'd the good man, his second father, ask'd

[1] An abbreviated form of ll. 5–57 of Addendum iv (43 lines for 53), with
slight variants, is also found in the *Alfoxden* note-book of 1798. But this
was almost certainly added later and probably only just before the insertion
of Addendum iv in MS. 18 A. For it is found at the end of the book, *after*
D. W. had taken it over for German exercises, and is the only poetic entry
in her hand, all the earlier entries being rough drafts in W.'s hand.

From him parental blessings, and assum'd
This lowly occupation. The good Pair
Offer'd up prayers and blessed him but with hearts
Foreboding evil.

This passage persists, with slight variants, through MSS. E, M, and P.

MS. E, a fair copy in the hand of D. W., with no heading but *Part First*, incorporates the important change noted above in Addendum iv to D. The Pedlar is brought back with different antecedents and a background further elaborated. The MS. can be assigned with some certainty to Dec.–March 1801-2. In D. W.'s *Journal*, from Dec. 21, 1801 to March 10, 1802, there are no less than twenty references to *The Pedlar*, as in all but one instance the poem is now called; of these the most significant are the following:

Dec. 21 (1801). Wm. sate beside me and read *The Pedlar*; He was in good spirits and full of hope of what he should do with it.

Dec. 22. Wm. composed a few lines of *The Pedlar*.

Dec. 27. Mary wrote some lines of the third part[1] of Wm.'s poem which he brought to read to us.

Jan. 26 (1802). [The next reference to the poem; the W.s had been away from Grasmere for nearly a month.] Wm. had tired himself with working—he resolved to do better. . . . We sate till we were both tired, for Wm. wrote out part of his poem, and endeavoured to alter it, and so made himself ill.

Jan. 30. Wm. worked at *The Pedlar* all the morning. He kept the dinner waiting till four o'clock. He was much tired.

Feb. 1. William worked hard at *The Pedlar*, and tired himself.

Feb. 5. William not well. Sate up late at *The Pedlar*.

Feb. 7. We sate by the fire and . . . read *The Pedlar*, thinking it done; but lo! though Wm. could find fault with no one part of it, it was uninteresting, and must be altered. Poor Wm.!

Feb. 11. Wm. sadly tired and working still at *The Pedlar*.

Feb. 12. I recopied *The Pedlar*, but poor Wm. all the time at work. . . . I almost finished writing *The Pedlar*; but poor Wm. wore himself and me out with labour.

Feb. 13. Still at work at *The Pedlar*, altering and refitting.

Feb. 16. Wm. was better, had altered *The Pedlar*.

Feb. 28. Wm. very ill, employed with *The Pedlar*.

March 3. I was so unlucky as to propose to rewrite *The Pedlar*. Wm. got to work and was worn to death.

March 6. I wrote *The Pedlar*, and finished it.

March 7. I stitched up *The Pedlar*.

[1] E is the first MS. which divides the poem into three parts (1–433, 434–604, 605–end). It is also the first which incorporates the final reconciling passage and ends substantially as text of *Exc.* i

March 10. William has since tea been talking about publishing the Yorkshire Wolds poem [i.e. *Peter Bell*] with *The Pedlar*. [This is interesting as showing that at this time W. still regarded *The Pedlar* as a poem complete in itself, and not as a part of *The Excursion*.]

E was probably the MS. almost finished on Feb. 12, the work done in later February and early March being represented by a MS. which I refer to as E², also written by D. W., a portion of which, ll. 1–356, is bound up with E.

MS. M is sufficiently described in *Prel.*, E. de S., p. xxx. It was transcribed by D. W., from MS. E², in March 1804. The first leaf containing ll. 1–58 of *The Pedlar* is missing.

MS. P, written by M. W., is the first that regards the poem as an integral part of a longer whole. The note-book contains the first three books of *The Excursion*. The MS. down to iii. 324 represents, probably, a fair copy of W.'s work in the summer of 1806 (*v.* p. 371 *supra*); but he has interlarded the fair copy with corrections and additions throughout. *v.* note to i. 435 (*app. crit.*) *infra*.

Since MS. B is given in full *supra* with variants from A and D, I have referred in my *app. crit.* mainly to the succeeding MSS., where, unless otherwise stated, MSS. stands for E to P inclusive.

p. 7. 1 *et seq.* "All that relates to Margaret and the ruined cottage, etc., was taken from observations made in the South West of England, and certainly it would require more than seven league boots to stretch in one morning from a Common in Somersetshire or Dorsetshire to the heights of Furness Fells and the deep valleys they embosom."— I. F.

It is significant that W. made no attempt to adjust the landscape of the original *Ruined Cottage* to the setting of the Langdale valleys which he adopts as the main scene of *The Excursion*. The hot, bare, waterless common, the thatched cottage (903–4) with its grass-grown walls (942–3) are as remote as possible from those rocky valleys with their many streams and waterfalls, slate-roofed farms, and naked walls.

2–3. glared Through a pale steam] Cf. *An Evening Walk*, 37–8:
When, in the south, the wan noon, brooding still,
Breathed a pale steam around the glaring hill.

12. A twilight of its own] Cf. *An Evening Walk*, 61: "And its own twilight softens the whole scene."

29. a brotherhood of lofty elms] Cf. *Sonnet composed at — Castle* (Vol. III, p. 83): "A brotherhood of venerable Trees."

51. (*app. crit.*) The alteration of 1845 is made to avoid the clash of final *th* with initial *th* "Beneath the . . .", cf. "Strange fits of passion" (Vol. II, p. 29), where "Beneath the evening moon" is altered to "Beneath an . . .". Quillinan writes, March 19, 1844: "Mr. Words-

worth has been working very hard lately, to very little purpose, to mend the versification of *The Excursion*." (*C.R.* ii, p. 548); *v.* also letter of M. W. to H. C. R., April 7, 1844 (*C.R.* ii, p. 551). But his alterations nearly always enliven the rhythm.

113–14. Cf. *Resolution and Independence*, ll. 97–8:

> Such as grave Livers do in Scotland use,
> Religious men, who give to God and man their dues.

118–300. Much of this passage can be closely paralleled by what W. relates in *The Prelude* of his own experiences as a boy. Lines 238–56 of MS. B were removed to *Prelude*, ii (*Text* A, 416–34).

148. liveliness of dreams] It is generally stated that the images of dreams are vague and indistinct and lack colour. W.'s experience was the opposite.

179. left half-told] Cf. *Il Penseroso*, 109–10:

> Or call up him that left half told
> The story of Cambuscan bold.

185–307. Cf. the poet's own experience as related in *Prelude*, iv. 231–55, 323–30.

206–7. his spirit drank The spectacle *etc.*] Note the physical metaphor; cf. Book IV. 1265, "Thus deeply drinking-in the soul of things", and *To my Sister*, 27–8:

> Our minds shall drink at every pore
> The spirit of the season.

248–50. A direct transcript, surely, from the experience of the youth Wordsworth: the poems he wrote as a schoolboy, and still more *An Evening Walk* and *Descriptive Sketches*, show the pervading influence of Milton upon his mind and ear. *v.* notes on these poems, Vol. I, and cf. Addendum, p. 362 *supra*.

253–4. For what W. thought of Mathematics *v. Prelude*, v. 56–140, and vi. 115–28.

266. sweet influence] Cf. "The Pleiades . . . Shedding sweet influence", *Paradise Lost*, vii. 375.

326. such travellers find their own delight] Cf. ii. 19–24.

341. much did he see of men] "At the risk of giving a shock to the prejudices of artificial society, I have ever been ready to pay homage to the aristocracy of nature; under a conviction that vigorous human-heartedness is the constituent principle of true taste. It may still, however, be satisfactory to have prose testimony how far a Character, employed for purposes of imagination, is founded upon general fact. I, therefore, subjoin an extract from an author who had opportunities of being well acquainted with a class of men, from whom my own personal knowledge emboldened me to draw this portrait.

"We learn from Caesar and other Roman Writers, that the travelling merchants who frequented Gaul and other barbarous countries, either newly conquered by the Roman arms, or bordering on the Roman conquests, were ever the first to make the inhabitants of those countries familiarly acquainted with the Roman modes of life, and to inspire them with an inclination to follow the Roman fashions, and to enjoy Roman conveniences. In North America, travelling merchants from the Settlements have done and continue to do much more towards civilizing the Indian natives, than all the missionaries, papist or protestant, who have ever been sent among them.

"It is farther to be observed, for the credit of this most useful class of men, that they commonly contribute, by their personal manners, no less than by the sale of their wares, to the refinement of the people among whom they travel. Their dealings form them to great quickness of wit and acuteness of judgment. Having constant occasion to recommend themselves and their goods, they acquire habits of the most obliging attention, and the most insinuating address. As in their peregrinations they have opportunity of contemplating the manners of various men and various cities, they become eminently skilled in the knowledge of the world. *As they wander, each alone, through thinly-inhabited districts, they form habits of reflection and of sublime contemplation.* With all these qualifications, no wonder, that they should often be, in remote parts of the country, the best mirrors of fashion, and censors of manners; and should contribute much to polish the roughness, and soften the rusticity of our peasantry. It is not more than twenty or thirty years since a young man going from any part of Scotland to England, of purpose *to carry the pack*, was considered as going to lead the life and acquire the fortune of a gentleman. When, after twenty years' absence, in that honourable line of employment, he returned with his acquisitions to his native country, he was regarded as a gentleman to all intents and purposes."—Heron's *Journey in Scotland*, vol. i, p. 89.—W. W.

345-7. Cf. *Preface to Lyrical Ballads*, 1800: "Low and rustic life was generally chosen, because, in that situation, the essential passions of the heart find a better soil in which they can attain their maturity, are less under restraint, and speak a plainer and more emphatic language; because in that situation our elementary feelings coexist in a state of greater simplicity, and, consequently, may be more accurately contemplated, and more forcibly communicated."

370-1. afford to suffer *etc.*] *The Tempest*, I. ii. 5-6:

O, I have suffer'd
With those that I saw suffer.

Cf. W.'s remark about Coleridge, quoted in Barron Field's "Memoirs of the Life and Poetry of W. W." (B.M. MS. Add. 41325-7): "It was poor dear Coleridge's constant infelicity that prevented him from being the poet that Nature had given him the power to be. He had always too much personal and domestic discontent to paint the sorrows of mankind. He could not afford to suffer with those whom he saw suffer"; and cf. W.'s account of himself (*Prelude*, xi. 276–7) ". . . withal a happy man, And therefore bold to look on painful things".

381–93. *v.* note to 435 *infra.*

415–16. The . . . teasing ways of children vexed not him] Cf. Addendum iv to MS. B, *supra*, p. 405.

422–33. For this portrait of the Pedlar W. made several fragmentary sketches, which are jotted down in the *Alfoxden* note-book (date Jan. 20–March 5, 1798). The most interesting are as follows:

> His eye was like the star of Jove
> When in a storm its radiance comes and goes
> As winds drive on the thin invisible cloud

> Some men there are who like insects *etc.*
> . . . dart and dart against the mighty stream
> Of tendency . . . others with no vulgar sense
> Of their existence, to no vulgar end
> Float calmly down

> there is a holy indolence
> Compared to which our best activity
> Is oftimes deadly bane

> They rest upon their oars,
> Float down the mighty stream of tendency
> In a calm mood of holy indolence
> A most wise passiveness.

> He lov'd to contemplate
> The mountains and the antient hills, to stand
> And feed his spirit in their solitudes.

> Transfigured by his feeling, he appeared
> Even as a prophet—one whose purposes
> Were round him like a light—sublime he seem'd,
> One to whom solitary thought had given
> The power miraculous by which the soul
> Walks through the world that lives in future things.

435. (*app. crit.*) The Pedlar of W.'s first conception (*v.* MS. B, 302–4) was still labouring in his vocation: that "weary load" (MS. B) "his pack of rustic merchandize" (MSS. D—P) is absent from the text of 1814, where the Pedlar has retired from business and now has no appendage but his staff. *v.* also l. 965 *app. crit.* It is in the revisions in W.'s hand to MS. P that these changes are effected, and the Pedlar of *The Ruined Cottage* becomes the Wanderer of *The Excursion.* Note that ll. 381–93 *supra* do not appear in the MSS. until W. W. makes a first draft of them in an addition to P.

513–19. These lines first became part of *The Ruined Cottage* in

MS. E, but a draft of them followed by another few lines about Margaret is found among fragments of blank verse in MS. 2 of *Peter Bell* (date 1799–1800):

> She was of quiet mood,
> Tender and deep in her excess of love,
> Not speaking much, pleased rather with the joy
> Of her own heart. By some especial care *etc., as text*
> . . . Should live on earth a life of happiness.
>
> > Her person and her face
> Were homely, such as none who pass her by
> Would have remembered, yet when she was seen
> In her own dwelling place a grace was hers
> And Beauty which beginning from without
> Fell back on her with sanctifying power.

546. And their place knew them not] Cf. *Paradise Lost*, vii. 144: "Whom their place knows here no more." Both passages derive from Psalm ciii. 16.

593. deepest noon] Cf. *The Waggoner*, 6: "In silence deeper far than that of deepest noon."

703. "trotting brooks"] From Burns, *Epistle to William Simpson*, xv: "Adoun some trotting burn's meander"; quoted by W. at the end of his first note on *The River Duddon* (Vol. III, p. 504).

708. bladed grass] Cf. *A Midsummer Night's Dream*, I. i. 211.

792. (*app. crit.*) The alteration here with its reversal of accent in the fourth foot was clearly made to strengthen the metrical effect of the line. Cf. variants at ii. 400 and 500, and v. 857 and 989; and *v.* note to i. 51 *supra*.

846–7. (*app. crit.*) The change in the text has been made to get rid of "towards" as a disyllable. Cf. *app. crit.* to ii. 586, 636–8, iv. 396, 862, *etc.* Mr. T. Hutchinson showed (*Academy*, Dec. 2, 1893) that W. first regarded this word as a disyllable, but from 1836 onwards used it invariably as a monosyllable. Even as early as 1814 he often used it as a monosyllable, spelling it "t'ward", or "t'wards" in the first edition of *The Excursion*.

871–916. These lines, the first written of *The Excursion* according to W. (*v.* I. F.), were quoted by S. T. C. in his letter of June 1797, and Mary Hutchinson had a copy of them. *v.* D. W. to M. H., March 5, 1798. The poem originally ended here.

916. Last human tenant] The significance of the words "*human tenant*" is impoverished by the withdrawal from the text of the earlier passage, in MS. B, 361–3, describing the *non-human* tenants of the Cottage—the wild colt, unstalled heifer, and Potter's Ass.

917–56. For Wordsworth's earlier attempt at a final reconciling passage *v. supra*, p. 400.

934–40. (*app. crit.*) no longer read The forms of things with an unworthy eye] A new significance is given to these words by the first placing of this passage in MS. B (*q.v. supra*, p. 390), 366–7 *app. crit.*, as 'an afterthought immediately following the lines which describe the desolate and ugly spectacle of the *rank spear-grass* and rotting nettles, symbols of neglect and decay (MS. B, 357–9). Seen in another mood the spear-grass is an image of beauty and tranquillity.

934–55. Note that the changes in the text of this passage were made as late as 1845. Possibly W. was moved by the charge brought against him by John Wilson in his chapter on Sacred Poetry in *Recreations of Christopher North*, publ. 1842, where he designates W.'s religion as "a very high religion", but "not Christianity", and illustrates his point from the Story of Margaret, quoting the above lines and deploring "the utter absence of Revealed Religion where it ought to have been all-in-all".

BOOK II

It seems likely that Book II was composed as a whole, though not in its final form, in the summer of 1806, but some parts of it were written earlier. Lines 1–26, originally intended as an opening for *Prelude*, viii, were composed in the spring of 1804 (*v. Prel.*, E. de S., p. lii).

A fair copy of the whole Book is found in MS. P (*v.* p. 410 *supra*). An early draft of the Book down to l. 725, together with a draft of ll. 741–62 on a separate page, is found in MS. X of *The Prelude*; *v. Prel.*, E. de S., p. xxxi. I refer to the variants it supplies as X in my *app. crit.* In MS. 58 (*v.* p. 371 *supra*) are found ll. 153–320, in a version intermediate between MS. X and MS. P. This last version, which I refer to as MS., corresponds closely with the printed text, though with some variants.

These MSS. make it clear that Book II as first conceived lacked two significant ingredients of the printed version: (1) the details of the story of the old man lost on the mountains, ll. 730–895 (*v.* notes *infra*); and (2) the facts of the Solitary's marriage and loss of his wife and children, ll. 185–210 (*v.* note *infra*), an addition to the Solitary's history made by W. after the death of his own two children in 1812 (*v.* introductory note to Book III).

p. 42. **25–7.** (*app. crit.*) Cf. note to i. 435 (*app. crit.*) *supra*.

41–6. Expert and pompous *réchauffé* of rejected passage in Book I *v. app. crit.* i. 415–22: "He lov'd them all chickens and household dogs . . .", *etc.* Note that the passage is a later addition to Book II, not present in the MSS.

92–6. mountains stern and desolate . . . with aerial softness clad] The suggestion of the contrast between mountains that are stern and desolate at close quarters, but fair with "aerial softness clad" when seen from a distance, comes perhaps from Dyer's *Grongar Hill*:

> As yon summits soft and fair,
> Clad in colours of the air

Which to those who journey near
Barren, brown, and rough appear.

It is to be noted that "aerial" is an epithet applied by Dyer to the sides of Cader Ydris (*Fleece*, Book III). Cf. W.'s sonnet on Dyer and note, Vol. III, pp. 10 and 421–2.

112. dark hill] i.e. Lingmoor Fell.

185–210. It is to be remarked that these lines do not appear either in X or in the draft of ll. 152–320 in MS. 58 referred to above. They occur in MS. P, M. W.'s fair copy, in a long passage written on pages which have been sewn into the book to replace earlier version removed; *v.* the introductory note to Book III, *infra*.

210–309. The whole of this passage should be compared with the account W. gives in *The Prelude* of his own experiences of the French Revolution.

231. regions opposite as heaven and hell] Cf. *Prelude*, x. 337–8.

314–15. "a world Not moving to his mind."] Nowell Smith has traced this quotation to George Dyer's *Lines on Gilbert Wakefield*.

324. dreary plain] Cf. *Paradise Lost*, i. 180: "Seest thou yon dreary Plain."

327–48. This passage is quoted by W. in his *Guide to the Lakes*, prefaced by the words: "The scene in which this small piece of water (Blea Tarn) lies suggested to the Author the following description, supposing the spectator to look down upon it, not from the road, but from one of its elevated sides."

373–93. Cf. D. W.'s account of a Grasmere funeral in her *Journal* of Sept. 3, 1800: "I then went to a funeral at John Dawson's. About 10 men and 4 women. Bread, cheese, and ale. They talked sensibly and chearfully about common things. The dead person, 56 years of age, buried by the parish. The coffin was neatly lettered and painted black, and covered with a decent cloth. They set the corpse down at the door; and, while we stood within the threshold, the men with their hats off sang with decent and solemn countenances a verse of a funeral psalm. The corpse was then borne down the hill, and they sang till they had got past the Town-End. I was affected to tears while we stood in the house, the coffin lying before me. There were no near kindred, no children. When we got out of the dark house the sun was shining, and the prospect looked so divinely beautiful as I never saw it. It seemed more sacred than I had ever seen it, and yet more allied to human life. The green fields, neighbours of the churchyard, were as green as possible; and, with the brightness of the sunshine, looked quite gay. I thought she was going to a quiet spot, and I could not help weeping very much. When we came to the bridge, they began to sing again, and stopped during four lines before they entered the churchyard." And see also her account of the funeral of the Greens, in her narrative *George and Sarah Green*, p. 56 (Oxford, 1936): "The funeral procession was very solemn—passing through

Easedale, and, altogether, I never witnessed a more moving scene. As is customary here, there was a pause before the bodies were borne through the Church-yard Gate, while part of a psalm was sung, the men standing with their heads uncovered."

381–2. *Shall in the grave . . . faithfulness?*] From metrical Version of Psalm lxxxviii. 11.

443. a novel of Voltaire] i.e. *Candide. ou l'Optimisme* (1759).

484. dull product of a scoffer's pen] Hazlitt and Lamb, among others, have criticized W: for this description of *Candide*. In his review of *The Excursion* in *The Examiner* Hazlitt remarked: "We cannot agree that *Candide* is dull. It is, if our Author pleases, 'the production of a scoffer's pen', or it is anything, but dull'"; and at Haydon's "immortal dinner", as Haydon reports, " 'Now', said Lamb, 'you old Lake poet, you rascally poet, why do you call Voltaire dull?' We all defended Wordsworth, and affirmed there was a state of mind when Voltaire would be dull." But Lamb himself, writing to W. in Sept. 1814, had said, "I dared say you never could relish *Candide*. I know I tried to get through it about a twelvemonth since, and couldn't for the dullness." But W. seems to have meditated changing "dull" to "vile"; *v. app. crit.*

500. (*app. crit.*) The correction is clearly made to enliven the dull metrical effect of the line.

550–2. Many precious rites *etc.*] Cf. I. F. note, quoted in note to v. 671.

692. two huge Peaks] The Langdale Pikes, Pike of Stickle and Harrison Stickle; they are not actually visible from the cottage.

738–826. he, whom this our cottage *etc.*] "The account given by the Solitary toward the close of the second Book, in all that belongs to the character of the Old Man, was taken from a Grasmere Pauper, who was boarded in the last house quitting the vale on the road to Ambleside; the character of his hostess, and all that befell the poor man on the mountain, belong to Paterdale; the woman I knew well; her name was Ruth Jackson, and she was exactly such a person as I describe. The ruins of the old Chapel, among which the old man was found lying, may yet be traced, and stood upon the ridge that divides Paterdale from Boardale and Martindale, having been placed there for the convenience of both districts. The glorious appearance disclosed above and among the mountains was described partly from what my friend Mr. Luff, who then lived in Paterdale, witnessed upon that melancholy occasion, and partly from what Mary and I had seen in company with Sir G. and Lady Beaumont above Hartshope Hall on our way from Paterdale to Ambleside."—I. F.

W. first heard the story here related during his excursion with Dorothy on the banks of Ullswater in Nov. 1805. Here is Dorothy's version of it: "Looked down into Boar Dale above Sanwick—deep and bare, a stream winding down it. After having walked a considerable way on the tops of the hills, came in view of Glenridding and the mountains at the head of Grisdale. Luff then took us aside, before we had begun to descend, to a small ruin, which was formerly a Chapel, or place of worship where the inhabitants of Martindale and Patterdale were accustomed to meet on Sabbath days. There are now no traces by which you could distinguish that the building had been different from a common sheepfold; the loose stones and the few which yet remain piled up are the same as those which lie elsewhere on the mountain; but the shape of the building being oblong is not that of a common sheepfold, and it stands east and west. Whether it was ever consecrated ground or not I do not know; but the place may be kept holy in the memory of some now living in Patterdale; for it was the means of preserving the life of a poor old man last summer, who, having gone up the mountain to gather peats together, had been overtaken by a storm, and could not find his way down again. He happened to be near the remains of the old Chapel, and, in a corner of it, he contrived, by laying turf and ling and stones in a corner of it from one wall to the other, to make a shelter from the wind, and there he sate all night. The woman who had sent him on his errand began to grow uneasy towards night, and the neighbours went out to seek him. At that time the old man had housed himself in his nest, and he heard the voices of the men, but could not make himself heard, the wind being so loud, and he was afraid to leave the spot lest he should not be able to find it again, so he remained there all night; and they returned to their homes, giving him up for lost; but the next morning the same persons discovered him huddled up in the sheltered nook. He was at first stupefied and unable to move; yet after he had eaten and drunk, and recollected himself a little, he walked down the mountain, and did not afterwards seem to have suffered."

741–62. A first draft of these lines appears in MS. X, on a blank page, between passages of *Prelude*, vii and viii. They appear to have been written later than the main draft of ii. 1–725 which occupies the last pages of the note-book.

BOOK III

The first rough draft was written in 1806, and a fair copy perhaps early in 1810 (*v*. p. 371 *supra*). But this version must have differed in one respect from the final text. I have already noted (*v*. note to ii. 185–210) that lines of Book II, which briefly recount the marriage of the Solitary and his loss of wife and children, were not in the original text; similarly all that part of Book III which deals at greater length (ll. 539–679) with the same theme appears to be a late addition, and no part of W.'s original conception of the Solitary's life and character. W. was led to imagine personal bereavement as a leading contributory cause of his despondency by his own passionate grief at the loss of his two children, Catharine in June 1812, and Thomas in the following December. There is much in the text, and especially in the first draft of these added passages (*v.* especially *app. crit.* l. 638 and ll. 645–9), to corroborate this—the loss of first the girl, by a sudden illness, and then the boy, the inclusion in the draft of the lines previously written about Catharine (*v. Characteristics of a Child Three Years Old*) but put into the past tense, the ages of the children (the Solitary had been married seven years when the blow fell upon him: Thomas W. was six when he died and Catharine four), the allusion to the boy's delight in playing in the churchyard (*v. app. crit.* 645–9 and *Maternal Grief* 67–72, and cf. D. W.'s letter to Mrs. Cookson [*M.Y.*, p. 529]: "his life latterly has been connected with the churchyard in the most affecting manner —there he played daily amongst his schoolfellows, and daily tripped through it to school"); whilst the death of the mother through the effects of grief is paralleled in the constant apprehensions of both Dorothy W. and the poet as to Mary's state of health. Cf. *M.Y.*, pp. 533, 529: "All this I could bear to see in another . . . but in her case it must be struggled against or it will destroy her. When Catharine died she was terribly shaken; for her body was not strong enough to bear up against the shock of the mind, and that corroding sorrow that followed. She was beginning to recover when this second shock came, and now she seems more feeble than ever. . . . I would not have us stay here (in Grasmere) if it were possible to do otherwise, for though she bears up with the greatest fortitude, I am sure that from the weakness of her body she would sink under depression of spirits, and her constitution would be slowly undermined." On Jan. 5, 1813, D. W. wrote to Mrs. Clarkson: "William has begun to look into his poem *The Recluse* within the two last days and I hope he will be the better for it. . . . It would have pitied the hardest heart to witness what he has gone through." On the blank page of a draft letter to Lord Lonsdale, dated Jan. 8, 1813, W. has written a first sketch of lines 584–98 of *Exc.* Book III. It was surely to this book that W. turned at the time, and made the addition to the Solitary's experience. As they stand in the draft (*v. app. crit.* 550–660) the lines bear evidence of their origin in deep personal emotion, but not emotion recollected in tranquillity so much as a hurried effusion with which to ease his passion, like the stanzas poured out soon after the loss of his brother John in 1805. Their later drastic revision cut out much that was hastily written, or too personal, as well as too discursive and out of proportion to the general scheme of the poem. This revision must have been among the latest in his preparation of the poem for press.

p. 75. **17–20.** A fragment of an early draft of this passage runs as follows:

> . . . Sequestered though it be with jealous care
> Is slenderly endowed, a little gem
> Which might by no incurious search be miss'd;
> But if discover'd and once seen 'tis then
> Seen to the heart and thoroughly possess'd:
> So saying round he look'd. . . .

69–73. For the image cf. Appendix B, IV. i, lines written in 1798.

93. timid lapse] "lapse" for the fall of streams is part of W.'s inheritance from Milton; *v. Paradise Lost,* viii. 263 "liquid Lapse of murmuring streams", and W.'s *The River Duddon,* xx. 4, and *Exc.* viii. 331 and note.

112. Lost in unsearchable eternity] Since this paragraph was composed, I have read with so much pleasure, in Burnet's "Theory of the Earth", a passage expressing corresponding sentiments, excited by objects of a similar nature, that I cannot forbear to transcribe it.

"Siquod verò Natura nobis dedit spectaculum, in hâc tellure, verè gratum, et philosopho dignum, id semel mihi contigisse arbitror; cùm ex celsissimâ rupe speculabundus ad oram maris Mediterranei, hinc æquor cæruleum, illinc tractus Alpinos prospexi; nihil quidem magìs dispar aut dissimile, nec in suo genere, magìs egregium et singulare. Hoc theatrum ego facilè prætulerim Romanis cunctis, Græcisve; atque id quod natura hîc spectandum exhibet, scenicis ludis omnibus, aut amphitheatri certaminibus. Nihil hîc elegans aut venustum, sed ingens et magnificum, et quod placet magnitudine suâ et quâdam specie immensitatis. Hinc intuebar maris æquabilem superficiem, usque et usque diffusam, quantum maximùm oculorum acies ferri potuit; illinc disruptissimam terræ faciem, et vastas moles variè elevatas aut depressas, erectas, propendentes, reclinatas, coacervatas, omni situ inæquali et turbido. Placuit, ex hâc parte, Naturæ unitas et simplicitas, et inexhausta quædam planities; ex alterâ, multiformis confusio magnorum corporum, et insanæ rerum strages: quas cùm intuebar, non urbis alicujus aut oppidi, sed confracti mundi rudera, ante oculos habere mihi visus sum.

"In singulis ferè montibus erat aliquid insolens et mirabile, sed præ cæteris mihi placebat illa, quà sedebam, rupes; erat maxima et altissima, et quà terram respiciebat, molliori ascensu altitudinem suam dissimulabat: quà verò mare, horrendúm præceps, et quasi ad perpendiculum facta, instar parietis. Prætereà facies illa marina adeò erat lævis ac uniformis (quod in rupibus aliquando observare licet) ac si scissa fuisset à summo ad imum, in illo plano; vel terræ motu aliquo, aut fulmine, divulsa.

"Ima pars rupis erat cava, recessusque habuit, et saxeos specus, euntes in vacuum montem; sive naturâ pridem factos, sive exesos mari, et undarum crebris ictibus: In hos enim cum impetu ruebant et fragore, æstuantis maris fluctus; quos iterum spumantes reddidit antrum, et quasi ab imo ventre evomuit.

"Dextrum latus montis erat præruptum, aspero saxo et nudâ caute; sinistrum non adeò neglexerat Natura, arboribus utpote ornatum: et prope pedem montis rivus limpidæ aquæ prorupit; qui cùm vicinam vallem irrigaverat, lento motu serpens, et per varios mæandros, quasi ad protrahendam vitam, in magno mari absorptus subito periit. Denique in summo vertice promontorii, commodè eminebat saxum, cui insidebam contemplabundus. Vale augusta sedes, Rege digna: Augusta rupes, semper mihi memoranda!"—Page 89. *Telluris Theoria sacra, etc. Editio secunda.*—W.

133. A Druid cromlech] W.'s interest in Druid remains goes back to his schooldays; *v. The Vale of Esthwaite*, 1. 32 and note (Vol. I, pp. 270 and 368).

240. With the American] K., in illustration of this passage, quotes from Falkner's *Description of Patagonia and the adjoining parts of South America* (1774): "They believe that their good deities made the world, and that they first created the Indians in their caves, gave them the lance, the bow and arrows, and the stone bowls, to fight and hunt with, and then turned them out to shift for themselves."

277–80. This is the plea of Spenser's Despayre, *F.Q.* i. ix. 40.

325–34. (*app. crit.*) purpureal sunshine] Cf. *Laodamia*, 106–8.

367–405. This passage occurs in a long desultory poem, never published by W., entitled *The Tuft of Primroses*, which he wrote in the spring of 1808. It will be found in Appendix C to this volume, p. 354 (*v.* ll. 265–96). W. seems first to have intended the passage for Book V; *v.* line 16 *app. crit.*

401–3. (*app. crit.*) Note the beautiful reading of C, unfortunately not adopted.

403. seasons' difference] From *As You Like It*, ii. i. 6.

532–49. The scenery here described, with its smooth lonely downs, green winding tracks, and sylvan combes is that of the Quantocks, which W. and D. W. delighted in at Alfoxden. *v.* D. W.'s letter Aug. 14, 1797; *E.L.*, p. 170.

549/50. (*app. crit.*) shading pencil] From *Paradise Lost*, iii. 509.

598–9. (*app. crit.*) The Spartan monarch] "Agesilaus among others had this special property, that he loved his children dearly; and a tale goeth of him, that he would play with them in his house when they were litle ones, and ride upon a litle cocke horse, or a reed, as on horsebacke: insomuch as a friend, taking him one day with the manner, playing among his children, he prayed him to say nothing, til he had litle children himself."—North's *Plutarch*.

617. progress] The reading of MS. and all the texts before 1850; with K., I take ";process" to be a printer's error.

638 and **645–9.** (*app. crit.*) some of the rejected lines of these passages appeared in the poem *Maternal Grief*, *q.v.* (Vol. II, p. 51, and *note*, p. 477).

669. heavy change] *Lycidas*, 36.

701. Went sounding on, a dim and perilous way] W. had already used this line in *The Borderers* (l. 1775). Lamb remembered it in his tender thought of the young chimney-sweeper when, as a child himself, he "pursued him in imagination as he went sounding on through so many dark stifling caverns": *Praise of Chimney Sweepers*.

720–2. A reference to the spectacle described in ii. 820–81. Line 720 is repeated from ii. 832.

726. the tree of Liberty] K. notes that the Jacobins planted the first tree of Liberty in Paris in 1790. During the American War of Independence trees had been planted as symbols of freedom.

744 (*v. app. crit.*) "burned" is clearly W.'s correction. He distinguished *burned* preterite from *burnt* past participle. Cf. *Written after the death of Charles Lamb*, 61, where the earlier reading should have been restored (Vol. IV, p. 274).

774. fiercer zealots] i.e. the Jacobins. Cf. *Prelude*, x, and notes.

776. As Brutus did to virtue] "Cf. Dion Cassius, xlvii. 49, where Brutus is represented as quoting this saying of Heracles (from an unknown source):

> ὦ τλῆμον ἀρετή, λόγος ἄρ' ἦσθ', ἐγὼ δέ σε
> ὡς ἔργον ἤσκουν. σὺ δ' ἄρ' ἐδούλευες τύχῃ.

Poor virtue! So thou wert after all a mere idea, while I practised thee as a reality; but thou wert Fortune's slave all the while."— (Nowell Smith.)

815. Which now, as infamous, I should abhor] *Paradise Lost*, iv. 392: "To do what else though damnd I should abhorre."

827. In Britain ruled a panic dread of change] Cf. *Prel.*, E. de S. (A text), x. 646–57 and note, p. 602.

928–40. Cf. lines 208–13 of a passage written for *The Prelude*, but rejected (*Prel.*, E. de S., p. 577).

931. Of Mississippi, *etc.*] "A man is supposed to improve by going out into the *World*, by visiting *London*. Artificial man does; he extends with his sphere; but, alas! that sphere is microscopic; it is formed of minutiæ, and he surrenders his genuine vision to the artist, in order to embrace it in his ken. His bodily senses grow acute, even to barren and inhuman pruriency; while his mental become proportionally obtuse. The reverse is the Man of Mind: he who is placed in the sphere of Nature and of God, might be a mock at Tattersall's and Brooks's, and a sneer at St. James's: he would certainly be swallowed alive by the first *Pizarro* that crossed him:—But when he walks along the river of Amazons; when he rests his eye on the un-rivalled Andes; when he measures the long and watered savannah; or contemplates, from a sudden promontory, the distant, vast Pacific

—and feels himself a freeman in this vast theatre, and commanding each ready produced fruit of this wilderness, and each progeny of this stream—his exaltation is not less than imperial. He is as gentle, too, as he is great: his emotions of tenderness keep pace with his elevation of sentiment; for he says, 'These were made by a good Being, who unsought by me, placed me here to enjoy them.' He becomes at once a child and a king. His mind is in himself; from hence he argues, and from hence he acts, and he argues unerringly, and acts magisterially; his mind in himself is also in his God; and therefore he loves, and therefore he soars."—From the notes upon "The Hurricane", a Poem, by William Gilbert.

The Reader, I am sure, will thank me for the above quotation, which, though from a strange book, is one of the finest passages of modern English prose.—W.

931. that northern stream] i.e. the St. Lawrence.

947. the melancholy Muccawiss] i.e. the Whip-poor-will (*v.* variant quoted in *app. crit.*), a popular name in U.S.A. and Canada for a species of goatsucker (*O.E.D.*). W. owed his knowledge of the bird to Carver's *Travels in N. America* (1772): "The Whipperwill, or as he is called by the Indiens, the Muckawiss, acquires its name by the noise it makes" (Carver). K. "entertains no doubt that W. first of all met with the name of this bird, whip-pow-will, in Waterton's *Wanderings in S. America*", but Waterton's book was not published till 1825. W. refers to the whip-poor-will again in *A Morning Exercise*, 16 (Vol. II, p. 124).

BOOK IV

There is no complete consecutive MS. of this Book. Lines 1–331 are not found in any extant note-book, but drafts of most of the remainder, in separate groups of lines, not in the order in which they were finally published, and generally without connecting links, survive in a note-book, MS. 58, already referred to (*v.* prefatory note, p. 371 *supra*). Since this note-book was subsequently used for early drafts of passages of Book II, it is clear that Book IV was largely conceived before Book II was completed, and the first draft of many important passages probably date from 1806. Other passages forming the basis of ll. 1150–1295 are found in a later MS., MS. 60 probably written in 1809–10, though some of these look like fair copies of earlier drafts. But perhaps the most interesting of all date back to a much earlier period, 1797–1800. And this is not surprising, since in this Book W. draws together the central ideas of his philosophy, rising to the "highth of his great argument". *v.* prefatory note on Chronology of *Exc.*, p. 369 *supra*, and notes to ll. 332–72, 402–12, 763–5, 958–68, 1158–87, 1204–97, and 1207 *infra*.

p. 110. **2–3.** commenced in pain, In pain commenced] an obvious imitation of the common Miltonic repetition; cf. *Paradise Lost*, ii. 7–8, 598–9, 1021–2; iii. 153–4, *etc.*

111. visionary powers] Cf. *Prelude*, ii. 311: "Thence did I drink the visionary power."

114–9. An allusion to the Wanderer's youthful experiences as described in i. 117–48. Cf. also W.'s own, as described in *Prelude*, iv. 320–30.

123. Those fervent raptures are for ever flown] Cf. *Tintern Abbey*, 83–5, and *Prelude*, xii. 280–2.

130–1. an easy task Earth to despise] See, upon this subject, Baxter's most interesting review of his own opinions and sentiments in the decline of life. It may be found (lately reprinted) in Dr. Wordsworth's "Ecclesiastical Biography".—W.

In C. W.'s *Ecclesiastical Biography*, published 1810 (Vol. V, p. 585), is found this extract from Part I of Richard Baxter's *Narrative of the most memorable Passages of his Life and Times*: "I find it comparatively very easy for me to be loose from the world, but hard to live by faith above. To despise earth is easy to me; but not so easy to be acquainted and conversant in heaven. I have nothing in this world which I would not easily let go; but to get satisfying apprehensions of the other world is the great and grievous difficulty."

136. 'tis a thing impossible to frame, *etc.*] Cf. *Convention of Cintra*: "The passions of men . . . do immeasureably transcend their objects. The true sorrow of humanity consists in this;—not that the mind of man fails but that the course and demands of action and of life so rarely correspond with the dignity and intensity of human desires."

205–6. Alas! . . . time] This subject is treated at length in the Ode *Intimations of Immortality.*—W.

245–50. Cf. *When to the attractions of the busy world*, 61–6, 98–110. Vol. II, pp. 121–2.

266. Could e'er, *etc.*] W.'s alteration of the word order in 1845 was clearly due to his wish to avoid a rhyme-ending. Cf. note to i. 51 *supra*.

293–4. Wisdom of her sons, *etc.*] Matthew xi. 19.

305–19. These lines were applied by D. W. in a letter to Mrs. Clarkson, to the attitude of the Government to Napoleon in April 1815: "If they had exercised half the understanding and zeal which the wicked have shewn in conducting their plots, things could never have been in this state. Refer to the 4th Book of the *Excursion*, and you will find an admirable comment upon the conduct of the Allies from beginning to end."—(*M.Y.*, p. 663.)

324–31. Knowing the heart of man is set to be, *etc.*] The passage quoted from Daniel is taken from a poem addressed to the Lady Margaret, Countess of Cumberland, and the two last lines, printed in italics, are by him translated from Seneca.[1] The whole poem is very

---

[1] Barron Field called W.'s attention to this in a letter dated Sept. 15,

beautiful. I will transcribe four stanzas from it, as they contain an admirable picture of the state of a wise Man's mind in a time of public commotion.

"Nor is he moved with all the thunder-cracks
Of tyrant's threats, or with the surly brow
Of Power, that proudly sits on others' crimes;
Charged with more crying sins than those he checks.
The storms of sad confusion that may grow
Up in the present for the coming times,
Appal not him; that hath no side at all,
But of himself, and knows the worst can fall.

"Although his heart (so near allied to earth)
Cannot but pity the perplexed state
Of troublous and distressed mortality,
That thus make way unto the ugly birth
Of their own sorrows, and do still beget
Affliction upon Imbecility:
Yet seeing thus the course of things must run,
He looks thereon not strange, but as fore-done.

"And whilst distraught ambition compasses,
And is encompassed, while as craft deceives,
And is deceived: whilst man doth ransack man,
And builds on blood, and rises by distress;
And th' Inheritance of desolation leaves
To great-expecting hopes: He looks thereon,
As from the shore of peace, with unwet eye,
And bears no venture in Impiety.

"Thus, Lady, fares that man that hath prepared
A rest for his desires; and sees all things
Beneath him; and hath learned this book of man,
Full of the notes of frailty; and compared
The best of glory with her sufferings:
By whom, I see, you labour all you can
To plant your heart! and set your thoughts as near
His glorious mansion as your powers can bear."—W.

332–72. A first draft of this passage written for *The Recluse*, Book I, is found in MS. R. *v.* note to *The Recluse*, i. 502–4 (*app. crit.*), Appendix A, p. 478, *infra*.

387. "feathery bunch"] Nowell Smith traced this quotation to *The Favorite Village* (1800) of James Hurdis (1763–1801, Professor of Poetry at Oxford 1793). His other poems were *The Village Curate* (1788) and *Tears of Affliction* (1792). He is described in the *D.N.B.* as "a friend of Cowper, of whom he was at best a pale imitation".

1837, where he gives the sentence from Seneca: "O quam contempta res est homo, nisi suprà humana se erexerit!"

394. A stray passage in MS. 58 was perhaps intended to follow here:

> Enlivening thoughts
> On this aerial voyager attend;
> By sympathy the wasted Spirits feel
> Soft renovations of admiring love,
> And boundless sovereignty participate
> Of innocent pleasures.

402–12. A draft of this passage occurs in MS. Y of *The Prelude* (*Prel.*, E. de S., p. 562). In the I. F. note to *To Joanna* W. writes: "There is in *The Excursion*, an allusion to the bleat of a lamb thus re-echoed and described, without any exaggeration as I heard it on the side of Stickle Tarn, from the precipice that stretches on to Langdale Pikes."

459. their clang] Cf. *Paradise Lost*, vii. 421–2.

489–504. In W.'s Commonplace Book of 1800 Thomas Wilkinson has written after the passage which suggested *The Solitary Reaper* (*v.* Vol. III, p. 445) the following: "But take courage, return to thy Father, rise with the lark, climb the summits of thy surrounding Hills, roll the Stone in thunder from the mountain, and follow with all thy might the Wild Goats of Ben Vorlach, so shalt thou return weary to thy Cottage, and thy rest will be as quiet as mine."

505–7 (*app. crit.*), 536–41 (*app. crit.*). It will be seen that Queen's College copy of *Exc.* 1814, a first issue, of which I know no other example, agrees with the MS. in omitting the poet's intervention 506–39, and in giving to the Wanderer the whole speech 418–549.

536–8. The language is clearly reminiscent of Shakespeare, cf. *King Lear*, iii. ii. 1–16 and *Troilus and Cressida*, i. iii. 92–8.

602. "the dreadful appetite of death"] No critic, so far as I am aware, has yet been able to trace this quotation.

637. Cf. *P.L.* xii. 629: "Gliding meteorous as Ev'ning Mist."

653–4. blaze of light Or cloud of darkness] Cf. *P.L.* iii. 377–80.

686–7. That Belus . . . to his splendid couch Descending] K. notes that W. is here indebted to Herodotus, i. 182, where he speaks of the temple of Belus: "On the topmost tower there is a spacious Temple, and inside the Temple stands a couch of unusual size, richly adorned, with a golden table by its side. There is no statue of any kind set up in the place. . . . The Chaldaeans, the priests of this god, declare—but I, for my part, do not credit it—that the God comes down nightly into this chamber and sleeps upon the couch" (tr. Rawlinson).

699. The planetary five] Mercury, Venus, Mars, Jupiter, and Saturn, called by W. "Mercuries" because they carry the "decrees and resolutions of the Gods" (704). In speaking of the heavenly bodies the Wanderer, who in youth had

> Gazed upon that mighty orb of song,
> The divine Milton,   (i. 249–50)

inevitably becomes Miltonic in phrasing. Cf. *P.L.* x. 656–8:

> To the blanc Moon
> Her office they prescrib'd; to th' other five
> Thir planetarie motions,

and *P.L.* vi. 6: "light and darkness in perpetual round".

719. sounding shores] Cf. *Lycidas*, 154, "shores and sounding seas"; and *Hymn*, 182, "the resounding shore".

745–50. Take, running river, take these locks of mine, *etc.*] Bishop Wordsworth directed K. to Pope's note on *Iliad*, xxiii. 175 as W.'s probable source here: "It was the custom of the ancients not only to offer their own hair, but likewise to consecrate that of their children to the river-gods of their country. This is what Pausanias shows in his Attica. Before you pass the Cephisus, says he, you find the tomb of Theodorus, who was the most famous actor of his time for tragedy; and, on the banks you see two statues, one of Mnesimachus, and the other of his son, who cut off his hair in honour of the rivers: for that this was in all ages the custom of the Greeks, may be inferred from Homer's poetry, where Peleus promises by a solemn vow to consecrate to the river Sperchius the hair of his son, if he returns safe from the Trojan war." Both Pope's Homer and Thomas Taylor's translation of Pausanias (1794) were in W.'s library.

753–62. Leigh Hunt, reviewing Keats's 1817 volume in the *Examiner*, noted how deeply Keats was influenced in his attitude to Greek mythology by W.'s treatment of it in this book of *The Excursion* (718–62; 847–87). The influence of these lines (753–62) upon the *Ode to the Nightingale*, vii is similarly evident. In B. R. Haydon's copy of *The Excursion*, now in the library of Cornell University, Haydon has written against lines 858–64: "Poor Keats used always to prefer this passage to all others."

763–5. We live by admiration, *etc.*] First found in a passage rejected from *Prelude*, viii.(*v. Prel.*, E. de S., p. 571):

> Two feelings have we also from the first
> [?   ] of grandeur and of tenderness;
> We live by admiration and by love
> And even as these are well and wisely fixed
> In dignity of being we ascend.

Neither in the MSS. nor in any of the texts published in W.'s lifetime is there any authority for the reading adopted by Dowden of "widely" for "wisely" in l. 764. Cf. also passage quoted from another MS. (*Prel.*, E. de S., p. 613):

> While he regulates
> His notions of the beautiful and grand
> In him will admiration be no weak
> Fantastic quality, that doth betray
> Its owner, but a firm support, a source
> Perennial of new faculties and powers.

800–5 The Shepherd lad, *etc.*] Cf. *Henry VI, Part 3*, II. v. 21–5:

> O God! methinks it were a happy life,
> To be no better than a homely swain;
> To sit upon a hill, as I do now,
> To carve out dials quaintly, point by point,
> Thereby to see the minutes how they run, *etc.*

847–87. Barron Field compared these lines with Boileau:

> Là, pour nous enchanter, tout est mis en usage;
> Tout prend un corps, une âme, un esprit, un visage.
> Chaque vertu devient une divinité:
> Minerve est la prudence, et Venus la beauté;
> Ce n'est plus la vapeur qui produit le tonnerre,
> C'est Jupiter armé pour effrayer la terre:
> Un orage terrible aux yeux des matelots,
> C'est Neptune en courroux qui gourmande les flots:
> Echo n'est plus un son qui dans l'air retentisse,
> C'est une nymphe en pleurs, qui se plaint de Narcisse.

910–11. Saint Fillan . . . Saint Anne . . . Saint Giles] Saints who were all specially revered in Scotland. St. Anne was the mother of the Virgin Mary; St. Fillan an Irish saint who came as a missionary to Scotland in the eighth century; Bruce is said by Boece to have attributed his success at Bannockburn to "the aid of God and St. Fillan . . ."; St. Giles was a Greek who settled in France and founded a Benedictine society there. He was the patron of cripples because he refused himself to undergo a cure for lameness, preferring to mortify the flesh. The parish church of Edinburgh was dedicated to him, and his arm-bone was among the church relics.

956. laughter at their work in heaven] Cf. *Paradise Lost*, xii. 59, "great laughter was in Heaven", at the "presumption" of the builders of the Tower of Babel and their discomfiture.

958–68. if 'twas ever meant, *etc.*] Originally part of the Wanderer's discourse at the close of *The Ruined Cottage*; *v.* Addendum to MS. B, ll. 58–68, p. 402 *supra*.

975. fearfully devised] Psalm cxxxix. 14, "I am fearfully and wonderfully made."

1132–40. I have seen A curious child] When malicious gossip attributed to W. the remark that Southey's poetry was "not worth five shillings a ream", Landor retorted by attacking W. for "clapping into his pouch" his simile of the sea-shell (*v. A Satire upon Satirists*, 284 *et seq.*). In the I. F. note to *Evening Voluntaries*, x. Wordsworth commented: "I was not a little surprised when I heard Mr. Landor had denounced me as a plagiarist from himself for having described a boy applying a sea-shell to his ear, and listening to it for intimations of what was going on in its native element. This I had done myself scores of times, and it was a belief among us that we could know from the sound whether the tide was ebbing or flowing." The passage in Landor is *Gebir*, i. 120–7:

> But I have sinuous shells, of pearly hue
> Within, and they that lustre have imbibed
> In the sun's palace porch; where, when unyoked
> His chariot wheel stands midway in the wave.
> Shake one, and it awakens; then apply
> Its polished lips to your attentive ear,
> And it remembers its august abodes,
> And murmurs as the ocean murmurs there.

Landor published a destructive criticism of W. in *An Imaginary Conversation between Southey and Porson* in Blackwood's *Edinburgh Magazine*, Dec. 1842. Quillinan replied, without W.'s knowledge, in a *Dialogue between Walter Savage Landor and the Editor of Blackwood's Magazine*, published in the same magazine, April 1843, where he defended W. from "the imputed plagiarism" in the matter of the shell. Landor made some amends in his *Imaginary Conversation between Archdeacon Hare and Walter Landor*, published 1853: "Truly he [Wordsworth] owes me little. My shell may be the prettiest on his mantelpiece; but a trifle it is at best."

1158–87. Two holograph passages in MS. 60 which appear to be copied from earlier drafts form the basis of these lines:

> (1) Come ye that are disturb'd, this steady voice
> Of streams, the stillness and the stiller sound
> Shall awe you into peace, this gleaming lake
> These glistening Cottages and hoary fields
> And in the midst above and underneath
> Shadowy recesses, bosoms, gloomy Holds
> Viewless, impenetrable, infinite
> And tranquil as the abyss of deepest sleep
> Or that dark world the untroubled home of death.
> Lo in the west a solemn sight, behold
> Upon yon craggy barrier's lofty ridge
> A Pageantry of darksome trees that stand
> Single in their aerial solitude,
> Stand motionless in solitary calm
> Yet greeted gently by the moving clouds
> That pass and pass, and ever are to come
> Varying their colours slowly in the light
> Of an invisible moon. Cloud follows cloud
> As thought [? succeeds] to thought, but now ensues
> A pause—the long procession seems to end,
> The breeze that was in heaven hath died away

> And all things are immoveably composed
> Save here and there an uncomplying Star
> That twinkles in its station self-disturbed.

(2) The second passage corresponds with ll. 1158–70 and 1177–87 with variants as in *app. crit.* The passage in *app. crit* at 1185 is a later working up of the closing lines of (1).

1173–4. rills . . . Inaudible by daylight] Cf. *An Evening Walk* (A) 433–4, and note (Vol. I, p. 332).

1175–87. Cf. D. W.'s Journal for July 27, 1800: "After tea we rowed down to Loughrigg Fell . . . . The lake was now most still, and reflected the beautiful yellow and blue and purple and grey colours of the sky. We heard a strange sound in the Bainriggs wood, as we were floating on the water; it *seemed* in the wood, but it must have been above it, for presently we saw a raven very high above us. It called out, and the dome of the sky seemed to echo the sound. It called again and again as it flew onwards, and the mountains gave back the sound, seeming as if from their center; a musical bell-like answering to the bird's hoarse voice. We heard both the call of the bird, and the echo, after we could see him no longer." *v.* also I. F. notes to *Evening Voluntaries*, vii (Vol. IV, p. 396) and W. W.'s letter to Mrs. Clarkson, Dec. 1814 (*M.Y.*, p. 619).

1204–97. An early draft (*v.* I. F. Note) of this passage was written in 1798 as part of the discourse of the Pedlar at the end of *The Ruined Cottage* (*v.* Addendum to MS. B, p. 400 *supra*). From this passage S. T. C. quotes the first 18 lines in a letter to his brother George, dated March 1798, introducing W.'s lines to clinch his own views, which are stated thus: "I devote myself to such works as encroach not on the anti-social passions—in poetry, to elevate the imagination and set the affections in right tune by the beauty of the inanimate impregnated as with a living soul by the presence of life. . . . I love fields and woods and mountains with almost a visionary fondness. And because I have found benevolence and quietness growing within me as that fondness has increased, therefore I should wish to be the means of implanting it in others and to destroy bad passions not by combating them but by keeping them in inaction."

1207. inarticulate language] In the *Alfoxden* MS., a note-book used by W. between Jan. 20 and Mar. 5, 1798, there are what appear to be first jottings for the passage in MS. B referred to in the preceding note (*v.* note to II. ii, Appendix B, *infra*, p. 479).

1264. (*first draft*, lines 57–76, *v.* p. 402) This majestic imagery . . . Affections, organs, passions] These lines were obviously indebted to two of Hamlet's speeches. Cf. II. ii. 318–27: "This most excellent canopy the air, look you, this brave and overhanging firmament, this majestical roof fretted with golden fire, why, it appears no other thing to me but a foul and pestilent congregation of vapours. What a piece of work is a man! how noble in reason! how infinite in faculty! in form, in moving, how express and admirable!—in action how like an angel! in apprehension how like a god!" and IV. iv. 33–9.

1268–9. strict necessity] For the thought cf. ix. 87 and note. The phrase is from Milton, *Paradise Lost*, v. 528.

1270–4 (*v. app. crit.*). I have restored to the text line 1272: "The humblest functions of corporeal sense ;" omitted, I believe by mistake, in 1845. The line stands clearly written in identical revised versions of this passage intended for *ed.* 1845, one in W.'s own hand in C, the other in M. W.'s hand in Q.

BOOK V

A fair copy of this book survives, written by M. W. in MS. 61. There are also rough drafts of most of it, which show that it underwent much re-handling. The first two hundred lines were probably written before the end of 1806 (*v.* prefatory note, p. 371 *supra*), but the main composition must belong to the second period of writing beginning in the winter of 1809–10 (*v.* p. 371–2 *supra*).

p. 153. **16.** (*app. crit.*) What impulse drove the Hermit . . .] *v.* note to iii. 367–405.

28/9. (*app. crit.*) sounding shores] *v.* note to iv. 719.

75–6. as a billow . . . sea] Barron Field criticized this simile as retirement "to anything but solitude and a covert, back to the ocean of life!" W. replied: "I cannot accede to your objection to the billow. The point simply is, he was cast out of his element and falls back into it, as naturally and necessarily as a billow into the sea. There is imagination in fastening solely upon that characteristic point of resemblance—stopping there, thinking of nothing else!" (*L.Y.*, p. 313.)

77–91. As the I. F. note (*supra*, p. 376) explains, the scene is now transferred, "as by the waving of a magic wand", from Little Langdale to Grasmere. But the "tufted trees" (81) which screened the church-tower had disappeared in 1807; *v.* D. W.'s letter to Mrs. Clarkson, July 19 (*M.Y.*, p. 138): "All the trees in Bainriggs are cut down, and even worse, the giant sycamore near the parsonage house, and all the finest fir-trees that overtopped the steeple tower."

80–3. The phraseology is from Milton *v. L'Allegro*, 77–8:

> Towers and Battlements it sees
> Boosom'd high in tufted trees.

96. A popular equality reigns here] Cf. *Prelude*, ix. 215–27.

141–3. A grateful coolness fell, *etc.*] *v.* Lamb's letter to W. of Aug. 9, 1814: "One feeling I was particularly struck with as what I recognised so very lately at Harrow Church on entering in it after a hot and secular day's pleasure,—the instantaneous coolness and calming, almost transforming, properties of a country church just entered—a certain fragrance which it has—either from its holiness, or being kept shut all the week, or the air that is let in being pure country—exactly what you have reduced into words but I am feeling I cannot."

264–73. In a note-book MS. 61 containing a rough draft of the bulk of Book V these lines are preceded by ll. 1–77 of the passage quoted below, which has been pieced together from pages of the same note-book. It is clear from the manner in which it is related to the final text that the passage was first written as a long speech of the Solitary, voicing his conception of a typical peasant's life, but it was never revised and was ultimately rejected as disproportionate. Some of the reflections are incorporated in the final text: cf. ll. 309–35 with v. 391–410, and ll. 344–57 with v. 431–9. The delightful picture of the peasant boy, of which ll. 150–65 *infra* are supplied from a stray sheet of another MS., seems to have been the germ of the whole. Lines 221–308 (To the Yoke . . . dreams) are also found in another note-book MS. 62ᴬ of which most of the contents appear in the 1815 volumes: this suggests that W. may have intended at that time to include the lines in these volumes as a fragment on a peasant's courtship and married life. The references in the right-hand margin are to *Excursion*, Book V.

"While here I stand

	And cast my eyes around these still abodes,	
	One I behold which hath to-day been filled	
	By a poor friendless Man—an aged Orphan	(885–6)
5	So call him, for humanity to him	
	No parent was,—the rest to me are mute,	
	I know no more what tenant each contains	
	Than doth the grass (sod) that roofs it.—Yet, methinks,	
	If mere imagination might presume	
10	To touch a theme that wants the steadier light	
	Of your experience—might I step before,	
	And with no better guide than chance regards	
	Or notice forced upon incurious ears,	(418)
	Attempt an honest sample to set forth	
15	Of those by doom of nature hither brought	
	From their sequestered Cottages—a race	
	Thrice favoured, uncorrupted men, who share	
	The elevation of a Christian land,	
	A land of peace and liberty and truth,	
20	Thus would I paint him—thus from morn to eve	
	From life's dim opening to its last decay	
	Would I retrace his history." At these words	
	A sudden influx of enlivening thought	
	Brightened the sick man's faded countenance.	

15–21 Of Nature's rustic offspring, here interred,
Thus from life's opening, *etc.* (*other draft*)

25 My expectation shaped for him a path
    On the plain ground inscribed, but his discourse
    Mounted aloft, and under many a cloud,
    And crossing many a streak of ether blue,
    Sailed high or low upon the inconstant wind
30 Part wheeling, blown about in part—with bold
    And not ungraceful struggles—"Let the house
    (Thus buoyantly did that discourse ascend)
    Where first he breathes the vital air be glad!
    For a Manchild is born. See weakness now
35 Impersonated here in human form,
    Assert her rights, and helplessness ensure
    From eager tendance all that it requires.
    Beneath the lowly (naked) rafters of the roof
    That shelters him, supine the (the breathing) Infant lies,
40 Senseless and powerless, yet a King of State,
    Of high observance and of prime concern,
    And every eye that enters turns to him
    Not less than if he were the destined Lord
    Of large domains, exultingly announced
45 With church-tower music rung in clamorous peal.
    Stooping as needs she must, let Fancy tell,
    But why? Though versed in sciences occult,
    Prognostics, tokens, planetary sway
    And fireside omens, far as skill can go,
50 What tongue, for this occasion competent,
    May trace the lore through all its curious maze,
    Or note the spells, the forms that must be kept
    Strictly, or not less scrupulously shunned,
    As each sage Gossip dictates, to protect,
55 For the unconscious object of their care
    And regent of their busy services,
    Body and mind from evil, and ensure
    A length of days by fortune's sunshine cheered.
    Nor fail their garrulous tongues to interpose
60 Brief words of ready prayer for honest ways,
    And God's good grace to aid and crown the whole.
    Meanwhile how pure or exquisite the bliss
    That from the touch or sensible approach
    Of her new Acquisition shall pervade
65 The languid Mother's heart, what yearning love
    What tender awe or pious gratitude
    To the still spirit may convey delight
    And lift it in this Sabbath of her rest   (*Prelude*, v. 261)
    Above the level of life's daily course,

43–5 The star unseen before that now hath risen. (*other draft*)

70   This is a mystery—a saintly lamp
       Burns here within its own peculiar shrine,
       Forbid to blend its light with common day.
       Due honour will the ensuing months obtain
       If we record that like his Brother Babes
75   Cradled in palaces, this Cottage nursling
       Learn'd in that tedious time to yawn, smile, sneeze,
       Though yet irrational of soul to grasp
       With tiny finger—to let fall a tear;   (265)
       And, as the heavy cloud of sleep dissolves,
80   To stretch his limbs, bemocking, as might seem
       The outward functions of intelligent Man;
       A grave proficient in amusive feats
       Of puppetry, that from the lap declare
       His expectations, and announce his claims
85   To that inheritance which millions rue
       That they were ever born to!   (273)

    ·   ·   ·   ·   ·   ·

87   So let our Rustic child, a freight in arms,
       Go forth besprinkled with their flattering [? dews],
       Nor be the jocund Peasants harshly judged
90   If that abode to which they turn, whose hearth
       Glows like a furnace with the festal flame
       Ere the day's light be wasted, shall resound
       With boisterous merriment and jests impure,
       Which even the Mother, whom her natural stress
95   Did lately fling upon a stiller shore,
       Is now not unprepared to greet with smiles
       Of arch complacence, or at least receive
       Without an altered cheek. With these to teach,
       Restrain him, fashion, foster, and inure,
100   The Peasant Boy from leading strings is freed
       And from the Go-cart's moving Prison escapes,
       Running and struggling wheresoe'r his feet
       Can totter with him,—on the perilous edge
       Of tempting fire, or deep and sullen pool,
105   Or rain-swoln flood that near the Cottage roars
       And harms him not; for stray where'er he will,
       Approving by the event the Mother's creed
       Confidingly received from age to age,
       Heaven's tender care protects him through all risks.
110   Risen with the Sun's first rising in the East,
       And to his aery loft and couch of straw
       Dismiss'd not seldom ere the sun retires,
       A day of many-weathered hours he sees

72 And may not mingle with the common day (*other draft*)

	Neglected, humoured, scolded, and caressed.
115	But health of body, strength, and prosperous growth,
	Thanks to fresh air and hardy liberty,
	He for himself provides, and though so late
	Of tendance due deprived, and those nice arts
	Which ease and opulence are free to give
120	Or purchase, he a firmer aspect shows
	Than his coevals of more high degree.
	Yet mark the recompense, no longer now
	By teazing incapacities detained
	And burthensome through helplessness, how soon,
125	Matched with these ornaments of wealthier flower,
	Hath he outstripped them all. Robust of limb,
	Bright-eyed and rosy cheeked, to my mind's eye
	I represent him such as once I marked
	In springtime sporting on the threshold step
130	And where the plot of weedless pavement fronts
	The door not often closed; and as I passed,
	Calling to mind the wan uncoloured face
	Which, in the mother's arms, mine eyes had seen
	With some slight touch of pitiful regard,
135	Encountered while dark winter chilled the plains,
	The florid Youngling which I now beheld
	With the warm light of April on his cheek
	Or basking on his hair, exposed like leaves
	Or clustering blossoms, to my thought appeared
140	Less like a Creature, heretofore oppressed,
	Whose state had undergone a balmy change,
	Than one created on that sunny day.
	Such he, so fair, and to the passing eye
	As rich in promise; what if yon low pile
145	Yon ancient edifice with fern-clad roof
	Where now upon his form, through half the day
	In durance seated, he a primer cons

117–21 ... and though the course
    Of pressing tasks which scanty means enjoin
    Full soon deprived him of that tendance strict
    Which on his first consignment to the world
    Nature exacted for him, with some help
    By vain officious novelty supplied,
    And hence his lot has been to lag behind,
    In thriving infant loveliness surpassed
    By his coevals of more high degree, (*other draft*)

145–8 Within whose walls, methinks, I see him sit,
    Conducting, to and fro, deliberate eyes
    Of close regard along the primer's page,
    Or thumbing earnestly a holier book (*other draft*)

With poring eyes, or thumbs a holier book,
Of his advancement make no proud report,
150 Yet in the glad hours when restraint hath ceased
The fields accept him as their genuine growth;
Sauntering he plays upon his sycamore pipe
Or with his Mates at the earliest season's call
Hies to some orchard-ground or household croft
155 Where blow the splendid daffodils of March
And from that bed his rusty hat entwines
With golden wreath—the plunderers ye may track
Each to his home. Their garland is dispersed
Almost as soon as woven—the gay spoil
160 So late in bunches proudly grasped is now
Slighted as burthensome, or only prized
As matter for destruction—leaves and stalks
Flung here and there bestrew the path and road,
To the brisk Traveller or to him who walks
165 Musing with downcast eyes a notice bright
But pensive, that the flowering Spring is come.
Nor will the musing Traveller reprove
The wanton mischief or deplore the waste
Of inoffensive beauty from such source
170 Proceeding; and hereafter, if the Thrush
Or mother Linnet in her hopeful nest
Be subject to worse injury, for the Bird
He grieves, regrets his loss, but spares meanwhile
That overnice humanity which would brand
175 Their enterprize and pleasure-seeking ways
Who ignorant of the law that calls forth [sin]
In pure activity of rustic childhood
Do range about rejoicing, while that joy
Is yet allowed them in that law's despite.
180 Hark what an uproar in the hills, and see—
Nay, do not smile—('Tis Fancy that must see
By virtue of her own creative eye
And Fancy's ear must listen to the sound)
Behold a fragment down the rugged breast
185 Of the steep mountain bounding, and aloft
Mark the bold hero of my tale, whose pains,
At length unsettling in its antient seat
The mass, hath sent it headlong from the brink
Of the steep mountain's dizzy eminence
190 Thundering and smoking, ploughing the green turf
Shattering and shatter'd. With delight sublime
By apprehension [? driv'n] the Boy surveys

189 Down the steep mountain's long declivity *(other draft)*

The ungovernable motion; with the speed
Of Thought he calculates, divines its course,
195 Assigns its period while the timid sheep
All unendangered, far and near disperse
With trepidations innocent and wild,
Not pacified though in the pool below
Already the huge block hath found repose,
200 Echo is hushed, and silence hath returned.
　　Thus undepraved by labour in excess
Imposed, or premature, and unappalled
By ghastly Poverty, the Peasant lad
Thrives, and exhibits in his homely wits
205 A flattering miniature of native man
Unruly, daring, active, indolent,
But sometimes not without a short-lived zeal
To useful services, but happiest then
When danger tempts him,—nay with serpent eye
210 Enthralls and fascinates; or when mischief pleads,
Restless ambition's advocate and guide.
His days are happy—think not so, no days
Of human life with happiness are blest,
But his are fraught with pleasures manifold,
215 Nor destitute of Nature's grace, a wild
And generous dignity. But livelier joy
Awaits his riper Station; the fresh breath
Of Independence eagerly assumed,
The first pure relish of life's personal cares,
220 And the free earnings of his sinewy arms,
To his own use for purposes applied
By his own will, these glittering novelties
With store of self-applause for shrewdness, pains,
Or steadiness applied before their time,
225 And mightier far than these, love rushing in
With perturbation. To the yoke he bends
Receives the chain from Nature's conquering hand
Not loth, nor sad, but inwardly rejoiced,
Like the thrilled Blackbird whistling in the grove,
230 Or lordly Eagle in the rocky wild,
By force of all-commanding Love sublime.
The stripling's day shews little, by that light
You cannot read him; into the hours of rest
His spirit's course of action overflows.
235 No ghost familiar with the night like him,
To this new service bound, his fervent zeal
The liveliest star outwatches, in mid heaven
Fixed, or slow travelling on the horizon's bound.

Happy if she for whom he wakes abide
240   Within the limits of his native vale,
The native vale of both, a common Home;
And not less happy if, need be, the Youth
Posts over hill and dale and mountain top,
Through wood and brook, across by shortest line
245   Hasting, and chiding oft the watry clouds
Which the sky breeds to blind his eager steps.
What sundry shapes of hazard, paths obscure
And length of indefatigable march,
Ere at the door the soft low tap be given,
250   Or from beneath the cottage eaves ascends
The stifled Cough, warning his chosen friend
That now, when sleep has hushed the world, he comes
For a brief taste of stealthy intercourse.
Ten thousand sparks do from this covert fire
255   Spring up at each incitement of the breeze
Vivid though noiseless,—blessed hours if doubt
Be not, and jealousy, but hours they are.
    But Time has wings, and Pleasure is Time's Slave,
He must depart, ere blush of morning's light,
260   With the far-wandering fox slink to his home
For short repose, or haply to commence
A long day's labour with the sun now risen.
    Each current stemmed of adverse circumstance,
The rock of absence either shunned or touched
265   Without a fatal shock, the uncertain shoals
Of jealousy triumphantly escaped,
And fancy's crosswinds, and her peevish squalls
All stoutly weathered, the trim vessel holds
Her port in open view. It dawns, the day,
270   The important day of lasting recompense,
Not unproceeded by a throng of cares,
Of frugal preparation intermixed
With inoffensive vanity and show.
    And see the orb, that animates the earth
275   And chears the frame and fills the spirit of man
With genial thoughts, upon that morning shine
In splendour, so that hill and dale reflect
The satisfaction of the festive troop
As they advance, or from the Church return;
280   Blithe company of Elders, Maids, and Youths,
And the blest pair for life's remaining course
Each given to each, indissolubly bound.
    This natural wedlock yields in season due
Fair fruit, most precious to the mother's heart

285   From the first hour, and to the Father's heart
        Doubly endeared, soon as the tender Babe
        By creeping years is strengthened to endure
        Rough fondness, and the gaiety of love
        In boisterous assault. Then ere he quits
290   His home, or as he enters from the fields,
        Lightly the vigorous Peasant at arm's length
        Tosses his lusty Boy aloft in air
        And laughs to see the laughing child at once
        Pleased and half frighted (daunted) by the dizzy height
295   Gain'd in a moment, in a moment lost.
            A seasonable gladness, a relief
        Occasional for six laborious days
        Is here prepared, and duly this resource
        Sweetens the day of leisure and repose
300   With innocent pastime. In a sheltered vale,
        Far from the gross contagion of the world,
        Thus are the earlier years of wedded life
        Adorned as Spring with flowers, and more to uphold
        The Pair, and favor them as they advance,
305   In later time, along their humble path,
        The Pitfalls of mistake they shall avoid
        By Prudence guarded, whose sure hand shall heal
        The hurts of unavoidable mischance,
        Immoderate Labour shall not sap their strength
310   Nor sickness overturn their plans, or thwart;
        Discord shall find no place by their fire-side,
        Nor shall the dread of Poverty oppress
        Their waking thoughts, nor guilt disturb their dreams.
            Ah, what avails it ? in the life of Man,
315   If to the Poetry of common speech   (391-)
        Faith may be given, we see as in a glass,
        A true reflection of the arching year
        With all its seasons. Grant that Spring is there
        Hopeful and promising with buds and flowers,
320   Yet where is glowing Summer's long rich day,
        That ought to follow, faithfully expressed ?
        And mellow Autumn charged with bounteous fruits
        Where is she imaged, in what favored soil
        Her lavish pomp and ripe magnificence ?
325   Yet while the better part is missed, the worse
        In Man's autumnal season is set forth
        With a resemblance not to be denied,   (405)

305/6 Oh! could a wish of mine avail, this Pair
        Should prove as blest as some whose [?]
        The pitfalls, *etc. but with* should *for* shall *throughout* (*other draft*)

And that contents him,—bowers that hear no more
The voice of gladness, less and less supply
330 Of outward sunshine and internal warmth,
And, with this change, they pass, and falling leaves,
Forerunning total Winter, blank and cold,
Form his torn wreath. Admit that restless hours
Revel and strife, and trembling eagerness,
335 And fitful gleams, and thriftless promises,
And hope, blithe hope, triumphant in the main,
Spring's natural Virtue and her dear delight,—
That these are all familiar to our youth,
Yet where is glowing Autumn's long rich day,   (398)
340 That ought to follow, faithfully expressed ?
     Spare then regret, misplace not your contempt,
If with no happier fate than others, born
Of Fortune's pure advantages, and reared
With Learning's boasted aid, this shepherd swain,
345 Albeit in Christian principles not unschooled,
And with an ear not ignorant of the threat
Denounc'd, the promise and the high command,
Do in his noiseless solitude partake
Man's general lot ; and lead a life whose course
350 Is fashioned like an ill-constructed Tale,   (432)
That in the outset wastes its gay desires,
Its fair adventures and its lively hopes
And pleasant interests. Thus far, step by step,
That life I have retraced ; and what remains,
355 What proof doth Manhood bring that now a scheme
Is rounded and complete, a promise kept,
A height attained, a noble growth matured ?
Day follows day, and year succeeds to year,
Old things repeating with diminished grace,
360 And all the high-prized novelties, at best
Imperfect substitutes, whose use and power
Evince the want or weakness whence they spring.   (439)
See for the gushing fount's continuous stream
The toiling engine's interrupted gifts,
365 Or joyless cistern's hoard, that fears the sun.
The sail that caught the help of every wind,
The sail abandoned for the creeping oar.
And on the basis of some goodly pile
Insensibly decayed, or with harsh hand
370 Demolished and subverted utterly,
Unsightly structure reared with needless pains.
     Why look with nearer view ? enough that he
Who, when a child, among the flowery fields

Convers'd, not lacking either eye or soul,
375   With Nature's beauty, on the dizzy height
Who stood in fearlessness a shepherd lad
And nursed the daring appetite of power,
Who skimmed the hills and dales as if on wings
A youthful Lover, and who, lastly, gained,
380   Following as no unworthy passion led,
A Husband's calm assurances, and reaped
The tender first-fruits of a Father's love,
That he, for all that to himself pertains
Of brief enjoyment, dignity, or power
385   Already ere the middle stage of life
Be passed, nay, fairly reached, doth walk the earth
In degradation. Man has breathed too long.
Ask of thyself, thou proud One of the world,
If this be not thy doom in life, than him
390   [?   ] and in worse degree. Toil, daily toil
Secures his vigorous health and tranquil sleep,
But time and custom overpower his soul,
Upon the tablet the bright colours fade,
The Image steals insensibly away,
395   And leaves a meagre outline in its place,
A ghost, a phantom.

With lines 231–48 *supra* cf. note to Robert Anderson's *Cumberland Ballads* (first published 1805) on the peasants' courtship customs: "A Cumbrian peasant pays his addresses to his sweetheart during the silence and solemnity of midnight. Anticipating her kindness, he will travel ten or twelve miles, over hills, bogs, moors, and mosses, undiscouraged by the length of the road, the darkness of the night, or the intemperature of the weather. On reaching her habitation, he gives a gentle tap at the window of her chamber, at which signal she immediately rises, dresses herself, and proceeds with all possible silence to the door, which she gently opens, lest a creaking hinge, or a barking dog, should awaken the family. On his entrance into the kitchen, the luxuries of a Cumbrian cottage—cream and sugared curds—are placed before him. . . . Next the courtship commences, previously to which the fire is darkened or extinguished, lest its light should guide to the window some idle or licentious eye. In this dark and uncomfortable situation (at least uncomfortable to all but the lovers), they remain till the advance of day, depositing in each other's bosoms the secrets of love."

292–308. It is to be noted that in the earlier draft these lines are given to the Solitary, and that 309–20 were added when they were transferred to the poet himself.

318. If to be weak is to be wretched—miserable] From *Paradise Lost*, i. 157.

329. graze the herb] The phrase is from Milton "Grasing the tender herb", *P.L.*, iv. 253.

417. chance-regards] Cf. chance-desires, *Ode to Duty*, 38; chance-temptation, *Duddon Sonnet*, xxx. 6; chance-sunbeam, *Liberty*, 102.

455–61. To an oak, *etc.*] *v.* I. F. note, p. 375 *supra*.

489. speculative height] Cf. Cowper, *The Task*, i. 289:

> Now roves the eye,
> And posted on this speculative height
> Exults in its command.

Both passages are reminiscent of Milton's "top of Speculation", *P.L.*, xii. 588–9, from which the Archangel offers Adam the monitory vision.

529. forbidding] I follow Nowell Smith in restoring the original reading, in place of "forbidden" which was printed in 1820, 1845, and 1850. "Forbidding" is clearly required by the context.

647. And have the dead around us]

> "*Leo.* You, Sir, could help me to the history
> Of half these graves ?
> *Priest.*   For eight-score winters past,
> With what I've witnessed, and with what I've heard,
> Perhaps I might ; . . . . .
> By turning o'er these hillocks one by one,
> We two could travel, Sir, through a strange round ;
> Yet all in the broad highway of the world."
>   See *The Brothers*.—W.

671. High on the breast, *etc.*] i.e. Hackett, above Little Langdale, and therefore not visible from Grasmere. That Hackett is referred to is confirmed by the I. F. note to *Misc. Sonnets*, I. viii (*v.* Vol. III, p. 420). Christopher W. has the following among his unpublished notes of W. W.'s conversation: "Betty Yewdale died this morning, Sunday, Jan. 12, 1834. She lived originally in Langdale, and was the woman who in my poem lights her husband Jonathan from the quarry. She talked the dialect of these parts in its purest and most ancient form. Much of her language is older than the Conquest."

"And now for a few words upon the Church, its Monuments, and the Deceased who are spoken of as lying in the surrounding Church-yard. But first for the one picture, given by the Pastor and the Wanderer, of the Living. In this nothing is introduced but what was taken from nature and real life. The cottage is called Hackett, and stands, as described, on the southern extremity of the ridge which separates the two Langdales ; the Pair who inhabited it were called Jonathan and Betty Yewdale. Once when our children were ill, of whooping-cough I think, we took them for change of air to this cottage, and were in the habit of going there to drink tea on fine summer afternoons, so that we became intimately acquainted with the characters, habits, and lives of these good, and, let me say, in the main, wise people. The matron had, in her early youth, been a servant in a house at Hawkshead, where several boys boarded, while I was a schoolboy there. I did not remember her as having served in that capacity; but we had many little anecdotes to tell to each other of remarkable boys, incidents and adventures which had made a noise in their day in that small town. These two persons afterwards settled at Rydal, where they both died.

"*Church and Churchyard.* The church, as already noticed, is that of Grasmere. The interior of it has been improved lately—made warmer by under-drawing the roof and raising the floor, but the rude and antique majesty of its former appearance has been impaired by painting the rafters; and the oak benches, with a simple rail at the back dividing them from each other, have given way to seats that have more the appearance of pews. It is remarkable that, excepting only the pew belonging to Rydal Hall, that to Rydal Mount, the one to the Parsonage, and I believe another, the men and women still continue, as used to be the custom in Wales, to sit separate from each other. Is this practice as old as the Reformation? and when and how did it originate? In the Jewish synagogues and in Lady Huntingdon's Chapels the sexes are divided in the same way. In the adjoining churchyard greater changes have taken place; it is now not a little crowded with tombstones; and near the school-house which stands in the Churchyard is an ugly structure, built to receive the hearse, which is recently come into use. It would not be worth while to allude to this building or the hearse-vehicle it contains, but that the latter has been the means of introducing a change much to be lamented in the mode of conducting funerals among the mountains. Now, the coffin is lodged in the hearse at the door of the house of the Deceased, and the corpse is so conveyed to the Churchyard gate: all the solemnity which formerly attended its progress, as described in the Poem, is put an end to. So much do I regret this, that I beg to be excused for giving utterance here to a wish that, should it befall me to die at Rydal Mount, my own body may be carried to Grasmere Church after the manner in which, till lately, that of every one was borne to that place of sepulture, namely, on the shoulders of neighbours, no house being passed without some words of a funeral Psalm being sung at the time by the attendants. When I put into the mouth of the Wanderer, 'Many precious rites and customs of our rural ancestry are gone, or stealing from us; this, I hope, will last for ever' [ii. 550–3], and what follows, little did I foresee that the observance and mode of proceeding, which had often affected me so much, would so soon be superseded. Having said much of the injury done to this Churchyard, let me add that one is at liberty to look forward to a time when, by the growth of the Yew Trees, thriving there, a solemnity will be spread over the place that will in some degree make amends for the old simple character which has already been so much encroached upon, and will be still more every year. I will here set down, by way of memorial, that my Friend, Sir G. Beaumont, having long ago purchased the beautiful piece of water called Loughrigg Tarn, on the banks of which he intended to build, I told him that a person in Kendal who was attached to the place wished to purchase it. Sir George, finding the possession of no use to him, consented to part with it, and placed the purchase-money, £20, at my disposal for any local use which I thought proper. Accordingly I resolved to plant Yew Trees in the Churchyard, and had four pretty strong large oak enclosures made, in each of which was planted, under my own eye, and principally if not entirely by my own hand, two young trees, with the intention of leaving the one that throve best to stand. Many years after, Mr. Barber, who will long be remembered in Grasmere, Mr. Greenwood (the chief landed proprietor), and myself had four other enclosures made in the Churchyard at our own expense, in each of which was planted a tree taken from its neighbour, and they all stand thriving admirably, the fences having been removed as no longer necessary. May the trees be taken care of hereafter when we are all gone, and some of them perhaps at some far distant time rival in majesty the Yew of Lorton and those which I have described as growing in Borrowdale, where they are still to be seen in grand assemblage."—I. F.

824–6. Note the change in the text made in 1845, and *v.* note to i. 934–55.

975. And "gentle Nature grieved, *etc.*] "And suffering Nature grieved that one should die."—SOUTHEY's *Retrospect.*—W.

978. And whence that tribute ? wherefore these regards ?] The sentiments and opinions here uttered are in unison with those expressed in the following Essay upon Epitaphs, which was furnished by me for Mr. Coleridge's periodical work, "The Friend ;" and as they are dictated by a spirit congenial to that which pervades this and the two succeeding books, the sympathising reader will not be displeased to see the Essay here annexed.[1]—W.

Essay upon Epitaphs

It need scarcely be said, that an Epitaph presupposes a Monument, upon which it is to be engraven. Almost all Nations have wished that certain external signs should point out the places where their dead are interred. Among savage tribes unacquainted with letters this has mostly been done either by rude stones placed near the graves, or by mounds of earth raised over them. This custom proceeded obviously from a twofold desire ; first, to guard the remains of the deceased from irreverent approach or from savage violation: and, secondly, to preserve their memory. "Never any," says Camden, "neglected burial but some savage nations, as the Bactrians, which cast their dead to the dogs; some varlet philosophers, as Diogenes, who desired to be devoured of fishes; some dissolute courtiers, as Mæcenas, who was wont to say, 'Non tumulum curo; sepelit natura relictos'.

"I'm careless of a grave:—Nature her dead will save."

As soon as nations had learned the use of letters, epitaphs were inscribed upon these monuments; in order that their intention might be more surely and adequately fulfilled. I have derived monuments and epitaphs from two sources of feeling: but these do in fact resolve themselves into one. The invention of epitaphs, Weever, in his Discourse of Funeral Monuments, says rightly, "proceeded from the presage or fore-feeling of immortality, implanted in all men naturally, and is referred to the scholars of Linus the Theban poet, who flourished about the year of the world two thousand seven hundred; who first bewailed this Linus their Master, when he was slain, in doleful verses, then called of him Œlina, afterwards Epitaphia, for that they were first sung at burials, after engraved upon the sepulchres".

And, verily, without the consciousness of a principle of immortality in the human soul, Man could never have had awakened in him the desire to live in the remembrance of his fellows: mere love, or the yearning of kind towards kind, could not have produced it. The dog or horse perishes in the field, or in the stall, by the side of his companions, and is incapable of anticipating the sorrow with which his surrounding associates shall bemoan his death, or pine for his loss; he cannot pre-conceive this regret, he can form no thought of it; and therefore cannot possibly have a desire to leave such regret or remembrance behind him. Add to the principle of love which exists in the inferior animals, the faculty of reason which exists in Man alone; will the conjunction of these account for the desire? Doubtless it is a necessary consequence of this conjunction; yet not I think as a direct result, but only to be come at through an intermediate thought, viz. that of an intimation or assurance within us, that some part of our nature is imperishable. At least the precedence, in order of birth, of one feeling to the other, is unquestionable. If we look back upon the days of childhood, we shall find that the time is not in remembrance when, with respect to our own individual Being, the mind was without this assurance; whereas, the wish to be remembered by our friends or kindred after death, or even in absence, is, as we shall discover, a sensation that does not form itself till the *social* feelings have been developed, and the Reason has connected itself with a wide range of objects. Forlorn, and cut off from communication with the best part of his nature, must that man be, who should derive the sense of immortality, as it exists in the mind of a child, from the same unthinking gaiety or liveliness of animal spirits with which the lamb in the meadow, or any other irrational creature is endowed; who should ascribe it, in short, to blank ignorance in the child; to an inability

arising from the imperfect state of his faculties to come, in any point
of his being, into contact with a notion of death; or to an unreflecting
acquiescence in what had been instilled into him! Has such an un-
folder of the mysteries of nature, though he may have forgotten his
former self, ever noticed the early, obstinate, and unappeasable
inquisitiveness of children upon the subject of origination? This
single fact proves outwardly the monstrousness of those suppositions:
for, if we had no direct external testimony that the minds of very
young children meditate feelingly upon death and immortality, these
enquiries, which we all know they are perpetually making concerning
the *whence*, do necessarily include correspondent habits of interroga-
tion concerning the *whither*. Origin and tendency are notions insepar-
ably co-relative. Never did a child stand by the side of a running
stream, pondering within himself what power was the feeder of the
perpetual current, from what never-wearied sources the body of
water was supplied, but he must have been inevitably propelled to
follow this question by another: "Towards what abyss is it in pro-
gress? what receptacle can contain the mighty influx?" And the
spirit of the answer must have been, though the word might be sea
or ocean, accompanied perhaps with an image gathered from a map,
or from the real object in nature—these might have been the *letter*,
but the *spirit* of the answer must have been *as* inevitably,—a recep-
tacle without bounds or dimensions;—nothing less than infinity. We
may, then, be justified in asserting, that the sense of immortality, if
not a co-existent and twin birth with Reason, is among the earliest
of her offspring: and we may further assert, that from these conjoined,
and under their countenance, the human affections are gradually
formed and opened out. This is not the place to enter into the recesses
of these investigations; but the subject requires me here to make a
plain avowal, that, for my own part, it is to me inconceivable, that
the sympathies of love towards each other, which grow with our
growth, could ever attain any new strength, or even preserve the old,
after we had received from the outward senses the impression of
death, and were in the habit of having that impression daily renewed
and its accompanying feeling brought home to ourselves, and to those
we love; if the same were not counteracted by those communications
with our internal Being, which are anterior to all these experiences,
and with which revelation coincides, and has through that coincidence
alone (for otherwise it could not possess it) a power to affect us. I
confess, with me the conviction is absolute, that, if the impression
and sense of death were not thus counterbalanced, such a hollowness
would pervade the whole system of things, such a want of correspon-
dence and consistency, a disproportion so astounding betwixt means
and ends, that there could be no repose, no joy. Were we to grow up
unfostered by this genial warmth, a frost would chill the spirit, so
penetrating and powerful, that there could be no motions of the life

of love; and infinitely less could we have any wish to be remembered after we had passed away from a world in which each man had moved about like a shadow.—If, then, in a creature endowed with the faculties of foresight and reason, the social affections could not have unfolded themselves uncountenanced by the faith that Man is an immortal being; and if, consequently, neither could the individual dying have had a desire to survive in the remembrance of his fellows, nor on their side could they have felt a wish to preserve for future times vestiges of the departed; it follows, as a final inference, that without the belief in immortality, wherein these several desires originate, neither monuments nor epitaphs, in affectionate or laudatory commemoration of the deceased, could have existed in the world.

Simonides, it is related, upon landing in a strange country, found the corse of an unknown person lying by the sea-side; he buried it, and was honoured throughout Greece for the piety of that act. Another ancient Philosopher, chancing to fix his eyes upon a dead body, regarded the same with slight, if not with contempt; saying, "See the shell of the flown bird!" But it is not to be supposed that the moral and tender-hearted Simonides was incapable of the lofty movements of thought, to which that other Sage gave way at the moment while his soul was intent only upon the indestructible being; nor, on the other hand, that he, in whose sight a lifeless human body was of no more value than the worthless shell from which the living fowl had departed, would not, in a different mood of mind, have been affected by those earthly considerations which had incited the philosophic Poet to the performance of that pious duty. And with regard to this latter we may be assured that, if he had been destitute of the capability of communing with the more exalted thoughts that appertain to human nature, he would have cared no more for the corse of the stranger than for the dead body of a seal or porpoise which might have been cast up by the waves. We respect the corporeal frame of Man, not merely because it is the habitation of a rational, but of an immortal Soul. Each of these Sages was in sympathy with the best feelings of our nature; feelings which, though they seem opposite to each other, have another and a finer connection than that of contrast. —It is a connection formed through the subtle progress by which, both in the natural and the moral world, qualities pass insensibly into their contraries, and things revolve upon each other. As, in sailing upon the orb of this planet, a voyage towards the regions where the sun sets, conducts gradually to the quarter where we have been accustomed to behold it come forth at its rising; and, in like manner, a voyage towards the east, the birthplace in our imagination of the morning, leads finally to the quarter where the sun is last seen when he departs from our eyes; so the contemplative Soul, travelling in the direction of mortality, advances to the country of everlasting life; and, in like manner, may she continue to explore those cheerful tracts,

till she is brought back, for her advantage and benefit, to the land of
transitory things—of sorrow and of tears.

On a midway point, therefore, which commands the thoughts and
feelings of the two Sages whom we have represented in contrast, does
the Author of that species of composition, the laws of which it is our
present purpose to explain, take his stand. Accordingly, recurring to
the twofold desire of guarding the remains of the deceased and pre-
serving their memory, it may be said that a sepulchral monument is
a tribute to a man as a human being; and that an epitaph (in the
ordinary meaning attached to the word) includes this general feeling
and something more; and is a record to preserve the memory of the
dead, as a tribute due to his individual worth, for a satisfaction to the
sorrowing hearts of the survivors, and for the common benefit of the
living: which record is to be accomplished, not in a general manner,
but, where it can, in *close connection with the bodily remains of the
deceased*: and these, it may be added, among the modern nations of
Europe, are deposited within, or contiguous to, their places of worship.
In ancient times, as is well known, it was the custom to bury the dead
beyond the walls of towns and cities; and among the Greeks and
Romans they were frequently interred by the way-sides.

I could here pause with pleasure, and invite the Reader to indulge
with me in contemplation of the advantages which must have attended
such a practice. We might ruminate upon the beauty which the
monuments, thus placed, must have borrowed from the surrounding
images of nature—from the trees, the wild flowers, from a stream
running perhaps within sight or hearing, from the beaten road stretch-
ing its weary length hard by. Many tender similitudes must these
objects have presented to the mind of the traveller leaning upon one
of the tombs, or reposing in the coolness of its shade, whether he had
halted from weariness or in compliance with the invitation, "Pause,
Traveller!" so often found upon the monuments. And to its epitaph
also must have been supplied strong appeals to visible appearances
or immediate impressions, lively and affecting analogies of life as a
journey—death as a sleep overcoming the tired wayfarer—of mis-
fortune as a storm that falls suddenly upon him—of beauty as a
flower that passeth away, or of innocent pleasure as one that may be
gathered—of virtue that standeth firm as a rock against the beating
waves;—of hope "undermined insensibly like the poplar by the side
of the river that has fed it," or blasted in a moment like a pine-tree
by the stroke of lightning upon the mountain-top—of admonitions
and heart-stirring remembrances, like a refreshing breeze that comes
without warning, or the taste of the waters of an unexpected fountain.
These, and similar suggestions, must have given, formerly, to the
language of the senseless stone a voice enforced and endeared by the
benignity of that nature with which it was in unison.—We, in modern
times, have lost much of these advantages; and they are but in a

small degree counterbalanced to the inhabitants of large towns and cities, by the custom of depositing the dead within, or contiguous to, their places of worship; however splendid or imposing may be the appearance of those edifices, or however interesting or salutary the recollections associated with them. Even were it not true that tombs lose their monitory virtue when thus obtruded upon the notice of men occupied with the cares of the world, and too often sullied and defiled by those cares, yet still, when death is in our thoughts, nothing can make amends for the want of the soothing influences of nature, and for the absence of those types of renovation and decay, which the fields and woods offer to the notice of the serious and contemplative mind. To feel the force of this sentiment, let a man only compare in imagination the unsightly manner in which our monuments are crowded together in the busy, noisy, unclean, and almost grassless churchyard of a large town, with the still seclusion of a Turkish cemetery, in some remote place; and yet further sanctified by the grove of cypress in which it is embosomed. Thoughts in the same temper as these have already been expressed with true sensibility by an ingenuous Poet of the present day.[1] The subject of his poem is "All Saints' Church, Derby": he has been deploring the forbidding and unseemly appearance of its burial-ground, and uttering a wish, that in past times the practice had been adopted of interring the inhabitants of large towns in the country:

"Then in some rural, calm, sequestered spot,
Where healing Nature her benignant look
Ne'er changes, save at that lorn season, when,
With tresses drooping o'er her sable stole,
She yearly mourns the mortal doom of man,
Her noblest work, (so Israel's virgins erst,
With annual moan upon the mountains wept
Their fairest gone,) there in that rural scene,
So placid, so congenial to the wish
The Christian feels, of peaceful rest within
The silent grave, I would have stray'd.
. . . . . ."

[1] Mr. Roger Coxon has pointed out that Grosart and E. de S. were wrong in identifying this poet as John Edwards (1751–1832), a Nottingham poet born in Ireland: "The true author was John Edwards (1772–1845), liquor merchant of Derby; born at Fulneck, Moravian Settlement near Leeds, and educated there with James Montgomery, a close friend in later life." T. R. Potter writes (*The Reliquary*, vol. xi, p. 159): "Wordsworth never passed Derby on his way to Sir George Beaumont at Coleorton without calling at a respectable liquor merchant in the Iron Gate to have an hour with its owner, a brother poet, John Edwards. It was once my good fortune to see W. and Montgomery in that humble home and to hear the pleasant table-talk of three brother bards, two of whom I could not help looking at with wonder."

—wandered forth, where the cold dew of heaven
Lay on the humbler graves around, what time
The pale moon gazed upon the turfy mounds,
Pensive, as though like me, in lonely muse,
'Twere brooding on the dead inhumed beneath.
There while with him, the holy man of Uz,
O'er human destiny I sympathised,
Counting the long, long periods prophecy
Decrees to roll, ere the great day arrives
Of resurrection, oft the blue-eyed Spring
Had met me with her blossoms, as the Dove,
Of old, returned with olive leaf, to cheer
The Patriarch mourning o'er a world destroyed:
And I would bless her visit; for to me
'Tis sweet to trace the consonance that links
As one, the works of Nature and the word
Of God."—

JOHN EDWARDS.

A village churchyard, lying as it does in the lap of nature, may indeed be most favourably contrasted with that of a town of crowded population; and sepulture therein combines many of the best tendencies which belong to the mode practised by the Ancients, with others peculiar to itself. The sensations of pious cheerfulness, which attend the celebration of the sabbath-day in rural places, are profitably chastised by the sight of the graves of kindred and friends, gathered together in that general home towards which the thoughtful yet happy spectators themselves are journeying. Hence a parish-church, in the stillness of the country, is a visible centre of a community of the living and the dead; a point to which are habitually referred the nearest concerns of both.

As, then, both in cities and in villages, the dead are deposited in close connection with our places of worship, with us the composition of an epitaph naturally turns, still more than among the nations of antiquity, upon the most serious and solemn affections of the human mind; upon departed worth—upon personal or social sorrow and admiration—upon religion, individual and social—upon time, and upon eternity. Accordingly, it suffices in ordinary cases, to secure a composition of this kind from censure, that it contain nothing that shall shock or be inconsistent with this spirit. But, to entitle an epitaph to praise, more than this is necessary. It ought to contain some thought or feeling belonging to the mortal or immortal part of our nature touchingly expressed; and if that be done, however general or even trite the sentiment may be, every man of pure mind will read the words with pleasure and gratitude. A husband bewails a wife; a parent breathes a sigh of disappointed hope over a lost child; a son utters a sentiment of filial reverence for a departed father or mother;

a friend perhaps inscribes an encomium recording the companionable qualities, or the solid virtues, of the tenant of the grave, whose departure has left a sadness upon his memory. This and a pious admonition to the living, and a humble expression of Christian confidence in immortality, is the language of a thousand churchyards; and it does not often happen that anything, in a greater degree discriminate or appropriate to the dead or to the living, is to be found in them. This want of discrimination has been ascribed by Dr. Johnson, in his Essay upon the epitaphs of Pope, to two causes; first, the scantiness of the objects of human praise; and, secondly, the want of variety in the characters of men; or, to use his own words, "to the fact, that the greater part of mankind have no character at all". Such language may be holden without blame among the generalities of common conversation; but does not become a critic and a moralist speaking seriously upon a serious subject. The objects of admiration in human-nature are not scanty, but abundant: and every man has a character of his own, to the eye that has skill to perceive it. The real cause of the acknowledged want of discrimination in sepulchral memorials is this: That to analyse the characters of others, especially of those whom we love, is not a common or natural employment of men at any time. We are not anxious unerringly to understand the constitution of the minds of those who have soothed, who have cheered, who have supported us: with whom we have been long and daily pleased or delighted. The affections are their own justification. The light of love in our hearts is a satisfactory evidence that there is a body of worth in the minds of our friends or kindred, whence that light has proceeded. We shrink from the thought of placing their merits and defects to be weighed against each other in the nice balance of pure intellect; nor do we find much temptation to detect the shades by which a good quality or virtue is discriminated in them from an excellence known by the same general name as it exists in the mind of another; and, least of all, do we incline to these refinements when under the pressure of sorrow, admiration, or regret, or when actuated by any of those feelings which incite men to prolong the memory of their friends and kindred, by records placed in the bosom of the all-uniting and equalising receptacle of the dead.

The first requisite, then, in an Epitaph is, that it should speak, in a tone which shall sink into the heart, the general language of humanity as connected with the subject of death—the source from which an epitaph proceeds—of death, and of life. To be born and to die are the two points in which all men feel themselves to be in absolute coincidence. This general language may be uttered so strikingly as to entitle an epitaph to high praise; yet it cannot lay claim to the highest unless other excellencies be superadded. Passing through all intermediate steps, we will attempt to determine at once what these excellencies are, and wherein consists the perfection of this species of composition.—It will be found to lie in a due proportion of the common or universal feeling of humanity to sensations excited by a distinct and clear conception, conveyed to the reader's mind, of the individual, whose death is deplored and whose memory is to be preserved; at least of his character as, after death, it appeared to those who loved him and lament his loss. The general sympathy ought to be quickened, provoked, and diversified, by particular thoughts, actions, images,—circumstances of age, occupation, manner of life, prosperity which the deceased had known, or adversity to which he had been subject; and these ought to be bound together and solemnised into one harmony by the general sympathy. The two powers should temper, restrain, and exalt each other. The reader ought to know who and what the man was whom he is called upon to think of with interest. A distinct conception should be given (implicitly where it can, rather than explicitly) of the individual lamented.—But the writer of an épitaph is not an anatomist, who dissects the internal frame of the mind; he is not even a painter, who executes a portrait at leisure and in entire tranquillity: his delineation, we must remember, is performed by the side of the grave; and, what is more, the grave of one whom he loves and admires. What purity and brightness is that virtue clothed in, the image of which must no longer bless our living eyes! The character of a deceased friend or beloved kinsman is not seen, no—nor ought to be seen, otherwise than as a tree through a tender haze or a luminous mist, that spiritualises and beautifies it; that takes away, indeed, but only to the end that the parts which are not abstracted may appear more dignified and lovely; may impress and affect the more. Shall we say, then, that this is not truth, not a faithful image; and that, accordingly, the purposes of commemoration cannot be answered ?—It *is* truth, and of the highest order; for, though doubtless things are not apparent which did exist; yet, the object being looked at through this medium, parts and proportions are brought into distinct view which before had been only imperfectly or unconsciously seen: it is truth hallowed by love—the joint offspring of the worth of the dead and the affections of the living! This may easily be brought to the test. Let one, whose eyes have been sharpened by personal hostility to discover what was amiss in the character of a good man, hear the tidings of his death, and what a change is wrought in a moment! Enmity melts away; and, as it disappears, unsightliness, disproportion, and deformity, vanish; and, through the influence of commiseration, a harmony of love and beauty succeeds. Bring such a man to the tombstone on which shall be inscribed an epitaph on his adversary, composed in the spirit which we have recommended. Would he turn from it as from an idle tale ? No ;—the thoughtful look, the sigh, and perhaps the involuntary tear, would testify that it had a sane, a generous, and good meaning; and that on the writer's mind had remained an impression which was a true abstract of the character of the deceased; that his gifts and graces were remembered in the simplicity in which they ought to be remembered. The composition and quality of the mind of a virtuous man, contemplated by the side of the grave where his body is mouldering, ought to appear, and be felt as something midway between what he was on earth walking about with his living frailties, and what he may be presumed to be as a Spirit in heaven.

It suffices, therefore, that the trunk and the main branches of the worth of the deceased be boldly and unaffectedly represented. Any further detail, minutely and scrupulously pursued, especially if this be done with laborious and antithetic discriminations, must inevitably frustrate its own purpose; forcing the passing Spectator to this conclusion,—either that the dead did not possess the merits ascribed to him, or that they who have raised a monument to his memory, and must therefore be supposed to have been closely connected with him, were incapable of perceiving those merits; or at least during the act of composition had lost sight of them; for, the understanding having been so busy in its petty occupation, how could the heart of the mourner be other than cold? and in either of these cases, whether the fault be on the part of the buried person or the survivors, the memorial is unaffecting and profitless.

Much better is it to fall short in discrimination than to pursue it too far, or to labour it unfeelingly. For in no place are we so much disposed to dwell upon those points of nature and condition, wherein all men resemble each other, as in the temple where the universal Father is worshipped, or by the side of the grave which gathers all human Beings to itself, and "equalises the lofty and the low". We suffer and we weep with the same heart; we love and are anxious for one another in one spirit; our hopes look to the same quarter; and the virtues by which we are all to be furthered and supported, as patience, meekness, good-will, justice, temperance, and temperate desires, are in an equal degree the concern of us all. Let an Epitaph, then, contain at least these acknowledgments to our common nature; nor let the sense of their importance be sacrificed to a balance of opposite qualities or minute distinctions in individual character; which if they do not, (as will for the most part be the case,) when examined, resolve themselves into a trick of words, will, even when they are true and just, for the most part be grievously out of place; for, as it is probable that few only have explored these intricacies of human nature, so can the tracing of them be interesting only to a few. But an epitaph is not a proud writing shut up for the studious: it is exposed to all—to the wise and the most ignorant; it is condescending, perspicuous, and lovingly solicits regard; its story and admonitions are brief, that the thoughtless, the busy, and indolent, may not be deterred, nor the impatient tired: the stooping old man cons the engraven record like a second horn-book;—the child is proud that he can read it;—and the stranger is introduced through its mediation to the company of a friend: it is concerning all, and for all:—in the churchyard it is open to the day; the sun looks down upon the stone, and the rains of heaven beat against it.

Yet, though the writer who would excite sympathy is bound in this case, more than in any other, to give proof that he himself has been moved, it is to be remembered, that to raise a monument is a sober and a reflective act; that the inscription which it bears is intended to be permanent, and for universal perusal; and that, for this reason, the thoughts and feelings expressed should be permanent also— liberated from that weakness and anguish of sorrow which is in nature transitory, and which with instinctive decency retires from notice. The passions should be subdued, the emotions controlled; strong, indeed, but nothing ungovernable or wholly involuntary. Seemliness requires this, and truth requires it also: for how can the narrator otherwise be trusted? Moreover, a grave is a tranquillising object: resignation in course of time springs up from it as naturally as the wild flowers, besprinkling the turf with which it may be covered, or gathering round the monument by which it is defended. The very form and substance of the monument which has received the inscrip- tion, and the appearance of the letters, testifying with what a slow and laborious hand they must have been engraven, might seem to reproach the author who had given way on this occasion to transports of mind, or to quick turns of conflicting passion; though the same might constitute the life and beauty of a funeral oration or elegiac poem.

These sensations and judgments, acted upon perhaps unconsciously, have been one of the main causes why epitaphs so often personate the deceased, and represent him as speaking from his own tomb-stone. The departed Mortal is introduced telling you himself that his pains are gone; that a state of rest is come; and he conjures you to weep for him no longer. He admonishes with the voice of one experienced in the vanity of those affections which are confined to earthly objects, and gives a verdict like a superior Being, performing the office of a judge, who has no temptations to mislead him, and whose decision cannot but be dispassionate. Thus is death disarmed of its sting, and affliction unsubstantialised. By this tender fiction, the survivors bind themselves to a sedater sorrow, and employ the intervention of the imagination in order that the reason may speak her own language earlier than she would otherwise have been enabled to do. This shadowy interposition also harmoniously unites the two worlds of the living and the dead by their appropriate affections. And it may be observed, that here we have an additional proof of the propriety with which sepulchral inscriptions were referred to the consciousness of immortality as their primal source.

I do not speak with a wish to recommend that an epitaph should be cast in this mould preferably to the still more common one, in which what is said comes from the survivors directly; but rather to point out how natural those feelings are which have induced men, in all states and ranks of society, so frequently to adopt this mode. And this I have done chiefly in order that the laws, which ought to govern the composition of the other, may be better understood. This latter mode, namely, that in which the survivors speak in their own persons, seems to me upon the whole greatly preferable: as it admits a wider range of notices; and, above all, because, excluding the fiction which is the groundwork of the other, it rests upon a more solid basis.

Enough has been said to convey our notion of a perfect epitaph; but it must be borne in mind that one is meant which will best answer the *general* ends of that species of composition. According to the course pointed out, the worth of private life, through all varieties of situation and character, will be most honourably and profitably preserved in memory. Nor would the model recommended less suit public men, in all instances save of those persons who by the greatness of their services in the employments of peace or war, or by the surpassing excellence of their works in art, literature, or science, have made themselves not only universally known, but have filled the heart of their country with everlasting gratitude. Yet I must here pause to correct myself. In describing the general tenour of thought which epitaphs ought to hold, I have omitted to say, that if it be the *actions* of a man, or even some *one* conspicuous or beneficial act of local or general utility, which have distinguished him, and excited a desire that he should be remembered, then, of course, ought the attention to be directed chiefly to those actions or that act: and such sentiments dwelt upon as naturally arise out of them or it. Having made this necessary distinction, I proceed.—The mighty benefactors of mankind, as they are not only known by the immediate survivors, but will continue to be known familiarly to latest posterity, do not stand in need of biographic sketches, in such a place; nor of delineations of character to individualise them. This is already done by their Works, in the memories of men. Their naked names, and a grand comprehensive sentiment of civic gratitude, patriotic love, or human admiration—or the utterance of some elementary principle most essential in the constitution of true virtue;—or a declaration touching that pious humility and self-abasement, which are ever most profound as minds are most susceptible of genuine exaltation—or an intuition, communicated in adequate words, of the sublimity of intellectual power;—these are the only tribute which can here be paid—the only offering that upon such an altar would not be unworthy.

> "What needs my Shakspeare for his honoured bones
> The labour of an age in piled stones,
> Or that his hallowed reliques should be hid
> Under a star-ypointing pyramid?

Dear Son of Memory, great Heir of Fame,
What need'st thou such weak witness of thy name ?
Thou in our wonder and astonishment
Hast built thyself a livelong monument,
And so sepulchred, in such pomp dost lie,
That kings for such a tomb would wish to die."—W.

BOOK VI

In two rough note-books, MSS. 60, 61, dating probably from 1809–12, are found drafts covering most of this book. But a manuscript of *The Recluse*, MS. B, written in the early months of 1800, includes the two stories found in lines 1080–191, *v. Recluse (app. crit.)* 383/4 in Appendix A, *supra*, and thus proves them to have been composed at 'that time. The first, and the latter half of the second, from 1150, are also preserved in another note-book in use in 1800, MS. R.

p. 186. **11.** beauty of holiness] A phrase which occurs four times in the Bible—1 Chron. xvi. 29, 2 Chron. xx. 21, Ps. xxix. 2, Ps. cx. 3.

19. And spires "whose silent finger points to heaven"] An instinctive taste teaches men to build their churches in flat countries with spire-steeples, which as they cannot be referred to any other object, point as with silent finger to the sky and stars, and sometimes, when they reflect the brazen light of a rich though rainy sunset, appear like a pyramid of flame burning heavenward. See "The Friend", by S. T. Coleridge, No. 14, p. 223.—W.

95–211. "And now for the persons that are selected as lying in the Churchyard. But first for the Individual whose grave is prepared to receive him. His story is here truly related : he was a school-fellow of mine for some years. He came to us when he was at least 17 years of age, very tall, robust, and full-grown. This prevented him from falling into the amusements and games of the school ; consequently he gave more time to books. He was not remarkably bright or quick, but by industry he made a progress more than respectable. His parents not being wealthy enough to send him to college, when he left Hawkshead he became a schoolmaster, with a view to preparing himself for holy orders. About this time he fell in love as related in the Poem, and everything followed as there described, except that I do not know exactly when and where he died. The number of youths that came to Hawkshead school, from the families of the humble yeomanry, to be educated to a certain degree of Scholarship as a preparation for the Church, was considerable, and the fortunes of these persons in after life various of course, and of some not a little remarkable. I have now one of this class in my eye who became an Usher in a preparatory school and ended in making a large fortune. His manners when he came to Hawkshead were as uncouth as well could be ; but he had good abilities, with skill to turn them to account; and when the Master of the School, to which he was Usher, died, he stept into his place and became Proprietor of the Establishment. He contrived to manage it with such address, and so much to the taste of what is called High Society and the fashionable world, that no school of the kind, even till he retired, was in such high request. Ministers of State, the wealthiest gentry, and nobility of the first rank, vied with each other in bespeaking a place for their sons in the seminary of this fortunate Teacher.[1] In the solitude of Grasmere, while living as a married man in a cottage of £8 per annum rent, I often used to smile at the tales which reached me of the brilliant career of this quondam clown, for such in reality he was in manner and appearance before he was polished a little by attrition with *gentlemen's* sons trained at Hawkshead, rough and rude as many of our families were. Not 200 yards from the cottage in Grasmere, just mentioned, to which I retired, this gentleman, who many years afterwards purchased a small estate in the neighbourhood, is now erecting a boat-house, with an upper story, to be resorted to as an entertaining-room when he and his associates may feel inclined to take their pastime on the Lake. Every passenger will be disgusted with the sight of this Edifice, not merely as a tasteless thing in itself, but as utterly out of place, and peculiarly fitted, as far as it is observed (and it obtrudes itself on notice at every point of view), to mar the beauty and destroy the pastoral simplicity of the Vale. For my own part and that of my household it is our utter detestation, standing by a shore to which, before the highroad was made to pass that way, we used daily and hourly to repair for seclusion and for the shelter of a grove under which I composed many of my poems, *The Brothers* especially, and for this reason we gave the grove that name.

> That which each man loved
> And prized in his peculiar nook of earth
> Dies with him, or is changed. [i. 471–3.]

So much for my old school-fellow and his exploits. I will only add that as the foundation has twice failed, from the lake no doubt being intolerant of the intrusion, there is some ground for hoping that this impertinent structure will not stand. (It has been rebuilt in somewhat better taste and much as one wishes it away it is not now so very unsightly. The structure is an emblem of the man,—perseverance has conquered difficulties and given something of form and polish to rudeness (*added in pencil*)."—I. F.

119–20. (*app. crit.*) and pined When he had told his love] Probably altered (in 1827) so as to avoid invidious comparison with Viola in *Twelfth Night*, ii. iv. 113–15, "She never told her love, But . . . pined in thought".

---

[1] Mr. Pearson *pencil note in MS.*

163. Love will not submit, *etc.*] Chaucer, *The Franklyn's Tale*, 36–8:

> Love wol nat ben constreyned by maistrye;
> Whan maistrie comth, the god of love anon
> Beteth his winges, and farewell! he is gon!

and Spenser, *F.Q.* III. i. 25:

> Ne may love be compeld by maisterie;
> For soon as maisterie comes, sweet love anone
> Taketh his nimble wings, and soone away is gone.

187. Shedding sweet influence] *Paradise Lost*, vii. 375.

212–61. "The Miner, next described as having found his treasure after twice ten years of labour, lived in Paterdale, and the story is true to the letter. It seems to me, however, rather remarkable that the strength of mind which had supported him through this long unrewarded labour, did not enable him to bear its successful issue. Several times in the course of my life I have heard of sudden influxes of great wealth being followed by derangement, and in one instance the shock of good fortune was so great as to produce absolute Idiotcy. But these all happened where there had been little or no previous effort to acquire the riches, and therefore such a consequence might the more naturally be expected than in the case of the solitary Miner. In reviewing his story one cannot but regret that such perseverance was not sustained by a worthier object. Archimedes leapt out of his bath and ran about the streets proclaiming his discovery in a transport of joy, but we are not told that he lost either his life or his senses in consequence."—I. F.

260. "Unshaken, unseduced, unterrified"]: *Paradise Lost*, v. 896.

273. mixture of Earth's mould] *Comus*, 244.

275–375. "The next character, to whom the Priest is led by contrast with the resoluteness displayed by the foregoing, is taken from a person born and bred in Grasmere, by name Dawson; and whose talents, disposition, and way of life were such as are here delineated. I did not know him, but all was fresh in memory when we settled in Grasmere in the beginning of the century."—I. F.

327. the wide-staring owl] Cf. Shakespeare, *Love's Labour's Lost*, v. ii. 927: "Then nightly sings the staring owl."

386. dividual being] *Paradise Lost*, xii. 85.

405–522. "From this point the conversation leads to the mention of two Individuals who, by their several fortunes, were, at different times, driven to take refuge at the small and obscure town of Hawkshead on the skirt of these mountains. Their stories I had from the dear old Dame with whom, as a schoolboy and afterwards, I lodged for nearly the space of ten years. The elder, the Jacobite, was named Drummond, and was of a high family in Scotland; the Hanoverian Whig bore the name of Vandepat, and might perhaps be a descendant of some Dutchman who had come over in the train of King William. At all events his zeal was such that he ruined himself by a contest for the representation of London or Westminster, undertaken to support his party, and retired to this corner of the world, selected, as it had been by Drummond, for that obscurity which, since visiting the Lakes became fashionable, it has no longer retained. So much was this region considered out of the way till a late period, that persons who had fled from justice used often to resort hither for concealment; and some were so bold as to, not unfrequently, make excursions from the place of their retreat, for the purpose of committing fresh offences. Such was particularly the case with two brothers of the name of Weston who took up their abode at Old Brathay, I think about 70 years ago. They were highwaymen, and lived there some time without being discovered, though it was known that they often disappeared in a way and upon errands which could not be accounted for. Their horses were noticed as being of a choice breed, and I have heard from the Relph family, one of whom was a saddler in the town of Kendal, that they were curious in their saddles and housings and accoutrements of their horses. They, as I have heard, and as was universally believed, were in the end both taken and hanged."—I. F.

421. Culloden] Prince Charles and his Highlanders were routed by the Duke of Cumberland at Culloden Moor on April 16, 1745.

532–3. too quick a sense Of constant infelicity] K. has traced this quotation to Jeremy Taylor's *Holy Dying*, I. v. 2: "How many people there are that weep with want and are mad with oppression, or are desperate with too quick a sense of a constant infelicity."

544. line of Thebes] *Il Penseroso*, 99, "Thebes or Pelops line".

550–1. pomp Of circumstance] *Othello*, III. iii. 354, "Pride, pomp and circumstance of glorious war."

594–8. (*app. crit.*) Cf. *Paradise Lost*, v. 185–7:

> Ye mists and *exhalations that now rise*
> From Hill or steaming Lake, duskie or gray
> *Till the Sun paint* your fleecie skirts, *etc.*

Note that in revising the passage W. clears it of its close Miltonic phrasing.

605–10. almost wholly free, *etc.*] Such was Grasmere Churchyard when W. first knew it. In the I. F. note to the *Epistle to Sir G. Beaumont—Upon perusing the foregoing* W. speaks of it as having, "during late years, lost much of its rustic simplicity by the introduction of iron palisades, to fence off family burying-grounds, and by numerous monuments, some of them in very bad taste, from which this place of burial was in my memory quite free; see the lines in the sixth Book of *The Excursion*, beginning 'Green is the churchyard'."

678, *etc.* Tall was her stature, *etc.*] "This person lived at Town End, and was almost our next neighbour. I have little to notice concerning her beyond what is said in the Poem. She was a most striking instance how far a woman may surpass in talent, in knowledge, and culture of mind, those with and among whom she lives, and yet fall below them in Christian virtues of the heart and spirit. It seemed almost, and I say it with grief, that in proportion as she excelled in the one, she failed in the other. How frequently has one to observe in both sexes the same thing, and how mortifying is the reflection!"—I. F. The woman was Aggy Fisher, sister-in-law of Molly, servant of the W.'s 1800–4. In D. W.'s *Journal* will be found a hint of her parsimony (May 16, 1800) and examples of her gift for conversation (June 3 and 21, 1802). She died in 1804.

766–74. (*v. app. crit.*) Note the definitely Christian addition to this passage made in 1845, and cf. note to i. 934–55.

778–9. Cf. "seats in the rude wall" of the Churchyard described in *An Evening Walk*, A. 49–52, *app. crit.* (Vol. I, p. 7).

787. "The story that follows was told to Mrs. Wordsworth and my Sister by the sister of this unhappy young woman; every particular was exactly as I have related. The party was not known to me, though she lived at Hawkshead, but it was after I left school. The Clergyman, who administered comfort to her in her distress, I knew well. Her Sister who told the story was the wife of a leading yeoman in the Vale of Grasmere, and they were an affectionate pair and greatly respected by every one who knew them. Neither lived to be old; and their Estate—which was perhaps the most considerable then in the vale, and was endeared to them by many remembrances of a salutary character not easily understood, or sympathised with, by those who are born to great affluence—passed to their eldest son, according to the practice of these Vales, who died soon after he came into possession. He was an amiable and promising youth, but was succeeded by an only brother, a good-natured man, who fell into habits of drinking, by which he gradually reduced his property; and the other day the last acre of it was sold, and his wife and children and he himself, still surviving, have very little left to live upon, which it would not perhaps have been worth while to record here but that, through all trials, this woman has proved a model of patience, meekness, affectionate forbearance, and forgiveness. Their eldest son, who, through the vices of his Father, has thus been robbed of an ancient family inheritance, was never heard to murmur or complain against the cause of their distress, and is now [1843] deservedly the chief prop of his mother's hopes."—I. F.

905. pang of despised love] *Hamlet*, III. i. 72.

919–20. He, at whose command the parchèd rock Was smitten] A reference to Numbers xx. 1–11.

945–51. (*app. crit.*) goodly thewes] From Spenser, *F.Q.* I. x. 4, "well upbrought In goodly thewes".

1005. Home to her mother's house] An unconscious reminiscence of the last line of *Paradise Regaind*: "Home to his Mother's house private return'd".

1080–191. As already noted, these two stories were written in 1800, as a part of *The Recluse*. Mr. Gordon Wordsworth was of opinion that the family described in the second of them was drawn from the Ashburners, W.'s near neighbours at Town End, to whom D. W.'s Grasmere *Journals* contain many references. Thomas Ashburner was not a widower, for he had a second wife, so that the story is in part at least imaginary or drawn from some other family.

1114. Here, it seems probable, W. intended to place the story of the Shepherd of Bield Crag. The scattered sheets of a MS. book (MS. 61) containing long passages from Books V, VI–IX of *The Excursion* reveal many abortive attempts to start this tale, which evidently was after W.'s heart:

(*a*) But fixing now his eye
    Upon a heap of turf that near him rose
    The Priest resumed

(*b*) Beneath this turf, this undistinguished Heap
    Which a brief tablet of memorial words
    Of warning and of pity well would grace

(*c*) Yet unregarded thee I will not pass,
    Thee, poor ill fated shepherd of Bield Crag
    Who next dost meet me—Thou wert longer used
    To range the Coves and Heights with different aim,
    Far different thoughts, and thou didst perish there
    —There was he doomed to breathe his latest breath:—
    More hapless than the old Man whom we this day
    Have given to the earth. But Arthur did not want
    House of his own, and lands and numerous flock,
    And wife and children to bewail his loss,
    And a dumb Friend and Servant, in its kind
    Loving as they, and marvellously true.
    The Tale with all its moving incidents
    Were long to tell—

The contrast drawn in lines 3–5 of (*c*) fits well with the story of Wilfred Armathwaite, *Exc.* vi. 1078–114.

Pieced together from the scattered sheets the whole tale reads as follows:

    Nor unregarded may I pass thee by
    Thee, poor ill-fated Shepherd of Bield Crag,
    Who next doth meet me. Oft-times we are stopped
    Wandering through antient churches among tombs
    By sculptur'd image of the buried Man
    Recumbent, Knight or Squire, with sword and shield
    And, at his feet, armorial figure couch'd

Lion, or Greyhound, Lamb, or gentle Fawn,
The bold or timid creature, each alike
Resting in duteous quiet, without fear
Of the sword's point and unoffending spurs
That deck the Warrior in his last repose;
So in a just Tradition that will long
Preserve in our unvarying solitude
No weak remembrance of that sad event,
So have I sometimes wished that o'er this ground
Like Sculpture might be placed albeit rude
And by some rustic hand uncouthly wrought
A Shepherd imaged in his mountain garb
And at his side the serviceable staff
With which he lightly bounds from crag to crag,
And couchant like a pillow at the soles
Of his unarmed feet the faithful Dog
That loved his Lord and clung to him in death.
The Tale with all its moving Incidents
Were long to tell. Behold that smooth blue steep
That sinks abruptly from the grassless crown
Of yon huge height. The man who here is laid
Venturing along the brink of that sheer edge
To take his well-known way, in eager quest
Of some endangered straggler from his flock
Slipped in the turmoil of a winter's storm
And far beneath by next day's light was found
A wounded coarse with face toward the snow
And Raiment by that long precipitous fall
Torn from his back—and there was found his Dog
In mournful Posture o'er the naked part
Couching as if to shield it from the cold.
Thither with sorrowful and decent care
A Bier was brought, and underneath the bier
The afflicted Creature from the fatal spot
Walk'd with her Master's Body, nor withdrew
Nor quitted the forlorn society
Of those remains till weeping Friends had laid them
Beneath this turf.

Bield Crag is on the side of Lingmoor Fell, at the head of Little
Langdale, named from the Bield Farm which lies at its foot. Mr.
R. C. K. Ensor, to whom I read the poem, and who thereafter ex-
plored the crag, writes: "Bield Crag exactly fits Wordsworth's story.
It has high black precipices below slippery sloping ledges . . .: at the
foot of the precipices is a high screes almost equally steep. A body
falling from above could easily roll some way down the screes, and
be much torn in the process."

W. needed the story of a typical Shepherd to complete the Pastor's character-studies of his flock. Why did he never publish this moving tale ? Another fragment reads :

> To thy sad mishap
> A word shall be devoted for the sake
> Of a dumb Friend and servant who though weak
> To save was marvellously true.

Perhaps W. concluded that the tale bore too close a resemblance to that of Gough and his faithful dog, which he had already told in *Fidelity*, published in 1807 (Vol. IV, p. 80).

BOOK VII

Drafts of most of this Book are found in a note-book (MS. 61) belonging, probably, to the years 1809–12 ; a few fragments are also extant, torn from another note-book (MS. 62) of the same period. An earlier version of ll. 242–91 forms part of *The Tuft of Primroses*, written in 1808 (*v.* note to iii. 367) ; *v.* also vii. 980–2 and note.

p. 231. 7–8. Snowdon . . . Cader Idris] In the summers of both 1791 and 1793 W. was staying in North Wales with his friend Robert Jones. For an account of his ascent of Snowdon *v. Prelude*, xiv.

31–3. (*app. crit.*) three contiguous vales . . . its own Compartment] The parish of Grasmere included three townships: (1) Grasmere, (2) Langdale, (3) Rydal, Loughrigg, and Ambleside (Above Stock): to each of these a part of the churchyard was assigned as burial ground.

36–7. encroaching On the smooth playground] At this time the Grasmere village school was in the building adjoining the lych-gate, and part of the churchyard was used as a school playground. *v. An Evening Walk*, *app. crit.* to A. 49–52 (Vol. I, p. 7).

38–291. "The Clergyman and his family described at the beginning of this [seventh] book were, during many years, our principal associates in the Vale of Grasmere, unless I were to except our very nearest neighbours. I have entered so particularly into the main points of their history, that I will barely testify in prose that—with the single exception of the particulars of their journey to Grasmere, which, however, was exactly copied from, in another instance—the whole that I have said of them is as faithful to the truth as words can make it. There was much talent in the family: the eldest son was distinguished for poetical talent, of which a specimen is given in my notes to the sonnets to the Duddon [Vol. III, p. 506]. Once, when in our cottage at Town End I was talking with him about poetry, in the course of conversation I presumed to find fault with the versification of Pope, of whom he was an enthusiastic admirer: he defended him with a warmth that indicated much irritation: nevertheless I would not abandon my point, and said, 'In compass and variety of sound

your own versification surpasses his.' Never shall I forget the change
in his countenance and tone of voice: the storm was laid in a moment;
he no longer disputed my judgment, and I passed immediately in his
mind, no doubt, for as great a critic as ever lived. I ought to add, he
was a clergyman and a well-educated man, and his verbal memory
was the most remarkable of any Individual I have known, except
a Mr. Archer, an Irishman, who lived several years in this neighbour-
hood, and who in this faculty, was a prodigy; he afterwards became
deranged, and I fear continues so, if alive."—I. F. The Rev. Joseph
Sympson, curate of Wytheburn for over fifty years, died at the age
of 92 and was buried in Grasmere churchyard on July 2, 1807. His
constant intercourse, and that of his family, with the W.s in their
early years at Town End is attested on nearly every page of D. W.'s
Grasmere *Journals*.

43. length of road] The road from Grasmere vale up to Dunmail
Raise. The "cottage" (52), where the Sympsons lived, still known as
Broadrain, is situated some 300 yards above the bridge over Tongue
Ghyll; the "vale beyond" (57) is Wytheburn.

162. three fair children] Joseph Sympson had, in fact, six children,
three boys and three girls. It will be noted that in the passage 241/2,
omitted after 1820, mention is made of "three leaving home" to seek
their fortune in the world, and of these the one, Bartholomew, who
returned "to till his father's glebe", did not die before his father, as
l. 260 would lead us to suppose, but lived till 1832. The youngest
daughter, Elizabeth Jane, was 36 years of age when she married
Julius Caesar Ibbetson, an artist, in Dec. 1803. She died in the
following September, and her child three months later. Mrs. Sympson,
who was eleven years younger than her husband, died in Jan. 1806.

242–91. A first version of this passage, quoted in the *app. crit.* as
T. of P., formed a part of *The Tuft of Primroses* (*q.v.*, pp. 351–2). On
the versos of the MS. of that poem are found portions of this first
version as adapted for *The Excursion*, ending "Were gathered to each
other", l. 291, after which is written "End of the Tale".

316–60. A priest] "Then follows the character of Robert Walker,
for which see notes to the Duddon."—I. F. (*v.* Vol. III, p. 510).

343. held] I have adopted the reading of C, "held" for "borne" at
the end of the line, a change made at the same time as W.'s revision
of ll. 351–2, where "borne" is introduced at the end of l. 351: he
clearly wished to avoid the repetitive effect.

395–481. "Then [follows the character of] the deaf man, whose
epitaph may be seen in the churchyard at the head of Haweswater,
and whose qualities of mind and heart, and their benign influence in
conjunction with his privation, I had from his relatives on the spot."
—I. F. W. used these lines to conclude his third essay *Upon Epitaphs*,
written by him in 1809–10 for *The Friend*, but not published till 1876,
when Grosart included it in the *Prose Works* (ii. 60–75). They were,

says W., "suggested by a concise epitaph which I met with some time ago in one of the most retired vales among the mountains of Westmoreland. There is nothing in the detail of the poem which is not either founded upon the epitaph or gathered from inquiries concerning the deceased, made in the neighbourhood." The MS. reading quoted in *app. crit.* are from Grosart's transcript (the MS. is lost); in l. 467 Grosart has "cross" for "crags"—an obvious misreading of the MS.

482–536. "The blind man, next commemorated, was John Gough, of Kendal, a man known, far beyond this neighbourhood, for his talents and attainments in Natural History and Science."—I. F. John Gough (1757–1825) became blind at the age of 3, as a result of small-pox; but at 8 years old he began to study plants by touch, and he became a distinguished botanist. S. T. C. commemorates him in *Omniana*, 1812, under the heading "The Soul and its Organs of Sense": "The every way amiable and estimable John Gough of Kendal is not only an excellent mathematician, but an infallible botanist and zoologist. He has frequently at the first feel corrected the mistakes of the most experienced sportsmen with regard to the birds or vermin which they had killed. . . . As to plants and flowers, the rapidity of his touch appears fully equal to that of sight; and the accuracy greater. Good heavens! It needs only to look at him! Why his face sees all over! It is all one eye! I almost envied him; for the purity and excellence of his own nature, never broken in upon by those evil looks . . . with which low cunning, habitual cupidity, presumptuous sciolism, and heart-hardening vanity, caledonianize the human face,—it is the mere stamp, the undisturbed *ectypon* of his own soul!" It is noteworthy that W. places him in the churchyard while he is still alive.

509–15. instinct with spirit] In his description of the blind man W. instinctively falls into Miltonic phraseology and rhythm; "instinct with spirit" is from *Paradise Lost*, vi. 752, "fancy and understanding" from *P.L.* v. 486, "stood abashed" from *P.L.* iv. 846; and cf. also Adam's eulogy of Eve, *P.L.* viii. 551–2, 557:

> All higher *knowledge in her presence* falls
> Degraded, wisdom in *discourse* with her
> Loses . . .
> Greatness of mind and nobleness . . . create an *awe.*

536. married to immortal verse] *L'Allegro*, 137.

543. adown a rugged slope] There is no "rugged slope" with a "steep descent" near Grasmere churchyard; here, "as by the waving of a magic wand", the poet takes us back to the church in Langdale.

595–624. (*app. crit.*) the seasons' difference] *As You Like It*, ii. i. 6.

617. That sycamore]

> "This Sycamore oft musical with Bees;
> *Such Tents* the Patriarchs loved."
> S. T. COLERIDGE.—W.

625–31. In a first version written on a stray sheet of MS. 62, W's description of the old woodman assumed that he was already dead:

> At length when he had stood a hundred years
> Firm as the finest Patriarch of the woods
> Lusty and green in age yet with dry top
>
> (v. vii. 626 [app. crit.])
>
> Hoary, but somewhat shrunken in the limbs,
> Yet by mishap unscath'd, from weakness free
> From all unsightly withering or decay,
> Himself without a moment's warning fell.
> Such and not seldom is the kindly end,
> Of spriteful, temperate, and industrious Men
> After long life among these healthy hills:
> So have I seen on some mild day of March
> When the bright sun was high in heaven refreshed
> With growth of vernal power, a splendid Pile
> Of ice and Icicles which lingering frost
> Against the surface of an upright rock
> In monumental shape serene and high
> Had reared, and more than monumental lustre;
> Meanwhile faint tricklings, as I gazed, were heard
> A voice of melting, that in whispers sang
> Of easy dissolution and decay
> By presence and by influence of soft air
> And flattering sunshine, when without a touch
> Insensibly the total fabric fell
> And spread a confused ruin at the feet
> Of the bare rock whose wall it had adorn'd
> But soon, while on the [frozen ?] ground it lies,
> Soon to depart and wholly disappear—
> Such was the bright decay (happy end) the sudden fate,
> Of that old man, the oldest of the vale.

This passage must have been written earlier than the description of the old clergyman, ll. 111–291 *supra*, to whom W. transfers the distinction of being "the oldest of the vale", ll. 242–3. It is therefore earlier than 1808, the year in which the story of the Sympsons was first written in *The Tuft of Primroses, v.* pp. 351–2 *supra*. For the image in the latter part of the passage cf. *Inscription*, xi. (Vol. IV, p. 204.)

632–95. "Of the Infant's Grave, next noticed, I will only say, it is an exact picture of what fell under my own observation; and all persons who are intimately acquainted with Cottage Life must often have observed like instances of the workings of the domestic affections."—I. F.

636–94. This refers to the Greens, an ancient and much respected

Grasmere family, who had lived for many generations at Pavement End at the head of the lake. The grandfather (l. 660) was John Green (1724–1806), and his wife's name was Margaret (l. 672). The father, another John Green (1758–1839), was a butcher, a man of integrity and much shrewdness. It was he who added on the rooms at Pavement End to accommodate his old parents (663–6). His sons, whether seven (636) or six (MS. 657), were notable men: two of them became parsons; one of them, Isaac, became master of Sedbergh School and was a close friend of Hartley Coleridge. Goldrill (637) was the name given by W. to the beck which runs past the farm at Pavement End into the lake; the name was suggested by the colour of the beck, stained by manure as it passed the farm. I owe the above information to Mrs. Rawnsley.

695–890. "This young volunteer bore the name of Dawson, and was younger brother, if I am not mistaken, to the Prodigal of whose character and fortunes an account is given towards the beginning of the preceding book. The Father of the family I knew well; he was a man of literary education and of experience in society much beyond what was common among the inhabitants of the Vale. He had lived a good while in the Highlands of Scotland, as a manager of ironworks at Bunaw, and had acted as clerk to one of my predecessors in the office of Distributor of Stamps, when he used to travel round the country collecting and bringing home the money due to Government in gold, which, it may be worth while to mention for the sake of my Friends, was deposited in the cell or Iron closet under the west window of the long room at Rydal Mount, which still exists with the Iron doors that guarded the property. This of course was before the time of bills and notes. The two sons of this person had no doubt been led by the knowledge of their Father to take more delight in scholarship, and had been accustomed in their own minds to take a wider view of social interests than was usual among their associates. The premature death of this gallant young man was much lamented, and, as an attendant at the funeral, I myself witnessed the ceremony and the effect of it as described in the Poem."—I. F. v. letter of D. W., July 19, 1807: "Many persons are dead . . . young George Dawson, the finest young man in the vale" (*E.L.*, p. 138).

695. On a bright day—so calm, so bright] Cf. Geo. Herbert, *Sunday*, "O Day, so calme, so bright"; and *Vertue*, "Sweet day, so cool, so calm, so bright".

745. (*app. crit.*) A delightful description of the lakeland fox-hunt on foot, unfortunately not adopted in the text.

751. glead] "glede or gled, the kite, now chiefly *northern*" (*O.E.D.*).

782–801. (*app. crit.*) At Austerlitz (1805) Napoleon, by defeating the Russians and Austrians, gained possession of the central and southern German states, north Italy, and the coast of the Adriatic.

At Jena, on Oct. 14, 1806, he routed the Prussians and thirteen days later entered Berlin.

814–15. When grove was felled, *etc.*] The Book of Judges vi. 25–34.

848. all hoping and expecting all] 1 Corinthians xiii. 7.

923–75. Tradition tells . . . the house is gone] "The Pillars of the Gateway in front of the mansion remained when we first took up our abode at Grasmere. Two or three cottages still remain, which are called Knott-houses from the name of the gentleman (I have called him a knight) concerning whom these traditions survive. He was the ancestor of the Knott family, formerly considerable proprietors in the district."—I. F.

980–2. Perish the roses and the flowers of kings, *etc.*] The "Transit gloria mundi" is finely expressed in the Introduction to the Foundation-charters of some of the ancient Abbeys. Some expressions here used are taken from that of the Abbey of St. Mary's Furness, the translation of which is as follows:

"Considering every day the uncertainty of life, that the roses and flowers of Kings, Emperors, and Dukes, and the crowns and palms of all the great, wither and decay ; and that all things, with an uninterrupted course, tend to dissolution and death: I therefore," *etc.*—W.

v. Tuft of Primroses, 357–9, Appendix C, p. 356, for an earlier version of these lines.

BOOK VIII

There is no complete consecutive manuscript of this Book, but rough drafts of all but ll. 487–519 are extant in note-books (MSS. 61, 62) which probably date from 1809–12. An early version of ll. 283–305, 315–32 is also found in a note-book, MS. 18 A (which contains MS. D of *The Ruined Cottage*), in the hand of D. W., dating from 1798–9.

p. 267. **50.** Cf. Milton's memorable line:

> For not to irksome toil but to delight
> He made us. (*Paradise Lost*, ix. 242.)

87, etc. An inventive age, *etc.*] "What follows in the discourse of the Wanderer upon the changes he had witnessed in rural life, by the introduction of machinery, is truly described from what I myself saw during my boyhood and early youth, and from what was often told me by persons of this humble calling. Happily, most happily, for these mountains, the mischief was diverted from the banks of their beautiful streams, and transferred to open and flat countries abounding in coal, where the agency of steam was found much more effectual for carrying on those demoralising works. Had it not been for this invention, long before the present time every torrent and river in this district would have had its factory, large and populous in proportion to the power of the water that could there have been commanded. Parliament has interfered to prevent the night-work which was once carried on in these mills as actively as during the daytime, and by necessity still more perniciously—a sad disgrace to the proprietors, and to the nation which could so long tolerate such unnatural proceedings. Reviewing at this late period, 1843, what I put into the mouths of my Interlocutors a few years after the commencement of the century, I grieve that so little progress has been made in diminishing the evils deplored, or promoting the benefits of education which the Wanderer anticipates. The results of Lord Ashley's labours to defer the time when Children might legally be allowed to work in factories, and his endeavours to limit still farther the hours of permitted labour, have fallen far short of his own humane wishes, and those of every benevolent and right-minded man who has carefully attended to this subject: and in the present session of Parliament (1843) Sir James Graham's attempt to establish a course of religious education among the children employed in factories has been abandoned, in consequence of what might easily be foreseen, the vehement and turbulent opposition of the Dissenters; so that, for many years to come, it may be thought expedient to leave the religious instruction of Children entirely in the hands of the several denominations of Christians in the Island, each body to work according to its own means and in its own way. Such is my own confidence, a confidence I share with many of my most valued friends, in the superior advantages, both religious and social, which attend a course of instruction presided over and guided by the Clergy of the Church of England that I have no doubt that, if but once its members, lay and clerical, were duly sensible of those benefits, their Church would daily gain ground, and rapidly, upon every shape and fashion of Dissent; and in that case, a great majority in Parliament being sensible of these benefits, the Ministers of the Country might be emboldened, were it necessary, to apply funds of the State to the support of Education on Church principles. Before I conclude, I cannot forbear noticing the strenuous efforts made at this time in Parliament, by so many persons, to extend manufacturing and commercial industry at the expense of agricultural, though we have recently had abundant proofs that the apprehensions expressed by the Wanderer were not groundless."—I. F.

100. thorpe and vill] Thorpe O.E. and M.E. for hamlet or village; vill O.F. for farm, country house, or village (*O.E.D.*).

111–12. Earth has lent Her waters, Air her breezes] In treating this subject, it was impossible not to recollect, with gratitude, the pleasing picture, which, in his Poem of the Fleece, the excellent and amiable Dyer has given of the influences of manufacturing industry upon the face of this Island. He wrote at a time when machinery was first beginning to be introduced, and his benevolent heart prompted him to augur from it nothing but good. Truth has compelled me to dwell upon the baneful effects arising out of an ill-regulated and excessive application of powers so admirable in themselves.—W.

The passage which follows was clearly suggested by the close of *The Fleece*, Book III, where Dyer describes the transport of wool not merely by road, but also

> Through every navigable wave . . .
> . . . through Tyne and Tees,
> Through Weare and Lune and merchandising Hull,
> And Swale and Aire, . . .
> Through Ken, swift rolling down his rocky dale
> Like giddy youth impetuous, . . .
> Through Towy, winding under Merlin's towers
> And Usk, that frequent under hoary rocks
> On her deep waters paints the impending scene,
> Wild torrents, crags and woods, and mountain snows. . . .
> The northern Cambrians . . . lay their bales
> In Salop's streets, beneath whose lofty walls
> Pearly Sabrina waits them with her barks
> And spreads the swelling sheet. For nowhere far
> From some transparent river's naval course
> Arise, and fall, our various hills and vales,
> Nowhere far distant from the masted wharf.

and Dyer goes on to suggest the digging of a canal to join Thames, Severn, and Trent. Thomson had also celebrated the development, in his day, of roads and canals in England:

> 'Tis not for me to paint, diffusive shot
> O'er fair extents of land, the shining road;
> The flood-compelling arch; the long canal
> Through mountains piercing and uniting seas.
>
> (*Liberty*, v.)

W.'s lines 115–16 have given critics some difficulty, but he does not mean that the canal is necessarily high up on the mountain's side, only that it passes along the lofty slope of a mountain. He is perhaps thinking of the Kendal to Lancaster canal, of which the construction began shortly after 1792, which winds along through hilly country with magnificent views, in places, of Morecambe Bay and the Lakeland fells.

220. Call Archimedes from his buried tomb] "The hint for this description comes from Cicero (*Tusculan Disputations*, lv. 23) who says that when he was Quaestor in Sicily he found the tomb of Archimedes, buried in brambles, *etc.*, and forgotten by the Syracusans themselves."—Nowell Smith.

283–7. (*app. crit.*) There is a law severe of penury] So begin the lines, headed "Fragment", towards the close of the note-book, MS. 18 A, into which D. W. copied *The Ruined Cottage* (MS. D, v. p. 404 *supra*), and *Adventures of Salisbury Plain, etc.* It corresponds with ll. 283–305, 315–32 of our text, and as there is a blank half-page in the MS. after the line corresponding with 305, it is reasonable to suppose that a draft of 306–14 was also written at the same time, 1798–9, but that D. W. was unable to decipher it, and left the space to be filled in when she could consult her brother.

283. Economists will tell you] Compare W.'s reference to *The Wealth of Nations* in *Prelude*, xiii. 78 and *Humanity*, 58–63.

297–302. W. was perhaps drawn into a special interest in the evils of child-labour in factories by conversations with John Thelwall, who visited him at Alfoxden in 1797. Cf. Thelwall's lines quoted by Professor Harper:

> the unwieldy pride
> Of Factory overgrown, when Opulence,
> Dispeopling the neat cottage, crowds his walls
> (Made pestilent by congregated lungs
> And lewd association) with a race
> Of infant slaves, brok'n timely to the yoke
> Of unremitting drudgery.

331. lapse of liquid element] Cf. note to iii. 93 *supra.*

389. vagrants of the gipsy tribe] Cf. *Gipsies*, Poems of the Imagination, xx, Vol. II, p. 226, for W.'s view of these "wild outcasts of society".

413. Christ-cross-row] "The alphabet, so called from the figure of the cross prefixed to it in hornbooks" (*O.E.D.*).

556–71. *v.* Shelley, *Peter Bell the Third*, 584–8, and Note.

BOOK IX

There is no complete continuous manuscript of this Book, but nearly all of it is covered by drafts found in different note-books, MSS. 60, 61, 62, presumably dating from 1809–12. Lines 1–26, 128–52 are also found under the heading *Fragment* in the same note-book, MS. 18 A, 1798–9, as contains lines from Book VIII (*v.* note to ll. 283–7 *supra*). The relation of thought expressed in them to that of *Lines composed . . . above Tintern Abbey*, written about the same time, is obvious enough.

p. 288. **59.** High peaks that bound the vale where now we are] This is more appropriate to Langdale than to Grasmere. But on the general topography of the poem *v.* I. F. note p. 375, *supra.*

87. the mighty stream of tendency] Hazlitt refers, in his essay on Malthus in *The Spirit of the Age*, to " 'the mighty stream of tendency' as Mr. Wordsworth in the cant of the day calls it". For the image cf. W.'s letter in reply to Mathetes in *The Friend*, 1809 (*v.* Vol. III, p. 35, ed. 1818), where he supports his conception of the progress of human nature towards perfection by the simile of a winding river. Hazlitt refers more than once to W.'s belief in the philosophical doctrine of necessity which, he suggests, he derived from Godwin:

v. Examiner, Aug. 21, 1814, which opens with a misquotation of *Lines composed above Tintern Abbey*, ll. 92–102,

> For I have learnt
> A sense sublime . . .
> A motion and a spirit that impels
> All thinking things, all objects of all thought
> And rolls through all things,

and continues: "Perhaps the doctrine of philosophical necessity was never more finely expressed than in these lines"; and *Spirit of the Age*: essay on Godwin: "Throw aside your books of Chemistry," said W. to a student in the Temple, "and read Godwin on Necessity". For the "cant of the day" about "inevitable progress", "tendency" towards the state of perfection, *etc.*, *v.* final chapter of Godwin's *Political Justice*, 1796. But W.'s phrase was his own; cf. fragment from the Alfoxden note-book quoted in notes to *The Prelude*, ed. E. de S., p. 548: "They rest upon their oars, Float down the mighty stream of tendency" (a description of the class of men to which the Wanderer belongs). The influence of a memorable passage in Burke's *Thoughts on the French Revolution* may perhaps be traced in both thought and image: "If a great change is to be made in human affairs, the minds of men will be fitted to it; the general opinions and feelings will draw that way. Every fear, every hope will forward it; and then they who persist in opposing *this mighty current in human affairs*, will appear rather to resist the decrees of Providence itself, than the mere designs of men." Cf. M. Arnold in *St. Paul and Protestantism*: "That *stream of tendency by which all things seek to fulfil the law of their being*, and which, inasmuch as our idea of real welfare resolves itself into this fulfilment of the law of one's being, man rightly deems the fountain of all goodness, and calls by the worthiest and most solemn name he can, which is God, science also might willingly own for the fountain of all goodness, and call God."

114–15. wherever man is made . . . a tool, *etc.*] Cf. viii. 283 and note.

134. chalice] altered from "vessel", because Barron Field objected that the "vessel" was ambiguous, and that by "vessel" he understood a ship. In his Memoir (B.M. MS. Add. 41325–7) B. F. notes: I have never been able to find such a line: Shakspeare has "Fills the wide vessel of the Universe", *Henry V* (Chorus to Act IV), and the "big round tears" in *As You Like It*.

151. human form divine] *Paradise Lost*, iii. 44, "Human face divine".

152. (*app. crit.*) And their eternal soul may waste away] In the 1798–9 MS. (MS. 18 A) which contains the first version of 1–26 (*v. app. crit.*) and 128–52, and with no break between the first version of 27–128 (*v. app. crit.*) and 128–52, the passage concludes as follows:

Oh never was this intellectual power
This vital spirit, in its essence free
As is the light of heaven, this mind that streams
With emanations like the blessed sun
Oh never was this [   ] existence formed
For wishes that debilitate and die
Of their own weakness, fears that live by search
Of knowledge, which they cannot find, for hopes
That have no blessing in them, blind regrets
And such desires as do but stir the heart
To waken consciousnesses of despair,
For hesitations, pining languors, cold
And dead suppressions, all the subtle host
Of feverish infirmities that give
Sad motion to the pestilential calm
Of negative morality, and feed
From day to day their never-ending life
In the close prison-house of human laws.

195–8. I spake of mischief . . . destroy] "The Chartists are well aware of this possibility, and cling to it with an ardour and perseverance which nothing but wiser and more brotherly feeling towards the many, on the part of the wealthy few, can moderate or remove."—I. F.

226–8. It is worth noting that this passage was added in 1845 (*v.* note to i. 934–55).

296. (*app. crit.*) A saintly youth] i.e. Edward VI.

299. Binding herself by statute] The discovery of Dr. Bell affords marvellous facilities for carrying this into effect; and it is impossible to over-rate the benefit which might accrue to humanity from the universal application of this simple engine under an enlightened and conscientious government.—W.

Dr. Andrew Bell (1753–1832) published in 1797 *An Experiment in Education made at the Asylum of Madras*, in which he advocated the use of pupil teachers. W. read the book in 1808 and was much impressed by it (*v. M.Y.*, p. 245), and both Coleridge and Southey became enthusiastic supporters of Bell's "discovery". In 1811 and 1812 Bell spent some time in the Lake district, and became intimate with the Wordsworth family. Joseph Lancaster, a Quaker, in his *Improvements in Education* (1803) admitted his debt to Bell for his own monitorial system, but when he pressed for widely spread free education "on general Christian principles" his position as a Quaker aroused the fears of the Tory and Church party, who rallied round Bell as the advocate of Church schools.

336. Calpe] The classical name for Gibraltar. W. alludes here to the almost total subjugation of the Continent to Napoleon at this time. Cf. ll. 409–12.

363–4. the fear Of numbers] A reference to the theory of Thomas

Malthus (1766–1834) whose *Essay on Population* had appeared in 1798 and was widely read. Hazlitt published *A Reply to the Essay on Population* in 1807.

431. shy compeer] Cf. Satan's "bold compeer", *Paradise Lost*, i. 127.

437–48. A version of this passage, written in 1804, occurs in MS. Y of *The Prelude* (1805), viii. 496/7. *v. Prel.*, E. de S., p. 562.

484. on thy bosom, spacious Windermere] Cf. *Prelude*, ii. 54–7.

519. Vouchsafe sweet influence] A Miltonic phrase: cf. "shedding sweet influence": *Paradise Lost*, vii. 375; the use of "sweets" in 544 also recalls Milton.

530–1. A choice repast, *etc.*] Cf. Milton, Sonnet XVII, "What neat repast shall feast us, light and choice". Barron Field criticized the earlier reading as "too much in the vein of Scriblerus. This is what I call poetic diction, in your bad sense. I would say, 'Merrily seated in a ring, drank tea'." W. replied "Drank tea" is too familiar. My line (I own) is somewhat too pompous, as you say. The line now stands, *etc.*, *as text*. W. wrote this in 1828, but the correction was not made before 1837 ed.

590–633. This description of the sunset is, significantly, full of Miltonic phraseology: thus *the orb* (593) for the sun. *v. Paradise Lost, passim*; *blue firmament* (596), *P.L.* xi. 206; *unapparent fount* (605), cf. *P.L.* vii. 103; *effluence of thyself* (617), cf. *P.L.* iii. 6; *paternal splendours* (620), *paternal glory*, *P.L.* vii. 219; *frail earth* (625), *frail World*, *P.L.* ii. 1030; *empyreal throne* (631), *P.L.* ii. 430.

609. from the grassy mountain's open side] "The point here fixed upon in my imagination is half-way up the northern side of Loughrigg Fell, from which the Pastor and his companions are supposed to look upwards to the sky and mountain-tops, and round the Vale, with the lake lying immediately beneath them."—I. F.

690–711. Cf. *Prelude*, xiii. 329–35; and for his early interest in the Druids, *Vale of Esthwaite*, 32 (Vol. I, p. 270 and note p. 368), and *Guilt and Sorrow*, 122 and 185–98 *app. crit.* (Vol. I, p. 104 and note p. 336).

704. Taranis] "Taranis is the name of a Celtic God, probably 'the Thunderer', mentioned by Lucan, *Pharsalia*, i. 446: Et Taranis Scythicae non mitior ara Dianae."—Nowell Smith.

743–7. (*app. crit.*) Cf. the combination in *Paradise Lost*, vi. 645, of rocks, waters, woods.

750. They know if I be silent, morn or even] *Paradise Lost*, v. 202, "Witness if I be silent, morn or eeven".

775. welcome promise made] "When I reported this promise of the Solitary, and long after, it was my wish, and I might say intention, that we should resume our wanderings, and pass the Borders into his native country, where, as I hoped, he might witness, in the society of the Wanderer, some religious ceremony—a sacrament, say, in the open fields, or a preaching among the mountains—which, by recalling to his mind the days of his early Childhood, when he had been present on such occasions in company with his Parents and nearest kindred, might have dissolved 'his heart into tenderness, and so done more towards restoring the Christian faith in which he had been educated, and, with that, contentedness and even cheerfulness of mind, than all that the Wanderer and Pastor, by their several effusions and addresses, had been able to effect. An issue like this was in my intentions. But, alas

" 'Mid the wreck of IS and WAS,
Things incomplete and purposes betrayed
Make sadder transits o'er thought's optic glass
Than noblest objects utterly decayed."
[*Malham Cove*, 11–14].—I. F.

Rydal Mount, June 24, 1843.
St. John Baptist day.

APPENDIX A

p. 313. THE RECLUSE, Book I. The lines quoted in the *app. crit.* to 170–1, "Thrice hath the winter moon been filled with light", *etc.*, show that W. was at work on the first book of *The Recluse* in late March 1800: he and D. W. arrived in Grasmere to take up their abode in Dove Cottage on Dec. 20, 1799 ; the moon was full on Jan. 10, 1800, again on Feb. 9, and for the third time on March 10. The full moon was important to them, for they walked much by moonlight (*v.* D. W.'s *Journals, passim*, and her letter, *M.Y.*, p. 85 *etc.*). References in the poem all corroborate the date of composition as between February and April: "Two months unwearied of severest storm" (181) ; "Soon will peep forth the primrose (514) ; "melted hoar-frost" on "the bare twigs" (564) ; *app. crit.* 544–9 ; and note to 658–9. There are four extant MSS. A is an incomplete early draft, a fair copy chiefly in W.'s hand but with 49 lines in the middle transcribed by M. H. It begins with the 26 lines quoted in *app. crit.* 151/2, "We will be free", *etc.* Its 27th line is l. 152 of D, the latest text ; its 25th is numbered 215, which proves A to be a fragment of which the first 190 lines are lost. It comes to an end at l. 376 of D, which in A is numbered 467. R, an interleaved copy of part of Coleridge's *Poems*, 1796, contains drafts, written by Wordsworth opposite to *Religious Musings*, of scattered passages, incorporated after revision, in *The Recluse*, Book I, and in *The Excursion*. It gives versions of *Recluse*, i. 427–539, 502–4 (*app. crit.* and note), 592–609, 532–642, 633–7, and the two stories *Recluse*, i. 383/4, afterwards used in *Exc.* vi.

B is the first complete text: it was probably written later in 1800. It begins as a fair copy transcribed by M. H. who writes to l. 383,. including lines in *app. crit.* 383/4: on the versos—and this continues throughout the MS.—W. scrawls on the rectos alternative drafts of passages afterwards inserted. The rest of the fair copy is in the hand of W. except for two pages by D. W. in the middle and a page and a half by M. H. at the end. It concludes with the passage used as a *Prospectus* of *The Excursion* (MS. 2 of the *Prospectus, supra*, p. 338) which begins at l. 954, "On Man, on Nature", *etc.*, and the last line is numbered 1047. D gives the final text, which I adopt in the present edition: it is in M. W.'s hand, and the corrections and revisions, some of them pasted over the original readings, are in her hand also. This MS. must be dated after 1814, for it comes to an end after "Musing in Solitude" (l. 2 of *Prospectus* to *The Excursion*) with the words (*see Preface to the Excursion to its conclusion*). But it does not follow that all the corrections embodied in it were made at so late a date. Possibly the MS. was written early in 1815 when D. W. and M. W. were anxious that W. should get to work upon *The Recluse*: "William has had one of his weeks of rest and we now begin to wish that he was at work again, but as he intends completely to plan the first part of *The Recluse* before he begins composition, he must read many Books before he will fairly set to labour again" (D. W. to S. H., Feb. 18, 1815). M. W. may have suggested making a copy of Book I to give him a start.

31–8. Cf. Spenser's *Muiopotmos*, 209–13:

> What more felicitie can fall to creature,
> Than to enjoy delight with libertie,
> And to be Lord of all the works of Nature,
> To raine in th'aire from earth to highest skie,
> To feed on flowers, and weeds of glorious feature.

The whole passage recalls Spenser's description of the flight of the Butterfly. Cf. *Prelude*, 1805, x. 838–9 and note (E. de S.).

52–3. damp and gloom Of the gay mind] Cf. *Yarrow Revisited, etc.*, xxvi (Vol. III, p. 280):

> that sweet and tender melancholy
> Which may itself be cherished and caressed
> More than enough ; a fault so natural
> (Even with the young, the hopeful, or the gay)

For the phrase cf. *Paradise Lost*, xi. 544, "a melancholy damp".

58. cloud-capt hills] Cf. *The Tempest*, IV. i. 152, "cloud-capp'd towers".

71–97 and **110–25.** were quoted from the MS. in the *Memoirs* of the poet, 1851 (*M.* i, pp. 157–8); ll. 122–5 were quoted from the MS. in his *Guide to the Lakes*, 1810.

80–2. Cf. *Lines . . . above Tintern Abbey*, 41–6:

> that serene and blessed mood
> In which the affections gently lead us on,
> Until the breath of this corporeal frame

And even the motion of our human blood
Almost suspended, we are laid asleep
In body, and become a living soul

151/2. An alternative to the last three lines of this passage from
A and B is found in a rough draft on one of the versos of B:

> A symbol of Eternity and heaven.

> Nor have we been deceived, thus far the effect
> Falls not below the loftiest of our hopes.
> This Vale these mountains cease not to put forth
> Fresh graces, new enjoyments to us here
>
> .   .   .   .   .   .
>
> The torrents murmur to my listening ear
> With unabated influence. So it is always
> So must be, termination is not here
> 'Tis not in holy Nature to betray
> Or disappoint her genuine Votary:
> My trembling heart acknowledges her Power
> To be divine, and therefore infinite.

Cf. *Lines . . . above Tintern Abbey*, 122–3:

> Knowing that Nature never did betray
> The heart that loved her.

152–67. First printed in *M.i.* 155. For a prose account of the
journey here described *v.* W. W.'s letter to Coleridge dated Christmas
Eve, 1799 (*E.L.*, pp. 234–42).

170–1. (*app. crit.*) Cf. *Hart-leap Well* (Vol. II, p. 249) and I. F.
note (Vol. II, p. 514). The writing of this passage was almost con-
temporary with that of *Hartleap Well*; the lines "Thrice hath the
winter moon", etc., dates its composition as late March 1800, *v. supra*
p. 475.

203–29. This passage was first printed in the fourth edition of
W.'s *Guide to the Lakes*, 1823, where it is introduced thus: "In winter
the lakes are sometimes resorted to by wild swans; and in that season
habitually by widgeons, goldings, and other aquatic fowl of the
smaller species. Let me be allowed the aid of verse to describe the
evolutions which these visitants sometimes perform, on a fine day
towards the close of winter."

> Mark how the feather'd tenants of the flood
> With grace of motion, *etc.*

Notice that the artificially phrased opening is not in the original text.
The extract was published in ed. 1827 among *Poems of the Imagination*
(Vol. II, p. 288). For the Miltonic echoes in the lines *v.* Vol. II, p. 522.

233. onward-looking thoughts] Cf. *Michael*, 148, "forward-looking
thoughts", written in the same year.

323-5. hound . . . among the lonely woods His yell repeating] Cf. *An Evening Walk*, 378, "Or yell, in the deep woods, of lonely hound".
334. *bield*] a refuge or shelter; W. italicizes it because it is a dialect word only found in Scotland and the north of England.
502-4. (*app. crit.*) These lines close a passage in MS. R evidently intended for this book of *The Recluse*, but afterwards rewritten for *Exc.* iv. 332-72. The whole passage runs as follows:

Happy is he who lives to understand,
Observes, explores, to the end (for this) that he may find
The law and what it is and where begins
The union and disunion that which makes
Degree or kind in every shape of being
The constitution powers and faculties
And habits and enjoyments, that do assign
To every class its office and abode
Through all the mighty commonwealth of things
Up from the stone or plant to sovereign man.
Such converse, if but fervent, teaches love
For knowledge is delight and such delight
Is love, yet suited as it rather is
To thought and to the climbing Intellect,
It teaches less to love than to adore
If that be not indeed the highest love.
And yet a something to our Nature cleaves
Which is not satisfied with this, and he
Is still a happier Man who, for those heights
Of speculation not unfit, descends
At Nature's call to walk in humbler ways,
Hath individual objects of regard
Among the inferior kinds, not merely those
Which he may call his own and which depend
Upon his care, from which he also looks
For signs and tokens of a mutual bond,
But others far beyond his narrow sphere
Which for the very sake of love he loves,
And takes the after-knowledge as it comes.
Nor is it a mean praise of rural life
And solitude that they do favour most,
Most frequently call forth and best sustain
These mild and pure affections, and to me
How much do they endear the quietness
Of this sublime retirement. I begin
Already to inscribe upon my heart
A liking for the small grey horse that bears
The paralytic Man . . .

521. Owlet-crag] I cannot trace this as a local name: perhaps W. invented it.

543/4 (*app. crit.*) underplace] A word (not in *O.E.D.*) characteristic of W. *v. Prel.*, E. de S., p. 622, note on "underpresence".

654. a Stranger of our Father's house] John W., who was at Grasmere from Jan. to Sept. 1800.

658-9. Sisters . . . Brother of our hearts] Mary Hutchinson and her sisters; and Coleridge. Coleridge was with them shortly before April 11; and before April 4 Mary Hutchinson had been with them for three weeks (*v.* letter of Lamb to Manning, April 5, 1800, and D. W. to R. W., *E.L.*, p. 242).

666. unreproved delight] W. uses the phrase in *Prelude*, v. 493; cf. *L'Allegro*, 40, "In unreproved pleasures free".

718-20. one . . . fronted multitudes in arms] A reminiscence of Abdiel in *Paradise Lost*, vi. 30:

who single has maintained
Against revolted multitudes the cause
Of truth, in word mightier than they in Armes

749-50. the hope to fill The heroic trumpet with the Muse's breath] Cf. *Prelude* (1805), i. 177-219.

APPENDIX B

p. 340. I. Yet once again, *etc.*: Holograph preserved in The Pierpont Morgan Library in New York; perhaps written as early as 1795, when W. first conceived the poem about the old Cumberland Beggar. It seems to record his return to Cockermouth on his way to Whitehaven in 1794, after his visit to Windy Brow.

p. 340. II. *Fragments from the Alfoxden note-book.* This note-book, used by W. between Jan. 20 and March 5, 1798 (*v. Prel.*, E. de S., p. xxv) contains drafts of passages of *The Old Cumberland Beggar* and fragments of blank verse, some of which were afterwards worked into *The Prelude* or *The Ruined Cottage*.

p. 340. i. *There would he stand, etc.* An early sketch of an experience of the Pedlar of *The Ruined Cottage*, afterwards the Wanderer of *The Excursion*, an experience akin to those which W. ascribes to himself in *The Prelude*, Books I and II.

p. 340. ii. *Why is it we feel, etc.* This looks like the first draft of the passage afterwards developed in the long addendum to MS. B of *The Ruined Cottage* (*v.* p. 400 *supra*) and finally incorporated in *Exc.* iv. 1204 *et seq.*; *v.* note. Cf. also the passage quoted as "an overflow" from Nutting, *Prel.*, E. de S., pp. 612-14.

p. 340. iii. *Of unknown modes of being, etc.* Cf. *Prelude*, i. 391 *et seq.* and *Exc.* ix. 13-15.

p. 342. II. ix. *Where truth Like some fair fabric, etc.* These lines clearly recall the building of Satan's palace:

> Anon out of the earth a Fabrick huge
> Rose like an Exhalation with the sound
> Of Dulcet Symphonies and voices sweet.
> (*Paradise Lost*, i. 710–12.)

p. 342. III. *There was a spot, etc.* Thése lines are found on a rough sheet, and are followed, after a line drawn across the page, by *Prelude*, x. 270. Lines 1–11 (instrument) occur also in the *Alfoxden* note-book.

p. 342. IV. *Fragments from a note-book containing the first extant MS. of* Christabel. This note-book was evidently in use from the early months of 1798. Several of the fragments, like those in the *Alfoxden* note-book, are of interest as attempts to describe at first hand the experience, and the far-reaching effect upon his mind, of his intercourse with Nature. He is at pains on the one hand to make careful note of forms and images that appealed especially to his imagination through eye and ear (*v.* II. vii ; III ; IV. i) and on the other to record as closely as possible the inward state to which Nature led him through his senses.

p. 342. IV. i. *Thou issuest from a fissure, etc.* Cf. note to *Exc.* iii. 69–73.

p. 343. IV. ii. *The leaves stir not, etc.* Cf. *Prelude* (1805), iii. 539 :

> Hush'd meanwhile
> Was the undersoul, lock'd up in such a calm
> That not a leaf of the great nature stirr'd.

p. 343. IV. iii, and II. iv, p. 341. These fragments taken together record an experience which was of vital importance to W.'s poetic life. Its foundation is a scene of quiet beauty (the stillness is an essential element)—of which the images affect the poet with sensations of delight. His deeper consciousness is stirred, and the first phase is marked by the presence *within* his mind of the images as though they had passed from external to internal existence. *v.* IV. iii: "things that are without Live in our minds as in their native home." Cf. *Prelude* (1850), ii. 348–52 :

> What I saw
> Appeared like something in myself, a dream
> A prospect in the mind.

The second phase is the passing from a dreamlike consciousness of images into a deeper state in which "the mind is called Into itself, by image from without Unvisited", *v.* II. iv *supra*, and *Prelude* (1850), ii. 305–6 :

> an elevated mood, by form
> Or image unprofaned.

The pulse of physical life seems suspended :

> I lived without the knowledge that I lived (II. iv *supra*.)

From such a trance-like mood springs the mystic vision. Cf. *Lines . . .
above Tintern Abbey*:

> the breath of this corporeal frame
> And even the motion of our human blood
> Almost suspended, we are laid asleep
> In body and become a living soul,
> While with an eye made quiet by the power
> Of harmony and the deep power of joy
> We see into the life of things.

p. 343. IV. iv. **3–5.** The ear hears not, *etc.*] A significant tribute to
the ear as that among the senses which has the most spiritual function.
p. 343. IV. vi. *There is creation in the eye, etc.*
6. godlike faculties] Cf. fragment IV. vii. 12, "the godlike senses".
One of the difficult paradoxes in W.'s thought is this: he knew the
power of the senses to lead the mind straight into the spiritual
intuition of life; and he also knew the "despotic" power of the senses
to shut off the mind from the deeper experience, cf. *Exc.* iv. 207
"domineering faculties of sense". (He thought the eye "the most
despotic of the senses", *v. Prelude*, xii. 128 ff.). Contrast the MS.
readings *Ode, Intimations of Immortality*, 191/2 *app. crit.*:

> *Divine indeed of sense
> A blessed influence*

and 153/4 (*app. crit.*):

> But for those first affections
> Those shadowy recollections
> Which be they what they may
> *Throw off from us, or mitigate the spell
> Of that strong frame of sense in which we dwell*

He was continually conscious of "the incumbent mystery of sense
and soul", *Prelude*, xiv. 286. Imagination is the saving power.
"Higher minds," he says, those which penetrate by imagination, are

> By sensible impressions not enthralled,
> But by their quickening impulse made more prompt
> To hold fit converse with the spiritual world.
>   (*Prelude*, xiv. 90–108).

Cf. note to *Prelude*, E. de S., xiii. 1–119, p. 621.
9–12. Cf. Coleridge, *The Nightingale a Conversation Poem*, ll. 24–9:

> Poet who had been building up the rhyme
> When he had better far have stretched his limbs
> Beside a brook in mossy forest-dell,
> By sun or moonlight, to the influxes
> Of shapes and sounds and shifting elements
> Surrendering his whole spirit . . .

Coleridge learnt this lesson from W., whose experience, however, went farther and deeper.

12–23. Cf. *Prelude*, ii. 315 *et seq.*; and Preface to *Lyrical Ballads*, 1800: "Poetry . . . takes its origin from emotion recollected in tranquillity; the emotion is contemplated till, by a species of reaction, the tranquillity gradually disappears, and an emotion kindred to that which was before the subject of contemplation is gradually produced and does itself actually exist in the mind."

p. 344. IV. ix. *For let the impediment, etc.* Also found in the note-book from which the next two passages are taken. It is obviously connected with *Prelude* (1805), xii. 194–201.

p. 345. V. i. *There are who tell us, etc.* An early draft of the passage first printed in *Prelude* (1805), v. 370–88.

p. 347. VII. i. Clearly intended for *The Prelude*.

p. 347. VII. ii. Perhaps intended for *The Recluse*: *v.* ll. 79–97, and the end of the passage from MS. B in *app. crit.* 70–9.

p. 347. VII. iii and iv. K. has arranged these lines in four separate groups, ending the first group at "sole proprietor", and beginning the second with the line "A moon among her stars, a mighty vale". His third group begins with the line "A multitude of little rocky hills", and his fourth with "Embowering mountains and the dome of Heaven". I conjecture that the lines *To the Evening Star over Grasmere Water* (dated by K. 1806, probably a mistake for 1800) ends at "stars" in l. 5, and that a new group of lines begins with "A mighty vale", this passage with the third and fourth of K.'s groups being in reality jottings for the description of Grasmere, *Recluse*, i. 117–28, in which one of the lines, "The multitude of little rocky hills", appears intact. I have therefore rearranged the lines on this understanding.

p. 347. VII. iv. **2–3.** Cf. D. W.'s *Journal*, May 1, 1802: "Oh the overwhelming beauty of the vale below, greener than green."

6. I find it difficult to make sense of "lonely there"—perhaps wrongly transcribed.

APPENDIX C

p. 348. THE TUFT OF PRIMROSES. These incomplete and discursive verses were written in the spring of 1808. The MS., in W.'s writing throughout, is preserved in an octavo note-book,[1] bound in marble boards, which also contains an early draft of the *Address to the Clouds* and the poem, not published by W., on *A Vision of St. Paul's*, which he described in a letter to Sir G. Beaumont dated April 8, 1808 (*v.* Vol. iv, p. 374). Internal evidence confirming the date is afforded by the fact that Mr. Sympson had died on June 27, 1807, during the absence of the W.s at Coleorton (*v.* ll. 143–85), that on July 19 of that

[1] An earlier draft of ll. 1–62 is also found on the reverse of some pages of the first MS. of *Peter Bell*, along with a draft of *Address to the Clouds* and *A vision of St. Paul's*: I refer to this as MS. A.

year D. W. had written to Mrs. Clarkson of the grief they had all felt on their return to Grasmere at the removal of the firs and sycamore near the church (ll. 81–109; v. M.Y., p. 138); and that in March and April of 1808 the W.s were seriously alarmed at Sara Hutchinson's state of health (v. ll. 37–48 and M.Y., pp. 177, 185, 201). The poem thus belongs to the interval between 1806 and 1809, when W. let *The Excursion* rest; and two passages from it (ll. 143–85, 265–96) were later developed for insertion in the longer work. The passage relating to the Chartreuse, ll. 510–71 corresponding to *Prelude*, vi. 424–71, which is almost free from correction in the MS., seems to have been copied in from another MS., but it will be noted that the lines were not found in the original *Prelude*; and they were probably first written for this poem, and only adapted for *The Prelude* when W. gave up the idea of completing or publishing *The Tuft of Primroses*. Our MS. has been copiously revised, and, as W. has often left two versions of the same passage undeleted, it is not always clear which he had decided to retain. My *app..crit.* only gives the more interesting of the variants.

7–19. The "Thou", "Thou art", and "thy" which occur in these lines have in most cases been altered in the MS. to "she", "she is", and "her", but as this change has not been carried farther into the poem, and even in these lines is not invariable, I have retained the original reading. The variants to 1–2, 4–7, quoted in the *app. crit.*, are obviously a part of this contemplated change from the second to the third person.

75. John W. had perished in 1805. From 1806 onwards S. T. C.'s gradual estrangement was felt. *v̇. A Complaint*, Vol. II, p. 34 and note p. 473.

103. blanc] The Miltonic spelling; v. *Paradise Lost*, iii. 48.

143–85. This is the first version of the story of the Sympsons, told in *Exc.* vii. 242–91. On the reverse of two pages of the MS. is found its first adaptation to *The Excursion*.

165. Emma] i.e. D. W.

265–95. Cf. *Exc.* iii. 367–405 and note.

296. St. Basil] A famous scholar and theologian of the fourth century. Born at Cesarea in A.D. 329, he studied first at Constantinople, then at Athens. After this he retired to a chosen spot in wild mountain country near Annesi in Pontus, where he began to organize a monastery on the lines of the cenobium or common life.

307. his Sister's voice] Basil's brother, Gregory of Nyssa, in his *Life of Macrina* says that it was his sister Macrina's persuasion and example which led Basil to devote himself to a life of self-denial.

318–420. This description of the Pontic solitude and Basil's appeal to Gregory Nazianzen are drawn from Basil's Letter XIV to Gregory his Friend (v. Library of Nicene Fathers, New Series, 8, St. Basil). The translation by Newman is as follows:

"... I must at once make for Pontus, where perhaps, God willing, I may make an end of wandering. After renouncing, with trouble, the idle hopes which I once had about you ... I departed into Pontus in quest of a place to live in. There God has opened on me a spot exactly answering to my taste, so that I actually see before my eyes what I have often pictured to my mind in idle fancy. There is a lofty mountain covered with thick woods, watered towards the North with cool and transparent streams. A plain lies beneath, enriched by waters which are ever draining off from it, and skirted by a spontaneous profusion of trees almost thick enough to be a fence. . . . Indeed it is like an island, enclosed as it is on all sides; for deep hollows cut off 2 sides of it; the river, which has lately fallen down a precipice runs all along the front and is impassable as a wall; whilst the mountain extending itself behind, and meeting the hollows in a crescent, stops up the path at its roots. There is but one pass, and I am master of it. Behind my abode there is another gorge, rising into a ledge up above, so as to command the extent of the plains and the stream which bounds it which is not less beautiful to my taste than the Strymon as seen from Amphipolis. For while the latter flows leisurely . . . and is too still to be a river, the former is the most rapid stream I know, and somewhat turbid too from the rocks just above, from which, shooting down, and eddying in a deep pool, it forms a most pleasant scene for myself or anyone else, and is an inexhaustible resource to the country people, in the countless fish which its depths contain. What need to tell of the exhalations from the earth, or the breezes from the river? Another might admire the multitude of flowers and singing birds; but leisure I have none for such thoughts. However the chief praise of the place is, that being happily disposed for produce of every kind, it nurtures what to me is the sweetest produce of all, quietness; indeed it is not only rid of the hustle of the city, but is even unfrequented by travellers, except a chance hunter. It abounds indeed in game, as well as other things, but not, I am glad to say, in bears or wolves, such as you have, but in deer, and wild goats, and hares and the like."

349. Nazianzen] W. had the works of Nazianzen in his library at Rydal Mount: *Gregorii, D. (A. C. 37) Cognomento Theologi Episcopi Nazanzeni Opera.* 1522.

356-8. the Roses and the flowers of kings, *etc.*] Cf. *Exc.* vii. 980-2 and W.'s note.

372-3. These lines contain obvious Miltonic echoes. Cf. *Paradise Lost*, i. 743, "from Noon to dewy Eve", and *Lycidas*, 178-9:

> There entertain him all the saints above
> In solemn troops and sweet societies

424-31. And Nazianzen fashioned a reply] Gregory's reply is his Epistle IV, in which he gives a satirically exaggerated account of the gloom and discomfort of the place, ending "This then is what I think of those Fortunate Islands and of you happy people".

434. Amphilochius] Bishop of Iconium in the fourth century, regarded as the foremost man in the Eastern Church after his friends, Basil of Cesarea, and Gregory of Nazianzus. Basil addresses him in his *De Spiritu Sancto* as "his brother Amphilocius, his dear friend most honoured of all" (*v. Saint Basil*, by W. K. Lowther Clarke).

449–53. In 359 St. Basil was called away from his Pontic solitude to take part in an important Council at Constantinople. This was a period of strife and confusion in the Church through the prolonged doctrinal battle initiated by the Arian heresy. In 370 he was made Bishop of Cesarea.

510–71. *Prelude*, vi. 424–71.

520–9. Cf. *Descriptive Sketches* (1793), ll. 53–79, a first version of W.'s impressions of the Chartreuse on his visit in 1790.

ADDENDA

p. 362. These lines, hitherto unpublished, are written in Wordsworth's early hand on the blank front page of a copy of *Paradise Lost* which is inscribed in the same hand *Wordsworth, Cambridge*. He must have given the copy later to his wife, for she has written her name, Mary Wordsworth, and the date August 27, 1822, under Wordsworth's name. On her death her two sons gave the book to Dr. John Davy with the following dedication inscribed on the verso of the title-page: "This copy of Paradise Lost, belonging to William Wordsworth when at College, is presented to Dr. Davy, as a Memorial of the Love of William and Mary Wordsworth, and of their long Friendship—Also, as an acknowledgement, from their Sons, of his most affectionate attention during the last illnesses of their beloved Parents.

John Wordsworth	Rydal Mount
Wm. Wordsworth	17th Jany. 1859."

The book is now in my possession, and will be given to Dove Cottage.

The lines breathe the spirit of his later allusions to Milton and his poetry: "the Bard, Holiest of Men" (MS. reading of Prospectus to *The Excursion*, 24–5), "that mighty orb of song, The divine Milton" (*Exc.* i. 249), "those trumpet-tones of harmony that shake Our shores in England" (*Prelude*, v. 205–6). Cf. note to *Exc.* i. 248–50.—H. D.

p. 412. i. 368. MS. B reads *within*: MS. P. reads *without*, and is followed by all printed texts. As Mr. H. J. F. Jones points out in *The Egotistical Sublime*, p. 114, *within* is the right 'reading, and I have restored it to the text.

p. 426. iv. 505–7. Dove Cottage Library now has a copy of the first issue.

p. 428. iv. 858–60.' These lines are marked by Haydon in his copy of *The Excursion*, 1814, now in the Library of Cornell University, with the note: *Poor Keats used always to prefer this passage to all others.*

CORRIGENDA AND ADDENDA

VOL. I

p. 10, *app. crit.*: 4th and 2nd line from bottom *for* Bandusia, Bandusian *read* Blandusia, Blandusian

p. 12, *app. crit.*: *after l.* 127 . . . *insert between ll.* 8 and 9: Blest are those spirits tremblingly awake

p. 27, *app. crit.*, *l.* 9: *for* charmed *read* charnel

p. 51, *app. crit.*, A. 138: *for* where *read* when   139: *for* as *read* 'tis

p. 226, I, *l.* 4: *for* it is *read* is it

pp. 232–3, *app. crit.*: for *so* 1836 *in each place*, except *l.* 21, *read so* 1845; and for 1807–15 *read* 1807–15, 1836–43: *at l.* 21 read *so* 1840; and *so* 1836 *but* spoke *for* spake

p. 236, X, *read* [Composed and Published 1798.]

p. 263, IV, *l.* 7: *for* waters *read* water. *l.* 11: *for* True time *read* True, true

p. 264, first line on page: *for* wave *read* waves

p. 270, *l.* 3: *for* Hark . . . Hark *read* Lark . . . Lark

p. 275, *l.* 242: *for* woods *read* wind's

p. 321, *l.* 28: *for* A. 155 read A. 85

p. 324, footnote: *for* pp. *read* ll.

p. 329, *l.* 5: *for* III *read* VII

p. 330, 15 lines from bottom: *for* xxxvii–l *read* xxxviii–l

p. 341, *l.* 15: *for l.* 30 *read l.* 630

p. 362, 14 lines from bottom: *after* p. 238 *insert* XI

p. 363, *l.* 10: *after* p. 241 *for* XI *read* XII

p. 365, at beginning of *l.* 17: *insert* XIX The Poet's Dream

p. 367, l. 15: *after Beauty and Moonlight insert* the original from which S.T.C. developed *Lewti, v. infra,* Vol. II, p. 531; and *l.* 27, *for* iii *read* iv; and 4 lines from bottom of page *for* 40 *read* 4

p. 369, *l.* 8: *for* 79 *read* 75

p. 371, 6 lines from bottom of page: *after* some French stanzas signed Anon. *insert L'education de l'Amour,* by Vicomte de Segur (*v.* article by Christensen, *M.L.N.* Vol. LIII. 280)

p. 374, *l.* 1: *for* 247 *read* 147

VOL. II

p. 8, *l.* 255 of text: *for* steps. *read* steps,

p. 17: *indent l.* 95

p. 27, *l.* 51: *read* listlessness

p. 52, *l.* 42: *delete comma after* worse

p. 65, *app. crit.*: *for* 1845 *read* 1840

p. 87, *app. crit.*, *l.* 207: *after* 1802–5 *add* and cancel leaf 1800 *but* household

p. 128: There should be no space between lines 11 and 12

p. 135, *app. crit.*: 7–8 *read so* 1807–32, 1840

p. 154: XX *read* [Composed 1842.—

p. 198, *l.* 30: *read* Beholds

p. 209. Airey Force Valley. *read* [Composed Sept. 1835.—

p. 250, *l.* 36: *for* soil *read* spoil

p. 264, *l.* 14 (7th line on the page): *after* seem'st *insert* now

p. 385, *footnote* 1: *read* a greater number

p. 409: *for footnote* 2 *substitute*, i.e. to the Preface to the second edition of *Lyrical Ballads, v.* W.'s *Poetical Works*, ed. 1836–7, Vol. III, p. 315. In 1815 The Essay Supplementary opens with a paragraph never reprinted referring to the 'senseless outcry which has been raised against these poems and their author'.

p. 432, insert footnote to *l.* 12: *for* human *read* common: emendation of N. C. Smith

p. 474, *l.* 17: *for* Monkouse *read* Monkhouse

p. 501, third line from bottom: *read* foundrous] The word is in the *O.E.D.* under founderous (cf 'founderous passages' in W.'s Letter to a friend of R. Burns): the *Dialect Dictionary*, &c.

VOL. III

p. 133, XVIII: *read* [Composed 1810.—

p. 195, *l.* 37: *read* upon solemn [*del.* the]

p. 283, third line: *read* Wife!

p. 361, *app. crit.*, I, 1–6, 23rd line: *for* perceive *read* preserve

p. 362, *app. crit.*, II, 1–14, *l.* 3: *for* also *read* else

p. 431, three lines from bottom: *for* Thurson *read* Thomson

p. 436, two lines from bottom, p. 54, XXXI: Lo! where she stands, &c., *insert* Sara Coleridge has written 'Dora Wordsworth' under this Sonnet in her copy of W.'s Poems, 1840.

p. 484, l. 12: *for* 189 *read* 223

p. 493, *l.* 5: *for* Marmetine *and* Marmetinus *read* Mamertine *and* Mamertinus

p. 501, *before l.* 7: In its published form, &c., *insert*: A draft of the sonnet in Longman MS. supplies the eleventh line: And do not that way turn thine arm severe;

p. 565, *l.* 15: *for* Chichester *read* Chicheley

p. 569, *l.* 17: *for* Ardworth *read* Cudworth

p. 573, *l.* 21: *for* unpractical *read* unpoetical

VOL. IV

p. 35, *app. crit.*, 8–9: *read* such (l.c.)

p. 81, *app. crit.*, 40: *read so* 1815: Sad sight! the Shepherd, &c.

p. 135, *app. crit.*: *read* pass'd]

p. 150, *app. crit.*: *for* 274–5 *read* 274–7

p. 274, *l.* 61: *for* Burnt *read* Burned

p. 473, *l.* 11: *for* translations *read* stanzas translated

INDEX TO VOLS. I TO V

Titles of Poems are given, and first lines where there are no titles (except in the case of Inscriptions, Vol. IV, pp. 195–208). Sonnets in series are not indexed individually but by the heading of the series: *Ecclesiastical Sonnets, National Independence and Liberty*, &c.

Translations are given under the name of the author translated. Vols. I to IV each contains a complete index of titles and first lines, including those of Poems hitherto unpublished or not found in Wordsworth's edition of 1849–50.